The Law of Transnational
Business Transactions

(Release #5, 9/86)

The Law of Transnational Business Transactions

Edited by
Ved P. Nanda

Volume 1
International Business & Law Series

Clark Boardman Company, Ltd.
New York, New York   1986

(Release #5, 9/86)

Library of Congress Cataloging in Publication Data

Main entry under title:

The Law of transnational business transactions.

(International business & law series; v. 1)
Includes index.
Contents: U.S. lawyers and international business transactions /
Donald W. Hoagland—Foreign business organization / Ralph
Lake—United States taxation of foreign investors / Herrick K.
Lidstone and Robert S. Rich—[etc.]
1. Commercial law—Addresses, essays, lectures. 2. International
business enterprises—Law and legislation—Addresses, essays,
lectures. 3. Foreign trade regulation—Addresses, essays, lectures.
4. Commercial law—United States—Addresses, essays, lectures. I.
Nanda, Ved P.
II. Series.
K1005.6.L38   346'.07   81-2392
ISBN 0-87632-342-5   342.67   AACR2

PUBLISHER'S NOTE

Clark Boardman's *International Business & Law Series* is the response to the perceived need for an integrated and comprehensive reference library of writings on international business and law. The Series begins at a time when the world economy is in a period of rapid transition, and when United States dominance in international trade has been seriously eroded.

Changing legal implications of international trade and transnational negotiations have obliged lawyers, both in the United States and other jurisdictions, to become aware of such effects in practice. The Clark Boardman *International Business & Law Series* is designed to provide accurate and authoritative information to lawyers who must advise clients in international transactions. Often a detailed knowledge of the national laws which may affect the international transaction must be obtained, a complex process involving interpretation of multiple legal disciplines.

Recent and important changes in international trade and customs laws of the United States signaled this as an opportune time to commence the *International Business & Law Series*. As a result of the passage of the Trade Act of 1974, the Customs Procedural Reform and Simplification Act of 1978, the Trade Agreements Act of 1979, and the Customs Courts Act of 1980, more changes in customs and international trade law were enacted than at any time in the past forty years. The establishment of the United States Court of International Trade is clearly attributable to the increased importance of international business transactions not only in the United States, but throughout the world as well.

The *International Business & Law Series*, it is anticipated, will in time focus on parallel business and legal developments in the industrialized nations of the world. Transnational practitioners will have available in looseleaf format, with periodic updating, the significant literature in the field of international law and business. It is hoped that this reference collection will be of considerable service to the bar and to businessmen throughout the world.

Clark Boardman Company, Ltd.

PREFACE

During the past decade, new centers of international commercial activity have arisen in every country. No longer does the specialized lawyer alone handle transnational transactions, for it is not uncommon for lawyers primarily in domestic practice to advise clients on issues and transactions which are transnational in scope.

It is the purpose of this book to provide assistance to attorneys and students at different levels of expertise, from international lawyers to those in domestic practice to students generally interested in the field. The authors bring varied backgrounds and rich experience to this project. They are associated with multinational enterprises, large and small law firms, law schools, and government agencies.

In planning the book, I made two decisions at the outset: first, to treat only selected aspects of the subject, and second, to discuss those aspects both from a theoretical point of view and in terms of their practical consequences.

During the two-year period it took to complete the book, my associates and former students at the University of Denver College of Law have been of significant help both as authors and advisers. Nancy Nones, Administrator of the International Legal Studies Program, and several of my research assistants, especially David Pansius and Christina Neslund, provided substantial aid which I gratefully acknowledge. I would like to thank Tom Costner, Vice-President, Publishing at Clark Boardman, to whom I am deeply indebted for his helpful suggestions, and William Cubberley, Administrative Editor, and his associates, for their assistance in the publication process.

Finally, this book is presented to the reader with an invitation that any suggestions regarding revision of these materials be forwarded to the editor.

Denver, Colorado   Ved P. Nanda

TABLE OF CHAPTERS

TABLE OF CONTENTS

Volume 1

CHAPTER 3
United States Taxation of Foreign Investors
Herrick K. Lidstone and Robert S. Rich

CHAPTER 3A
Foreign Tax Provisions of the 1984 Tax Act
Robert S. Rich

CHAPTER 4
Selected Clauses in Transnational Contracts
Mark S. Caldwell

CHAPTER 5
International Technology Transfers
Robert Y. Peters

CHAPTER 6
International Technology Transfer Agreements
Michael Bard and Robert Y. Peters

CHAPTER 7

Foreign Natural Resource Investment
James E. Horigan

CHAPTER 8
Forum-Selection and Choice-of-Law Clauses in International Contracts   Ved P. Nanda

CHAPTER 10
Jurisdictional Problems in the Application of the Antitrust Laws David K. Pansius

TABLE OF CONTENTS

Volume 1A

CHAPTER 11
Enforcement of the European Community's Antitrust Laws—The Single Enterprise Theory
Lillian Heimke Filegar and Lisa L. Helling

CHAPTER 13
International Boycotts   Stephen J. Doyle

CHAPTER 15
Dismissals in Europe   Roel Nieuwdorp

CHAPTER 16
Regulation of Multinational Enterprises: International Codes of Conduct   Paula R. Rhodes

CHAPTER 17
International Economic Institutions
David A. Chaikin

CHAPTER 1

U.S. Lawyers and Transnational Business Transactions—An Introduction

DONALD W. HOAGLAND*

This freshly revised volume offers a reference work for U.S. lawyers who are experienced in domestic commercial practice, but who need a briefing on new issues that arise when the transaction has transnational aspects. The authors of each chapter generally deal with discrete subjects. Several new ones have been added since the first edition. The book is not designed to develop any common policy theme, nor to embrace the whole of a very large field. Rather, in anticipating the needs of such a practitioner the authors are looking for the new issues he or she might not think of without this kind of help—for example, the varying intensities of economic nationalism; the effect of treaties; the foreign exchange implications of a proposed transaction; the possible extraterritorial application of one state's laws; the risk of facing a dispute governed by a foreign law, in a foreign language and in a foreign court— the kinds of subjects that are on the bridge between the national law systems of the participants in a transnational transaction.

There are also new and possibly unexpected internal law questions in foreign countries. Assistance of effective local counsel is not always available. Even if it is, complete reliance on an attorney from another country may not always be desirable. If a United States business is going to try to function in

---

*B.A., Yale; LL.B., Columbia, 1948. Senior Partner, Davis, Graham and Stubbs, Denver, Colorado.

a foreign country, what different substantive and regulatory patterns is it likely to encounter? How does one set up a distribution system in a country that may limit sales commissions? What are the applicable trade regulation and antitrust principles in countries that may value central planning above competition? What are the accepted and enforceable methods of transferring technology without losing control of it?

If a foreign investor is undertaking a venture in the United States, most of the substantive legal problems will be familiar ground to U.S. practitioners. But even in the internal U.S. law there are traps for the unwary, with one critical question standing out: How will the U.S. income tax laws apply to the foreign investor?

These and many more fundamental questions are dealt with in this volume. Some preliminary issues, however, deserve attention before examining the substantive materials. The lawyer's role itself is the foremost of these. It will be a very different role if he is advising an established U.S. client going abroad than it will be if he is sought out by a foreign client considering some business activity in the United States.

When a U.S. lawyer is advising a familiar American client about the legal implications of going abroad, the lawyer and client know and trust each other, speak the same language and share a common understanding of what the lawyer's job is. But even with this base of common understanding, there can be misunderstandings about responsibility for the coverage of the new elements in the problems faced by the client. As appears from the revised chapter treating the Arab boycott, the possibility of commercial contact with nations who are hostile to each other brings emotionally charged foreign policy issues into the mix of considerations on which the client will need current advice.

To the extent that U.S. foreign policy has been expressed in legislation, it is clearly the American lawyer's job to find the legislation and see that his client is advised about it. To the extent that significant policy considerations are expressed in local law in the foreign countries where contact will occur, the job of the U.S. lawyer will include obtaining competent local counsel. Economic nationalism, differences in political philosophy and the disturbing proliferation of "act of state" cases can introduce unexpected and important host-country legal risks or requirements. The coordinating (and interpreting) function of the U.S. lawyer in dealing with local law questions abroad is essential because of the risk of the "wrong question syndrome," and, also, because of the need to coordinate the legal requirements of foreign jurisdictions with the U.S. legal requirements to develop a workable pattern of organization and operation. The new chapters on multinational enterprises, proposed codes of conduct and antitrust law emphasize the integrating function to be performed by the U.S. lawyer when his client goes abroad. Similarly, the ebb and flow of extraterritorial assertions of jurisdictions by the U.S. (both its courts and its administrative agencies) represents forces in an area requiring constant alertness by U.S. counsel.

In the gap between explicit U.S. legislation and host country laws there is an area of great potential misunderstanding between lawyer and client. Questions of procedure and custom will arise concerning foreign exchange, customs, insurance, banking, loading and shipping, licensing, personal relationships, problems of interpretation of language and intention, anticipation of favorable and unfavorable business climates and even how long it takes in different cultures to become acquainted and negotiate an agreement. All of these subjects and more can become critically important in a transnational business project. They do not come in packages labelled "legal problem." The U.S. lawyer's initial responsibility is to be sure someone is covering them for his client; he may not be expected to cover them all, but he must anticipate the need for attention to all of these considerations.

A different set of problems is presented to a U.S. lawyer advising a foreigner about a possible business venture in the U.S. Here the job is not only to give reliable advice about internal U.S. law, but to do two more things: first, to find those elements of U.S. law which deal particularly with foreigners (such as the intricate tax considerations summarized in Chapter 3) and, second, to anticipate the areas of possible misconception, or erroneous assumptions, which might otherwise create problems.

The first potential misconception is the role and cost of legal services in the U.S. Some foreign business people expect a commercial lawyer to be primarily a scrivener or expediter, *i.e.*, to write agreements as instructed or to obtain governmental approvals and to do what he is told to do without asking questions. Others may wish total representation, even including business judgments, something close to a general agent. Between these extremes lie infinite gradations. Because the range is so great the U.S. lawyer should try to reach an early understanding with a foreign client about the nature of his responsibilities and how he plans to charge for his work. The role he probably prefers, that of a constructive counsellor testing all assumptions of business proposals before acting on them, will not be expected by many foreign clients, and may not be wanted by some. As the cost of legal services rises, some foreign business people may well arrive with a reborn conviction that society's ancient prejudice against lawyers is justified. They will have read horror stories about the way some U.S. lawyers run up huge bills for research and analysis not expected by the client. They may want to minimize the lawyer's role, seek "standard" documents, and limit the amount of information the lawyer is given. The challenge to the lawyer then is to make a responsible, professional exploration of the utlty of his services and of the dangers of proceeding on uninformed advice or untested assumptions. The client is entitled to be satisfied on such questions, and so is U.S. counsel. Both parties to the engagement will be well advised to clarify these issues at the outset.

A closely associated issue of the greatest delicacy concerns ethical standards. Corruption is no stranger to the United States. Unofficially supplementing the income of governmental officials is regarded very differently in different places, but the occasions for considering such actions can arise anywhere. The accepted attitudes toward telling the truth to the government, toward facilitating government actions by strategically placed payments and toward paying all of one's taxes differ in different countries. It is by no means simple for a U.S. lawyer to pick his way through these bramble bushes with his domestic clients. It is a diplomatic challenge of the first order, however, for a U.S. lawyer to determine whether he and his foreign client have the same general approach to these subjects. If the project is in the United States, the American lawyer can expect his views to be given considerable credibility in these areas. If the scene is abroad, his task is more difficult. Our badly-named Foreign Corrupt Practices Act accentuates the difficulty.

Some elements of the U.S. scene as to which the U.S. lawyer must anticipate possible misconceptions are not so philosophical, and are much more technical. Most of the commerce in the world is carried on in countries which do not have common law or Anglo-Saxon legal traditions. The roles in the U.S. of such persons as notaries public and corporate directors will need to be discussed, because they are different in civil law countries. Some quirks in corporate organization may cause confusion. For example, some foreign jurisdictions do not recognize the freedom observed in U.S. law to sell shares of stock in newly organized corporations for more than par value, with the balance assigned to surplus. Differing accounting practices may have to be reconciled by communications between accounting firms in the two countries involved. (Fortunately the major U.S. accounting firms are well established in international practice.) All phases of entity organization will be different in nomenclature and in detail. In this area particularly, the U.S. lawyer needs to prepare himself for a searching cross-examination on the precise legal meaning and practical implications of such concepts as par value, quorum, conflict of interest, notice, stock subscriptions, preferred stock, limited partnership, transfer restrictions and many other features of U.S. law that are not predictably to be found in foreign legal systems.

The U.S. lawyer working in a domestically-based international transaction becomes much more deeply involved in political and foreign policy issues than he does when he is working on a purely domestic transaction. Although many branches of domestic practice such as resource development and labor relations develop significant domestic political dimensions, there are many transactions such as real estate purchases and organization of companies, and the financing of both, which proceed in domestic practice with very little attention to national policy issues.

These same transactions can become politically supercharged when the source of funds is foreign. On an unpredictable pattern of local initiatives, several states in the U.S. have begun to limit foreign ownership of land. This has happened in previous eras in U.S. history and it is happening again. States such as Oklahoma, Alaska, and Mississippi have enacted (or are reinterpreting) state laws restricting foreign ownership of land or mineral resources. The United States Supreme Court has recently declined to prohibit such legislation. Proposals have appeared in the U.S. Congress to limit foreign ownership of agricultural land, and the United States now requires reporting of some agricultural land and commercial enterprise acquisitions. Some forms of subsidized developmental financing are not available to foreign-owned enterprises. Federal mineral leases cannot be issued to certain foreigners. All of this is not new in U.S. law, but much of it is new, and the older requirements are being enforced more strictly. In many cases the mere formation of a U.S. entity as a vehicle for foreign owned enterprises may not defeat such restrictions, especially those based on national defense considerations.

If the project is not domestic, but is either an export or a foreign investment, then the need to probe unfamiliar political territory is intensified. The economic nationalism which is stirring in the United States is in full bloom in many parts of the rest of the world. Europe seems somewhat less obsessed by it now than was apparent, for example, in France in the recent past, but the over 51 percent local ownership approach has been prominent in the development regimes of such countries as India, Mexico, Peru and Indonesia. Local content requirements, maximum expatriate employment and severe penalties for terminating host country employees are common.

The concern that multinational corporations may overwhelm the regulatory capabilities of some nations is growing, as the new Chapter 17 well illustrates. It describes the slow evolution of codes of conduct being proposed to cope with, to some, the alarming potential strength of multinational enterprises. The effort to develop these codes continues in international bodies such as the OECD and the UN Commission on Transnational Corporations; so much so that even if they do not soon become binding law they must be regarded as prime indicators of the directions in which law in this area is being pressed to develop.

United States counsel who do not rely entirely on local counsel in such situations and instead travel to the host country to participate in investigations and negotiations may find themselves in the unaccustomed role of defender of the policy underpinning of U.S. commercial practices and procedures which they generally take for granted. The focal debate over freedom of management to make decisions without governmental participation continues and will continue. The equitable distribution of profits will always be a central issue. The degree of corporate democracy may well be debated. Other and narrower issues arise. For example, an entity organized under German law can operate in the United States through a branch without forming a controlled entity organized under U.S. law. We permit this because we assume in the U.S. that our qualification and jurisdictional statutes will give domestic creditors as much access to the information they need, or to the assets they seek judgment against, as they would have if a new U.S. entity were required. Some foreign nations do not share this view. Indonesia is an example, and the U.S. lawyer asserting the correctness of the U.S. view will need to be fluent in due process fundamentals to have any hope of avoiding the requirements, and with them the discomfort of operating through entities with strange or unpredictable characteristics.

Making intelligent use of facilities offered through the U.S. government is another area in which U.S. lawyers need to inform themselves. This volume does not investigate this area, in part, because the U.S. government itself is active in offering such information, and in part, because excellent private publications are becoming available. One example is the handy volume by Delphos, W.A., *Washington's Best Kept Secrets: A U.S. Government Guide to International Business*. New York: Wiley & Sons, 1983.

The role of the U.S. government in connection with foreign business activities of American citizens is reasonably well publicized in such areas as the Arab boycott legislation, (dealt with in Chapter 13), tariff levels, anti-dumping, and the Russian embargoes. More obscure but often helpful are the U.S. government's programs to facilitate U.S. investment in developing countries. In the mid-1960's these programs were part of a reasonably consistent government-wide policy to encourage direct investment in the friendly Third World countries. In 1965 the President's foreign assistance proposals even included a proposed 30 percent tax credit for direct investment in Less Developed Countries (LDCs). Since then, the policy has become less consistent and has lost considerable public support. The labor movement has shifted its attitude out of a fear that jobs might be exported through foreign investment. Host country governments themselves are no longer uncritical about their welcome to foreign enterprises, out of a debatable impression that the earnings of foreign companies seemed to flow back to the home country of the project's foreign investors without leaving commensurate benefits behind. The general public in the U.S. is even less sure than it was twenty years ago that the economic development of friendly but poor nations deserves a claim on U.S. resources. The violent impact of oil price increases has skewed all the pre-1973 classifications of developed and developing nations and complicated their relationships. Nevertheless, recent federal policy has re-established a bureau of private enterprise in the Agency for International Development (AID), and there is reason to believe that this office, together with the Overseas Private Investment Corporation (OPIC), will be more able to facilitate private investment in the developing countries.

Other U.S. government resources, are supporting U.S. business activity abroad—especially in LDCs. The Export-Import Bank is a substantial source of assistance to U.S. exporters. The World Bank and its various agencies are still contributing to the strengthening of LDC economies (and societies) in many ways. The United States contributes substantially to the U.N. agencies and other regional banking institutions which may lend direct or indirect support to private business activity in developing countries. OPIC is offering insurance against the risks of war damage, expropriation, and inconvertibility of currency. These coverages have been gradually broadened, since the first was introduced in 1957, to cover the results of insurrection and civil disturbances under the war coverage, and to cover "creeping" expropriation. Even certain stages of oil and gas exploration investment and some aspects of contractor's risk are now covered.

The insurance for oil investment is relatively new: it first appeared in 1977 in connection with an oil exploration project in Jordan. This project offered the exciting possibility of the discovery of oil in a non-OPEC area, beneath the floor of the Dead Sea, a hope that has not yet been realized. OPIC's policy (and the policy of predecessor U.S. agencies managing this program since 1957, including AID) had been to withhold political risk insurance from oil exploration investment on the theory that the oil multinationals did not need this kind of financial assistance, and that its availability was not likely to change their investment decisions. By 1977 however, the policy changed, presumably because of the new significance of finding non-OPEC sources of oil in the developing countries, and perhaps because of a recognition of the value of encouraging independent oil companies to explore for oil in such places instead of leaving the field to the largest oil companies.

The key requirement for U.S. lawyers to keep in mind is that OPIC insurance cannot be applied for *after* the investment has been committed. It is authorized by Congress as an incentive to the covered forms of investment, and if the investment is committed before the application for insurance is registered, it would be very hard to say that the availability of the insurance contributed to the investment decision. Some private insurance of this character also exists.

Americans pride themselves on their ability to make friends easily. We generally bank on openness and practical rationality. We start, however, with a serious disadvantage which is getting more serious all the time—our inadequate language skills. Fluency in any foreign language is rare among American lawyers who are not active international law specialists. Fluency in three to five languages is commonplace for business people in most other parts of the world. Although English is the second language most commonly studied around the world, we cannot expect commerce always to be conducted in English. Even if an agreement is to be drafted in English, or if the other parties to a negotiation can speak English, a lawyer who has some facility in the language of the foreign parties involved can use that skill to break drafting deadlocks, ease the social situation, avoid confusion, and minimize the adversary and formalized character of a negotiation carried on through interpreters.

The willingness of foreign parties to make concessions to U.S. educational shortcomings may decline. The U.S. economy is attractive now to Japanese, German, French, Belgian, Swiss, and Canadian investors because our political system (whatever our tunnel vision may lead us to think about it) looks stable by world standards. Four or five years ago this presented an ideal combination for a capital exporting nation's investors: a weakened dollar with a stable political system offered cheap but secure investments. Although investments in the United States look attractive from abroad, the dollar has strenghtened and our prices are up.

The deference to which Americans have grown accustomed in international business situations since 1945 is fading. The atomic bomb is no longer our monopoly. Our share of the gross value of goods and services produced worldwide is less than half what it was in 1945. Plants originally slated for construction by U.S. firms are now likely to be built by German and French firms. It's a new world.

Even the vaunted U.S. predominance in management skills is seriously challenged. We are reaching for joint ventures with Japanese and European manufacturers. The inability of our automotive, steel, and textile industries to match the creative productivity of foreign sources may be due to some extent to forces (especially government decisions) beyond management's control. Nevertheless, "management" means coping with whatever has to be dealt with, and to some European and Japanese managers many major U.S. companies have become ossified, bureaucratic, and ineffective.

All of this puts U.S. lawyers to the test: Can we keep pace with the sophisticated demands of international commerce? Can we contribute something as lawyers to support the creative efforts of private entrepreneurs attempting to function productively in today's environment? As in most other aspects of our work, preparation is the key. No one volume can meet the entire need, and many excellent works are available to assist us in the process. This volume is offered in the hope that it will be materially helpful to our fellow practitioners.

CHAPTER 2

Foreign Business Organization

RALPH B. LAKE*

*Legal Counsel—Europe and Middle East, Holiday Inns Inc., LL.M., London School of Economics, London, England; B.A., Wake Forest; M.B.A., J.D., Denver. This chapter was prepared with the invaluable assistance of Gerald K. Fisher of the Ohio Bar and J.W.F. Faircloth of the D.C. Bar.

　　　　　[ii]　Société à Responsibilité Limiteé
　　　　　[iii]　Partnerships
　　[c]　Federal Republic of Germany
　　　　　[i]　Aktiengesellschaft (AG)
　　　　　[ii]　Gesellschaft mit beschränkter Haftung
　　　　　　　(GmbH)
　　　　　[iii]　Partnerships

§ 2.01　Introduction and General Considerations

This chapter treats the legal relationships and entities which are employed in the distribution of products abroad. The vehicles for foreign product distribution are surprisingly few in number although each is capable of numerous permutations and combinations with others. They may be generally classified as those which do not involve the legal presence of the U.S. manufacturer abroad (agency and distributor relationships) and those which do (foreign branches and foreign subsidiaries).

A combination of commercial and legal factors influence the decision as to which vehicle a U.S. manufacturer uses for its sales in a particular foreign country. The size and complexity of a foreign operation is perhaps the most important commercial consideration. Indeed, the distribution of products abroad can be viewed as a progression characterized by the increasing degree of foreign activity by a U.S. manufacturer, and a correspondingly increasing degree of legal complexity. Such a progression often represents a normal course of events as a U.S. manufacturer's foreign sales expand over time and its foreign operations mature. The simplest method is an export sale without any foreign presence of the U.S. manufacturer and without any foreign intermediary. The next step often involves the appointment of a foreign commission agent or representative, followed perhaps by the appointment of an independent foreign distributor. A major commitment to a particular foreign market usually involves the establishment of a legal presence in the country by either a direct branch of the U.S. manufacturer or a sales subsidiary incorporated abroad. At the end of the progression is a foreign manufacturing facility to serve foreign markets or to be integrated with U.S. manufacturing facilities. Such a move involves a substantial financial investment, and almost invariably brings numerous foreign regulatory schemes into play. The degree of legal complexity is therefore appreciable. Firms which have extensive international operations customarily use all of these methods.

A second important commercial consideration is the psychological impression a foreign organization makes on foreign customers and foreign regulatory bodies. In this respect a locally incorporated subsidiary is often considered to be an effective marketing tool irrespective of its legal implications since it is perceived as being less "foreign" than, for example, a branch. In some countries the appointment of a local distributor is thought to create a favorable impression for the same reason.

Although each country is unique with respect to the factors determining the best business organization for it, it seems useful to identify a few legal considerations of general import. They can be conveniently grouped in the following categories.

First, there are always U.S. legal implications. The most obvious of these is federal taxation. That subject is treated briefly in the sections which follow. Federal regulation of international trade is already pervasive, and is increasing.[1] Lawyers contemplating a foreign business organization should pay particular attention to the possible effects of the U.S. antitrust laws,[2] the U.S. securities regulation laws,[3] the Foreign Corrupt

---

[1] The response to this development abroad has been generally critical. See Hacking, "The Increasing Extraterritorial Impact of U.S. Law: A Cause for Concern Amongst Friends of America," 1 Northwestern J. Int'l L. & Bus. 1 (1979); Bradfield, "United States Extraterritorial Commerce Regulations," in Private Investors Abroad—Problems and Solutions in International Business 19 (V. Cameron ed. 1976). Some countries, including France, West Germany, Switzerland and the United Kingdom have enacted so-called "blocking" statutes to prevent extraterritorial application of the U.S. antitrust laws. See Marcuss and Richard, "Extraterritorial Jurisdiction in United States Trade Law: The Need for a Consistent Theory," 20 Colum. J. Trans. L. 439 (1981); Sornarajah, "The Extraterritorial Enforcement of U.S Antitrust Laws: Conflict and Compromise," 31 Int'l & Comp. L.Q. 127 (1982).

[2] See Chapter 12 infra.

[3] See Chapter 9 infra.

Practices Act of 1977,[4] and the U.S. antiboycott laws.[5] These laws can in some circumstances virtually mandate a particular form of foreign organization.

Second, the law of the host country regarding the conduct of business by foreigners must be considered. Of primary importance in this respect are the statutes and judicial doctrines which deal with the degree of activity in a country which constitutes "doing business" or "conducting business" and thus require the establishing of a local legal presence. Also, most countries regulate foreign investment in some manner. Such regulation occurs in both the less developed and the developed countries, and is an immensely complex and controversial subject.[6] For the purposes of this chapter it is sufficient to note that many countries simultaneously encourage and discourage foreign activity in their economies,[7] and that foreign investment laws can significantly affect the type of organizational vehicle a foreign investor selects.[8] Among a host of

---

[4] Foreign Corrupt Practices Act of 1977, 15 U.S.C.A. Sec. 78a note, 78m, 78dd-1, 78dd-2, 78ff. *See generally* W. Surrey & R. Von Mehren, *Corporate Conduct Overseas* (1978); Note, "Congressional Response to the Problem of Questionable Corporate Payments Abroad: The Foreign Corrupt Practices Act of 1977," 10 Law & Pol'y Int'l Bus. 1253 (1978).

[5] Export Administration Amendments of 1977, Pub. L. No. 95-52, 91 Stat. 235 (1977) amending the Export Administration Act of 1969, 50 U.S.C. app sec. 2401, *et seq.* (1970) (as amended 1974, 1979); Tax Reform Act of 1976, Pub. L. No. 94-455 Sec. 504, 90 Stat 1563, Sec. 1061-64, codified at I.R.C. Sec. 908, 952 (a) as amended 995 (b)(1) as amended Sec. 999 (1976). *See generally* "Symposium: The Arab Boycott and the International Response," 8 Ga. J. Int'l & Comp. L. 527 (1978); The Anti Boycott Bulletin (all issues).

[6] A classic argument for restricting foreign investment in less developed countries is found in Hirschman, "How to Divest in Latin America and Why," in *76 Essays in International Finance* 4 (1969); *See also* Loehr, "The Uneasy Case for Private Investment in Developing Countries," 2 Denver J. Int'l L. & Policy 179 (1972). For approaches taken in the developed countries see Cranston, "Foreign Investment Restrictions: Defending Economic Sovereignty in Canada and Australia," 14 Harv. J. Int'l L. 345 (1975).

[7] The approach taken by Thailand is not atypical. See R. Robinson, *National Control of Foreign Business Entry* 55 (1976); Comment, "Foreign Investment in Thailand: The Effect of Recent Legislation," 3 Denver J. Int'l L. & Policy 304 (1973).

[8] A good example of direct regulation which affects business organization is found in Nigeria which prohibits the use of branches, and mandates ownership by Nigerian nationals of some portion of the equity of corporations

means of foreign investment regulations used by various countries, the prominent ones include regulatory schemes, controls of foreign exchange, local taxation, local customs laws, and controls of technology transfer.[9]

Finally, foreign business organization law which is not specifically aimed at foreigners may itself suggest a preferable means of local operation. An example is the wide variety of limited liability entities available in many civil law countries. The business planner is able to select the one most propitious for a given situation. Also, the usual factors which encourage the use of the corporate form of doing business are no less relevant in foreign countries than in the United States.

There are a variety of means of doing business abroad which do not involve the traditional organizational methods. These include:

1. Turn-key operations, in which a U.S. manufacturer performs all functions associated with the establishment of a foreign manufacturing or agricultural enterprise including technology licensing, training of personnel, construction, initial supply of equipment and management; and turns the entire operation over to a foreign customer when it is completed. The foreign company receives a fee for this service and possibly sales and royalty income.

2. Contractual joint ventures by which a U.S. manufacturer and a foreign entity agree to perform different functions for a common result in a foreign country. The

---

organized under Nigerian law. Nigerian Enterprises Promotion Decree 1977, Decree No. 3 (1977); Nigerian Companies Decree of 1968. See generally, Megwa, "Foreign Direct Investment Climate in Nigeria: The Changing Law and Development Policies," 21 Colum. J. Trans. L. 487 (1983). Donovan, "Nigeria: Still Safe for U.S. Investors?" 10 Vanderbilt J. Trans. L. 601 (1977); Blankenheimer, "The Foreign Investment Climate in Nigeria," 10 Vanderbilt J. Trans. L. 589 (1977).

[9] Mexico strictly regulates technology transfers. Colloquium on Certain Legal Aspects of Foreign Investment in Mexico: "Regulation of Capital Investment, Patents and Trademarks and Transfer of Technology," 7 Ga. J. Int'l & Comp. L 1 (1977). Brill, "Transfer of Technology in Mexico," 4 Denver J. Int'l L & Policy 51 (1974).

responsibilities and liabilities of such operations are governed by contract and there is no formal foreign organization.

3. Management and technical assistance agreements by which U.S. companies perform the management of a foreign organization in which they have no ownership. U.S. companies customarily receive a fee for these services based on the profits of the enterprise.

4. Production sharing agreements in extractive industries and in agricultural projects by which U.S. companies operate a foreign enterprise in return for a share of this production.

5. Franchise agreements where a "system" and trademarks are granted to a foreign organization for a fee.

The above arrangements are often preferred over the traditional foreign organizations in socialist countries and those less developed countries where economic nationalism is prevalent.

§ 2.02 Forms Not Involving a Foreign Presence

[1] Agency Arrangements

The appointment of a foreign agent is often the first step taken by a U.S. manufacturer in developing its international business. Commercially, a distributor relationship is usually more advantageous than an agency relationship to a U.S. manufacturer since distributors take title to goods and bear the financial and commercial risks of subsequent sale. The use of agents by foreign companies occurs primarily for foreign governmental sales, where an on-going commercial operation is not contemplated; in relatively small markets; and in the Middle East, where the role of intermediaries is an important aspect of local cultures.[10]

There are a number of legal considerations which should be addressed by lawyers counseling U.S. manufacturers which appoint foreign agents.

---

[10] R. Patai, *The Arab Mind* 228-246 (1976).

[a] Nature of the Relationship

The term "agent" is widely used in international business to characterize a number of relationships which would not strictly be agency relationships in the United States. As a general proposition, agents do not buy and sell for their own account, but receive commission income for sales made by their principals. They may or may not be granted the authority to accept orders or to otherwise contractually obligate their foreign principals. Often included in the term are brokers; distributing agents, who are really distributors; "del credere" agents, who are liable to their principals for non-payment by purchasers[10.1] and sponsors. Perhaps a better term is "representative," since it is neutral, and does not imply a particular legal relationship, at least to U.S. lawyers.

There are some significant differences between the common and civil laws of agency, which bear examination prior to the appointment of a foreign agent.[11] The liability of a principal for the acts of undisclosed agents is a concept unique to the common law world. Legal relationships between principals and third parties are not created by agreements with agents who act in their own names in civil law countries.

Civil codes often clearly distinguish between different types of agents, and the agency law is often more closely connected with the labor law of civil law countries than in the United States. The commercial code of West Germany, for example, provides for three forms of agency which are distinguished by function and authority.[12] It is significant that when authority is defined by the commercial code, it may not be restricted

---

[10.1] *See generally* G. LaVilla & M. Caetella, *The Italian Law of Agency and Distributorship Agreements* 91-94 (1977).

[11] *See generally* II K. Zweigert & H. Koetz, *An Introduction to Comparative Law* 99–108 (1977); H. de Vries, *Civil Law and the Anglo-American Lawyer* 368 (1976); Yiannopoulos, "Brokerage, Mandate, and Agency in Lousiana: Civilian Tradition and Modern Practice," 19 La. L. Rev. 777 (1959); Muller-Freienfels, "Law of Agency," 6 Am. J. Comp. L. 165 (1957).

[12] *See generally* I B. Rüster, ed., *Business Transactions in Germany*, chapter 13 (1984); N. Horn, H. Kötz and H. Leser, *German Private and Commercial Law: An Introduction* 225-35 (1982); F. Staubach, *The German Law of Agency and Distributorship* (1977).

contractually. Holders of *Prokura* and *Handelsvollmacht* authority are employees of the principal. The former is a very broad, almost unrestricted, authority to represent the principal, which is generally related to anything connected to the running of an enterprise. The latter authority is more restricted, being generally related to the conduct of a particular business. The *Handelsvertreter* is the true commercial agent in the U.S. sense and is an independent businessman, not an employee. A *Handelsvertreter* may be given the authority to conclude contracts or only the authority to negotiate them, but in other respects generally has the authority to engage in transactions which are customary for a principal's particular business. A *"Kommissionär"* buys and sells goods in his own name but for the account of another. Since the relationship is undisclosed, the *Kommissionär* is not a true agent under German law.

In France, there are two types of statutory agents. The "agent commercial" and the "VRP." The latter is an abbreviation for "voyager, representant et placier," a nineteenth century functional classifications now better described by the term "representative."[12.1]

Sponsors are unique to the Middle East. In return for a commission, which is normally less than the commission paid to a commercial agent, a sponsor merely legitimizes the presence of a foreign seller in a particular country. Goods are imported in the name of the sponsor, but business is conducted directly by the principal by means of a "commercial establishment" which bears the name of the sponsor. Unlike the foreign commercial agent, the sponsor is not really a part of a U.S. manufacturer's international marketing effort.

It is most important to note that in many countries, the appointment of a commercial agent which has the authority to accept orders and/or conclude contracts on behalf of a foreign principal constitutes "doing business" and subjects the foreign principal to local jurisdiction and taxation. Commissions paid

---

[12.1] *See generally* I Simeon, Moquet, Borde & Associés, ed., *Doing Business in France*, chapter 4 (1985); J. Guyenot, *The French Law of Agency and Distributorship Agreements* (1976).

to foreign sales representatives are deductible for U.S. tax purposes.[13]

[b] Foreign Laws Affecting Agency Relationships

In addition to provisions in foreign civil codes and common law doctrines governing the relationship of agent and principal, many countries have adopted specific legislation which affects the contractual relationship between a U.S. manufacturer and its agent in those countries.

[i] Requirement of Local Representation

Some Middle Eastern countries require the use of local agents for sales made to customers located in those countries.[14] Such countries almost always require that local agents be nationals of the country.[15] Finding a competent local agent which does not already represent competitors may be quite difficult in small countries in which commercial activity is often conducted principally by foreigners. The requirement can be met by making sales through a local trading corporation in which nationals of the country own a specified portion of the equity. Indeed, the trend in the Middle East seems to be to emphasize such arrangements in preference to agency rela-

---

[13] I.R.C. Sec. 162(c) Reg. 162-18(a)(2).

[14] Countries which require the use of local agents or representatives for at least some purposes include Bahrain, Egypt, Jordan, Kuwait, Libya, Qatar, Saudi Arabia, and the United Arab Emirates. In Libya, the agent must be a government agency. Saudia Arabia formerly acquired the use of local agents only for commercial sales, but now seems to require them for government sales as well. Taylor and Weissman, "Middle East Agency Law Survey," 14 Int'l Law. 351 (1980).

[15] Law No. 12 of 1964, as amended by Decree No. 25 of 1966, of Qatar states the requirement that agents for sales in Qatar must be Qatari nationals or local companies in which Qatari nationals must own at least 51 percent of the equity. As a practical matter, registration of agents is only permitted for companies in which 100 percent of the equity is owned by Qatari nationals. Egypt and Indonesia have similar requirements.

[16] (Reserved)

tionships as the economies of the countries in that region mature.

[ii]   Prohibition of Local Agents

Some countries, particularly those with socialist or putatively socialist economies, prohibit the use of local agents for certain types of sales.[17] In many socialist countries, imports must be transacted through local state trading corporations, which are in effect government-owned agencies.

[iii]   Registration and Disclosure

Many countries require that contracts with local intermediaries be registered with a governmental authority, and that certain elements of the relationship be disclosed.[18] The usual disclosure is the amount of the commission.

[iv]   Limitation of Commissions

Increasingly, foreign countries tend to limit the amount of a commission which may be paid to a local agent.[19] Such limitations work to the benefit of foreign sellers, of course, and ingenious arrangements may be proposed to increase the compensation a local agent receives. Such arrangements should be

---

[17] Algeria seems to prohibit the use of local agents altogether. Algerian Law 78-02 of February 11, 1978, 2 Int'l Lawyers Newsletter 8 (1980). Iraq and Syria prohibit their use in Government procurement.

[18] Decree No. 23 of October, 1975 of Bahrain, for example, requires that an authenticated copy of an agency contract be registered with the Ministry of Commerce.

[19] Beginning in 1978, Saudi Arabia, for example, limited commissions to 5 percent of the contract price for sales to the Saudi Arabian government. Taylor, "Alternative Legal Structures for Doing Business in Saudia Arabia: Distributorships, Agency, Joint Venture and Professional Office," 12 Case Wes. Res. J. Int'l L. 77 (1980); Cartwright & Hamza, "The Saudi Arabian Services Agents Regulations," 34 Bus. Law 475 (1979).

examined very carefully to ensure not only that local law is not violated, but that the arrangement for an increased foreign commission does not raise questions under U.S. law.[20]

[v] Exclusivity

Some countries require that local agents be granted exclusive rights to represent a foreign seller in the country. As a practical matter, most reputable agents in the Middle East are not willing to accept any arrangement other than exclusivity.

[vi] Restrictions on Termination

In addition to whatever termination compensation is required by the agreement between a foreign agent and a U.S. manufacturer, in some countries restrictions are placed by law on the termination of agents.[21] These countries tend to be the most important trading partners of the United States. Since legislation often resembles protective legislation covering distributors, the discussion regarding distributors in the following section is relevant. If an agent is considered to be "dependent," despite contractual language to the contrary, an agent may be regarded as the employee of the principal. In such cases, the employer may be required to give notice before termination. Similarly, other benefits of the local labor law, which often may be available to the agent, include the requirement to pay a lump sum termination indemnity.

---

[20] *See* the Foreign Corrupt Practices Act of 1977, 15 U.S.C.A. 78a Note, 78m, 78dd-1, 78dd-2, 78ff.

[21] *See generally,* Vorbrugg and Mahler, "Agency and Distributorship Agreements under German Law," 19 Int'l L. 607 (1985); Sales, "Termination of Sales Agents and Distributors in France," 17 Int'l L. 741 (1983); Simons, "Termination of Sales Agents and Distributors in Belgium,"17 Int'l L. 752 (1983); Juncadella, "Agency, Distributions and Representation Contracts in Central America and Panama," 6 Law. Am. 35 (1974); Cowles, "Indemnities for Terminating Foreign Representatives," 53 B.U.L. Rev. 278 (1973); Jones, "Practical Aspects of Commercial Agency and Distribution Agreements in the European Community," 27 Bus. Law. 543 (1972).

Irrespective of labor codes, some countries have enacted specific protective legislation which places restrictions on the termination of local agents.[22] Such legislation may require the payment of a termination indemnity usually based upon the duration of the agency relationship. The extent to which protective legislation is waivable or contractually avoidable varies widely.

The degree of protection granted a local agent is often dependant upon the classification of the relationship under local law. In France, for example, non-renewal of a commercial agent's contract does not give rise to an indemnity, whereas the non-renewal of a "VRP's" contract does. The extent of compensation varies widely as well. It should be noted that the amount of compensation is usually determined by the case law, and greatly exceeds statutory minimums.

Moreover, there are international moves toward unifying protective agency legislation. The European Economic Council, as a part of the EEC efforts to harmonize the commercial law of its member countries, has proposed draft legislation[23] which would require either notice for the termination of an agent in the EEC or the payment of a commission in lieu of notice. The draft also provides for the payment of a goodwill indemnity where agents have increased a principal's business or have brought new customers to the principal. Unlike some dealer termination laws, the draft EEC legislation is not specifically aimed at foreign principals.

[c]   Representation Agreement Form

The form which follows is intended to be read in conjunction with the preceding text. A number of assumptions are

---

[22] Such countries include Austria, Bahrain, Brazil, Colombia, Costa Rica, Dominican Republic, El Salvador, France, Federal Republic of Germany, Guatemala, Honduras, Italy, Jordan, Kuwait, Lebanon, Luxembourg, Morocco, Netherlands, Nicaragua, Norway, Oman, Panama, Puerto Rico, Spain, Sweden, Switzerland, and the United Arab Emirates (Abu Dhabi and Dubai).

[23] Text published in the Official Journal of the European Communities of January 18, 1977, No. C 13, page 2. Vanderhaege and Jones, "Current Developments in European Agency Law," 12 Int'l Law. 671 (1978).

made which may not be applicable to particular arrangements. For example, there is no provision for service and repair by the representative, no reference to competing products and the agreement is non-exclusive. Representation agreements for the sale of products to governments customarily contain provisions relating to the representative's specific services with respect to local officials.

REPRESENTATION AGREEMENT

This Agreement made as of the _____ day of _____ 19 ____, between _____ (hereinafter referred to as "Company") and _____ (hereinafter referred to as "Representative"),

WITNESSES THAT

WHEREAS, Company is organized for the purpose, among other things, of the international sale of its products and,

WHEREAS, Company believes that such sales can best be accomplished in the Republic of Ruritania (hereinafter referred to as the "Territory") by the appointment of a non-exclusive representative, and

WHEREAS, Representative desires to be Company's non-exclusive representative in the Territory.

THE PARTIES AGREE AS FOLLOWS:

APPOINTMENT

1. a) Subject to the terms and conditions of this Agreement and subject to such implementing rules and instructions as Company may issue from time to time, Company hereby appoints Representative its non-exclusive representative in the Territory for those products identified in Schedule 1 of this Agreement (hereinafter referred to as the "Products").
   b) Unless terminated sooner pursuant to Article 7 hereof, this Agreement shall have a term of three years. Thereafter, either party may terminate the Agreement upon written notice to the other party of not less than 180 days.

COMPENSATION

2. a) As consideration for its services hereunder and in reimburse-
        ment of all costs and expenses incurred by it pursuant to this
        Agreement, and for such additional services as may be agreed
        to by the parties, Representative shall receive, on orders
        placed by customers within the Territory, a fee of ____% cal-
        culated on the FOB (port of shipment) price of the Products,
        after full payment has been received by Company for the
        Products sold.
    b) (1) Company shall pay the above-mentioned fee to Represent-
        ative in (currency) by bank transfer, check, or other accepta-
        ble means, which shall be effected in compliance with any
        exchange control regulations or other applicable laws of the
        Territory within thirty (30) days after receipt by Company of
        any payment from a customer upon which the fee is to be
        calculated as owing to Representative. Payment will be made
        to Representative at the address stated herein as Representa-
        tive's principal place of business, which Representative repre-
        sents is the country from which it regularly and normally
        conducts its business.
        (2) No fee shall be due and owing by Company to Representa-
        tive on any sale of the Products by Company for which full
        payment has not been received.

OBLIGATIONS AND SERVICES OF REPRESENTIVE

3. a) Representative shall use its best efforts actively and effectively
        to enhance the reputation of Company within the Territory,
        and to maintain good relations with customers and potential
        customers during the term of this Agreement.
    b) Representative shall, on request, report fully and promptly to
        Company on the sales activities of competitors of Company,
        and advise on sales and marketing strategies.
    c) Representative shall maintain communications throughout
        the term of this Agreement with designated personnel of
        Company in order to facilitate the promotion and sale of the
        Products.
    d) Representative shall send to Company not later than thirty
        (30) days after the end of each calendar quarter a full report
        relating to Representative's activities pursuant to this Agree-
        ment during that quarter.
    e) Representative shall take such action as may be required and
        shall perform such services as may be necessary to enable

Company to obtain and keep current all applicable government licenses, permits, and approvals, including any registration of this Agreement, which are necessary or advisable for Company to carry out its activities with respect to the Products in the Territory.

f) Representative shall comply with all laws and regulations of the Territory as may be applicable to this Agreement and to all transactions and activities to be performed hereunder (unless such compliance would be contrary to, or cause Company to incur financial detriment under the laws of the United States; and shall keep Company informed of any laws or regulations of the Territory which may affect the promotion, sale, services, or maintenance of the Products in order that Company will not violate any such laws or regulations through ignorance thereof.

g) Representative shall render such other additional services in furtherance of its obligations hereby created as may reasonably request, including, but not limited to, the collection of any accounts in the Territory which are delinquent.

h) Representative shall give Company access at reasonable times to any business premises of Representative in order that Company may inspect same and verify compliance by Representative with its obligations under this Agreement.

EXPENSES

4. Representative shall be solely responsible for all its expenses in its performance of this Agreement, except as may otherwise be agreed with Company in writing. Any claim for reimbursement of expenses specifically assumed in advance by Company shall be accompanied by a detailed description of such expenses and a copy of the Company letter authorizing such expenditure.

ASSISTANCE OF COMPANY

5. a) Company shall provide Representative with reasonable amounts of such sales literature, advertising and other promotional materials as Company has prepared for the Products. Representative will be responsible for the expense of any translation, reproduction and printing necessary to make the data suitable for use in the Territory.

b) Company shall provide to Representative the assistance of Company's employees as may in the judgement of Company be required from time to time to assist in the promotion and sale of the Products.

REPRESENTATIONS OF REPRESENTATIVE

6. a) Representative represents and warrants that:

   (1) any fees paid by Company to Representative shall be for actual services rendered and no part of any fees and expenses paid to Representative by Company will be paid to or accrue for the benefit of, directly or indirectly, anyone who is an official, agent, or employee of, or in any manner connected with, any government or governmental entity in the Territory or any political subdivision thereof, or who is an officer, agent, or employee of a political party or who is a candidate for political office, or who is a director, officer, employee or shareholder of any private customer or prospective customer, or when such payment or accrual would be illegal under the applicable laws of the United States or the Territory;

   (2) neither this Agreement, the relationship created hereby, nor the performance hereof is contrary to the current laws, rules or regulations of the Territory.

   b) If Representative's representations and warranties under Article 6. a) of this Agreement are breached, this Agreement will be null and void and any fees then owed to Representative shall be forfeited by Representative and no further payments shall be made for Representative's account.

TERMINATION

7. a) Notwithstanding Article 1 b) hereof, if any of the sovereign entities or political subdivisions in the Territory enacts legislation relating to the relationship created by this Agreement which grants rights to Representative which are not granted by this Agreement, this Agreement shall terminate automatically one day prior to the date such legislation becomes effective.

   b) Notwithstanding Article 1 b) hereof, either party may terminate this Agreement by written notice effective immediately if the other party makes any extraordinary arrangement with its creditors generally, commits an act of bankruptcy, goes into liquidation or winding-up, has execution or distress levied upon any of its assets, or becomes unable to pay its debts, including its debts to the other party, as they fall due. Such party shall promptly and fully inform the other party of the imminence or occurrence of any event described in paragraph b) of this Article.

c) Notwithstanding Article 1 b) hereof, either party may terminate this Agreement upon thirty (30) days written notice to the other party in the event of a material default in the performance of the Agreement by such other party.

d) Notwithstanding Article 1 b) hereof, Company may terminate Representative's right to represent Company for certain of the Products and Representative's right to certain parts of the Territory as its area of primary responsibility for any reason upon ninety (90) days' written notice at any time.

e) Upon termination of this Agreement in any manner, the following provisions shall take effect:

    i.   All rights granted to Representative under or pursuant to this Agreement shall cease, and where appropriate, revert to their owner;

    ii.   Representative shall immediately cease acting on behalf of Company and shall cease its activities concerning the Products. Representative also promptly shall return all sales literature, sales brochures, samples, and other materials or facilities furnished by Company for the use of Representative hereunder;

    iii.   The provisions of this Agreement which are expressed to survive this Agreement or to apply notwithstanding termination hereof shall be observed by Representative.

TERMINATION—LIMITATION OF LIABILITY

8. Upon the termination of this Agreement in any manner and for any reason, neither party shall be liable to the other party, either for fees, expenses, other compensation, or damages of any kind or character whatsoever, whether on account of the loss by Company or Representative of present or prospective profits or fees on sales or anticipated sales, or expenditures, investments, or commitments made in connection therewith, or in connection with the establishment, development, or maintenance of the business of any party, or on account of any other cause or thing whatsoev-

er, provided that such termination shall not prejudice or otherwise affect the rights or liabilities of any party with respect to:

    i.   the Products theretofore sold by Company hereunder,
except that any such rights of Representative to compensation for Products sold shall apply only to sums
received by Company for a period of 12 months after
the date of any termination, or

    ii.   any indebtedness owing by either party to the other
party at the time of termination.

INFRINGEMENT OF PATENTS

9. (Patent Protection Clause)

TRADEMARKS

10. (Trademark Protection Clause)

CONFIDENTIALITY

11. Representative shall treat as confidential and appropriately safeguard both during the life of this Agreement and thereafter until
such time as the information properly comes into the public domain technical information identified as confidential and all information pertaining to Company or any part of Company's pricing,
business or assets which are received at any time from Company
for the purpose of this Agreement.

FORCE MAJEURE

12. Neither party shall be liable to the other party for any loss, damage, delay or failure of performance resulting directly or indirectly from any cause beyond its reasonable control, including force
majeure, strikes, or the laws, regulations, acts, or failure to act of
any governmental authority.

DISCLOSURE

13. This Agreement may be discussed with, shown to, and filed with
any governmental agency or official as determined to be appropriate by either party.

DISPUTE SETTLEMENT

14. This Agreement (is made and) shall be construed (interpreted)
according to the laws of (state), and any controversy arising under

or in relation to this Agreement shall be settled (by arbitration to be held) in (place and state). The courts and authorities of (state) shall have exclusive jurisdiction over all controversies which may arise under or in relation to this Agreement, especially with respect to the execution, interpretation, and compliance of this Agreement, the parties hereto waiving any other venue to which they might be entitled by virtue of domicile, habitual residence or otherwise.

AGREEMENT INCLUSIVE

15. This Agreement covers all contracts and agreements relating to the Territory between the parties relating to the subject matter hereof. All other contracts between the parties which relate to the subject matter of this Agreement are hereby terminated. In order to be binding upon Company or Representative any amendment, modification supplementation, extension, renewal, ratification, recision, discharge, abandonment or waiver of this Agreement, or any of the provisions hereof, must be in writing signed by the party sought to be bound.

ASSIGNMENT

16. Neither party shall, directly or indirectly (whether by succession, amalgamation, merger, or otherwise), assign this Agreement or any of its rights or obligations hereunder, without the prior written approval of the other. Representative shall not appoint subrepresentatives without the prior written permission of Company.

WAIVER OF BREACH

17. No waiver of breach of any of the provisions of this Agreement shall be construed to be a waiver of any succeeding breach of the same or any other provision.

LANGUAGE

18. The English language text, and American usage thereof, shall control the interpretation of this Agreement and of all other writings between the parties.

NOTICES

19. Any notice, demand, acknowledgement or other communication which under the terms of this Agreement or otherwise must be given or made by either party shall, unless specifically otherwise provided in this Agreement, be in writing and shall be given or made by telegram, telex or similar communication or by certified or registered mail addressed to the respective parties as follows:

To Representative:

To Company:

Such notice, demand, acknowledgement or other communication shall be deemed to have been given or made in the case of telegram or similar communication when sent and in the case of certified or registered mail when deposited postage prepaid in the mail. The above addresses may be changed at any time by giving thirty (30) days prior written notice as above provided.

IN WITNESS WHEREOF, the parties have respectively signed this Agreement as of the day and year first written above.

[2] Distributorships

The appointment of a distributor[24] usually represents an involvement in a foreign market by a U.S. manufacturer, and

---

[24] *See generally* Emory, "Checklist for International Distribution Contracts," 7 Int'l Lawyer's Newsletter No. 1 (1985); Vorbrugg and Mahler, *supra* N. 21; Simons, *supra* N. 21; Simeon, Moquet, Borde & Associés, *supra* N. 12.1; B. Rüster, *supra* N. 12; Bauman, "International Sales Representation and Distributorship Agreements," 3 N.C.J. Int'l L. & Com. Reg. 141 (1978); "Negotiating Distributorship Contracts and Licensing Agreements," in D. Nelson and R. Rendell, *Legal Aspects of Exporting* (PLI 1978); Juncadella, "Agency, Distribution and Representation Contracts in Central America and Panama," 6 Law. Am. 35 (1974); Cowles, "Indemnities for Terminating Foreign Representatives," 53 B.U.L. Rev. 278 (1973); Jones, "Practical Aspects of Commercial Agency and Distribution Agreements in the European Community," 27 Bus. Law. 543 (1972); Moore, "Agreements for the Transmission of Technology Abroad: The Distributor Relationship," 45 Denver L.J. 43 (1968); Meek, "Overseas Distributorship Agreements," 21 Bus. Law. 661 (1966); Johnson, "International Distributorship and Agency Agreements," in Southwestern Legal Foundation, *Negotiating and Drafting International Commercial Contracts* (1966).

certainly by the distributor, which is appreciably more extensive than the involvement represented by making simple export sales or by appointing an agent. Since a distributor takes title to goods and maintains an inventory, a substantial financial investment must often be made. A financial investment is particularly necessary for distributors of technologically sophisticated products for which installation and maintenance constitute an important aspect of the business, necessitating the expensive training of service employees, often at locations in the U.S. In return for this investment, the foreign distributor customarily receives the exclusive right to sell the U.S. manufacturer's products within a foreign geographic area: a right which has considerable value.

The decision to appoint a foreign distributor is often made to avoid a financial investment by the U.S. manufacturer or to avoid the active management of a foreign operation. These are by no means the only criteria, however. As is the case with all forms of overseas business organization, the distributorship may be mandated by local governmental policies. Moreover, direct operations in some countries are so difficult due to local commercial, labor, or logistical conditions that distributorships are the only practical means of doing business. U.S. manufacturers often increase their participation in such markets by the use of management and technical assistance agreements under which the U.S. manufacturer contributes those services to the distributorship in return for a fee.

The sections which follow discuss the principal legal considerations pertinent to the appointment of a foreign distributor. Since sales to foreign distributors are transnational sales to an unrelated entity, the legal considerations relevant to all transnational sales should thus be considered in regard to sales to distributors. A form of a distributorship agreement is included at the end of the section.

[a] Nature of the Relationship

In international commercial parlance the distinction between an agent or representative on the one hand and a distributor on the other is clearly drawn, despite the facts that the word "distributor" is not explicitly defined in U.S. legal terminology, and that some major U.S. multinationals refer to their foreign distributors as "agents." The legal distinction is not unlike the Securities Act distinction between "brokers" and "dealers."[25] A foreign agent or representative does not take title to goods, and merely receives a commission on sales made by his principal as a result of the agent's efforts. A distributor, however, is an independent contractor who purchases for his own account and bears the risk of the subsequent disposition of the goods.[26] In Anglo-American commercial usage, the "dealer" and "distributor" are synonymous. The nature of the relationship created should be explicitly stated in an instrument which appoints a distributor for two basic reasons: first, legislation which protects local agents and distributors in countries which have such legislation often provides for different protection for agents and distributors. Since agents are often afforded greater protection, U.S. manufacturers should make a distributor's status very clear. Second, an important motivation for the choice of a distributor, as opposed to an agent, is the fact that a distributor cannot contractually commit a U.S. manufacturer and consequently has to bear the risk of subsequent sales and relations with foreign purchasers.

---

[25] 15 U.S.C. Section 78C(a)(4) and (5).

[26] " 'Distributor' means a person who buys goods and resells them on his own account independently of the person selling the goods to him." Drysdale and Stephens-Ofner, "Distributorship and Agency Agreements," 1973 New L. J. at 728, citing Lamb v. Goring, [1932] 1 KB 710 at 716–722. The German Federal Supreme Court in 1970 said, "a distributorship agreement is a contract of a special nature for a specified or unspecified period, by which one party (the dealer or distributor) undertakes to sell the goods of another (the manufacturer or supplier) in his own name and on his own account, and by which the dealer is integrated into the sales organization of the manufacturer." F. Staubach, *The German Law of Agency and Distributorship Agreements* 229 (1977).

[b] Exclusivity

While some distribution arrangements are non-exclusive, the granting of an exclusive distributorship for a particular country is the more common situation. Territorial exclusivity is a two-headed coin. It protects the foreign distributor from competition within the territory and also protects other distributors, and, indeed, a U.S. manufacturer's own selling organizations in other territories from competition from the distributor. The latter situation is usually not a major consideration since most U.S. manufacturers charge a higher price to distributors than to their own selling organizations. Furthermore, the additional freight and customs associated with two export transactions make export sales by distributors uncompetitive. The situation can arise, however, as a result of regional integration where countries within a group have lower tariffs among themselves than with the United States; disparate corporate income tax rates; and varying prices charged by U.S. manufacturers for the same product abroad.

Exclusivity may be enforced by a variety of means. Sales outside a distributor's territory may be defined as an incident which allows a U.S. manufacturer to terminate a distributorship agreement, but such a provision may be unenforceable in a particular country, or even prohibited under the antitrust or other laws of a given jurisdiction. There are U.S. antitrust considerations of exclusive territories,[27] and the anti-monopoly law of the European Economic Community (Article 85(1) of the Treaty of Rome) can in many circumstances severely restrict or prohibit exclusive territories unless exempted.[28] Some

---

[27] The U.S. Department of Justice has indicated that exclusive foreign territories without some further anticompetitive conduct are permissible where the foreign distributors who have exclusive rights in those territories are not competitors of the U.S. supplier. U.S. Dep't of Justice, *Antitrust Guide for International Operations* (1977) 46.

[28] *See infra* § 9.03[2][d]; V. Korah, in *Introductory Guide to EEC Competition Law and Practice* 62-70 (2d ed. 1981); B. Hawk, *United States, Common Market and International Antitrust: A Comparative Guide*, 577-594 (1979); Salzman, "Analogies Between United States and Common Market Antitrust Law in the Field of Distribution," 13 Int'l Law. 47 (1979); Osterweil, "Developing EEC Antitrust Law in the Field of Distribution under Article 85 of the Treaty of Rome," 8 Law & Pol. Int'l Bus. 77 (1976).

2-23

national laws restrict exclusivity. French law, for example, restricts exclusive distributorships to a period of ten years.[28.1] A less drastic method to ensure some degree of exclusivity is to contractually require that some or all of the sales price of goods sold outside a distributor's territory be paid to the distributor or company organization having the exclusive right to sell in that territory.[29] Noncompetition within a territory is related to exclusivity, and in this regard reasonable agreements by distributors not to sell competing products during the life of an agreement are enforceable in most jurisdictions.

[c] Payments

United States manufacturers understandably desire to be paid in U.S. currency, and an instrument appointing a distributor should so specify. Payment terms may be specifically addressed in a distributorship agreement or left to the discretion of the U.S. manufacturer. Since manufacturers often grant increasingly more lenient terms of payment as their relationships with distributors mature, some degree of flexibility should be given to the manufacturer in a distributorship agreement. The customary payment methods seem to be by open account or by a blanket letter of credit opened by the distributor.

[d] Prices

Foreign distributors often desire some sort of protection against major price increases which could render their distributorships uncompetitive. Most U.S. manufacturers insist upon the absolute right to alter their prices at their discretion. Some degree of relief may be afforded to the distributor by a

---

[28.1] Ordonnance N° 45-1438 of 30 June, 1945; Carbonneau, "Exclusive Distributors in French Law," 28 Int'l & Comp. L.Q. 91, 96 (1979).

[29] It should be noted, however, that conduct which significantly limits reexports to the United States could pose U.S. antitrust problems. *Antitrust Guide, supra* N. 27, at 48.

provision exempting orders already placed from higher prices, or by a notice requirement for price changes. Fixing the price at which a foreign distributor may resell a product does not seem to be prohibited by U.S. laws,[30] but is prohibited by the domestic laws of some countries.[31] Furthermore, fixing the resale price raises the possibility of a distributor's being characterized as an agent under the domestic law of some jurisdictions.

[e] Termination

Instruments appointing foreign distributors are in a sense not unlike antenuptial agreements; a divorce should be considered before a marriage is performed. A careful consideration of the termination provisions of such an instrument, as well as the effects of local law are perhaps the most important contributions of a counsel.

A distributorship agreement can, by its terms, provide a number of protections for a U.S. manufacturer, but such provisions may sometimes be nullified by the domestic law of the country in which a foreign distributor is located. Distributors are often understandably reluctant to make a major investment if their right to a product line may be contractually terminated at the will of a manufacturer. U.S. firms, on the other hand, perceive the need to retain flexibility, and are reluctant to wed themselves to an unproven foreign distributor for more than a trial period, particularly in light of the onerous protective statutes present in some countries. A common compromise is the granting of a term during which a manufacturer may not terminate the relationship absent the occurrence of certain events. Aside from the expected incidents of termination (default and bankruptcy) a U.S. manufac-

---

[30] Hawk, *supra* N. 28, at 195.

[31] French law, for example, absolutely prohibits the practice in the absence of an individual exemption. Article 37(4) of Price Ordinance No. 45-1483 of 30 June, 1945. German law permits recommendations in the case of brand name products, but prohibits contractual resale price maintenance. Sections 15 and 38(a) Gesetz gegen Wettbewerbsbeschränkungen of 1957.

turer may protect itself by requiring that certain standards be met. These can include sales quotas, required sales growth increments and defined promotional activities by the distributor.

From the perspective of a U.S. manufacturer, it is important that a distributorship agreement eliminate the possibility of a distributor becoming a competitor after termination of the agreement. To this end it is advisable that a distributorship agreement give the U.S. manufacturer the right to re-purchase a distributor's inventory upon termination.

Drafters of distributorship agreements should consider including contractual provisions which give the U.S. manufacturer the power to bring about at least a partial termination of the distributorship relation aside from a formal termination clause. Such provisions include an express negation of any obligation of the manufacturer to accept orders, the right of the manufacturer to modify the extent of a distributor's territory or the number of products covered by the agreement, and even making the distributorship non-exclusive.

As in the cases of agents and representatives, the accusation has often been made abroad that foreign suppliers appoint distributors as a means of initially entering a market, and terminate them after the distributor has developed the market to a degree sufficient to induce the foreign supplier to wish to operate in it directly. Partly as a response to this accusation, the law of some countries can affect or supersede the contractual agreement between a U.S. manufacturer and a distributor located in those countries.[32]

The ways foreign law affects the termination provisions of distributorship agreements can be roughly divided into four categories of countries. First, the law of those countries with a common law tradition is normally based upon freedom of

---

[32] Countries which have legislation or judicial doctrines which substantially affect distributorship terminations include Bahrain, Belguim, Brazil, Columbia, Costa Rica, Dominican Republic, El Salvador, Federal Republic of Germany, Guatemala, Honduras, Nicaragua, Panama, Puerto Rico, Lebanon, Oman, and the United Arab Emirates. Countries which have less stringent legislation or judicial doctrines regarding distributorship terminations include Austria, the Netherlands, Norway, Philippines, Switzerland, Thailand and Turkey.

contract and has no effect. Second, although freedom of contract is the general basis of the civil law of contract, the law of some countries requires that compensation be given a terminated distributor if the termination is "abusive." This abusiveness is sometimes more readily found by foreign courts than by U.S. courts.[33] Similarly, some civil law jurisdictions expressly require that a prescribed notice be given to a distributor prior to termination, and in others the granting of a reasonable notice of termination is itself sufficient to avoid "abusiveness."

The law of a third group of countries is likely to require the payment of an indemnity, which can be substantial, to terminated distributors based upon their juridical characterization as something other than distributors. Distributors can be found to be agents of their foreign suppliers or even their employees. The effect of the former situation is to bring distributors under the umbrella of legislation designed to protect local agents.[34] Since there are a number of countries which provide legislative protection to agents and not to distributors, such a characterization can have severe financial results for the foreign manufacturer. The characterization of a distributor as an agent can arise as a result of the perhaps unintentional lack of differentiation in some foreign agency legislation between agents and distributors.[35] More significantly, it can arise from the nature of the distributor's relations with the supplier, *i.e.*, when a distributor is subordinate to, under the control of, or dependent upon a supplier.[36]

The labor laws of many European and Latin American coun-

---

[33] Jones, *supra* N. 24, at 553.

[34] *See* text at § 2.02[2], *supra*.

[35] The agency legislation of Oman, for example, treats agents and distributors identically. Spoliansky, "Modern Business Law in the Sultanate of Oman," 13 Int'l Law. 101, at 112 (1979). In many Middle Eastern countries the term "agent" encompasses the distributor relationship or is ambiguous. United Arab Emirates Federal Act No. 18 of 1981 defines a "commercial agency" as the "representation of the principal by an agent for distribution, sale, display or provision of any commodity or service within the state in consideration of any commission or profit."

[36] Staubach, *supra* N. 12, at 240. In some countries a supplier's requirment that stated hours of work be maintained by a distributor is sufficient to create a subordinate relationship.

tries require that employees be given a lump sum payment upon termination of their employment, sometimes even if this termination is made by the employee. The size of this payment is customarily based upon the length of an employee's service. Some Latin American countries treat local distributors as employees for purposes of these termination indemnities if certain employment-like elements in the distributor/manufacturer relationship are present. These elements are as a rule the existence of the above mentioned subordinate relationship, the receipt by the distributor of remuneration which resembles a salary, and the rendering by the distributor of services for the supplier.[37] It should be noted that countries which tend to treat distributors as employees do so only in the case of distributors who are natural persons. The use of a corporate form by a distributor thus generally eliminates the potential application of a country's labor laws.[38]

A fourth group of countries has enacted legislation which provides protection for local distributors. These statutes customarily provide for the payment of indemnities if a termination does not meet certain standards. If a manufacturer/distributor relationship has existed for some time, the indemnities can be so large as to effectively prohibit the termination of the local distributor. The distributor protection statute of Costa Rica[39] is one of the most stringent of such statutes, and since it contains most of the elements found in other terminations statutes, an examination of its provisions seems useful. The statute, which is non-waivable, requires that an indemnity equal to four months' average gross profit for each year or fraction thereof that a distributor agreement has been in force be paid to a distributor in the event of a unilateral termination by a foreign supplier, or in the event of the refusal of a foreign supplier to renew a distributorship agreement for a definite

---

[37] Meek, *supra* N. 24, at 665.

[38] *Id.*

[39] Costa Rican Law No. 6209 of April 3, 1978. "Law for the Protection of Representatives of Foreign Firms." The statute applies to agents and representatives as well as to distributors.

term at the expiration of that term.[40] The maximum indemnity is nine years' average gross profit of the distributor. Moreover, foreign suppliers must re-purchase the inventory of terminated distributors at prices determined by the Costa Rican government.[41]

A Costa Rican distributor may terminate a distributorship agreement and claim compensation for a variety of reasons including:

a. The placement of "unjustified" sales restrictions on the distributor.
b. The unilateral modification by a foreign supplier of the distributorship agreement if the local distributor is injured thereby.
c. Any "serious offense" that damages the legal rights of the local distributor.[42]

A foreign supplier may avoid application of the statute only for "just cause," a concept present in most foreign protective statutes. Situations creating "just cause" include:

a. Crimes committed by the distributor against the foreign supplier.
b. The judicial declaration (by a Costa Rican Court) of negligence or ineptitude on the part of the distributor if sales are stagnant or decreasing. The use of quotas by a foreign supplier can provide the basis of a prima facie case of the absence of negligence or ineptitude.
c. Breach of the obligation of confidence by a distributor.[43]

The application of the Costa Rican statute seems to be virtually impossible to avoid contractually, but there are contractual provisions which may render inapplicable, or at least

---

[40] *Id.*, Article 2.
[41] *Id.*, Article 3.
[42] *Id.*, Article 4.
[43] *Id.*, Article 5.

ameliorate, the effect of both foreign protective statutes and foreign judicial doctrines in other countries. These include:

a. The inclusion of a notice period for unilateral termination. Such periods are often required by statute or judicial doctrine.

b. The insistance by a U.S. manufacturer of the use of the corporate form by foreign distributors.

c. A contractual provision for the automatic termination of the distributorship agreement one day before the effective date of a new protective statute in the country of the distributor.

d. A specific contractual list of obligations of a distributor which, if not met, may be used to define "just cause." Such a list may include sales quotas or objectives.

e. The express waiver by the distributor of the benefits of local protective legislation.

f. The choice of the law of the country of the foreign manufacturer, or of a third country which does not have protective legislation or judicial doctrine.

g. The use of an indefinite term, or a specific term. The laws of some countries are by their terms inapplicable to contracts of indefinite term or contracts for a specific term.

h. The use of a provision that requires that enhancements to the value of a distributor's goodwill inure to the benefit of the foreign manufacturer.

i. The use of a provision expressly stipulating that the foreign distributor is neither the employee nor the agent of the U.S. manufacturer.

j. The appointment of a non-exclusive distributor. Some foreign termination laws only apply to exclusive distributorships. Furthermore, the right to appoint a second distributor can obviate the necessity of terminating a distributorship agreement in the first place.

k. The express provision for the existence and amount of a termination indemnity.

Obviously, the efficacy of any of the above methods will vary from country to country, and the laws of each country must be carefully examined prior to the negotiation of a distributorship agreement.

[f] International Distributorship Agreement Form

The form which follows is intended to be read in conjunction with the preceding text. The form makes a number of assumptions which may not be valid for a particular appointment, and is intended to provide a significant degree of flexibility for the manufacturer. For example, implementing rules are permitted to be made by the manufacturer, the manufacturer retains the right to reject orders for any reason, and the general terms of sale are placed in an easily modified schedule. Local law must be carefully examined, however, to ascertain whether such flexibility may create a dependent status and thus subject a U.S. manufacturer to termination indemnities.

Since the agreement requires the distributor to provide service for the products it distributes, it provides for a specific term during which the manufacturer may not terminate the relationship absent a breach of the agreement by the distributor. Where a distributor is not required to perform service activities (and is not required to make a substantial investment in the distributorship), the mutual right to terminate the agreement upon a relatively short notice should be considered.

DISTRIBUTORSHIP AGREEMENT

This Agreement made as of the _____ day of _____, 19 ____ between _____ (hereinafter referred to as "Company") and _____ (hereinafter referred to as "Distributor"),

Witnesses that

WHEREAS, Company is organized for the purpose, among other things, of the international sale of its products and,

WHEREAS, Company believes that such sales can best be accomplished in the Republic of Ruritania (hereinafter referred to as the "Territory") by the appointment of an exclusive distributor, and

WHEREAS, Distributor desires to be Company's exclusive distributor in the Territory.

The parties agree as follows:

APPOINTMENT

1. a. Subject to the terms and conditions of this Agreement and subject to such implementing rules and instructions as Company may issue from time to time, Company hereby appoints Distributor its exclusive distributor in the Territory for those products identified in Schedule 1 of this Agreement (hereinafter referred to as the "Products").
   b. Unless terminated sooner pursuant to Article 15 hereof, this Agreement shall have a term of three years. Thereafter, either party may terminate the agreement upon written notice to the other party of not less than 180 days.
   c. The rights granted to Distributor under this Agreement are personal in character and are not assignable without the written consent of Company. Any attempted assignment absent the written consent of Company shall be void. Distributor shall inform Company of its underlying ownership structure at every level, and shall give Company prior notification of all changes in excess of 5 percent in any calendar year at any level of its ownership structure in a manner such that Company will at all times be fully aware of the actual ownership and control of Distributor at each tier in any ownership hierarchy which may exist.

NO AGENCY CREATED

2. The relationship of the parties under this Agreement shall be and at all times remain one of independent contractors, and Distributor is neither an employee nor an agent of Company. Distributor shall have no authority to assume or create obligations on Company's behalf with respect to the Products or otherwise, and shall not take any action which has the effect of creating the appearance of its having such authority.

ORDERS

3. a. Company shall fill with all practicable dispatch all orders which it accepts under this Agreement, but reserves the right to reject any orders for any reason.

   b. Distributor shall reimburse Company for any additional costs incurred by Company for Products ordered by Distributor which are ordered changed or cancelled by Distributor after the manufacturing process of Products has begun.

   c. Company shall not be liable to Distributor for any delay in filling orders, due to causes beyond its reasonable control including, by way of example but not limited to, delays caused by force majeure, strikes, backlog of prior orders, and delay in payments by Distributor.

   d. All Products shall be sold upon Company's terms and conditions of sale in force at the date of acceptance of the relevant order, subject only to the provisions of this Agreement which shall prevail in the event of any inconsistency between this Agreement and those terms and conditions. The terms and conditions currently in force are attached hereto as Schedule 2. Company shall give written notice of not less than thirty days of any change to such Schedule.

   e. Subject to such limitations as are imposed by this Agreement, Distributor may specify the time of shipment and destination of any Products ordered.

PRICES

4. The prices to be paid by Distributor for Products purchased pursuant to this Agreement shall be those established by Company from time to time. Company shall give Distributor reasonable notice of any changes in such prices.

PAYMENTS

5. Distributor shall promptly make all payments due under this Agreement by certified irrevocable letter of credit guaranteed by a U.S. bank, or upon such other terms as may be determined by mutual agreement. Payments for Products shall be made in U.S. Dollars, or otherwise as may be determined by mutual agreement.

TITLE TO PRODUCTS

6. Unless otherwise agreed by the parties in writing, on all sales by Company to Distributor the parties shall designate on each order a point at which the beneficial and legal title to, ownership of, right to possession of and control over, and risks of loss and damage to, all Products sold by Company to Distributor under a particular order shall pass.

OBLIGATIONS OF DISTRIBUTOR

7. Distributor shall:
   a. Use its best efforts to promote and expand the sale of Products within the Territory;
   b. Maintain an adequate business location, together with an adequate storage facility for the Products;
   c. Maintain adequate stock levels;
   d. Maintain a competent sales personnel to solicit orders for the sale of the Products within the Territory;
   e. Maintain an advertising program for the Products. No advertising and promotional materials shall be used by Distributor, however, prior to Distributor's receipt of Company's prior written approval of such materials;
   f. Comply with all applicable laws and regulations in the Territory unless such compliance would be contrary to, or cause Company to incur financial detriment under U.S. law; and comply, without limitation, with any requirements for the registration or recording of this Agreement with governmental entities in the Territory;
   g. Arrange for and ensure the prompt and efficient maintenance and warranty replacement or repair, subject to the liabilities of Company under its product warranty, of all Company's Products sold by Distributor, and maintain the necessary maintenance and repair personnel, and stock levels of spare parts to enable Distributor to perform such maintenance services effectively;
   h. Give proper consideration and weight to the interests of Company in all dealings and abide by any proper and reasonable rules or instructions notified by Company to Distributor;
   i. Prepare and provide Company with such reports of Distributor's activities in furtherance of Company's business in the Territory as Company may reasonably request;
   j. Not take any action which will cause Company to be in violation of any law of any jurisdiction in the Territory or the

United States including but not limited to the U.S. Foreign Corrupt Practices Act of 1977, the U.S. Export Control laws and the U.S. Anti-Boycott laws;

k. Provide requested data in reasonable detail on the overall marketplace, market segments, market potentials, and other information as an aid in measuring Company's potential and planning its efforts in the Territory;

l. Meet the sales objectives identified in Schedule 3 to this Agreement. *(Optional)*

SALES OUTSIDE THE TERRITORY AND COMPETITIVE SALES

8. a. Although Distributor is not prohibited from selling in other areas, it is mutually understood and agreed that Company's policy may be to require that some or all of the price of Products sold by Distributor outside the Territory be paid to the person whose area of primary responsibility is such area outside the Territory. It is further understood and agreed that in such event Company's policy shall also be to require that Distributor be paid some or all of the price of Products sold by other persons in the Territory.

b. Absent the written consent of Company, Distributor shall not itself, or in association with others, sell or assist in the sale of any new or used products of the kind described in Schedule 1 hereof, except those sold to it by Company.

INFRINGEMENT OF PATENTS

9. (Patent Protection Clause.)

TRADEMARKS

10. (Trademark Protection Clause.)

WARRANTY

11. The terms of the warranty which Distributor extends to its customers shall be no less favorable than the warranty terms which Company extends to Distributor for the same Product.

PROMOTIONAL MATERIALS

12. Company shall, at Company's expense, furnish Distributor with such quantities as shall be determined by Company to be reasonable, of standard information and marketing literature in the

English language relating to the Products, and thereafter upon the request and at the expense of Distributor at prices then being charged generally by Company to its distributors plus the costs of shipment. Upon termination of this Agreement, Distributor will return all manuals, product information letters, and similar material supplied to Distributor by Company.

PURCHASES FROM RELATED COMPANIES

13. Company may, from time to time, cause Distributor's purchases of Products to be supplied directly by Company's affiliated companies in the United States or elsewhere.

CONFIDENTIALITY

14. Distributor shall treat as confidential and appropriately safeguard both during the life of this Agreement and thereafter until such time as the information properly comes into the public domain technical information identified as confidential and all information pertaining to Company or any part of Company's pricing, business or assets which are received at any time from Company for the purpose of this Agreement.

TERMINATION

15. a. Notwithstanding Article 1(b) hereof, if any of the sovereign entities or political subdivisions in the Territory enacts legislation relating to the relationship created by this Agreement which grants rights to Distributor which are not granted by this Agreement, this Agreement shall terminate automatically one day prior to the date such legislation becomes effective.

   b. Notwithstanding Article 1(b) hereof, either party may terminate this Agreement by written notice effective immediately if (i) any of the sovereign entities or political subdivisions in the territory, whether by legislation or decree, prevents payments being made pursuant to Article 5 of this agreement or (ii) the other party makes any extraordinary arrangement with its creditors generally, commits an act of bankruptcy, goes into liquidation or winding-up, has execution or distress levied upon any of its assets, or becomes unable to pay its debts, including its debts to the other party, as they fall due. Such party shall promptly and fully inform the other party of the imminence or occurrence of any event described in paragraph (b) of this Article.

c. Notwithstanding Article 1(b) hereof, either party may terminate this Agreement upon thirty (30) days' written notice to the other party in the event of a material default in the performance of the Agreement by such other party.

d. Notwithstanding Article 1(b) hereof, Company may terminate Distributor's right to sell certain of the Products and Distributor's right to certain parts of the Territory as its area of primary responsibility for any reason upon ninety (90) days' written notice at any time.

e. Upon termination of this Agreement in any manner, the following provisions shall take effect:

(i)   All rights granted to Distributor under or pursuant to this Agreement shall cease, and where appropriate, revert to their owner;

(ii)   The provisions of this Agreement which are expressed to survive this Agreement or to apply notwithstanding termination hereof shall be observed by Distributor;

(iii) Company at its option shall have the right to inspect and repurchase all or any Product then owned by Distributor at whichever is the lower of the original price paid by Distributor or Company's export price at the date of termination, less a reasonable inspection and repacking charge. Company shall have the right to assign such option to repurchase to any other person whom it may designate.

In the event of cancellation of part of the Territory, Company's option to repurchase shall refer to those Products located in such part of the Territory. In the event of termination of Distributor's right to certain of the Products, the option to repurchase shall refer to those certain Products.

TERMINATION—LIMITATION OF LIABILITY

16. Upon termination of this Agreement in any manner, neither party shall be liable to the other, either for compensation or for damages of any kind, whether on account of the loss by Company or Distributor of present or prospective profits on present sales or prospective sales, investments or goodwill, and the parties hereby waive any rights which may be granted to them by sovereign entities or political subdivisions in the Territory which are not granted to them by this Agreement. Termination of this Agreement shall not prejudice or otherwise affect the rights or

liabilities of the parties with respect to Products theretofore sold hereunder, or any indebtedness then owing by either party to the other; nor shall this clause relieve the parties of any obligations imposed by provisions of this Agreement which are expressed to survive this Agreement or any liability for damages resulting from a breach of such provisions.

EXPENSES

17. All of the expenses incurred by Distributor relating to the sale of the Products and the provision of related services will be borne by Distributor except as otherwise expressly provided herein or by written instrument signed by Company.

TECHNICAL ASSISTANCE

18. Company will provide or arrange for reasonable amounts of technical assistance and training with regard to sales, installation, maintenance and repair of the Products upon such terms, conditions and prices as the parties shall mutually agree.

TAXES AND OTHER CHARGES

19. Distributor will in all cases be responsible for the payment of all shipping, handling, insurance, brokerages, taxes, customs and other governmental charges however designated imposed in the Territory and other costs and expenses after passage of title.

FORCE MAJEURE

20. Neither party shall be liable to the other party for any loss, damage, delay or failure of performance resulting directly or indirectly from any cause beyond its reasonable control, including force majeure, strikes, or the laws, regulations, acts, or failure to act of any governmental authority.

DISCLOSURE

21. This Agreement may be discussed with, shown to, and filed with any government agency or official as determined to be appropriate by either party.

DISPUTE SETTLEMENT

22. This Agreement (is made and) shall be construed (interpreted) according to the laws of (state), and any controversy arising under

or in relation to this Agreement shall be settled (by arbitration to be held) in (place and state). The courts and authorities of (state) shall have exclusive jurisdiction over all controversies which may arise under or in relation to this Agreement, especially with respect to the execution, interpretation, and compliance of this Agreement, the parties hereto waiving any other venue to which they might be entitled by virtue of domicile, habitual residence or otherwise.

AGREEMENT INCLUSIVE

23. This Agreement covers all contracts and agreements relating to the Territory between the parties relating to the subject matter hereof. All other contracts between the parties which relate to the subject matter of this Agreement are hereby terminated. In order to be binding upon Company or Distributor, any amendment, modification supplementation, extension, renewal, ratification, recision, discharge, abandonment or waiver of this Agreement, or any of the provisions hereof, must be in writing signed by the party sought to be bound.

WAIVER OF BREACH

24. No waiver of breach of any of the provisions of this Agreement shall be construed to be a waiver of any succeeding breach of the same or any other provision.

LANGUAGE

25. The English language text, and American usage thereof, shall control the interpretation of this Agreement and of all other writings between the parties.

NOTICES

26. Any notice, demand, acknowledgment or other communication which under the terms of this Agreement or otherwise must be given or made by either party shall, unless specifically otherwise provided in this Agreement, be in writing and shall be given or made by telegram, telex or similar communication or by certified or registered mail addressed to the respective parties as follows:

To Distributor:

To Company:

Such notice, demand, acknowledgment or other communication shall be deemed to have been given or made in the case of telegram or similar communication when sent and in the case of certified or registered mail when deposited postage prepaid in the mail. The above addresses may be changed at any time by giving thirty (30) days' prior written notice as above provided.

IN WITNESS WHEREOF, the parties have respectively signed this Agreement as of the day and year first written above.

§ 2.03   Forms Involving a Foreign Presence

When activity in a foreign country reaches a relatively high level, the establishment of a legal presence in the country is often desirable or legally required. In this respect it should be noted that many countries permit the physical presence of employees and some commercial activities without the establishment of any local presence. Such exceptions are usually found in statutes, and are often granted to permit the performance of government contracts. The commercial incentive for a foreign presence usually arises from the desire to locate the employees of a U.S. firm abroad or from the preference of the host country itself. The legal incidents of a foreign presence involve the submission of the U.S. firm to general foreign jurisdiction and specifically to foreign taxation. A foreign presence may be established by means of a branch of the U.S. firm or its subsidiary. Also included in this section is a brief discussion of foreign liaison offices, which, strictly speaking, do not involve foreign legal presence, but are a hybrid organizational form allowing certain direct activities in a foreign country without generally subjecting the firm to foreign legal jurisdiction.

[1]   Liaison Offices

Liaison offices are a form of business organization which permits the residence of a foreign company's employees in a country, but which does not submit the foreign company to the general legal jurisdiction of the country in which a liaison office is registered. The establishment of a liaison office does not generally constitute "doing business" in a country, and liaison offices are thus not subject to foreign taxation. Although the extent of activities in which liaison offices may engage varies from country to country depending upon the local law of what constitutes "doing business," countries which provide for them intend that they be used for activities which fall short of "doing business" such as conducting market surveys, quality control, and sales promotion. When sales promotion personnel are housed in a liaison office, they are not usually allowed to book orders or to receive payment for goods sold. In some countries, liaison offices are designed to house personnel who are resident in the country temporarily or itinerantly. Liaison offices are perhaps best seen as short-term vehicles by which the cognizance of a foreign government of relatively limited activities of a U.S. firm is gained.[44]

The registration of a liaison office is customarily simple and inexpensive, involving the submission of information about the registering company and the appointment of a "liaison officer."[45]

---

[44] Article 386 of the Company Law of the Republic of China (Taiwan) requires the filing of a (liaison office) report by "[a] foreign company which has no intention to transact business continuously within the territory of China, has not applied for admission in China, but occasionally sends its representative for the performance of juristic acts in the territory of China." It should be noted however, that the establishment of a liaison office in the ROC may establish the basis of local taxation despite the language of Article 386. The Company Law is contained in D.C.C. Kang, *A Compilation of the Laws of the Republic of China* (1971).

[45] In South Korea, for example, the procedures for the registration of a liaison office are identical to those for the establishment of a branch. The registering company must simply file with the district court in the geographic location of the proposed liaison office, the jurisdiction under which it is organized and the name and residence of the liaison officer. Yoon, "Legal Aspects of Doing Business in and with the Republic of Korea," in J. Haley, ed., *Current Legal Aspects of Doing Business in Japan and East Asia* (1978).

[2] Branches

The simplest method of overseas operation is the establishment of a branch of a U.S. manufacturer in a foreign country. A foreign branch constitutes the direct legal presence of a U.S. company abroad and thus theoretically exposes the company's U.S. assets to the jurisdiction of the foreign country as well as the branch assets to U.S. jurisdiction.[46] Since the jurisdictional reach of U.S. courts seems to exceed that of most foreign countries,[47] the jurisdictional dangers of foreign branches may initially appear greater than reality warrants, at least with respect to the unwilling involvement of a U.S. company in foreign litigation.

The courts of some countries apply a sort of *quasi in rem* jurisdiction to the branches of foreign countries; *i.e.*, only assets located within the country are considered to be subject to local jurisdiction. The jurisdiction dangers of foreign branches can usually be ameliorated by housing them in a U.S. or offshore holding subsidiary.

As is the case with other forms of foreign organizations, the use of a branch may be required or prohibited by local law or by local commercial necessity. For example, some countries prohibit the establishment of foreign branches altogether (Nigeria and India). Others require extensive local ownership of local limited liability entities, which may make the use of a branch obligatory if total control is desired (South Korea, Ku-

---

[46] Heininger, "Liability of U.S. Banks for Deposits Placed in their Foreign Branches," 11 L. & Pol. Int'l Bus. 903 (1979). Although the considerations of jurisdiction of banks are different than those of sales branches, the thorough analysis in the article is very useful.

[47] *See, e.g.,* Public Administrator of the County of New York v. Royal Bank of Canada, 19 N.Y.2d 127, 224 N.E.2d 329, 278 N.Y.S.2d 378 (1967), in which the separately incorporated French subsidiary of a Canadian bank was found to be subject to the jurisdiction of New York on the theory that the French operation was in effect a branch and that since New York had jurisdiction over the New York branch of a Canadian bank, it had jurisdiction over the bank's other branches also. The New York courts have rather frequently found subsidiaries of foreign corporations to be in effect branches, and have held the parent corporations subject to in personem jurisdiction in New York. Taca International Airlines, S.A., v. Rolls-Royce of England, Ltd., 15 N.Y.2d 97, 204 N.E.2d 329, 256 N.Y.S.2d 129 (1965).

wait, and Taiwan). Commercially, some foreign governments regard local selling subsidiaries as middlemen and prefer to do business directly with foreign branches (Iraq and Algeria). Branches seem to be used frequently in the Middle East, often in conjunction with a local agent.

Typically, a foreign branch is established or "registered" by application to a foreign commercial registry administration. The registration process, compared with the establishment of a limited liability entity, is usually rather simple and inexpensive, involving the submission of certain documents of an informational nature and a power of attorney delineating the authority of the branch manager.[48] Some countries statutorily grant certain powers to the branch managers of foreign companies.[49] In general, however, branch managers must be given specific authority by their employers. In this respect a branch manager's power of attorney becomes quite important, and in some countries an act as elementary as receiving registered mail requires the production of a power of attorney. Foreign branch managers are customarily given rather broad legal authority to act for their employers. A form for power of attorney for a foreign branch manager is included at the end of this section. It should be noted that the distinctions between branches and subsidiaries abroad are often less important from the perspective of foreign investment regulatory authorities than from the perspective of lawyers, and those authorities sometimes treat them identically with respect to reporting and local foreign investment regulation.

In countries with a federal system, the selection of the city in which a foreign branch is registered can have important consequences. In West Germany, for example, there are lim-

---

[48] In Greece, for example, a branch of a foreign company may be registered merely by filing evidence that the company has been incorporated in accordance with the laws of its governing jurisdiction, a legalized copy of the Company's Articles of Association, and a legalized power of attorney for the branch manager with the Greek Ministry of Commerce. Greek Law 2190/1920, as amended, Article 50. This has to be done in the Greek language.

[49] Article 614 of the Commercial Code of the Republic of Korea grants to foreign branch managers the legal authority to bind the company in Korea.

itations on the ability of claimants to use venues other than that of the location of a foreign branch's registration.

The use of a foreign branch may be advantageous from the U.S. income tax standpoint, particularly where initial losses in a foreign country are anticipated.[50] Because a branch (U.S. or foreign) has no legal identity separate from that of the U.S. corporation that registers it, and because U.S. corporations are taxed on their worldwide income, the profit or loss of the foreign branch is immediately includable in the U.S. corporation's income for tax purposes. In contrast, a foreign subsidiary may have its profit (but not its losses) treated as immediately includable in the income of its U.S. parent only if the subsidiary falls into the category of a controlled foreign corporation generating so-called "Subpart F" income.[51] If a foreign branch is later converted to a limited liability entity, certain recoveries of losses taken must be made in order to obtain a "tax free" conversion under I.R.C. section 367.[51.1]

On the other hand, under a provision added to the IRC by the Tax Reform Act of 1976,[52] the losses of the foreign branch may also have an immediate and adverse impact on the U.S. corporation's capacity to claim a credit against its U.S. tax liability for the income taxes it pays in all the foreign countries in which it operates; whereas, the losses of a foreign subsidiary would not have that immediate effect on the U.S. corporation's foreign tax credit. There may be some foreign tax benefits associated with the use of a foreign branch. In some countries, for example, remittances of earnings from a branch are not subject to a dividend withholding tax. The tax planner must thus carefully weigh both the U.S. and foreign tax impacts of a branch registration.

Branches possess the desirable qualities of being totally owned and totally controlled by the foreign company which registers them. They are relatively simple to establish and do not require more than a very moderate corporate secretarial

---

[50] J. Bischel and R. Feinschreiber, *Fundamentals of International Taxation*, 31–33 (1977).

[51] *See* I.R.C. sections 951 *et. seq.*

[51.1] *See generally,* 3 International Lawyers Newsletter, No. 3 at 15 (1981).

[52] I.R.C. section 904(f).

function. Moreover, they are often easier to dismantle than foreign subsidiaries should a direct operation decision be temporary or erroneous, and they can sometimes be used to shelter a foreign investor from undesirable local laws. Nevertheless, foreign branches seem to have fallen into disfavor with international business planners. Their uncertain and potentially dangerous jurisdictional nature together with the reduction of the U.S. tax benefits associated with their use have rendered them a relatively undesirable means of doing business overseas. There are other problems as well. The registration of a foreign branch may require the disclosure of the financial details of a manufacturer's worldwide operations. It may result in a greater foreign tax liability since all income regarded by foreign taxing authorities as having a source in their country usually becomes subject to foreign taxation by virtue of the registration of a branch. Some such income (royalty income for example) might otherwise be exempt from taxation. The use of a foreign branch may also result in the inability of the U.S. company which registers it to repatriate interest or royalty income from the foreign branch. Some countries take the position that since a branch has the same legal personality as the company which registers it, permitting a foreign company to lend to or license its own branch is tantamount to allowing it to lend to or license itself and hence impermissible.

POWER OF ATTORNEY

KNOW ALL MEN BY THESE PRESENTS

That _____, a corporation organized under the laws of the State of _____, U.S.A., with its principal place of business in the city of _____, _____, said State and Country ("Company"), DOES HEREBY MAKE CONSTITUTE AND APPOINT effective (date), (name), a (citizenship) citizen residing in the city of (city), its true and lawful attorney, for it, and in its name, place and stead to represent it and to manage and conduct its business in the Republic of Ruritania ("Ruritania") with the powers delineated below:

FIRST: To do and perform all acts and things necessary or required to secure or maintain its proper admission and registration to do business in Ruritania.

SECOND: To conduct generally the business for and on behalf of the Company in Ruritania, directing, and administering the same; and for this purpose to represent the Company before any person or persons or any officials of the Government of Ruritania, to comply with regulations or laws governing the operation of the foreign corporations in Ruritania;

THIRD: To demand, recover, collect, effect payment of and receive any and all manner of goods, chattels, debts, claims, demands, choses in action, duties, rents, sums of money, whatsoever, due or hereafter to become due to it in Ruritania, on any account whatsoever, by any person or persons or other legal entity, or their successors, assigns or legal representatives, and upon receipt of the same, or any part or parts thereof, to make, execute and deliver all proper receipts, releases or other discharges of and for the same, under seal or otherwise;

FOURTH: To open bank accounts in the name of the Company and close same, and to sign checks pertaining to the various accounts which the Company may have in the banks located in Ruritania;

FIFTH: To represent the Company before all administrative authorities in Ruritania; to deal with matters of customs and shipping; to pay duties; to file and prepare bills of lading and declarations; to receive merchandise which may be imported by the Company; to sign and execute letters, bills or other documents on behalf of and required by any customhouse; to withdraw and take charge of in the post offices, telegraph and telephone offices and agencies, any and all communications, and to forward any letters, packages, registered or unregistered, addressed to or destined for it or any of its representatives; and to deal with all other governmental or municipal authorities in matters concerning its business;

SIXTH: To attend, on behalf of the Company, meetings of creditors for the composition of any person, persons, firms or companies in whose affairs the Company may be interested prior to or after bankruptcy, and to accept or deny such composition or to take any other measures as the attorney may deem proper;

SEVENTH: To apply for and obtain marine, fire, theft, workmen's compensation, public liability and any other kind of insurance whatsoever for the proper protections of the Company's property, business, or undertakings in Ruritania and for these purposes to sign any applications or other documents necessary for obtaining such insurance;

EIGHTH: To represent the Company before every class of court in Ruritania, to institute, maintain and prosecute to the highest tribunals any legal or other action which the attorney may deem necessary for the protection of the Company's legal or equitable interests, and to follow all such suits through all their proceedings without restrictions whatsoever; to accept process on behalf of the Company and to appear in defense of the rights of the companies before any or all judges, tribunals, courts, being empowered to apply for preliminary and final attachments; propound and answer interrogatories; take oaths; settle disputes; agree to awards of arbitrators and referees; appoint arbitrators and referees; attend verbal summons; appoint experts; and intervene in all matters that may arise in consequence thereof;

NINTH: To compound and compromise any debts which may be owing by or to the Company, and to waive any rights which may be necessary in carrying out these powers;

TENTH: To rent or lease, at such rent or other consideration, and subject to such covenants and conditions as he may think reasonable, any premises which he considers necessary for its business in Ruritania;

ELEVENTH: To revoke, cancel, and annul any powers of attorney heretofore granted by the Company in Ruritania, and to perform all acts necessary to register this Power of Attorney before the appropriate governmental authorities of Ruritania.

IN WITNESS WHEREOF, (Company) has caused its corporate name to be ascribed hereto by (Name) by order of its Board of Directors at _____, United States of America this _____ day of _____, 19____.

[3] Foreign Subsidiaries

[a] General

Since the formation and operation of a foreign subsidiary is somewhat more complex than the use of other organizational forms, the decision to select an incorporated form for doing business overseas can only be legitimately made after an informed consideration of multiple factors.[53] These factors arise not only from the legal and business environment of the investing country, but also from the investment climate of the host country and from the anticipated transnational flow of capital, labor, products, and technologies underlying the particular investment.

As is the case with other foreign organizational forms, the overall tax effect is often the single most important consideration. For example, the home tax situation of the investing company may dictate that currently taxable foreign-source income or currently deductible losses are desirable; hence a branch, partnership, or joint venture operation may be the preferred alternative. If that is not the situation, most—though not all—foreign corporate forms offer deferral tax planning opportunities. That is, the profits from the subsidiary will generally not be taxed in the U.S. until actually remitted to the parent corporation, provided (with certain technical exceptions) the subsidiary operates solely in the foreign country of incorporation.

The host country's tax rules similarly cannot be overlooked. Similarity of effective tax rates for companies, branches, and partnerships should be considered as should the existence of a tax treaty bridging the home-host taxing systems, and thus eliminating to the extent possible nonproductive double taxation or withholding requirements. The U.S. foreign tax credit regulations should be carefully considered.[54]

From a nontax perspective, local incorporation *may* provide

---

[53] *See generally* Bardack and Wright, "Corporate and Tax Aspects of European Sales Subsidiaries," 33 Bus. Law. 49 (1977); L. Theberge, ed., *Multinational Corporation Checklist for Subsidiaries* (1975); Bruno, "Checklist for Formation of a Foreign Subsidiary," 24 Bus. Law. 493 (1969).

[54] *See generally* W. Streng, *International Business Transactions—Tax and Legal Handbook* (1978); D. Watt, R. Hammer and M. Burge, *Accounting for the Multinational Corporation* (1977); J. Bischel and R. Feinschreiber, *supra*, N. 50. The following looseleaf services are useful. U.S. Taxation of International Operations (Prentice Hall); [Tax Treaties] Federal Taxes (Prentice Hall); Tax Treaties (Commerce Clearing House); Tax Management—Foreign Income Portfolios (Bureau of National Affairs).

1. A better local marketing image than an extension (branch) of a foreign firm;
2. Legal insulation in bankruptcy or product liability proceedings;
3. Access to local securities markets;
4. More local management flexibility;
5. More opportunities in financing the investments;
6. The ability to create licensing arrangements with a separate entity;
7. Better access to local courts (collections, etc.);
8. Eligibility for local incentive programs;
9. A structure which can be transferred in whole or part easily (*i.e.*, sale of shares);
10. Some insulation from home country laws; and
11. The ability to afford local investors the opportunity to participate in the enterprise.

The above list is by no means exhaustive, and merely points to areas which require thorough investigation before any conclusions may be drawn.

Multi-tiered structures are often useful and are widely employed. Second-tier subsidiaries may be more acceptable in countries which have political difficulties with the home country of the parent company. The use of an intermediary entity located in a tax haven jurisdiction or in a country with a highly developed system of tax treaties, such as Sweden or the Netherlands, or a domestic international sales corporation ("DISC") or another U.S. subsidiary may create a more favorable overall tax effect for the U.S. parent.

The increased complexity of the corporate form requires a relatively greater corporate secretarial function,[55] and often creates significantly more extensive U.S. and foreign governmental regulation. Whereas other organizational forms remain relatively less regulated, foreign corporation law, as well as that of the United States, seem to be moving toward greater

---

[55] *See generally* L. Theberge, ed., *supra* N. 53. The careful observance of the formalities of corporate governance tends to be very important in many foreign jurisdictions. Torem and Rau, "The Subsidiary in France: Problems of Control under French Law," 8 Texas Int'l L.J. 137 (1973).

disclosure, more detailed reporting and enhanced protection of minority interests.[56] Many rules relating to company structures, particularly in developing countries, provide restrictions with respect to maximum foreign equity limits, minimum number of local shareholders and directors and their nationality, and so forth. Of course, astute planning and drafting, particularly through the use of nominee shareholder techniques, may be useful in dealing with some of these rules, but as a general proposition creative methods of circumventing local foreign investment laws should be approached with great caution.

While the decision of whether to incorporate is significant, the choice of how to incorporate, what legal personality to create, also requires careful analysis. The law of most foreign countries provides for more than one limited liability entity. In addition to the stock company, which is usually intended for large public corporations, many corporation statutes provide for the limited liability company, which is designed for a limited number of shareholders, and is often well suited to the needs of the foreign investor.[57] Although limited liability companies have most of the characteristics of U.S. corporations, their essential nature in legal systems which provide for them is that of a contract, as opposed to a government charter. This contractual nature gives business planners wide flexibility in structuring a relationship. For this reason, limited liability companies are particularly useful to house joint ventures where substanial protections are likely to be negotiated by minority shareholders. Table A indicates the names of these entities in selected countries. A brief review of a few forms should provide a reasonable legal sampler of factors to be considered when attempting to reach an informed decision. The alternatives available in France and Germany are reasonable

---

[56] See generally Comment, "The Protection of Minority Shareholders in a Konzern under German and United States Law," 18 Harv. Int'l L.J. 151 (1977); Munton, "Shareholders' Rights in the Common Market: A Comparative Study," 9 Cornell Int'l L.J. 191 (1976); Berger, "Shareholder Rights under the German Stock Corporation Law of 1965," 38 Ford. L. Rev. 687 (1970).

[57] See generally Eder, "Limited Liability Firms Abroad," 13 U. Pitt. L. Rev. 193 (1952).

choices, since they afford a brief look into incorporated entities with civil law underpinnings used extensively by transnational enterprises. Table B is a list of the various organizational forms in France and Germany, and their rough U.S. equivalents.

[b] France

French law provides for a number of business entities through which one can structure an investment.[58] French company law has two principal forms of business organization of common usage that should be somewhat familiar to American counsel, the *société anonyme* (SA) and the *sociéte à responsabilité limitée* (SARL), which share some common attributes with an American corporation and closely-held corporation, respectively. These entities are principally regulated by the Commercial Code of France and in particular the Law No. 66-537 of July 24, 1966, and the Decree of March 23, 1967, as amended and supplemented. It is critical to note that the prior approval of the Ministry of Economy, specifically the Department of Treasury (*Direction du Tresor*), is required as a condition precedent to the making of a foreign direct investment, *i.e.*, organizing a company, in France.[59] This approval is by no means automatic and can cause substantial delays.

[i] Société anonyme

Societe anonyme: SAs may be either publicly or privately held and have a legal charter *(statuts)* which is the functional equivalent of both the articles of incorporation and the by-laws

---

[58] *See generally* I Simeon, Moquet, Borde & Associés, *supra* N. 12.1, chapter 5; S. Frommel and J. Thompson, eds., *Company Law in Europe* 169-227 (1975); Rawlings, "French Company Law: Choice of Corporate Forms Available to the Foreign Investor," 30 Bus. Law. 1251 (1975); J. LeGall, *French Company Law* (1974).

[59] *See generally* I Simeon, Moquet, Borde & Associés, *supra* N. 12.1, chapter 3; Torem and Craig, "Developments in the Control of Foreign Investment in France," 70 Mich. L. Rev. 285 (1971); Torem and Craig, "Control of Foreign Investment in France," 66 Mich. L. Rev. 669 (1968).

of an American company. A public SA typically has shares or debentures quoted on a French stock exchange. This discussion, however, will focus on the characteristics of a private, unquoted SA, which form is used extensively by transnational companies structuring an investment in France.

The life of an SA may not exceed ninety-nine years, must be expressed in the *statuts*, and may be extended by the shareholders *(actionnaires)*, of which there must be seven either juristic or natural persons. Contributions in kind, given in exchange for shares, as well as shareholder preferences detailed by the *statuts*, are the subject of a special review by *commissaries aux apports*, expert appraisers, prior to the registration of the *statuts* and assorted incorporation documentation with the clerk of the commercial court, the commercial registry, and the tax and other administrative authorities. The appropriate commercial court for registration is found in the *departement* where the company has its *siege social*, its registered office. To be filed the documents must have been approved by a notary for compliance with paid-in capital requirements, statutory formalities, and the like. The minimum amount of capital for a publicly held SA is 500,000 francs, for a private SA 100,000 francs. The company comes into existence after the completion of the filing requirements with registration in the commercial register.

Share certificates are no longer issued, having been replaced by book entries in 1984. Each share must have the right to one vote with certain exceptions for preferred classes as per the *statuts*. Personal shareholder liability is limited to the par value of the shares held. There are special conditions which must be met by a private company prior to the issuance of any debentures.

Shares must be fully issued and subscribed, and cash contributions to capital must be at least 25 percent paid-up at the time of subscription. Contributions in kind must be fully paid initially and no contributions of skills or services qualify. Registered shares can be transferred by the execution of a transfer form, or by endorsement, and registration thereof in the SA's share transfer records; bearer shares are transferable by mere delivery. Note that there are special depositary requirements for bearer shares. A typical restriction in private SA *statuts* is the necessity of consent before stock transfers can be made to third parties. The transfer of shares among existing stockholders is not restricted. An SA may purchase its own shares only to reduce capital or for employee stock plans.

The *statuts* of an SA may provide for management either by a *conseil d'administration* (board of directors) in conjunction with various board-selected officers, or a *conseil de surveillance* (supervisory council) and *directoire* (directorate) regime. The SA *conseil d'administration* has from three to twelve members, each of which must be a shareholder. Shareholder nominee techniques are sometimes used to fulfill this qualifying requirement, as well as minimum shareholder numerical requirements. Members need not be French nationals and may be removed by the shareholders without cause and indemnity.

The *conseil d'administration* has broad powers limited only by the *statuts* and those items expressly reserved to the shareholders in the company laws. One board member will be elected by the board to be president, who can be relieved of his duties at will and will be the chief operation executive of the company. He is subject to personal liability for certain acts of mismanagement. Any contracts between SA and management are subject to certain disclosure and/or prior authorization requirements to prevent self-dealing and other conflict of interest situations.

The other management alternative which may be selected for an SA consists of the *conseil de surveillance* (supervisory council), whose initial members are also named in the *statuts*, which in turn selects a *directoire* (directorate) composed of two to five members. The members of the *directoire* need not be shareholders and cannot be members of the *conseil de surveillance*. The *directoire* manages the SA on a daily basis. The *conseil de surveillance* is generally more passive in nature than the *conseil d'administration*, yet both have similar powers. The *directoire* has generous powers of management when dealing with third parties.

There are detailed secretarial requirements for SAs, as well as extensive disclosure requirements to auditors, shareholders, and the public.

For both SAs and SARLs, there are generally no restrictions on the repatriation of capital or dividends, excepting some exchange control limitations and situations involving partial or total liquidations.

[ii]   Société à responsabilité limitée

All of the *parts sociales, i.e.,* ownership in a SARL by deed, which are not represented by share certificates or other negotiable instruments and cannot be the subject of any public offering, must be fully issued, subscribed, and paid-in by the participants (*associes*) prior to the SARL's effective registration with the commercial registry. The *associes* may contribute cash or contributions in kind, excluding skills and services, to the initial capitalization. Contributions in kind must be independently appraised by a *commissaire au compte,* and the *associes* remain personally liable after the SARL's formation for over-valuation problems. The liability of the *associes* extends only to the extent of their capital contribution.

The minimum capital required is F20,000, and the minimum par value for *parts sociales* is F100. If the registered capital exceeds F300,000 the SARL must appoint an independent auditor. Rules affecting the increase, decrease, or repair of the capital account are similar to that of an SA.

The basic filing requirements for a SARL are quite similar to that of a private SA in terms of documentation and costs, but with less financial information. The *statuts* to be filed must indicate the *parts sociales* held by each *associe.* There must be at least two *associes* but no more than fifty; they may be individuals or entities of any nationality. The term of the SARL is limited to ninety-nine years, unless extended by affirmative action by the *associés.*

The SARL is managed by one or more *gérants* (managers), not by a board of directors or other supervisory council. *Gérants* need not be an *associé* and have a term of office coextensive with the life of the SARL. Removal (by the *associés) of a gérant* without cause may give rise to liability to the dismissed manager for damages. *Gérants* have full powers of commercial representation when dealing with third parties. Restrictions in the *statuts* or in the employment agreement with a *gérant* may not be effective against claims by third parties. *Gérants* may be held personally liable, individually or jointly, for exceeding the authority granted them in the *statuts* or by law.

Transfers of *parts sociales* can only be accomplished by written instrument signed by the transferor and transferee submitted to the company. There is generally free transferability among *associés* and their families, with certain restrictions which may be contained in the *statuts*. Transfers to third parties generally require the prior consent of a prescribed percentage of *associés* both in terms of number and percentage of registered capital. There are minimal disclosure and reporting requirements for SARLs. The annual accounts must be approved at an annual meeting by the *associés*. The *associés* can be required to repay dividends paid that were not legally distributable.

[iii] Partnerships

French law provides for three types of partnerships. By far the most frequently used by foreign investors is the general partnership (*société en nom collectif,* abbreviated SNC). French taxation of foreign branches is very high. An SNC, like a branch, is fiscally transparent; its profits or losses flow directly to the partners. Partners in a SNC have unlimited liability, but they may be limited liability entities. There are no minimum capitalization requirements, and unlike SAs and SARLs, there is no requirement that financial statements be publically disclosed. The partners have wide authority to structure the management as they see fit. There are two forms of limited partnership in France—the *société en commandite simple* and the *société en commandite par actions*. Neither is frequently used because of their complexity of operation.

[c]   Federal Republic of Germany

Formation of a company in the Federal Republic of Germa-ny,[60] by a foreign individual or entity is not subject to any prior German direct investment restrictions presently, nor are there exchange controls on future repatriations. Basically, foreign-owned enterprises are subject to the same company law regulations as locally-owned firms. Two common forms of organization are the *Aktiengesellschaft* (AG), which is in essence a stock corporation, and a limited liability company form called a *Gesellschaft mit beschraenkter Haftung* (GmbH). This latter entity is selected most frequently by foreign investors. The GmbH law dates from the 1890s, although there are current government proposals for reform in light of the company law harmonization presently occurring within the EEC. The GmbH entity has served as the model for small, limited liability companies throughout the world.

[i]   Aktiengesellschaft (AG)

The AG form of business organization is typically only suitable for large investments. A minimum of five incorporators must contract to form an AG before a notary. The articles and bylaws are usually contained in one document called the *Satzung,* wherein the supervisory board *(Aufsichtsrat)* is appointed. This supervisory board will subsequently appoint a board of management *(Vorstand).*

The legal existence of an AG commences with the completion of registration with the local trade registry. Documents to be filed include the incorporators' contract, the initial balance sheet, the notarized *Satzung,* and certain information relating to the paid-in capital.

The shareholder's liability in an AG is limited to the par value of his shareholdings. In order to protect creditors, there

---

[60] *See generally* II Rüster, *supra* N. 12, chapter 23; S. Frommel and Thompson, eds., *supra* N. 58, at 229-68; N. Horn, et al., *supra* N. 12 at 239-81; H. Wurdinger, *German Company Law* (1975); Kutschelis, "Doing Business in the Federal Republic of Germany," 3 Denver J. Int'l L. & Pol. 197 (1974).

is a statutory legal reserve which must be set aside out of earnings up to a specified percentage of the paid-in capital. There is a minimum capital requirement of DM100,000 of which 25 percent must be paid-in at the initial incorporation. Capital stock may be issued at a premium but not a discount. Capital contributions may be in cash or in kind, which is interpreted to mean any property which has an ascertainable value with certain limitations as to contributions concerning services.

Certificates are issued to represent the shares and may be either bearer or registered in form. The *Satzung* may create multiple classes of shares with various preferences as to voting and liquidation rights, for example. Shares of an AG may be traded on a German stock exchange if properly registered. Shares in an AG are generally freely transferable unless the *Satzung* provides otherwise. Shareholders may be either an individual or a legal entity, either resident or nonresident, and of any nationality.

The supervisory board, which consists of from three to twenty-one members, functions as the principal policy-making board and deals principally with selecting of managers, advising the board of management, and safeguarding the interests of shareholders and employees. Depending on the size of the AG in terms of financial means and labor force, certain members of the supervisory board will be elected by the employees.

The board of management consists of the main operating officers and is selected by the supervisory board. The board has full powers in dealing with third parties in the company's commercial matters. The composition of the board of management is also affected by the German co-determination (*Mitbestimmung*) law, which mandates that certain members be elected by the employees of the AG. The co-determination aspect of the management of German companies is a source of concern from the American viewpoint because of a lack of experience with such legislation. The German experience with co-determination, however, has been relatively uneventful in terms of serious operating difficulties for German companies.[61]

---

[61] Gruson and Meileke, "The New Co-determination Law in Germany," 30 Bus. Law. 571 (1977). Co-determination is required by the laws of several

An AG is subject to very extensive accounting, secretarial, and other statutory requirements in the administration and conduct of its business. Audited financials are a regular requirement as well as a dependency report for those companies which are controlled by another company.

[ii]   Gesellschaft mit beschräenkter Haftung (GmbH)[62]

The GmbH was the first limited liability company, being authorized by an 1892 statute. Unlike limited liability companies in other countries, a GmbH may be formed by one person (*Gesellschafter*). This ability, which was granted in a 1980 amendment to the GmbH law,[63] is significant in that while it represents an acknowledgement that many small businesses in Germany are conducted by one person, it is a sharp derogation from the basic concept of the GmbH's being a contract and not a charter. The statutes of a GmbH are still called the *Gesellschaftsvertrag,* which translates as "corporate contract," but, of course, a contract must have two parties.

A GmbH comes to juridical life upon registration in the commercial registry. The *Gesellschaftsvertrag* must be notarized and must specify the name (*Firma*), the domicile, the purpose, the initial capital, and the capital division among the initial shareholders. The German *Notar,* like his equivalents in other civil law countries, is quite different in terms of function, authority and remuneration from the American notary public. There is an initial capital requirement of DM 50,000 which must be fully subscribed and at least 25 percent paid-in. Contributions in kind must be appraised and fully delivered to the GmbH prior to registration. The *Gesellschaftsvertrag* may

---

other European countries and has been seriously proposed in several other countries and by the EEC Commission. *See generally* Steuer, "Employee Representation on the Board: Industrial Democracy or Interlocking Directorate," 16 Columb. J. Trans. L. 255 (1977).

[62] *See generally* M. Peltzer & J. Brooks, *German Law Pertaining to Companies with Limited Liability* (1981); DeVries and Juenger, "Limited Liability Contract, The GmbH," 64 Colum. L. Rev. 866 (1964).

[63] Gesetz betreffend die Gesellschaften mit Beschraenker Haftung vom 20 April, 1892 (RGBI.S.477) as amended July 4, 1980 (GmbH Law).

contain the name of the first manager (*Geschaeftsfuehrer*) or managers.

There are no basic restrictions on who may be a shareholder in a GmbH. There are minimal filing requirements. Shares in a GmbH may be represented by certificates, but such is not required. Only transfers duly authenticated by a notary in writing and reported to the company are binding. There can be no public trading of GmbH shares. Since the GmbH was designed for small business, preemptive rights are customarily included in the statutes. A GmbH may be organized very quickly, the major delay being the obtaining of the approval of the German Cartel authority.

The manager (*Geschaeftsfuehrer*), like his French cousin the *gerant,* has wide authority to represent the GmbH which may not be restricted by the *Gesellschaftsvertrag.* The manager must be a natural person, and, since 1980, may not have been convicted of a felony within the preceding five years.[64] The manager must manage the company with the care of an ordinary prudent businessman, and is personally liable for failures to do so.[65] As a kind of balance for this responsibility, a manager is entitled to significant indemnities upon being dismissed. Since managers of foreign owned GmbH's are often not resident in Germany, efficient management practice dictates that someone resident in Germany be granted a *Prokura* [66] to execute contracts and generally represent the company.

The ultimate decision-making authority of a GmbH lies with its shareholders, and certain matters, such as the appointment of managers and the distribution of profits, must be determined by the shareholders. A supervisory board may or may not be created. Co-determination applies to GmbH's as well as AG's.

There are generally no statutory audit requirements or requirements to publish financial information that are applicable to a GmbH, assuming it is of moderate size. The laws relating to the GmbH may be significantly affected by company law

[64] GmbH Law, section 6.
[65] GmbH Law, section 43.
[66] *See supra,* § 2.02[1][a].

developments within the EEC, as current reforms would require greater protections for creditors, and minority shareholders, *inter alia*. This would include the imposition of more stringent financial reporting requirements.

Selected attributes of an AG and GmbH are generally compared in Table C.

[iii]   Partnerships[67]

German law recognizes three types of commercial partnerships, all of which are governed by the Commercial Code (*Handelsgesetzbuch*). The general partnership (*Offene Handelsgesellschaft*, abbreviated OHG) is very similar to a common law general partnership. It is used most frequently by small enterprises. Partners are individually liable for partnership obligations, but the partnership may perform legal acts as a judicial entity.

The silent partnership (*Stille Gesellschaft*) form permits the identity of some partners not to be publically disclosed. Since the partnership agreement governs the external liability of the partners, the use of the form permits some partners to be liable only to the extent of their contributions.

The partnership form most likely to be encountered by foreigners is the limited partnership (*Kommanditgesellschaft*, abbreviated KG). Like limited partners in a common law limited partnership, the limited partners of a KG (*Kommanditisten*) are liable for the obligations of the KG only to the extent of their contributions. There must be a general partner with unlimited liability, but German law permits the general partner to be a limited liability entity. The normal KG construction is thus the so-called "GmbH & Co. KG" which is not a separate statutory creature, but merely a KG in which the general partner is a GmbH. KGs are very widely used, and because tax losses flow directly to the limited partners, they seem to be a particularly useful vehicle for real estate investments.

---

[67] II Ruester, *supra* N. 12, chapter 22.

TABLE A

	STOCK CORPORATIONS	LIMITED LIABILITY COMPANIES
Argentina	Sociedad Anonima (SA)	Sociedad De Responsibilidad Limitada (SRL)
Austria	Aktiengesellschaft (AG)	Gesellschaft mit Beschraenkter Haftung(Ges.mbH)
Belgium	Naamloze Vennootschap (NV)/ Societe Anonyme (SA)	Personenvennootschap met Beperkte Aansprakelijkheid (PvbA)/Societe de Personnes a Responsabilite Limitee (SPRL)
Brazil	Sociedade Anonima (SA)	Limitada
Chile	Sociedad Anonima (SA)	Sociedad de Responsibilidad Limitada
Colombia	Sociedad Anonima (SA)	Sociedad de Responsibilidad Limitada (SRL)
Costa Rica	Sociedad Anonima (SA)	Sociedad de Responsibilidad Limitada (SRL) or Limitada (LTDA)
Denmark	Aktieselskabet (A/S)	Anpartsselskab (APS)
France	Societe Anonyme (SA)	Societe a Responsabilite Limitee (SARL)
Germany	Aktiengesellschaft (AG)	Gesellschaft mit Beschraenkter Haftung (GmbH)

TABLE A (cont'd)

	STOCK CORPORATIONS	LIMITED LIABILITY COMPANIES
Italy	Societa Per Azioni (SPA)	Societa a Responsibilita Limitata (SRL)
Japan	Kabushiki Kaisha	Yugen Kaisha
Republic of Korea	Chusik Hoesa	Yuhan Hoesa
Luxembourg	Societe Anonyme (SA)/ Aktiengesellschaft (AG)	Societe a Responsibilite Limitee (SARL)/Gesellschaft mit Beschraenkter Haftung.(GmbH)
Netherlands	Naamloze Vennootschap (NV)	Besloten Vennootschap met Beperkte Aansprakelijkheid (BV)
Spain	Sociedad Anonima (SA)	Sociedad de Responsabilidad Limitada (SRL)
Switzerland	Aktiengesellschaft (AG)/ Societe Anonyme (SA)	Gesellschaft mit Beschraenkter Haftung (GmbH)/Societe a Responsabilite Limitee (SARL)
Turkey	Anonim Sirkit	Limited Sirket

TABLE B

UNITED STATES	GERMANY	FRANCE
Companies		
Corporation	Aktiengesellschaft	Societe Anonyme
Closely Held Corporation	Gesellschaft mit beschraenkter Haftung	Societe a Responsibilite Limitee
Capital Investment Company	Kapitalanlagegesellschaft	
Partnerships, Joint Ventures & Civil Companies *		
General Partnership	Offene Handelsgesellschaft	Societe en nom Collectif
Limited Partnership	Kommanditgesellschaft	Societe en Commandite Simple
Limited Partnership/ Quasi-Corporation	Kommanditgesellschaft Auf Aktien	Societe en Commandite par Actions
Silent Partnership/ Joint Venture	Stille Gesellschaft	Societe en Participation
Joint Venture		Groupment D'Intret Economique
Association	Gesellschaft Buegerlichen Rechts	Societe Civile
Branch		
Branch	Zweigniederlassung	Succursale
Individual		
Sole Proprietor		Entreprise Individuell

* Omitted are special purpose organizations which can be formed for certain investments, real property, export, regional development, and oil and gas R&D purposes. These forms are regulated by special legal and tax statutes.

TABLE C

	AG	GmbH
Incorporators	Minimum of 5	Minimum of 2
Shareholders	Need only 1	Need only 1 (Maximum of 50)
Minimum Capital	DM100,000	DM50,000
Formalities of Formation and Operation	Extensive	Presently simple
Management	Board system impacted by co-determination principles	Single manager is possible
Audited and Published Financials	Yes	No, except for large operations
Share Transfers	Generally freely transferred	Restricted
Public Issue of Securities	Yes	No
Ownership	Bearer or registered shares	Registered

2-64

CHAPTER 3

United States Taxation of Foreign Investors

HERRICK K. LIDSTONE*
ROBERT S. RICH**

*Harvard LL.B. 1948; member, New York and Colorado bars.
**Yale LL.B. 1963; member, New York and Colorado bars.

This chapter covers the United States taxation of foreign investors in the United States on the basis of the law in effect in July, 1980. It focuses on the Federal income tax, which is the most important tax in terms of both general applicability and revenue raised, but state and local taxes and Federal estate and gift taxes also are briefly reviewed. This chapter also discusses the principal provisions of tax treaties, because the bilateral tax treaties, which the United States has entered into with other countries, generally overrule contrary provisions in the Federal tax law.[1]

§ 3.01 Federal Income Taxation of Foreign Investors

In view of the complexity of the Federal income tax law,[2]

(Text continued on page 3-5)

---

[1] IRC §§ 894(a), 7852(d).

[2] The Federal income tax law is included in Title 26 of the United States Code, 68A United States Statutes at Large (Pub. L. No. 591, Ch. 736, 68A Stat.), and is officially known as the "Internal Revenue Code of 1954."

Throughout this chapter the Internal Revenue Code of 1954 will be referred to as the "Code." Citations and other references to the Code will be primarily to sections, *e.g.,* IRC § 61. In addition to the Code, the Federal income tax law is found in the decisions of the Federal courts of which a decision of the United States Supreme Court is the law and binding on all other courts unless overturned by either an act of Congress or a reversal by the Supreme Court of its previous decision. Until reversed by an act of Congress or a decision of the Supreme Court, a decision of one of the eleven Circuit Courts of Appeals (by the time this volume is published, the Court of Appeals for the Fifth Circuit may have been split into two Circuits thereby raising the number to twelve) is binding on the courts the decisions of which would be appealed to the Circuit Court (*i.e.,* on the Federal district courts within the Circuit and on the United States Tax Court if an appeal from a Tax Court decision would be to the specific Circuit). A decision of one Circuit Court is not binding on any other Circuit, but generally it is persuasive. The Tax Court, the various Federal district courts, and the Court of Claims generally follow their own decisions, subject, of course, to the preceding rules of higher authority.

In addition to the Code and decisions of the courts, the Federal income tax law is found in the Treasury's regulations, some of which, because of the delegation of authority by Congress, have the force of law (*e.g.,* the Congress, in IRC § 385, delegated to the Secretary of the Treasury the authority "to prescribe such regulations as may be necessary or appropriate to determine whether an interest in a corporation is to be treated for purposes of this title as stock or indebtedness").

The Internal Revenue Service, the agency of the United States Treasury charged with the administration of the Internal Revenue laws, publishes revenue rulings, revenue procedures, etc., to inform taxpayers and their advisors of the position that it is taking on the matters described in the publication. Similarly, the IRS (in this chapter the Internal Revenue Service will be referred to as the "IRS" or as the "Service") publishes "acquiesences" and "nonacquiesences" of decisions of the Tax Court to inform taxpayers and their advisors of the Service's intention to continue or not to continue to litigate one or more of the issues covered by the Tax Court's decision. Although revenue rulings, acquiesences, and nonacquiesences are for the information of taxpayers, they are instructions to and binding on the Service's personnel who deal with taxpayers' returns.

Finally, in most cases, the IRS will issue both private letter rulings to taxpayers who request advice on the tax consequences of specific proposed transactions and technical advise memoranda to taxpayers and revenue agents who request advice on the tax consequences of completed transactions. Although Letter Rulings ("LR") and technical advice memoranda are made publicly available and are published by private publishing firms, they are binding on the IRS only with respect to the specific taxpayer requesting the advice, and, then, only in the absence of fraud or incomplete or misleading data submitted by the taxpayer. Although the private written determina-

the scope of this volume permits only a summary discussion of the law and its application to foreign investors. The reader is cautioned, therefore, that further research may be necessary to understand the application of the law to any given facts or circumstances and that exceptions to the general rules may be discussed only in footnotes or entirely omitted. Moreover, since this chapter was completed in mid-July, 1980, it may not reflect the law at the time of reading because the Federal income tax law is subject to change as a result of legislative or administrative action or court decisions. For example, the scheme of taxation of foreign investors in real estate and natural resources located in the United States probably will be changed by Congress in 1980, or shortly thereafter, and the United States probably will impose a tax on capital gains derived by foreign investors from direct or indirect holdings of United States real estate and natural resources in many situations that currently escape Federal income tax.[3]

The general principle of Federal income taxation is simply stated: The taxable income of individuals, trusts, and estates[4] and of corporations[5] for each taxable year[6] is subject to the Federal income tax. Taxable income means the taxpayer's gross income less the deductions allowed by the Code.[7] "Gross

---

tions are helpful to other taxpayers and their advisors because they show the IRS thinking on the specific subject, a private "written determination may not be used or cited as precedent." IRC § 6110(j)(3).

[3] *See* the Foreign Investment in Real Property Tax Act of 1980, contained in Subtitle E, of Title II, of H.R. 7652, 96th Cong., 2d Sess. (1980), which was being considered by Congress in July, 1980. *See* the discussion in § 3.05[2] *infra*. It is expected that, in order to comply with the new U.S. law, the treaty provisions which exempt treaty country nationals from capital gains tax with respect to U.S. real estate and natural resources probably will be renegotiated or phased-out over a period of years.

[4] IRC § 1 prescribes the rates of Federal income tax on individuals, trusts, and estates.

[5] IRC § 11 prescribes the rates of Federal income tax on corporations.

[6] A taxable year is the taxpayer's annual accounting period; and it may be either a calendar year or a fiscal year. It is the calendar year if the taxpayer keeps no books of account or has no annual accounting period. IRC § 441(b). A fiscal year means a period of twelve months ending on the last day of any month other than December. IRC §§ 441, 7701(a)(23), (24).

[7] IRC § 63.

income means all income from whatever source derived. . . ."[8]

Notwithstanding the general principle that the United
States imposes its income tax at graduated tax rates[9] on each
taxpayer's worldwide taxable income (*i.e.*, on his or its worldwide gross income less allowed or allowable deductions[10]),
nonresident aliens[11] and foreign corporations[12] are subject to
Federal income tax on only two categories of gross income,
namely

1. Gross income that is derived from sources within the
    United States but not effectively connected with the
    conduct of a trade or business within the United States
    is taxed at a flat rate of 30 percent, unless the tax is
    reduced or eliminated by treaty; and
2. Gross income that is effectively connected with the con-
    duct of a trade or business within the United States is
    taxed, after allowable deductions, at graduated tax
    rates.[13]

---

[8] IRC § 61.

[9] The rates range from 14 percent to 70 percent on the taxable income
of individuals, trusts, and estates (IRC § 1) and from 17 percent to 46 percent
on the taxable income of corporations (IRC § 11).

[10] The distinction between allowed and allowable deductions is usually
not important. In the case of depreciation, amortization, and cost depletion,
however, it is possible that a taxpayer may claim a deduction that is less than
the law would allow. In such a case, the taxpayer's adjusted basis in the
property is computed by deducting from acquisition cost or adjusted basis
the greater of the amount of the depreciation, amortization, or cost depletion deduction that was allowed or the amount that was allowable.

[11] Resident aliens and United States citizens, wherever resident, are subject to tax each taxable year on their worldwide taxable incomes. Treas. Regs.
§§ 1.1-1(a)(1), 1.1-1(b), 1.871-1(a).

[12] A foreign corporation is defined as one that is not a domestic corporation. IRC § 7701(a)(5). A domestic corporation is defined as one "created or
organized in the United States or under the laws of the United States or of
any State" (IRC § 7701(a)(4)) or of the District of Columbia (IRC §
7701(a)(10)). This chapter does not cover investment in the United States by
foreign corporations owned, directly or indirectly, by U.S. corporations or by
U.S. citizens or resident aliens.

[13] IRC §§ 872(a) (relating to nonresident alien individuals), 882(b) (relating
to foreign corporations). If a nonresident alien or foreign corporation is

The first category of gross income includes only certain types of U.S. source income, notably fixed or determinable annual or periodical gain, profits and income (*e.g.*, salaries, wages, dividends, interest, rents, and royalties). In the case of a nonresident alien (but not of a foreign corporation), the first category also includes capital gains if the nonresident alien is physically present in the United States for a period or periods aggregating 183 days or more during the taxable year.

[1] Basic Definitions

The concept of "gross income" in the case of nonresident alien individuals and foreign corporations presents basic definitional problems that must be examined before the rules applicable to the taxation of nonresident alien individuals and foreign corporations can be understood, to wit: First, what is the source of the foreign investor's income and deductions? Second, is the foreign investor engaged in a trade or business within the United States? Third, if the foreign investor conducts a trade or business within the United States, what portion of the foreign investor's income and deductions is effectively connected with the conduct of the trade or business within the United States?[14]

---

subject to tax under both regimes in a taxable year, the tax is calculated separately with respect to each regime (Treas. Regs. §§ 1.871-8(a), 1.882-1(a)), and the nonresident alien or foreign corporation is not subject to higher rates of tax on his or its effectively connected income because he or it also has income subject to flat rates of tax (*i.e.*, the income subject to flat rates of tax is not taken into account in determining the rates of tax applicable to the effectively connected income). Treas. Regs. §§ 1.871-8(b)(2)(i), 1.882-1(b)(2)(i).

[14] "The term 'United States' when used in a geographical sense includes only the States and the District of Columbia." IRC § 7701(a)(9). The "seabed and subsoil of those submarine areas [*i.e.*, the continental shelf] which are adjacent to the territorial waters of the United States and over which the United States has exclusive rights, in accordance with international law, with respect to the exploration and exploitation of natural resources" are included within the geographical United States, with respect to mines, oil and gas wells, and other natural deposits. IRC § 638(1).

[a]   What Is the Source of the Foreign Investor's Gross
      Income and Deductions?

The Code establishes source rules for determining whether
specified items of income and deduction are from sources within[15] or without[16] the United States; and it also deals with the
allocation or apportionment of items of income and deductions
that are not specified as being from sources within or without
the United States.[17]

[i]   Interest

The source of interest income is usually the place of the
debtor's residence. Thus, interest from the United States or the
District of Columbia,[18] and interest on bonds, notes or other
interest bearing obligations of U.S. residents, corporate or otherwise, constitutes U.S. source income.[19] Interest paid by a
resident alien individual or a domestic corporation usually constitutes U.S. source income.[20] Interest paid by a foreign corpo-

---

[15] IRC § 861.

[16] IRC § 862.

[17] IRC § 863.

[18] Interest on obligations of a State, Territory, or possession or of any
political subdivision of any of the foregoing is excluded from the gross income of all taxpayers. IRC § 103(a)(1). Curiously, although IRC § 103 excludes from gross income "interest on . . . the obligations . . . of the District
of Columbia," IRC § 861(a)(1) apparently includes interest on obligations of
the District of Columbia as U.S. source income that is subject to the 30
percent tax imposed by IRC § 871(a)(1)(A).

[19] IRC § 861(a)(1). IRC § 862(a)(1) provides that interest, other than as
provided for in IRC § 861(a)(1), "shall be treated as income from sources
without the United States. . . ." Apparently, interest paid by a resident
partnership (*i.e.*, a partnership, whether domestic or foreign, which is engaged in a U.S. trade or business) constitutes income from sources within the
United States. IRC § 861(a)(1); and Treas. Regs. §§ 1.861-2(a)(2), 301.7701-5.
Arguably, at least in the case of a foreign partnership, the interest from U.S.
sources should be only the amount that bears the same ratio to such interest
as the partnership's income which is effectively connected with its U.S. trade
or business bears to its gross income from all sources.

[20] IRC § 861(a)(1)(B). Interest paid by a resident alien individual or a
domestic corporation constitutes foreign source income if less than 20 per-

ration (other than interest paid or credited by a domestic branch of a foreign corporation, if the branch is engaged in the commercial banking business) constitutes U.S. source income, if for the three years preceding the taxable year of the payor's payment of interest, 50 percent or more of the gross income from all sources of such foreign corporation was effectively connected with the conduct of a trade or business within the United States, but only in an amount which bears the same ratio to such interest as the gross income of such foreign corporation for such period which was effectively connected with the conduct of a U.S. trade or business bears to its gross income from all sources.[21]

If not effectively connected with the conduct of a trade or business within the United States, interest received by a nonresident alien individual or a foreign corporation on a deposit with a bank or savings institution (or on money held by an insurance company if the insurance company has agreed to pay interest thereon) does not constitute interest from sources within the United States.[22]

[ii] **Dividends**

Dividends paid by a domestic corporation usually constitute U.S. source income.[23] Dividends paid by a foreign corporation constitute U.S. source income only if 50 percent or more of its gross income from all sources was effectively connected with the conduct of a trade or business within the United States and

---

cent of the gross income from all sources of such individual or corporation was derived from sources within the United States. IRC § 861(a)(1)(B).

[21] IRC §§ 861(a)(1)(C) and (D). Interest paid on an obligation of a resident of the United States by a nonresident alien or foreign corporation whose payment is made as guarantor of the obligation of the resident is treated as income from sources within the United States. Treas. Regs. § 1.861-2(a)(5).

[22] IRC § 861(c). See N. 89, *infra*.

[23] IRC § 861(a)(2)(A). If for the three-year-period ending with the taxable year preceding the declaration of the dividend in question, less than 20 percent of the gross income of a domestic corporation is derived from sources within the United States, the dividend will be considered as non-U.S. source income.

then only in an amount which bears the same ratio to the dividends as its gross income that was effectively connected with the conduct of a trade or business within the United States bears to its gross income from all sources.[24]

[iii]   **Personal Services**

Compensation for labor or personal services performed in the United States constitutes income from sources within the United States.[25] This rule applies regardless of the identity of the payor, the place in which the contract for service was made, or the place of payment.[26] Compensation for labor or

---

[24] IRC §§ 861(a)(2)(B), 862(a)(2). Rev. Rul. 72-230, 1972-1 Cum. Bull. 209, holding that dividends eliminated in computing consolidated return income constitute gross income for the 80:20 source rule computation, may be read as contrary to IRC § 861(a)(2)(B).

[25] IRC § 861(a)(3). Compensation paid to a nonresident alien under a contract not to compete in the United States has been held to constitute income from U.S. sources. Korfund Co., 1 T.C. 1180 (1943). *See* Rev. Rul. 74-108, 1974-1 Cum. Bull. 248.

[26] Treas. Regs. § 1.861-4(a)(1). IRC § 861(a)(3) grants a "commercial traveler" type exception to the general rule, *i.e.*, compensation for labor or services performed by a nonresident alien who is temporarily present in the United States for a period not exceeding ninety days is treated as non-U.S. source income, if the compensation does not exceed $3,000 in the aggregate and if the services are performed for a foreign employer. IRC § 861(a)(3)(A) through (C). If the compensation exceeds $3,000, the full amount is income from U.S. sources. Rev. Rul. 69-479, 1969-2 Cum. Bull. 149. This exemption, which is expanded in most income tax treaties (*see, e.g.*, Articles III of the U.S.-Canada Income Tax Treaty), applies whether the compensation is paid in dollars or in foreign currency; if paid in foreign currency, the currency is converted at the current official dollar rate of exchange in effect at the time the payment is made. Rev. Rul. 55-472, 1955-2 Cum. Bull. 381.

Compensation for labor or personal services presumably would include cost of living allowances, such as housing and schooling allowances, home leave travel allowances, and other employee benefits, whether paid in cash or in kind. Treas. Regs. § 1.61-2. *Cf.* IRC § 913. A nonresident alien, who is required to include in gross income compensation paid to him for services in the United States, may be entitled to deduct some of his U.S. living expenses to the extent that they qualify as away from home expenditures. IRC § 162(a)(2). Compensation also includes property (*e.g.*, corporate stock, a partnership interest, or an interest in a resources property) received in

personal services performed without the United States, on the other hand, constitutes foreign source income.[27]

[iv] Rentals and Royalties

Rentals or royalties from property located in the United States, including real estate and natural resources, or from any interest in such property, and rentals or royalties for the use of, or for the privilege of using in the United States, patents, copyrights, secret processes and formulas, good will, trademarks, trade brands, franchises and other like property, constitute income from sources within the United States.[28] Rentals or royalties from property located without the United States constitute income from sources without the United States.[29]

[v] Sale or Exchange of Real Property

Gains, profits, and income from the sale or exchange of real property located in the United States constitute income from sources within the United States.[30] Conversely, gains, profits

---

connection with the performance of services, to the extent that the fair market value of such property exceeds the amount paid for such property. IRC § 83. *See* Diamond v. Comm'r, 492 F.2d 286 (7th Cir. 1974); United States v. Frazell, 335 F.2d 487 (5th Cir. 1964), *reh'g denied,* 339 F.2d 885 (5th Cir. 1965), *cert. denied,* 380 U.S. 961 (1965).

Federal income tax may apply to compensation (including a pension) paid to a nonresident alien in a year in which the nonresident alien is no longer performing services and is not physically present in the United States, if the compensation is paid in respect of services the nonresident alien previously performed in the United States. In such a case, the compensation would constitute income from sources within the United States. *See* William N. Dillin, 56 T.C. 228 (1971), *acq.,* 1975-1 Cum. Bull. 1. In a year in which the nonresident alien is not engaged in a U.S. trade or business, presumably the tax would be at 30 percent of the gross compensation payments. *Cf.* Treas. Regs. § 1.864-4(c)(6)(ii).

[27] IRC § 862(a)(3).

[28] IRC § 861(a)(4).

[29] IRC § 862(a)(4).

[30] IRC § 861(a)(5). Thus, gain from the sale or exchange of an oil lease that constitutes real property under local law constitutes gain from sources with-

and income from the sale or exchange of real property located without the United States constitute income from sources without the United States.[31]

[vi] Sale or Exchange of Personal Property

Purchase and Sale of Personal Property

Gains, profits, and income derived from the purchase of personal property without the United States and its sale or exchange within the United States constitute income from sources within the United States.[32] Conversely, gains, profits, and income derived from the purchase of personal property within the United States and its sale or exchange without the United States constitute income from sources without the United States.[33] Thus, income from the purchase and sale of personal property is treated as derived entirely from the country in which the property is sold.[34]

A sale of personal property takes place at the time when, and the place where, the rights, title and interest of the seller in, and the risk of ownership of, the property are transferred to the buyer.[35] Thus, where a foreign corporation sold crude petroleum to a buyer with title and delivery to, and possession

---

in the United States, even though the sale or exchange is consummated outside the United States. Texas-Canadian Oil Corp. Ltd., 44 B.T.A. 913 (1941).

[31] IRC § 862(a)(5).

[32] IRC § 861(a)(6).

[33] IRC § 862(a)(6).

[34] Treas. Regs. § 1.861-7(a). Rev. Rul. 55-677, 1955-2 Cum. Bull. 289, applied the place of sale test without reference to the method of acquisition of the property. Curiously, even though the function of purchasing is not considered in determining the source of income of property sold within or without the United States, purchasing constitutes a trade or business activity to which income might be allocated in the absence of IRC § 862(a)(6). To eliminate any potential confusion, most income tax treaties specifically provide that an office within one treaty country that is limited to the purchase of goods will not be considered as a permanent establishment. *See, e.g.,* U.S.-Netherlands Income Tax Treaty (1965), Art. II(1)(i)(C)(iv); U.S.-United Kingdom Income Tax Treaty (1975), Art. 5(3)(d).

[35] Treas. Regs. § 1.861-7(c).

of, the oil passing to the buyer at a foreign port on the basis of an F.O.B. or C.I.F. contract of firm sale, the income constituted foreign source income, even though the contract was negotiated and payments were made in the United States.[36] If the sales "transaction is arranged in a particular manner for the primary purpose of tax avoidance," however, the foregoing title passage test will not be applied; and, instead, all factors of the transaction, such as the place of negotiation and execution of the agreement, the location of the property, and the place of payment, will be considered, and the sale will be treated as having been completed at the place where the substance of the sale occurred.[37]

If title to goods shipped from the United States to a foreign country passes to the buyer while the goods are in transit in international waters, the IRS has ruled that the income is from sources within the United States on the theory that the situs of goods in transit remains at their original situs until such time as they have acquired a permanent situs elsewhere.[38] Presumably, if goods are shipped from a foreign country to the United States with title passing on the high seas, the income would constitute foreign source income.

Production and Sale of Personal Property

Gains, profits and income from the sale of personal property (a) that is produced (in whole or in part) by the taxpayer within and sold or exchanged without the United States or (b) that is produced (in whole or in part) by the taxpayer without and sold or exchanged within the United States are treated as derived partly from sources within and partly from sources without the United States.[39]

Income derived from the ownership or operation of a farm, mine, oil or gas well, other natural deposit, or timber, located within the United States, whether the producer's sale of the products thereof occurs within or without the United States, ordinarily constitutes gross income from sources within the

---

[36] East Coast Oil Co. v. Comm'r, 85 F.2d 332 (5th Cir. 1936). *See* Ronrico Corp., 44 B.T.A. 1130 (1941).

[37] Treas. Regs. § 1.861-7(c).

[38] Rev. Rul. 70-304, 1970-1 Cum. Bull. 163.

[39] IRC § 863(b)(2). *See* Rev. Rul. 71-387, 1971-2 Cum. Bull. 264.

United States.[40] In certain cases, however, if peculiar conditions of production, sale, or other reason exist, gross income derived from natural resources located within the United States may be apportioned to sources partly from within and partly from without the United States.[41] Conversely, income of a foreign corporation from the mining and processing a natural resource in a foreign country and the sale of the product in the United States, without further treatment or processing outside the foreign country, probably constitutes gross income from sources without the United States.[42]

Sale or Exchange of Corporate Stock

Gain from the exchange of stock in a domestic corporation was held to constitute income from sources in the country of the exchange when the holder of the stock had no control over the location of the exchange.[43] If a transaction is arranged in separate steps so that no step independently attracts Federal income tax, however, the IRS and the courts may examine the entire transaction to determine whether it is subject to Federal income tax.[44]

---

[40] Treas. Regs. § 1.863-1(b).

[41] Treas. Regs. §§ 1.863-1(b)(1), (2).

[42] Rev. Rul. 67-194, 1967-1 Cum. Bull. 183.

[43] Rev. Rul. 75-263, 1975-2 Cum. Bull. 287. Gain from the exchange of stock in a domestic corporation for stock of a foreign corporation was treated as income from sources without the United States, where the exchange took place outside the United States. Hay v. Comm'r, 145 F.2d 1001 (4th Cir. 1944), *cert. denied* 324 U.S. 863 (1945). Query whether gain from the liquidation of a domestic corporation, which is treated as gain from the sale or exchange of stock, would be treated as foreign source income, if the liquidation could be arranged to take place outside the United States. In *Hay, supra,* the Court held that the source of income on the liquidation of a corporation is the same as the source of income on the distribution of a dividend by such corporation. In De Nobili Cigar Co. v. Comm'r, 143 F.2d 436 (2d Cir. 1944), a capital gain redemption was held not taxable to a foreign shareholder. *But see* Rev. Rul. 72-87, 1972-1 Cum. Bull. 274, which requires withholding in such a case even though the gain would not be taxable to the foreign shareholder.

[44] *Cf.* Rev. Rul. 77-83, 1977-1 Cum. Bull. 139, where, under IRC § 482, income was allocated from a foreign parent corporation to the distributing subsidiary in spite of IRC § 311, which provides to the contrary.

Sale or Exchange of Partnership Interests

It is unclear whether gain from the sale or exchange by a nonresident alien individual or a foreign corporation of an interest in a partnership that owns real property (*e.g.*, real estate or mineral leases) located within the United States and that is engaged in a U.S. trade or business, constitutes foreign source income, even if the disposition takes place without the United States. Gain from the sale or exchange of a partnership interest by a foreign partner probably constitutes ordinary income from sources within the United States to the extent of the gain attributable to the recapture of depreciation or the recapture of intangible drilling costs in respect of property located within the United States and used in a U.S. trade or business of the partnership.[45]

[vii] **Source of Deductions**

The source rules for deductions provide only that "[t]here shall be deducted [from the items of gross income discussed above as being income from United States sources] the expenses, losses, and other deductions properly apportioned or allocated thereto and a ratable part of any expenses, losses or other deductions which cannot be definitely allocated to some item or class of gross income."[46]

---

[45] IRC § 751. A foreign partner is considered as being engaged in a U.S. trade or business if the partnership of which the foreign person is a member is so engaged. IRC § 875(1). Thus, in the year of sale, the foreign partner would be deemed engaged in a U.S. trade or business, but, in the years after the year of sale, he would no longer be deemed engaged in a U.S. trade or business (assuming that he has no other partnership interests or other U.S. trade or business). Accordingly, payments received on the installment method in subsequent years should not be subject to Federal income tax, even though such income constitutes ordinary income from U.S. sources. Treas. Regs. §§ 1.864-3(a), 1.871-8(c), 1.872-1(b), 1.881-1(b)(1), 1.881-2(a)(1), 1.1441-2(a)(3).

[46] IRC §§ 861(b), 862(b), 863. Treas. Regs. § 1.861-8 describe, in a long and complex form with many examples, the allocation and apportionment rules.

[b] Is the Foreign Investor Engaged in a Trade or
      Business Within the United States?

As important as the source of income rules to the Federal
income taxation of foreign investors is whether the foreign
investor is engaged in a trade or business within the United
States.

[i] Trade or Business Under the Code

The Code itself does not define the term "trade or business
within the United States," except with respect to the performance of personal services and trading in securities or commodities.[47] Under the Code, the performance of personal services
within the United States at any time within the taxable year
constitutes a trade or business within the United States. There
is a limited exception, known generally as the "commercial
traveler" exception, for the performance by a nonresident
alien of services in the United States for a foreign employer
that is not engaged in a trade or business within the United
States, if the nonresident alien employee is temporarily
present in the United States for a period or periods not exceeding ninety days during the taxable year and the compensation
does not exceed $3,000.[48] This exception is broadened in vari-
ous income tax treaties with respect to the number of days
within the United States, the amount of compensation, or
both.[49]

In 1966, to assist the balance of payments, the Congress
amended the Code to provide that trading in securities or
commodities through a resident broker, commission agent,
custodian or other agent, even if the agent has discretionary

---

[47] IRC § 864(b).

[48] IRC § 864(b)(1). *See* discussion in N. 26, *supra*.

[49] *See*, for example, Article VII of the 1942 U.S.-Canada Income Tax
Treaty, where the period of presence in the U.S. is increased from 90 days
to 183 days and where exemption from taxation is granted if the Canadian
meets either of two tests: (i) the compensation (no limit) is for personal
services performed as an officer or employee of a Canadian resident corporation or for the Canadian permanent establishment of a U.S. enterprise or (ii)
the compensation for personal services in the U.S. does not exceed $5,000.

authority to make decisions in effecting the transactions, does not constitute a trade or business within the United States.[50] This amendment was particularly significant because, also as part of the 1966 amendments, known as the Foreign Investors Tax Act of 1966, Congress abandoned the "Force of Attraction" doctrine and substituted the "Effectively Connected Income" concept.[51] Under the Force of Attraction doctrine, if a foreign person was engaged in a U.S. trade or business, all of his U.S. source income was subject to Federal income tax at graduated tax rates.[52] For example, under the old law, if a nonresident alien or a foreign corporation were engaged in the oil and gas business in the United States, any U.S. source dividends and capital gains from investments in publicly traded stocks and securities would have been added to the oil and gas income and subjected to the graduated income tax rates of the Federal income tax, even if the dividends and capital gains were totally unconnected with the oil and gas business. Under the "Effectively Connected Income" concept, only income that is "effectively connected" with the U.S. trade or business of a nonresident alien individual or a foreign corporation is subjected to graduated income tax.[53] In the previous example, but under the new law, the capital gains of the foreign investor from trading in U.S. stocks or securities would not be subject to U.S. income tax if the gains are not effectively connected with a U.S. trade or business. In the case of a nonresident alien individual foreign investor who is present in the United States for 183 days or more in the taxable year, however, the gains would be taxed at a flat 30 percent rate.[54]

Generally, a single, isolated transaction will not cause a tax-

---

[50] IRC §§ 864(b)(2), as added by § 102(d) of the Foreign Investors Tax Act of 1966, P.L. 89-809.

[51] IRC § 864(c), as added by § 102(d) of the Foreign Investors Tax Act of 1966, P.L. 89-809.

[52] IRC § 871(c) before its elimination by the Foreign Investors Act of 1966, P.L. 89-809, § 103(a)(1).

[53] IRC §§ 872(a)(2) (nonresident alien individuals), 882(b)(2) (foreign corporations).

[54] IRC § 871(a)(2). The tax on capital gains may be eliminated by treaty. *See* Article VIII of the 1942 U.S.-Canada Income Tax Treaty and IRC § 894(b).

payer to be treated as engaged in a trade or business within the United States.[55] Furthermore, ownership of rental real estate and the receipt of rent under net leases of the property probably do not constitute the conduct of a trade or business in the United States.[56] The management of U.S. real estate, if done through a resident agent, however, probably constitutes the conduct of a U.S. trade or business, particularly if the management is considerable, continuous and regular.[57]

A nonoperating or nonworking interest in a U.S. oil and gas property (*e.g,* a royalty or net profits interest) probably does not constitute the conduct of a trade or business within the United States,[58] but a foreign investor holding an operating or working interest in a U.S. oil and gas property probably would be treated as engaged in the conduct of a U.S. trade or business, even if he is not the operator.[59]

A foreign investor is considered as being engaged in a U.S. trade or business if the partnership of which the foreign investor is a member is so engaged.[60] Moreover, even if the foreign person is only a limited partner in a U.S. limited partnership which is engaged in a U.S. business, he will be considered to

---

[55] *See* Continental Trading, Inc. v. Comm'r, 265 F.2d 40 (9th Cir. 1959), *cert. denied,* 361 U.S. 827 (1959); Jorge Pasquel, T.C. Dkt. No. 38425, 12 T.C.M. 1431 (1953). *Cf.,* George Buono, 74 T.C. — No. 15 (1980).

[56] Evelyn M. L. Neill, 46 B.T.A. 197 (1942); Rev. Rul. 73-522 Cum. Bull. 226; *see* Letter Rulings 7826039 (March 29, 1978) and 7731043 (May 6, 1977). But note that a taxpayer who derives income from U.S. real estate, the ownership of which does not constitute a U.S. trade or business, may elect to treat such income as effectively connected with a United States business. IRC §§ 871(d) (nonresident alien individuals), 882(d) (foreign corporations). *See* discussion in § 3.01[1][c][ii], *infra.*

[57] *See* Amos R. E. Pinchot v. Comm'r, 113 F.2d 718 (2d Cir. 1940); and Jan Casimir Lewenhaupt, 20 T.C. 151 (1953), *aff'd on another issue,* 221 F.2d 227 (9th Cir. 1955). *See also* Investors' Mortgage Security Co., T.C.Dkt. No. 2278, 4 T.C.M. 45 (1945).

[58] *See* Rev. Rul. 69-355, 1969-1 Cum. Bull. 65; and Rev. Rul. 73-419, 1973-2 Cum. Bull. 436. Query whether a taxpayer who holds a royalty interest which he retained in an oil and gas farm-out and which is convertible into a working interest after payout would be treated as engaged in a U.S. trade or business. *Cf.* Rev. Rul. 77-176, 1977-1 Cum. Bull. 77.

[59] *See* Bush #1, 48 T.C. 218 (1967), *acq.,* 1968-2 Cum. Bull. 2; Rev. Rul. 58-166, 1958-1 Cum. Bull. 324.

[60] IRC § 875(1).

be engaged in the U.S. business of the partnership and taxable on his distributive share of partnership income.[61]

[ii]   Trade or Business Under Treaty—Permanent Establishment

Generally, under an income tax treaty, the question is not whether the foreign investor is engaged in a trade or business within the United States, but whether he has a permanent establishment in the United States.[62] Although the concepts of "engaged in trade or business" and "permanent establishment" are similar, they are not synonymous; and a taxpayer may be engaged in a U.S. trade or business, but not be found to have a U.S. permanent establishment.[63]

Generally, income tax treaties provide that a U.S. subsidiary corporation is not treated as a permanent establishment of its foreign parent corporation.[64]

[iii]   Trade or Business—Annual Determination

Whether a foreign investor is engaged in a trade or business in the United States is separately determined for each taxable year.[65] If at any time during the taxable year the foreign investor is engaged in a U.S. trade or business, he is considered to be engaged in a U.S. trade or business during the entire taxable year. If he is not engaged in a U.S. trade or business at any time

---

[61] Rev. Rul. 75-23, 1975-1 Cum. Bull. 290. *See* Donroy, Ltd. v. Comm'r, 301 F.2d 200 (9th Cir. 1962).

[62] *See, e.g.,* Article II of the U.S.-Netherlands Treaty.

[63] In two Tax Court cases, foreign investors were found not to have permanent establishments in the U.S. in respect of their ownership and leasing of real property. Inez de Amodio, 34 T.C. 894 (1960), *aff'd per curiam,* 299 F.2d 623 (3d Cir. 1962) (under the U.S.-Swiss Income Tax Treaty); Elizabeth Herbert, 30 T.C. 26 (1958), *Acq.,* 1958-2 Cum. Bull. 6 (under the U.S.-British Income Tax Treaty).

[64] *See, e.g.,* Article 4(6) of the U.S.-France Income Tax Treaty; Article II(1)(i)(F) of the U.S.-Netherlands Income Tax Treaty.

[65] Treas. Regs. § 1.871-8(c)(1).

during the taxable year, no income is treated as being effectively connected with the conduct of a U.S. trade or business for any part of the taxable year, even though some or all of the income may have been effectively connected with the conduct of a U.S. trade or business for a previous taxable year.[66] On the other hand, income that is treated as effectively connected for a taxable year with the conduct of a U.S. trade or business generally will be treated as effectively connected for a subsequent taxable year if the foreign investor is engaged in a U.S. trade or business during any part of the subsequent year, even though such income is not effectively connected with the conduct of the trade or business carried on in the U.S. during such subsequent year. For example, if a foreign investor is engaged in a U.S. trade or business from January 1 through August 31, 1980, at which time he ceases his U.S. trade or business, installment payments in respect of U.S. sales received during September through December, 1980, would be treated as effectively connected income, but installment payments in respect of U.S. sales received in 1981 would not be treated as effectively connected income because he would not be engaged in a U.S. trade or business at any time during 1981.[67] If, in 1982, the foreign investor commences a new U.S. trade or business, even though it is unrelated to his previous U.S. trade or business, the installment payments he receives in 1982 in respect of the previous trade or business will be treated as effectively connected income.[68] Based upon the foregoing rules, if a foreign investor disposes of a U.S. trade or business on the installment basis, installments received in years following the year of sale and while he is no longer engaged in a U.S. trade or business would not be subject to U.S. income tax.[69]

---

[66] Treas. Regs. §§ 1.864-3(a), 1.871-8(c)(2) *Example* (2).

[67] Treas. Regs. §§ 1.864-3(a), 1.864-3(b), *Example* (1), 1.871-8(c)(1).

[68] Treas. Regs. § 1.871-8(c)(1).

[69] *Id.* Future payments would be subject to Federal income tax only if they constitute fixed or determinable annual or periodical gains, profits or income from U.S. sources. IRC §§ 871(a)(1), 881(a)(1). Interest on the installment payments would constitute fixed or determinable annual or periodical income. Interest would be imputed, if not stated in the obligation. IRC § 483. Although perhaps not free from doubt, principal payments probably do not

[c] What Is Effectively Connected Income?

[i] Background

As noted above, a nonresident alien individual or a foreign corporation is subject to Federal income tax on only two categories of income, namely (i) certain income from sources within the United States that is not effectively connected with the conduct of a trade or business within the United States;[70] and (ii) all income that is effectively connected with the conduct of a trade or business within the United States.[71]

This scheme of taxation of foreign persons was adopted by Congress in 1966, as part of the Foreign Investors Tax Act of 1966, to replace the "Force of Attraction" doctrine.

Under the prior scheme, if a foreign investor were engaged in a U.S. trade or business, all his U.S. source income would have been subject to tax at graduated tax rates. Under the present scheme, only the effectively connected income of a foreign investor is subject to graduated income tax rates; and his other taxable U.S. source income is subject to withholding tax at a flat rate of 30 percent, unless such tax is reduced or eliminated by treaty.[72] Prior to the 1966 amendments, foreign investors were subject to U.S. income tax only on U.S. source income, whether or not they were engaged in the conduct of a trade or business.[73] Under the 1966 amendments, effectively

---

fall within the concept of fixed or determinable annual or periodical income. Treas. Regs. §§ 1.871-8(c)(2), *Example* (2), 1.881-2(a)(1), 1.1441-2(a)(3). The conclusion set forth in the preceding sentence is based on the assumption that, if the foreign seller is a nonresident alien individual, he would not be present in the U.S. for 183 days or more in any year after the sale of his trade or business. IRC § 871(a)(2).

[70] Generally, this category of income falls within the general term "fixed or determinable annual or periodical income," which includes interest, dividends, rents, royalties, salaries, wages, premiums, annuities, compensations, remunerations, and emoluments. IRC §§ 871(a)(1)(A), 881(a)(1).

[71] IRC §§ 871(b), 882(a).

[72] *Id. See* N. 13, *supra.*

[73] IRC §§ 872(a) and 882(b), prior to the 1966 amendments.

connected income can include certain limited types of foreign source income.[74]

[ii]   Foreign Investor Not Engaged in U.S. Trade or Business

In General

If a nonresident alien individual or a foreign corporation is not engaged in a trade or business within the United States at any time during the taxable year, no income, gain, or loss is treated as being effectively connected with the conduct of a trade or business within the United States.[75] This rule applies even though the income, gain or loss would have been treated as effectively connected with the conduct of a trade or business within the United States if such income or gain had been received or accrued, or such loss had been sustained, in an earlier taxable year when the taxpayer was engaged in a U.S. trade or business.[76]

Real Property Election

In General. A nonresident alien individual or a foreign corporation may elect to treat income from real property as income that is effectively connected with a U.S. trade or business and, thus, subject the taxable income therefrom (*i.e.,* gross income less applicable deductions) to tax at graduated income tax rates.[77] This election applies to income (*e.g.,* to rents or royalties) that, but for the election, would be taxed at a flat rate of 30 percent on gross income because it would not be treated as income effectively connected with the conduct of a trade or business within the United States.[78] Often a tax at 30 percent of gross rental or royalty income would be greater than a tax of 46 to 70 percent of the taxable income from rent or royal-

---

[74] IRC § 864(c)(4). *See* text accompanying Ns. 96-102, *infra.*

[75] IRC § 864(c)(1)(B).

[76] Treas. Regs. §§ 1.864-3(a), 1.864-3(b), *Example* (1), 1.871-8(c)(1). *See* N. 69, *supra.*

[77] IRC §§ 871(d) (for nonresident alien individuals), 882(d) (for foreign corporations). A similar rule exists that permits foreign investors to treat income from certain aircraft and vessels as income from sources within the U.S. IRC § 861(e). This chapter excludes discussion of the special tax rules applicable to insurance and transportation.

[78] IRC § 871(d)(1)(B).

ties, *i.e.*, gross rental or royalty income less the applicable deductions for ordinary and necessary business expenses, interest, taxes, depreciation, and depletion.[79]

Types of Income Covered. The election covers income from real property held for the production of income and located in the United States or from any interest in such real property, including (1) gains from the sale or exchange of the real property or an interest therein; (2) rents or royalties from mines, wells or other natural deposits; and (3) gains from timber, coal or iron ore with a retained economic interest described in Code Sections 631(b) and (c). The election, however, may not be made with respect to only one class of such income, but must apply to all income from real property.[80] Thus, if the election is made, income from U.S. real property, which would not otherwise be subject to U.S. income tax, will be subject to U.S. income tax.[81] On the other hand, an election does not cause a foreign person not engaged in trade or business in the U.S. during the taxable year to be treated as engaged in a U.S. trade or business during the taxable year.[82] Except for income covered by the real property election, a foreign investor may not treat income (*e.g.*, interest) that is not effectively connected with the conduct of a U.S. trade or business as so connected.[83]

Binding Election. Under the Code. The election once made

---

[79] The individual foreign investor-owner of a building who receives $500,000 of rental income and who has agent's fees of $35,000, repair and maintenance expense of $50,000, custodial expenses of $15,000, real estate taxes of $70,000, mortgage interest of $90,000, and depreciation of $40,000 would suffer a 30 percent withholding tax of $150,000 as opposed to paying a tax of no more than $140,000 even if the entire $200,000 of taxable rental income ($500,000 less $300,000 of expenses) were taxed at the maximum 70 percent rate for individuals. The difference in the case of a foreign corporation is much more dramatic, *i.e.*, $92,000 if the entire $200,000 of taxable rental income were taxed at the maximum 46 percent rate for corporations, as compared to $150,000 of withholding tax at the flat 30 percent rate.

[80] Treas. Regs. § 1.871-10(b)(1). For purposes of the election, income from real property does not include interest on a debt obligation secured by a mortgage on real property. Treas. Regs. § 1.871-10(b)(2).

[81] *Id.*

[82] Treas. Regs. §§ 1.871-10(c)(1), 1.882-2(c).

[83] *See* Rev. Rul. 74-63, 1974-1 Cum. Bull. 374.

for a taxable year remains in effect for all subsequent years, unless revoked with the consent of the Commissioner with respect to any taxable year.[84] Moreover, once revoked, a new election cannot be made for any taxable year before the fifth taxable year following the year of revocation, unless the IRS consents to a new election.[85]

Under Treaties. Since the provisions of an income tax treaty generally override any contrary provisions of the Code,[86] nationals and corporations of a treaty country may be permitted to make the real property elections annually. Under the income tax treaty with the Netherlands, for example, a Netherlands corporation or a nonresident alien who resides in the Netherlands and who derives from U.S. sources (1) royalties in respect of the operation of mines, quarries or natural resources or (2) rentals from real property may make a new election each year to be taxed on a net basis; that is, the election the Dutch foreign investor makes for any one year is not binding on future years.[87]

Partnership. If a foreign investor is a member of a partnership that has real property income, the election to be taxed on a net basis in respect of the partnership's real property income must be made by the foreign partner and not by the partnership.[88]

[iii]   Foreign Investor Engaged in U.S. Trade or Business

For purposes of determining what income is effectively con-

---

[84] IRC §§ 871(d)(1), 882(d)(1).

[85] IRC §§ 871(d)(2), 882(d)(2).

[86] IRC §§ 894(a), 7852(d).

[87] United States-Netherlands Income Tax Treaty (1965), Art. X. A similar provision applies in the case of the Netherlands Antilles, except that the provision was modified by Protocol in 1963 to make it clear that the election pertains only to U.S. taxation of the rental and royalty income referred to in the Article and not to other income from U.S. sources. Article II of the Protocol. *See* Rev. Rul. 77-174, 1977-1 Cum. Bull. 414, which provides that the treaty election is an annual election under the Canadian and French treaties.

[88] Treas. Regs. § 1.871-10(d)(3).

nected income in the case of a nonresident alien individual or a foreign corporation that is engaged in a trade or business within the United States during a taxable year, the taxpayer's income falls into three categories, namely (1) periodical income and capital gains from U.S. sources; (2) other U.S. source income; and (3) foreign source income.[89]

Periodical Income and Capital Gain from U.S. Sources.

In the case of income from sources within the United States that consists of (1) fixed or determinable annual or periodical gains, profits and income (*e.g.*, interest, dividends, rents, and royalties) or (2) gain or loss from the sale or exchange of capital assets, certain factors are taken into account in order to determine whether the fixed or determinable annual or periodical income or the capital gain or loss is effectively connected for the taxable year with the conduct of a trade or business in the United States. The principal factors are (a) whether the income, gain or loss is derived from assets used in, or held for use in the conduct of the trade or business in the United States (the so-called assets-use test); and (b) whether the activities of the trade or business conducted in the United States were a material factor in the realization of the income, gain, or loss (the so-called business-activities test).[90]

Asset-Use Test. The asset-use test ordinarily applies in making a determination with respect to income, gain, or loss of a passive type where trade or business activities as such do not give rise directly to the realization of the income, gain, or loss. The asset-use test is of primary significance where, for example, interest or dividend income is derived from sources within the United States by a nonresident alien individual or foreign corporation that is engaged in the business of manufacturing or selling goods in the United States.[91] For example, if the U.S. branch of a foreign corporation is required to hold a large

---

[89] IRC § 864(c). Although interest on United States bank accounts, etc. (*see* discussion in the text, *supra*, at N. 22) is usually considered to be non-U.S. source income, for the purpose of determining whether such interest is effectively connected income, "such interest shall be treated as income from sources within the United States. . . ." Treas. Regs. § 1.864-4(c)(1)(iii).

[90] Treas. Regs. § 1.864-4(c)(1)(i).

[91] Treas. Regs. § 1.864-4(c)(2)(i).

current cash balance for business purposes, but the amount of the cash balance so ⌐ quired varies because of the fluctuating seasonal nature of the branch's business, interest on U.S. Treasury Bills purchased when large cash balances are not required constitutes effectively connected income.[92]

Business-Activities Test. The business-activities test ordinarily applies in making a determination with respect to income, gain, or loss which, even though generally of the passive type, arises directly from the active conduct of the taxpayer's trade or business in the United States. The business-activities test is of primary significance, for example, where (a) dividends or interest are derived by a dealer in stocks or securities, (b) gain or loss is derived from the sale or exchange of capital assets in the active conduct of a trade or business by an investment company, (c) royalties are derived in the active conduct of a business consisting of the licensing of patents or similar tangible property, or (d) service fees are derived in the active conduct of a servicing business.[93]

Other U.S. Source Income.

All income, gain or loss from sources within the United States, other than fixed or determinable annual or periodical income and capital gains, derived by a nonresident alien individual or a foreign corporation engaged in a trade or business in the United States is treated as effectively connected with the conduct of a trade or business within the United States.[94] This income, gain, or loss is treated as effectively connected for the taxable year with the conduct of a trade or business in the United States, whether or not the income, gain, or loss is derived from the trade or business being carried on in the United States during the taxable year.[95]

---

[92] Treas. Regs. § 1.864-4(c)(2)(iv), *Example* (1). Similarly, interest on a bank certificate of deposit, which would otherwise be treated as non U.S. source income (§§ 861(a)(1)(A), 861(c)), would be treated as effectively connected interest to be included in the foreign investor's gross income. See N. 89, *supra.*

[93] Treas. Regs. § 1.864-4(c)(3).

[94] IRC § 864(c)(3).

[95] Treas. Regs. § 1.864-4(b).

Foreign Source Income.

Although much attention has been given to the change made by the Foreign Investors Tax Act of 1966 to include foreign source income as one of the categories of effectively connected income, only three types of income, gain, or loss from sources without the United States can be treated as effectively connected with the conduct of a trade or business within the United States, and, then, only if the nonresident alien individual or foreign corporation has an office or other fixed place of business within the United States to which such income, gain, or loss is attributable.[96] The three types of income consist of (a) rents or royalties from the use of, or gains from the sale of, intangible property (*e.g.*, patents, copyrights, secret processes, trademarks, or franchises) located outside the United States, if such income is derived in the active conduct of a licensing business; (b) dividends, interest, or gain or loss from the sale or exchange of stocks, securities, bonds, or notes, if such income is derived in the active conduct of a banking, financing or similar business or received by a foreign investment company; and (c) income from the sale or exchange of personal property which constitutes inventory or other property held primarily for sale to customers in the ordinary course of business, but only if such property is sold through a U.S. office or other fixed place of business of the taxpayer and, if the property is sold for use, consumption or disposition outside the United States, an office or other fixed place of business of the taxpayer outside the United States did not participate materially in the sale.[97]

In determining whether a nonresident alien individual or a foreign corporation has an office or other fixed place of business within the United States, an office or other fixed place of business of an agent shall be disregarded unless the agent (i) has the authority to negotiate and conclude contracts in the name of the nonresident alien individual or foreign corporation and regularly exercises that authority or has a stock of merchandise from which he regularly fills orders on behalf of the foreign investor and (ii) is not a general commission agent,

---

[96] IRC § 864(c)(4).
[97] IRC § 864(c)(4)(B).

broker or other agent of independent status acting in the ordinary course of his business.[98] Income, gain, or loss shall not be considered as attributable to an office or other fixed place of business within the United States unless the office or fixed place of business is a material factor in the production of the income, gain, or loss and the office or fixed place of business regularly carries on activities of the type from which the income, gain, or loss is derived.[99]

Foreign source income is exempt from Federal income tax if required by a treaty, even if the income, in the absence of a treaty exemption, would be treated as effectively connected with the conduct of a trade or business within the United States.[100] For example, under the U.S.-Switzerland Income Tax Treaty, if a Swiss enterprise has a permanent establishment situated in the United States, the United States may impose Federal income tax on its industrial and commercial profits, but only on income from sources within the United States.[101] The IRS has ruled that, notwithstanding the 1966 amendments to the Code which impose Federal income tax on certain types of foreign source income, such taxation is not permitted if contrary to a treaty obligation.[102]

Computation of Taxable Income from U.S. Sources

Taxable income effectively connected with the conduct of a trade or business within the United States is determined by deducting from the gross income effectively connected with the conduct of a trade or business within the United States both (a) the expenses, losses and other deductions properly apportioned or allocated thereto and (b) a ratable part of any expenses, losses or deductions that cannot definitely be allocated to some item or class of gross income.[103] The Treasury Regulations contain extensive rules for the computation of

---

[98] IRC § 864(c)(5)(A).

[99] IRC § 864(c)(5)(B).

[100] Rev. Rul. 74-63, 1974-1 Cum. Bull. 374.

[101] Article III(1)(a) of the U.S.-Switzerland Income Tax Treaty. *See also* Article III(1) of the U.S.-Australia Income Tax Treaty.

[102] Rev. Rul. 74-63, *op. cit.*, N. 100, *supra.*

[103] IRC § 861(b). Deductions and credits are allowed, however, only if the foreign taxpayer files a true and accurate return. IRC §§ 874(a), 882(c)(2).

taxable income from sources within the United States,[104] the most controversial of which are those that require the allocation and apportionment of interest and research and experimental expenditures to non-U.S. source income as well as to U.S. source income of the taxpayer.[105]

In computing income effectively connected with the conduct of trade or business within the United States, a nonresident alien individual is allowed the deduction for one personal exemption of $1,000.[106]

The Code and most treaties contain provisions that permit the IRS to distribute, apportion, or allocate income, gain, loss, deductions, and credits among related persons (whether or not incorporated, whether or not organized in the United States, and whether or not affiliated), if the IRS determines that "such distribution, apportionment, or allocation is necessary in order to prevent evasion of taxes or clearly to reflect the income of any of such organizations, trades, or businesses."[107]

[2] Federal Income Taxation of Individual Foreign Investors

[a] General Scheme of Taxation

A foreign individual is either a nonresident alien or a resident alien for Federal income tax purposes. A resident alien is subject to Federal income tax basically in the same manner as a U.S. citizen, that is, he is subject to tax on his worldwide taxable income (*i.e.*, gross income less allowable deductions) at

---

104 Treas. Regs. § 1.861-8.

105 Treas. Regs. §§ 1.861-8(e)(2), (3).

106 IRC § 873(b)(3). Additional exemptions allowed by IRC § 151 are available only to nationals of the United States, and to residents of a contiguous country or if authorized by a treaty.

107 IRC § 482. The workings of IRC § 482 are far beyond the scope of this chapter. Suffice it to say that the IRS will scrutinize intercompany loans, intercompany service agreements (*e.g.*, marketing, managerial, administrative or technical agreements), intercompany licenses, and intercompany sales of goods. Treas. Regs. § 1.482-2.

graduated tax rates ranging from 14 to 70 percent.[108] A non-resident alien, on the other hand, is subject to Federal income tax on only two categories of gross income: (i) gross income derived from sources within the United States but *not* effectively connected with the conduct of a trade or business within the United States, which is subject to tax at a rate of 30 percent[109] unless the rate is reduced or eliminated by treaty; and (ii) gross income effectively connected with the conduct of a trade or business within the United States, which, after allowable deductions, is taxed at graduated tax rates ranging from 14 to 70 percent.[110] The first category includes only certain types of U.S. source income, notably (i) fixed or determinable annual or periodical gains, profits, and income (*e.g.*, salaries, wages, dividends, interest, rents, and royalties); (ii) gains from the sale of timber, coal or iron ore where the taxpayer retains an economic interest in such timber, coal or iron ore; and (iii) capital gains, but only if the nonresident alien is physically present in the United States for a period or periods aggregating 183 days or more during the taxable year.[111] If a nonresident alien has both categories of income in a taxable year, he calculates his

---

[108] Treas. Regs. §§ 1.1-1(b), 1.871-1(a).

[109] IRC §§ 871(a), IRC § 1441. Treas. Regs. § 1.871-7(a)(1). IRC § 1441(a) imposes the duty of withholding the 30 percent or reduced treaty rate of tax on "all persons, in whatever capacity acting (including lessees or mortgagors of real or personal property, fiduciaries, employers, and [indeed] all officers and employees of the United States) having control, receipt, custody, disposal, or payment of any ["fixed or determinable, annual or periodical" income] items . . . (to the extent any . . . constitutes gross income from sources within the United States) of any nonresident alien individual or foreign partnership. . . ." IRC § 1442 applies the withholding requirement to payments to foreign corporations. Since the problems of withholding are generally technical and since the duty to withhold is usually imposed on U.S. persons, the subject will not be further discussed in this chapter.

[110] IRC § 871(b). *See* Treas. Regs. § 1.871-1(a).

[111] IRC §§ 871(a)(1), (2). If a nonresident alien meets the 183-day physical presence test during a taxable year, capital gains arising during the period or periods of the taxable year in which he is not present are also subject to tax. Treas. Regs. § 1.871-7(d)(2)(i). If the nonresident alien does not meet the 183-day physical presence test during the taxable year, none of his capital gains derived during the taxable year is subject to U.S. income tax, unless they are effectively connected with a U.S. trade or business. Treas. Regs. § 1.871-7(d)(2)(ii).

Federal income tax separately with respect to each income category; and the nonresident alien is not subject to higher rates of tax on his effectively connected income because he also has income subject to flat rates of tax. Thus, income subject to flat rates of tax is not taken into account in determining either the rate or amount of tax on his effectively connected income that is subject to the graduated tax.[112]

[b] Nonresident and Resident Alien Defined

[i] General Rule

An alien is presumed to be a nonresident alien.[113] An alien who is physically present in the U.S. and who is not a mere transient or sojourner, however, is treated as a U.S. resident for Federal income tax purposes.[114] Whether an alien is a transient or sojourner depends on his intentions as to the length and nature of his stay. A mere floating intention, indefinite as to time, to return to another country is not sufficient to constitute transient or sojourner status. On the other hand, an alien who comes to the U.S. for a definite purpose, which in its nature may be promptly accomplished, is a transient.

Generally, an alien whose presence in the United States is limited by his entry visa is not a U.S. resident. On the other hand, an alien, who enters the United States for a fixed purpose, but later determines that an extended stay is necessary to accomplish the purpose of his entry and, to that end, makes his home temporarily in the U.S., may become a resident for Federal income tax purposes, even though his intention at all times is to return to his foreign home when he completes or abandons his project.[115]

---

112 Treas. Regs. § 1.871-8(b)(2)(i).

113 Treas. Regs. § 1.871-4(b).

114 Treas. Regs. § 1.871-2(b). The fact that an alien is illegally or working illegally in the United States does not prevent him from being treated as a U.S. resident for income tax purposes. *See* A. Budhhuani, 70 T.C. 287 (1978).

115 Treas. Regs. § 1.871-2(b); M. H. Siddiqi, 70 T.C. 553 (1978). The IRS has ruled that a presumption of residence arises if the alien has resided in the U.S. for one year. Rev. Rul. 69-611, 1969-2 Cum. Bull. 150.

An alien who has acquired U.S. residence retains his resident status until he actually departs from the U.S. and abandons his previous resident status.[116] Indeed, a resident alien may not lose resident status for tax purposes even though he has left the country and remained outside the United States beyond the expiration of his reentry permit.[117]

An alien may be treated as a U.S. resident for Federal income tax purposes, even if he also is treated as a resident of a foreign country and, therefore, is a dual resident.[118]

[ii]　Taxable Year; Dual Status Tax Year

As explained earlier in this chapter, the Federal income tax is computed on the basis of an annual accounting period known as the taxable year.[119] A foreign investor may be treated both as a resident alien and a nonresident alien for the same taxable year (*e.g.*, the year of arrival of a nonresident alien who becomes a resident alien or the year of departure of a resident alien who becomes a nonresident alien). In such a year, known as a dual status tax year, the foreign investor files one return, on which he computes his Federal income tax as a resident alien for the portion of the taxable year that he is a resident alien and as a nonresident alien for the portion of the taxable year that he is a nonresident alien.[120]

Generally, the taxable year the taxpayer uses to compute his Federal income tax is the calendar year.[121] In certain circumstances, a taxpayer may compute his income tax on a fiscal year, which means a period of twelve months ending on the

---

[116] Treas. Regs. § 1.871-5.

[117] James T. Tracy, T.C. Memo 1973-28, 32 T.C.M. 102 (1973). *Cf.* Kazuko S. Marsh, 68 T.C. 68 (1977), *aff'd* without opinion (4th Cir. Oct. 25, 1978); Rev. Rul. 64-149, 1964-1 (Part I) Cum. Bull. 233.

[118] Sutton v. United States, 79-1 USTC ¶ 9293 (D.C. Tenn. 1979).

[119] IRC §§ 441, 7701(a)(23). *See* N. 6, *supra.*

[120] Reg. §§ 1.871-13, 1.6012-1(b)(2)(ii); U.S. Tax Guide for Aliens, IRS Publication 519, Chapter Four (Rev. Nov. 79).

[121] IRC § 441(b)(2).

last day of any month other than December,[122] if he is a new taxpayer and if he regularly keeps his books on such fiscal year.[123] The IRS has taken the position, however, that a nonresident alien who receives income from sources within the United States for the first time in a taxable year is not a new taxpayer in such year.[124] Moreover, the IRS probably would challenge an attempt by a foreign investor to use a taxable year other than a calendar year, unless he has a bona fide nontax purpose for doing so.[125]

[iii] Expatriation

A nonresident alien who gives up his United States citizenship nevertheless remains subject to Federal income tax at graduated rates on his income from U.S. sources for the ten-year-period following his loss of citizenship, unless he can prove that his loss did not have for one of its principal purposes the avoidance of Federal income, estate, and gift taxes.[126] For this purpose, U.S. source income is defined to include income from property located in the United States (*e.g.*, real estate) and income from stocks or bonds of domestic corporations.[127]

---

[122] IRC §§ 441(e), 7701(a)(24).

[123] IRC § 441(c).

[124] LR 7844042 (April 25, 1978).

[125] *See* IRC § 871(a)(2), last sentence, which generally prevents a nonresident alien from adopting a fiscal year to avoid the 183 day rule with respect to the taxation of capital gains.

[126] IRC § 877; Max Kronenberg, 64 T.C. 428 (1975).

[127] IRC § 877(c). The Service has ruled that the expatriation rules apply to a former U.S. citizen who becomes a resident of a foreign country with which the United States has an income tax treaty, even though the income tax treaty does not specifically preserve the right of the United States to impose tax under the expatriation provisions. It is sufficient, according to the IRS, that the treaty contain a provision (a "saving clause") that permits the United States to tax its citizens as though the treaty had not come into effect. Rev. Rul. 79-152, 1979-1 Cum. Bull. 237.

[3]   **Classification of Business Organizations for Federal Tax Purposes**

[a]   **General Rules**

A nonresident alien individual may invest directly in the United States, or he may invest through a business entity. Generally, for Federal income tax purposes, the business entity will be classified as a corporation or as a partnership[128] that can be either a domestic or a foreign entity.[129]

The standards or tests to classify a business entity for Federal income tax purposes, whether the entity is domestic or foreign, are determined under the Code, not under local law.[130] Thus, a business entity may be classified as a partnership under the laws of a state or country and as an association taxable as a corporation for Federal income tax purposes.[131]

Since corporations and partnerships share the two common characteristics of associates and an objective to carry on business and divide the gains from the business,[132] the Treasury Regulations provide that a partnership-type business entity (as opposed to a trust-type entity[133]) shall be classified as an association taxable as a corporation if it has at least three of the

---

[128] Trusts which conduct an active business generally would be classified as associations taxable as corporations or as partnerships for Federal income tax purposes. Treas. Regs. § 301.7701-4(b).

[129] A domestic corporation or partnership means a corporation or partnership created or organized in the United States or under the law of the United States or of any state or the District of Columbia. IRC §§ 7701(a)(4), (10). A foreign corporation or partnership means a corporation or partnership which is not domestic. IRC § 7701(a)(5).

[130] Treas. Regs. § 301.7701-1(b).

[131] Treas. Regs. § 301.7701-1(c). *See* William F. Buckley, 22 T.C. 1312 (1954), *aff'd*, 231 F.2d 204 (2d Cir. 1956); Arundel v. United States, 102 F.Supp. 1019 (Ct. Cl. 1952).

[132] Treas. Regs. § 301.7701-2(a)(2).

[133] Generally, the test applied to a trust is to determine whether the purpose "is to vest in trustees responsibility for the protection and conservation of property for beneficiaries who cannot share in the discharge of this responsibility and, therefore, are not associates in a joint enterprise for the conduct of a business for profit." Treas. Regs. § 301.7701-4(a). *See* Treas. Regs. § 301.7701-2(a)(2).

following four corporate characteristics, namely (1) continuity of life; (ii) centralized management; (iii) limited liability; and (iv) free transferability of interests.[134] If the business entity has less than three of these four corporate characteristics, it will be classified as a partnership for Federal income tax purposes.[135]

Although the Code rather than local law governs the standards to be applied to determine the classification of a business entity for Federal income tax purposes, local law governs the nature of the legal relationships that have been established as a result of the formation and operation of the organization.[136] For example, local law governs whether the investors have limited liability and whether the organization has unlimited life.

[b] Classification of Hybrid Entities

Generally, for Federal income tax purposes, there is not much doubt that a business entity created as a corporation under the corporation law of one of the states will be classified as a corporation or that a general partnership created under a statute corresponding to the Uniform Partnership Act will be classified as a partnership.[137] Recently, however, questions have been raised as to the classification of limited partnerships for Federal income tax purposes.[138] For example, the IRS has ruled that, notwithstanding the U.S.-German Income Tax Treaty that defines a United States corporation as a corporation created or organized under the laws of the United States

---

[134] Treas. Regs. §§ 301.7701-2(a)(1), (3).

[135] Treas. Regs. § 301.7701-2(a)(3). *See* Rev. Rul. 79-106, 1979-1 Cum. Bull. 448; Phillip G. Larson, 66 T.C. 159 (1976), appeal to 9th Cir. *dism'd* January 15, 1978. It should be noted, however, that these Regulations are controversial and they may be changed by administrative action (*see* Treas. Dept. News Release, Jan. 14, 1977) or the law may be changed by Congress as suggested in President Carter's Tax Message to Congress in 1978.

[136] Treas. Regs. § 301.7701-1(c). *See* Rev. Rul. 73-254, 1973-1 Cum. Bull. 613.

[137] The test applied is similar to the one used by the Supreme Court Justice to whom is attributed a statement that he could not define pornography, but that he knew it when he saw it.

[138] *See* Phillip G. Larson, *op. cit.* N. 135, *supra.*

or any state, a U.S. limited partnership with German resident limited partners and a U.S. general partner was an association taxable as a corporation.[139]

Some state laws and a great many foreign laws contain optional provisions that can be used to modify the character of a business entity with the result that a business entity, which otherwise would be treated as a corporation for Federal income tax purposes, will be treated as a partnership; or *vice versa.* Although it is relatively clear that a French Societe Anonyme, a German Aktiengesellschaft, a Mexican Sociedad Anonima, or a Brazilian Sociedade Anomina, will be treated as a corporation for Federal income tax purposes, there often is uncertainty as to whether a French Societe a Responsabilite Limitee, a German Gesellschaft mit beschraenkter Haftung, a Mexican Sociedad de Responsibilidad Limitada, or a Brazilian Sociedade por Quotas de Responsabilidade Limitada will be treated as a corporation or partnership for Federal income tax purposes.[140] Similarly, there is doubt as to the Wyoming Limited Liability Company, which can assume the characteristics of a partnership or corporation for Federal income tax purposes.[141]

For tax planning purposes, it may be possible to design a business entity that, for Federal income tax purposes, constitutes an association taxable as a corporation, but, for foreign law purposes, constitutes a partnership, or *vice versa.* Such a hybrid entity may be useful, for example, in a situation where the foreign investors wish to avoid being treated as partners engaged in a U.S. trade or business (*e.g.,* to avoid filing U.S. income tax returns), but wish to pass through deductions for

---

[139] Rev. Rul. 76-435, 1976-2 Cum. Bull. 490.

[140] The IRS has published a list with the classification of about two-hundred forms of business entities used in about forty-five countries. Exhibit 600-8, Foreign Forms of Business Organization, Internal Revenue Manual, referred to in I CCH Internal Revenue Manual (Audit) ch. 671, 673, at 7283-72.

[141] Wyo. Stat. § 17-15-101 *et seq.* (1977). It is understood that the IRS is considering a ruling request on the classification of a Wyoming Limited Liability Company, but there is now no published authority on the tax status of such an entity.

foreign income tax purposes.[142]

Although there is no technical reason why a foreign business entity may not be treated "as one kind of taxpayer under foreign law but [as] a different class of taxpayer under U.S. law," there is dictum in a recent case that a "[t]axpayer may not escape liability in a foreign nation's courts under one theory and then seek an advantage in this nation's courts by contending the opposite."[143] Thus, the IRS and the courts may be reluctant to permit a business entity to have a different tax status under U.S. law than under foreign law, particularly in a case of tax avoidance. In addition, under certain circumstances the IRS may treat a business entity as a nominee, dummy or sham, and, therefore, ignore it for Federal income tax purposes.[144]

There are certain legal forms of organization under foreign law which have been classified contrary to the expectation of the foreign investors utilizing such forms of organization. For example, if the grantor of a Liechtenstein Anstalt has the power to revoke the entity and recover the assets, the Alstalt might be classified as a grantor trust rather than as a corporation.[145] If the Anstalt holds U.S. real property, the U.S. estate tax might apply on the death of the grantor[146] and U.S. gift tax might apply on an intervivos disposition of Anstalt interests to family members,[147] contrary to the expectation of the foreign investor/grantor. Foreign investors, therefore, should seek specific advice as to the classification for Federal income tax purposes of the business organizations they desire to utilize to

---

[142] *Cf.*, Abbott Laboratories International Co. v. Comm'r, 267 F.2d 940 (7th Cir. 1959).

[143] United States v. Elot H. Raffety Farms Inc., 511 F.2d 1234, 1239 (8th Cir. 1975). *See* "Foreign Entity Characterization," 35 Tax L. Rev. 167, 195 (1980).

[144] *See* Fillman v. United States, 255 F.2d 632 (Ct. Cl. 1966). *See also* Aiken Industries, 56 TC 925 (1971), where the Tax Court upheld the IRS that had ignored a treaty country corporation which was interposed between a U.S. borrower and a foreign lender solely to avoid withholding tax on interest payments. *See* discussion, *infra*, § 3.02[3][b], following N. 237.

[145] *See* Rev. Rul. 79-116, 1979-1 Cum. Bull. 212.

[146] IRC § 2103.

[147] IRC § 2511(a).

hold U.S. property or to conduct a trade or business in the United States.

[4] Federal Income Taxation of Foreign Corporations

[a] General Rules

A corporation is treated for Federal income tax purposes as a taxable entity separate from, and independent of, its shareholders.[148] The rates of the Federal corporation income tax are as follows:[149]

17 percent of the first $25,000 of taxable income
20 percent of the second $25,000 of taxable income
30 percent of the third $25,000 of taxable income
40 percent of the fourth $25,000 of taxable income
46 percent of taxable income in excess of $100,000.

Although domestic corporations are taxable on their world-wide taxable income, a foreign corporation is subject to Federal income tax in a fashion similar to the taxation of a nonresident alien individual, namely, it is subject to Federal income tax on only two categories of gross income: (i) gross income that is derived from sources within the United States but is not effectively connected with the conduct of a trade or business within the United States is subject to a flat rate of tax of 30 percent, unless such tax is reduced or eliminated by treaty; and (ii) gross income that is effectively connected with the conduct of a trade or business within the United States and

---

148 IRC § 11(a). A foreign investor cannot utilize a Subchapter S corporation, which, similar to a partnership (see § 3.01[5], infra), permits income and loss to flow through to its shareholders, because Subchapter S status is available only to a domestic corporation, and a domestic corporation itself cannot qualify if it has a corporation or a nonresident alien individual as a shareholder. IRC § 1371(a).

149 IRC § 11(b). A foreign investor may not use multiple corporations in order to use the lesser graduated tax rates and, therefore, reduce the Federal income tax on the first $100,000 of taxable income of each corporation. IRC §§ 1551, 1561.

that, after allowable deductions, is taxed at the corporate tax rates applicable to domestic corporations.[150]

The first category of income includes only certain items of income, notably dividends, interest, rents, royalties, and other fixed or determinable annual or periodical income, and gains from the sale of timber, coal or iron ore where the taxpayer retains an economic interest in such timber, coal or iron ore.[151] Unlike a nonresident alien individual, who, if physically present in the U.S. for 183 days or more during the taxable year, is taxable on capital gains which are not effectively connected with the conduct of a trade or business within the United States, a foreign corporation is not subject to tax on capital gains unless the capital gains are effectively connected with the conduct of a U.S. trade or business.[152]

[b] Accumulated Earnings Tax and Personal Holding Company Tax

A domestic corporation may be subject to a special penalty tax, in addition to the regular corporate income tax, on its accumulated taxable income to the extent that the earnings of the corporation are permitted to accumulate beyond the reasonable needs of the business.[153] A domestic corporation may be subject to an almost confiscatory penalty tax on its personal holding company income, if at least 60 percent of its adjusted ordinary gross income for the taxable year is personal holding company income (*e.g.*, passive income) and more than 50 per-

---

[150] IRC §§ 881, 882(b), and Treas. Regs. §§ 1.11-1(a), 1.882-1. *But see* IRC § 891. If a foreign corporation has both categories of income, the non-effectively connected income is not taken into account in determining either the rate or amount of tax on the effectively connected income. Treas. Regs. § 1.882-1(b)(2).

[151] IRC §§ 881(a)(1), (2).

[152] IRC § 871(a)(2) includes capital gains as an item of U.S. source, non-effectively connected income of a nonresident alien individual who has met the 183 days physical presence test. IRC § 881, which specifies the items of noneffectively connected income on which a foreign corporation is taxed, does not list capital gains. *See* Treas. Regs. § 1.882-3(b).

[153] IRC §§ 531 *et seq.*

cent in value of its outstanding stock is owned, directly or indirectly, by not more than five individuals.[154] If the corporation constitutes a personal holding company, the accumulated earnings tax does not apply.[155]

A foreign corporation may be liable for the accumulated earnings tax or the personal holding company tax, but not both, with respect to income derived by the corporation from sources within the United States, whether or not the foreign corporation is engaged in trade or business within the United States.[156] The accumulated earnings tax is not applicable, however, if none of the shareholders of the foreign corporation is subject to U.S. income tax on dividend distributions by the corporation.[157] The personal holding company tax does not apply to a foreign corporation if during the last half of the taxable year, all of the corporation's stock is owned, directly or indirectly, by nonresident alien individuals.[158]

---

[154] IRC §§ 541 *et seq.* There is a special, limited exception from the personal holding rules for a corporation that derives 50 percent or more of its adjusted ordinary gross income from either rents or royalties from minerals, oil, and gas. IRC § 543(a)(2).

[155] IRC § 532(b)(1).

[156] Treas. Regs. §§ 1.881-1(e)(1), (2), 1.532-1(c), 1.541-1(b). These Regulations all were adopted in the 1950s, prior to the 1966 addition of the effectively connected concept. Presumably, both the accumulated earnings tax and the personal holding company tax would apply to foreign source income of a foreign corporation that is effectively connected to a U.S. trade or business.

[157] Treas. Regs. § 1.532-1(c). In this connection, under some income tax treaties, dividends paid by a treaty country corporation to a shareholder other than a U.S. citizen or resident are exempt from all income taxes imposed by the United States. *See* Article XII(1) of the 1942 U.S.-Canada Income Tax Treaty; and Article XII of the U.S.-Netherlands Income Tax Treaty. In addition, under some treaties, the accumulated earnings tax may not apply to a treaty country corporation. *See* Article XIII of the 1942 U.S.-Canada Income Tax Treaty.

[158] IRC § 542(c)(7); Treas. Regs. § 1.541-1(b). (*But see* N. 225, *infra*, for an exception to the general rule.) Some income tax treaties exempt foreign corporations from the personal holding company tax. *See* Article XIII of the 1942 U.S.-Canada Income Tax Treaty, which extends the exemption to Canadian corporations more than 50 percent of the stock of which is owned directly or indirectly by individual residents of Canada who are not U.S. citizens.

[c] Capitalization of Corporations

A corporation may be capitalized with equity or debt. Generally, the use of debt permits tax benefits because (i) interest, even if paid to shareholders, is deductible;[159] (ii) the payment of interest to foreign lenders may not be subject to U.S. withholding tax;[160] and (iii) the repayment of principal is not subject to Federal income tax. Furthermore, Congress is considering an amendment to the Code which would exempt from tax interest paid to certain foreign lenders.[161] On the other hand, dividends are not deductible and are subject to withholding tax of 30 percent, or a reduced treaty rate. No treaty totally exempts dividends from withholding tax.

There is a substantial risk, however, that, in the case of a "thin" corporation, loans from principal shareholders or loans guaranteed by principal shareholders will be treated as equity.[162] The Treasury's recently proposed regulations suggest that, if a corporation's debt:equity ratio does not exceed 1:1, intercompany loans will not be subject to scrutiny as equity and that, if the debt:equity ratio exceeds 10:1, generally the debt will be treated as stock.[163] If intercompany debt is treated as equity, both the payment of interest and the repayment of principal are treated as corporate distributions with respect to stock. A corporate distribution with respect to its stock constitutes a dividend, however, only to the extent of the current and accumulated earnings and profits of the corporation.[164] Thus, if the intercompany advances are repaid prior to the first taxable year in which the corporation has its first earnings and profits, the payment of interest and principal should not attract Federal income tax, even though interest deductions may be disallowed.

---

[159] IRC § 163.

[160] Under some income tax treaties, interest paid to a foreign lender organized as a treaty country corporation (*e.g.*, a Dutch finance subsidiary) is exempt from U.S. withholding tax. *See* Article VIII, U.S.-Netherlands Income Tax Treaty.

[161] H.R. 7553, 96th Cong., 2d Sess. (1980).

[162] IRC § 385.

[163] Prop. Treas. Regs. §§ 1.385-2(d)(2), 1.385-8(a).

[164] IRC § 316.

[5] Federal Income Taxation of Partnerships and Partners

[a] General Scheme

For Federal income tax purposes, a partnership includes a syndicate, group, pool, joint venture, or other unincorporated organization through or by means of which any business, financial operation, or venture is carried on, and which is not a corporation or a trust.[165]

A partnership, whether domestic or foreign, is not subject to Federal income tax.[166] The partners take into account, in their separate or individual capacities, their distributive shares of the partnership's income, gain, losses, deductions and credits.[167] Although the computation of the taxable income of a partnership and certain elections are made at the partnership level, a partnership is considered to be a tax transparency or a pass-through entity.[168] Moreover, the character of any item of income, gain, loss, deduction, or credit included in a partner's distributive share is determined as if the item were realized by the partner directly from the source from which it was

---

[165] IRC §§ 761(a), 7701(a)(2). A partner means a member in such a syndicate, group, pool, joint venture, or organization. IRC §§ 761(d) and 7701(a)(2).

[166] IRC § 701.

[167] IRC § 702. A partner's distributive share of income, gain, loss, deduction, or credit is determined by the partnership agreement. IRC § 704(a). Income, gain, loss, deductions, or credits may be specially allocated among the partners, if the allocation has substantial economic effect. IRC § 704(b)(2). In some partnerships between U.S. persons and foreign persons, an attempt has been made to allocate the deductible items (e.g., intangible drilling and development costs) to the U.S. partners (in order to shelter unrelated income of such U.S. partners subject to Federal income tax), and to allocate the non-deductible items (e.g., leasehold costs) to the foreign partners (who do not have other income subject to Federal income tax). The question of whether a special or functional allocation has substantial economic effect is beyond the scope of this chapter. See Staff of the Joint Committee on Taxation, "General Explanation of the Tax Reform Act of 1976" (U.S. Gov't Printing Office, Washington: 1976), p. 95, note 6; LR 8008054 (November 28, 1979).

[168] IRC § 703.

realized by the partnership.[169]

A nonresident alien individual or a foreign corporation is considered as being engaged in a trade or business within the United States if the partnership, whether domestic or foreign, of which such individual or corporation is a member is so engaged.[170] This rule applies to a foreign person who is a limited partner of a limited partnership.[171]

A nonresident alien partner or a foreign corporate partner of a partnership that is engaged in a U.S. trade or business generally is required both to obtain a taxpayer identification number and to file a Federal income tax return.[172]

[b] Taxable Year of a Partnership

A new partnership must adopt the same taxable year as the taxable year of its principal partners, unless the partnership obtains the consent of the IRS to adopt a different taxable year.[173] If all of its principal partners are not on the same taxable year,[174] a partnership must adopt the calendar year, unless it obtains the consent of the IRS to adopt a different taxable year.[175] In computing the taxable income of a partner for a taxable year, the partner includes his distributive share of partnership income and loss for the taxable year of the partnership ending within or with his own taxable year.[176]

Although the Code and the Treasury Regulations restrict the freedom of individuals and partnerships in the selection of taxable years, a new corporation, whether foreign or domestic,

---

[169] IRC § 702(b).

[170] IRC § 875(1). The test of whether a partnership is engaged in trade or business within the United States is the same as that for a nonresident alien individual or foreign corporation. Treas. Regs. § 1.875-1.

[171] Rev. Rul. 75-23, 1975-1 Cum. Bull. 290.

[172] Treas. Regs. §§ 1.6012-1(b)(1)(i) and 1.6012-2(g)(1)(i). Rev. Proc. 63-22, 1963-2 Cum. Bull. 755.

[173] IRC § 706(b).

[174] A principal partner is one with a 5 percent or more interest in the partnership. IRC § 706(b)(3).

[175] Treas. Regs. § 1.706-1(b)(1)(ii).

[176] IRC § 706(a).

generally can adopt as its first taxable year a calendar year or any fiscal year, merely by timely filing its first return for such period.[177] If a taxpayer, having selected a taxable year, desires to change it, he must obtain the IRS's approval.[178] In certain circumstances, however, a corporation may change its taxable year without the IRS's approval.[179]

§ 3.02   Treaties and Their Effect on Federal Income Taxation of Foreign Investors

[1]   Background

Generally, treaty provisions are superior to any contrary provisions of the Internal Revenue Code.[180] If income is exempt from Federal income tax by treaty, it is not included in gross income for Federal income tax purposes.[181]

The United States has bilateral income tax treaties with twenty-eight countries, and some of these treaties have been extended to overseas territories (some of which are now independent) of some treaty countries.[182]

---

[177] Treas. Regs. § 1.441-1(b)(3).

[178] IRC § 442.

[179] Treas. Regs. § 1.442-1(c).

[180] United States Constitution, Article VI, Clause 2. *See* Cook v. United States, 288 U.S. 102 (1933). It should be noted, however, that, since a treaty or a treaty provision may be superseded by subsequent acts of Congress, most tax legislation includes a savings clause such as Section 110 of the Foreign Investors Tax Act of 1966, which states, "No amendment made by this title shall apply in any case where its application would be contrary to any treaty obligation of the United States."

[181] IRC § 894(a). *Cf.* IRC § 7852(d).

[182] For example, the 1948 treaty between the U.S. and the Netherlands was extended to the Netherlands Antilles, by a 1955 Protocol. It should be noted that the 1948 treaty, as extended to the Netherlands Antilles, was modified by a 1963 Protocol; and that the 1948 treaty, as it applies to the Netherlands (but not as extended to the Netherlands Antilles), was amended in 1965. The 1963 Protocol that modified the application of the 1948 Netherlands Treaty to the Netherlands Antilles contains restrictions on the treaty benefits for interest, dividends and royalties paid to Netherlands Antilles holding companies. It also should be noted that the future status of the benefits now available to Netherlands Antilles corporations is uncertain be-

The primary purpose of most bilateral income tax treaties is to mitigate double taxation in situations where a national (individual or corporation) of one treaty country derives income from the other treaty country, and where, but for the treaty, the income may be taxable by both countries.[183] There are several methods by which double taxation is avoided under the treaties. For example, the treaty may require that the country of source either not tax the income or tax it at a reduced rate. This method generally applies to investment income, such as interest, dividends, and capital gains. The treaty also may provide that the national's country either not tax the foreign source income or allow a credit for the tax imposed by the country of source. This method generally applies to income from real property.

[2] Treaty Provisions

For purposes of briefly reviewing and illustrating the operation of important treaty provisions and concepts, reference will be made to the 1948 United States-Netherlands Income Tax Convention, as amended in 1965 and brought into force in 1966.[184]

---

cause negotiations are being conducted between the United States Treasury and the Netherlands Antilles Inspector of Taxation for the purpose of agreeing on a new income tax treaty between the U.S. and the Netherlands Antilles. Treas. Dept. News Release M-551 (June 18, 1980); see BNA Daily Tax Report #119, at G-4 (June 18, 1980).

[183] Even in the absence of a treaty, the United States mitigates the effect of double taxation by giving United States taxpayers a credit for part or all of the foreign income tax paid on foreign source income that is included in the taxpayer's gross income for Federal income tax purposes. IRC §§ 33, 901 et seq. Note that, although IRC § 164(a)(4) allows a deduction for foreign income taxes, IRC § 275(a)(4) disallows the deduction if the foreign tax credit is claimed. The foreign tax credit is extended, subject to certain limitations (see, e.g., IRC § 861(a)(2)(B)), to foreign taxes on the effectively connected foreign source income of nonresident alien individuals and foreign corporations engaged in a trade or business within the United States. IRC §§ 901(b)(4), 906.

[184] Treas. Regs. § 505.101. The U.S.-Netherlands Income Tax Treaty is based on the 1963 Draft Double Tax Convention on Income and Capital,

[a]   Taxes Covered

The Treaty applies only to the Federal income tax; it does not apply to State or local taxes.[185] As a result of the recent efforts by state legislators and tax collectors to collect more taxes, notably through application of the "unitary" or world-wide business concept,[186] state and local taxes may become a subject for treaty coverage. Indeed, the British negotiators had persuaded the U.S. Treasury negotiators to include a provision in the recently concluded income tax treaty between the United States and the United Kingdom that would have precluded the states from applying the unitary formula in calculating state income tax of a British enterprise. The United States Senate, however, refused to ratify the Treaty with the provision that restricted the rights of a state to define the taxable income base of its income tax.[187]

[b]   Permanent Establishment

Perhaps the key provision of most income tax treaties is the concept and the definition of a "permanent establishment." Under the Treaty, if a Netherlands enterprise does not have a permanent establishment in the United States, it is not subject to Federal income tax on its industrial or commercial profits

---

prepared by the Organization for Economic Co-Operation and Development (O.E.C.D.). The Treaty, as amended in 1965, adopts the effectively connected income concept (subsequently included in the Code as a result of the Foreign Investors Tax Act of 1966) in place of the old force of attraction doctrine on which the 1948 Treaty was based. Hereafter, all references to the Treaty, as amended in 1965, will be "Treaty Art."

[185] Treaty Art. I(1)(a).

[186] *See* Mobil Oil Corp. v. Vermont, 445 U.S. —, 100 S.Ct. 1223 (1980); Exxon Corp. v. Wisconsin, — U.S. —, 100 S.Ct. 2109 (1980); ASARCO, Inc. v. Idaho, — U.S. —, 100 S.Ct. 1333 (1980).

[187] Subsequently, after a Third Protocol, dated March 15, 1979, that restricted the application of the Treaty to Federal income taxes (excluding from the Treaty the accumulated earnings tax and the personal holding company tax) and the tax on insurance premiums of foreign insurers, the Treaty was ratified and entered into force on April 25, 1980.

from United States sources.[188] If a Netherlands enterprise has a permanent establishment in the U.S., it is subject to Federal income tax on the income effectively connected to such permanent establishment.[189]

A permanent establishment is defined as a fixed place of business in which a business is wholly or partly carried on,[190] and includes especially a branch; an office; a sales outlet; a factory; a workshop; a mine quarry or other place of extraction of natural resources; and a building site or construction or assembly project which exists for more than twelve months.[191] A permanent establishment is also deemed to exist if a Netherlands enterprise engages in business in the United States through an agent who has authority to conclude contracts in the name of the enterprise and regularly exercises that authority in the U.S., unless the exercise of authority is limited to the purchase of goods or merchandise for the account of the enterprise.[192] A permanent establishment does not exist, however, if the Netherlands enterprise is engaged in trade or business in the United States through a broker, general commission agent or any other agent of independent status, "where such persons are acting in the ordinary course of their business."[193] The Treaty provides that certain activities, such as the maintenance of a fixed place of business for the purpose of purchasing goods or merchandise, or for collecting information, for the Dutch enterprise[194] or for the use by a Dutch enterprise of facilities or the maintenance of a stock of goods for storage, display or delivery,[195] shall not constitute a permanent establishment. The fact that a Netherlands investor owns or controls a U.S. subsidiary or affiliate (or is controlled by a United States corporation or any foreign corporation that is engaged in United States trade or business through a permanent establishment) is not taken into account in determining

---

[188] Treaty Art. III(1).
[189] Id.
[190] Treaty Art. II(1)(i)(A).
[191] Treaty Art. II(1)(i)(B)(i) through (vii).
[192] Treaty Art. II(1)(i)(D).
[193] Treaty Art. II(1)(i)(E).
[194] Treaty Art. II(1)(i)(C)(iv).
[195] Treaty Art. II(1)(i)(C)(ii). *See* Rev. Rul. 62-31, 1962-1 Cum. Bull. 367.

whether such person has a U.S. permanent establishment.[196]

As discussed earlier, the Foreign Investors Tax Act of 1966 amended the Code to replace the force of attraction doctrine with the effectively connected income concept. Many U.S. income tax treaties existing at that time, particularly the older ones (*e.g.*, the Canadian and British treaties), were based upon the force of attraction doctrine rather than the effectively connected income concept. As part of the 1966 changes, the Code was amended to provide that, even though the treaty in force would deny the treaty benefits because of the existence of a U.S. permanent establishment, in applying any exemption from, or reduction of, any tax as provided for in a treaty with respect to income which is not effectively connected with the conduct of a trade or business within the United States, a nonresident alien or a foreign corporation shall not be deemed to have a U.S. permanent establishment.[197] In effect, therefore, the United States unilaterally extended to countries with which it had treaties based on the old force of attraction doctrine the benefits of the newer effectively connected income concept.

[c]   Industrial or Commercial Profits

Industrial or commercial profits means income derived from the active conduct of a trade or business and profits derived from the furnishing of services of employees or other personnel.[198] The term "industrial or commercial profits" does not include dividends, interest, royalties, and capital gains, unless such income is effectively connected with a permanent establishment. Moreover, the U.S. source industrial or commercial profits of a Dutch enterprise are taxable by the U.S. only if they are attributable to a U.S. permanent establishment

---

[196] Treaty Art. II(1)(i)(F).

[197] IRC § 894(b). *See* Rev. Rul. 79-56, 1979-1 Cum. Bull. 459.

[198] Treaty Art. III(5). No significance should be attached to the use of the differing terms "income" and "profits" in Treaty Art. III(5).

of the Dutch enterprise.[199] The result of the Treaty is that, if any item of U.S. source income of a Dutch enterprise (even if the Dutch enterprise has a U.S. permanent establishment) does not fall within the concept of industrial or commercial profits or one of the specific items of income covered by the treaty (see discussion below infra this section), it is not subject to Federal income tax.[200]

[d] Other Types of United States Source Income Covered by Treaties

[i] United States Source Real Property Income

Income from real property (including gains derived from the sale of such property, but not including interest from mortgages or bonds secured by real property) and royalties from the operation of mines, quarries, or other natural resources may be taxed in the country in which the property is situated, without regard to whether the taxpayer has a permanent establishment in such country.[201] This provision merely permits the country where the property is located to tax the income from such property, it does not require or impose taxation.

Under U.S. internal law at July, 1980, capital gain from the sale of real property is not subject to tax unless (i) the gain is effectively connected with the conduct of a U.S. trade or business or (ii) the seller is a nonresident alien individual who is present in the United States for 183 days during the taxable year. If, as appears likely, the Foreign Investment in Real

---

[199] Treaty Art. III(1). If a U.S. permanent establishment engages in transactions with an affiliated company, the permanent establishment is attributed the same industrial and commercial profits that it would be expected to derive in transactions with independent enterprises, dealing at arm's length. Treaty Art. III(2). *See also* Treaty Art. IV.

[200] London Displays Co. N.V., 46 T.C. 511 (1966), *acq.*, 1967-1 Cum. Bull. 2.

[201] Treaty Art. V. Note that the 1948 Treaty as extended to the Netherlands Antilles includes "interest from mortgages secured by real property" within the concept of income from real property." 1948 Treaty Art. V. *See also* 1948 Treaty Art. VIII(1). Rev. Rul. 79-251, 1979-2 Cum. Bull. 271.

Property Act of 1980 is adopted, the U.S. could impose tax on capital gain derived by Dutch persons from U.S. real property without the necessity of amending the treaty with The Netherlands. On the other hand, the current (1942) treaty with Canada, which exempts all capital gains from Federal income tax,[202] including gain from the alienation of real property, must be amended or terminated with respect to U.S. source capital gains from real estate of Canadians in order to impose tax on capital gains derived by Canadians from U.S. real property. The present Bill that may become the Foreign Investment in Real Property Act of 1980 provides that any treaty exemption with respect to the taxation of gain from U.S. real property will no longer be effective after December 31, 1984.[203]

[ii]   **United States Source Real Property Income—Net Election**

A Dutch resident or corporation, deriving from sources within the United States royalties in respect of the operation of mines, quarries or other natural resources, or rentals from real property, may elect for any taxable year to be subject to Federal income tax on a net basis, that is, as if the Dutch resident or corporation were engaged in a trade or business within the United States through a permanent establishment.[204] This provision permits a Dutch investor who derives U.S. source rental or royalty income that, because it would not be deemed effectively connected with a U.S. permanent establishment, would otherwise be subject to a flat 30 percent rate

---

[202] 1942 U.S.-Canada Income Tax Treaty, Art. VIII.

[203] Section 275(c) of H.R. 7652, 96th Cong. 2d Sess. (1980). The authors understand that negotiations are being conducted to revise the 1942 U.S.-Canada Income Tax Treaty, and that one of the new provisions will allow gain from real property, including natural resources, to be taxed in the country where the property is located. It is expected that another provision will permit a step-up in basis to the fair market value of such property as of a treaty valuation date, if the gain from the disposition of such property would not be treated as effectively connected income under the old law. *See* § 3.05[2], *infra*.

[204] Treaty Art. X.

of tax on gross rental or royalty income to elect to pay regular tax rates on the net rental or royalty income (*i.e.*, gross rental or royalty income less allowable deductions for ordinary business expenses, interest, taxes, depreciation and depletion). Although the real property election under the Code provides that the election is irrevocable without the consent of the IRS,[205] the Treaty provides that a Dutch investor may make the election on an annual basis.[206] Thus, a Dutch investor can determine at the time for filing a return for each year whether or not to make the election. If the net election is made for a taxable year, capital gains derived from the alienation of real property during such year probably would be subject to tax as income effectively connected with a U.S. permanent establishment, although installments received in years in which the election is not in effect and the taxpayer is not engaged in a U.S. trade or business should (under current law) be free from Federal income tax.[207]

[iii] Dividends

Domestic Corporation
Dividends paid by a domestic corporation to a Netherlands shareholder are subject to a maximum withholding tax of 15 percent, which is further reduced to 5 percent in certain cases.[208] The reduced rate of tax, however, does not apply if the dividends are effectively connected with a U.S. permanent establishment of the recipient.[209]

Dutch Corporation
Dividends paid by a Dutch corporation to its shareholders

---

[205] IRC §§ 871(d)(1), 882(d)(1). *See* § 3.01(1)(c)(ii), *supra.*

[206] Rev. Rul. 77-174, 1977-1 Cum. Bull. 414.

[207] Treas. Regs. §§ 1.864-3(a), 1.871-8(c), 1.872-1(b), 1.881-1(b)(1), 1.882-(a)(1).

[208] Treaty Art. VII(1), (2).

[209] Treaty Art. VII(3). In such case, the dividends would be included in the gross income of the recipient and subject to graduated rates of tax; in the case of a corporate shareholder, however, the dividends received deduction would be available. IRC § 243.

are exempt from U.S. income tax, unless the recipient share-holder is a citizen, resident, or corporation of the United States.[210] This provision can be of great benefit, because the Dutch corporation can distribute its profits to foreign share-holders, including non-Dutch shareholders, without U.S. tax on the dividends. It eliminates the need to finance the corpora-tion with debt rather than equity, always a risky under-taking.[211] Moreover, it permits the corporation to engage in intercompany transactions without the risk of the IRS deter-mining that the corporation had paid a constructive dividend, subject to withholding tax; to operate without regard to the personal holding company tax, because it can distribute divi-dends free of U.S. withholding tax; or to retain earnings with-out regard to the accumulated earnings tax.[212]

[iv] Interest

Domestic Obligor
Interest on bonds, notes, debentures, securities, deposits, or any other form of indebtedness (including interest from mort-gages on bonds secured by real property) paid to a Dutch resident or corporation is exempt from Federal income tax, as long as the interest is not effectively connected with a U.S. permanent establishment of the recipient.[213]

Dutch Corporate Obligor
Interest paid by a Netherlands corporation is exempt from Federal income tax, except where the recipient is a citizen,

---

[210] Treaty Art. XII.

[211] *See* IRC § 385, discussed *supra,* § 3.01[4][c].

[212] Treas. Regs. § 1.532-1(c). This provision has led to the formation of the so-called Netherlands or Netherlands Antilles "Sandwich," that, is, the cre-ation of a Netherlands or Netherlands Antilles holding company between the foreign investor and the Dutch operating company, so that dividends can be paid free of withholding tax from the operating company to the holding company and accumulated by the holding company.

[213] Treaty Art. VIII. As explained earlier in N. 201, *supra,* the treaty exemption for interest under the Netherlands Antilles Treaty does not apply to interest on mortgages secured by U.S. real property.

resident or corporation of the United States.[214]

[v] Royalties

Royalties paid to a resident or corporation of The Netherlands are exempt from U.S. withholding tax, unless the royalties are effectively connected with a U.S. permanent establishment of the recipient.[215] Royalties mean royalties, rentals, or other consideration paid for the use of, or the right to use (i) copyrights, artistic or scientific works, patents, designs, plans, secret processes, or formulae, trademarks, motion picture films, films or tapes for radio or television broadcasting, or other like property or rights or (ii) information concerning industrial, commercial, or scientific knowledge, experience, or skill.[216]

[vi] Interest and Royalties—Requirements for Arm's Length Payments

The Treaty provides that, if interest or royalties paid to a related person exceed a fair and reasonable consideration for the indebtedness or property licensed, the exemptions apply only to the fair and reasonable amounts.[217] Presumably, the excess would be treated as dividends, which are not deductible and which are subject to withholding tax.

[vii] Capital Gains

Gains derived by a resident or corporation of the Nether-

---

[214] Treaty Art. XII. The combination of Treaty Articles VIII and XII have permitted the use of subsidiaries created under the laws of the Netherlands (and in some cases the Netherlands Antilles—but see the 1963 Protocol to the Netherlands Antilles treaty) to act as finance companies to provide loans to U.S. operations.

[215] Treaty Art. IX(1), (3).

[216] Treaty Art. IX(2). See Rev. Rul. 73-419, 1973-2 Cum. Bull. 436.

[217] Treaty Art. VIII(3), IX(4).

lands from the alienation of a capital asset (other than gain from the alienation of real property and royalties from natural resources) are exempt from Federal income tax, unless the capital gain is effectively connected with a U.S. permanent establishment of the Dutch resident or corporation.[218] The capital gain exemption is not applicable to an individual Dutch resident who is present in the United States for 183 days or more during the taxable year, if the asset alienated was held by such person for six months or less.[219]

[viii] Compensation for Personal Services

An individual resident of the Netherlands is exempt from Federal income tax with respect to U.S. source income from personal services if he is present within the United States for a period or periods not exceeding in the aggregate 183 days during the taxable year, and, in the case of employment income, (i) the Dutch individual is not an employee of a resident or corporation of the United States or is an employee of a permanent establishment of a resident or corporation of the United States located outside the United States and (ii) such income is not deducted in computing the profits of a permanent establishment in the United States.[220] The term "income from personal services" includes employment income and income earned by an individual from the performance of personal services in an independent capacity. The term "employment income" includes income from services performed by officers and directors of corporations, but does not

---

[218] Treaty Art. XI(1), (2). Note that the English language version of the Treaty uses the broad expression alienation instead of either the "sale or other disposition" language of IRC § 1001(a) or the more restrictive "sale or exchange" language used in most other sections of the Code. The Netherlands Antilles Treaty does not contain a provision with respect to capital gains.

[219] Treaty Art. XI(3).

[220] Treaty Art. XVI(1).

include income from personal services performed by partners.[221]

Private pensions and life annuities derived from the United States and paid to individuals in the Netherlands are exempt from United States taxation.[222]

[e] Exemption from United States Accumulated Earnings and Personal Holding Company Taxes

The Treaty, as presented to the U.S. Senate, contained a provision to exempt a Netherlands corporation from the U.S. accumulated earnings and the personal holding company taxes, if individuals who were residents of the Netherlands (other than U.S. citizens) controlled, directly or indirectly, throughout the last half of the taxable year, more than 50 percent of the entire voting power in such corporation.[223] The U.S. Senate, in ratifying the treaty, rejected and eliminated this provision. Notwithstanding the absence of this provision, a Netherlands corporation owned by non-U.S. persons is subject neither to the accumulated earnings tax[224] nor to the personal holding company tax.[225] In addition, these taxes could be avoided by dividends because dividends distributed by a Netherlands corporation to non-U.S. persons are exempt from U.S. income tax.[226]

---

[221] Treaty Art. XVI(2). *Cf.* IRC §§ 861(a)(3) and 864(b)(1), which provide a more limited exemption under the Code for personal services income. *See* discussion *supra,* in N. 26 and in the text at Ns. 48 and 49.

[222] Treaty Art. XV(2), (3).

[223] Treaty Art. XIII, as presented to the U.S. Senate.

[224] Treas. Regs. § 1.532-1(c).

[225] IRC § 542(c)(7) exempts all income from the personal holding company tax except certain personal service contract income covered by IRC § 543(a)(7), a matter beyond the scope of this chapter. The 1942 U.S.-Canada Income Tax Treaty, on the other hand, does exempt Canadian corporations owned by Canadian residents from the accumulated earnings tax and the personal holding tax. Article XIII of the 1942 U.S.-Canada Income Tax Treaty.

[226] Treaty Art. XII. *See* N. 212, *supra.* In addition, U.S. internal law might exempt Canadian corporations owned by Canadians from these penalty taxes. Treas. Regs. § 1.532-1(c); IRC § 542(c)(7).

[f]   Savings Clause and Tax Credit

The United States has reserved the right to tax its citizens and residents and domestic corporations on all items of income taxable under the Federal income tax laws as if the Treaty had not come into effect.[227] The Treaty includes, as a correlative provision, a requirement that the United States allow a credit, subject to applicable limitations, to its citizens and residents and domestic corporations against Federal income tax for income taxes paid to the Netherlands.[228]

[g]   Requirement for Nondiscrimination

If a citizen or corporation of one country is a resident of, or has a permanent establishment in, the other country, the citizen or corporation shall not be subjected in the other country to more burdensome taxes than is a citizen or corporation of the other country carrying on the same activities.[229] In addition, a corporation of one country that is wholly or partly owned by one or more citizens or corporations of the other country shall not be subjected in the former country to more burdensome taxes than is a corporation of the former country which is wholly owned by one or more citizens of the former country.[230]

[h]   Exchange of Information, Competent Authority Procedure and Mutual Assistance Provisions

Tax treaties usually provide that the competent authorities

---

[227] Treaty Art. XIX(1). A similar right was retained by the Netherlands with respect to its citizens, residents and corporations.

[228] Treaty Art. XIX(2). *See* Rev. Rul. 59-66, 1959-1 Cum. Bull. 737. As discussed earlier in N. 183, the U.S. has long mitigated the effects of double taxation by offering its taxpayers the choice of either a credit or a deduction for foreign income taxes. IRC §§ 38, 164(a)(3), 275.

[229] Treaty Art. XXV(2), (3).

[230] Treaty Art. XXV(4). *See* Rev. Rul. 72-598, 1972-2 Cum. Bull. 451. *Cf.* IRC § 891.

of tax treaty countries will exchange such information as is necessary for carrying out the provisions of the treaty, for the prevention of fraud, or for the administration of statutory provisions against legal avoidance in relation to the taxes which are the subject of the treaty.[231] The two countries also undertake to lend assistance and support to each other in the collection of taxes that are the subject of the treaty.[232]

A citizen, resident or corporation of one country may request that the competent tax authority of his country meet with the competent tax authority of the other country, if the citizen, resident or corporation can prove that the action of the tax authorities of the two countries has resulted or will result in taxation not in accordance with the treaty.[233] In particular, the competent authorities will consult together to endeavor to agree (a) to the same attribution of industrial or commercial profits to a permanent establishment in one of the countries of an enterprise of the other country or (b) to the same allocation of profits between related enterprises.[234]

[3] Treaty Shopping and Treaty Abuse

[a] Treaty Shopping

The income tax benefits afforded by income tax treaties, purportedly to avoid double taxation, are available to treaty country nationals (citizens, residents or corporations). Many treaties, including the Netherlands Treaty, make treaty benefits available to corporations created under the laws of the other country, without regard to whether such corporations

---

[231] Treaty Art. XXI.

[232] Treaty Art. XXII.

[233] Treaty Art. XXIV. The IRS has published procedures to be followed when a taxpayer desires to request competent authority assistance in order to resolve issues arising under an income tax treaty between the United States and a foreign country. Rev. Proc. 77-16, 1977-1 Cum. Bull. 573; and Rev. Proc. 79-32, 1979-1 Cum. Bull. 599. *See also* Rev. Proc. 70-18, 1970-2 Cum. Bull. 493.

[234] Treaty Art. XXIV(2).

are owned by citizens or residents of the other country.[235] Thus, third country nationals can create a treaty country corporation (*e.g.*, a Netherlands or a Netherlands Antilles corporation) and obtain the tax treaty benefits.[236]

[b] Treaty Abuse

On the other hand, some treaties specifically preclude treaty tax benefits to certain persons, and the IRS and the Courts have denied, or have attempted to deny, treaty benefits in cases of tax evasion or where it could be demonstrated that the treaty country corporation served no business purpose other than tax avoidance. As noted earlier in this § 3.02, as a result of the 1963 Protocol, certain benefits of the Netherlands Antilles Treaty are not available to investment or holding companies or to other entities which are entitled to certain special tax benefits under Netherlands Antilles tax law, unless (a) the entity is owned by individual residents of the Netherlands or the Netherlands Antilles or solely by Netherlands corporations, or (b) the payer of the U.S. source income is a U.S. corporation which satisfies certain tests as to its income and stock ownership.[237]

The Courts have denied treaty benefits to corporations which were created merely to obtain treaty benefits. In *Aiken Industries, Inc.*[238] a Bahamas corporation held the note of a U.S. obligor. Interest paid on the note by the U.S. obligor to the Bahamian holder would have been subject to 30 percent U.S.

---

[235] *See* Treaty Art. II(1)(a) through (h) of the U.S.-Netherlands Income Tax Treaty.

[236] The IRS has ruled that a Netherlands Antilles corporation owned by individuals and corporations of foreign countries other than the Netherlands or the Netherlands Antilles qualified for the tax treaty benefits of The Netherlands Treaty as extended to the Netherlands Antilles. Rev. Rul. 75-23, 1975-1 Cum. Bull. 290.

[237] *See* N. 182, *supra.* The Luxembourg Treaty also contains a provision excluding holding companies entitled to special tax status under Luxembourg law from tax treaty benefits. Article XV of the U.S.-Luxembourg Income Tax Treaty.

[238] 56 T.C. 925 (1971).

withholding tax. Thus, the Bahamas corporation sold the note to an affiliated Honduras corporation for a note of the Honduran corporation the terms of which were identical to the note of the U.S. corporation. The Honduras corporation received payments of principal and interest from the U.S. obligor and repaid the exact amount on its own note to the Bahamas corporation. Under the then existing U.S.-Honduras treaty,[239] interest was exempt from withholding tax. The Tax Court recognized the separate existence of the Honduras corporation, but treated the Honduran corporation as a mere conduit or collection agency for the Bahamas corporation and not the beneficial owner of the U.S. corporation's note. The Court determined that, because the Honduran corporation was an affiliated corporation that received no profit, the interest paid by the U.S. corporation was not received by the Honduran corporation, but, instead, was received by the Bahamas corporation. The interest, therefore, was subject to the usual, non-treaty 30 percent withholding tax.[240]

§ 3.03 State and Local Taxes

Most states impose an income tax on income generated from the conduct of a trade or business within the state. State income taxes generally are imposed at low rates, however, and are deductible in computing Federal taxable income.[241] For example, a corporation pays Colorado income tax at the rate of 5 percent on its taxable income; and an individual pays Colorado income tax at graduated rates, the highest of which

---

[239] Honduras terminated the Treaty, effective December 31, 1966, pursuant to notice given in accordance with Article XXI(2). A similar notification provision is found in all treaties. *See e.g.*, Art. XXIV of the U.S.-Netherlands Treaty.

[240] *See also* Johansson v. United States, 336 F.2d 809 (5th Cir. 1964), where the courts refused to recognize a Swiss corporation created by Ingemar Johansson in an attempt to avoid income tax on the proceeds of world heavyweight boxing championship fights held in the United States between Johansson and Floyd Patterson.

[241] IRC § 164(a)(3).

is 8 percent of taxable income.[242]

Theoretically, a state imposes its income tax on the income derived from business activity within the state.[243] A problem may arise, however, if a corporation conducts business both within and without the state or if it is a member of a corporate group that conducts business both within and without the state. In such a case, it is necessary to determine the amount of income which is attributable to the state for purposes of the state income tax. Generally, income is apportioned to a state based upon a two- or three-factor formula.[244] Recently, however, some states have attempted to apply a so-called "unitary" or worldwide formula in computing the total income subject to apportionment. For example, in *Mobil Oil Corp. v. Vermont*,[245] Vermont was permitted to include dividends received by Mobil Corporation, a multinational oil conglomerate headquartered in New York, from Mobil's overseas subsidiaries, in Mobil's income base subject to apportionment to Vermont. This approach may greatly increase the state tax burden of a multinational corporation.

Lately, state and local governments have become more aggresive in collecting other taxes. For example, state and local tax collectors have attempted to broaden the definition of property subject to sales and use taxes (computer software). In addition, state and local tax collectors have attempted to apply use tax to tangible property located only temporarily in the taxing jurisdiction (to property or equipment which is located in the jurisdiction only for temporary use by the taxpayer or

---

[242] Colorado Revised Statutes (hereafter "C.R.S.") 1973 §§ 39-22-104 and 39-22-301. Taxable income for Colorado income tax purposes is Federal taxable income with adjustments, the most important of which is the substitution of the Federal income tax as a deduction in lieu of State and local income taxes. Colorado also imposes an additional 2 percent surtax on the gross dividend and interest income of individuals in excess of $15,000. Some states, *e.g.*, Wyoming and Texas, do not impose any income tax.

[243] *See* C.R.S. 1973 § 39-22-301.

[244] *See* C.R.S. 1973 § 39-22-303. For example, the total taxable income of the corporation subject to apportionment to the state is determined, than a portion of such income is apportioned to the state based upon the ratio of (i) sales within the state to total sales; (ii) property within the state to total property; and (iii) payroll within the state to total payroll.

[245] 445 U.S. —, 100 S.Ct. 1223 (1980). *See* N. 186, *supra*, for other cases.

which is stored in the jurisdiction pending shipment to other jurisdictions for temporary use in such other jurisdictions).[246] Although many states have long imposed excise or severance taxes on the extraction of minerals within their jurisdictions, state legislatures recently have expanded the types of minerals covered by the taxes and have increased the rates of such taxes.[247]

§ 3.04 Federal Gift and Estate Taxes

Although most of the states have estate or inheritance taxes, they will be ignored in this chapter which discusses briefly and in summary fashion only the Federal estate and gift taxes.[248]

[1] Direct Ownership of U.S. Tangible Property

A nonresident alien individual who directly owns tangible property situated within the United States (*e.g.*, real estate) is subject to the Federal gift tax on a gift of an interest in such property[249] and to the Federal estate tax (with no marital deduction and only a $3,600 estate tax credit) upon his death.[250] The United States has concluded estate tax treaties with some countries, but generally these treaties do not preclude the imposition of the Federal estate tax on the tangible property

---

246 In Japan Line Ltd. v. County of Los Angeles, 441 U.S. 434 (1979), the U.S. Supreme Court held that a Los Angeles, California county tax on instrumentalities of foreign commerce was unconstitutional.

247 *See* C.R.S. 1973 § 39-29-10 *et seq.*

248 If property included in the Federal gross estate of a decedent has been subjected to an estate, inheritance, legacy, or succession tax of any State or the District of Columbia, all or a portion of the tax *actually paid* may be credited against the Federal estate tax. IRC § 2011. Indeed, some States, such as Colorado, provide that their state death tax will be the amount of the credit allowed by IRC § 2011(b), which ranges from 8/10 of 1 percent of the Federal taxable estate in excess of $100,000 to 16 percent of the Federal taxable estate in excess of $10,000,000.

249 IRC §§ 2501 *et seq.*

250 IRC § 2101 *et seq.* IRC § 2101(c)(2)(B) provides for a greater credit in certain cases.

of foreign domiciliaries that is situated within the United States. The estate tax treaties may authorize exemptions (or perhaps the credit that was substituted for the exemption in 1976) in computing the Federal estate tax; and they may authorize a credit to the foreign domiciliary in the foreign country for any Federal estate tax on the U.S. property.[251]

[2] Federal Estate and Gift Taxation of Partnership Interests

The application of Federal estate and gift taxes to nonresident alien individuals who own interests in partnerships which in turn own U.S. property or which are engaged in trade or business within the United States is not clear. If a partnership interest is treated as intangible property, the Federal gift tax would be inapplicable, whether the partnership is treated as a domestic or foreign partnership.[252]

The Federal estate tax applies to the property of a nonresident alien which is situated in the United States at the time of his death.[253] The IRS has ruled that "a partnership interest at the time of a partner's death is not in the nature of a debt although it may accrue as a debt after death"; and that the situs of a partnership interest is not determined by where the individual items of the partnership assets are located.[254] In the absence of a treaty, the IRS may take the position that the situs of a partnership interest is where the partnership business is carried on. Presumably, an allocation would be made if the partnership conducted business both within and without the

---

[251] *See* the U.S.-French Estate Tax Treaty; and the U.S.-Netherlands Estate Tax Treaty. The United States has concluded gift tax treaties that provide rules for the determination of the situs of property and for the allowance of credits and deductions in computing gift taxes. *See* the U.S.-Australian Gift Tax Treaty of 1953.

[252] IRC § 2501(a)(2). *Cf.*, Sections 25 and 26 of the Uniform Partnership Act; and Blodgett v. Silberman, 277 U.S. 1 (1928).

[253] IRC § 2103.

[254] Rev. Rul. 55-701, 1955-2 Cum. Bull. 836. *Cf.* Sections 25 and 26 of the Uniform Partnership Act.

United States.[255] If an analogy were made between the ownership by a nonresident alien of an interest in a partnership and the ownership of stock of a corporation, an interest in a domestic partnership would be subject to Federal estate tax, but an interest in a foreign partnership would not.[256] Some estate tax treaties provide, however, that a partnership interest has a taxable situs at the principal place of business of the partnership.[257]

[3] Ownership of Shares of Stock of U.S. Corporations

Although a gift by a nonresident alien of shares of stock of a U.S. corporation generally is not subject to U.S. gift tax,[258] U.S. expatriates are subject to the Federal gift tax on gifts of shares of stock of domestic corporations for the ten-year-period after loss of citizenship. The Federal estate tax applies to shares of stock in a U.S. corporation owned by a nonresident alien at the time of his death, or transferred other than as a result of a bona fide sale for full and adequate consideration within three years of death.[259]

[4] Ownership of Shares of Stock of Foreign Corporations

Neither Federal gift tax nor Federal estate tax applies to shares of stock in a foreign corporation owned by a nonresident alien, although the Federal estate tax may apply to U.S.

---

[255] See Rev. Rul. 55-701, op. cit. N. 254.

[256] See IRC §§ 2104(a), 2107.

[257] See, e.g., Article II(h) of the U.S.-Canada Estate Tax Treaty.

[258] IRC §§ 2501(a)(2), 2511(a); IRC §§ 2501(a)(3), 2511(b). See also IRC § 2107.

[259] IRC §§ 2104(a), (b). Some recent estate tax treaties exclude shares of stock of a U.S. corporation from the taxable estate of a treaty alien decedent. See the Netherlands, the United Kingdom, and the proposed French Estate Tax Treaties.

expatriates with respect to the shares of stock of certain controlled foreign corporations.[260]

§ 3.05 Summary and Proposed Legislation

[1] Current Law

Under current (July, 1980) U.S. tax law (Code and treaties),
foreign investors are subject to a favorable tax climate in the
United States. Foreign investors generally are not treated as
engaged in a U.S. trade or business as a result of trading in U.S.
securities or commodities, even if the trading is accomplished
through resident brokers or agents.[261] Furthermore, even if a
foreign investor is otherwise engaged in a U.S. trade or business, his income from securities or commodities generally will
not be treated as effectively connected with such trade or
business.[262] In addition, foreign direct investors in U.S. real
estate or natural resources usually can structure their investments so that they pay little or no tax both on current income
from the property while they are holding the property and on
gain from the sale, exchange or other disposition of the property.

One technique used by foreign investors to minimize U.S.
taxes on investments in U.S. real estate or natural resources is
to invest through a Netherlands Antilles corporation. One benefit is that, since it is a foreign corporation, the foreign investor
can avoid Federal gift and estate taxes.[263] Other benefits are
that the Netherlands Antilles does not impose its income tax
on income from U.S. real property or natural resources;[264] U.S.
withholding taxes do not apply to dividends or interest paid to
foreign persons by a Netherlands Antilles corporation, even if
all of the corporation's income is effectively connected with

---

[260] IRC §§ 2104(a), 2107, 2511(a).

[261] IRC § 864(b)(2).

[262] IRC § 864(c)(2).

[263] IRC §§ 2104(a), 2501(a)(2).

[264] Article V of the U.S.-Netherlands Antilles Income Tax Treaty, as inter-
preted by the Netherlands Antilles tax authorities, notwithstanding Article
XIX(1) of the U.S.-Netherlands Antilles Income Tax Treaty (*i.e.*, the Savings
Clause). *See* N. 227, *supra.*

the conduct of a trade or business within the United States;[265] there are no withholding taxes in the Netherlands Antilles;[266] there are no estate, gift or inheritance taxes in the Netherlands Antilles;[267] and a Netherlands Antilles corporation can obtain the benefits of the U.S.-Netherlands Antilles income tax treaty, even if the corporation is owned by foreign investors from countries other than the Netherlands or the Netherlands Antilles.[268] This favorable tax result generally can be achieved whether the Netherlands Antilles corporation itself owns the U.S. property directly or whether its interest is through a partnership or joint venture.

Foreign investment in U.S. real property or natural resources may or may not constitute the conduct of a trade or business within the United States. If the investment does not constitute a trade or business (e.g., a net lease of real property or a royalty, net profits, or other nonworking interest in natural resources),[269] the Netherlands Antilles corporation presumably would elect annually under the U.S.-Netherlands Antilles treaty to pay tax on a net basis on its rental or royalty income, so that its U.S. source gross income can be reduced or eliminated by deductions for interest, real estate, severance and similar taxes, depreciation, depletion, and general business expenses.[270] In the year of disposition, the corporation would not make the election, so that the gain on disposition would consti-

---

[265] Article XII of the U.S.-Netherlands Antilles Income Tax Treaty.

[266] Kramer, Roeloffs, and Walboom, 263 T.M. *Business Operations in the Netherlands Antilles,* A-4(1972).

[267] *Id.*

[268] Rev. Rul. 75-23, 1975-1 Cum. Bull. 290.

[269] Rev. Rul. 73-522, 1973-2 Cum. Bull. 226; Rev. Rul. 69-355, 1969-1 Cum. Bull. 65; Rev. Rul. 73-419, 1973-2 Cum. Bull. 436; and Rev. Rul. 58-166, 1958-1 Cum. Bull. 324.

[270] Article X of the U.S.-Netherlands Antilles Income Tax Treaty. An election to pay U.S. income tax on a net basis must be in effect to avoid a U.S. withholding tax (presumably withheld by the lessee or operator) of 30 percent on gross rents, royalties, etc., unless the tax is reduced or eliminated by treaty. Moreover, the rents or royalties are grossed-up by real estate taxes and other expenses of the lessor that are usually paid by the lessee as additional rental expense of the lessee under a net lease. Rev. Rul. 73-522, *op cit.,* N. 269.

tute a tax-free gain.[271] If it is preferable to maintain the net election in the year of sale in order to shelter the rental and royalty income received until the date of sale, the sale could be made on the installment basis. Although the gain on the installment received in the year of sale would be subject to tax, installments received after the year of sale would constitute tax-free gain.[272] If the investment in U.S. real property or natural resources constitutes a U.S. trade or business, the corporation would automatically be taxed on a net basis while it held the property.

The property could be disposed of with significant tax savings in several ways. The easiest method would be for the foreign investors to realize a tax-free capital gain by selling the shares of stock of the Netherlands Antilles corporation. Presumably, the purchaser of the shares would liquidate the corporation in order to step-up the basis in the property from the depreciated basis of the corporation to the fair market value of the property.[273] Thus, the sales price would be reduced from fair market value to reflect the purchaser's costs of liquidation and any recapture of depreciation, intangible drilling costs, investment tax credit, and other recapture items. If the foreign investor expects to sell the property in the near future, his Netherlands Antilles corporation, in order to minimize recapture, might not claim accelerated depreciation or elect to deduct intangible drilling costs. Although U.S. persons who dispose of shares of stock in corporations that own U.S. real estate or natural resources are subject to potential application of the collapsible corporation provisions,[274] nonresident alien individual or foreign corporate selling shareholders can ignore the collapsible corporation provisions, because these provisions merely recharacterize what, absent Section 341, would have been capital gain as "ordinary income." The recharacterization of the gain as ordinary income does not cause the gain

---

[271] IRC §§ 871(a)(2), 881(a).

[272] Treas. Regs. §§ 1.864-3(a), 1.871-8(c), 1.872-1(b), 1.881-1(b)(1), 1.881-2(a)(1).

[273] IRC §§ 334(b)(2), 1012.

[274] IRC § 341.

to be taxable to foreign shareholders if it is not otherwise taxable.[275]

Instead of selling the shares of stock of the Netherlands Antilles corporation to the purchaser, the Netherlands Antilles corporation might sell the property to the purchaser. If the Netherlands Antilles corporation is treated as engaged in a U.S. trade or business in the year of sale, because of its actual business activities or because of a net election, the corporation could sell the property on the installment basis. As noted above, installment payments received in the year of sale would be taxable, but installments received in subsequent years, when the corporation is no longer engaged in a U.S. trade or business, would not be subject to Federal income tax.[276] Accordingly, the selling corporation might receive a small down payment in the year of sale (*e.g.*, 10 percent of the purchase price) and the remainder in the following year or years, including a balloon in the first month of the following year.[277]

Consideration might be given to a sale of the property by the Netherlands Antilles corporation in a so-called twelve-month liquidation under Code Section 337. There are several exceptions, however, to the application of Code Section 337, and the liquidating corporation will recognize gain if it distributes installment obligations in a taxable year in which it is engaged in the conduct of a trade or business within the Unit-

---

[275] IRC § 64; Treas. Regs. §§ 1.881-2(a)(1), 1.1441-2(a)(3).

[276] *See* N. 272, *supra.*

[277] In the year of sale, all or a portion of the gain which is taxable in such year may be taxable as ordinary gain rather than as capital gain, because of the recapture rules. IRC §§ 1245, 1250, 1254. Also, there may be recapture of investment tax credits. IRC § 47. If interest is not charged on installment payments due more than six months after the sale or exchange, a part of the installment payments will be imputed as interest. IRC § 483. Interest paid (or imputed as paid) to a Netherlands Antilles corporation by a U.S. obligor is subject to U.S. withholding tax at the rate of 30 percent, if the obligation is secured by a mortgage on U.S. real property or if the 1963 Netherlands Antilles Protocol to the 1948 Treaty applies. There may be methods for avoiding the U.S. withholding tax on the interest, however, such as using an intermediate Netherlands or Netherlands Antilles finance company, but these schemes must pass the tests of sham, tax avoidance, and no business purpose. *See Aiken Industries, supra,* at N. 238.

ed States.[278] Thus, the twelve-month period must straddle two taxable years, with the sale of the property occurring in the first taxable year when the corporation is engaged in the U.S. business and the distribution of the installment obligations occurring in the second taxable year when the corporation is not engaged in a U.S. trade or business.

Another, but more cumbersome, method of disposition would be for the corporation to exchange the U.S. property for foreign property in a tax-free like-kind exchange, and, at a later time, dispose of the foreign property.[279] Since a key requirement of a tax-free like-kind exchange is that the property acquired on the exchange be held either for productive use in a trade or business or for investment, the IRS undoubtedly will attempt to ignore the like-kind exchange if the disposition of the foreign property is prearranged. The foreign property, therefore, must be held for investment for a period of time.

If the foreign investors expect to hold interests in more than one property, consideration might be given to placing separate properties in separate corporations because it is probable that the properties will not all be disposed of at the same time. Moreover, if there is any risk that the accumulated earnings tax or the personal holding company tax may be imposed, a holding company could be created to hold the shares of stock of the one or more Netherlands Antilles corporations which hold U.S. property. Dividends paid by a Netherlands Antilles corporation, even if all of the corporation's income is effective-

---

[278] IRC §§ 337(c)(1) and (2), 453(d). IRC § 337 does not apply to a collapsible corporation, as defined in IRC § 341(b), even if the corporation is owned by foreign shareholders. IRC § 337(c)(1)(A). *But see* IRC § 341(e)(4); Rev. Rul. 63-125, 1963-2 Cum. Bull. 146; and *Leisure Time Enterprises*, 56 T.C. 1180 (1971). Section 337 also does not apply to most liquidations of a subsidiary corporation if Code Section 332 applies (*i.e.*, if the Netherlands Antilles corporation is 80 percent or more owned by another corporation. IRC § 337(c)(2). Moreover, IRC § 332 cannot be avoided by the failure to obtain a ruling under Code Section 367. *See* Temp. Regs. 7-367(a)-1(g); Rev. Rul. 64-177, 1964-1 (Part 1) Cum. Bull. 141. It should also be pointed out that recapture applies on the sale of property by the liquidating corporation in an IRC § 337 liquidation. IRC §§ 1245, 1250, 1254.

[279] IRC § 1031. Rev. Rul. 68-363, 1968-2 Cum. Bull. 336. Recapture, except for investment credit recapture, does not apply to a like-kind exchange. IRC §§ 1245(b)(4), 1250(d)(4), 1254(b)(1).

ly connected with a U.S. trade or business, are free of U.S. withholding tax by treaty.[280] There is a risk, however, that the IRS would challenge multiple corporations, particularly if there is no business purpose for their separate existences.

[2] Proposed Legislation and Treaty Modifications

At July, 1980, there are several proposals in the Congress to amend the scheme of taxation applicable to foreign investors in U.S. real estate and natural resources.[281] The legislation is designed to impose U.S. income tax on gains from the disposition of U.S. real estate and natural resources that currently escape U.S. income tax. The purposes are to eliminate the tax advantages held by foreign investors vis-a-vis U.S. investors with respect to gain from the disposition of U.S. real estate and natural resources; to reduce the inflow of foreign capital into U.S. real estate and natural resources; and to reduce the escalation in the price of U.S. real estate, particularly farm land, purportedly created by foreign investment.

It is expected (although significant revisions are possible) that the proposed legislation would treat gain from the disposition of a United States real property interest by a nonresident alien individual or a foreign corporation as if the gain were effectively connected with the conduct of a U.S. trade or business of the foreign person, whether or not such person was engaged in a U.S. trade or business. A "United States real property interest" would include an interest in real property (including an interest in a mine, well or other natural deposit) or an interest in a "United States real property holding organization."[282] A United States real property holding organiza-

---

[280] Article XII of the U.S.-Netherlands Antilles Income Tax Treaty.

[281] *See*, for example, Foreign Investment in Real Property Tax Act of 1980, contained in Subtitle E, of Title II, of H.R. 7652, 96th Cong., 2d Sess. (1980). *See also Taxation of Foreign Investment in U.S. Real Estate*, prepared by the Department of the Treasury, U.S. Govt. Printing Office, Stock Number 048-000-00327-3 (May, 1979), prepared pursuant to Section 553 of P.L. 95-500, the Revenue Act of 1978.

[282] Publicly held corporations may be excluded from the definition of a "United States real property holding organization."

tion would include a corporation, partnership or trust, whether domestic or foreign, if the fair market value of its United States real property interests equals or exceeds 50 percent of the fair market value of its total assets, with special rules for the ownership of real property through subsidiaries. Gain from the disposition of a United States real property interest, including gain from the sale of shares of stock of a foreign corporation that constitutes a United States real property holding organization, would constitute U.S. source income. There also would be special rules which would limit the extent to which nonrecognition rules would apply to the disposition of a United States real property interest. Detailed reporting and withholding provisions also are expected.

It is not known whether Federal gift and estate taxes would be made applicable to interests in a United States real property holding organization.

The proposed new legislation also would provide that, after December 31, 1984, gains from the disposition of real property subject to tax under the new law would not be exempt from Federal income tax by reason of any treaty obligation of the United States. Because of this latter provision, it is expected that some treaties (*e.g.*, the 1942 U.S.-Canadian Treaty) will be renegotiated prior to December 31, 1984. It is anticipated, however, that as part of the treaty negotiations some foreign governments will obtain for their nationals who own U.S. real property a step-up in the basis of the U.S. real property to the fair market value as of a certain date, *e.g.*, the date of enactment of the legislation, so that only appreciation after that date would be subject to Federal income tax. It is not know whether the U.S. legislation will have a transitional rule to allow such a step-up for all foreign investors, but the current bills do not contain such a rule.

[3] Conclusion

Although the Federal income tax law (July, 1980) affords a favorable tax climate to foreign investors in U.S. real property and natural resources, it is expected that this favorable climate soon will be terminated. Since foreign investment in United States assets is motivated by many factors other than taxes, including the desire to move capital out of countries deemed politically or economically unstable, the enactment of legislation to tax foreign investors on gains from the sale of real property and natural resources is not expected to impede foreign investment in the United States.

The proposed new U.S. tax law will not discriminate against foreign investors. Instead, the purpose of the proposed legislation is to put U.S. and foreign investors in real estate and natural resources on an equivalent basis. Indeed, many other countries treat foreign investors the same as domestic investors with respect to the taxation of gain from real property located within the country. Thus, the proposed law merely will impose a tax on gains from the disposition of interests in U.S. real property at capital gains rates (except to the extent that a portion of the gain is taxable at ordinary rates because of recapture) with the result that foreign investors will continue to realize a substantial return after taxes from investment in U.S. real property and natural resources.

CHAPTER 3A

Foreign Tax Provisions of the 1984 Tax Act[*]

ROBERT S. RICH**

---

* Prepared in mid-June, 1984, and derived substantially from the Senate Finance Committee's Explanation of the Deficit Reduction Tax Bill of 1984, issued April 2, 1984, and the Committee on Ways and Means' Supplemental Report on H.R. 4170, and Tax Reform Act of 1984, issued March 5, 1984.
** Partner, Davis, Graham and Stubbs, Denver, Colorado.

§ 3A.01 Taxation of Certain Transfers of Property Outside
the United States (IRC §§ 367, 1492, 1494, 7477,
7482 and new section 6038B)

[1] Present Law

[a] Taxation of U.S. and Foreign Corporations

U.S. corporations are taxed on their worldwide income, but
foreign corporations are taxed only on their income that is
effectively connected with the conduct of a trade or business
within the United States and on certain U.S. source income
that is not effectively connected.[1] Thus, a U.S. taxpayer can
defer tax on foreign source income if derived through a foreign
corporation until such income is repatriated as dividends or
shares disposed.

---

[1] Reg. § 1.11-1(a); IRC §§ 881 and 882.

[b] Tax-free Transfers and Perceived Abuse

Certain transfers of appreciated property in a corporate organization, reorganization or liquidation are tax-free both to the corporation and to its shareholders.[2] Thus, through literal application of the provisions providing for the tax-free organization and liquidation of corporations, tax might be avoided on the transfer of appreciated property to a foreign corporation.

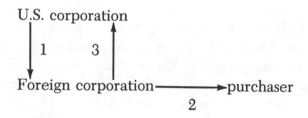

[c] Correction of Abuse

In 1932, in order to prevent an apparent loophole in the case of the organization, reorganization or liquidation of foreign corporations, the predecessor to IRC § 367 was adopted.[3] Section 367 requires that in order for certain tax-free transactions involving foreign corporations to be tax-free, a ruling must be obtained that the exchange does not have as one of its principal purposes the avoidance of Federal income tax.

Arguably, section 367 has been unnecessary to prevent this abuse, as the sham transaction, business purpose doctrine or IRC § 482 should apply.[4]

---

[2] IRC §§ 332, 351, 354, 355, 356, and 361.

[3] H.R. Rep. No. 708, 72d Cong., 1st Sess. 51-52 (1932); and S. Rep. No. 665, 72d Cong., 1st Sess. 55-56.

[4] *See* Gregory v. Helvering, 293 U.S. 465 (1935), which involved a 1928 transaction. *See also* Rev. Rul. 77-83, 1977-1 C.B. 139, which applied IRC § 482 notwithstanding the nonrecognition provision of IRC § 336.

[d] IRS Rulings Guidelines

In 1968, the IRS published rulings guidelines as to when a section 367 ruling ordinarily would be issued.[5]

[i] Active Conduct of a Trade or Business

One guideline is that the assets be devoted by the foreign transferee corporation to the active conduct of a trade or business in a foreign country. *But see Dittler Bros., Inc.,*[6] where the Tax Court held that a taxpayer was entitled to a section 367 ruling, even though the rulings guideline that the transferee devote the transferred property to the active conduct of a trade or business was not satisfied, because the taxpayer was found to have valid business reasons for the transfer.

It should be noted that for many years the IRS ruled favorably on the transfer of nonoperating working interests in oil and gas properties by a U.S. corporation to a foreign corporation.[7] Recently, however, the IRS has ruled that the transfer of nonoperating working interests does not satisfy the active trade or business test of the Guidelines.[8] On the other hand, the IRS also has recently ruled that the holder of a nonoperating working interest in an oil and gas property is subject to self-employment tax, even though the taxpayer has an inactive role, on the theory that the income is from a trade or business.[9] The IRS stated that the taxpayer would be deemed engaged in a trade or business because of the activities performed in his behalf.[10]

---

[5] Rev. Proc. 68-23, 1968-1 C.B. 821.

[6] 72 T.C. 896 (1979).

[7] *See* LR 8319014, LR 8245013 and LR 8151061.

[8] *See* LR 8415037 and LR 8406059.

[9] LR 8416019, citing Rev. Rul. 58-166.

[10] *Cf.* Reg. § 1.612-4(a), which allows a deduction for intangible drilling costs to the holder of a non-operating interest in an oil and gas lease.

[ii] Tainted Assets/Toll Charge

If certain "tainted assets" are transferred to a foreign corporation, the transferor must agree to recognize as income, as a toll charge, the gain attributable to such tainted assets as a condition of a favorable ruling, even though such assets would be used in the active conduct of a trade or business.

[e] Tainted Assets

Tainted assets include:

(a) Inventory, certain copyrights.
(b) Accounts receivable, installment obligations, and similar property where the income has been earned by the transferor.
(c) Property that is expected to be disposed of by the transferee.
(d) Property leased or licensed by the transferor.
(e) Property that is expected to be leased or licensed by the transferee, with certain exceptions.
(f) Certain U.S. and foreign patents.
(g) Stock and securities, with certain exceptions.[11]

[f] Recapture of Foreign Losses

As noted above, U.S. corporations are subject to worldwide taxation, but foreign corporations are not subject to U.S. tax on foreign income. Accordingly, a U.S. corporation might commence foreign operations as a branch, thus claiming the foreign branch losses against U.S. income, and convert to a

---

[11] *But see* Kaiser Aluminum & Chemical Corp., 76 T.C. 325 (1981), *Acq.* 1982-2 C.B.1, where the Tax Court held, under the facts, that the stock transferred "was closely akin to operating assets," because the holder of the stock was entitled to a source of supply of raw materials, and the stock was not readily marketable, *i.e.*, the stock was not a portfolio investment providing for a passive return.

foreign subsidiary when operations go from loss to profit, thus shielding the foreign income from U.S. income tax.

In 1978, in order to combat this apparent loophole, the IRS announced a further toll charge as a condition for a favorable section 367 ruling. Beginning in 1978, in order to obtain a favorable ruling on the incorporation of a foreign branch, the U.S. transferor must recapture its foreign branch losses.[12]

The IRS has had some difficulty in applying its toll charge to recapture foreign branch losses. In *Hershey Foods Corp.*,[13] the Tax Court rejected the Commissioner's determination that tax avoidance existed unless the taxpayer agreed to include in its gross income its historical branch losses, stating that "Congress never intended section 367 to be used to recapture past losses when a branch is incorporated in a foreign country." In addition, the IRS initially failed to reconcile its foreign loss recapture with IRC § 904(f), which was enacted in 1975 and which recaptures foreign losses through a reduction in the foreign tax credit.[14] Moreover, the IRS has had to refine its branch loss recapture where a taxpayer operated abroad through several branches where some were profitable and others were not, and where some were incorporated and others were not.[15] Lastly, the IRS had to modify its rule where the gain on the transfer was less than the losses of the foreign branch.[16]

[g] Intangible Assets; Research and Development

U.S. taxpayers are entitled to current deductions and credits for expenditures for research, experimentation and development that produce assets (*e.g.*, patents and know-how) that have a useful life beyond the current year.[17] The IRS is concerned that the transfer of intangible assets to foreign trans-

---

[12] Rev. Rul. 78-201, 1978-1 C.B. 91.
[13] 76 T.C. 312 (1981).
[14] Rev. Rul. 80-246, 1980-2 C.B. 125.
[15] Rev. Rul. 81-82, 1981-1 C.B. 127.
[16] Rev. Rul. 82-146, 1982-2 C.B. 84.
[17] IRC §§ 174 and 44F.

ferees for use in a foreign trade or business will permit the U.S. transferor to claim deductions and credits but avoid tax on the income derived from the fruits of the research. *Cf.* LR 8409009, where recently the IRS required a taxpayer to recapture research and development expenses on the sale of patents and know-how, by treating a portion of the gain as ordinary income. The IRS relied upon the tax benefit rule as discussed in the recent U.S. Supreme Court decision of *Hillsboro National Bank.*[18]

[h] Advance Ruling; Judicial Review

[i] Advance Ruling

Section 367, as initially enacted and until 1976, required that U.S. taxpayers obtain a ruling in advance of the transaction. This created a serious problem where the transaction could not wait a ruling. Thus, in 1976, section 367 was amended to permit taxpayers to apply for a ruling up to 183 days after the transaction.

[ii] Judicial Review

Another problem with section 367 was that taxpayers had no recourse if the IRS ruled adversely. In 1976, section 367 was further liberalized to permit taxpayers to litigate adverse IRS determinations in section 367 ruling requests through declaratory judgment procedures in the Tax Court.[19] Curiously, the IRS has lost all reported declaratory judgment cases.[20]

---

[18] 103 S. Ct. 1134, 75 L. Ed. 2d 130 (1983).

[19] IRC § 7477.

[20] *See* Kaiser Aluminum & Chemical Corp., *supra;* Dittler Bros., Inc., *supra;* and Hershey Foods Corp., *supra.*

[2] Reasons for Change

[a] Principal Purpose to Active Trade or Business

The Congressional committees feel that the Tax Court's interpretation of the phrase, "a principal purpose," to mean "first in rank, authority, importance or degree" is too narrow and has caused the IRS difficulty in administering section 367.[21]

Thus, the Bill replaces the principal purpose test with an "active trade or business test." That is, under the proposed new law, a transfer of property by a U.S. person to a foreign person will be taxable unless the property is transferred for use by the foreign corporation in the active conduct of a trade or business outside the United States.[22]

[b] Tainted Assets

The proposed new law to a great extent, but with certain exceptions, codifies the 1968 IRS rulings guidelines.[23] Thus, except as to be provided in regulations, the transfer of certain liquid or passive investment assets ("tainted assets") will not be tax-free, unless the U.S. tax on the potential earnings from such assets is paid or preserved for future payment. In addition, the new law adapts the IRS position on the recapture of foreign branch losses.

---

[21] *See* Dittler Brothers, Inc., 72 T.C. 896, at 915 (1979). *Cf.* Malat v. Riddell, 383 U.S. 569 (1966), where the U.S. Supreme Court held that the word "primarily" as used in IRC § 1221(a) means "principally" or "of first importance."

[22] Prop. IRC § 367(a)(3)(A).

[23] Rev. Proc. 68-23.

[3]   Explanation of New Law

[a]   Elimination of Ruling Requirement

The major change is that the mandatory ruling requirement, long a feature of section 367, would be eliminated. The
Committee feels that the elimination of the principal purpose
test and the codification of the rulings guidelines renders the
need for a ruling unnecessary. Thus, taxpayers would no longer need advance or post-transaction IRS clearance. Transfers
to foreign corporations will be tax-free or will involve the payment of an appropriate toll charge in accordance with the
substantive rules set forth in section 367. Of course, taxpayers
nevertheless may apply for rulings, if they desire some certainty, although the issuance of such rulings will be discretionary
with the IRS.

As the counterpart to the repeal of a mandatory ruling, the
Bill repeals the declaratory judgment procedure for Tax Court
review of section 367 rulings.

[b]   Notification Requirement

[i]   Notification

A second major change in the Bill is the establishment of a
notification requirement for section 367 transfers and a set of
penalties for failure to comply with the requirement.[24] The
purpose is to permit the IRS to continue to be informed of
outbound transfers of property subject to IRC § 367. The Committee does not believe that the normal IRS audit procedure
would be sufficient to detect outbound transfers of property
subject to IRC § 367. The information to be furnished and the
time for filing is to be provided by regulations. Curiously, the
Committee failed to note IRC § 6046, which since 1963 has
required the filing of returns upon the organization or reorganization of foreign corporations. Presumably, the IRS will

---

[24] Prop. IRC § 6038B.

take into account IRC § 6046 in adopting regulations to section 6038B.

[ii]   Penalty

Failure to comply with the notification requirements without reasonable cause shall subject the taxpayer to a penalty equal to 25 percent of the amount of gain which is realized on the exchange.

[iii]   Statute of Limitations

The three year statute of limitations with respect to the collection of any tax imposed by section 367 is extended if the taxpayer fails for any reason to give the required notice. The statute is extended to three years after the IRS is notified. Thus, in effect, the statute is extended indefinitely if the taxpayer fails to give notice.

[c]   Active Trade or Business

Transfers of property from the United States to abroad will be tax-free only if the transferee foreign corporation will use the property in the active conduct of a trade or business outside of the United States.[25] However, the Secretary, by regulations, may provide for the recognition of gain in the case of certain transfers, generally in cases of transfers involving the potential of tax avoidance.[26]

---

[25] Prop. IRC § 367(a)(3).
[26] Prop. IRC § 367(a)(5).

[d] Assets Ineligible for Active Trade or Business Treatment

The transfer of certain assets ("tainted assets") will be taxable even if transferred for use in an active trade or business, although no gain will be recognized on the transfer of assets other than tainted assets.[27] Tainted assets include:

(a) Inventory and copyrights.
(b) Installment obligations; accounts receivable.
(c) Foreign currency and property denominated in foreign currency.
(d) Property leased by the transferor.

[e] Intangibles

[i] Taxable

A transfer of intangible property by a U.S. person to a foreign corporation in an exchange described in IRC §§ 332, 351, 354, 355, 356 or 361 will be treated as a taxable sale. The tax will apply on an annual basis over the useful life of the property, as though payments were received under an exclusive licensing agreement.[28] Presumably, regulations will provide guidelines for determination of the amount of the "annual payment."

[ii] Defined

Intangible property is defined as any:

1. Patent, invention, formula, process, design, pattern, or know-how.
2. Copyright, literary, musical, or artistic composition.
3. Trademark, tradename or brand name.

---

[27] Prop. IRC § 367(a)(3)(B).
[28] Prop. IRC § 367(d).

4. Franchise, license, or contract.
5. Method, program, system, procedure, campaign, survey, study, forecast, estimate, customer list, or technical data.

[iii] Correlative Rules

Earnings and profits. The earnings and profits of the transferee foreign corporation are reduced by the amount of income required to be included in gross income by the transferor U.S. corporation.[29]

U.S. source income. Amounts included in gross income under this rule for intangibles are treated as ordinary income from sources within the United States.[30] Arguably, the income should be characterized as foreign source income, if the income is deemed derived from a foreign license.

Disposition. If the stock of the foreign transferee is disposed, the gain attributable to the transferred intangibles is treated as U.S. source income. If the foreign transferee disposes of the intangible assets, the U.S. transferor is treated as having received a payment with a U.S. source.

[f] Stock and Securities

[i] Active Business Exception

Generally, stock and securities will constitute tainted assets. However, certain transfers of stock and securities by a U.S. person to a foreign corporation will fall within the active trade or business rule and will, therefore, be free of U.S. tax.[31] The Committee report provides that transfers of stock such as that in the *Kaiser* case, *supra* (where stock was found akin to a direct interest in producing assets) should fall within the exception. This rule also might apply where the transferee owns

---

[29] Prop. IRC § 367(d)(2)(B).
[30] Prop. IRC § 367(d)(2)(C).
[31] Prop. IRC § 367(a)(2).

substantial stock in the company whose stock is transferred, or where the business activities of the foreign transferee are integrated with the business of the corporation whose stock is transferred.

[ii]   Closing Agreement

Proposal

The Committee Report suggests that the IRS should set forth regulations whereby, where appropriate, the IRS would not impose tax on the transfer of stock, provided that the transferor agrees that the stock will not be disposed of by the transferee (or any other person) for a substantial period of time (*e.g.*, fifteen years) following the year of the transfer. The transferor would be taxed on any income or gain from a disposition of the stock as if the disposition occurred in the year of the original transfer at the fair market value of the stock at the time of the original transfer. Interest would be added to the tax for the period from the initial transfer to the subsequent transfer.

Prior Law

Curiously, the IRS has consistently refused to enter into closing agreements with respect to transfers in connection with section 367 rulings, notwithstanding that a closing agreement might obviate any principal tax avoidance purpose. The IRS has refused because of the perceived administrative burden of concluding such agreements and possible difficulties in enforcing them. *See Kaiser, supra,* where the IRS' failure to enter a closing agreement was disapproved by the Tax Court. The Committee believes that the burdens of enforcing compliance with closing agreements do not outweigh the benefit of closing agreements. However, the Committee suggests that the regulations provide for an annual waiver of the statute of limitations and that the IRS might require security to ensure that any tax will be paid.

[g]   Other Assets

[i]   Goodwill

The Committee Report suggests that ordinarily no gain will be recognized on the transfer of goodwill or going concern value for use in an active trade or business.

[ii]   Marketing Intangibles

The Committee Report also expects that regulations will provide that gain will not be recognized on transfers of marketing intangibles (*e.g.*, trademarks or tradenames) in appropriate cases.

[iii]   Leased Property

The transfer of property (*e.g.*, tangible property) that will be leased by the transferee in the active conduct of a leasing business generally should fall within the active trade or business rule, provided the property is not to be leased in the United States and the transferee has need for a substantial investment in the type of property transferred.[32]

[iv]   Partnerships

Aggregate Theory
A transfer by a U.S. person of a partnership interest to a foreign corporation in a section 367 exchange is to be treated as a transfer of the U.S. person's pro rata share of the partnership's assets.[33]

---

[32] *See* Rev. Proc. 80-14, 1980-1 C.B. 617.
[33] Prop. IRC § 367(a)(4).

Limited Partnerships

The foregoing rule will not apply to most transfers of interests in limited partnerships. The Committee believes that limited partnership interests represent passive interests comparable to stock and securities and should be treated like stock or securities for section 367 purposes.

[h] Foreign Branch Losses

Upon the incorporation of a foreign branch by a U.S. corporation, gain shall be recognized in an amount equal to the lesser of (a) any gain on the transfer and (b) the excess of losses incurred by the foreign branch before the transfer and with respect to which a deduction was allowed to the U.S. taxpayer over the amount of such losses that is treated as income from sources within the United States under section 904(f).[34] That is, to the extent that a U.S. taxpayer has incurred an overall foreign loss in years prior to the incorporation that has not previously been recaptured, any gain on incorporation of the foreign branch, to the extent of prior unrecaptured losses, is includible in gross income and is recharacterized as U.S. source income. Although unclear, it appears that the gain recognized will have the same character as the prior branch losses.

[i] Regulations

The IRS is given broad authority to adopt regulations in connection with IRC § 367.[35]

---

[34] Prop. IRC § 367(a)(3)(C).
[35] Prop. IRC § 367(a)(5).

[j]   **Effective Date**

[i]   **Post 1984 Transfers**

Both the House and Senate Bill apply the new law to transfers or exchanges made after December 31, 1984, but the Senate Bill provides that the new law shall not apply to transfers or exchanges with respect to which a ruling request under section 367 was filed with the IRS before March 1, 1984. However, transfers of intangibles after June 6, 1984, may be subject to a special rule.

[ii]   **Regulations**

The Committee suggests that, prior to January 1, 1985, the Treasury will issue regulations presenting the standards to be used in determining whether property is transferred for use in the active conduct of a trade or business within the meaning of the Bill. However, the Committee Report further provides that if Regulations are not issued before January 1, 1985, current IRS practice as reflected in IRS ruling policy will determine the existence of an active trade or business.

§ 3A.02   **DISC to FSC (Prop. IRC §§ 921 to 927)**

[1]   **Present Law—DISC**

[a]   **Tax Deferral**

The Revenue Act of 1971 provided a system of tax deferral to Domestic International Sales Corporations (DISCs) and their shareholders.[36] A DISC typically is a wholly-owned subsidiary of a U.S. company engaged in exporting. Under the system, a DISC is not subject to taxation, but its shareholders are taxable on distributions and deemed distributions from the

---

[36] IRC § 991 *et seq.*

DISC.[37] Until 1976, the DISC system permitted a deferral of tax on 50 percent of a DISC's income. Since 1976, the deferral has been limited to 42.5 percent of the DISC's income, and the deferral is calculated only on the incremental export income of the DISC, except for small DISCs. Federal income tax is deferred on the remaining portion of the DISC's taxable income until the income is actually distributed to the DISC's shareholders, the shareholders dispose of their stock, the DISC is liquidated or the corporation no longer qualifies as a DISC.

[b] DISC Defined

A DISC is a domestic corporation that satisfies certain tests as to its gross receipts and gross assets.[38] However, basically, a DISC is a paper corporation for which the normal rules of corporate substance are reduced.[39] Under special inter-company pricing rules, without regard to whether the DISC conducts any activity or has any employees, the taxable income of a DISC may equal the greater of 4 percent of the gross export receipts or 50 percent of the combined taxable income of the DISC and its related supplier (normally its parent).[40]

[c] Purposes of DISC Legislation

The purposes of DISC legislation are:

(1) To stimulate exports.
(2) To create a disincentive to the shift of manufacturing abroad.
(3) To redress the tax treatment to U.S. exporters in face of the more favorable tax treatment provided by other trading nations for their exports.

---

[37] IRC §§ 991 and 995.
[38] IRC § 992(a).
[39] Reg. § 1.992-1(a). See Rev. Rul. 72-166, 1972-1 C.B. 220. See also Durbin Paper Stock Company, 80 T.C. 252 (1983).
[40] IRC § 994(a).

[2] Reasons for Change

[a] GATT Violation

Since its enactment, several European member countries of the General Agreement on Tariffs and Trade (GATT) have contended that the DISC provisions are an illegal export subsidy in violation of GATT. In 1976, a GATT panel determined that the DISC had the characteristics of an illegal export subsidy.

[b] U.S. Response

The U.S. has consistently denied that DISC violates GATT, but in 1981 the U.S. agreed to modify its law to satisfy the concern of other GATT members.

[c] GATT Rules

The GATT is not violated by an exemption from taxation for economic activities occurring outside the territory of a member nation.

[3] Explanation of Provisions—FSC

[a] In General

Under U.S. tax law, income of a foreign corporation derived outside the United States is not subject to U.S. income tax.[41] Thus, the proposal is for the creation of a foreign sales corporation (FSC), which will be exempt from U.S. income tax on a portion of its eligible export income.[42] An exemption from U.S. tax on foreign income satisfies the GATT principle of territorial taxation.

---

[41] IRC §§ 881 and 882.
[42] Prop. IRC § 921(a).

[b] Foreign Presence

In order to satisfy both the GATT principle of territorial taxation and the U.S. principle that foreign source income of a foreign corporation is exempt from U.S. income tax, a FSC must satisfy a foreign presence test. This test has six requirements.

Foreign Corporation

A FSC must be incorporated under the laws of a foreign country or possession of the United States. The foreign country must be a party to an agreement or tax treaty with the U.S. that contains a satisfactory exchange of information procedure.[43]

Shareholders

A FSC can have no more than 25 shareholders.[44]

Preferred Stock

A FSC cannot issue preferred stock, but can have more than one class of common stock.[45]

Foreign Office

A FSC must maintain an office outside the United States and maintain a set of its permanent books of account at such office. The office should meet the tests for a permanent establishment under U.S. tax treaty principles. However, a FSC may share an office with another FSC, and the office may be outside the country of incorporation of the FSC.[46]

Directors

A FSC must have at least one director that is not a U.S. resident, although the individual may be a U.S. citizen.[47]

Controlled Group

A FSC may not be a member of a controlled group in which

---

[43] Prop. IRC § 922(a)(1)(A).
[44] Prop. IRC § 922(a)(1)(B).
[45] Prop. IRC § 922(a)(1)(C).
[46] Prop. IRC § 922(a)(1)(D).
[47] Prop. IRC § 922(a)(1)(E).

a DISC is a member.[48]

[c] Exempt Foreign Trade Income

A FSC is exempt from federal income tax on its exempt foreign trade income. Its exempt foreign trade income is equal to 34 percent of the foreign trade income of the FSC.[49] Alternatively, under a special administrative pricing rule, exempt foreign trade income is 17/23 of the foreign trade income derived from a transaction.[50] Exempt from trade income is an exclusion from gross income of the FSC. Deductions are allocated and apportioned between exempt and nonexempt income.[51] Nonexempt foreign trade income will be taxable to the FSC as income effectively connected with a U.S. trade or business of the FSC.

[d] Foreign Trade Income

Foreign trade income is gross income of a FSC attributable to foreign trading gross receipts. Such income can be from profits earned by the FSC or from commissions earned by a FSC on products or services exported by others.

Foreign Trading Gross Receipts (Prop. IRC § 924)
(a) Sale of export property.
(b) Lease or rental of export property.
(c) Engineering and architectural services on foreign construction projects.
(d) Export management services.

Excluded Receipts (Prop. IRC § 924(g))
(a) Income attributable to patents and other intangibles which do not constitute export property.

---

[48] Prop. IRC § 921(a)(1)(F).
[49] Prop. IRC § 923(a)(2).
[50] Prop. IRC § 923(a)(3).
[51] Prop. IRC § 921(b).

(b) Income from export property or services destined for ultimate use in the U.S.

(c) Transactions supported by U.S. subsidy.

[e] Foreign Management

A FSC must be managed outside the United States.[52]

(a) Meetings of directors and shareholders must be outside the U.S.

(b) Principal bank account maintained outside the U.S.

(c) Dividends, legal and accounting fees and salaries disbursed out of foreign bank account.

[f] Foreign Economic Processes

Certain economic processes of a FSC must occur outside the U.S.[53]

Sales Portion of Transaction. The solicitation, negotiation or making of the transaction must occur outside the U.S. A FSC treated as conducting such processes if processes conducted by an agent for the FSC.

Direct Costs. A FSC may not earn foreign trading gross receipts unless the foreign direct costs incurred by the FSC attributable to the transaction equals or exceeds 50 percent of the total direct costs or 85 percent of the costs from two of five enumerated categories of foreign activities.[54] The costs of an agent acting on behalf of a FSC count.[55] Five categories of activities are:

1. Advertising and sales promotion;
2. Processing orders and arranging for delivery;
3. Transportation;

---

[52] Prop. IRC § 924(b)(1)(A) and (C).
[53] Prop. IRC § 924(b)(1)(B) and (d).
[54] Prop. IRC § 924(d).
[55] Prop. IRC § 924(d)(3)(A).

4. Determination and transmittal of invoice or statement of account and receipt of payment;
5. Assumption of credit risk.

[g] Transfer Pricing Rules (Prop. IRC § 925)

[i] Administrative Transfer Pricing Rule

If the foreign economic processes requirements discussed above (*e.g.*, sales solicitation and negotiation, and direct costs requirements) are satisfied, a special administrative pricing rule may apply. If the administrative pricing rule applies, the taxable income of a FSC may be based on a transfer price that allows a FSC to derive taxable income attributable to the sale in an amount that does not exceed the greater of (i) 1.83 percent of the foreign trading gross receipts from the sale; (ii) 23 percent of the combined taxable income of the FSC and the related person; or (iii) the actual sales price subject to the principles of section 482.

[ii] Adjustments After Year-End

A FSC and its related supplier may make adjustments upward or downward in the transfer price following the close of the taxable year in which the FSC sells the goods.

[iii] No Loss Rule

The transfer price cannot create a loss to the related supplier.

[h] Taxation of a FSC

Generally

A FSC is not subject to tax on its exempt foreign trade income. A FSC is subject to federal income tax on the remainder of its taxable income—which includes nonexempt foreign trade income and other income *e.g.*, interest, dividends, royalties).[56]

ITC

A FSC will not be entitled to an investment tax credit or other credits.

Foreign Tax Credit

A FSC will not be allowed a foreign tax credit with respect to exempt foreign trade income, but it will be allowed a foreign tax credit on its nonexempt foreign trade income.[57]

Tax Treaties

A FSC cannot claim benefits under a U.S. income tax treaty.

[i] Distributions to Shareholders

Distributions will be treated as being made first out of earnings and profits attributable to foreign trade income and then out of other earnings and profits.[58]

[j] Dividends from FSC

A domestic corporation will be allowed a 100 percent dividends received deduction for amounts distributed from a FSC out of earnings and profits attributable to foreign trade income. Thus, there is no corporate level tax on exempt foreign trade income and only a single level corporate tax (at the FSC level) on foreign trade income other than exempt foreign

---

[56] Prop. IRC § 921(d).
[57] Prop. IRC § 921(c).
[58] Prop. IRC § 926(a).

trade income. However, no dividends received deduction will be allowed for dividends to corporate shareholders that are not attributable to foreign trade income.

FSC dividends attributable to foreign trade income probably will not be treated as foreign personal holding company income. FSC dividends to individual shareholders that are not attributable to foreign trade income will be subject to tax in the same manner as dividends from a foreign corporation.

[k]   Export Property (Prop. IRC § 927(a))

Fifty Percent U.S. Content. Export means property manufactured, produced, grown or extracted in the United States by a person other than a FSC, held primarily for sale, lease or rental. Not more than 50 percent of the fair market value of the property can be attributable to articles imported into the U.S.

Excludes Patents and Intangibles. Export property does not include patents and other intangibles.

Includes Depletable Products. Coal and uranium products, and other depletable products, other than oil and gas, can constitute export property. Depletable products were excluded under the DISC rules.

[l]   Election (Prop. IRC § 927(f))

Generally. A corporation may elect to be a FSC for a taxable year at any time during the 90 day period immediately preceding the taxable year.

New Corporation. A new corporation may elect to be a FSC within the first 90 days of its taxable year.

[m] Small Business (Two Alternatives)

[i] Interest Charge DISC (Prop. IRC § 995(f))

Deferral on $10 Million. A DISC may continue to defer tax on income attributable to $10 million or less of qualified export receipts. Deemed distributions will be eliminated. Thus, substantially all of a DISC's income attributable to $10 million or less of qualified export receipts may be deferred. Income of a DISC in excess of $10 million will be deemed distributed. Thus, if export receipts exceed $10 million, the DISC would not be disqualified; there merely would be no deferral of tax on income attributable to the excess receipts.

Interest Charge. An interest charge will be imposed on the shareholders of the DISC. The amount of interest will be based on the tax otherwise due on the deferred income computed as if the income were distributed. The interest rate will be based on the T-bill rate. The interest is paid at the time the shareholders' regular tax is required to be paid.

[ii] Small FSC

Relaxed Requirements. A FSC may elect to be a small FSC. In such case, neither the foreign management nor the foreign economic process requirements need be met.[59]

Five Million Dollar Maximum. Gross receipts in excess of $5 million are not taken into account in determining exempt foreign trade income.[60] If gross receipts of a small FSC exceed $5 million, the small FSC may select the gross receipts to which the limitation is allocated.[61]

---

[59] Prop. IRC § 922(b).
[60] Prop. IRC § 924(b)(2)(B)(i).
[61] Prop. IRC § 924(b)(2)(B)(ii).

[n]   Taxable Year of DISC and FSC

The taxable year of any DISC or FSC must conform to the taxable year of the majority shareholder as determined by voting power.[62] Under the former DISC rules, a DISC's taxable year did not have to conform to the taxable year of any of its shareholders. Thus, an eleven-month deferral was possible by having the DISC's year end one month after its parent's year.

[o]   Transition Rules

Taxable Year

The taxable year of any DISC which begins before January 1, 1985, and which would otherwise include January 1, 1985, will close on December 31, 1984.

Accumulated DISC Income

Accumulated DISC income that is derived before January 1, 1985, will be exempt from tax. This result will be achieved by treating such income as previously taxed income.[63] This provision for the indefinite deferral of tax on accumulated DISC income has caused certain members of Congress, including Rostenkowski, to be noncommittal in supporting the FSC legislation.

[p]   Transfers from DISC to FSC

Except as provided in regulations, section 367 will not apply to transfers made before January 1, 1986, by a DISC to a FSC, of qualified export assets held on August 4, 1983, in a transaction to which section 351 or 368(a)(1) would apply.

---

[62] Prop. IRC § 441(h).

[63] *See* IRC § 996.

[q] **Effective Date**

The FSC provisions will apply after December 31, 1984.

§ 3A.03 Repeal of 30 Percent Withholding on Interest Paid to Foreign Persons (IRC §§ 864, 871, 881, 1441, 1442 and 2105)

[1] **Present Law**

[a] **In General**

Foreign persons who are not engaged in a U.S. trade or business but receive interest (and other fixed or determinable annual or periodical income) from U.S. sources are subject to a withholding tax of 30 percent on such amounts, unless the tax is reduced or eliminated by treaty or a special exemption applies.[64] Under the treaty with the Netherlands Antilles, interest received by a Netherlands Antilles corporation from U.S. sources is exempt from U.S. tax, unless the obligation is secured by a mortgage on real property.[65]

[b] **Eurobond Market and International Finance Subsidiaries**

A major capital market exists outside the United States, known as the Eurobond market. Both U.S. and foreign issuers, both private and public, issue bonds through this market. When Texaco acquired Getty Oil last winter, it issued $1.5 billion of convertible Eurobonds. It is anticipated that $83.7 billion of new-issue Eurobonds will be offered in 1984, of which $61.3 billion will be Eurodollar bond issues.[66] Eurodollars are dollars held abroad, accumulated because of the U.S. balance of payment deficits.

---

[64] IRC §§ 871(a)(1), 881(a)(1), 1441 and 1442.
[65] U.S.-Netherlands Antilles Income Tax Treaty, Article VIII.
[66] *See Wall Street Journal,* May 29, 1984, p. 1.

Eurobonds generally are issued free of withholding taxes on interest. Thus, in order for a U.S. corporation to raise funds in the Eurobond market, an international finance subsidiary must be established, generally in the Netherlands Antilles. The IFS issues its bonds in the Eurobond market and relends the funds to its U.S. parent. There is no U.S. withholding tax on the interest paid by the U.S. parent by operation of the U.S.-Netherlands Antilles Treaty; there are very low taxes in the Antilles on the spread between interest received and interest paid; and there are no Netherlands Antilles withholding taxes on interest paid to the Eurobond holders.

[c] IRS Attack

Most international finance subsidiaries are paper companies, with their Eurobonds guaranteed by the U.S. parent corporations. Thus, the IRS has challenged the arrangements, apparently in at least twenty-five situations.[67] The IRS challenge is based upon *Aiken Industries, Inc.*,[68] which may support the argument that the U.S. parent is the true obligor and that the paper subsidiary is a mere conduit interposed for tax avoidance; and *Plantation Patterns, Inc.*,[69] which may support the argument that the guarantor is the true obligor where the subsidiary is thinly capitalized.

[2] Reasons for Change

The Senate Finance Committee believes that it is important that U.S. businesses have access to the Eurobond market as a source of capital. It further believes that the imposition of U.S. withholding tax, and the costs and risks of attempting to avoid such tax, impair the ability of U.S. corporations to raise money in the Eurobond market. Thus, the Senate Finance Committee proposes the repeal of the 30 percent withholding tax on inter-

---

[67] 46 *Taxes International* 13 (August, 1983).

[68] 56 T.C. 925 (1971).

[69] 462 F.2d 712 (5th Cir. 1972).

est paid to foreign lenders by U.S. borrowers. There is no such proposal in the House bill, although the House Ways and Means Committee has scheduled hearings on proposals to eliminate the 30 percent withholding rules.

[3] Explanation of Provision

[a] Phase-out of Withholding

The 30 percent withholding tax on interest (and original issue discount) paid by a U.S. borrower on portfolio debt investments where the interest is received by nonresident aliens or foreign corporations would be phased-out.[70] The phase-out would be as follows:

	Percent
From Date of Enactment	5
1985	4
1986	3
1987	2
Jan. - June, 1988	1
July 1, 1988 and thereafter	0

The purpose of the phase-out or transitional period is to prevent sudden substantial negative impact on the economy of the Netherlands Antilles. It might be noted that the Netherlands Antilles has stated that the proposed repeal of the 30 percent withholding tax on interest constitutes an abrogation of the Treaty.

[b] Categories of Debt Obligations Qualified

1. *Bearer Instruments (Prop. IRC § 871(h)(3)(A)).* See IRC § 163(f), which denies a deduction for interest on certain bearer bonds.

---

[70] Prop. IRC § 871(h).

(a) If arrangements designed to insure issue only to non-U.S. persons.

(b) Interest must be payable outside the U.S. and its possessions.

(c) The instrument on its face must state that any U.S. person who holds it will be subject to U.S. income tax laws.

2. *Registered Instruments (Prop. IRC § 871(h)(3)(B)*

(a) U.S. payor must receive statement that beneficial owner of the obligation is not a U.S. person, although security owner need not be identified.

(b) Statement must be made by beneficial owner or a securities clearing organization, a bank or a financial institution. Prop. IRC § 871(h)(5).

3. *Obligations assumed by U.S. Corporations (Prop. IRC § 871(h)(3)(C))*

(a) Obligation must be assumed after the date of enactment.

(b) Obligation must have been issued on or before the date of enactment.

(c) At the time of issuance, the assumed obligation must have been guaranteed by a U.S. person and must have been issued pursuant to arrangements reasonably designed to ensure that it would be sold only to non-U.S. persons.

(d) The assuming U.S. corporation must meet certain reporting requirements that would be imposed on the corporation from which the obligations would be assumed were the latter corporation to continue to hold the obligation.

[c] **Ineligible Persons**

[i] **Ten Percent Equity Interest in Payor**

Interest paid to a foreign person owning directly, indirectly or constructively 10 percent or more of the total combined voting power of the U.S. corporate payor. If the domestic payor is a partnership, the interest is ineligible if the foreign payee owns a 10 percent or more capital or profits interest in the partnership. The attribution rules of IRC § 318(a) apply, with certain exceptions.[71]

[ii]   Foreign Banks

Foreign banks are not eligible for the phase-out with respect to interest on bearer or registered instruments on an extension of credit pursuant to a loan agreement entered into in the ordinary course of their banking business. Foreign banks qualify for the phase-out on interest paid on obligations of the United States.

[iii]   CFCs

A controlled foreign corporation is not entitled to the phase-out, to prevent U.S. persons from indirectly taking advantage of the new law.

[d]   Estate Tax

Obligations held by nonresident alien individuals will be exempt from U.S. estate tax if the income on such obligations would be eligible for the phase-out of withholding upon receipt by the decedent at the time of death.[72]

[e]   Prevention of Tax Evasion

If the IRS determines that the U.S. is not receiving adequate information from a foreign country to prevent evasion of U.S. income tax by U.S. persons, the IRS may provide that the phase-out of withholding tax will not apply to payments of

---

[71] Prop. IRC § 871(h)(4)(C).
[72] Prop. IRC § 2105(b)(3).

interest addressed to or for the account of persons within that country for issuances of debt obligations after the date of publication of the determination.[73] The termination will continue until the IRS determines that the exchange of information between the U.S. and that country is adequate to prevent the evasion of U.S. income tax by U.S. persons. Any termination for interest will also apply to terminate the exemption from estate tax.

[f] Obligation of U.S. Payors

The duty to withhold tax at 30 percent will arise only if the person otherwise subject to the duty knows, or has reason to know, that the interest is subject to tax at the 30 percent rate because the recipient is a controlled foreign corporation, has a direct ownership interest in the U.S. payor, or is a bank and the interest is received on an extension of credit made pursuant to a loan agreement entered into in the ordinary course of the bank's business. However, the IRS can require that the payor withhold in cases where the payor does not know the identity of the beneficial owner with respect to which the interest is paid.

[g] Effective Date

The phase-out of withholding will take effect for interest paid after the date of enactment. The estate tax exclusion will apply to estates of decedents dying after the date of enactment.

-----

[73] Prop. IRC § 871(h)(6).

§ 3A.04 Withholding on Disposition by Foreigners of U.S. Real Property Interests (IRC §§ 6039C and new 1444)

[1] Present Law

In 1980, Congress adopted the Foreign Investment in Real Property Tax Act, known as FIRPTA, requiring that foreign persons who dispose of U.S. real property interests pay tax on any gain realized on the disposition.[74] U.S. real property interests include direct interests in U.S. real property and stock of a corporation if the fair market value of its U.S. real property interests equals or exceeds 50 percent of the fair market value of its U.S. and foreign real property interests and its other assets used or held for use in a trade or business.[75]

The 1980 Act rejected withholding and provided for enforcement a system of information reporting designed to identify foreign owners of U.S. real property interests.[76]

[2] Reasons for Change

[a] Evasion

Tax returns are not filed until after the end of the year, and foreign sellers can take the proceeds of sale out of the U.S. and be beyond the jurisdiction of the U.S.

[b] Reporting

The IRS has had difficulty in developing regulations to cover the reporting prescribed by FIRPTA. Final regulations have not yet been issued and no reporting is yet required.[77] Moreover, the Senate believes that withholding is preferable to

---

[74] IRC § 897.

[75] IRC § 897(c).

[76] IRC § 6039C.

[77] T.D. 7940, filed January 31, 1984.

enforcement through reporting—it reduces paperwork and it reduces fear of disclosure by foreign investors who risk political consequences in their home countries.

[3] Explanation of Provisions

[a] Amount Withheld

In the case of any acquisition of a U.S. real property interest from a foreign person, the transferee, the transferee's agent or any settlement officer must withhold the lower of (a) 28 percent of the sales price in the case of a corporate transferor and 20 percent in the case of a noncorporate transferor; (b) the transferors maximum tax liability; or (c) the fair market value of the portion of the sales proceeds which is within the withholding agent's control.[78] The calculations are complex.

[b] Time of Withholding

Withholding applies when a U.S. real property interest is acquired from a foreign person.

[c] Withholding Agent

Withholding is imposed on the transferee, a transferee's agent or a settlement officer, but only if, before each payment of consideration with respect to the acquisition of a U.S. real property interest, they know or have received notice from either the transferor or any agent of the transferor that the transferor is a foreign person.[79]

---

[78] Prop. IRC § 1444(a).
[79] Prop. IRC § 1444(b)(1).

[d] Transferor's Notice

The transferor is required to give notice to the transferee, the transferee's agent and the settlement officer that the transferor is a foreign person.[80] A transferor's agent is also required to notify the transferee that the transferor may be a foreign person if the agent has reason to believe that the transferor may be a foreign person.

[e] Liability of Transferor's Agent

If the transferor's agent fails to make a reasonable inquiry about the transferor's status, he is required to notify the transferee that the transferor may be foreign. However, the transferor's agent is relieved of any responsibility to give notice to a transferee if he relies in good faith on a written statement of the transferor that the transferor is a U.S. person. A transferor's agent who does not fulfill his obligation to provide notice is required to withhold the appropriate amount from any of the transferee's consideration he has within his control, including any compensation received by him in connection with the transaction. A transferor's agent includes a person who represents a foreign transferor in negotiations preceding the transaction or at a settlement of the transaction. A person who at the transferor's request procures the services of an agent for negotiations or settlement is also an agent of the transferor. Thus, lawyers, accountants and real estate agents all may constitute agents of a transferor and be liable for giving notice or for withholding.

[f] Exemptions from Withholding

Principal Residence Under $200,000. Withholding is not required if the transferee is to use the real property as his principal residence and the purchase price is $200,000 or less.

Qualifying Statement. Withholding is not required if the

---

[80] Prop. IRC § 1444(c).

transferor obtains a qualifying statement from the Treasury that he is exempt from tax or has provided adequate security for payment of the tax, or has otherwise made arrangements with Treasury for the payment of the tax.

Traded Stock. Withholding is not required if the property being transferred is stock of a corporation and the transfer takes place on an established U.S. securities market.

[g]   Partnerships

Special rules are provided for withholding by a domestic partnership (and domestic trusts and estates) on amounts which such entities have in their custody and which are attributable to the disposition of a U.S. real property interest, but only if the amounts are income of a nonresident alien or foreign corporation, partnership, trust or estate.[81]

[h]   Effective Date

The withholding requirements apply to payments of consideration with respect to the acquisition of a U.S. real property interest that are made more than thirty days after the date of the bill's enactment. Note that the sale may have occurred prior to the bill's enactment.

[i]   Repeal of FIRPTA

By separate bills in the Senate and House (S. 1915; H.R. 5673), proposals have been introduced to repeal FIRPTA, that is, to repeal the capital gains tax on the disposition of investments in U.S. real property by foreign persons.

---

[81] Prop. IRC § 1444(f).

§ 3A.05 Resident Alien Defined (IRC § 7701(b))

[1] Present Law

[a] Taxation of Aliens

Resident aliens are taxed like U.S. citizens, that is, they are taxed on their worldwide income at regular graduated tax rates. Nonresident aliens are taxed only on U.S. source income and on income effectively connected with a U.S. trade or business.

[b] Definition

The Internal Revenue Code does not define the term "resident alien" or "nonresident alien." The Treasury Regulations generally apply a subjective test and define the terms on the basis of an alien's intentions with regard to the length and nature of his stay.[82] A mere transient or sojourner is not a resident, but living in the U.S. with no definite intention as to the length or nature of his or her stay makes an alien a resident.

[2] Reasons for Change

The House Ways and Means Committee (there is no Senate provision) believes that the tax law should contain a more objective definition of residence for income tax purposes.

[3] Explanation of Provision

[a] Generally

The Bill provides a definition of resident alien for U.S. in-

---

[82] Reg. § 1.871-2.

come tax purposes.[83] The Bill does not affect the definition of resident for federal estate or gift tax purposes. Aliens who do not meet the definition will be nonresident aliens.[84]

[b] General Test of Residence

An individual will be considered a resident alien with respect to any calendar year if:

[i] Green Card

He is a lawful permanent resident of the U.S. at any time during the calendar year (the "Green Card Test"); or

[ii] Substantial Presence

He is present in the U.S. for 31 or more days during the current calendar year and has been present in the U.S. for a substantial period of time. Apparently, a loophole exists in the legislation because under the so-called 31 day de minimus rule, a resident alien could become a nonresident alien for a taxable year by remaining outside the U.S. for 334 days in such year.

The substantial presence test is satisfied if the number of days that the individual was present in the United States during the calendar year and the preceding two years equals or exceeds 183 days, computed as follows: (1) the days present during the current calendar year, (2) one-third of the days present during the preceding calendar year, and (3) one-sixth of the days present during the second preceding calendar year. Thus, an average of 122 days of presence over three years will trigger the test. There are special rules for the first and last year of residency.

---

[83] Prop. IRC § 7701(b).
[84] Prop. IRC §7701(b)(1)(B).

[c] Less than 183 Days—Closer Connections Test

[i] 183 Day Test

If an individual is present in the U.S. for fewer than 183 days during the calendar year, and if the individual establishes that he or she has a closer connection with a foreign country than with the U.S., and has a tax home in that country for the year, the individual generally will not be treated as a resident for such year on account of his substantial presence. If an individual is present in the U.S. for as many as 183 days during a year, this closer connections/tax home exception will be unavailable.

[ii] Tax Home

A "tax home" means the individual's home for purposes of IRC § 162(a)(2) relating to travel expenses while away from home. Thus, maintenance of a U.S. abode will not automatically prevent an individual from establishing a foreign tax home.

[iii] Change of Status

An alien who has an application pending to change his or her status to permanent resident or who has taken other steps to apply for status as a lawful permanent U.S. resident will not be eligible for the closer connections/tax home exception.

[d] Exempt Individual

An individual shall not be treated as being present for purposes of the substantial presence test if he is an exempt individual.

[i]   Foreign Government—Related Individual

An individual who is temporarily present in the U.S. by reason of diplomatic status or visa; is a full-time employee of an international organization; or is a member of the immediate family of such an individual. An international organization is one entitled to the benefits of the International Organizations Immunities Act.[85]

[ii]   Teacher or Trainee

An individual who is temporarily present in the U.S. as a teacher or trainee under section 101(15)(J) of the Immigration and Nationality Act. An individual cannot be exempt as a teacher or trainee if he or she has been exempt as a teacher, trainee or student for any part of two of the six preceding calendar years.

[iii]   Student

An individual who is temporarily present in the U.S. as a student under section 101(15)(F) or (J) of the Immigration and Nationality Act. An individual cannot be exempt as a student if he or she has been exempt as a teacher, trainee or student for more than five calendar years, unless the individual establishes that he or she does not intend to reside permanently in the U.S. and that he or she has substantially complied with the requirements of a student visa.

[e]   Annual Statements

The IRS may require exempt individuals to submit an annual statement setting forth the basis on which they claim such status.

---

[85] *See* IRC § 7701(a)(18).

[f] Medical Condition

An individual who cannot physically leave the U.S. because of a medical condition that arose after the individual's presence in the U.S. is eligible for the closer connections/home exception to the substantial presence test even if present in the U.S. for more than 182 days during the fiscal year.

[g] Fiscal Year

An alien who has not established a taxable year for any prior period will be taxed on a calendar year basis. An alien who establishes a fiscal year will nevertheless determine residence on a calendar year basis, and will be subject to tax as a resident for any portion of his fiscal year within the calendar year of residence.

[h] Treaties

If the definition of residence in the bill conflicts with the definition in an existing treaty, the treaty shall prevail.[86]

[i] Effective Date

The provisions will apply to taxable years beginning after December 31, 1984. However, pre-1985 presence of an alien who was not a resident under current law at the close of 1984 will not count in the substantial presence test; and pre-1984 presence of an alien will count only if that individual was a resident under current law at the end of both 1983 and 1984.

---

[86] *See* IRC §§ 894(a) and 7852(d).

§ 3A.06   Factoring Trade Receivables (IRC §§ 553, 861, 954 and 956)

[1]   Present Law

[a]   Factoring Income

If a seller of goods or services takes back a receivable as payment and sells the receivable to a third party (a "factor") at a discount, the factor (rather than the seller) realizes the income equal to the difference between the amount the factor paid for the receivable and the amount received upon collection of the receivable (the "discount income").

[b]   Character of Discount Income

The Tax Court has held that discount or factoring income derived in an active factoring business is not interest income within the meaning of personal holding company income.[87] The IRS has ruled that factoring income is not interest income for purposes of subpart F.[88]

[2]   Reason for Change

On the assumption that discount income does not constitute interest income, a U.S. parent corporation can sell its accounts receivable to a foreign subsidiary at a discount and avoid tax on the discount income. If the discount income constituted interest income, such income would be taxable to the U.S. parent corporation as subpart F income.[89]

According to LR 8338043, *supra,* the discount income is services income. However, if the foreign subsidiary conducts all its activities in the foreign country of its incorporation, such

---

[87] Elk Discount Corp., 4 T.C. 196 (1944).
[88] LR 8338043; GCM 39220.
[89] IRC § 954(c).

income would not constitute subpart F services income.[90] Moreover, if the services are performed abroad, such income would constitute foreign source services income, so no withholding would be required.[91]

It should be noted that arguably the purchase of receivables by a foreign subsidiary from its U.S. parent corporation constitutes a proscribed investment in U.S. property and would be taxable to the U.S. parent under IRC § 956. This issue was raised but not resolved in LR 8338043.

[3]   Explanation of Provision

[a]   Foreign Personal Holding Company Income

[i]   Trade or Services Receivable

A new category of foreign personal holding company income is created, namely, income from trade or service receivables.[92] A trade or service receivable means an account receivable or evidence of indebtedness arising from the disposition of property described in section 1221(1) (*e.g.*, inventory), or the performance of services, by a related person.[93] A related person is defined in section 267(b), and can be a foreign or United States person.[94] Thus, the U.S. shareholders of a foreign personal holding company or a controlled foreign corporation will be taxable currently on income from trade or service receivables.

[ii]   Ten Percent De Minimus Rule Inapplicable

The so-called 10:70 rule with respect to subpart F income is amended so that income from trade receivables constitutes

---

[90] IRC § 954(e)(2).
[91] LR 8338043.
[92] Prop. IRC § 553(a)(8)(A).
[93] Prop. IRC § 553(a)(8)(B).
[94] Prop. IRC § 553(a)(8)(C).

foreign base company income even if such income is less than 10 percent of the gross income of a controlled foreign corporation.[95]

[iii]   Exception for Certain Related Party Transfers

A controlled foreign corporation will not derive subpart F income from a trade or service receivable that is acquired from a related person which (i) is created or organized under the laws of the same foreign country in which the factor is organized, and (ii) has a substantial part of its assets used in its trade or business located in that same foreign country.[96]

[b]   Investment in U.S. Property

[i]   U.S. Property

The term "United States property" for purposes of section 956 is amended to include any trade or service receivable as defined in Prop. IRC § 553(a)(8)(B) acquired directly or indirectly from a related person who is a United States person.[97] That is, the new law treats certain factoring transactions as though they were loans from a controlled foreign corporation to a related U.S. shareholder. Therefore, the U.S. shareholders of a controlled foreign corporation will be taxable currently on the amount that is paid for factoring trade or service receivables (up to the amount of the controlled foreign corporation's earnings and profits).

[ii]   Indirect Investment

The Committee Report states that it is intended that a loan by a foreign subsidiary to a second foreign subsidiary of the

---

[95] Prop. IRC § 954(b)(3)(A).
[96] Prop. IRC § 954(c)(4)(A).
[97] Prop. IRC § 956(b)(3)(A).

same parent, which factors the receivables of the parent, shall be treated as an investment by the first foreign subsidiary in U.S. property for purposes of IRC § 956.[98]

[iii]   Exception for Export Property Receivables

Trade or service receivables which arise out of the disposition or rental of export property (within the meaning of IRC § 993(c) - DISC provisions), the income from which would be treated as qualified export receipts under the DISC provisions, shall not constitute U.S. property.[99] However, this exception shall not apply to any receivable arising out of transactions involving a DISC or a FSC, without regard to whether the export property disposed or rented is held by the DISC or FSC.[100]

[c]   Possessions Corporations

Income from a trade or service receivable is not eligible for the possessions tax credit and is not eligible for the reduction of Virgin Islands tax.[101]

[d]   Source of Income

[i]   Factoring Income

Income from factoring trade or service receivables acquired from a related U.S. person will be treated as income from sources within the United States, although income from factoring certain export receivables will be treated as 50 percent income from sources within the United States and 50 percent

---

[98] *See* Rev. Rul. 76-192, 1976-1 C.B. 205.
[99] Prop. IRC § 956(b)(3)(B).
[100] *Id.*
[101] Prop. IRC §§ 936(d)(4) and 934(b).

income from foreign sources.[102]

[ii] Distributions

Any distribution from a foreign corporation and any amount included in gross income under section 951, to the extent attributable to factoring income, will be treated as income from sources within the United States, although any distribution or amount included in gross income under section 951 that is attributable to factoring of certain export receivables will be treated as 50 percent income from sources within the United States and 50 percent foreign source income.

[e] Effective Date

These provisions will apply to accounts receivable and evidences of indebtedness transferred after March 1, 1984, in taxable years ending after such date.

§ 3A.07 Decontrol of Foreign Corporations (IRC § 1248)

[1] Present Law

Generally, but with exceptions, gain from the sale or exchange of stock is capital gain. One exception is that gain derived by a U.S. shareholder from the sale or exchange of stock of a controlled foreign corporation is a dividend, to the extent of the post-1962 earnings and profits of the controlled foreign corporation attributable to the stock sold.[103] Thus, if a U.S. corporation wholly owns a foreign subsidiary, gain derived by the U.S. corporation from the sale or exchange of the stock of the foreign corporation is treated as a dividend to the extent of the CFC's post-1962 earnings and profits. The rule is designed to prevent the controlled foreign corporation

---

[102] Prop. IRC § 862(a).
[103] IRC § 1248(a).

from accumulating earnings and profits tax-free and repatriating such earnings and profits as capital gain. The Tax Reform Act of 1976 extended the rule of section 1248 to tax-free dispositions under sections 311, 336 and 337. Thus, a U.S. parent corporation recognizes dividend income on dispositions of stock of a controlled foreign subsidiary that would otherwise be tax-free under sections 311, 336, or 337.

[2] Reason for Change

Although unclear, it appears that section 1248 does not apply to a U.S. parent corporation where a controlled foreign corporation acquires a majority interest in the stock of the U.S. parent in exchange for shares of stock of the CFC and a small amount of cash. Presumably, this scheme is used where the shareholders of the U.S. parent corporation have a loss or have little or no gain in their stock of the U.S. parent corporation, because any gain on the exchange would be recognized.[104] Moreover, this scheme is used only if the U.S. parent corporation is widely held or at least sufficiently broadly held so that the foreign subsidiary is no longer a CFC after the exchange. A foreign corporation is a CFC only if more than 50 percent of its voting stock is owned by U.S. shareholders, and only shareholders who own 10 percent or more of the foreign corporation's voting stock are counted for this purpose.[105]

As a result of this so-called decontrol of a foreign corporation, its earnings and profits escape U.S. income tax, if the scheme works.

[3] Explanation of Provision

In order to prevent the perceived abuse, if a shareholder of a U.S. shareholder corporation of a foreign corporation in which the U.S. corporation owns 10 percent or more of the voting stock exchanges stock of the U.S. shareholder corpora-

---

[104] IRC § 1001.
[105] IRC §§ 957(a) and 951(b).

tion for the stock of the foreign corporation, for purposes of IRC § 1248, the stock of the foreign corporation received in the exchange shall be treated as if it had been (1) issued to the U.S. shareholder corporation, and (2) then distributed by the U.S. shareholder corporation to its shareholder in redemption of his stock.[106] Thus, the U.S. corporate shareholder would be required to recognize dividend income.[107] The amount of the dividend is equal to the difference between the fair market value of the stock of the foreign corporation received by the shareholders of the U.S. parent corporation and the U.S. parent corporation's basis for its stock in the foreign corporation, subject to the post-1962 earnings and profits limitation.[108]

[4] Effective Date

The Senate bill would apply section 1248 to exchanges after the date of enactment, whereas the House bill would apply to transfers made after December 31, 1984.

§ 3A.08   Stapled Stock (New IRC § 269B)

[1] Present Law

Taxpayers have devised schemes for tax avoidance by "stapling" or "pairing" the stock of two or more corporations (*i.e.*, the stock of one corporation cannot separately be transferred; the shares of stock of both corporations trade together).

A foreign subsidiary of a U.S. corporation is a controlled foreign corporation, thus imposing the subpart F and anti-boycott rules, among others. However, if the foreign subsidiary is owned by the same shareholders as the U.S. corporation, and its shares are sufficiently widely-held, the foreign corporation will not constitute a controlled foreign corporation.

---

[106] Prop. IRC § 1248(i).
[107] IRC § 1248(f).
[108] IRC § 1248(f)(1).

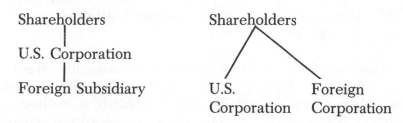

Shareholders | U.S. Corporation | Foreign Subsidiary

Shareholders | U.S. Corporation | Foreign Corporation

[2]　Reason for Change

The Committee believes that the stapling of stock is a simple means to attempt to avoid certain tax rules, such as the controlled foreign corporation or anti-boycott rules.

[3]　Explanation of Provision

[a]　General Rule

If a foreign corporation is stapled to a domestic corporation, the foreign corporation will be treated as a domestic corporation.[109] Therefore, the foreign corporation will be subject to U.S. tax on its worldwide income. The Committee Report indicates that section 367 will not apply because distributions from the new domestic corporation will be subject to U.S. tax.

[b]　Stapled Entities

Stapled entities means any group of two or more entities if more than 50 percent in value of the beneficial ownership in each of such entities consists of stapled interests. Two or more interests are stapled if, by reason of form of ownership, restrictions on transfer, or other terms or conditions, in connection with the transfer of one of such interests the other such interests are also transferred or required to be transferred.

---

[109] New IRC § 269B(a)(1).

[c] Election to Treat Stapled Foreign Entities as Subsidiaries

In the case of any foreign corporation and domestic corporation which as of June 30, 1983, were stapled entities, such domestic corporation may elect to be treated as owning all interests in the foreign corporation which constitute stapled interests with respect to the stock of the domestic corporation. The election must be made no later than 180 days after the date of enactment of the new law. If the election is made, the foreign corporation will not be treated as a domestic corporation. If the election is made, the new foreign subsidiary would constitute a controlled foreign corporation, and cause subpart F to be applicable. However, stock of the foreign corporation held by foreign persons will not be subject to the election and earnings attributable to stock of a foreign shareholder will not be subject to U.S. tax.

[d] Treaties

The stapled stock provision generally will override treaty provisions that otherwise would exempt the income of a foreign corporation from U.S. income tax. A grandfather clause will permit treaty benefits for entities stapled on June 30, 1983.

§ 3A.09 Foreign Investment Companies (IRC §§ 535 and 1246)

[1] Present Law

U.S. Shareholders	U.S. Shareholders	U.S. Shareholders
		Foreign Parent Corp.
U.S. Corporation	Foreign Corporation	Foreign Subsidiary Corp.

[a] **U.S. Taxation of Foreign Corporations**

U.S. corporations are taxed on their worldwide income. Foreign corporations are subject to U.S. tax only on income from a U.S. business or on certain passive U.S. source income.[110] Moreover, income of foreign corporations from trading in U.S. securities or commodities is not subject to U.S. income tax, if properly organized.[111] Dividends received by a foreign corporation from a second foreign corporation are not subject to tax unless more than 50 percent of the paying corporation's income is effectively connected with a U.S. trade or business.[112] Moreover, under certain treaties, dividends from foreign corporations, even if such corporations are engaged in a U.S. trade or business, are exempt from tax.[113]

[b] **Taxation of U.S. Shareholders of Foreign Corporations**

A U.S. shareholder of a foreign corporation is not subject to tax on the income of the foreign corporation unless the foreign corporation is a controlled foreign corporation or a foreign personal holding company.[114] Gain derived from the disposition of stock of a foreign corporation is capital gain, unless the foreign corporation is a controlled foreign corporation or a foreign investment company.[115] A foreign corporation owned equally by eleven unrelated U.S. persons would be neither a controlled foreign corporation nor a foreign personal holding company.[116] A foreign investment company is a foreign corpo-

---

[110] IRC §§ 881 and 882.
[111] IRC § 864(b)(2).
[112] IRC § 861(a)(2)(B).
[113] See Article XII of the U.S.-Netherlands Income Tax Treaty.
[114] IRC §§ 551 and 951.
[115] IRC §§ 1248 and 1246.
[116] IRC §§ 552(a)(2) and 957(a).

ration (a) registered under the Investment Company Act of 1940, or (b) engaged primarily in investing or reinvesting in securities and more than 50 percent of its stock is owned by U.S. persons.[117] Commodities do not constitute securities for purposes of determining whether a foreign corporation is a foreign investment company.

[c] Accumulated Earnings Tax

The accumulated earnings tax applies to U.S. or foreign corporations formed or availed of for the purpose of avoiding the U.S. individual income tax on shareholders by accumulating earnings at the corporate level rather than distributing such earnings to shareholders as dividends.[118] However, the accumulated earnings tax applies only to U.S. source income of a foreign corporation.[119]

Thus, a foreign subsidiary that derives income from trading in securities or commodities in the U.S. would be subject to the accumulated earnings tax, but a foreign parent corporation that receives only dividends from such foreign subsidiary would not be subject to the accumulated earnings tax, because such dividends would not constitute U.S. source income.[120]

[2] Reasons for Change

Based upon the foregoing tax rules, U.S. persons can establish a structure to invest in U.S. securities or commodities and avoid tax on the trading income and pay only capital gains tax when they dispose of their stock in the investment vehicle.[121]

---

[117] IRC § 1246(b).

[118] Reg. § 1.532-1(a)(1).

[119] Reg. § 1.532-1(c).

[120] IRC § 861(a)(2)(B).

[121] *See* Kepke and Powers, *Commodity Futures Trading Through an*

The structure would involve a foreign parent corporation and a foreign subsidiary corporation. The foreign subsidiary would not be subject to U.S. income tax on its trading income.[122] The foreign subsidiary would avoid the accumulated earnings tax by distributing dividends to its foreign parent corporation. The foreign parent corporation would not be subject to U.S. income tax or accumulated earnings tax on the dividends.[123] The U.S. investors would obtain capital gain upon the disposition of their shares in the foreign parent corporation, assuming that the foreign parent corporation is neither a controlled foreign corporation nor a foreign investment company.

[3]   Explanation of Provisions

[a]   Foreign Investment Company

The definition of foreign investment company is expanded to include not only trading in securities, but trading in commodities.[124] However, a foreign corporation will not constitute a foreign investment company if less than 50 percent of its stock is held by U.S. persons.[125]

[b]   Effective Date

The provision will apply to sales and exchanges after October 31, 1984. However, in the case of shares held on October 31, 1984, the new law will not apply for one year if such shares are disposed by the person who was the owner of the shares on October 31, 1984.

Offshore Investment Corporation, P-H, U.S. Taxation of International Operations, ¶ 6016 (1980).

[122] IRC § 864(b)(2)(B).
[123] IRC § 861(a)(2)(B).
[124] IRC § 1246(b)(2).
[125] IRC § 1246(b)(2).

[c] Accumulated Earnings Tax

U.S. persons will not be able to use two or more foreign corporations to avoid the accumulated earnings tax. For purposes of the accumulated earnings tax, if more than 10 percent of the earnings and profits of any foreign corporation for any taxable year are derived from U.S. sources or are effectively connected with a U.S. trade or business, then any distribution received by a United States-owned foreign corporation out of those earnings and profits will be treated as derived by the receiving corporation from United States sources. That is, the earnings and profits retain their U.S. source in the hands of the receiving corporation, so that they are subject to the accumulated earnings tax.

A United States-owned foreign corporation means a foreign corporation if 50 percent or more of its stock is held, directly or indirectly, by U.S. persons. Thus, a less than 50 percent U.S. owned foreign corporation avoids the new rule.

§ 3A.10 Miscellaneous Changes to Foreign Personal Holding Company Provisions (IRC §§ 551, 552, 553, 554 and 951)

[1] Present Law

[a] In General

In 1937, Congress adopted the foreign personal holding company provisions, to prevent U.S. persons from creating foreign corporations to accumulate investment income tax-free until repatriated.[126] A foreign personal holding company is a foreign corporation that satisfies both a stock ownership test and a gross income test.[127]

---

126 IRC § 551.
127 IRC § 552.

Stock Ownership Test

More than 50 percent in value of its stock is owned by five or fewer individuals who are U.S. citizens or residents.

Gross Income Test

At least 60 percent of its gross income is foreign personal holding income (*i.e.* passive income, such as dividends, interest, royalties and gains from the sale or exchange of stock or securities).[128] The 60 percent gross income test decreases to 50 percent for taxable years after the 60 percent test is first satisfied.[129]

[b] Technical Problems

During the past few years, several technical problems have arisen with respect to the interpretation of the foreign personal holding company provisions. The purpose of the proposed changes is to correct these problems.

[2] Attribution Rules

[a] Current Rule

The foreign personal holding company provisions contain constructive ownership rules that determine whether five or fewer U.S. citizens or residents own more than 50 percent in value of a foreign corporation.[130] These rules treat an individual as owning the stock owned, directly or indirectly, by or for his or her partners, brothers and sisters, spouse, ancestors and lineal descendants.

---

[128] IRC § 553.
[129] IRC § 552(a)(1).
[130] IRC § 554.

[b]   Problem

Under the literal language of the Code, stock owned by a nonresident alien individual is treated as owned by a U.S. citizen or resident if the nonresident alien is a partner or a family member of the U.S. citizen or resident. For example, the IRS treated a foreign corporation as a foreign personal holding company where it was owned 60 percent by two Canadian sisters and 40 percent by an unrelated U.S. person, because the two sisters had a U.S. citizen brother.[131] Thus, the unrelated U.S. person would be subject to tax under the foreign personal holding company provisions on his 40 percent share of the corporation's foreign personal holding company income. The same result could occur if a nonresident alien shareholder in a foreign corporation had a partner who was a U.S. citizen or resident.

[c]   Family Attribution

For purposes of the stock ownership test, the bill repeals the rules that attribute ownership of stock actually owned by a nonresident alien individual to the alien's U.S. brothers and sisters, ancestors and lineal descendants.[132] Attribution will continue to apply from a nonresident alien spouse. Note that attribution will not apply even if the U.S. family member also owns stock in the foreign corporation, although this rule may be changed by the conference committee.

[d]   Partner Attribution

The bill also repeals the attribution of ownership of stock from a nonresident alien to the alien's U.S. partners, but only if the alien's U.S. partners do not own, directly or indirectly,

---

[131] *See* Estate of Nellie S. Miller, 43 T.C. 760 (1965), nonacq., 1966-1 C.B. 4.

[132] Prop. IRC § 554(c)(1).

stock in the foreign corporation.[133]

[3] Coordination of Subpart F with Foreign Personal Holding Company Provisions

[a] Background

In 1962, to supplement the foreign personal holding company rules, Congress adopted Subpart F, which imposes tax on U.S. shareholders of a controlled foreign corporation. Subpart F income includes, but is not limited to, passive income, such as foreign personal holding company income.[134]

The Subpart F rules provide that if a U.S. shareholder is subject to tax under the foreign personal holding company rules, he will not be subject to tax under Subpart F.[135] This has created a loophole, because a taxpayer who is subject to tax under the foreign personal holding company rules is then arguably not subject to tax under the more expansive Subpart F rules. For example, if a foreign corporation is both a foreign personal holding company and a controlled foreign corporation, a U.S. shareholder who is subject to tax on dividends or interest income of the foreign corporation under the foreign personal holding company provisions arguably would not be subject to tax on any investment in U.S. property by the foreign corporation in the same taxable year. The courts are split on this issue.[136]

[b] New Law

The bill repeals IRC § 951(d) which provides that the foreign personal holding company provisions have priority when

---

[133] Prop. IRC § 554(c)(2).

[134] IRC § 954.

[135] IRC § 951(d).

[136] *Compare* Whitlock, 494 F.2d 1297 (10th Cir. 1974), *cert. denied*, 419 U.S. 839 (holding the taxpayer liable for tax under Subpart F), *with* Lovett, 621 F.2d 1130 (Ct. Cl. 1980)(holding that no Subpart F tax was due).

there is an overlap with the Subpart F rules. Under the new law, the Subpart F income of a CFC will be taxable under Subpart F and not under the foreign personal holding company rules, to the extent that such income would be taxable under both sets of rules.[137] Income includible under only one set of rules will be includible under that set of rules. A U.S. shareholder who is taxable under Subpart F on amounts other than Subpart F income will be taxable under Subpart F whether or not he is also subject to tax under the foreign personal holding company provisions.

[4] Same Country Dividend and Interest Rule

[a] Problem

Under both the foreign personal holding company provisions and the Subpart F provisions, dividends and interest are taxable to U.S. shareholders.[138] However, under the Subpart F rules, dividends and interest from (1) a related corporation, (2) organized in the same country as the recipient corporation, and (3) having a substantial part of its assets used in its trade or business located in that same foreign country, are not treated as Subpart F income.[139] This "same country" exception has no counterpart in the foreign personal holding company provisions.

[b] Correction

For both Subpart F and the foreign personal holding company rules, dividends and interest that satisfy the "same country" test will not constitute foreign personal holding company income.[140] Note that these dividends and interest also will be excluded in determining non-foreign personal holding compa-

---

[137] IRC § 951(d).
[138] IRC §§ 553(a)(1) and 954(c)(1).
[139] IRC § 954(c)(4)(A).
[140] Prop. IRC § 553(a)(1).

ny income.[141] That is, for purposes of the threshold fraction for determining whether a foreign corporation meets the gross income requirement for foreign personal holding company purposes, such income will be excluded from both the numerator and denominator.[142]

[5] Income Inclusion Through Foreign Entity

[a] Problem

Interposition of a foreign partnership or a foreign corporation other than a foreign personal holding company (or certain estates and trusts) between a U.S. shareholder and a foreign personal holding company arguably may allow for avoidance of the personal holding company rules.

[b] Correction

The bill adds a so-called tracing rule that makes it clear that U.S. taxpayers cannot interpose foreign corporations or foreign partnerships or other entities between themselves and a foreign corporation to avoid the foreign personal holding company rules.

§ 3A.11   Foreign Collapsible Corporations (IRC § 341)

[1] Present Law

Gain from the sale or exchange of stock of a collapsible corporation is taxed as ordinary income.[143] However, section 341(f) permits a shareholder to obtain capital gains treatment

---

141 Prop. IRC § 552(a)(1).

142 *Cf.* IRC § 543(b)(1)(A) and (B), which excludes capital gains and section 1231 gains from both the numerator and denominator of the gross income test for personal holding companies.

143 IRC § 341(a).

if the corporation consents to recognize gain on the disposition of its subsection (f) assets, even if such gain is not otherwise recognized.[144]

[2] Reasons for Change

There is concern that if a foreign corporation gives a section 341(f) consent, enforcement of the consent may be impractical because, for example, the foreign corporation is not engaged in a U.S. trade or business. Nevertheless, it is believed that in certain situations it may be appropriate to allow a foreign corporation to give a consent.

[3] Proposed Change

To the extent provided in regulations, a section 341(f) consent given by a foreign corporation shall not be effective.[145] This new rule also applies to tax-free transactions between the consenting corporation and a transferee under section 341(f)(3), if the transferee is a foreign corporation.

[4] Effective Date

The provision is effective on the date of enactment.

§ 3A.12 Other Changes in Foreign Provisions

A. Original Issue Discount and Coupon Stripping—Foreign Investors (IRC §§ 871 and 881)
B. Source of Transportation Income (IRC § 863)
C. Use of Territories to Avoid U.S. Tax on Foreign Investors (IRC §§ 881 and 7651)

---

[144] IRC § 341(f)(2).
[145] Prop. IRC § 341(f)(8).

D. Recharacterization of U.S. Income as Foreign Income (IRC § 904)
E. Recharacterization of Interest Income as Dividend Income (IRC § 904)
F. Technical Corrections to TEFRA-IRC § 907
   1. Recapture of foreign oil losses
   2. Definition of foreign oil-related income
G. Technical Change to IRC §§ 959 and 1248
   1. Earnings and Profits Adjustment
   2. Foreign Tax Credit Adjustment
H. Insurance of Related Parties by a Controlled Foreign Corporation (IRC § 954(e))
I. Excise Tax On Insurance Premiums Paid to Foreign Insurers and Reinsurers (IRC §§ 4371-74)
J. Limitation on Cover Over (Payment) of Certain Federal Excise Taxes to Puerto Rico and the Virgin Islands (IRC § 7652)
K. Treatment of Community Property Income of Nonresident Aliens (IRC § 879)
L. Ordinary Income Treatment on Disposition of Stock of Certain Foreign Corporations (IRC § 1248)
M. Foreign Currency Contracts (IRC § 1256(3))—technical correction
N. Extension of Moratorium on R&D Allocation Rules (Reg. § 1.861-8)
O. Treasury Study on Foreign Taxation of Certain U.S. Services (section 889 of Senate Bill).

CHAPTER 4

Selected Clauses in Transnational Contracts

MARK S. CALDWELL*

---

*B.A., J.D., University of Denver. Assistant Director, Program of Advanced Professional Development, University of Denver, College of Law.

§ 4.01 Introduction

Recent advances in the means of transportation and communication have resulted in shrinking distances between nations. The effect this has had on the business community is staggering. More and more companies are transacting business abroad. Implicit in this trend is an increasing need for more law firms and lawyers to be conversant with transnational commercial law.

The foundation of any commercial transaction is the contract. However, a transnational contract is by no means the same creature as a domestic contract. All too often, the courts are littered with the remains of agreements that were drafted without considering international ramifications. Every attorney who practices in this area has heard at least one horror story involving a domestic-type contract that was used in a transnational setting. There may be significant differences between agreements performed within the United States and those performed abroad. The attorney engaged in transnational contracts should be sensitive to these differences, or he may be committing malpractice.

Contract drafting is no different from drafting any other kind of document; certain rules of form and style are to be followed. The transnational agreement, however, demands that special consideration be given to certain contract practices. The following rules, most of which are preparatory to the actual drafting of the agreement, are helpful in offering the needed perspective for transnational agreements.

Among the special features which distinguish a transnational agreement from a domestic one are the different types of pressure brought to bear on international agreements. Domestic business enterprises expect certain stresses in their day-to-day operations. Pressures such as new legislation and government regulation, inflation, stockholder disputes, and strikes are predictable. Lawyer and client alike know and understand these problems. They are part and parcel of business and transactions may be designed around them. However, the business environment abroad is fraught with pressures that are entirely different. Mandatory local stock ownership, labor participation in management, cartels, expropriation, tariff barriers, and exchange controls are just a few examples. To compound problems, these pressures may originate from outside sources. The two most prevalent situations where these additional stresses might arise are within member nations of either the Andean Common Market (ANCOM) or the European Economic Community (EEC). Two recent examples from the EEC are the introduction of the European Patent and the European Company. Thus, the first rule to bear in mind is that an attorney can ill afford to confine his inquiry exclusively to the laws of the state in question.

Second, an attorney should consider, evaluate, and understand his client's position. In businesses newly entering the international marketplace, a typical scenario is that of an inexperienced client working with an attorney who is familiar with the economic, legal, and political problems of a particular area of the world. This combination of experience and inexperience provides an ideal setting for the wrong question syndrome.[1] Consider a situation where an inexperienced client, misinformed about the laws of the country where business is to be conducted, predetermines his own legal needs based upon such misinformation. The client then requests the attorney to perform a service. Since the services requested by the client may be completely inappropriate to his actual needs, it is the duty of the attorney not to take the request at face value and perform the services as requested, for a costly mistake might be made. It is preferable for the attorney to objectively consider the client's initial request and develop some background information. In that way, the attorney can insure that the service performed is what is actually needed.

Third, the entire transaction should be in writing. All too often, certain parts of the negotiation are only oral. If a disagreement later arises, the problems already present in a transnational agreement are compounded. The wonders of modern communication are truly helpful in business transactions. However, they should not be left to stand on their own. The best way to conduct transnational business is in writing.

---

[1] E. Murphy, Jr., "An Overview: Special Considerations in Representing Clients Abroad," *International Law for General Practitioners*, A-3 (1977).

It is worth emphasizing that all elements of the agreement should be in writing. If it is necessary to use telephone, telegram or telex, the attorney should still ask that confirmation be made in writing.

Fourth, the attorney should make sure that each agreement is considered to be a separate entity. Although standard form contracts may be preferred, especially in highly repetitive situations, to provide a convenient solution to an otherwise expensive problem, the question that always must be considered is, "do the facts in this particular situation warrant special attention in drafting?" Since no two fact situations are exactly the same, the attorney must evaluate the facts and recommend how the contract can be drafted to fit specific needs.

These four simple preparatory rules will help to insure that the contract is tailored to the client's needs. The remainder of this chapter will consider some of the specialized clauses that may be used in a transnational agreement. Space considerations preclude the inclusion of every clause that might be found in an international contract. Additionally, a separate chapter deals with the choice of laws and choice of forum in transnational agreements. Therefore, the choice is limited to those clauses which in the author's judgment should be considered for inclusion in every agreement.

§ 4.02   Definitions and Standardized Terms

The preamble and introductory sections of a contract are used to set the stage for the body of the agreement. The first major clause of the transnational contract will be the definition section.

Completeness and precision in the terms of the contract are clearly the most important aspects of all commercial transactions. In domestic situations, bodies of legislation, such as the Uniform Commercial Code (UCC), are designed to provide the rules to regulate rights and obligations of the parties when they are not specified in the body of a contract. While these matters may be specifically set out by the parties if they choose, it is more common to simply define certain terms, leaving the remainder to be determined by reference to the applicable law. This is such a common domestic practice that it is often taken for granted.

This, however, is not the situation in a transnational contract. Unfortunately, there is not a uniform body of law such as the UCC in effect throughout the world. Parties to a contract may not be familiar with each other's legal system. Even if a choice of law clause, which would include the UCC or a similar code, is part of the agreement, it is best to create a private code that will at least cover the most important parts of the contract. It may also be that the subject of the contract is so specialized that it is not covered by any of the uniform laws that may be available. A clear understanding of any essential term is what will make the contract work.

This is not to say that every time a contract is drafted a personal version of the UCC should be included. The ideal situation is to develop a balance between the business interest of a short form contract with the attorney's desire to meet all possible problems and resolve them.

There are many trade terms that at first blush have a standard meaning, e.g., C.I.F., F.O.B., and F.A.S. Closer examination shows that this may not be true. Courts and trade associations in various nations have adopted different interpretations of the same trade terms.[2] These differences in understanding of the same terms by the parties often have lead to difficulties.[3]

One method of resolving this problem has been used in conjunction with the sale of goods. Export contracts often incorporate by reference a set of standard terms published elsewhere. The parties to the contract simply agree to bind themselves to terms that are defined elsewhere than in the documents which pass between them.[4]

There are several sets of standard terms being used in inter-

---

[2] *See, e.g.,* International Chamber of Commerce, *Trade Terms* (1953), which contains annotated synoptic tables of the meanings of various trade terms in eighteen countries.

[3] M. Meek and I. Feltham, "Foreign Sales Distribution, Licensing and Joint Venture Agreements," 17 De Paul L. Rev. 46, at 51 (1967).

[4] *Id.*

national commerce. The two most popular are *Incoterms 1953* and the *Revised American Foreign Trade Definitions 1941* (R.A.F.T.D.). *Incoterms* was prepared by the International Chamber of Commerce, while a joint committee of representatives from the Chamber of Commerce of the United States, the National Council of American Importers, Inc., and the National Foreign Trade Council adopted the R.A.F.T.D. *Incoterms* is probably the more comprehensive of the two as it has been reviewed and updated several times since its initial publication.

One of the greatest selling points of these standardized terms is that they may be used as a compromise when parties cannot agree as to whose terms, buyer's or seller's, they will accept. Both have been approved by important trade organizations.

Neither of these sets of terms is comprehensive. While they provide a degree of certainty to terms such as F.A.S., F.O.B., C.I.F., etc., they should not be relied on by themselves without careful analysis of the remainder of the contract. Thus, they should not be used as a substitute for a carefully drawn definitions clause.

Draftsmen should also be aware of the danger of altering one of the standard trade definitions. Variations in the standard terms may destroy the specific nature of the term as it relates to the contract.[5]

Standardized trade terms will not be available to all contracts. Therefore, before the contract is drafted, its subject and the relationship of the parties should be discussed with the client. Careful consideration should be given to several factors: (1) Is the subject matter of the contract unique? (2) Are there any unusual business practices involved? (3) Are there any special terms of art?, etc. If the answer to any of these questions is in the affirmative, there should be some provision in the definition section describing the special nature. For example, does the other nation use the Gregorian or Georgian calendar? If one of the nations involved uses the Gregorian

---

[5] Meek and Feltham, *supra* N. 2, at 54. Comptoir d' Achat et de Vente du Boerenbend Belge S.A. v. Luis de Ridden, Limitada [1949] A. C. 293.

calendar, a definition more particularly describing the dates is in order.

Careful attention to definitions will insure the parties are in agreement and assist in the smooth performance of the agreement.

§ 4.03   Choice of Language Clause

Parties to transnational contracts often do not speak the same language. While they may be conversant in a common language, the highly complex and specialized terms in an agreement might prove to be beyond the parties' comprehension, possibly giving rise to differing interpretations. It is likely that a commonly used word in one language might not even exist in another. Thus, what was believed to be a clear understanding of the contract at the time of its execution could be transformed into a monstrous problem.

In drafting the transnational contract, the draftsman should follow the example set by many complex domestic agreements. After many drafts, the final form of the domestic contract is identified as the official form. Only the language in this official form may be relied upon. None of the other drafts is binding or has any legal effect. The transnational contract should also have *one* official draft. This official document should have *one* official language.

Occasionally, a draftsman, moved by equitable consideration, inserts a clause authorizing two official versions of the contract, one in English and the other in a different language. However, if a problem develops and the contract must go to litigation, numerous evidentiary and linguistic problems may be raised. Each side will try to prove that its version of the contract is the one the finder of fact should consider and accept. There may also be difficulties with the parole evidence rule.

A choice of law clause may resolve this problem to some extent. The conflict of laws rules of the named jurisdiction should state which version will be controlling. Likewise, an arbitration clause could leave the choice to the arbitrators.

None of these solutions is particularly appealing. In fact, any such decision could open the door to appeal, thus lengthening the litigation process further. The best solution is simply to designate one official language.[6]

Naturally, in representing the client to the best of his ability, the draftsman will specify his client's language as the official language. It is critical that the draftsman also be technically fluent in this language. If this is not the situation, outside counsel, with fluency in the language, should be retained as co-counsel.

Model Choice of Language Clause

This Agreement is signed in two (2) originals in the English language, which shall be regarded as the authoritative and official text. (Any matters referred to arbitration will also be in the English language, which will be the official language used in arbitration.)

In situations where, either from a weak negotiating position or by action of law, a language other than English is the official language of the contract,[7] the rule for keeping one official language still holds true. To lessen the impact of this problem, an official translation of the contract should be provided for in the agreement. This official translation should be ratified by the parties. If disagreement does arise concerning the contract, it can be asserted that even though the foreign language is controlling, reliance on the official translation was reasonable.

Model Choice of Language Clause with Translation Provision

This Agreement is signed in two (2) originals in the _____ language, which shall be regarded as the authoritative and official text. Parties hereto agree to provide an official translation of this Agreement in the English language. This translation will be ratified by both parties and it may be

---

[6] Meek and Feltham, *supra* N. 2, at 58.

[7] For example, in all transactions with Saudi Arabia any document must be in Arabic by action of law.

relied upon as being an accurate representation of the official form.

Another possible method of avoiding this problem would be to include an arbitration clause in the contract. The arbitration clause would then provide for English to be the official language of the arbitration.[8]

After choosing one official language, it is essential that the wording of the document be clear and concise. Throughout the United States, a trend is developing that emphasizes the use of simple and plain language. Some jurisdictions are enforcing this trend by enacting legislation that requires the contract to be comprehensible to the average person.[9] The transnational contract should model itself on these plain-speaking domestic relatives. The goal of every contract is to be so clear and understandable that all parties can perform smoothly and efficiently without the assistance of counsel. In the event the agreement must be translated, this plain language will certainly reduce the possibility of misunderstanding.

§ 4.04 Payment Clauses

[1] General

The terms and manner of payment have always been a matter of concern when transacting business overseas. For many years payment in United States dollars was the standard. The current economic situation has recently bought the possibility of change. What was once a standard "boiler plate" clause is now a negotiating point. It is more important than ever to be

---

[8] It is not known whether this method has been employed successfully. On its face it appears that it would satisfy government regulations specifying other languages and still allow for the use of English.

[9] Plain language legislation has been introduced in twenty-four states. *See generally* W. O. Connor, Jr., "Plain English," 34 Bus. Law. 1453 (1979). *But see* E. Burke, "Simply Put, Plain English Drive Stalls," The National Law Journal, Monday, June 9, 1980, at 1, col. 4

sure to draft this clause to meet the client's particular desires and needs.

It is of prime importance to determine in which currency payment is to be made. Some nations, *e.g.*, the Soviet Union, will not permit their currency to leave the country. If an invoice is paid to a local agent in one of these restricted currencies, the business will be locked into a situation in which the money paid for goods or services cannot effectively be used. It is essential, therefore, to elect a readily usable form of currency.

Similar to restriction of currency is the situation where the foreign government has statutes limiting the repatriation of money. In these situations the invoice (contract price) may be paid in the elected currency, but the client is unable to take the money out of the country. If the money can ever be repatriated it may take years to withdraw the entire amount. The contract should specify, either in the payment clause or in the governmental approval clause, that it is the responsibility of the promisee to secure approval for payment in specified currency (usually U.S. dollars) in a specified place (usually the United States) before the contract will be honored.

Another factor of equal concern in transnational agreements relates to problems of inflation. The operations of many transnational contracts have been distorted by spiraling costs. The certainty of value that once existed is no longer present. The international marketplace has seen the devaluation of the dollar twice since 1972. There are daily erratic fluctuations in the value of various important foreign currencies as they relate to the dollar. All of these factors have made payment of obligations created by contract an uncertainty.

Contract law in the United States is based on a theory of nominalism.[10] The assumption has been that the value of the subject matter remains constant. The current distortion of the economy has placed this theory in question. To reduce the problems created by such distortion, contracts increasingly contain clauses that account for inflation. A discussion of these various clauses follows.

---

[10] Rosenn, "Protecting Contracts from Inflation," 33 Bus. Law. 729, 730 (1978).

[2] Open-Price Clauses

The open-price clause leaves the determination of price to a later point in time, usually the time of delivery or performance. This protects against changes in cost between the time of ratification and performance.

Open-price clauses are most often used in the sale of homogeneous commodities or for services that are regularly bought and sold in an active market. This type of clause is not suited to a manufactured product that contains a variety of materials or components and substantial labor costs.

An open-price clause is also not favored by the buyer. This is understandable in that there is an inability to ascertain costs at the time of agreement. It is difficult for the seller to overcome this uncertainty. Convincing the buyer that this type of clause is a "good deal" is often impossible.

In addition to the purchaser's dislike of this type of clause, the courts of the United States have also demonstrated a clear hostility. Two arguments against the open-price clause have been voiced. The first argument states that this clause is simply an agreement to agree at a later date.[11] The second claims that the Statute of Frauds bars use of this type of clause.[12] The majority of jurisdictions in the United States regard the contract price as an extremely critical provision. The courts have been loath to try to reconstruct the parties' presumed intent as to the determination of price.[13]

However, courts have upheld contracts that contain a formula for the determination of price at the time of performance.[14] This determination could be based on the seller's cost, the price in the marketplace, a price established in a trade journal, or the price charged by competing sellers.

If the contract involves the sale of goods the Uniform Commercial Code may control. Section 2-305 states that an agree-

---

[11] *See, e.g.,* Livingston Waterworks v. City of Livingston, 53 Mont. 1, 162 P. 381 (1916).

[12] *See, e.g.,* Hanson v. Marsh, 40 Minn. 1, 1 N.W. 841 (1888).

[13] Hurst, "Drafting Contracts in an Inflationary Era," 28 U. Fla. L. Rev. 879, at 884 (1976).

[14] *Id.* at 885.

ment to agree is permissible and not void for indefiniteness. The intent of this section appears to be to overrule case precedent. However, Comment 3 of this section does stress that the final price must be reasonable.

Use and validity of the open-price clause may be based on two factors. First is the bargaining position of the party wishing to use such a clause. If the buyer has a stronger position he will surely demand a set, predetermined price.[15] Second, if such a clause is to be used, care must be exercised in drafting a definite formula to determine price.[16]

[3] Cost-Plus Clauses

In a cost-plus clause the price is computed by determining the seller's cost of production and adding a profit (usually a fixed sum or a percent of the production cost). The cost-plus clause is most often seen in the sale of goods to the government.

In most instances this type of clause has been enforced by the courts. However, there have been situations where a court has refused to accept such a clause because of uncertainty, *e.g.*, where a definition of cost was undeterminable.[17]

The major problem with a cost-plus clause is arriving at an accurate definition of the word "cost." Some commentators have described this type of clause as the worst of all inflation hedges for this reason.[18] A glance at the *Armed Forces Procurement Regulations* will demonstrate the problems of defining cost.[19]

If a cost-plus clause is to be used the attorney should phrase the clause so as to provide for an increase in price in proportion

---

15 *Id.* at 886.

16 Compare the problems encountered in: New York Overseas Co. v. China, Japan & S. A. Trading Co., 206 App. Div. 242, 200 N.Y.S. 449 (1923); Abshine v. Smith, 86 Ind. App. 354, 156 N.E. 408 (1927); and Ford v. Norton, 32 N.M. 518, 260 P. 411 (1927).

17 *See, e.g.*, Dwight Bros. Paper Co. v. Ginzburg, 238 Ill. App. 216 (1925).

18 *See* Hurst, *supra* N. 12, at 889.

19 32 C.F.R. §7.203-04.

to any increase in material and labor costs that exceed the current market price.

[4] Gold Clauses

Gold clauses have been reinstated in the United States as a valid means of payment since 1974.[20] There are two basic types of gold clauses: (1) where payment is made in a specified number of ounces of gold or number of gold coins of a set quality; or (2) where payment is based on an index that takes into account changes in the value of gold.

The second of these is preferable because it avoids the problems of transportation and assaying that are present in the first.

The major drawback with gold clauses is the speculative nature of gold. The price of gold tends to fluctuate wildly. For example, the price of gold jumped from $200 to $800 to $600 within the span of a few months in 1979-80. A more telling example covers the period from December, 1974 to July, 1976 when the price of gold fell from $200 to $110. While the price of gold fell 45 percent, the Consumer Price Index (CPI) rose 9 percent. If a gold clause were in use in a contract during this time there could have been an overall 54 percent loss on the contract price.[21]

If a gold clause is to be used, it should state precisely how and where the price is to be determined and that when a price is set it will be the average price taken over several days rather than the spot price on a single day.

[5] Foreign Currency Clauses

Payment under a foreign currency clause should be made in a relatively stable "hard" currency, e.g., the Japanese yen or the Deutsche mark. A common form of foreign currency clause is the multiple currency clause, which gives the creditor

---

[20] 86 Stat. 116; 87 Stat. 352; 91 Stat. 1229; and Executive Order 11825, 40 Fed. Reg. 1003 (1974).

[21] Hurst, *supra* N. 12, at 895.

the option of receiving payment in one of several predetermined currencies. This is a common technique for shifting exchange risks in transnational agreements. While at one time United States courts would not enforce multiple currency clauses with the dollar as one of the choices,[22] all forms of currency clauses are now enforceable.[23]

The major problem with currency clauses is that they often fail to make provisions for the rate of inflation in the "hard" currency.

[6] Stabilization Clauses

This type of clause ties the underlying value of the obligation to the price of a commodity or group of commodities rather than to money. There are several types of stabilization clauses, ranging from those that use commodities as both the measure of value and as payment, to those that use a general price index that measures value but leaves payment in currency.

Generally, the former are regarded as a crude maintenance of value device. They are subject to volatile price fluctuations of the commodity (e.g., silver) and do not have any relation with purchasing power. The latter are considered by many commentators to be the best means of reducing the risks of inflation.[24] The most common usage of this type of clause is in collective bargaining agreements. In one form or another, this style of clause is used in Austria, Belgium, Brazil, Canada, Chile, Denmark, France, Great Britain, Israel, Luxembourg, the Netherlands, New Zealand, Switzerland, and the United States.

These clauses are well received in the courts.[25] However,

---

[22] See, e.g., Guaranty Trust Co. v. Henwood, 307 U.S. 247 (1939); and Bethlehem Steel Co. v. Zurich Ins. Co., 307 U.S. 265 (1939).

[23] English Transcontinental, Ltd. et al. v. Puebla Tramway, Light and Power Co., 186 Misc. 481, N.Y.S.2d 356 (Sup. Ct., N.Y. City 1946).

[24] See Hurst, supra N. 12, at 893 and Rosen, supra N. 9, at 738.

[25] See, e.g., Culcasiew Paper Co. v. Memphis Paper Co., 32 Tenn. App. 293, 222 S.W.2d 617 (1949).

problems have arisen when an index is no longer published.[26] This problem is foreseeable and can be corrected by careful drafting. For example, provision can be made in the arbitration clause of the contract for resolution of the problem in arbitration.[27]

Other problems may also be found with this style of clauses. The buyer may be unwilling or unable to keep pace with the changes. Additionally, this clause may necessitate frequent and inconvenient revisions. This latter problem may be avoided by providing for changes only if the index increases by a certain minimum percentage in a given time period or by semi-annual raises.

When drafting any of these clauses there are rules that should be followed. First of all, simplicity is the key. If a formula is to be used, it should not be excessively complex. Second, the most appropriate index should be chosen to fit the circumstances. The Consumer Price Index (CPI) or the Wholesale Price Index (WPI) are two good alternatives. The index must accurately represent a true change in the contract price. Third, the index should be carefully described. There should be provisions accounting for change; either a substitute index or the basis on which the contract may be renegotiated. Fourth, the method for making adjustments should be specified. It is wise to indicate a time setting, *e.g.*, annually, quarterly or monthly.

[7] Sample Clauses

Gold Clause, with a Currency Clause included

It is a condition of this agreement that payment shall be made by (Promisee) in cash in (location) (in currency stated in the invoice, either U.S. dollars, British pounds, Deutche marks, or Japanese yen, etc.).

It is a further condition that if before payment is made the weight of the United States gold dollar is altered, from 15-5-21 grams of gold, nine-tenths fine or the price at which the United

---

[26] Domhoff & Joyce Co., v. Hamilton Furnace Co., 108 Ohio St. 25, 140 N.E. 485 (1923).

[27] *See* Hurst, *supra* N. 12, at 892.

States Government or any authorized agent thereof offers to buy or sell gold shall rise above (42.22 United States dollars per fine Troy ounce), or if the United States Government shall terminate, suspend or limit its present policy of freely buying and selling gold, or the United States dollar is otherwise devalued in relation to gold, the sale is automatically cancelled.

Commodity Clause

This sale is conditioned upon payment by (promisee) in United States dollars in (location).

It is a further condition of this sale that the price stipulated in this agreement shall be subject to increase based upon any rise in (state the index to be used, *e.g.*, Consumer Price Index). This increase shall be based upon the following formula (in detail give the formula). If the (index) specified above is modified or no longer used the (second choice of index) shall be substituted.

Adjustments in the contract price shall be made (time of computation, *e.g.*, quarterly) beginning with the date of ratification.

§ 4.05   Force Majeure and Supravening Law Clause

Force majeure clauses have traditionally been included in transnational contracts. The term *force majeure* is French, meaning an irresistible or superior force. Used in the context of a contract it would mean protection for the promisor from contingencies beyond his control. In the past, this type of clause has mainly been used as a safeguard from some natural interruption of performance. More recently, the thrust of the force majeure clause has been to protect against political upheavals and/or inflation. The revolution in Iran and the Soviet invasion of Afghanistan are the best recent examples of situations where contracts have been suspended by political actions. The unprecedented high rate of inflation in the United States in early 1980 is an example of where inflation made some contracts impossible to perform.

Although many standard "boiler plate" clauses are available, care should be taken in choosing or drafting the correct clause for the situation. An improperly drawn clause may create more problems than it solves.

The force majeure clause should be broadly drawn. It should contain a list of items which are deemed to be of sufficient supravening force to excuse performance under the contract. Elements commonly included are: fires; floods; riots; strikes; labor disputes; freight embargos or transportation delays; shortage of labor; inability to secure materials, supplies, or power at reasonable prices or on account of shortages; and acts of God or the public enemy.

In addition to these general types of excusable events there are some special considerations that should be considered. The OPEC oil embargo forced the disruption of many contracts. Therefore, inability to secure fuel may be a valid excuse for nonperformance. The rate of inflation may drive costs beyond the selling price of contracted goods. Some sellers have relied upon a force majeure clause to excuse their performance when costs became unmanageable. Impossibility may be a valid excuse under a force majeure clause, however, it would be prudent to also include a pricing clause that deals with inflation. This double security would insure the client's protection.

Before any transnational contract is drafted there should be a study of the other nation's political and economic situation. This is especially important for use when drafting the force majeure clause. A quick check on the stability of the government, the rate of inflation, and any existing or pending legislation that affects the contract will insure that any contingency is provided for. This study of the foreign nation should be made regardless of the status of the nation, either developed or developing. Lebanon is a good example of a "secure" nation that deteriorated very quickly.

There are some major problem areas that should be considered when drafting a force majeure clause. First, should the clause delay the seller's duty of performance or should it terminate the contract? The *Restatement of Contracts* section 462 takes the position that temporary impossibility suspends the promisor's duty to perform unless the delay would create a greater burden than would have been imposed had there been no impossibility. The clause should expressly provide for either continuation or termination. Second, what is the degree of impossibility or impracticability that will discharge performance? Care should be taken to define what will amount to a complete discharge. Third, how should the cause of impossibility be determined? Reasonability should be the guide here. A good test would be if performance would force the promisor to secure parts, services, or supplies at a rate that was unforeseeable at the time of drafting. Finally, if the promisor can give part performance, should he do so? Allocation of supplies in times of shortages is becoming a common practice. There is some question as to whether such allocation amounts to a breach. Section 2-615(b) of the Uniform Commercial Code imposes a duty of allocation with the sale of goods. The possibility of allocation must be discussed with the client and such possibility should be stipulated in the clause.

Two Sample Force Majeure Clauses

1. The parties hereto shall not be liable for failure of performance hereunder if occasioned by war, declared or undeclared, fire, flood, interruption of transportation, inflation beyond the expected rate, embargo, accident, explosion, inability to procure or shortage of supply of materials, equipment, or production facilities, prohibition of import or export of goods covered hereby, governmental orders, regulations, restrictions, priorities or rationing by strike lockout or other labor troubles interfering with production or transportation of such goods or with the supplies of raw materials entering into their production or any other cause beyond the control of the parties. If, by any of the above mentioned causes, an allocation of supplies must be made the parties are hereby informed that such allocation will be fairly made.

Any suspension of performance by reason of this article shall be limited to the period during which cause of failure exists, but such suspension shall not affect the running of the period of this contract as heretofore defined.

2. Notwithstanding anything contained in this agreement to the contrary, the obligations of the parties hereto and of their subsidiaries shall be subject to all laws, both present and future, of any government having jurisdiction over the parties hereto or

their respective subsidiaries, and to orders, regulations, directions or requests of any such government, or any department, agency, or corporation thereof, and to war, acts of God, or any causes of like or different kind beyond the control of the parties and, except as hereinafter provided in this section, the parties hereto shall be excused from any failure to perform any obligation hereunder to the extent such failure is caused by any law, order, regulation, direction, request, or contingency.

§ 4.06 Government Approval, Local Taxation, and Fees

Frequently, the approval of a contract must be secured from one or more governments before performance may take place. More often than not, this approval must come from foreign governments. However, there are occasions when it is necessary to secure approval from the United States government. Various U.S. Government agencies regulate the exportation of goods and technology of United States origin.[28]

---

[28] The Department of Commerce is the main agency that regulates exports. However, several other agencies also control exports. To illustrate:

Arms, ammunition, and implements of war are regulated by the Office of Munitions Control, U.S. Department of State.

Narcotic drugs and marijuana are regulated by the Bureau of Narcotics and Dangerous Drugs, U.S. Department of Justice.

Specified materials and facilities related to the production of atomic energy are regulated by the Division of State and Licensee Regulations, U.S. Energy Research and Development Agency, except that components for the facilities are regulated by the Office of Export Administration.

Watercraft owned by citizens of the United States are regulated by the U.S. Maritime Administration; but additional approval is required by the Department of State for vessels of war, as defined in the U.S. munitions list, and by the Office of Export Administration if the watercraft is to be reduced to scrap metal.

Natural gas and electric power are regulated by the Federal Power Commission.

Tobacco seeds and live tobacco plants are regulated by the Consumer Marketing Services, U.S. Department of Agriculture.

Migratory birds and endangered native fish and wildlife are protected

It is not necessary to document here the bias that may exist when a foreigner attempts to secure approval in any number of nations. There are even instances where national law requires local registration by citizens of that nation.[29] The simple solution to what could be a significant problem is to require the party from the nation requiring approval to register for and secure any necessary documents.[30] The skilled attorney will make this clause two-edged, with his client responsible for any application and approval from the United States. The use of dual responsibility promotes a sense of equity in the agreement to both parties' satisfaction.

Similar to governmental approval is the requirement of payment of any fees or taxes; often governmental approval entails some type of license, permit or grant. Likewise, there may be some form of taxation that accompanies the transaction. This taxation may be in the guise of a duty or tariff, a stamp tax, a registration fee, a surtax, or any number of other taxes. As with seeking governmental approval, the contract should make the payment of such fees or taxes the responsibility of the party whose country is assessing the charge.

A useful negotiating strategy may be the offer to pay all such fees and taxes (excluding income tax), and to build these costs into the actual cost of the goods or services. To successfully use this technique, two prices must be prepared before the negotiations begin. The local tax and fee provisions must be discussed before the price is negotiated. However, such negotiation might be risky and should only be used after careful consideration.

Some sample clauses follow:

Governmental Approval Provisions Clause

Any approval of this agreement by (foreign government) which

---

by the Bureau of Sport Fisheries and Wildlife, Fish and Wildlife Service, U.S. Department of the Interior.

[29] For example, nations in the Andean Common Market (ANCOM) often require such registration.

[30] This approval would be a condition precedent to validation of the agreement. This should prevent complications with repatriation, work permits, duration of the agreement, etc.

is required to enable (promisee) to enter into this agreement, perform under the terms of this agreement, do business with (promisor), or to make payments to (promisor) hereunder in United States dollars in the United States of America shall be secured by (promisee). Any approval of this agreement required by the Government of the United States will be secured by the (promisor).

Local Taxes and Fees Provisions Clause

Any and all governmental charges relating to or arising out of this agreement, or any amendment hereto, in the form of registration fees, surtax, stamp duties, income tax, or other governmental rates, taxes, or charges of any nature whatsoever shall be paid (1) by the (promisee) when such charges are due under any national or local law of (country of promisee), and (2) by the (promisor) when such charges are due under any Federal, State, or local law of the United States of America.

(Promisee) undertakes to indemnify (promisor) and to be substituted for (promisor) for any assessments that might be made against (promisor) under the terms of this agreement by (country of promisee).

§ 4.07 Special Problems with Distributorship or Agency Agreements

While the subject of distributorships was discussed in the previous chapter, the author wishes to add some thoughts on the subject.

Distribution agreements can be formal and complex, or very informal, leaving many details to be settled as business develops. In either form, several important considerations may be left out. It is important that the contract include the following provisions: (1) the date and place of execution of the contract; (2) a choice of law clause specifying the manufacturer/exporter's own law as the one to govern interpretation of the agreement; (3) English as the official language; (4) designation of currency in which payment will be made; and (5) any prohibitions set by United States laws that may limit sales.[31]

Unlike the laws of the United States, the laws of many nations limit in varying degrees the freedom of the manufacturer to terminate the agency or distributorship agreement or even to simply allow the agreement to expire. In fact, it is possible that the manufacturer/exporter will incur substantial liability by termination.

Limitation of liability by the manufacturer/exporter is the key to successful distributorship or agency agreement. There are three main categories of foreign laws which may be encountered. The first of these are the laws of countries with a common law background, *e.g.*, England, Canada, and Australia. Contracts with distributors in these countries may contain any termination provision that suits the parties. There are no overriding statutes which place greater obligations or control over the parties.

The second group includes Belgium, France, and Puerto Rico, which have enacted laws for the protection of agents and distributors. The most stringent are the Belgian laws. A Belgian statute[32] provides that a manufacturer/exporter cannot terminate an exclusive distributorship agreement entered into for an indefinite term unless reasonable notice or fair compensation is given, "fixed by the parties at the time of notice of termination." If the parties are unable to reach a settlement, the courts will determine an equitable settlement. In addition to the settlement, the distributor is also entitled to compensation that takes into account: (1) the increase in sales to customers secured by the distributor who remain customers after termination; (2) expenses the distributor incurred in developing the distributorship; and (3) sums which the distributor must pay to employees he dismisses as a result of the termination. This law is based on the idea that the distributor becomes dependent on the status conferred by the manufacturer/exporter and that the work of the distributor has benefitted the

---

[31] T. Johnson, *International Distributorship and Agency Agreements*, 230 (1967).

[32] Law of July 30, 1963, Concerning Sales Contracts; Law of July 27, 1961, Concerning the Termination of Exclusive Sales Concessions.

manufacturer/exporter. Using a short term contract subject to renewal will not avoid this statute if it is apparent that the distributorship has continued for several terms.[33]

In France, dependent agents are entitled to the benefit of labor law principles which provide for substantial notice or indemnification for cancellation.[34] Independent distributors are not entitled to this compensation but have been awarded damages on the basis of a tort action based on "abuse of right." This recovery has been based on a contract that is terminated too abruptly.

A third group of countries, most notably those in Latin America, employ a labor law type of approach. The test for this type of law is whether the distributor would qualify as an employee, *i.e.*, is the distributor dependent on or subordinate to the manufacturer/exporter. If a degree of independence can be proved, these laws will not apply.

The best means of avoiding the problems inherent in the latter two groups is to deal only with incorporated distributors and not with individuals.[35] Among other means of limiting the risks of this type of agreement, the following are worth consideration: (1) include a choice of law clauses that specifies United States law; (2) give the manufacturer/exporter the right to terminate on a year-by-year basis (caveat—this loses effectiveness the longer the agreement continues); (3) spell out what "just cause" for termination of the agreement will be; (4) make equitable provisions for the handling of and compensation for orders placed by the distributor prior to receipt of notice and during the notice period; (5) provide for the handling of and compensation for the liquidation of any supply of finished products, spare and replacement parts, sales literature, service manuals, etc; (6) dispose of any outstanding service contracts; and (7) specifically state that the distributor is a separate, individual principal and *not* an employee, agent, or legal representative of the manufacturer/exporter.

A point for special consideration is the advisability or neces-

---

[33] T. Johnson, *supra* N. 30, at 231.

[34] Decree of December 23, 1958, Concerning Agents.

[35] M. Meek, "Overseas Distributorship Agreements," 21 Bus Law 661 (1966).

sity of requiring the distributor to furnish lists of customers, either periodically during the contract or upon termination. This feature will certainly be considered if an idemnity is sought by the distributor.

Special Model Clauses for Distributorship Agreements

Representative Status

[Distributor] is an independent contractor under the terms of this agreement, and is not a partner co-venturer, agent, employee, or legal representative of [Exporter], and is acting in the ordinary course of business. [Distributor] shall have no authority to conclude contracts or extend warranties on behalf of [Exporter].

Tenure and Termination Provision

This Agreement shall commence on the first day of [January], 19[80], and shall terminate on the last day of [December], 19 [80]. [Exporter] will advise [Distributor] of its desire to renew this Agreement for another one year term within sixty (60) days of the termination of this Agreement.

If this Agreement is terminated under the terms of this article, [Distributor] shall continue to receive commissions thereafter pursuant to the terms of this Agreement for a period of six (6) months from the date of termination.

§ 4.08   Arbitration Clauses

[1]   General

Arbitration agreements may be of two types: either contemporaneous with or prospective to a commercial dispute. The first type of agreement is an attempt by parties to an existing dispute to resolve that dispute by arbitration. The latter, an arbitration clause, is an understanding by the parties that any future disputes that may arise will be referred to arbitration. Since the focus of the chapter is dealing with drafting contracts, it will not discuss arbitration agreements entered into after a contract dispute arises.

Whether or not an arbitration clause belongs in the contract is primarily a business decision that must be made by those who will be performing the day to day administration of the contract. However, it is the responsibility of the attorney drafting the agreement to present all options to his client. The facts of each particular situation may warrant totally different decisions and perhaps totally different arbitration clauses. Therefore, it is essential to understand the range of options in a specific situation and make them available to the client for a final decision. The attorney's opinion is likely to affect this decision since it is important that all the pertinent material be presented as objectively as is humanly possible.

To better understand what an arbitration clause is, a definition is in order. International commercial arbitration may be defined as "an agreement between two parties to a transnational commercial transaction to submit differences arising between them to the decision of a third party and to abide by that decision.[36] In essence, the parties are removing jurisdiction from the courts by voluntary agreement and placing it in the hands of an independent party who usually has expertise in resolving ordinary commercial disputes. Simply put, it is an alternative method of problem-solving, designed to settle a conflict out of court while maintaining both cordial relations between the parties and operation of the contract.

[2] Should an Arbitration Clause Be Included?

The first question that should be addressed when determining if an arbitration clause will be included in the agreement is whether an arbitration clause is needed. The prime argument presented by opponents of arbitration is that it simply adds steps to the litigation process. For example, in several English cases, an arbitrator's award was taken to an appeals board within the trade association, then to the regular courts—first the High Court, then the Court of Appeal, and finally to

---

[36] C. Evans and R. Ellis, "International Commercial Arbitration: A Comparison of Legal Regimes." 8 Tex. Int'l L.J. 17 (1973).

the House of Lords.[37] In these cases, two extra steps, with accompanying expenses, were added to the litigation process. From this perspective, it is clear why both the courts and commentators are critical of the use of arbitration clauses without careful advance consideration by the parties.

Another factor to be weighed in addition to higher costs is the amount of time required for arbitration. If the contract is of limited duration, arbitration could unreasonably lengthen the term of the contract. The resultant inconvenience to the parties might prove to be a greater loss than simple termination of the agreement.

Finally, there may be no means of appeal for an agrieved party after an award has been made. Both English and Canadian Courts have ruled that if a specific point of law is referred to arbitration, the parties are bound by the decision of the arbitrators, even if the interpretation is wrong.[38] While this is not often the case, it certainly bears consideration. If any of these possibilities are present, the client should be cautioned about the advisability of an arbitration clause.

On the other side of the coin, there are many advantages to including an arbitration clause. The risk of losing a contract as a result of a failure to agree on some minor point should be enough to interest the parties in arbitration, since the purpose of every agreement is to carry out the intentions of the parties smoothly and without problems. The majority of agreements will come to a successful conclusion without any dispute or resort to law. The parties would never have reached the point of drafting a contract without a mutual desire to do business.

If a dispute should arise in the performance of a contract, an arbitration clause should help to keep relations between the parties amicable while problems are resolved. Arbitration does not have the adversary nature of a court action, in which communication between the parties is restricted. This crucial difference in the level of communication could save the contract.

A second positive feature of an arbitration clause is that it

---

[37] Ross T. Smyth & Co., Ltd. v. Bailey, [1940] 3 All E. R. 60, 62; Peter Cassidy Seed Co., Ltd. v. Osuustukkukauppa I. L., (1957) 1 All E. R. 484, 489; *see generally* Meek and Feltham, *supra* N. 2, at 56.

[38] Russell, *Arbitration*, 316 (17th Ed. 1963).

may provide for continued performance under the contract while differences are settled. This is a possibility that is not present in litigation. With arbitration, a technical dispute can be settled even as performance continues, satisfying the needs of all concerned. This is especially important when performance under the contract must be continuous, *e.g.*, supply of raw materials or components to a manufacturer.

Another important element of arbitration is that it permits a flexibility in interpretation that is impossible under the law. The strict construction applied to the contract by a court may not take into consideration the intent of the parties. However, the arbitrator named by the parties may be more familiar with usual business practices and therefore able to mold the terms to fit the actual situation. This is especially so where a form contract has been used in place of an individually drafted agreement.

Work done to prepare for arbitration will be substantially similar to trial preparation. While arbitration may add a step to the appeals process, it certainly does not add time to the discovery process. In fact, any work done for arbitration can take the place of some pretrial preparation. This will help defer some of the legal fees to the client and perhaps make the arbitration process more economically feasible.

Finally, arbitration clauses may be helpful in determining issues regarding jurisdiction and choice of laws. If the parties agree to submit disputes to an arbitration tribunal constituted in a particular jurisdiction, it may be construed that the parties have also agreed that the contract will be governed by the laws of that jurisdiction. This stipulation for arbitration can therefore be another method of localizing the contract with respect to governing law.[39]

[3] Choice of Arbitration Clauses

Once the decision to include an arbitration clause has been made, there are several available options. This choice should be made only after careful consideration of the facts. There are

---

[39] 2 Rabel, *The Conflict of Laws: A Comparative Study*, 387-8 (1960).

several different arbitration groups who have developed their own rules of procedure. The two most prominent groups are the American Arbitration Association (AAA) and the International Chamber of Commerce (ICC). In addition to these two, there has been some interest in the new rules developed by the United Nations Commission on International Trade Law (UNCITRAL).

The facts surrounding the contract should help in the selection of an appropriate model clause or form. Under no circumstances should a clause be used without a working knowledge of the rules and procedures of the particular arbitration group. Failure to understand the arbitration procedure could be compared to starting a trial in a foreign jurisdiction without looking at the rules of procedure. Not only is this bad form, it could also be considered malpractice. It is advisable to be familiar with the rules of both the American Arbitration Association and the International Chamber of Commerce.

Following are four model clauses suggested by three of the main arbitration associations.

[4] Model Clauses

American Arbitration Association (AAA) Model Clause

Any controversy or claim arising out of or relating to this contract, or any breach thereof, shall be settled by arbitration in accordance with the Rules of the American Arbitration Association, and judgment upon award rendered by the arbitrator(s) may be entered in any court having jurisdiction thereof.

International Chamber of Commerce (ICC) Model Clause

All disputes arising in connection with the present contract shall be finally settled under the Rules of Conciliation and Arbitration of the International Chamber of Commerce by one or more arbitrators appointed in accordance with the Rules.

Joint AAA-ICC Model Clause

Any controversy or claim arising out of or relating to this contract or the breach thereof shall be finally settled by arbitration conducted either outside of the United States of America in accordance with the Rules of Arbitration of the International Chamber of Commerce or in the United States of America in accordance with the Rules of the American Arbitration Association. If the parties fail to agree in writing on the place where the arbitration is to be conducted, final and binding determination of this question shall be made by a Joint Arbitration Location Committee, consisting of three persons, one of whom shall be appointed by the ICC, one by the AAA, and one by agreement between the ICC and AAA.

UNCITRAL Model Clause

Any dispute, controversy or claim arising out of or relating to this contract, or the breach, termination or invalidity thereof, shall be settled by arbitration in accordance with the UNCITRAL Arbitration Rules as at present in force.

[5] Recommended Sample Clause

While all of the above model clauses are acceptable and are often considered to be standard "boiler plate," there are several inherent problems that must be considered before using them.

First, none of these clauses states where arbitration will take place should it be needed. The implication in the American Arbitration Association clauses is that disputes will be arbitrated in the United States. Likewise, the International Chamber of Commerce clause could lead one to believe that arbitration will be held outside of the United States. The UNCITRAL clause makes no mention whatsoever of location. Even the joint clause is somewhat ambiguous regarding "the place where the arbitration is to be conducted." Similarly, it is unclear as to what law will govern. The problem with this lack of selection is the resulting lack of predictability. Even with the forum and choice of law clauses in the body of the contract, it may be that the arbitrators will choose to apply local law to the arbitration. If there is disagreement with the arbitrators' findings, the resultant problems are multiplied if an unexpected set of laws are introduced.

Although the choice of the governing law may be inferred from a separate choice of law clause in the contract, or it may be assumed that the laws of the place of arbitration will apply, there are instances where a specific stipulation regarding the governing law might be useful. For example, in a licensing agreement between a United States company and a citizen of Mexico, where Mexican law specifies that in any transfer of technology involving a Mexican citizen, the laws of Mexico will govern the contract,[40] by inserting an arbitration clause specifying use of the laws of the United States, perhaps the requirement of using the more stringent Mexican law could be avoided.

Second, none of these clauses specifically states who the arbitrators will be. Since all that is specified is that arbitrators shall be appointed in accordance with either AAA or ICC rules, the only criterion for the appointment is that the arbitrators be familiar with the rules of arbitration. Many arbitrable disputes revolve around a working knowledge of business practices. Without an understanding of customary business practices, the conclusions reached by an arbitrator might yield unexpected or seemingly arbitrary results.

Similarly, if a point of law regarding the contract must be understood to reach a decision and the arbitrator has no legal background, the final ruling of the arbitrator could be erroneous at law and still binding on the parties.

The UNCITRAL model clause deserves additional consideration. Following the publication of a sample clause in the rules, the report does suggest that parties may wish to consider adding additional clauses, such as:

(a) The appointing authority shall be _____ (name of institution or person);

(b) The number of arbitrators shall be _____ (one or three);

(c) The place of arbitration shall be _____ (town or country);

---

[40] Law on the Registration of the Transfer of Technology and the Use and Exploitation of Patents and Trademarks, Diario Oficial, Dec. 30, 1972.

(d) The language(s) to be used in the arbitral proceedings shall be _____.[41]

By adding one or all of these additional phrases, the clause becomes much more complete and yields a greater degree of predictability.

There is nothing actually wrong with any of the clauses. In fact, their use may best fit a client's needs. However, the ambiguities just discussed should be indicated to the client.

More often than not, the client's needs will require a more complex clause. Utilizing either the American Arbitration Association or the International Chamber of Commerce rules and the above suggestions a sample clause would read:

All disputes arising in connection with this agreement shall be finally settled in accordance with the rules then in force of (the AAA or ICC). The location of this arbitration shall be _____ and its proceedings will be governed by the laws of _____. The arbitrator or the majority of such arbitrators shall be individuals skilled in the legal and business aspects of the subject matter of this agreement. (Arbitrators are to be selected by the parties, each side choosing one. In case the two arbitrators so selected cannot agree, they shall select a third and the decision of any two of the three shall be binding upon the parties. In case the two arbitrators so selected cannot agree upon the selection of the third arbitrator, such third arbitrator shall be appointed by the (AAA or ICC) upon a reference being made to such body.) The costs of the arbitration shall be in the discretion of the arbitrators, provided, however, that no party shall be obliged to pay more than its own costs and the cost of a third arbitrator. Judgment upon the award rendered may be entered in any Court having jurisdiction or application may be made to such Court for a judicial acceptance of the award and an order of enforcement, as the case may be.

There are some instances where the subject matter of a contract is so unique that the usual arbitration provisions are

[41] UNCITRAL Report, 31 U.N. GAOR Supp. (No. 17), 34 U.N. Doc. A/31/17 (1976). For further discussion, *see* A. McClelland, "International Arbitration: A Practical Guide to the System for the Litigation of Transnational Commercial Disputes," 17 Va. J. Int'l L. 730 (1977).

inadequate. To this end, the concepts of "amiables com-positeurs" and "astreinte" may be used.

"Amiables compositeurs" is a concept widely used in the Common Market although not familiar in Great Britain or the United States. It permits arbitrators flexibility where they are not required to decide in accordance with substantive rules of law or to adjudicate disputes *ex aequo et bono.* The amicable compositor, therefore, is free to base his decision on considera-tions other than strict legal principles. Trade customs or busi-ness practices common to the particular transaction may play as great a role as the law. This does not mean, however, that the rules of arbitration may be disregarded. The amicable compositor, no matter what his reasoning, is still an arbitrator and, as such, will be governed by the rules of law that apply to arbitration. For example, the arbitrator-amicable composi-tor will be required to state the reasons for the award. Amica-ble composition, therefore, adds a high degree of flexibility to the arbitral procedure while still preserving the basic rights of the parties.

The French Civil Code concept of "astreinte" provides for both specific performance and payment of damages until the specific performance is carried out. The damages serve as a type of punishment or an incentive to perform as quickly as possible. If the party that must perform refuses, then the award of damages will at least ease any problems created.[42]

Combining these two concepts into a clause would look like this:

> All disputes arising under this Agreement concerning its inter-pretation and enforcement shall be resolved by a final and binding decision of an arbitral tribunal in accordance with the general principles of equity and the terms of the Agreement, provided, however, that no act of the tribunal can compel any party hereto to violate any treaty, law or regulation of its gov-ernment. Should any dispute be submitted to arbitration by [first party], arbitration shall be performed in _____, in a place designated by [first party]. Should any dispute be sub-mitted to arbitration by [second party], arbitration shall be per-

---

[42] De laume, *Transnational Contracts: Applicable Law and Settlement of Disputes,* § 13.11 (1979).

formed in any place in _____ designated by [second party]. Arbitration shall be conducted by three arbitrators to be appointed pursuant to the rules of the International Chamber of Commerce (American Arbitration Association), and said arbitration shall be conducted in accordance with the rules of said group. The arbitrators shall decide as *amiables compositeurs*. Each of the parties hereto recognizes that the subject matter of this Agreement is unique, that damages may not be adequate under given circumstances and, for these reasons, agrees that the arbitrators are hereby expressly empowered to decree specific performance. Since it is possible that such a decree may not be enforced by a court in which a party hereto may find it necessary to seek enforcement of the arbitration decision, the parties hereto expressly authorize the arbitrators to give an award in the nature of *astreinte* which shall be given concurrently with any decree for specific performance as an alternative remedy.[43]

Some clients are especially hesitant in accepting arbitration as a preferred mode of resolving disputes. The typical hesitation lies in the fear that the arbitrators' decision might have an impact over more than one contract; *e.g.*, a binding arbitral decision in a licensing agreement that holds a patent invalid. One possible way of easing the client's fears and still providing for arbitration is to restrict the issues subject to arbitration. In many ways, this is a preferable method of separating the technical and quality aspects of the contract. Several commentators, however, have cautioned against using this type of clause.[44] The main problem appears to be the difficulty inherent in defining precisely what can and cannot be arbitrated. Careful drafting and special attention to what the client sees as the special facts of his particular trade should help alleviate this potential problem. A sample of such a clause, taken from a licensing agreement is as follows:

All disputes arising in connection with this Agreement shall be

---

[43] The author wishes to thank Roland P. Campbell, Esq. for his comments and sample clause.

[44] Meek & Feltham, *supra* N. 2, at 57; *but see* J. Moore, "Contemporary Issues in an Ongoing Debate: The Roles of Congress and the President in Foreign Affairs," 7 Int'l Law. 733, 741 (1973).

finally settled under the Rules of Conciliation and Arbitration
of the International Chamber of Commerce by one or more
arbitrators appointed in accordance with the Rules. The arbitrator or the majority of such arbitrators shall be individuals
skilled in the legal and business aspects of the international
licensing of industrial property rights. *The arbitrators shall not
decide any issue concerning the validity of any Letters Patent.*
Judgment upon award rendered may be entered in any Court
having jurisdiction or application may be made to such Court
for a judicial acceptance of the award and an order of enforcement, as the case may be.

Being more specific in an arbitration clause enhances predictability if a problem develops with the contract. By inserting more exact language, many procedural problems can be
avoided and the attorney's time can be spent in preparation
for the actual arbitration. This additional certainty can be used
to make the client more comfortable with the idea of arbitration.

[6] Enforceability of Arbitration Clauses

If an arbitration clause is part of a contract and the contract
is governed by United States law, it can be assumed that arbitration must be completed before the matter can be appealed
to the courts. This has not always been the case. Historically,
American courts regarded agreements to arbitrate with suspi-
cion. Courts in the nineteenth and early twentieth centuries
usually struck down these agreements as being against public
policy.[45] This policy, known as the "ouster doctrine," was applicable until the mid-1920s. The Arbitration Act of 1925[46]
gave a Congressional mandate to arbitration clauses. The
enactment of this law directed courts to stay proceedings
where there was an issue referrable to arbitration when (1)

---

[45] Sudbury v. Ambi Verwaltung, etc., 213 App. Div. 94,210 N.Y.S. 164 (1st
Dept. 1925); Sliosberg v. New York Life Ins., 217 App. Div. 685, 217 N.Y.S.
226 (1st Dept. 1926); Carbon Black Export, Inc. v. The S. S. Monrosa, 254
F.2d 297 (5th Cir. 1958), *cert. dismissed* 359 U.S. 180 (1959).

[46] 9 U.S.C. § 1 *et seq* (1970).

there has been a written agreement for such arbitration, and (2) one of the parties to that agreement moved for a stay of the proceedings until arbitration had been perfected.[47] The court's interpretation of this law in the case of *Wm. H. Miller & Co. v. Swedish American Line*,[48] developed a standard of "reasonableness" in view of the circumstances of the case.[49] More recently, two cases have interpreted and applied the reasonableness doctrine. In *M/S Bremen v. Zapata Off-shore Co.*,[50] a case involving a forum selection clause (not an arbitration clause), the Supreme Court held that a party seeking to avoid such a clause must show that enforcement would be unreasonable, unfair, or unjust. The importance of this decision lies in the recognition by the Court that businessmen with equal bargaining power should be permitted to stand by their reasonable contractual selection of a forum.

This perception of equal bargaining power in international agreements was specifically extended to arbitration clauses in *Scherk v. Alberto Culver Co.*,[51] a case involving a question of securities fraud. Justice Stewart, writing for the majority, discussed the "parochial" approach to the resolution of disputes in international commerce, if judicial restraints were to be placed on arbitration agreements. While Justice Stewart did not specifically refer to the reasonableness doctrine, he quoted the section of the *Bremen* case that held a forum clause should control unless there were strong reasons for it to be set aside.[52]

The *Scherk* case, in some ways, marks a departure from what is perceived to be the traditional American public policy —that there are several areas where the subject matter of a contract is not arbitrable.[53] *Scherk* has carved out an exception to this rule of non-arbitrability. Even though there were questions of securities fraud, the Court felt the transnational aspects of the agreement were overriding.

---

[47] 9 U.S.C. § 3 (1970).

[48] Wm. H. Miller & Co. v. Swedish American Line, Ltd., 224 F.2d 806 (2d Cir. 1955), *cert. denied* 350 U.S. 903 (1955).

[49] *Id.* at 808.

[50] 407 U.S. 1 (1972).

[51] 417 U.S. 506 (1974).

[52] *Id.* at 518.

[53] Arbitration Act of 1970, 9 U.S.C. §§ 1-14, 201-08 (1970).

This, however, has not proved to be the case in antitrust matters. Actions by a party that are alleged to be in violation of United States antitrust laws are *not* subject to arbitration.[54] The difference between securities matters and antitrust problems has been suggested by a commentator: "Under antitrust laws, an injured competitor suing on behalf of both itself and the public, is a situation different from that under the securities laws, where each injured investor may sue on its own behalf."[55]

Based on these precedents, it seems that, absent an antitrust problem, an arbitration clause included in the contract will ensure an arbitration proceeding.

To conclude this discussion, while arbitration is a means of resolving contractual problems without destroying the agreement, it is not a panacea to be included in all contracts. The costs of arbitration may prove to be the same or greater than litigation.[56] Likewise, the length of time involved in the arbitration process may be comparable to a court proceeding. Finally, an award or judgment in favor of the client is small consolation if it cannot be satisfied by the defaulting party. If there are no assets to attach, enforcement will be meaningless. The client in such a situation is in no different position than if he had taken legal action.[57]

---

[54] *See, e.g.*, Societe National Pour La Recherche, La Production, Le Transport, La Transformation et La Commercialisation des Hydrocarbures v. General Tire and Rubber, 430 F.Supp. 1332 (S.D.N.Y. 1977). *See also*, De laume, *supra* N. 41, at § 6.10.

[55] Nissen, "Antitrust and Arbitration in International Commerce," 17 Harv. Int'l L.J. 110, 117 (1976).

[56] For example, the cost of arbitration proceedings under the International Chamber of Commerce is based on a graduated percentage of the amount of the dispute. A case involving a claim of $1.2 million which is decided before three arbitrators would cost between $39,125 and $110,350, including registration fees, arbitration fees, and administrative charges. This amount does not include additional attorney fees, expert witness fees, travel expenses, etc. *See* De laume, *supra* N. 41, at 23 n27.

[57] This is a situation where it is advisable to have a portion of the clause that permits the arbitration award to be treated as a judgment. This will at least secure a judgment with hope that sometime a portion of the award will become collectible.

CHAPTER 5

International Technology Transfers

ROBERT Y. PETERS*

---

*Attorney, AT&T; Member of the District of Columbia, New York, Pennsylvania, and North Carolina Bars; B.E.E., University of Detroit; J.D., Georgetown University; LL.M., George Washington University. I am grateful to my colleagues at AT&T and Western Electric for their valuable assistance in the preparation of this chapter.

§ 5.01 Introduction

Technology is power. As the driving force behind both rapid and sustained economic growth, it is the very foundation of our industrial society. Although technology is sometimes viewed as a threat to existing social norms, it offers hope for the future and is indeed a key to human well-being.[1] The availability of technology often makes the difference between living and dying, winning and losing, and building and destroying.

The key role of technology helps explain the shroud of controversy surrounding its international transfer, or lack of it, especially between the developed and less developed countries. Without a transfer of technology it is sometimes difficult, even impossible, to engage in international trade. Some countries insist that a major transfer of manufacturing technology accompany large purchases. Also, the requirements of some countries for local manufacturing and exporting, especially in certain markets such as autos, necessitate international technology transfers.

A simple way to describe technology is to view it as a means (including tools and machines, processes and ideas) by which man controls his material environment (*e.g.,* matter, energy, space and their interactions) for his own benefit. Technology is related to science which deals with man's understanding of his material environment. This relationship between science and technology is best explained by a brief look at the history of technology. Man's control of his environment was initially achieved by craft in the form of trial and error but toward the end of the 18th century technology became applied science, with astonishing results in the 19th and 20th centuries. Now, the line between technology and science is blurred. And, for convenience, technology is used in the broad sense in the context of this chapter to encompass science.

No definition of technology satisfactorily describes the com-

---

[1] *See generally* D. Hamilton, *Technology, Man and the Environment* (1973); R. Forbes, *The Conquest of Nature: Technology and Its Consequences* (1968); G. Foster, *Traditional Cultures: and the Impact of Technological Change* (1962).

bination of skills and rights embraced within its concept.[2] Therefore, it is preferable to indicate what technology involves in the context of its international transfer. In general, it involves the results of creative thinking to control the material environment. Technology includes the ability to put things together, to make them work, to develop and satisfy customers, and to do all of these efficiently.[3] It may be represented by material items such as factories, machines, products, and infrastructures (laboratories, transportation systems, storage facilities, water sources, etc.). Technology may also be represented by non-material items such as patents, technical information, know-how or organizational forms. Sometimes technology is even considered to include the wherewithal to effectively use the results of creative thinking, such as capital, manufacturing and purchasing information, assemblies, subassemblies, components, tools, test sets, and the like.

Technology in the form of creative thinking often receives some form of protection under various laws of various nations and sometimes such protectable creative thinking is called "intellectual property." It is property in that it costs money to create, it produces money, and in some forms can be bought, sold, and licensed.[4]

It is apparent that technology is vitally important to the economic life of all nations of the world; hence, the international transfer of technology among the nations is likewise vitally important. The transfer of technology to recipients of various nations is charged with controversy.[5] Many less developed countries are demanding that technology suited to their particular needs be transferred to them on their terms, either free or for a royalty or fee they deem reasonable. And many of the developed countries are insisting that the less developed

---

[2] See Technology Transfer and the Developing Countries, Chamber of Commerce of the U.S., April, 1977, at 3.

[3] Id.

[4] Id.

[5] See International Transfer of Technology: Sources of Conflict, Chamber of Commerce of the U.S., Oct., 1976, at 5. See also Carey, "Science and the Politics of Development," 205 Science 4412 (Sept. 1979), and Goekjion, "Legal Problems of Transferring Technology to the Third World," 25 Am. J. Comp. L. 565, 566 (1977).

countries pay a proportionate share of the development costs of the technology and preserve its proprietary nature by maintaining it in confidence until it properly passes into the public domain.

In international commerce, "technology transfer" is in common parlance, though it may not be well defined.[6] Many countries require that agreements for the transfer of technology be approved by and registered with certain governmental agencies.[7] Such approval may result in the modification of an agreement for the transfer of technology.[8] Also, such countries sometimes have foreign exchange control laws that make it difficult for patent royalties or technical information fees to be paid for the use of the technology.[9] The tax laws of such countries may greatly reduce such royalties and fees. Thus, it is apparent that the governments of these countries play a key role in technology transfer, including not only its meaning but also its effect.

Although there is disagreement and uncertainty as to what actually is a technology transfer,[10] in a broad sense the transfer arguably includes the conveyance of any means whereby man understands his material environment and controls it for his own benefit. This includes tools, machines, processes, and ideas. And if such means flow across national boundaries the technology transfer is international in scope. A technology transfer is also what the various laws relating to it define it as being. A technology transfer in the international sphere typically involves, although not always, one or several of the following, which usually takes the form of one or a combination of several agreements:

1.   A patent assignment or license.

---

[6] *See* Perry, Jr., "U.S. Foreign Policy and Emerging Legal and Policy Issues of Technology Transfer," 70 Proc. Am. Soc'y Int'l L. 1 (1976). *See also, e.g., Presidency of the Republic (Venezuela), Carlos Andres Perez,* Decree No. 2442, Nov. 8, 1977.

[7] *Id.* at art. 63.

[8] *Id.* at art. 65.

[9] *Id.* at art. 32.

[10] *See International Transfer of Technology: Sources of Conflict, supra* N. 5, and Perry, Jr., *supra* N. 6.

2. A license for technical and other information useful in business, including, *e.g.*, engineering, manufacturing, purchasing, operation, maintenance, repair, marketing and management information.
3. A computer software license.
4. A joint development project.
5. A trademark license.
6. A joint venture.
7. A sale of assemblies, subassemblies, components and parts.
8. A sale of manufacturing tools and test sets.
9. Technical and management assistance.
10. Training, and
11. The establishment of a manufacturing facility, sometimes called a "turnkey operation."

A technology transfer may include a complete package in the form of one agreement of virtually everything that is required to manufacture a product, for this is what the recipient of the technology really wants. But it may be advantageous to split the package into separate agreements, such as supply or service agreements, that do not use technology transfer terminology. By doing this, under some circumstances it might be possible to avoid some foreign legal constraints, and possibly some foreign tax, with respect to the technology transfer. Also, if the package is so split and if the technology owner is a separate legal entity from the supplier of assemblies and other hardware, the technology owner may be able to avoid signing the supply agreements and thereby avoid liability under them. On the other hand, the use of technology transfer terminology is often useful from a public relations viewpoint. Such terminology represents what foreign customers, especially governments, deem absolutely necessary for industrialization.

The next chapter discusses in more detail the items enumerated above along with several model agreements.

§ 5.02 Why a Technology Transfer?

It is helpful to consider why an owner of technology might desire to transfer it internationally. Such a transfer is voluntary and while it may be forbidden or discouraged, it cannot be compelled.[11]

An important consideration is whether the transfer will result in a fair return to the owner.[12] Will there be an adequate sharing of the cost of developing the technology? The return might result not only from patent royalties or technical information fees but also from sales of various items and services in support of the technology transfer.

The owner may use the technology transfer to penetrate a foreign market and thereby open it for additional sales of components and products, both related and unrelated to the technology. This penetration is particularly important when the owner's products might not be competitive in foreign markets due, for example, to various factors such as shipping costs, tariffs, taxes, consular fees, and the like.[13] An advantage of this type of market penetration is that it can be done without the owner having to risk his capital in the foreign country.

Another reason for transferring technology from the viewpoint of its owner is that this may be the only way of making sales in a particular foreign country. For example, Australia, Brazil, Mexico and Spain require a high percentage of local content in autos sold in their countries.[13.1] Sometimes governments require a transfer of manufacturing technology in public requests for tenders, especially for large purchases.

---

[11] *Supra* N. 2 at i.

[12] *See* Radway, "Negotiating Technology Transfer Agreements with Latin American Governments," *Licensing Law and Business Report,* Vol. 2, No. 8, at 198 (Mar. 1980).

[13] *See generally* Steiner and Vagts, *Transnational Legal Problems: Materials and Text,* 1209 (2d ed. 1976).

[13.1] A local content law with export performance requirements for the U.S. auto industry was introduced in the U.S. Congress as H.R. 5133, 97th Cong., 1st Sess. (1981). Apparently, more than thirty nations currently apply local content requirements to their auto industry. 41 Economic Developments L-5 at L-6 (Mar. 2, 1982).

§ 5.03 Legal Restraints

Of at least equal importance with a fair return to the technology owner is whether there are any legal restraints on the technology transfer or restraints that might reduce the advantages associated with the transfer. These restraints must be viewed from the standpoint of the law of the country of the owner of the technology as well as from the standpoint of the law of the country of the recipient of the technology, coupled with any applicable treaties that might control or affect these laws. Also, the owner must not make any assumptions that the laws of the recipient country are similar to the laws of his country; he must specifically consider the laws of the recipient country. Knowledge of only the laws of the owner's country may point toward incorrect answers. For example, it can be dangerous to draw conclusions under foreign law based on a knowledge of U.S. laws alone.

[1] Taxes

A primary consideration is the extent to which taxes might reduce the return to the technology owner for the technology transfer. In some countries the owner can require in the agreement for the technology transfer that the recipient pay taxes, such as corporate income taxes of the recipient country, while in other countries this cannot be done.[14] And, of course, even if the owner has to pay the taxes, he may be able to qualify for a foreign tax credit.

Shifting the tax burden to the recipient is not without problems. For example, if the recipient is required by the agreement to pay taxes on royalties or fees, this might be considered to increase such royalties or fees to such an extent that governmental approval of the agreement by the recipient country cannot be obtained. Nevertheless, taxes of the recipient country are often shifted to the recipient in the agreement except

---

[14] *See* Radway, *supra* N. 12 at 201, indicating "yes" for Mexico and "no" for Venezuela.

to the extent such taxes are allowed as a credit against taxes in the technology owner's country.

Not only must U.S. tax laws be considered with respect to a U.S. technology owner but also those of the recipient country along with any applicable treaties. Adding to the complexity is the necessity of considering the laws of the recipient country concerning repatriation of profits, royalties, and fees.

More specifically, a problem might arise because of the manner in which the recipient or the recipient-country's taxing authorities designate a fee for research and development to make a product more suitable to the recipient country. A problem might also arise due to the designation of a fee for gathering technical information. For example, such fees might be designated as royalties instead of fees for a service. As a result, under the laws of the recipient country, it might not be possible to deduct expenses incurred in performing the research and development or in gathering the information. Another important consideration is whether the fees are subject to withholding and, if so, whether the withholding is measured by the gross amount of the fees or by the net income derived.

Whether the recipient country mandates a tax year other than the calendar year can also be an important consideration. Such a mandate can have an impact on the timing established for receipt of the royalties or fees so that receipts can be matched with the incurrence of associated expenses.

[2] Export License

Assuming the technology owner is domiciled in the United States, consideration must be given to whether the U.S. Government will grant an export license to the owner who desires to transfer the technology internationally. The export law[15] and regulations[16] of the United States prohibit the export of

---

[15] The Export Administration Act of 1979, as Amended, 50 U.S.C.A. App. 2401-20 (1982). *See generally A Lawyer's Guide to International Business Transactions*, 151-64, Pt. I (2d ed. 1977).

[16] Export Regulations of the Department of Commerce, 15 CFR Parts 368-99 (1981).

non-military technology, as represented by products and technical data, unless they can be exported under a general license or a validated license. This law and these regulations are based, at least in part, on national interests including those related to security. The degree of restrictiveness of the regulations in permitting exports of products and data depends upon the type of products and data and the country group to which export is proposed. These regulations, which are issued by the U.S. Department of Commerce, provide general licenses for some products and data, and therefore, no written application for a license is required. For example, unrestricted published data is covered by a general license. Also covered by a general license is unpublished data which may be exported to specified friendly countries under certain restrictions (*e.g.*, accompanied with a letter of assurance concerning reexport).

However, many products and data cannot be exported except under a validated license, which requires a written application to the Department of Commerce. For example, unpublished technical data cannot be exported to specified unfriendly countries without first obtaining a validated export license. Also, reexport of technical data is prohibited except for certain reexports of generally licensed data.

As to the export of military technology, it is controlled by a separate law and regulations, which also provide a licensing procedure.[16.1] Such licensing is handled by the U.S. State Department.

[3] **Protectability of Technology**

Another important consideration is whether the technology is protectable in the recipient country. The technology is often represented by patents and proprietary information (including trade secrets and proprietary industrial know-how). Patents and rights based on patents exist almost everywhere in the world and the protection is generally territorial in scope.

[16.1] The International Security Assistance and Arms Export Control Act, 22 U.S.C.A. 2751-96 (1982); International Traffic in Arms Regulations, 22 CFR Parts 121-30 (1981).

However, the protection varies among the various nations in a number of important respects, such as the expiration date of the patents or the class of goods patentable. In some countries, certain items relating to nuclear energy, food, medicine, surgical or curative devices are not patentable.[17] While proprietary information is also widely recognized,[18] some countries limit the period during which it may be held secret, for example, five years.[19] Also, some countries are more likely than others to enforce patent and proprietary information rights.

[4] Government Intervention

Another consideration is whether, and to what extent, a government agency of the recipient country might intervene in an agreement for the technology transfer. For example, in some countries such agreements are required to be approved by and registered with a governmental agency which might include a bank.[20] If such agreements are not so approved and registered, they may be unenforceable in such a country,[21] and it may be difficult to repatriate royalties and fees received for the transfer.[22]

Another concern is whether, and to what extent, such agency might modify, or attempt to modify, the agreement.[23] The agency might limit the period that the proprietary information may be protected by keeping it in confidence.[24] Various clauses that such agency deems too restrictive might be deleted, and royalties or fees might be reduced. One possible way to reduce the risks of having an agreement so modified is to

---

[17] The U.S. is illustrative of the non-patentability of items related to nuclear energy and Italy is illustrative of the non-patentability of items, even with respect to processes, related to the remaining items.

[18] *See generally* A. Wise, *Trade Secrets and Know-how Throughout the World*, Vols. 1-5 (1974, rev. 1980).

[19] *See, e.g.,* Decree No. 2442, *supra* N. 6 at art. 65(e).

[20] *Id.* at art. 63.

[21] *Id.* at art. 72.

[22] *Id.* at art. 32.

[23] *Id.* at art. 65.

[24] *Id.* at art 65(e).

include a clause in the agreement that it is void if so modified. Of course, the agreement will then have to be renegotiated and resubmitted to the involved agency for approval. But some concessions may be obtained to at least partially counteract the modifications of the agency.

Whether, and to what extent, the technology owner might be able to negotiate with the recipient government is another important consideration.

[5] Competitive Effects

The technology owner must consider the possible competitive effects of the technology transfer. The technology recipient might plan to manufacture in his country products using the technology and to not only sell the products in his country but also export them, possibly even to the owner's country.

An important consideration is whether the owner might lose technological superiority to the technology recipient who might improve or completely redesign a licensed product covered by the technology.[25] In regard to this consideration, of importance is the anticipated time when the technology being transferred will become obsolete and will be replaced by newly developed technology. Another important consideration is whether the owner has his technology adequately protected in his own country, for example, by patents, and whether he has refrained from granting the recipient a license to the technology in the owner's country. In this way the owner can place some restraints on his potential competition by preventing the importation of infringing products or products contrary to the terms of a patent license agreement.[26]

---

[25] See Firms Giving Away Technological Superiority, Bank Official Says, Washington Report (July 21, 1980).

[26] See generally Payne et al., "U.S. Antitrust Aspects of the International Transfer of Technology," N.C.J. Int'l L. & Com. 91, 115-16 (Winter 1980).

[6] Antitrust Laws

Other legal restraints on an international technology transfer are the domestic and foreign antitrust laws.[26.1] Technology transfer agreements, especially those relating to the licensing of patents and proprietary information, must be carefully reviewed with respect to these laws. Such a review is particularly important if the technology owner seeks to restrain some activities of the recipient licensee.

Whether the U.S. antitrust laws reach technology transfers must be considered. If one or both parties to a technology transfer agreement are U.S. citizens, the U.S. antitrust laws clearly apply. Where the use of technology outside the United States has a substantial effect on the import or export of goods and services to or from the United States, these laws also apply.[27] Where the challenged conduct has had an impact upon U.S. commerce, a U.S. court has jurisdiction over the subject matter of a claim asserted under the Sherman Act.[27.1] If there is a close connection between activities which occur in a foreign country and their effect on U.S. commerce, and the effect is substantial and is a direct and foreseeable consequence of these activities, such activities are subject to the U.S. antitrust laws.[28]

The antitrust laws may reach contracts or combinations made abroad if they are intended to restrain U.S. foreign commerce and actually do affect it.[29] Also, when foreign transactions have a "substantial and foreseeable effect on U.S. commerce," the U.S. Department of Justice indicates that the antitrust laws apply.[30] According to the Justice Department,

---

[26.1] *See generally* chapter 9 of this volume and specifically § 9.02[3] with respect to U.S. antitrust laws.

[27] *Id.* at 94.

[27.1] United States v. U.S. Alkali Export Ass'n, 86 F. Supp. 59 (S.D.N.Y. 1949); United States v. Minnesota Mining & Mfg., et al., 92 F. Supp. 947 (D. Mass. 1950).

[28] *Restatement (Second) of Foreign Relations Law of the U.S.* § 18 (1965). *See also* Payne, *supra* N. 26 at 94.

[29] United States v. Aluminum Co. of America, 148 F.2d 416 (2d Cir. 1945).

[30] *See* U.S. Department of Justice, *Antitrust Guide for International Operations* 6 (Jan. 26, 1977).

the antitrust laws do not apply to foreign activities that have no direct or intended effect on either U.S. consumers or export opportunities.[31] However, controversy continues to grow regarding the extraterritorial application of the U.S. antitrust laws. Some countries have even adopted special legislation to protect themselves from enforcement of the U.S. antitrust laws. Also, U.S. businessmen are seeking a relaxation of antitrust restrictions on export trading, but the Justice Department has yet to change its posture.[32]

If the technology owner seeks to restrain foreign activities of the technology recipient, the antitrust laws of the recipient country must be carefully considered. In some countries where there is a contract, including a licensing agreement, in restraint of trade or an exclusive dealing, an authorization may be obtained from a governmental agency. The test for granting the authorization is whether the agency believes that the contract or exclusive dealing is likely to result in a substantial benefit to the public.[33] Also, such an agency may grant a clearance for contracts and exclusive dealings which the agency considers are not likely to have a significant effect on competition.[34] Proceedings before such an agency may, however, be costly and time consuming.

Considering U.S. statutory antitrust laws which must be considered with respect to technology transfers subject to U.S. jurisdiction, Section 1 of the Sherman Act[35] prohibits contracts, combinations and conspiracies in restraint of trade. Section 2 of this Act[36] prohibits monopolies or attempts or conspiracies to monopolize. However, the proscription of Section 1 cannot be taken literally. Every contract or combination by definition restrains trade. Therefore, qualification of the "restraint" was essential. The U.S. Supreme Court read into the Sherman Act the "rule of reason." Certain restraints the Supreme Court has found unreasonable *per se*, that is, anticom-

---

[31] *Id.* at 7.

[32] *See* 102 *Daily Report for Executives* C-1 to C-3, BNA (May 23, 1980).

[33] *See, e.g.,* Hewison, "Licensing Situation in Australia," XII-3 Les Nouvelles 182, 188-89 (Sept. 1977).

[34] *Id.*

[35] 15 U.S.C.A. § 1 (1982).

[36] 15 U.S.C.A. § 2 (1982).

petitive activity which has such a "pernicious effect on competition and lack of any redeeming virtue . . . [so as to be] conclusively presumed to be unreasonable and therefore illegal."[37] These restraints include activities that could be related to technology transfers, such as allocation of territories, horizontal price fixing, and tying agreements.

Another antitrust law that should be considered is the Clayton Act.[38] This Act prohibits restraints or acts, which substantially lessen competition or tend to create a monopoly. Section 5 of the Federal Trade Commission Act, as amended,[39] should also be considered with respect to technology transfers. This Section proscribes "unfair methods of competition in commerce, and unfair or deceptive acts . . . in commerce. . . ."

Section 337 of the Tariff Act of 1930[40] authorizes the U.S. International Trade Commission to bar unlicensed foreign goods from entry into U.S. commerce under certain circumstances. These include those situations where such goods infringe a U.S. product patent or have been produced abroad by a process subject to either a U.S. patent or trade secret. Proposed licensing agreements entered into by parties in controversies before the commission are subject to commission regulations.[41]

A detailed discussion of restraints in technology transfer or licensing agreements and their legality is beyond the scope of this chapter.[42] However, under U.S. antitrust law each restraint should be considered in view of (1) whether it has an anticompetitive effect, (2) what is the relevant market, and (3) what effect does the restraint have in the relevant market. A brief outline of some of the more typical restraints and general

---

[37] Standard Oil Co. v. United States, 221 U.S. 1 (1911); Chicago Board of Trade v. United States, 246 U.S. 231 (1918).

[38] 15 U.S.C.A. § 12-27 (1982).

[39] 15 U.S.C.A. § 45 (1982).

[40] 19 U.S.C.A. § 1337 (1982); 19 U.S.C.A. § 1337(a) (1973).

[41] *See International Technology Transfer: A Review of Related Legal Issues,* 24 (U.S. International Trade Commission Publ. 935, Jan. 1979).

[42] For a more detailed review of these restraints, including extensive case citations, *see* N. 26 at 98-117 and N. 41 at 24-28 *supra.*

indications of their legality follows:[42.1]

1. Tie-Ins. These occur when one party to an agreement,
    using some leverage he has on one item, forces the
    other party to the agreement to take another item as a
    condition to obtaining the first. Tie-ins occur only when
    the licensee must take the unwanted item. They do not
    occur when the licensee voluntarily buys the item.
    Tying restraints are generally illegal.[43]
2. Tie-Outs. These occur when the technology owner re-
    stricts the freedom of the technology recipient from
    buying or selling competing items. Tie-outs usually
    have the same anticompetitive effect as tie-ins and have
    been held *per se* illegal.[44]
3. Package Licenses. These occur when a licensing party
    requires the other licensing party to take a license
    under more than one patent or other form of technolo-
    gy. If such a license is for the convenience of the parties,
    it is legal. If it is the result of coercion, it is usually illegal
    and unenforceable.[45]
4. Post Expiration Royalties. These occur when payment
    of royalties is required beyond the life of the technolo-
    gy, *e.g.*, after patents expire or proprietary information
    passes into the public domain. Such a requirement is
    unenforceable in the area of patents. If the royalties,
    however, relate to a pre-expiration use, payment after
    the patent expires appears proper. Also, payment pur-
    suant to an arm's length agreement to pay for use of

[42.1] The current thinking and likely enforcement policy of the Antitrust
Division of the U.S. Department of Justice does not completely correspond
to the indications of legality of the outline. *See* Lipsky, "DOJ Official's Address on Patent Licensing, Antitrust," Vol. IV, No. 25 Legal Times of Washington 18 (Nov. 23, 1981). However, most of the U.S. antitrust law
concerning technology transfers is based, not on Department of Justice cases
but instead on private patent infringement or trade secret violation cases.

The outline is mainly offered as a checklist to aid in the study of some of
the more typical restraints in technology transfers.

[43] *See* N. 26 at 100-101 and N. 41 at 26 *supra,* both citing cases.

[44] *See* N. 26 at 103-104 and N. 41 at 26 *supra,* both citing cases.

[45] *See* N. 26 at 105-106 and N. 41 at 26 *supra,* both citing cases.

proprietary information after it passes into the public domain is proper.[46]

5. Total Sales Royalties. These result when a licensing party is required to pay a royalty based on the sale of all items that he sells that are covered by transferred technology. This is generally permissible if voluntary but illegal if coerced.[47]

6. Grant-Backs. These result when the recipient of the technology agrees to grant the technology owner rights to technology developed by the recipient. Grant-backs are tested by the rule of reason. Generally, exclusive grant-backs are suspect while non-exclusive grant-backs are not illegal.[48]

7. Field of Use Restrictions. These result when the technology owner limits the product line or industrial use of the technology. Although this received some court approval in a 1938 case, it has been attacked by the U.S. Justice Department.[49] But recently patent owners have been allowed substantial freedom to license, one appellate court indicating that licensing restrictions should be judged on the basis of whether they are reasonable profit-maximizing techniques which harmonize competing interests of the antitrust and patent laws.[49.1]

8. Territorial Restrictions. These result when the technology owner restricts the geographical territory in which the recipient can use the technology or market items incorporating it. Regarding such restrictions, patent owners have recently had substantial freedom to license.[49.2] Whether these restrictions are legal depends

---

[46] See N. 26 at 104 and N. 41 at 26 supra, both citing cases.

[47] See N. 26 at 106-107 supra, citing cases.

[48] See N. 26 at 108-109 and N. 41 at 25 supra, both citing cases.

[49] See N. 26 at 111-112 and N. 41 at 25 supra, both citing cases.

[49.1] United States v. Studiengesellschaft Kohle et al., 670 F.2d 1122, 212 U.S.P.Q. 889 (D.C. Cir. 1981), rev'g 200 U.S.P.Q. 389 (D.D.C. 1978). The court rejected the Government's contention that any restraint on products produced by a process patent is outside the protection of the patent laws and illegal "per se."

[49.2] United States v. Mitsubishi et al., 648 F.2d 642 (9th Cir. 1981).

on the underlying facts.[50]

9. Nondiminishing Royalties. These occur when the same royalty is paid throughout the term of the technology transfer even though some of the technology expires. This is legal if not coerced.[51]

10. Veto Power. This occurs when either the owner or the recipient is restrained from granting further licenses to the technology without the express permission of the other party. This has been held *per se* illegal.[52]

11. Quantity or Volume Restrictions. These result when the technology owner fixes the minimum or maximum number of products that can be made with the transferred technology. Such restrictions are generally tested under the rule of reason.[53]

12. Resale Restrictions. These occur when the technology owner places a restriction on the sale or use of items made with the technology after the technology recipient has parted with title of the products. Such restrictions are tested by the rule of reason.[54]

13. Royalty Discrimination. This occurs when the technology owner charges different recipients of it different royalty rates. This has been held to violate Section 5 of the Federal Trade Commission Act.[55]

[7] International Accords

There are several treaties, agreements or cooperative arrangements involving the United States and a number of other countries which should be considered by a U.S. technology owner with respect to restrictive practices in internationally transferring the technology. For example, the United States has signed a number of treaties of friendship, commerce and

---

[50] *See* N. 26 at 113-114 and N. 41 at 25 *supra*, both citing cases.

[51] *See* N. 26 at 107 *supra*, citing cases.

[52] *See* N. 26 at 109-110 and N. 41 at 27 *supra*, both citing cases.

[53] *See* N. 26 at 110-111 and N. 41 at 26 *supra*, both citing cases.

[54] *See* N. 26 at 116-117 and N. 41 at 25 *supra*, both citing cases.

[55] *See* N. 41 at 27 *supra*, citing a case.

navigation which include a restrictive business practice clause
This clause provides that one country upon the request of the
other agrees to consult with the other on restrictive business
practices and take such measures as it deems appropriate to
eliminate the harmful effects of such practices. The United
States also maintains antitrust cooperation arrangements with
Canada and West Germany.[56]

The antitrust provisions of the European Economic Community (EEC), should be considered with respect to technology transfers into or out of the countries of the EEC. These
provisions, which are reminiscent of the Sherman Act and
certain sections of the Clayton Act,[57] are contained in Articles
85 and 86 of the Treaty of Rome. Article 85 prohibits certain
"concerted practices . . . which have as their object or effect
the prevention, restriction or distortion of competition."
These practices include (1) price fixing; (2) limiting or controlling production, markets, technical development or investment; (3) sharing markets or sources of supply; (4) applying
dissimilar conditions to equivalent transactions with other
trading parties; and (5) tying arrangements. This article contains exceptions for certain restrictive practices of any agreement that "contributes to improving the production or
distribution of goods or to promoting technical or economic
progress while allowing consumers a fair share of the resulting
benefit. . . ."

Article 86 of this Treaty prohibits "any abuse by one or more
undertakings of a dominant position." This article sets forth
the following as particularly offensive: (1) directly or indirectly
imposing unfair purchase or selling prices or other unfair trading conditions; (2) limiting production, markets, or technical
development to the prejudice of consumers; (3) applying dissimilar conditions to equivalent transactions with other trading parties; and (4) tying arrangements that have no
connection with the subject of the contracts.[58]

The Andean Common Market (ANCOM) has established the
Andean Foreign Investment Code for technology transfer.

---

[56] *See* N. 41 at 22 *supra*.
[57] *See* Steiner & Vagts, *supra* N. 13, at 1343 and N. 41 *supra* at 37.
[58] *See* N. 41 *supra* at 37.

This Code is designed not so much to promote competition as to promote the growth of local technology and to prevent precious foreign exchange from being spent on technologies which are not useful in the development of the Andean countries.[59]

The Code requires that in every contract of sale there must be included the value of each element concerned with technology transfer. The Code prohibits tying arrangements (except in unusual circumstances), the fixing of the sale or resale prices of products made with the technology, restrictions on the volume and structure of production, restraints on the use of technology, full or partial purchase options on the part of the technology owner, obligations on the part of the technology recipient to transfer to the owner any inventions or improvements, and requirements for payments for royalties to the owner for patents which are not used, and restraints on exporting products made by the technology.[60] Later adopted decisions of the Andean Pact require an applicant for a proposed technology transfer agreement to present data concerning alternate technology, explaining why the selected technology is appropriate. Also, licensing agreements are required to expire after five years.[61]

In the multilateral setting, the United Nations Conference on Trade and Development (UNCTAD) provided a forum for the proposals of a number of nations on technology transfer. The proposals reflect the desires of three major groups of UNCTAD: the Group of 77 (the Third World nations), Group B (the Western nations and Japan), and Group D (the Socialist countries).[62] The desires of these three groups differ substantially. A fundamental difference between Group B and the Group of 77 is exemplified by the view of the Group of 77 that technology belongs to all nations. Group B countries, on the other hand, emphasize that technology the developing countries seek has been developed at great expense by private

---

[59] See N. 41 supra at 39.
[60] Id.
[61] Id.
[62] See N. 41 supra at 50.

companies in the developed nations,[63] and these companies should receive a fair return for the use of such technology.

Concerning choice of law and forum selection, Group B countries believe the choice should be made by the parties to a contract, so long as the chosen law and forum are not unduly burdensome and there is a reasonable basis for the selection. In contrast to this, the Group of 77 would give the recipient country exclusive jurisdiction over dispute settlement.[64] However, both Group B and the Group of 77 are in general agreement that there should be guarantees that the information of the technology be full and complete and be fit and suitable for the purpose for which it was intended.[65] Also, the Group of 77 and Group B agree that the confidentiality of trade secrets should be maintained.[66] More recently, under UNCTAD's auspices, a group of governmental experts has drafted a Restrictive Business Practices Code, entitled, "A Set of Multilaterally Agreed Equitable Principles and Rules for the Control of Restrictive Business Practices Having Adverse Effects on International Trade, Particularly that of Developing Countries, and on the Economic Development of These Countries."[67]

[8] Selected Countries

[a] In General

In the forefront of legislation concerning the transfer of technology are Japan, Mexico, and Brazil.[68] Australia and Venezuela are illustrative of other approaches having some aspects in common with these three countries.

Mexico, Brazil, and Venezuela, which have recently experienced rapid growth, still remain in the "developing"

---

[63] *See* N. 41 *supra* at 51.

[64] *Id.*

[65] *See* N. 41 *supra* at 52.

[66] *Id.*

[67] *See generally* Davidow, "The UNCTAD Restrictive Business Practices Code," 13 Int'l Law. 587 (1979); Gill, "The UNCTAD Restrictive Business Practices Code for Competition," *Id.* at 607.

[68] *See* N. 41 *supra* at 39.

group of nations and have tightened their controls on technology transfers. Japan, on the other hand, which is now becoming an exporter of technology, is easing its restrictions on the technology transfer.[69] Australia, although a young country, is not overly restrictive on technology transfers.[70] However, all of these countries have one thing in common: they require the approval of international technology transfer agreements by some governmental agency.[71]

[b] Japan

In this country, the required procedure has two main steps. The first, which precedes the granting of an effective date for the agreement, is initiated by filing the agreement with the Bank of Japan which has the authority to consult with pertinent agencies such as the Ministry of International Trade and Industry (MITI). In the typical case, if no question is raised by the Bank, the agreement is considered automatically approved at the expiration of two weeks from the date of filing. If a question is then raised, until the agreement is approved, it is not deemed valid and, if the parties begin to operate under a license granted by the agreement without first receiving approval, they may become subject to prosecution as violators of the foreign exchange and trade control laws.[72] The second step requires that, within thirty days after the effective date, the agreement be filed with the Japanese Fair Trade Commission which examines the agreement to determine whether it conforms to the Antimonopoly Act.[73]

Under present Japanese practice, the following restrictions are permitted: limitations on the amount of production in both exclusive and non-exclusive licensing agreements, the fixing of a minimum price at which a licensee may sell a licensed

---

[69] *Id.* at 40.

[70] *See* N. 33 *supra* at 186.

[71] *See* N. 41 *supra* at 40 concerning Japan, Mexico, and Brazil.

[72] Eckstrom, *Licensing in Foreign and Domestic Operations,* Vol. 3 "Licensing Operations in Japan," § 31.09 (1980 Rev.).

[73] *Id.* at § 31.10.

product, and limitations on the field of use of a licensed
product. However, the Japanese laws do not allow the setting
of resale prices at the wholesale or retail levels or tying arrangements that are not indispensable to working a patent.
Restrictions on the use of competing products or technology
are allowed insofar as a licensee agrees, beginning at the time
of the agreement, not to use competing products or different
technology.[74] It is believed that the validity of these restrictions and others may become questionable as the Japanese
licensee gains expertise. The Japanese Fair Trade Commission
has begun to disapprove older restrictions, once considered
valid, when they continue to be applied to such a licensee.

A restriction that is not permitted is that a licensor cannot
require a licensee to discontinue practices already established.[75]

[c] Mexico

Here, there are substantial restrictions on the international
transfer of technology. The law for the transfer of technology,[75.1] which is entwined with the law on inventions and
trademarks, is complex. In general, agreements for the transfer of technology in any form must be registered with the
National Registry for the Transfer of Technology.[76] Such
agreements requiring registration include those for licensing
a patent, Certificate of Invention, trademark, and technical
information and computer software or providing technical assistance, engineering plans or services to operate a business.

---

[74] See N. 41 supra at 40.

[75] Id.

[75.1] Law on the Control and Registration of Transfers of Technology and
Use and Exploitation of Patents and Trademarks (Mexico), effective Feb. 10,
1982 [hereinafter cited as Mexican Technology Transfer Law].

[76] Id. at art. 2, Mexican Technology Transfer Law. Also see Soberanis,
"Legal Aspects Concerning the Technology Transfer Process in Mexico," 7
Ga. J. Int'l & Comp. L. 17, 19 (1977), and Brill, Jr., "Transfers of Technology
in Mexico," 4 Den. J. Int'l L. & Pol'y 51, 53 (1974). See generally Eckstrom,
Licensing in Foreign and Domestic Operations, Vol. 3 "Licensing in Mex-
ico," Chapter 26 (1980 Rev.).

Failure to so register such an agreement renders it unenforceable in Mexico and may subject the involved parties to criminal penalties.[77]

To register technology transfer agreements with the Registry, the agreements must be filed with the Ministry of Industry and Commerce within sixty days from the date of their execution.[78] However, agreements containing certain provisions cannot be registered with the Registry, and, as previously mentioned, agreements that are not registered are unenforceable in Mexico. These provisions include a price for the technology that does not represent the technology acquired or that is an unjustified or excessive burden on the Mexican economy.[79]

Such provisions also include, in the view of the Ministry, an unreasonable term. With respect to obligations of the technology recipient, such term must not exceed the term of the technology transfer agreement, must not be excessive and must not in any case exceed ten years.[79.1]

Also, to be registrable technology transfer agreements must contain certain provisions. For example, the technology owner must assume responsibility for infringement of patents of third parties resulting from the recipient's use of the transferred technology.[79.2] In addition, the owner has to guarantee the quality of, and the results achieved with, the transferred technology.[79.3] Mexican law and courts must be used to resolve any disputes under the agreement.[79.4]

However, the Mexican Ministry of Industry and Commerce has discretion to register agreements with the Registry that contain prohibited, or do not contain required, provisions

---

[77] *Supra* N. 75.1 at arts. 11 and 19, Mexican Technology Transfer Law. *Also see* Soberanis, *supra* N. 76 at 21; Brill, Jr., *supra* N. 76 at 54; and Eckstrom, *supra* N. 76 at § 26.02[4].

[78] *Supra* N. 75.1 at art. 10, Mexican Technology Transfer Law. *Also see* Eckstrom, N. 76 *supra* at § 26.02[3].

[79] *Supra* N. 75.1 at arts. 15-16; *Id.* at § 26.02[4].

[79.1] *Supra* N. 75.1 at art. 15, XI and art. 16, III, Mexican Technology Transfer Law.

[79.2] *Supra* N. 75.1 at art. 15, XII, Mexican Technology Transfer Law.

[79.3] *Supra* N. 75.1 at art. 15, XIII, Mexican Technology Transfer Law.

[79.4] *Supra*, N. 75.1 at art. 16, IV, Mexican Technology Transfer Law.

when the technology transferred is of special interest to the country.[80]

It may be possible in some cases to reduce the impact of the Mexican technology transfer law on such information. For example, if improvement technology were transferred at future intervals, the ten-year confidentiality period would run from each transfer, and in this way it would appear that such period could be effectively extended. Also, if a foreign owner of the information enters into a joint venture agreement with Mexican interests to form a Mexican affiliate, a majority of the shares of which are owned by the Mexican interests, as required by Mexican law, it may be possible to include some limitations in such agreement to protect the information. These limitations may include requiring a vote of a two-thirds majority of the shares before the information may be released outside the affiliate without restrictions. Thus, the information may be protected even after the ten-year confidentiality period has expired, or after the expiration of an agreement transferring the information to the affiliate.

Mexican patent law grants in addition to patents, Certificates of Invention which may cover non-patentable inventions.[81] An unusual feature is that anyone can use the invention of the Certificate if he signs a royalty agreement for the use of the invention.[82] A government agency has the right to review the royalty and set terms of the agreement if the parties fail to agree.[83]

The Mexican law attempts to ensure that patents granted thereunder are worked in Mexico. To do this, the law sets forth a three-year time limit in which a patent must be used. If, for example, a licensee fails to so use the patent, compulsory licenses may be awarded to others and a governmental board may establish a suitable royalty.[84]

---

[80] *Supra* N. 75.1 at art. 17, Mexican Technology Transfer Law; *supra* N. 78 at § 26.02[4].

[81] Medina, "Significant Innovations of the New Mexico Law of Inventions and Trademarks," 7 Ga. J. Int'l & Comp. L. 5, 6 (1977)

[82] *See* N. 41 *supra* at 40.

[83] *Id.* at 41.

[84] *Id. See also* Medina, N. 81 *supra* at 9.

[d]   Brazil

This country's law relating to technology transfers is in some ways similar to that of Mexico. Technology transfers include agreements for licensing patents and trademarks and for furnishing industrial technology and technical industrial cooperation. The agreements must be registered with the Brazilian Patent Office.[85]

Patent and trademark license agreements are limited to the period of protection of patents and trademarks, which varies from ten to fifteen years. In the case of agreements for technical industrial cooperation, the term is limited to a maximum of five years, starting from the actual commencing of production. Concerning agreements for furnishing industrial technology and for industrial cooperation, contractual obligations, presumedly including those relating to preserving confidentiality of technical information, must be limited to a term set forth in the agreement.[86]

[e]   Australia

Here, there are no major obstacles to technology transfers. Patents and proprietary information are protected and may be licensed under Australian laws.[87] Australia does not impose specific limitations on the time that information can be held in confidence. However, technology transfer agreements must not operate against the public interest. In this regard the Australian Trade Practices Act,[88] which is based on the Sherman Act and its judicial interpretations, must be considered. This law makes certain restrictive trade practices unlawful.

The Trade Practice Act is administered by the Trade Practice Commission. The Commission has the power to grant "au-

---

[85] *See* N. 41 *supra* at 41. *See also* Eckstrom, *Licensing in Foreign and Domestic Operations,* Vol. 3 "Licensing in Brazil," Chapter 29 (1980 Rev.).

[86] *See* Eckstrom, *supra* N. 85 at § 29.06[3].

[87] *See* Eckstrom, *supra* N. 85 at Vol. 3 "Licensing in Australia," § 25.01 (1980 Rev.).

[88] *Id.* at § 25.08.

thorizations" for certain contracts in restraint of trade and exclusive dealings. The test for granting an authorization is whether the Commission believes that the contracts or exclusive dealings are likely to result in substantial benefits to the public. The Commission is also empowered to grant "clearances" for contracts or exclusive dealings which the Commission considers are not likely to have a significant effect on competition.[89]

In Australia, agreements for technology transfer must be approved by the Australian Reserve Bank for exchange control of foreign currency movement. Aside from this, no other approvals are required; there is no registry for technology transfer agreements.[90]

[f] Venezuela

In this country, agreements to import technology must be approved and registered by the Superintendency of Foreign Investments (SIEX).[91] Restrictions on royalties and fees are imposed on majority foreign-owned subsidiaries and certain clauses may not be included in the agreements.[92] Failure to obtain such approval and registration results in the agreements being void and unenforceable. Such failure may also result in the inability to make payments of royalties and fees under the agreement.[93]

In general, agreements to preserve the confidentiality of proprietary technical information may not extend beyond the term of agreement or five years, whichever is less. In some cases the period may be extended to fifteen years with appropriate governmental approvals.[94] It is speculated that if the Venezuelan government deems certain information to be critically important to the country, it may be possible to

---

[89] *Id. See also* N. 33 *supra.*

[90] *Id.* at § 25.09.

[91] *See* N. 6 *supra* at Art. 63. *See also* Carl et al., "Venezuela and the Andean Common Market," 7 Den. J. Int'l L. & Pol'y 151, 178 (1978).

[92] *Id.* at 191.

[93] *Id.* at 178. *See also* Decree No. 2442, *supra* N. 6 at art. 32.

[94] *See* Carl *et al.*, N. 92 *supra* at 191.

negotiate more advantageous terms, especially in view of recent developments concerning SIEX.[95]

§ 5.04 Conclusion

A mere glimpse into the intriguing and complicated field of technology transfer has been offered here. The checklist provided here is designed merely to guide the attorney in advising a client interested or engaged in a technology transfer as to the nature and scope of the issues he is likely to confront. Each of these issues demands thorough research and understanding which alone can ensure a skillful handling of a client's needs.

---

[95] *See New York Times,* July 15, 1980, at D1 and D11.

CHAPTER 6

International Technology Transfer Agreements

MICHAEL BARD*
ROBERT Y. PETERS**

---

*Attorney, American Telephone & Telegraph Co.; Member of the District of Columbia, Michigan, Massachusetts, and North Carolina Bars; B.M.E., The City College (N.Y.) School of Technology; J.D., The American University.

**Attorney, American Telephone & Telegraph Co.; Member of the District of Columbia, New York, Pennsylvania, and North Carolina Bars; B.E.E., University of Detroit; J.D., Georgetown University; LL.M., George Washington University.

§ 6.01   Aspects of International Technology Transfer Agreements

In Chapter five it was noted that technology transfer typically involves one or several of the following,[1] usually taking the form of one or a combination of several agreements:

1. A patent assignment or license.
2. A license for technical and other information useful in business, including, *e.g.*, engineering, manufacturing, purchasing, operation, maintenance, repair, marketing and management information.
3. A computer software license.
4. A joint development project.
5. A trademark license.
6. A joint venture.
7. The sale of assemblies, subassemblies, components, and parts.
8. The sale of manufacturing tools and test sets.
9. Technical and management assistance.
10. Training, and
11. The establishment of a manufacturing facility, sometimes called a "turnkey operation."

Various aspects of international technology transfer agreements will now be discussed with respect to each of these forms.

[1]   Patent Assignment or License

Probably the most common form of a technology transfer is a patent assignment or license. Patents, a form of intellectual property, are one of the principal ways for the transfer and dissemination of technology, especially by licensing the patents in the developed countries. In many developed countries, such as the United States, a patent grants its owner the right to prevent or exclude others for a limited time from making,

---

[1] *See* "International Technology Transfers," Chapter 5, this volume.

using, or selling the subject matter claimed in the patent.[2] But a special word of caution—a patent generally does not confer on its owner the right to make, use or sell the subject matter covered by the patent. It simply gives him the right to prevent others from doing so.

To help describe how a patent assignment or license affects a technology transfer, consider a specific example involving two countries: the United States and Germany. Assume that a U.S. citizen makes an invention and that he wants to market it in the United States and Germany. To enhance his market position and protect his developmental investment in his invention, he wants to patent his invention in the United States and Germany. He would be required to make a full and complete disclosure of his invention to the United States[3] and German Patent Offices.[4] His invention would have to fulfill other legal requirements of such countries, such as novelty,[5] unobviousness[6] or inventiveness[7] and utility.[8] It would also have to fall within the legally defined statutory classes[9] or patent categories[10] of inventions for these countries. For the disclosure, the U.S. government would grant him a patent which would give him a seventeen-year period of exclusive control in the United States.[11] The German government would grant him a twenty-year period of exclusive control from the date of filing the

---

[2] 35 U.S.C.A. §§ 154, 271, 281, 283, 284 (1982).

[3] 35 U.S.C.A. § 112.

[4] Laws of the Federal Republic of Germany, The Patent Act, as amended to Jan. 1, 1978 [hereinafter the "German Patent Act"] § 1. *See* Schulte, Annotation 33 to § 1 of the German Patent Act (Heymann's Ed., Cologne Germany 1978). *See generally* Vol. 1 *Manual for the Handling of Applications for Patents, Designs and Trade Marks Throughout the World, Federal Republic of Germany* 1-15 (Sup. No. 37, Aug. 1978).

[5] 35 U.S.C.A. § 102 (1982) for the United States, and German Patent Act, § 2. *See also* Schulte, N. 4 *supra*, Annotation 1 to § 2.

[6] 35 U.S.C.A. § 103 (1982).

[7] German Patent Act, § *See also* Schulte, N. 4 *supra*, Annotation 5 to § 1.

[8] 35 U.S.C.A. § 101 (1982) and German Patent Act § 1. *See also* Schulte, N. 4 *supra*, Annotation 28 to § 1.

[9] 35 U.S.C.A. § 101 (1982).

[10] German Patent Act § 1. *See also* Schulte, N. 4 *supra*, Annotations 79-100 to § 1.

[11] 35 U.S.C.A. § 154 (1982).

German application.[12] When the patent is granted in the United States or the application is filed in Germany, the description is published in the United States and Germany for anyone to study, the word "patent" meaning open to the public.

During the seventeen years in the United States and twenty years in Germany, the patent owner gets the relative peace of mind that others cannot pirate or capitalize on his ingenuity and hard work without paying tribute to him. After the patent time limitations of both countries expire, the invention passes into the public domain, and may be further used or sold by anyone. So, the inventor gets seventeen years of protection in the United States and twenty years in Germany, and the public gets the benefit of the inventive knowledge. If the invention is actually marketed, the public gets the opportunity to buy and use the invention, the opportunity to further develop the invention, and finally, when the patent expires, the opportunity to freely make and use it.

Since a patent is clearly an embodiment of technology, the international assignment or licensing of a patent results in an international technology transfer. The assignment results in a transfer of title to or ownership rights in the patent while the licensing of it results in the transfer of something less.[13]

A patent license conveys the right to make, use or sell the subject matter of the patent without being sued for patent infringement.[14] In a patent license, the licensee gets no right to sue in his own name for patent infringement,[15] while in a patent assignment, the assignee gets such a right.

In the example, if the U.S. owner of the invention is successful in obtaining a German patent, and if he assigned it to a German firm, this would result in an international technology transfer. The transfer would occur, in a broad sense, first upon the filing of the application in Germany for a patent and then, in a narrower sense, the transfer would become more effica-

---

[12] German Patent Act, § 10. *See* Schulte, N. 4 *supra*, Annotation 2.

[13] Waterman v. Mackenzie, 138 U.S. 252 (1891).

[14] *See* Landis (Chairman), *Patent, Copyright, Trademarks and Trade Secrets for Corporate Counsel and General Practitioners,* 377 (PLI 1980).

[15] 138 U.S. at 255.

cious upon assigning the patent in Germany to have the invention manufactured in that country.

The international licensing of patents is of greater concern than their assignment because licensing occurs much more frequently and is involved in a greater number of international transfers of technology. In the example, if the U.S. owner of the German patent licensed it to a German firm this would also result in an international transfer of technology.

Typically, the recipient of such a technology transfer desires the very latest and most sophisticated technology in such vital areas ranging from steel fabrication to telecommunications. A technology transfer often includes many patents involving several countries. What the recipient is usually most interested in is the manufacture, use, and sale of a product. Toward that end he needs both information and freedom to use that information. As a consequence of such needs, it is not at all unusual to find the recipient licensed under patents to manufacture, use, sell, lease, and import a particular product or class of product. Thus, for example, a technology recipient who desires to establish a nationwide telecommunication system in Egypt may very likely need a license under all the technology owner's patents covering all or portions of switching systems. If the recipient desired to procure components or parts from sources outside of Egypt, he might very likely need licenses under related patents of the licensor in the United States, the Common Market, and elsewhere.

Often, the recipient must make a large investment and financial commitment to manufacture the product. This venture usually will be in a technological area in which the recipient has developed an expertise. Can the recipient risk that the technology owner might make a technological breakthrough which will make his product obsolete and one for which he will not have the necessary patent licenses? By the same token, would an owner be comfortable with transferring a large portion of its hard-earned technology to a recipient only to have its own information stimulate the recipient into inventing improvements and obtaining patent protection therefor under which the owner would not be licensed?

It is because of considerations such as these that in the case

of significant international technology transfers the parties frequently will cross-license each other. The parties usually extend licenses to each other not only under their existing patent
portfolios covering the product to be made, but also under all
patents covering the relevant technological area that each
party obtains within a specified future time period.[16]

Additional considerations involved in formulating the patent license agreement include the manner of payment. Should
there be a running royalty calculated on the basis of the value
of goods manufactured and sold under the license? Should
there be a lump sum paid-up license, or should there be a
commuted rate whereby a recipient will pay a royalty on all
goods of a particular type he manufactures and sells, independent of whether the particular goods are covered by one or
more of the owner's patents? To answer these questions would
require a knowledge of the potential market, the recipient's
business practices and the relevant international laws including those relating to taxes.

[2] License of Technical and Other Information Useful in Business

Another principal way for transferring technology is an
agreement for furnishing technical and other information useful in business, including industrial know-how. Often this type
of information, which has not been published or is not otherwise in the public domain, is protectable under the laws of
many countries, especially the developed ones.[17]

In the United States, this information is commonly known as
"trade secrets." It is also known as "private," "confidential,"
"industrial know-how" or simply "secret information." Because under U.S. law it is capable of being owned, it is some-

---

[16] *See, e.g,* §§ 2.01 and 2.02 of Sample Patent License Agreement, p. *infra.*
See also definition of "LICENSEE'S PATENTS" and "LICENSOR'S PAT-
ENTS" in "GENERAL DEFINITIONS APPENDIX" of Sample Patent Li-
cense Agreement, *infra.*

[17] *See generally* A. Wise, *Trade Secrets and Know-How Throughout the
World* (1974 rev. 1981).

times referred to as "proprietary information," and will be referred to here as such or as trade secrets. It is information that the owner uses or plans to use in his business that gives him an advantage over actual or potential competitors who do not know about it.[18] It may be generated by the owner or developed by someone else, such as a consultant, for the owner's use.

Proprietary information is not limited to information concerning items that may be patentable. The scope of proprietary information extends beyond patentable items and includes machine drawings, process instructions, production programs or schedules, manufacturing costs, manufacturing and testing specifications, and many other items of information. Even information respecting the direction in which the owner's technology is moving or his use of a certain approach may be proprietary. Knowing what does not work may be a valuable property right because it may eliminate a costly choice in research and development. To make an analogy with the oil industry, because of the cost of drilling it can be almost as important knowing where not to drill—where the dry holes are likely to be—as it is to know where to drill.

There may be various degrees of proprietary information and its value may vary accordingly. In any case, information that gives the owner a significant competitive advantage, or, in the development of which the owner has spent or is likely to spend large sums of money, may be highly proprietary and deserving of substantial efforts, including contractual mandates, to control its use and disclosure.

The information may also be highly proprietary if it results in a significant cost advantage, or makes something economical to manufacture that would not otherwise be economical. Similarly, if the information covers something that its owner would not like an employee to leave his employ with, it may be highly proprietary. If the information sets a new direction to a major technical problem or represents a new solution, it may likewise be highly proprietary.

In transferring information internationally, especially if it is highly proprietary, steps must be taken, usually in an agree-

---

18 Restatement, Torts, § 757, Comment b (1939).

ment, to safeguard such information. But equally important, the laws of the recipient country must permit this protection to be realized, especially by a foreign transferor who owns such information.

The main thing to remember is that proprietary information is legally protectable in many countries,[19] including the United States, so long as the information is not published, released without restriction, or commonly known. In other words, it is protectable in these countries only so long as it is maintained generally secret.

As in the case of patent license agreements, most technical information agreements are concerned with significant amounts of extremely valuable or highly complex information. Many important decisions have to be made in approaching such an agreement. For example, the question of payment must be squarely faced. Is there to be a single lump sum payment to be made regardless of how extensively the licensee uses the information? Is there to be a running fee based on the licensee's production using the information?[20] If the latter is the case, is there any time or quantity limit affecting the licensee's payments?[21]

Are there to be any restrictions on the types of goods the licensee produces with the information? This latter point may prove to be quite significant. Consider a licensee who receives a large amount of information relevant to a new electric vehicle having both a novel engine and a power supply. Suppose the license permits him to use the information to make vehicles, engines, and power supplies with a fee of 5 percent payable on sales of vehicles, engines, and power supplies manufactured during a five-year period. Suppose that the licensee initially manufactures only power supplies during the five-year period and thereafter significantly increases his production of power supplies and commences production of engines and complete vehicles as well. Will the licensee now be able to escape having to pay fees on completed vehicles and engines?

Would it not be far better to eliminate the problem in the

---

[19] *See generally* N. 17, *supra* Vol. 1 at v.

[20] *See* Sample Technology Transfer Agreement, § II-3.02, *infra*.

[21] *Id.* (*see* definition of "BASE PERIOD").

first instance by providing that in any period where the production does not exceed a given threshold, that period will not count as part of the five-year period?[22] Similarly, would it not be far better to provide separate five-year periods for each of vehicles, engines, and power supplies? Further, if the licensee is licensed to manufacture (for an unlimited future period) using the information throughout the world for a 5 percent fee on sales, for say a five-year period in each country of manufacture, and thereafter produces engines in France using the information, is he then free to manufacture in Germany five years later without further payment?[23]

In addition to some of the same legal constraints concerning proprietary information as are present with respect to patent license agreements, particular attention must be paid to the trade secret laws of the countries in which the technical information will be used as well as those of the licensor's domicile. For example, will the licensor lose all his valuable technical information after five years if he licenses a company in Venezuela to use the same?[24] Will a U.S. licensor be in violation of the U.S. export regulations if he exports technical information on photographic equipment to South Africa?[25]

Certainly restrictive trade practices must be carefully looked at. Consider whether it would be permitted to refuse to provide technical information absent the licensee's agreement to purchase components from the licensor?[26]

---

[22] *Id.*

[23] *See generally,* Centrafarm BV v. Sterling Drug, Inc., 14 Common Market L. Rep 480 (1974); *see also,* Terrapin v. Terranova, 2 Common Market L. Rep. 482 (Case 199/75, June 22, 1976); Merck v. Stephar, 3 Common Market L. Rep. 463 (Case 187/80, July 14, 1981).

[24] Presidency of the Republic (Venezuela), Carlos Endres Perez, Decree No. 2442, Nov. 8., 1977.

[25] *See* Export Administration Regulations 15 CFR § 385.4 (s) and consider whether photographic equipment may be characterized as "particularly useful in crime control."

[26] Compare Section 1 of the Sherman Act (15 U.S.C.A. § 1 (1982)), Section 2 of the Sherman Act (15 U.S.C.A. § 2 (1982)), Section 3 of the Clayton Act (15 U.S.C.A. § 14 (1982)), and Section 5(a)(a) of the Federal Trade Commission Act (15 U.S.C.A. § 45 (a)(1) (1982)). Compare also International Business Machines Corp. v. United States, 298 U.S. 131 (1936), with Siegel v. Cluilsen Delight, Inc. 171 U.S.P.Q. 269 (9th Cir. 1971). *See also* § 5.03[6] of this volume.

6-9

[3] Computer Software License

Computer software is frequently essential in a technology transfer because of the ever increasing use of micro-processors and mini-computers in all areas of technology from automotive products to telephony. In addition to its use in products such as stored program controlled switching systems, computer software is frequently used in manufacturing equipments and test sets.

Computer software licensing carries with it all of the problems inherent in a transfer of other technology, including technical information, as well as many unique problems, some of which will now be explored.

Software programs are machine readable by computers when recorded on magnetic tape, discs, punch cards or similar mediums. Such programs are commonly classified as being in either the object code format or source code format. Object code is limited to the actual list of instructions required by the computer to operate as desired. The object code does not disclose sufficient information to permit a programmer to substantially modify or understand the underlying makeup of the program. On the other hand, the source code discloses a great deal of information which would be valuable to a programmer in modifying the program or developing new programs.

Because it is easier to make new editions from source code than object code and because the underlying theory behind the program is discernible by the programmer from the source code, a greater scope of technology transfer results from a transfer of source code than from a transfer of object code. Therefore, the owner of the source code frequently will require greater protection of it than of object code and will probably be reluctant to permit its transfer to a foreign country if adequate protection for it is not available under the laws of such country.

A technology transfer may also involve an agreement for the sale, lease or license of computer software either in the form of object code, source code or both. Under the laws of some countries if such sale, lease or license is associated with the sale or lease of a computer (frequently referred to as hardware), there is a possibility that such sale, lease or license, while a technology transfer in essence, may not be considered to be subject to the technology transfer laws of the recipient country. Also, under the laws of some countries the argument might be made that if software is being sold or leased rather than licensed, such software will not be considered subject to those countries' stringent laws on technology transfer. Therefore, it is apparent that the laws of the particular recipient country should be carefully studied before transferring technology there.

It was mentioned earlier that a transfer of computer software frequently carries with it problems in addition to those extant in a transfer of other technology. This is due, at least in part, to the dual legal nature of computer software. Computer software may exist in the form of a proprietary trade secret.[27] As such it would be licensed (never "sold") for use with the express requirement that it be maintained in confidence. The normal considerations of fee, duration of secrecy, and the trade secret and other laws of the licensor's and the licensee's jurisdiction, which are present in the case of a transfer of other technology, will also apply to the transfer of software.

Even when being licensed as a trade secret, however, computer software can present some unique problems. As was mentioned earlier, the software might be used in the end product itself. In such a case any sale of a complete end product will provide a useless mechanism to the purchaser unless the manufacturing transferee is able to somehow transfer the necessary software to his using customer. Fortunately, the using customer does not normally need to obtain the highly valuable source code and a transfer of the machine readable object code is all that is required. In such a situation careful consideration must be given to the necessary terms and conditions to be placed not only in the agreement transferring software to the manufacturer but also in a separate agreement to be executed by his customer.

Computer software has another legal nature or form in which it may exist as a valuable proprietary asset. The software

---

[27] *See, e.g.,* University Computing Co. v. Lykes-Youngstown Corp., 504 F.2d 518 (5th Cir. 1974).

may be publicly known but it may be the subject of a valuable claim of copyright.[28] As such it may be possible to sell copies of the program and to license the recipient to make copies thereof for his customers. The law of copyrights as applied to computer software is not well-developed.[29] As a precautionary note one should carefully consider the developing law of the various jurisdictions involved. Also, careful attention must be paid to any information which is embodied in or discernible from the software to be copyrighted.

Recently, the law in the United States and elsewhere has evolved that a publication of a work such as a computer program is no longer necessary to secure a copyright.[30] Even where a publication is required to maintain or enforce a claim of copyright, there are decisions which suggest that a "publication" for such a purpose does not amount to such a publication as would destroy a claim of trade secret in the work.[31] Thus, there is an impressive body of opinion building, at least in the United States, that one may simultaneously enjoy both copyright and trade secret protection in the same work, such as a computer program.

Since it is not necessary in this country to "publish"[32] (in the sense of a public disclosure or any other sense) to initially secure a copyright in the computer software, it would appear desirable to consider placing a copyright notice on a computer program while contracting with the recipient to maintain it in confidence.[33]

---

[28] *Cf.* 17 U.S.C.A. § 101 (1982) ("literary works") with 17 U.S.C.A. § 102 (a) (1982).

[29] Milgrim, *Trade Secrets* (1978), § 2.06 A[5][c].

[30] 17 U.S.C.A. § 302(a) (1982).

[31] *Cf.* Nimmer, 1 *Nimmer on Copyright* § 4.13 [A] (1980) with Milgrim, *supra* N. 29 at § 2.06 A[2][b] n. 52; *see also* B. Niblett, *Legal Protection of Computer Programs,* at 41-59 (London 1980).

[32] *See* N. 43 *supra.*

[33] *Cf.* Milgram, N. 29 *supra* at § 2.06 A [2] [a] n. 47 and § 2.06 A [3] n. 73 with Ladd v. Oxnard, 75 Fed. 703 (D.C. Mass 1896).

[4] Joint Development Project

Not infrequently, a prospective recipient of a technology transfer may face technological requirements in his market which are quite different from those which the products of the technology owner must conform to. These requirements may amount to little more than a conversion from English to metric sizing, but all too often they are far more complex.[34] Different voltages, frequencies, signalling standards, and customer needs in a prospective recipient's market will often necessitate extensive changes in both the hardware and software of the end product. These changes will necessarily involve fundamental changes and new developments in the technical information, know-how and software to be transferred.

Obviously, developments in this area may lead to the making of inventions by one or more of the parties. Who will own these inventions? What rights will each of the parties have in information and inventions developed in such an undertaking? Will the parties jointly participate in such an undertaking and on what basis, or will one of the parties fund the other to do the work? Where will the development work be done? What happens if the development is unsuccessful? Is there a time period in which the work is to be completed or the project terminated? These possibilities should be provided for in the agreement.[35]

In view of the foregoing, the parties to a prospective technology transfer often find it necessary to enter into a joint development contract covering the above questions, and the terms and conditions of such an agreement must be meshed with those of the various other necessary agreements such as the Patent License Agreement, the Technical Information Agreement, etc.

---

[34] In the case of telecommunications equipment, for example, there may be differences in line frequencies, desired output functions, ringing current, voltage, etc.

[35] *See* §6.02, *infra.*

[5] Trademark License

Frequently the recipient of a technology transfer desires to capitalize on the goodwill and established name of the owner of the technology, and as an adjunct to other forms of technology transfer, requests a trademark license or user agreement.

A trademark is a word, symbol, or often a shorthand means used on an article or product of commerce to identify its source which may not be expressly designated. Trademarks are used publicly as marketing devices; they do not, strictly speaking, result in a transfer of technology.[36] But, since they are used on products manufactured pursuant to a technology transfer agreement, they are considered here.

First, it must be determined whether it would be advantageous to identify the product made pursuant to a technology transfer agreement with the trademark of the owner of the technology. For example, the trademark may be neutral or even repulsive in the recipient country. On the other hand, it may be well-known in the recipient country and its registration may enhance sales there. The mark may be a signal to a customer of the maintenance of known standards of quality.[37] Another important concern is whether the mark is protectable in the recipient country, and if so what steps are required to protect it? Must the mark be registered? Is a registered user agreement required? Must any special marking be used on the product or on other descriptive material?

Since a trademark identifies source, and since at least implicit with source is an indication of quality, some assurance of quality is normally required by law. Therefore, a trademark license agreement normally requires a specification for controlling the quality of the involved product along with quality assurance inspections pursuant to the specification. This specification and the inspections made pursuant to it often result in a transfer of technology.

As previously mentioned, the mark may be an indication to a customer of a quality standard. While this may be desirable

---

[36] *See Technology Transfer and the Developing Countries,* Chamber of Commerce of the U.S., April 1977, at 4.
[37] *Id.*

to the recipient in a technology transfer arrangement, it is not without its hazards to the transferor. For example, there is a growing body of product liability law which imposes liability on a trademark licensor[38] which arises from the duty to assure quality of the end product imposed on the licensor by the trademark law in the recipient's country. Therefore, a trademark licensor must satisfy himself that it is practical for him to control the quality standard of the licensee. He must be satisfied that the market in the country of the licensee will support the addition to the price of the product of not only fees based on any patent license, technical information license, and computer software license, but also fees based on the use of the trademark. These fees should compensate the licensor for the risks (*e.g.*, product liability) he is assuming as well as the costs he will encounter in assuring the quality of the licensee's end product.

[6] Joint Venture

Another way to internationally transfer technology is to establish an international joint venture. In the typical case, the owner of technology, who is also a manufacturer of certain products using that technology in his own country, enters into a legal relationship with a company of another country, the recipient country. Pursuant to the relationship, they establish a separate joint venture company in the recipient country to manufacture the same products using the technology. In this model, both the transferor of the technology and its recipient have an ownership interest in the joint venture company. Thus, the transfer is to a related party, contrasted with the other situations already noted where it is usually to an unrelated party.

Although ownership and management will be joint, a crucially important consideration, of course, is who will have the controlling interest in the joint venture company. The laws of

---

[38] *See, e.g.,* Connelly v. Uniroyal, Inc., et al, No. 50358, Supreme Court of Illinois, January 26th, 1979. Note also the cases referred to at 51 A.L.R. 3d 1344 (1973).

the recipient country must be consulted, for various countries have different requirements for local ownership.

Another consideration is what will the parties to the joint venture arrangement contribute? The owner of the technology might contribute his technology in the form of patent licenses, technical information, technical and management assistance, and the like. The recipient country party might contribute capital, labor, and similar items.

If the owner of the technology is a U.S. company, the U.S. tax laws must be carefully considered, for there may be serious tax consequences to the transfer of the technology. For example, if the U.S. owner of technology, as its capital contribution to the joint venture company, grants the joint venture company a license for a certain period, then such owner would be subject to the U.S. income tax on the present value of the royalties under the present interpretation of Section 367 of the IRS Code of 1954.[39] Hence, the effect would be to accelerate taxes, contrary to the usual desire to defer taxes.

Additionally, various United States laws might be of concern, including the premerger notification statute.[40] Significant problems may be faced because of existing obligations of a joint venture company if it is not a newly formed entity, but one previously in existence that is to be reorganized. It may be necessary to draft a joint venture or shareholders agreement, new articles of incorporation and one or more letters of intent.

Not infrequently, representations may have to be made to appropriate agencies of the recipient government which may have a binding effect between the parties. Indeed, in the final analysis, a complete legal audit of all commitments, assets and understandings of any existing entity and its key employees may ultimately prove necessary.

---

[39] *See, e.g.,* DuPont v. United States, 471 F.2d 1211 (Ct. Cl. 1973).
[40] *See* 15 U.S.C.A. § 18 (1982).

[7] Sale of Assemblies, Subassemblies, Components, and Parts

To make a transfer of technology efficacious, it is often not enough to merely transfer the technology in the form of patents and technical and other information useful in business. It is also necessary to sell the recipient of the technology assemblies, subassemblies, components and parts so that the recipient can manufacture products using the technology within a reasonable time. In addition, or as an alternative to such sale, the transferor of the technology may provide as part of the technical information, purchasing information including purchasing specifications and sources.

In some cases, the product to be manufactured with the technology may include one or more components such as highly sophisticated integrated circuits which the recipient is neither qualified to nor desires to manufacture. It may happen that the only source of such components is the owner of the technology. To further complicate the situation, assume that the owner may desire to protect the manufacturing information for such a component, not allowing the recipient to obtain such information for its own or its supplier's use. It may even be that the component embodies proprietary information not belonging to the owner of the balance of the technology and the owner is not free to pass such information to the recipient. Then, it may be necessary for the owner to sell the components themselves to the recipient or, in appropriate cases, to license its own supplier to sell such components to the recipient.

[8] Sale of Manufacturing Tools and Test Sets

To further enhance the technology transfer and help the recipient manufacture the products using the technology within a reasonable time, the transfer may also include the sale of manufacturing tools and test sets, and information concerning purchasing the same from third parties.

[9] Technical and Management Assistance

The technology transfer may also involve the owner's providing the recipient with technical and management assistance. This assistance may be performed in either the owner's country, the recipient's country, or both. Such assistance is another means of making the transfer more effective and helping the recipient manufacture products using the technology within a reasonable time.

The assistance may also include research, development, and engineering effort to adapt the technology to the recipient's country. Consideration must be given to how this will be paid for, the effect of tax laws on the return to the owner, and how the patent and proprietary information resulting from this effort will be divided between the parties. It is important to note that in addition to considerations of the amount of assistance, the duration of same, the fees for such assistance and the personnel to provide it, problems must be faced with respect to local laws, such as those relating to workers' compensation and the like.

[10] Training

As in the case of technical and management assistance, the training may take place in either or both the owner's or recipient's countries. This training is often an important part of the technology transfer and is another of many ways of making the transfer more effective. Similar considerations apply here as in the case of technical and management assistance with an added note of caution in both of these areas to consider the scope of any training or assistance as it may affect or effect any warranty obligations.

[11] Establishment of Manufacturing Facility

An international technology transfer may result from an owner company of one country establishing a manufacturing facility in another, the recipient country. If the facilities turned over to the recipient are to be complete and ready to manufacture products, they are often termed a "turnkey" operation. This type of transfer may be to a related party, such as a subsidiary or a joint-venture company, or an unrelated party such as a foreign company or government.

The manufacturing facility may be associated with a technology transfer agreement that includes other items necessary for production in the recipient country such as licenses of patents and technical and other business information. The manufacturing facility might also result from a direct investment in the recipient country. For example, the technology owner may desire to reduce custom's duty on products it exports to the recipient country and would be able to do this by manufacturing or assembling in the recipient country.[41]

§ 6.02 Model Agreements

[1] Patent License Agreement

The model Patent License Agreement reproduced as Appendix 6A at the end of this chapter typifies a broad bilateral exchange of patent licenses between a Licensor domiciled in the United States and a Licensee domiciled in the Commonwealth of Australia. This Agreement may in some cases stand alone as a technology transfer, in and of itself. In some cases an agreement such as this might accompany a Technology Transfer Agreement. It should be noted that the grant of licenses back to the Licensor are royalty-free and therefore an appropriate royalty rate to the Licensee should take this into consideration.

---

[41] *See generally* "Truck Plant," *Washington Post,* April 8, 1980, Business & Finance Section.

[2] Technology Transfer Agreement

This Agreement covers the transfer of technology in the form of proprietary information, software, technical assistance, and other services as well as sales of products. The Agreement reproduced as Appendix 6B at the end of this chapter is drawn for a United States domiciliary Licensor and a transferee domiciled in the Commonwealth of Australia. It is not contemplated that this Agreement would stand alone, and it is to be used with a Patent License Agreement such as the model which precedes it as Appendix 6A.

A detailed discussion of the individual clauses of the model Agreements is beyond the scope of this chapter and such clauses should be used as a guide in recognizing various problems and possible solutions.

Appendix 6A: Sample Patent License Agreement

PATENT LICENSE AGREEMENT

between

. . . .

and

. . . .

Effective as of . . . .

SAMPLE-070180-082180

PATENT LICENSE AGREEMENT

Effective only upon APPROVAL, and then as of . . . . ,
. . . . , a
. . . . corporation ("LICENSOR"), having an office at
. . . . , United States of America,
and . . . . ,
a corporation organized under the laws of . . . .
and having its registered office at . . . .
("LICENSEE"), agree as follows:

ARTICLE I

DEFINITIONS

1.01   Terms in this agreement (other than technical terms, names of parties, companies and Article headings) which are in capital letters shall have the meanings specified in the General Definitions Appendix, and technical terms in this agreement which are in capital letters shall have the meanings specified in the Technical Definitions Appendix.

ARTICLE II

GRANTS OF LICENSES AND IMMUNITIES

2.01   LICENSOR grants to LICENSEE under LICENSOR'S PATENTS nonexclusive licenses for products of the following kinds:

Combinations of any or all items specified separately above in this Section 2.01;

SAMPLE-070180-082180

2.02   LICENSEE grants to LICENSOR, under LICENSEE'S PATENTS, nonexclusive royalty-free licenses for products of the following kinds;

.

Combinations of any or all items specified separately above in this Section 2.02;

2.03   All licenses herein granted shall commence on the effective date hereof and, except as provided in Article VI and notwithstanding the expiration of the FIVE YEAR PERIOD, shall continue for the entire terms that the patents under which they are granted are in force or for that part of such terms for which the grantor has the right to grant such licenses.

2.04   The licenses granted for LICENSED PRODUCTS are licenses to make, have made, use, lease, sell and import such LICENSED PRODUCTS. Such licenses include the rights to maintain LICENSED PRODUCTS, to practice methods and processes involved in the use of LICENSED PRODUCTS and to make and have made, to use and have used, to import, and to maintain machines, tools, materials and other instrumentalities, and to use and have used methods and processes, insofar as such machines, tools, materials, other instrumentalities, methods and processes are involved in or incidental to the development, manufacture, installation, testing or repair of LICENSED PRODUCTS.

2.05   The grant of each license to either party hereto includes the right to grant sublicenses within the scope of such license to such parties' SUBSIDIARIES. Such right of either party may be exercised at any time prior to termination of the corresponding license under the provisions of Article VI. Any such sublicenses granted to any present SUBSIDIARY may be made effective, retroactively, as of the effective date hereof, and any such sublicenses granted to any future SUBSIDIARY may be made effective, retroactively, as of the date such company became a SUBSIDIARY.

2.06   Concerning a LICENSED PRODUCT (or maintenance part therefor) manufactured, used, leased, sold or imported for the services of the Australian Government in accordance with, and under authorization by the Commonwealth or a State pursuant to, the provisions of Sections 125 to 130, inclusive, of the Patent Acts, 1952-1976, of Australia, or any statutory modification or reenactment thereof, the term LICENSOR'S PATENTS shall be deemed not to include any patents issued in Australia unless (i) the payment of royalty on said LICENSED PRODUCT (or part) in accordance with this agreement is authorized by said Commonwealth or said State, or (ii) all the licenses granted in this agreement for said LICENSED PRODUCT are at a royalty rate of zero percent (0%). LICENSEE shall reasonably assist LICENSOR in connection with LICENSOR'S negotiations with said Commonwealth or said State pursuant to said Acts.

ARTICLE III

ACQUISITION AND WARRANTY

3.01 LICENSOR and LICENSEE shall each acquire rights to inventions made during the FIVE YEAR PERIOD which relate to the subject matter of licenses granted and are made, in the course of their employment, either solely or jointly with anyone, by its or its SUBSIDIARIES' employees who are employed to do research, development or other inventive work, such that each grantee shall, by virtue of this agreement, receive in respect of patents issued for such inventions, licenses and rights of the scope and upon the terms herein provided to be granted to such grantee.

3.02 LICENSOR and, except as may be stated in a letter from LICENSEE to LICENSOR referring to this agreement and delivered before or concurrently with the execution hereof by LICENSOR, LICENSEE each warrants that there are no commitments or restrictions which will limit the licenses and rights granted by it under patents issued at any time for inventions owned at any time during the FIVE YEAR PERIOD by it or any of its SUBSIDIARIES.

3.03 It is recognized that either party or any of its SUBSIDIARIES may have entered into or may hereafter enter into a contract with a national government to do development work financed by such government and may be required under such contract (either unconditionally or by reason of any action or inaction thereunder) to assign to such government its rights to grant, or may now or hereafter be restrained by such government from granting, licenses to others than its SUBSIDIARIES under patents for inventions arising out of such work or covered by such contract. The resulting inability of such party to grant the licenses purported to be granted by it under patents for such inventions shall not be considered to be a breach of this agreement, if

(i) such contract is for the benefit of such government's military or national defense establishment, the Department of Energy of the United States Government, the National Aeronautics and Space Administration of the United States Government, the Commonwealth Scientific Industrial Research Organization of the Australian Government or the Atomic Energy Commission of the Australian Government, or

(ii) in cases other than (i), such contract is with the United States Government or the Australian Government or any agency of and within either such Government, and any such requirement or restraint is pursuant to a statute or officially promulgated regulation of either such Government or agency applicable to such contract;

provided, however, that

(iii) such party (or, if a SUBSIDIARY thereof has entered into such contract, such SUBSIDIARY) shall exert its best efforts to enable such party to grant, or to cause to be granted by another, the licenses herein purported to be granted by it under such patents.

ARTICLE IV

ROYALTY

4.01   LICENSEE shall pay to LICENSOR royalty, at the applicable rate hereinafter specified, on each LICENSED PRODUCT, and maintenance part therefor, which is a ROYALTY-BEARING PRODUCT, and

(i)   which is sold, leased or put into use by LICENSEE or any of its SUBSIDIARIES while any license acquired hereunder by LICENSEE with respect to such ROYALTY-BEARING PRODUCT shall remain in force, or

(ii)   which is made by or for, or imported by, LICENSEE or any of its SUBSIDIARIES while any such license shall remain in force and is thereafter sold, leased or put into use by LICENSEE or any of its SUBSIDIARIES,

whether or not such SUBSIDIARIES are sublicensed pursuant to Section 2.05, such royalty rate to be applied, except as provided in Section 4.05, to the NET SELLING PRICE of such ROYALTY-BEARING PRODUCT if sold for a separate consideration payable wholly in money and in all other cases to the FAIR MARKET VALUE thereof. The royalty rates applicable to LICENSED PRODUCTS of the kinds specified in Section 2.01, and maintenance parts therefor, are as follows:

(iii) *LICENSED PRODUCTS*	*Applicable Royalty Rates (in %)*
Combinations of any or all items specified separately above in this Section 4.01	Weighted Average

The term "Weighted Average" means the royalty rate determined by dividing the sum of the royalties computed on the FAIR MARKET VALUES of those LICENSED PRODUCTS of a combination on which royalty rates are specified, treating such products as if they were subject to royalty at the rates specified therefor herein, by the aggregate of the FAIR MARKET VALUES of such products.

SAMPLE-070180-082180

4.02 (a) If a LICENSED PRODUCT is a ROYALTY-BEARING PRODUCT solely on account of one or a limited number of LICENSOR'S PATENTS issued in any one country, LICENSEE may elect to reduce the amount of royalty otherwise payable hereunder on said LICENSED PRODUCT by a royalty reduction percentage, and as of an effective date, established by LICENSOR. Upon written request from LICENSEE identifying the LICENSED PRODUCT and each relevant patent, LICENSOR will inform LICENSEE of the royalty reduction percentage applicable in respect of said LICENSED PRODUCT and patent or patents and the effective date thereof.

(b) If a LICENSED PRODUCT is a ROYALTY-BEARING PRODUCT on account of patents of more than one country, LICENSEE may elect to treat said LICENSED PRODUCT as being a ROYALTY-BEARING PRODUCT in each of such countries separately, calculate the royalty payable in respect of the patents of each such country by applying any royalty reduction afforded pursuant to Section 4.02(a) in respect of the applicable patents of such country and pay the sum of such royalties as one royalty under this agreement.

4.03 A LICENSED PRODUCT, or maintenance part therefor, which is made and sold by LICENSEE or any of its SUBSIDIARIES and which is a ROYALTY-BEARING PRODUCT hereunder on account of one or more of LICENSOR'S PATENTS, may be treated by LICENSEE as not licensed and not subject to royalty hereunder if all of the following conditions are met:

(i) the purchaser is licensed under the same patent or patents, pursuant to another agreement, to have said LICENSED PRODUCT or part made;

(ii) the purchaser expressly advises LICENSEE or its SUBSIDIARY, whichever effects the making and sale, in writing at or prior to (but in no event later than) the time of such sale that, in purchasing said LICENSED PRODUCT or part, it is exercising its own license or licenses under said patent or patents to have said LICENSED PRODUCT or part made; and

(iii) LICENSEE retains such written advice and makes it available to LICENSOR at the latter's request.

4.04 Only one royalty shall be payable hereunder in respect of any ROYALTY-BEARING PRODUCT. Royalty shall accrue hereunder on any LICENSED PRODUCT, or maintenance part therefor, upon its first becoming a ROYALTY-BEARING PRODUCT, and the royalty thereon shall become payable in accordance with the provisions of this Article IV upon the first sale, lease or putting into use thereof.

4.05 If any sale of a ROYALTY-BEARING PRODUCT shall be made by LICENSEE or a SUBSIDIARY thereof to an AFFILIATED COMPANY, royalty payable hereunder shall be computed on the FAIR MARKET VALUE of such ROYALTY-BEARING PRODUCT.

4.06 Concerning any LICENSED PRODUCT of the kinds specified in Section 2.01, or maintenance part therefor, which is sold in any country (whether or not for export to another country) by LICENSEE or any of its SUBSIDIARIES, no license or right is granted or agreed to be granted, expressly or impliedly, under LICENSOR'S PATENTS issued in any other country for the sale, lease, use or importation of said LICENSED PRODUCT or part unless LICENSEE has paid, or become obligated hereunder to pay, royalty on said LICENSED PRODUCT or part in an amount not lower than as prescribed in this agreement as applicable in respect of such sale of such LICENSED PRODUCT or part in the former country and a deemed simultaneous sale of such LICENSED PRODUCT or part made by the selling company in each such latter country, or unless such deemed sale would be royalty-free.

4.07 If any LICENSED PRODUCT of a kind specified in Section 2.01 is included in a larger LICENSED PRODUCT of a different kind specified in said Section 2.01, and such included LICENSED PRODUCT is a ROYALTY-BEARING PRODUCT on account of patents which are not otherwise applicable to the larger LICENSED PRODUCT, LICENSEE may elect to exercise its licenses for such included LICENSED PRODUCT and in so electing, report and pay royalty on the FAIR MARKET VALUE of such included LICENSED PRODUCT and disregard such patents in determining whether the larger LICENSED PRODUCT is a ROYALTY-BEARING PRODUCT; if such election is made, and if such larger LICENSED PRODUCT is a ROYALTY-BEARING PRODUCT otherwise than on account of such patents, LICENSEE may, in exercising its licenses for such larger LICENSED PRODUCT, disregard such patents in determining the amount of any royalty reductions available with respect to such larger LICENSED PRODUCT pursuant to Section 4.02. Any royalty payable on the larger LICENSED PRODUCT shall be based, nevertheless, on the NET SELLING PRICE or FAIR MARKET VALUE, as the case may be, of such larger LICENSED PRODUCT, including therein such included LICENSED PRODUCT, notwithstanding that a separate royalty will also be payable as aforesaid on such included LICENSED PRODUCT.

4.08 If LICENSEE or any of its SUBSIDIARIES shall make or have made for installation and use at a location any LICENSED PRODUCT which is a ROYALTY-BEARING PRODUCT hereunder by rebuilding, modifying or enlarging any product which has been installed and in use in such location, the completion of the work shall be deemed to be a sale of the LICENSED PRODUCT. If such product has theretofore been licensed under LICENSOR'S PATENTS, LICENSEE may elect to compute royalty on the NET SELLING PRICE or the FAIR MARKET VALUE, as the case may be, of such rebuilding, modification or enlargement (including costs of labor necessary thereto whether or not characterized as costs of installation), treating such rebuilding, modification or enlargement as a ROYALTY-BEARING PRODUCT having the same royalty rate as such LICENSED PRODUCT.

SAMPLE-070180-082180

ARTICLE V

REPORTS AND PAYMENTS

5.01 LICENSEE shall keep full, clear and accurate records on ROYALTY-BEARING PRODUCTS. LICENSOR shall have the right through its accredited auditing representatives to make an examination and audit, during normal business hours, not more frequently than annually, of all such records and such other records and accounts as may under recognized accounting practices contain information bearing upon the amount of royalty payable to it under this agreement. Prompt adjustment shall be made by the proper party to compensate for any errors or omissions disclosed by such examination or audit. Neither such right to examine and audit nor the right to receive such adjustment shall be affected by any statement to the contrary, appearing on checks or otherwise, unless such statement appears in a letter, signed by the party having such right and delivered to the other party, expressly waiving such right.

5.02 (a) Within sixty (60) days after the end of each semiannual period ending on June 30th or December 31st, commencing with the semiannual period during which this agreement first becomes effective, LICENSEE shall furnish to LICENSOR a statement, in form acceptable to LICENSOR, certified by a responsible official of LICENSEE:

(i) showing all ROYALTY-BEARING PRODUCTS, by kinds of LICENSED PRODUCTS, which were sold, leased or put into use during such semiannual period, the NET SELLING PRICES of such ROYALTY-BEARING PRODUCTS or (where royalty is based on FAIR MARKET VALUES) the FAIR MARKET VALUES thereof and the amount of royalty payable thereon (or if no such ROYALTY-BEARING PRODUCT has been so sold, leased or put into use, showing that fact);

(ii) identifying, if royalty is reduced under provisions of Section 4.02, each LICENSED PRODUCT by its type and the patent or patents involved in such royalty reduction;

(iii) showing, by purchasers and kinds of LICENSED PRODUCTS, the monetary totals of the sales, to each purchaser exercising its own "to have made" license or licenses, of LICENSED PRODUCTS and maintenance parts in transactions of the character described in Section 4.03;

(iv) identifying all transactions of the character described in Section 4.05;

(v) identifying, in the case of any election under the provisions of Section 4.07, the larger LICENSED PRODUCTS to which such election pertains, the ROYALTY-BEARING PRODUCTS included in such larger LICENSED PRODUCTS and the patents applicable to such included ROYALTY-BEARING PRODUCTS, and showing the quantities of such larger LICENSED PRODUCTS, the quantities and FAIR MARKET VALUES of such included ROYALTY-BEARING PRODUCTS, and the amounts of royalties payable with respect to such included ROYALTY-BEARING PRODUCTS; and

SAMPLE-070180-082180

(vi) identifying, if any tax of the character described in exception (ii) of Section 5.05 was withheld or deducted by LICENSEE, such tax and showing the amount withheld or deducted.

(b) Within such sixty (60) days LICENSEE shall, irrespective of its own business and accounting methods, pay to LICENSOR the royalties payable for such semiannual period.

(c) Notwithstanding the provisions of Section 7.04(a) (v), LICENSEE shall furnish whatever additional information LICENSOR may reasonably prescribe from time to time to enable LICENSOR to ascertain which LICENSED PRODUCTS (and maintenance parts therefor) sold, leased or put into use by LICENSEE or any of its SUBSIDIARIES are subject to the payment of royalty to LICENSOR, and the amount of royalty payable thereon.

5.03 Royalty payments provided for in this agreement shall, when overdue, be subject to a late payment charge calculated at an annual rate of one percent (1%) over the prime rate or successive prime rates in effect in New York City during delinquency; provided, however, that if the amount of such late payment charge exceeds the maximum permitted by law for such charge, such charge shall be reduced to such maximum amount.

5.04 Payment to LICENSOR shall be made in United States dollars to LICENSOR'S Treasury Organization at   ,
United States of America, or at such changed address as LICENSOR shall have specified by written notice. If any royalty for any semiannual period referred to in Section 5.02 is computed in other currency, conversion to United States dollars shall be at the prevailing rate for bank cable transfers on New York City as quoted for the last day of such semiannual period by leading banks dealing in the New York City foreign exchange market.

5.05 LICENSEE shall bear all taxes, however designated, imposed as a result of the existence or operation of this agreement, including, but not limited to, any tax on or measured by, any payment or receipt of payment hereunder, any registration tax, any tax imposed with respect to the granting or transfer of licenses or other rights or considerations hereunder, and any tax which LICENSEE is required to withhold or deduct from payments to LICENSOR, except (i) any such tax imposed upon LICENSOR by any governmental entity in the United States, and (ii) any such tax imposed upon LICENSOR in the country in which the aforesaid office of LICENSEE is located if such tax is allowable as a credit against United States income taxes of LICENSOR. To assist LICENSOR in obtaining such credit, LICENSEE shall furnish LICENSOR with such evidence as may be required by United States taxing authorities to establish that any such tax has been paid.

SAMPLE-070180-082180

ARTICLE VI

TERMINATION

6.01   Any termination under the provisions of this Article VI by one party of licenses and rights of the other party shall not affect the licenses and rights of the terminating party and its sublicensees, nor the obligations of LICENSEE under the provisions of Articles IV and V if it is the terminating party.

6.02   (a) If either party shall fail to fulfill one or more of its obligations under this agreement, the other party may, upon election and in addition to any other remedies that it may have, at any time terminate all licenses and rights granted to the party in breach hereunder, by not less than six (6) months' written notice to such party specifying any such breach, unless within the period of such notice all breaches specified therein shall have been remedied.

(b) Termination by LICENSOR of licenses and rights granted to LICENSEE shall terminate the obligations of LICENSEE under the provisions of Articles IV and V relating to such terminated licenses and rights, except such obligations as to ROYALTY-BEARING PRODUCTS made, sold, leased, put into use or imported prior to such termination.

6.03   (a) By written notice to LICENSOR, specifying any of LICENSOR'S PATENTS by country, number and date of issuance, LICENSEE may terminate all licenses and rights granted to it under, or under all of LICENSOR'S PATENTS except, such specified patent or patents or under any specified invention or inventions thereof. LICENSEE may also terminate all licenses and rights granted to it for any specified products under, or under all of LICENSOR'S PATENTS except, any such specified patent or patents or invention or inventions by designating in such notice any such specified products for which such termination shall be effective. Such termination shall be effective as of a date specified in said notice which shall not be more than six (6) months prior to the date of giving said notice. With respect to any licenses terminated by such notice, as of said effective date, such specified patent or patents or invention or inventions for which licenses have been terminated shall cease to be among, or among the inventions of, LICENSOR'S PATENTS for the purposes of this agreement without affecting obligations in respect of royalties accrued prior to said effective date.

(b) By written notice to LICENSOR, LICENSEE may reinstate any licenses terminated pursuant to Section 6.03(a). Such reinstated licenses shall be effective as of a date specified in said notice which shall not be more than six (6) months prior to the date of giving said notice and shall be at the royalty rates specified herein for such licenses.

SAMPLE-070180-082180

6.04 (a) Every sublicense granted by a party shall terminate with termination of its corresponding license.

(b) Any sublicenses granted shall terminate if and when the grantee thereof ceases to be a SUBSIDIARY of the grantor. Each LICENSED PRODUCT and each maintenance part, made by or for, or imported by, a SUBSIDIARY of LICENSEE, and on which royalty has accrued but which remains not sold, leased or put into use at the time such SUBSIDIARY ceases to be a SUBSIDIARY of LICENSEE, shall be deemed to have been put into use by such SUBSIDIARY immediately prior to such time at the place said LICENSED PRODUCT or part is then located.

6.05 Licenses and rights with respect to each LICENSED PRODUCT, and each maintenance part, made, sold, leased, put into use or imported prior to any termination under the provisions of this Article VI shall survive such termination.

ARTICLE VII

MISCELLANEOUS PROVISIONS

7.01 With respect to patents or inventions owned by LICENSEE, any of its SUBSIDIARIES, any of the employees of any of such companies, or any plurality of them, jointly with any other person or persons who has or have granted, or who shall hereafter grant, to LICENSOR, licenses or other rights thereunder, LICENSEE, to the extent that the licenses and rights so granted do not exceed the scope of the licenses and rights herein granted by LICENSEE, gives for itself, and, at LICENSOR'S request, will obtain from its SUBSIDIARIES and such employees, any consent required to make full and effective as to LICENSOR such licenses and rights granted by such other person or persons.

7.02 (a) Each party shall, upon written request from the other party sufficiently identifying any patent by country, number and date of issuance, inform the other party as to the extent to which any such patent is subject to the licenses and rights granted to such other party.

(b) If such licenses or rights under any such patent are restricted in scope, copies of all pertinent provisions of any contract (other than provisions of a contract with a government to the extent that disclosure thereof is prohibited under that government's laws or regulations) creating such restrictions shall, upon request, be furnished to the party making such request.

7.03 (a) Nothing contained in this agreement shall be construed as

(i)   requiring the filing of any patent application, the securing of any patent or the maintaining of any patent in force; or

(ii) a warranty or representation by any grantor as to the validity or scope of any patent; or

(iii) a warranty or representation that any manufacture, sale, lease, use or importation will be free from infringement of patents other than those under which and to the extent to which licenses are in force hereunder; or

(iv) an agreement to bring or prosecute actions or suits against third parties for infringement; or

(v)   an obligation to furnish any manufacturing or technical information or assistance; or

(vi) conferring any right to use, in advertising, publicity or otherwise, any name, trade name or trademark, or any contraction, abbreviation or simulation thereof; or

SAMPLE-070180-082180

(vii)   conferring by implication, estoppel or otherwise upon any grantee any license or other right under any patent, except the licenses and rights expressly granted to such grantee; or

(viii) an obligation upon any grantor to make any determination as to the applicability of any patent to any product of any grantee or any of its SUBSIDIARIES.

(b) Neither party makes any representations, extends any warranties of any kind or assumes any responsibility whatever with respect to the manufacture, sale, lease, use cr importation of any LICENSED PRODUCT, or part therefor, by any grantee, any of its SUBSIDIARIES, or any direct or indirect supplier or vendee or other transferee of any such company, other than the licenses, rights and warranties expressly herein granted.

7.04   There are countries in which the owner of an invention is entitled to compensation, damages or other monetary award from another for the latter's unlicensed manufacture, sale, lease, use or importation involving such invention prior to the date of issuance of a patent for such invention but on or after a certain earlier date, such earlier date being hereinafter referred to as the invention's "protection commencement date". For the purposes of this agreement, an invention which has a protection commencement date in any such country shall be deemed to have had a patent issued therefor in such country on such date, which patent shall be deemed to have been in force in such country on and from such protection commencement date until the date of issuance of an actual patent on the application filed in such country for a patent for such invention (whether or not other inventions are covered by such actual patent) or until such application has been withdrawn, abandoned or finally rejected. Provided, however, that the reporting and paying of any royalty, or any portion of royalty, which is attributable solely to such an invention before the issuance of an actual patent therefor, may be postponed until after, and if postponed shall be unnecessary unless, such actual patent issues; in the royalty statement for the semiannual period in which such actual patent issues, and within the time specified in Section 5.02 for reporting and paying royalties for such semiannual period, LICENSEE shall furnish the information required by said Section 5.02 to account for, and shall pay to LICENSOR, any deficiencies in royalties for prior semiannual periods attributable to such invention and the applicability of this Section 7.04.

7.05   Neither this agreement nor any licenses or rights hereunder, in whole or in part, shall be assignable or otherwise transferable.

7.06   Any notice, request, information or royalty statement shall be deemed to be sufficiently given when sent by registered mail addressed at its office above specified or at such changed address as the addressee shall have specified by written notice.

7.07 This agreement sets forth the entire agreement and understanding between the parties as to the subject matter hereof and merges all prior discussions between them, and neither of the parties shall be bound by any conditions, definitions, warranties, understandings or representations with respect to such subject matter other than as expressly provided herein, or in any prior existing written agreement between the parties, or as duly set forth on or subsequent to the effective date hereof in writing and signed by a proper and duly authorized representative of the party to be bound thereby.

7.08 The construction and performance of this agreement shall be governed by the law of the State of New York.

7.09 There are countries wherein it is necessary that certain agreements, by which licenses and rights are granted under patents issued in such countries, be registered. Accordingly, LICENSEE hereby agrees to register or cause to be registered, at its sole expense or at the expense of any of its SUBSIDIARIES, any such agreements wherein sublicenses or rights are granted by LICENSEE to any of its SUBSIDIARIES under LICENSOR'S PATENTS issued in such countries. LICENSEE hereby waives any and all claims or defenses, arising by virtue of the absence of such registration, that might otherwise limit or affect its royalty obligations to LICENSOR.

7.10 LICENSOR, for itself and for its present SUBSIDIARIES, hereby releases LICENSEE and its present SUBSIDIARIES and all purchasers and users of products (and maintenance parts therefor) of the kinds herein licensed as of the effective date hereof to LICENSEE, from all claims, demands and rights of action which LICENSOR or any of its present SUBSIDIARIES may have on account of any infringement or alleged infringement of any patent issued in any country of the world by reason of the manufacture or any past or future use, lease, sale or importation of any of such products or parts which, prior to the effective date hereof, were used or furnished by LICENSEE, its present SUBSIDIARIES or any of them.

7.11 LICENSEE, for itself and for its present SUBSIDIARIES, hereby releases LICENSOR and its present SUBSIDIARIES, and all purchasers and users of products (and maintenance parts therefor) of the kinds herein licensed as of the effective date hereof to LICENSOR, from all claims, demands and rights of action which LICENSEE or any of its present SUBSIDIARIES may have on account of any infringement or alleged infringement of any patent issued in any country of the world by reason of the manufacture or any past or future use, lease, sale or importation of any of such products or parts which, prior to the effective date hereof, were manufactured by or for, or used, furnished or imported by, LICENSOR, its present SUBSIDIARIES or any of them.

SAMPLE-070180-082180

IN WITNESS WHEREOF, each of the parties has caused this agreement to be executed in duplicate originals by its duly authorized representatives on the respective dates entered below.

By . . . .

Attest:

[SEAL]

. . . .
    Secretary

. . . .
    Date

The Common Seal of

. . . .

was hereunto affixed
in the presence of:

. . . .

                    Directors   [SEAL]

. . . .

. . . . Secretary

. . . . Date

GENERAL DEFINITIONS APPENDIX

AFFILIATED COMPANY means, with respect to a sale, lease or putting into use of a product,

(i) any company of which LICENSEE is a SUBSIDIARY at the time of such sale, lease or putting into use, or

(ii) LICENSEE or a SUBSIDIARY thereof or any other SUBSIDIARY of a company of which LICENSEE is a SUBSIDIARY at the time of such sale, lease or putting into use.

APPROVAL means the granting by the Australian Reserve Bank of all necessary approvals, authorizations and clearances for all agreements between LICENSOR and LICENSEE stated to have an effective date of   and all agreements which refer to such agreements.

FAIR MARKET VALUE means the NET SELLING PRICE which LICENSEE or any of its SUBSIDIARIES, whichever effects the sale, lease, or use of the product, maintenance part, component or material, would realize from an unaffiliated buyer in an arm's length sale of an identical product, maintenance part, component or material in the same quantity and at the same time and place as such sale, lease or use.

FIVE YEAR PERIOD means the period commencing on the effective date of this agreement and having a duration of five years.

LICENSED PRODUCT means, as to any respective grantee,

(i) any product as such, or

(ii) any product which is any specified combination,

of the kinds listed in Section 2.01 or 2.02 of this agreement. Although the term does not mean, and although licenses are not granted for, any other combination, a LICENSED PRODUCT

(iii) shall not lose its status as such on account of, and

(iv) shall not cause an unlicensed combination to infringe the grantor's patents (i.e., LICENSOR'S PATENTS or LICENSEE'S PATENTS, as the case may be) solely on account of,

such LICENSED PRODUCT being made, sold, leased, put into use or imported as part of an unlicensed combination.

SAMPLE-070180-082180

LICENSEE'S PATENTS means all patents (including utility models) issued at any time in any or all countries of the world for

(i)   inventions made prior to the termination of the FIVE YEAR PERIOD and owned or controlled at any time during the FIVE YEAR PERIOD by LICENSEE or any of its SUBSIDIARIES,

(ii) inventions made during the FIVE YEAR PERIOD, solely or jointly with anyone, and in the course of their employment by employees of any such company who are employed to do research, development or other inventive work, and

(iii) any other inventions made prior to the termination of the FIVE YEAR PERIOD, with respect to which and to the extent to which any such company shall at any time during the FIVE YEAR PERIOD have the right to grant the licenses and rights which are herein granted by LICENSEE.

LICENSOR'S PATENTS means all patents (including utility models) issued at any time in any or all countries of the world for

(i)   inventions made prior to the termination of the FIVE YEAR PERIOD and owned or controlled at any time during the FIVE YEAR PERIOD by LICENSOR or any of its SUBSIDIARIES,

(ii) inventions made during the FIVE YEAR PERIOD, solely or jointly with anyone, and in the course of their employment by employees of any such company who are employed to do research, development or other inventive work, and

(iii) any other inventions made prior to the termination of the FIVE YEAR PERIOD, with respect to which and to the extent to which any such company shall at any time during the FIVE YEAR PERIOD have the right to grant the licenses and rights which are herein granted by LICENSOR.

NET SELLING PRICE means the gross selling price of the ROYALTY-BEARING PRODUCT in the form in which it is sold, whether or not assembled (and without excluding therefrom any components or subassemblies thereof, whatever their origin and whether or not patent impacted), less the following items but only insofar as they pertain to the sale of such ROYALTY-BEARING PRODUCT by LICENSEE or any of its SUBSIDIARIES and are included in such gross selling price:

(i)   usual trade discounts actually allowed (other than cash discounts, advertising allowances, or fees or commissions to any employees of any AFFILIATED'COMPANY);

(ii) packing costs;

(iii)   import, export, excise and sales taxes, and customs duties;

(iv)   costs of insurance and transportation from the place of manufacture to the customer's premises or point of installation;

(v)   costs of installation at the place of use;

(vi)   costs of special engineering services not incident to the design or manufacture of the ROYALTY-BEARING PRODUCT; and

(vii)   costs of any product of the following kinds unless it includes, or its manufacture or use employs, any invention of any of LICENSOR'S PATENTS in force at the time and in the country of the manufacture, sale, lease or use of the ROYALTY-BEARING PRODUCT, or unless it upon importation includes, or its manufacture prior to such importation has employed, any invention of any of LICENSOR'S PATENTS in force in the country of such importation at the time of such importation or of any subsequent sale, lease or putting into use of such ROYALTY-BEARING PRODUCT in such country if the law of such country entitles LICENSOR to compensation for such importation, sale, lease or putting into use (in all cases other than patents or inventions excluded from the ROYALTY-BEARING PRODUCT definition with respect to the sold ROYALTY-BEARING PRODUCT):

ROYALTY-BEARING PRODUCT means any LICENSED PRODUCT of the kinds specified in Section 2.01 of this agreement (other than any LICENSED PRODUCT for which all the licenses granted in this agreement are at a royalty rate of zero percent (0"ₙ)), and any maintenance part therefor,

(i)   which upon manufacture includes, or the manufacture of which employs, any invention of any of LICENSOR'S PATENTS in force at the time and in the country of such manufacture, or

(ii)   which upon importation includes, or the manufacture of which prior to such importation has employed, any invention of any of LICENSOR'S PATENTS in force in the country of such importation at the time of such importation or of any subsequent sale, lease or putting into use of such LICENSED PRODUCT or part in such country if the law of such country entitles LICENSOR to compensation for such importation, sale, lease or putting into use, or

(iii)   which includes when sold, leased or put into use, or the use of which employs, any invention of any of LICENSOR'S PATENTS in force at the time and in the country of such sale, lease or use,

SUBSIDIARY means a company the majority of whose stock entitled to vote for election of directors is now or hereafter controlled by the parent company either directly or indirectly, but any such company shall be deemed to be a SUBSIDIARY only so long as such control exists.

SAMPLE-070180-082180

TECHNICAL DEFINITIONS APPENDIX

Appendix 6B: Sample Technology Transfer Agreement

TECHNOLOGY TRANSFER AGREEMENT

(To accompany a separate Patent License Agreement)

between

. . . .

and

. . . .

Effective as of. . . . .

TTA SAMPLE-070280

TECHNOLOGY TRANSFER AGREEMENT

AGREEMENT, effective only upon APPROVAL, and then as of . . . . ,
between . . . . ,
("LICENSOR"), having an office at . . . . ,
. . . . ,
United States of America, and . . . .
. . . .
("LICENSEE"), a corporation organized under the laws of . . . . ,
Australia, and having its registered office at . . . . ,
Australia.

DEFINITIONS

As used in this agreement, the term "patent" includes in its meaning any instrument in respect of which rights are granted by a government to an applicant in consideration of disclosure thereby of an invention. Other terms in this agreement appearing hereinafter (other than names of parties, Article and Chapter headings) which are in capital letters shall have the meanings specified in the Definitions Appendix.

CHAPTER I

RESEARCH AND DEVELOPMENT PROJECT

ARTICLE I-1

PROJECT DESCRIPTION AND TERM

I-1.01 LICENSOR shall undertake hereunder a Research and Development Project, and, in furtherance thereof, shall, as specified in Section I-3.01, exchange certain existing technical information with LICENSEE in the field of   to develop products (and further technical information and software therefor) which are intended to satisfactorily meet LICENSEE'S technical performance specifications and commercial goals.

I-1.02 (a) It is anticipated that such Project will culminate, within the term of this Chapter I, in the development of certain   (and further technical information and software therefor) in the form of EQUIPMENTS having features presently identified by LICENSOR as   , but which equipments have been modified to be certifiable by the Australian Governmental Commission for use in Australia.

(b) LICENSEE agrees to use its best efforts to secure promptly TYPE CERTIFICATION for such   EQUIPMENTS so developed.

I-1.03 The provisions of this Chapter I respecting this Research and Development Project shall continue in force for a term of   years from the effective date hereof, except as otherwise provided herein.

ARTICLE I-2

PROJECT SUPPORT

I-2.01 LICENSEE will, upon APPROVAL, forthwith make a payment to LICENSOR in the sum of   United States dollars ($ U.S.) in support of the Project.

TTA SAMPLE-070280-082180

I-2.02 Support for the Project in excess of that provided by LICENSEE pursuant to Section I-2.01 will be furnished by LICENSOR, in the form of personnel, facilities, materiel and other items, at such times and in such manner as LICENSOR in its sole judgment deems appropriate, provided, however, that the value of such support provided by LICENSOR (as determined solely by LICENSOR) shall not exceed the sum of   United States dollars ($ U.S.).

I-2.03 Nothing in, or done under, this Chapter I shall confer upon LICENSEE any right, title or interest in anything other than certain information and software, developed or acquired in the course of the Research and Development Project.

ARTICLE I-3

PROJECT INFORMATION

I-3.01 For purposes of advancing the Project, LICENSOR and LICENSEE shall disclose to each other such of their respective information, including that on inventions, relative to the field of   ,
and available prior to the undertaking hereunder of the Project, as the disclosing party in its sole discretion believes will be useful in furtherance of the Project and which it has the right to disclose.

I-3.02 Section II-2.01 sets forth terms and conditions relating to the use and communication of DEVELOPMENT INFORMATION furnished for or developed in the course of the Project.

I-3.03 Any information which may be disclosed to personnel of LICENSEE by LICENSOR'S personnel in the course of their performance under this Chapter I shall remain the property of LICENSOR and shall be deemed to be DEVELOPMENT INFORMATION furnished to LICENSEE.

ARTICLE I-4

FILING PATENT APPLICATIONS

I-4.01 (a) Neither LICENSEE nor LICENSOR shall be required under this agreement to file any patent application or to secure any patent or to maintain any patent in force.

(b) The following provisions of this Article I-4 shall be effective with respect to any inventions made by one or more of LICENSEE'S employees or agents jointly with one or more of LICENSOR'S employees or agents during the period of said Research and Development Project.

(i)   In the case of any such invention, LICENSOR shall promptly notify LICENSEE whether or not LICENSOR elects to file a patent application thereon in the United States.

(ii)   LICENSEE shall have the right to file a patent application in the United States claiming such invention in cases in which LICENSOR does not elect to file pursuant to subdivision (i) of this Section I-4.01(b).

(iii)   The party which elects to file a patent application on such invention in the United States shall have the first right of election to file a corresponding patent application in each foreign country or, where applicable, community of countries. Such party shall notify the other party of those foreign countries, if any, in which it elects to file such patent applications. The other party shall have the right to file patent applications on such invention in all other foreign countries.

(iv)   The expenses for preparing, filing and prosecuting each application, and for issue of the respective patent, shall be borne by the party which prepares and files the application. The other party shall furnish, at its sole expense, the filing party with all documents, information or other assistance, that may be necessary for the preparation, filing and prosecution of each such application.

(v)   In the case of an application for patent which is filed in a foreign country which requires the payment of taxes or annuities on a pending application or on an issued patent, the party which files the application may pay such taxes or annuities, and in the event such party does not wish to pay any particular tax or annuity such party shall so notify the non-filing party, in writing, at least two (2) months before the due date for payment of such tax or annuity, and the non-filing party may pay such tax or annuity. The failure of the filing party to pay any such tax or annuity shall not affect such party's rights in such application or patent under this agreement.

(vi)   The parties shall each have an equal title interest in each application and patent for such an invention, with LICENSEE holding an undivided one-half (1/2) interest and LICENSOR holding an undivided one-half (1/2) interest.

(vii)   LICENSOR and LICENSEE shall each have the right individually to grant nonexclusive licenses (including the right to sublicense) under applications and patents covering such inventions, each party hereby consenting to the grant of such licenses by the other party, and each party shall retain all royalties that it receives for such licenses, without accounting therefor to the other party.

TTA SAMPLE-070280-082180

(viii) Any patent covering any such invention shall be disregarded in respect of such invention for purposes of computing any royalty payable by LICENSEE under the Patent License Agreement stated to become effective only upon APPROVAL, and then as of   , hereinafter the "Patent License Agreement", relating to and various other products.

ARTICLE I-5

EMPLOYEES

I-5.01 LICENSEE represents that with respect to each of its employees and agents who is or may be engaged in work under the Project, it will use its best efforts to obtain (1) assignment to LICENSEE, or its nominee or nominees, without expense to LICENSOR, of all inventions made by such employee or agent during the course of his employment or association with LICENSEE, and (2) execution, acknowledgment and delivery of all papers, including applications for patents, that may be necessary to obtain patents for said inventions in any and all countries and to vest title thereto in LICENSEE.

CHAPTER II

MANUFACTURING AND IMPLEMENTATION INFORMATION

ARTICLE II-1

FURNISHING OF MANUFACTURING AND IMPLEMENTATION INFORMATION

II-1.01 Within   weeks after APPROVAL and receipt of written request from LICENSEE, LICENSOR will commence furnishing MANUFACTURING and IMPLEMENTATION INFORMATION to LICENSEE.

II-1.02 With the delivery of any of the MANUFACTURING and IMPLEMENTATION INFORMATION, LICENSOR shall also furnish to LICENSEE a list which completely identifies the MANUFACTURING and IMPLEMENTATION INFORMATION so being delivered. LICENSOR and LICENSEE shall promptly notify each other of any inaccuracies in the list. Each such list shall be deemed to be a part of the definition of MANUFACTURING and IMPLEMENTATION INFORMATION with the following qualification: If, within thirty (30) days after receipt of any such list, LICENSEE shall give LICENSOR written notice specifying particular information and software identified therein which was not actually received, the mention of such specified information and software shall be deemed deleted from such list until such information and software is actually received by LICENSEE.

II-1.03 During the   year period subsequent to   , LICENSOR shall notify LICENSEE of any revisions, deemed significant by LICENSOR, to the MANUFACTURING and IMPLEMENTATION INFORMATION previously furnished and, at LICENSEE'S request, furnish all such revisions so requested to LICENSEE for an appropriate payment and within a reasonable time after such payment. All such revisions so furnished shall be deemed to be part of the MANUFACTURING and IMPLEMENTATION INFORMATION.

ARTICLE II-2

GRANTS OF RIGHTS TO USE MANUFACTURING, DEVELOPMENT, AND IMPLEMENTATION INFORMATION

II-2.01 (a) LICENSOR grants to LICENSEE for itself and its SUBSIDIARIES a personal, nontransferable and nonexclusive right to use: (i) in Australia and New Zealand the MANUFACTURING INFORMATION and DEVELOPMENT INFORMATION, solely for the manufacture in such countries in factories of LICENSEE or its SUBSIDIARIES of   ; and (ii) throughout the world the IMPLEMENTATION INFORMATION solely in connection with the installation, operation, maintenance and repair of LICENSED PRODUCTS manufactured under this agreement with the use of the MANUFACTURING INFORMATION or furnished by LICENSOR.

(b) The aforesaid personal, nontransferable and nonexclusive right includes the right to: (i) communicate portions of the MANUFACTURING INFORMATION and DEVELOPMENT INFORMATION (hereinafter referred to as "procurement information") to suppliers in the United States of America, Australia, New Zealand and any other countries as may be hereafter requested by LICENSEE and approved in writing by LICENSOR, solely for the procurement by LICENSEE or its SUBSIDIARIES of materials, manufacturing facilities, parts and components, described in such procurement information, for use in the manufacture of   ; and (ii) communicate to customers or, where necessary, to the appropriate governmental authority (subject to the provisions of Sections V-1.04 and V-6.01 hereof) four copies of the appropriate IMPLEMENTATION INFORMATION with each LICENSED PRODUCT manufactured by LICENSEE hereunder or furnished to LICENSEE by LICENSOR, and which is furnished by LICENSEE to such customers.

ARTICLE II-3

FEES

II-3.01   LICENSEE shall forthwith pay to LICENSOR, upon APPROVAL: (a) the sum of   United States dollars ($ U.S.) for the cost of LICENSOR'S services in gathering and reproducing any MANUFACTURING and IMPLEMENTATION INFORMATION to be furnished to LICENSEE pursuant to Section II-1.01.

II-3.02   LICENSEE shall pay to LICENSOR, a fee, at the rate of percent (%), on each article of a kind hereinafter specified in this Section II-3.02, and on each maintenance part therefor, which is an ITEM SUBJECT TO FEE and which is sold, leased or put into use prior to two years after the expiration of the BASE PERIOD therefor, such fee rate to be applied, except as provided in Section II-3.04, to the NET SELLING PRICE of such ITEM SUBJECT TO FEE if sold for a separate consideration payable wholly in money and in all other cases to the FAIR MARKET VALUE thereof. The aforementioned kinds of articles are as follows:

Articles

CLASS (1)   EQUIPMENTS made in Australia.

CLASS (2)   EQUIPMENTS made in New Zealand.

CLASS (3) Other
    made in Australia.

CLASS (4) Other
    made in New Zealand.

II-3.03   Only one fee shall be payable hereunder in respect of any ITEM SUBJECT TO FEE. Such fee shall become payable in accordance with the provisions of this Article II-3 upon the first sale, lease or putting into use of such ITEM SUBJECT TO FEE.

TTA SAMPLE-070280-082180

II-3.04   If any sale of an ITEM SUBJECT TO FEE shall be made by LICENSEE or a SUBSIDIARY thereof to

(i)   any company of which LICENSEE is a SUBSIDIARY at the time of such sale, or

(ii)   LICENSEE or a SUBSIDIARY thereof or any other SUBSIDIARY of a company of which LICENSEE is a SUBSIDIARY at the time of such sale,

the fee payable hereunder on such ITEM SUBJECT TO FEE shall be computed on the FAIR MARKET VALUE thereof.

ARTICLE II-4

REPORTS AND PAYMENTS

II-4.01   LICENSEE shall keep full, clear and accurate records with respect to ITEMS SUBJECT TO FEE. LICENSOR shall have the right through its accredited auditing representatives to make an examination and audit, during normal business hours, not more frequently than annually, of all such records and such other records and accounts as may under recognized accounting practices contain information bearing upon the amounts of fees payable to it under this agreement. Prompt adjustment shall be made by the proper party to compensate for any errors or omissions disclosed by such examination or audit. Neither such right to examine and audit nor the right to receive such adjustment shall be affected by any statement to the contrary, appearing on checks or otherwise, unless such statement appears in a letter, signed by the party having such right and delivered to the other party, expressly waiving such right.

TTA SAMPLE-070280-082180

II-4.02 Within sixty (60) days after the end of each semiannual period ending on June 30th or December 31st, commencing with the semiannual period during which this agreement first becomes effective, LICENSEE shall furnish to LICENSOR a statement, in form acceptable to LICENSOR, certified by a responsible official of LICENSEE, showing all ITEMS SUBJECT TO FEE, which were sold, leased or put into use during such semiannual period, the NET SELLING PRICES of such ITEMS SUBJECT TO FEE or (where fees are based on FAIR MARKET VALUES) the FAIR MARKET VALUES thereof and the amounts of fees payable thereon. If no such ITEM SUBJECT TO FEE has been so sold, leased or put into use, that fact shall be shown on such statement. Each such statement shall also identify transactions of the character described in Section II-3.04. If any tax of the character described in exception (ii) of Section V-8.01 was withheld or deducted by LICENSEE, each such statement shall identify such tax and shall show the amount withheld or deducted. Within such sixty (60) days LICENSEE shall, irrespective of its own business and accounting methods, pay to LICENSOR the fees payable for such semiannual period. LICENSEE shall furnish whatever additional information LICENSOR may reasonably prescribe from time to time to enable LICENSOR to ascertain which articles (and maintenance parts therefor) sold, leased or put into use by LICENSEE or any of its SUBSIDIARIES are subject to the payment of fees to LICENSOR, and the amounts of fees payable thereon.

ARTICLE II-5

TERMINATION

II-5.01 If LICENSEE shall fail to fulfill one or more of its obligations under this Chapter II, LICENSOR may, upon election and in addition to any other remedies that it may have, at any time terminate all the rights granted by it pursuant to said Chapter II by not less than two (2) months' written notice to LICENSEE specifying any such breach, unless within the period of such notice all grounds specified therein for termination pursuant to this Section II-5.01 shall have been remedied. In addition, if any of the provisions of this Chapter II shall be rendered unenforceable pursuant to any change to the applicable law of any country in which manufacture is authorized hereunder, LICENSOR may, upon election and in addition to any other remedies that it may have, immediately terminate all the rights granted by it under this Chapter II by written notice to LICENSEE of such termination.

II-5.02 In the event that all of the MANUFACTURING INFORMATION becomes generally known to the public through acts not attributable to LICENSEE or any of its SUBSIDIARIES, LICENSEE may, upon written notice to LICENSOR, terminate all rights to use MANUFACTURING INFORMATION granted pursuant to this Chapter II. Such termination shall be effective as of the date of giving such notice but shall not relieve LICENSEE of its obligation to pay any fee with respect to any ITEM SUBJECT TO FEE manufactured prior to such date, whether or not any such ITEM SUBJECT TO FEE is first sold, leased or put into use prior to or subsequent to such date.

TTA SAMPLE-070280-082180

CHAPTER III

TECHNICAL ASSISTANCE

ARTICLE III-1

SERVICES TO BE PROVIDED

III-1.01 LICENSOR shall furnish to LICENSEE at LICENSEE'S request the services of personnel of LICENSOR or its agents, hereinafter in this Chapter III referred to as LICENSOR'S personnel, to give technical assistance and information for the start-up of a manufacturing facility for certain
. Such facility shall be constructed and said certain
shall be manufactured by LICENSEE with the use of information furnished to LICENSEE under Chapters I and II hereof and the use of which is authorized hereunder. It will be LICENSEE'S responsibility to provide LICENSOR'S personnel with suitable working quarters and adequate clerical and other assistance in order to facilitate the performance of their services.

III-1.02 Such services shall be available to LICENSEE at reasonable times and for reasonable intervals agreeable to LICENSOR during a   year period commencing on the effective date of this agreement.

III-1.03 Unless otherwise agreed to in writing by LICENSOR, the total of services to be provided by LICENSOR'S personnel hereunder, exclusive of travel time, shall not exceed   man-days, based on an eight (8) hour workday schedule.

III-1.04 Such services normally shall be furnished at one or more locations of LICENSEE designated by LICENSEE and will involve consultation between LICENSOR'S personnel and LICENSEE'S personnel either by telephone or by visits by LICENSOR'S personnel to such location(s). At the sole discretion of LICENSOR, such services may also be furnished at one or more locations designated by LICENSOR and involve one or more visits of LICENSEE'S personnel to such location(s).

III-1.05 LICENSOR shall (without charge and in addition to the provisions of Section III-1.03) provide training, relating to   , at LICENSOR'S plant to personnel of LICENSEE at LICENSEE'S request.

III-1.06 Such training shall be available to LICENSEE at reasonable times, and for reasonable intervals, agreeable to LICENSOR, during the   year period commencing on the effective date of this agreement.

III-1.07 LICENSEE'S personnel to be trained shall be limited to no more than   persons at any one time and their cumulative training shall not exceed   man-days in each   year of the   year period, based on the normal workday schedule at said plant.

III-1.08 Promptly after APPROVAL, LICENSOR and LICENSEE shall each appoint an employee to administer activities and performance under this Chapter III and will notify each other of the name, address and telephone number of such employee. All requests for services under this Chapter III and arrangements for providing services will be coordinated by such appointed employees.

III-1.09 LICENSOR and LICENSEE shall at all times retain the administrative supervision of their respective personnel.

ARTICLE III-2

PAYMENT

III-2.01 LICENSEE shall pay to LICENSOR for the work performed pursuant to Section III-1.01, including travel time outside of the Continental United States, by each of LICENSOR'S personnel, of the level of Senior Engineer, providing services hereunder the sum of   United States dollars ($ U.S.) for each day or fraction thereof worked in the year   .

Rates for other levels of LICENSOR'S personnel and for later years will be set by agreement of LICENSOR and LICENSEE.

III-2.02 LICENSEE shall also reimburse LICENSOR for actual expenditures for travel, living and other expenses incurred by LICENSOR'S personnel performing services under this Chapter III.

III-2.03 LICENSOR shall render to LICENSEE invoices for all payments to be made under this Chapter III, and LICENSEE shall make payment of all amounts so billed within thirty (30) days after date of invoice.

ARTICLE III-3

INFORMATION

III-3.01 Any information which may be disclosed to personnel of LICENSEE by LICENSOR'S personnel in the course of their performance under this Chapter III shall be deemed to be ASSISTANCE INFORMATION furnished to LICENSEE.

ARTICLE III-4

TERMINATION

III-4.01 All of LICENSOR'S obligations under this Chapter III shall terminate effective with any termination of the rights of LICENSEE pursuant to Chapter II of this agreement without affecting any of LICENSEE'S obligations under any other Chapter.

TTA SAMPLE-070280

CHAPTER IV

FURNISHING ITEMS

ARTICLE IV-1

ORDERS

IV-1.01   LICENSEE may by letter, telex or other means, request of LICENSOR a proposal providing specific information regarding ITEMS which LICENSEE is interested in obtaining, and, also, a quotation with regard thereto. Each request for a proposal shall specify: (1) quantity and type of ITEM; (2) requested delivery schedule; (3) packaging and marking requirements; (4) method of shipment; (5) place of delivery and acceptance; (6) reference to this Chapter IV; and (7) any other information necessary to prepare the proposal.

IV-1.02 LICENSOR shall, at its sole discretion, and after each such request by LICENSEE, furnish, through its DULY AUTHORIZED REPRESENTATIVE, a written proposal providing specific information regarding ITEMS which LICENSEE is interested in obtaining. Such proposal shall include: (1) unit and total price or fee for use for ITEMS; (2) delivery schedule; (3) duration of the proposal; (4) terms and conditions regarding dissemination and use of ITEMS; and (5) any other information, requested by LICENSEE and deemed essential to the proposal by LICENSOR. Orders placed pursuant to a proposal are termed "proposal orders." Issuance, through its DULY AUTHORIZED REPRESENTATIVE, of a proposal order by LICENSEE and receipt by LICENSEE of written notification of acceptance of the proposal order by LICENSOR shall create a binding agreement for furnishing the ITEMS specified therein.

IV-1.03 Orders not placed pursuant to a proposal are termed "unilateral orders." Unilateral orders may be issued by LICENSEE and each such order shall constitute a binding agreement when there is receipt by LICENSEE of written notification of acceptance by LICENSOR through LICENSOR'S DULY AUTHORIZED REPRESENTATIVE. LICENSOR reserves the right to reject any unilateral order for any reason. Unilateral orders issued shall be in writing, serially numbered, dated and signed by a DULY AUTHORIZED REPRESENTATIVE of LICENSEE. They shall set forth the ITEMS, quantities to be furnished, delivery schedule, packaging and marking requirements, and shipping instructions.

IV-1.04   LICENSEE and LICENSOR shall each designate to the other one or more DULY AUTHORIZED REPRESENTATIVES.

ARTICLE IV-2

PAYMENT

IV-2.01   On proposal orders, the prices and use fees paid by LICENSEE for ITEMS shall be those prices and use fees set forth in the proposal under which such order is being placed. On unilateral orders, the prices and use fees to be paid by LICENSEE for ITEMS shall be those established by LICENSOR from time to time. LICENSOR shall exercise reasonable efforts to provide LICENSEE with thirty (30) days advance notice of changes in prices and use fees for ITEMS.

IV-2.02   Sales prices, use and other fees are quoted pursuant to this Chapter IV in United States dollars and invoices shall be payable in United States currency. For each order in which payment due is   United States dollars ($ U.S.) or more, LICENSEE shall open an irrevocable documentary letter of credit ("credit") in the form attached hereto as Exhibit B. The letter of credit shall be issued or confirmed by a Domestic United States bank acceptable to LICENSOR and shall be made payable at:

Bank:
Address:

Cable: Telex:

naming LICENSOR as beneficiary. Each credit shall be issued within fifteen (15) days after the receipt by LICENSEE of written notification of LICENSOR'S acceptance of the order. Each credit shall have a validity extending thirty (30) days beyond the anticipated final shipping date and shall, if necessary, be extended at the written request of LICENSOR, and shall be payable at sight against presentation of shipping documents in the amount of one hundred percent (100",,) of the value of any shipment as specified in the invoice therefor. The documentary letter of credit shall provide that: (a) partial shipments are permitted; and (b) transshipments are permitted. It is understood that all charges associated with the letter of credit shall be paid by LICENSEE.

Sales prices, use and other fees per order of less than   United States dollars ($ U.S.), shall be payable cash against documents.

TTA SAMPLE-070280-082180

ARTICLE IV-3

MISCELLANEOUS

IV-3.01   If there is any conflict between the provisions of this Chapter IV and any order issued pursuant to the provisions of this Chapter IV, the provisions of this Chapter IV shall control. If there is any conflict between the provisions of this Chapter IV and the provisions of any Exhibit to it, the provisions of this Chapter IV shall control. If there is any conflict between or among the provisions of the Exhibits, the provisions of the Exhibits of the latest date shall control.

IV-3.02   LICENSOR warrants ITEMS manufactured by LICENSOR and furnished by LICENSOR hereunder to be free from defects in design, workmanship and material and to be fit for the purposes for which designed. With respect to ITEMS not manufactured by LICENSOR and so furnished, LICENSOR extends the warranties and affords the remedies to LICENSEE given to LICENSOR by its vendor of said ITEMS to the extent such warranty and remedies are assignable. Within a period of one (1) year from the date title passes to LICENSEE for any ITEM covered by such warranty, LICENSEE shall immediately notify LICENSOR of any failure of such ITEM to be as warranted above; otherwise LICENSEE unconditionally waives its rights under this warranty clause in respect of such ITEM. Solely with respect to ITEMS manufactured by LICENSOR, and upon notification to, and verification by LICENSOR of such failure, LICENSOR will, at its option, either repair or replace ITEMS not as warranted above without charge to LICENSEE or render credit thereon in such an amount as, in LICENSOR'S judgment, the situation may reasonably require. If LICENSOR determines that any ITEMS should be returned to it, LICENSEE will follow LICENSOR'S instructions regarding such return. *The foregoing is in lieu of and excludes all other express and implied warranties, including but not limited to warranties of merchantability and fitness for a particular purpose.*

The foregoing warranty does not extend to any ITEM which has been: (i) subjected to misuse, neglect, accident or abuse; (ii) wired, repaired or altered by anyone other LICENSOR or a party approved in writing by LICENSOR; (iii) improperly installed, stored or maintained by anyone other than LICENSOR or a party approved in writing by LICENSOR; (iv) used in violation of LICENSOR'S instructions; or (v) removed from its original site of installation.

IV-3.03 Except as expressly agreed otherwise in any orders accepted hereunder, beneficial and legal title to, ownership of, right to possession of, any control over, and risks of loss and damage to all ITEMS which are sold pursuant to this Chapter IV shall remain with LICENSOR until the shipment physically arrives ex-carrier (ship or aircraft, whichever is applicable), port of entry, country of destination. The time of payment, the place or medium of payment, the method of shipment, the manner of consignment, or the terms of any document related to sales by LICENSOR to LICENSEE, shall in no way limit or modify the rights of LICENSOR as the legal and beneficial owners of the goods and its right to possession of such goods until they physically arrive ex-carrier, port of entry, country of destination. Any use of such terms as "F.O.B.", "F.A.S.", "C.&F.", or "C.I.F." shall apply to price only and not to title.

IV-3.04 (a) LICENSOR will, subject to the conditions and exceptions stated herein, defend at its own expense all suits alleging infringement of any patent (except any patent of Australia or New Zealand) by reason of the use of any ITEM furnished by it to LICENSEE, and will save LICENSEE harmless from all payments which by final judgments therein may be assessed against LICENSEE on account of such infringement; and if such use shall be enjoined, LICENSOR will (the various alternatives being at LICENSOR'S option) replace the enjoined ITEM furnished hereunder with suitable materiel free of the infringement, or modify it so that it will be free of the infringement, or will procure for LICENSEE'S benefit a license or other right to use the same, or will remove the enjoined ITEM and refund to LICENSEE the amount paid to LICENSOR therefor less a reasonable allowance for use, damage and obsolescence; provided, that LICENSOR shall have had immediate written notice of all claims of such infringement and of all such suits and full opportunity and authority to assume the sole defense thereof, including appeals, and to settle such suits, and shall be furnished upon LICENSOR'S request and at its expense all information and assistance available to LICENSEE for such defense; and provided further, that no undertaking of LICENSOR herein shall extend to any infringement or claim of infringement (1) arising from adherence to specifications or drawings which LICENSOR is directed by LICENSEE to follow as to any ITEM (other than infringement residing in ITEMS of LICENSOR'S own design or selection or the same as LICENSOR'S commercial merchandise); (2) residing in ITEMS furnished by LICENSEE to LICENSOR for use hereunder; (3) to any infringement or claim of infringement not wholly inherent in the ITEM itself; or (4) to any infringement or claim of infringement relating to use of an ITEM furnished by LICENSOR in combination with other apparatus not furnished by LICENSOR. In the foregoing cases numbered (1) through (4), LICENSEE will defend and save LICENSOR harmless subject to the conditions and exceptions stated above with respect to LICENSOR'S undertakings.

TTA SAMPLE-070280-082180

(b) The liability of LICENSOR with respect to any and all infringement of patents, because of or in connection with, any ITEM furnished hereunder, shall be limited to the specific undertakings contained in this Section IV-3.04.

IV-3.05   The provisions of this Chapter IV shall continue in force for the lesser of a term of   years from the effective date of this agreement or until the provisions of Chapter II cease to be in force and effect. During said   year term LICENSEE shall exercise reasonable efforts to develop its own manufacturing capability or sources of supply for ITEMS.

TTA SAMPLE-070280-082180

CHAPTER V

GENERAL PROVISIONS
FOR CHAPTERS I-IV, INCLUSIVE

ARTICLE V-1

INFORMATION AND RELATED MATTERS

V-1.01   This agreement shall prevail in the event of any conflicting terms or legends which may appear on documents or ASSISTANCE INFORMATION, IMPLEMENTATION INFORMATION, MANUFACTURING INFORMATION, LICENSED SOFTWARE or DEVELOPMENT INFORMATION furnished hereunder.

V-1.02   LICENSOR believes that MANUFACTURING INFORMATION, IMPLEMENTATION INFORMATION, LICENSED SOFTWARE and DEVELOPMENT INFORMATION furnished hereunder will be true and accurate, but LICENSOR shall not be held to any liability for errors or omissions therein.

V-1.03   Neither the execution of this agreement nor anything in it or in the ASSISTANCE INFORMATION, MANUFACTURING INFORMATION, IMPLEMENTATION INFORMATION, LICENSED SOFTWARE, DEVELOPMENT INFORMATION or other information, furnished hereunder shall be construed as

(i)   an obligation upon LICENSOR to furnish any person, including LICENSEE and its SUBSIDIARIES, any assistance, except as provided in Chapter III hereof, of any kind whatsoever, or, except as otherwise expressly provided in this agreement, any information other than such MANUFACTURING INFORMATION, LICENSED SOFTWARE, IMPLEMENTATION INFORMATION, ASSISTANCE INFORMATION, DEVELOPMENT INFORMATION or to revise, supplement or elaborate upon such MANUFACTURING INFORMATION and IMPLEMENTATION INFORMATION except as otherwise provided in Section II-1.03; or

(ii)   providing or implying any arrangement or understanding that LICENSOR will make any purchase, lease, examination or test or give any approval with respect to any product or manufacturing facility.

V-1.04   LICENSEE agrees:

(i)   that neither LICENSEE nor its SUBSIDIARIES will use any LICENSED SOFTWARE, ASSISTANCE INFORMATION, DEVELOPMENT INFORMATION, IMPLEMENTATION INFORMATION or MANUFACTURING INFORMATION except as herein provided and as set forth on or on material associated with, such information;

TTA SAMPLE-070280-082180

(ii) that LICENSEE and its SUBSIDIARIES shall, except as otherwise expressly provided in this agreement, keep all LICENSED SOFTWARE, DEVELOPMENT INFORMATION, ASSISTANCE INFORMATION, IMPLEMENTATION INFORMATION and MANUFACTURING INFORMATION confidential, except for portions of such MANUFACTURING INFORMATION, LICENSED SOFTWARE, IMPLEMENTATION INFORMATION, ASSISTANCE INFORMATION and DEVELOPMENT INFORMATION (a) which were previously known to LICENSEE or its SUBSIDIARIES free of any obligation to keep confidential, or (b) which are or become generally known to the public, provided that such public knowledge is not the result of any acts attributable to LICENSEE or its SUBSIDIARIES, or (c) which LICENSOR explicitly agrees in writing need not be kept confidential, and that the obligation of LICENSEE and its SUBSIDIARIES under this Section V-1.04 (ii) shall survive and continue after any termination of rights under this agreement;

(iii) that neither LICENSEE nor its SUBSIDIARIES will, except as otherwise expressly provided in this agreement, without LICENSOR'S express written permission, make or have made, or permit to be made, any copies of the LICENSED SOFTWARE, nor more copies of any of the MANUFACTURING INFORMATION, IMPLEMENTATION INFORMATION or ASSISTANCE INFORMATION furnished hereunder than are necessary for its or their use hereunder, and that each such necessary copy shall contain the same proprietary notices or legends which appear on such MANUFACTURING INFORMATION, IMPLEMENTATION INFORMATION and ASSISTANCE INFORMATION;

(iv) that neither LICENSEE nor its SUBSIDIARIES will (a) make any procurement information contained in any MANUFACTURING INFORMATION or DEVELOPMENT INFORMATION furnished hereunder available to suppliers or prospective suppliers; or (b) make any IMPLEMENTATION INFORMATION, available to customers; except on the agreement in writing (of which a copy will be furnished by LICENSEE to LICENSOR if requested) of (1) such supplier, prospective supplier or customer that it shall keep such procurement information or IMPLEMENTATION INFORMATION confidential, except under conditions corresponding to those specified in paragraph (ii) of this Section V-1.04, and, in the case of procurement information, that the supplier or prospective supplier will not use it except in the United States of America, Australia, New Zealand, and any other countries as may be hereafter requested by LICENSEE and approved in writing by LICENSOR for the purpose of supplying to LICENSEE or its SUBSIDIARIES materials, manufacturing facilities, parts or components described therein, and will return all such procurement information and all copies thereof on demand of the company from which it was received; and (2) such customer that it will not use any IMPLEMENTATION INFORMATION with other than the specific LICENSED PRODUCT with which it is furnished by LICENSEE;

(v) that when a SUBSIDIARY'S relationship to LICENSEE changes so that it is no longer a SUBSIDIARY of LICENSEE, (a) such former SUBSIDIARY shall promptly deliver to LICENSEE all documents and other materiel containing any of the MANUFACTURING INFORMATION, DEVELOPMENT INFORMATION or ASSISTANCE INFORMATION and all copies thereof then under such former SUBSIDIARY'S control, and (b) each ITEM SUBJECT TO FEE manufactured by such SUBSIDIARY and which remains not sold, leased or put into use at the time such SUBSIDIARY ceases to be a SUBSIDIARY of LICENSEE, shall be deemed to have been put into use by such SUBSIDIARY immediately prior to such time at the place said ITEM SUBJECT TO FEE is then located; and

(vi) that all documents and information furnished hereunder shall remain the property of LICENSOR, and that upon termination of all rights granted to LICENSEE hereunder pursuant to Article II-5, LICENSEE shall upon request deliver to LICENSOR all documents and other materiel containing any of the MANUFACTURING INFORMATION, DEVELOPMENT INFORMATION, ASSISTANCE INFORMATION, or software source code furnished hereunder and all copies thereof then under LICENSEE'S, its SUBSIDIARIES' or its or their suppliers' control.

V-1.05 (a) LICENSEE shall, at reasonable charge to LICENSOR, disclose and furnish promptly to LICENSOR any and all software and information useful in manufacturing or testing, or otherwise relating to, originated or developed within   years from the effective date of this agreement by LICENSEE'S or its SUBSIDIARIES' employees, solely or jointly with anyone other than LICENSOR'S or its agents' personnel, as a result of performance under this agreement or of receiving from LICENSOR, DEVELOPMENT INFORMATION or, from LICENSOR or its agents, other information hereunder.

(b) LICENSOR shall have unrestricted, nonexclusive, royalty-free rights for all purposes to reproduce, use, have used, license and disclose, in whole or in part, such software and information so originated or developed without accounting to anyone.

(c) LICENSEE shall use its best efforts to acquire rights to such software and information so that LICENSOR shall receive the rights provided in this Section V-1.05.

(d) Any and all information and software useful in manufacturing or testing, or otherwise relating to,   originated or developed within   years of the effective date of this agreement jointly by one or more of LICENSEE'S or its SUBSIDIARIES' personnel and one or more of LICENSOR'S or its agents' personnel shall be and remain the joint property of LICENSOR and LICENSEE; and LICENSOR and LICENSEE shall each have unrestricted nonexclusive royalty-free rights for all purposes to reproduce, use, have used, license, sell and disclose, in whole or in part, such information and software without accounting to one another.

TTA SAMPLE-070280-082140

V-1.06 It is recognized that during the performance of this agreement, LICENSOR'S and its agents' and LICENSEE'S personnel may unavoidably receive or have access to private or confidential software and information of the other party which is neither DEVELOPMENT INFORMATION, ASSISTANCE INFORMATION, IMPLEMENTATION INFORMATION, LICENSED SOFTWARE, MANUFACTURING INFORMATION nor any software or information referred to in Section V-1.05 as being originated or developed. LICENSOR and LICENSEE shall not have any obligation to preserve said private or confidential software and information in confidence except with respect to such software and information that they know, or have been informed, is private or confidential and with respect to such software and information they shall accord such information the same degree of care and restricted access used to protect their own software and information of like character.

ARTICLE V-2

DISCLAIMER OF GENERAL WARRANTY

V-2.01 Except as otherwise expressly provided in Sections IV-3.02 and IV-3.04 hereof, LICENSOR makes no representations or warranties, expressly or impliedly, with respect to any subject matter furnished hereunder or any undertaking hereunder or product resulting from such undertaking. By way of example but not of limitation, LICENSOR makes no representations or warranties of merchantability or fitness for any particular purpose, or that the use of any MANUFACTURING INFORMATION, or other information or software, furnished hereunder or any of it will not infringe any patent, copyright or trademark of any third party, and it shall be the sole responsibility of LICENSEE to make such determination as is necessary with respect to the acquisition of licenses under patents of third parties. LICENSOR shall not be held to any liability with respect to any patent infringement or any other claim made by LICENSEE, its SUBSIDIARIES, or any third party on account of, or arising from, the use of any MANUFACTURING INFORMATION, ASSISTANCE INFORMATION, DEVELOPMENT INFORMATION, LICENSED SOFTWARE, IMPLEMENTATION INFORMATION or other information or software, furnished hereunder or any of it or on account of, or arising from, or involving, any such subject matter, undertaking or product.

ARTICLE V-3

LIMITATIONS ON PROPRIETARY RIGHTS

V-3.01   (a) Neither LICENSEE nor its SUBSIDIARIES will, without LICENSOR'S express written permission, (a) use in advertising, publicity, manufacture, marketing, or otherwise any trade name, trademark, trade device, service mark, symbol, or any other identification or any abbreviation, contraction or simulation thereof owned or used by LICENSOR, or (b) represent, directly or indirectly, that any product produced in whole or in part with the use of any of the MANUFACTURING INFORMATION, or other information of LICENSOR, is a product of LICENSOR, or is made in accordance with or utilizes any information or documentation of LICENSOR; provided that nothing in this Section V-3.01 shall be construed as prohibiting LICENSEE or its SUBSIDIARIES from representing that any product produced hereunder is manufactured pursuant to a license from LICENSOR.

(b) No advertising or publicity matter having any reference to any of the parties to this agreement shall be published, disseminated or distributed by any other party to the agreement, or anyone in such other party's behalf, unless and until such matter shall have first been submitted to and approved in writing by the company referred to in the advertising or publicity matter.

V-3.02   Nothing contained herein shall be construed as conferring by implication, estoppel or otherwise any license or right under any patent, whether or not the exercise of any right herein granted necessarily employs an invention of any existing or later issued patent.

V-3.03   Except as otherwise expressly provided herein, nothing contained herein shall be construed as conferring by implication, estoppel or otherwise any license or right in respect of any DEVELOPMENT INFORMATION, ASSISTANCE INFORMATION, MANUFACTURING INFORMATION, LICENSED SOFTWARE, IMPLEMENTATION INFORMATION or other information or software, whether or not any performance hereunder or resulting product necessarily employs or embodies any such information or software.

ARTICLE V-4

PERSONNEL

V-4.01   LICENSEE shall be solely responsible for the remuneration of its personnel and for their travel, living and other expenses, including such remuneration and expenses incurred in visiting locations designated by LICENSOR. LICENSEE shall also be solely responsible for any tax or other governmental charge, however designated, which is imposed on LICENSEE or its personnel by the United States or by any agency or political subdivision thereof as a result of the existence or operation of this agreement or as the result of the activities of LICENSEE'S personnel.

TTA SAMPLE-070280-082180

V-4.02   (a) LICENSOR'S and its agents' personnel shall, while on any location of LICENSEE, comply with LICENSEE'S rules and regulations with regard to safety and security. LICENSOR shall have full control over their respective personnel and over personnel of their agents and shall be entirely responsible for their complying with LICENSEE'S rules and regulations. LICENSOR agrees to indemnify and save LICENSEE harmless from any claims or demands, including the costs, expenses and reasonable attorney's fees incurred on account thereof, that may be made by (i) anyone for injuries to persons or damage to property resulting solely from acts or omissions of LICENSOR'S or its agents' personnel; or (ii) LICENSOR'S or its agents' personnel under Workmen's Compensation or similar laws. LICENSOR agrees to defend LICENSEE, at LICENSEE'S request, against any such claim or demand.

(b) LICENSEE'S personnel shall, while on any location of LICENSOR, comply with LICENSOR'S rules and regulations with regard to safety and security. LICENSEE shall have full control over such personnel and shall be entirely responsible for their complying with LICENSOR'S rules and regulations. LICENSEE agrees to indemnify and save LICENSOR harmless from any claims or demands, including the costs, expenses and reasonable attorney's fees incurred on account thereof, that may be made by (i) anyone for injuries to persons or damage to property resulting solely from acts or omissions of LICENSEE'S personnel; or (ii) LICENSEE'S personnel under Workmen's Compensation or similar laws. LICENSEE agrees to defend LICENSOR against any such claim or demand.

ARTICLE V-5

NON-TRANSFERABILITY

V-5.01   Except as provided in Sections I-4.01(b) (vii) and V-1.05(d) hereof, any assignment or other transfer of this agreement or licenses or rights existing or arising under this agreement, in whole or in part, or of any interest therein, by either party without the written consent of the other party shall be void.

ARTICLE V-6

EXPORT

V-6.01   (a) LICENSEE and LICENSOR hereby assure each other that they do not intend to and will not knowingly, without the prior written consent of the Office of Export Administration of the U.S. Department of Commerce, Washington, D.C. 20230, transmit directly or indirectly:

(i)   any information or software obtained pursuant to this agreement; or

(ii) any immediate product (including processes and services) produced directly by the use of such information or software; or

(iii) any commodity produced by such immediate product if the immediate product of such information or software is a plant capable of producing a commodity or is a major component of such plant;

to any Q, W, Y or Z country specified in Supplement No. 1 to Section 370 of the Export Administration Regulations issued by the U.S. Department of Commerce. LICENSEE and LICENSOR agree to promptly inform one another in writing of any such written consent by the Office of Export Administration.

(b) LICENSEE agrees that neither it nor its SUBSIDIARIES will, without the prior written consent of LICENSOR, transmit, directly or indirectly, the DEVELOPMENT INFORMATION, MANUFACTURING INFORMATION, ASSISTANCE INFORMATION, LICENSED SOFTWARE, IMPLEMENTATION INFORMATION or any portion thereof (or any other information or software obtained pursuant to this agreement, or any portion thereof) to any country outside of the United States of America, New Zealand, and the Commonwealth of Australia.

ARTICLE V-7

OBLIGATIONS, LIABILITIES AND LIMITATIONS THEREON

V-7.01 LICENSOR shall not be held responsible for any delay or failure in performance hereunder caused by fires, strikes, embargoes, government requirements, civil or military authorities, acts of God or by the public enemy, or other Force Majeure, inability to secure materiel, or transportation facilities, acts or omissions of carriers or other causes beyond its control.

V-7.02 LICENSOR shall not be liable for incidental or consequential loss or damages of any nature, however caused.

V-7.03 In the event of any breach of this agreement by LICENSOR, or of any loss or injury to LICENSEE arising out of this agreement, for which LICENSOR is liable to LICENSEE, LICENSOR'S total cumulative liability to LICENSEE for all such breaches, losses and injuries shall be the lesser of (i) the actual value of the injury or loss to LICENSEE or (ii) the sum of   United States dollars ($ U.S.).

V-7.04 The expiration or termination of this agreement or portions thereof shall not affect the respective rights of or relieve either party of any obligation arising under this agreement and which shall have accrued prior to such expiration or termination.

TTA SAMPLE-070280-082180

ARTICLE V-8

TAXES

V-8.01 LICENSEE shall bear all taxes, however designated, and other governmental charges imposed on LICENSOR, its agents, and its or their personnel as a result of the existence or operation of this agreement, including, but not limited to, any tax or charge upon, with respect to or measured by, any payment or receipt of payment hereunder, any registration tax or charge, any tax or charge imposed with respect to the granting or transfer of rights or considerations hereunder, and any tax or charge which LICENSEE is required to withhold or deduct from payments to LICENSOR, except (i) any such tax or charge imposed upon LICENSOR by any governmental entity in the United States, and (ii) any such tax or charge imposed LICENSOR in the country in which the aforesaid office of LICENSEE is located if such tax or charge is allowable as a credit against United States income taxes of LICENSOR. To assist LICENSOR in obtaining such credit, LICENSEE shall furnish LICENSOR with such evidence as may be required by United States taxing authorities to establish that any such tax or charge has been paid.

ARTICLE V-9

INTEREST AND PLACE OF PAYMENT

V-9.01 Payments by LICENSEE to LICENSOR provided for in this agreement shall, when overdue, bear interest at an annual rate of one percent (1%) over the prime rate or successive prime rates in effect in New York City during delinquency.

V-9.02 Payments under this agreement to LICENSOR shall be identified as to the applicable Chapter(s) hereof and shall be made in United States dollars to its Treasury Organization at   , United States of America, or at such changed address as it shall have specified by written notice. If any fee for any semiannual period referred to in Section II-4.02 is computed in other currency, conversion to United States dollars shall be at the prevailing rate for bank cable transfers on New York City as quoted for the last day of such semiannual period by leading banks dealing in the New York City foreign exchange market.

ARTICLE V-10

NOTICE, CONSTRUCTION AND GOVERNING LAW

V-10.01 Any notice, request, information, document or fee statement shall be deemed to be sufficiently given or provided when sent by registered mail addressed to the addressee at its office above specified or at such changed address as the addressee shall have specified by written notice.

TTA SAMPLE-070280-082180

V-10.02   This agreement sets forth the entire agreement and understanding between the parties as to the subject matter hereof and merges all prior discussions between them, and neither of the parties shall be bound by any conditions, definitions, warranties, understandings or representations with respect to such subject matter other than as expressly provided herein, or in any prior existing written agreement between the parties, or as duly set forth on or subsequent to the effective date hereof in writing and signed by a proper and duly authorized representative of the party to be bound thereby.

V-10.03   The construction and performance of this agreement shall be governed by the law of the State of New York.

ARTICLE V-11

APPROVAL

V-11.01   (a) All agreements between LICENSOR and LICENSEE stated to become effective upon APPROVAL, and then as of   , and all agreements which refer to such agreements, shall be submitted for approval to the Australian Reserve Bank ("the Bank") in accordance with the rules of the Bank then applicable. LICENSEE hereby agrees to effect, within fourteen (14) days of the execution of this agreement by LICENSOR and LICENSEE, the aforesaid submission.

(b) In the event that the Bank issues a ruling, decision, statement or communication of any kind relating specifically to any of the agreements specified above, which sets forth any reason for its withholding of any necessary approval or which recommends any modification, the parties hereto agree to enter immediately into negotiations in good faith to make any modification(s) suggested by the Bank believed necessary to obtain any necessary approval of the Bank, and, if agreed upon, to have LICENSEE submit such modifications to the Bank upon reaching such agreement. If all such modifications cannot be agreed upon within sixty (60) days of the commencement of negotiations, this agreement shall be automatically terminated, effective as of the expiration of such sixty (60) days.

(c) LICENSEE shall provide LICENSOR with copies of all documents submitted to the Bank in accordance herewith. LICENSEE and LICENSOR shall provide each other with copies of all documents provided to them by the Bank in response to any submissions or requests made pursuant hereto.

TTA SAMPLE-070280

IN WITNESS WHEREOF, each of the parties has caused this agreement to be executed in duplicate originals by its duly authorized representatives on the respective dates entered below.

By . . . .

Attest:

[SEAL]

. . . .
Secretary
. . . .
Date

The Common Seal of

. . . .

was hereunto affixed
by the authority of
the Board of Directors:

. . . .
Directors

[SEAL]

. . . .

. . . . Secretary

. . . . Date

DEFINITIONS APPENDIX

APPROVAL means the granting by the Australian Reserve Bank of all necessary approvals, authorizations and clearances for all agreements between LICENSOR and LICENSEE stated to have an effective date of   and all agreements which refer to such agreements.

ASSISTANCE INFORMATION means any information furnished to LICENSEE pursuant to Chapter III hereof.

BASE PERIOD means for all articles included in each class of articles designated in Section II-3.02 (and maintenance parts therefor), the   year period commencing on the first day of the calendar month in which occurs the first manufacture by LICENSEE or any of its SUBSIDIARIES of any article which is an ITEM SUBJECT TO FEE included in such class; provided, however, that if in one or more periods of twelve (12) or more consecutive calendar months there shall be no production of any article which is an ITEM SUBJECT TO FEE included in such class, such period or periods of nonproduction shall not be taken into account in determining the expiration of said   year period for such class.

DEVELOPMENT INFORMATION means any information or software disclosed to LICENSEE pursuant to Chapter I hereof, whether or not developed in the course of the Research and Development Project.

EQUIPMENT means a   , which is substantially similar to such a system manufactured by LICENSOR (in accordance with LICENSOR'S MANUFACTURING INFORMATION, including drawings:

DULY AUTHORIZED REPRESENTATIVE means that or those person(s) authorized in writing to act on behalf of LICENSEE or LICENSOR with respect to matters arising under Chapter IV of this agreement.

FAIR MARKET VALUE means the NET SELLING PRICE which LICENSEE or any of its SUBSIDIARIES, whichever effects the sale, lease or use of the ITEM SUBJECT TO FEE, would realize from an unaffiliated buyer in an arm's length sale of an identical ITEM SUBJECT TO FEE in the same quantity and at the same time and place as such sale, lease or use.

IMPLEMENTATION INFORMATION means INSTALLATION AND MAINTENANCE INFORMATION, OPERATIONAL INFORMATION, OPERATIONAL SOFTWARE and REPAIR INFORMATION.

INSTALLATION AND MAINTENANCE INFORMATION means that information owned and used by LICENSOR as of the effective date hereof relating to the installation and maintenance of   EQUIPMENT, and identified as the following of LICENSOR'S drawings and the associated technical information referred to thereon (LICENSOR reserves the right to substitute, in its sole discretion):

ITEM means any product, component, part, software programs (in object code format) and associated documentation, service, manufacturing tool, and test set of a kind identified in Exhibit A of this agreement.

ITEM SUBJECT TO FEE means any article of any of the kinds specified in Section II-3.02, and any maintenance part therefor, which is manufactured by LICENSEE or any of its SUBSIDIARIES prior to the expiration of the BASE PERIOD applicable to such article with the use of any of the MANUFACTURING INFORMATION (including any such article, and any maintenance part therefor, manufactured by any such company with manufacturing facilities made with the use of any of the MANUFACTURING INFORMATION), other than (i) demonstration models and articles and maintenance parts produced in the course of, or intended for use in connection with, research, development or experimental undertakings of LICENSEE or any of its SUBSIDIARIES, and (ii) articles and maintenance parts therefor furnished to LICENSOR. An article shall not be an ITEM SUBJECT TO FEE solely because it contains another article of a kind specified in Section II-3.02, which other article is an ITEM SUBJECT TO FEE, or solely because it contains another such article which would be an ITEM SUBJECT TO FEE hereunder except for the expiration of the BASE PERIOD for such other article.

LICENSED PRODUCT means a
as defined in the Patent License Agreement, and not anything else which may be the subject of licenses under the Patent License Agreement.

LICENSED SOFTWARE means the software programs and the associated documentation, or any portions thereof, either specifically listed in Exhibit A of this agreement or identified in, and forming a part of, the MANUFACTURING INFORMATION.

MANUFACTURING INFORMATION means information owned and used by LICENSOR as of the effective date hereof relating to the manufacture (including testing) and maintenance of   , such information being more fully identified as the following of LICENSOR'S drawings and the associated technical information referred to thereon:

Description   **Drawing No.**

such MANUFACTURING INFORMATION includes:

(a) technical specifications respecting components, subassemblies, and manufacturing and testing facilities;

(b) information respecting the purchasing of components and manufacturing and testing facilities;

(c) software and shop information used in component, subassembly, continuity and system testing; and

(d) drill tables and artwork respecting printed wiring boards.

NET SELLING PRICE, as the term is applied to an ITEM SUBJECT TO FEE, means the gross selling price thereof in the form in which it is sold, whether or not assembled (and without excluding therefrom any components or subassemblies thereof, whatever their origin), less the following amounts but only insofar as they pertain to the sale of such ITEM SUBJECT TO FEE by LICENSEE or any of its SUBSIDIARIES and are included in such gross selling price:

(i) usual trade discounts actually allowed (other than cash discounts, advertising allowances, or fees or commissions to any employees of LICENSEE, a SUBSIDIARY of LICENSEE, a company of which LICENSEE is a SUBSIDIARY at the time of the sale, or any other SUBSIDIARY of a company of which LICENSEE is a SUBSIDIARY at the time of such sale);

(ii) packing costs;

(iii) import, export, excise and sales taxes, and customs duties;

(iv) costs of insurance and transportation from the place of manufacture to the customer's premises or point of installation;

(v) costs of installation at the place of use; and

(vi) costs of special engineering services not incident to the design or manufacture of ITEMS SUBJECT TO FEE.

OPERATIONAL INFORMATION means that information owned and used by LICENSOR as of the effective date hereof relating to the operation of EQUIPMENT, and identified as the following and the information contained therein:

OPERATIONAL SOFTWARE means LICENSED SOFTWARE associated with, or with the operation of, any LICENSED PRODUCT furnished hereunder to LICENSEE by LICENSOR or manufactured by LICENSEE pursuant to rights granted under Chapter II hereof.

REPAIR INFORMATION means that information owned and used by LICENSOR as of the effective date hereof relating to the repair of EQUIPMENT, and identified as the following drawings and specifications and the information contained therein:

SUBSIDIARY means a company the majority of whose stock entitled to vote for election of directors is now or hereafter controlled by the parent company either directly or indirectly, but any such company shall be deemed to be a SUBSIDIARY only so long as such control exists.

TYPE CERTIFICATION means, in respect of any equipment, certification by the Australian Governmental Commission that its   design objectives, as set forth in its Specification   , have been complied with.

TTA SAMPLE-070280

EXHIBIT A (CHAPTER IV APPENDIX)

ITEMS determined by LICENSOR, in its sole discretion, to be necessary for the manufacture, installation, maintenance, repair and operation of EQUIPMENTS provided with features corresponding to the following identified software and feature packages:

and such other ITEMS as mutually agreed upon by LICENSEE and LICENSOR.

EXHIBIT B (CHAPTER IV APPENDIX)	**Irrevocable Documentary Letter of Credit**	
. . . . (Address) Cable Address . . . . Telex Number	Date of Issue (For Bank Use)	
	Issuing Bank Letter of Credit No (For Bank Use)	Advising Bank Letter of Credit No (For Bank Use)

Issuing Bank

(For Bank Use)

Applicant

LICENSEE

Beneficiary	Expiry Date (Presentation at our counters)		
LICENSOR Attention: Director of Administration	Day	Month	Year
	(To be completed per terms in Article IV-2.)		

Currency	Amount
U.S.$	Appx. (For Bank Use)

We hereby advise this documentary Letter of Credit in your favor which is available against beneficiary's draft at
drawn on .... Bank, (Address)
bearing the clause "Drawn under documentary Letter of Credit Number   " Accompanied by the following documer

1. Signed commercial invoice in three (3) copies. (Legalized, if necessary.)
2. Full set clean on board bills of lading to order (specify LICENSEE's bank)
   marked "notify LICENSEE" and also "freight collect" (if applicable) to be
   dated not later than (date) or whichever of the following is applicable:
   air way bills, or charter bills of lading, or forwarding agent's bills of
   lading, or forwarding agent's house air way bills, each cosigned to ( )
   and each marked "notify LICENSEE" and also "freight collect" (if applicable)
   to be dated not later than (date).

Purporting to Cover (Specify as applicable)

(Specify shipping terms)

Shipment From	U.S.A.	Partial Shipments	Transshipments
To	(Specify port of destination)	PERMITTED	PERMITTED
Special Conditions			

Storage on deck authorized (if applicable)

We hereby engage with the bona fide holders of all drafts drawn and/or documents presented under and in compliance with the terms of this letter of credit that such drafts and/or documents will be duly honored upon presentation to us
The amount of each drawing must be endorsed on the reverse of this letter of credit by the negotiating bank

☐ This is an irrevocable letter of credit of the above mentioned issuing bank and is transmitted to you without any responsibility or engagement on our part

☒ We confirm the credit and hereby undertake to honor drafts and documents if presented in accordance with the terms and conditions of the credit

When presenting document please include an extra copy of your invoice. Always refer to our reference number when communicating with us on this transaction.

Very Truly Yours,

North Carolina National Bank

SPECIMEN

Authorized Signature

NON–NEGOTIABLE

Except so far as otherwise expressly stated this documentary letter of credit is subject to the Uniform Customs and Practice for Documentary Credits (1974 Revision) the International Chamber of Commerce Document No 290

COPY

CHAPTER 7

Foreign Natural Resource Investment

JAMES E. HORIGAN*

---

*J.D., University of Oklahoma, 1949; Vice President and General Counsel, Charterhall America, Inc., Denver, Colorado. The author is an international petroleum lawyer best known for pioneer legal work related to the North Sea (1963-75) and the Java Sea, Indonesia (1966-69). In 1979-81 he was a Partner in the Denver firm of Holland & Hart. From 1970 to 1975, he was Senior Resident Partner of the London office of the Houston law firm, Vinson & Elkins. From 1963 to 1969, he was General Counsel of Hamilton

§ 7.01 Introduction and Objectives

From the time of ancient civilizations, man has explored in distant lands for natural resources. Seldom have indigenous supplies been adequate either to satisfy local requirements or the enterprising quest abroad for exploration and reward. Nature was not so kind as to neatly provide for the deposition of resources in geographical areas that coincide with man-made areas of political jurisdiction. In an historical sense alone, the extraterritorial search for resources has been a significant phenomenon in shaping the political or economic character of many human societies.

The legal practitioner who represents the large or small multinational company in the business of exploration and development of nature's bounties in foreign countries is faced with a complex challenge. "Going abroad" is a substantially different undertaking from that of simply going from one state of the U.S. to another to conduct petroleum exploration or mining activities. The applicable laws, regulations, and basic terms and conditions governing the exercise of rights are usually quite dissimilar to those encountered on the domestic scene. The lawyer must adapt to a new language that was quite unknown to the advisors of ancient resource explorers. It includes such modern-day concepts and terms as "nationalism," "sovereignty," "sanctity of contract," "coup," "foreign tax credit," "antitrust," "royalties," "off-shore drilling," "expropriation," "project financing," "technology transfer," "boycotts," "foreign exchange," and so on.

In most foreign petroleum producing countries, constitutional rights on the basis of an American model are unknown. In fact, the judiciary itself may not be an independent branch of government. Situations are also found where, absent protective provisions for an external arbitration or judiciary, the government or one of its agencies or entities may sit in judgment on a claim against itself. In a general sense, this does not necessarily mean that a given foreign nation's laws should command

Brothers Oil Co., and earlier was a senior attorney for Mobil Oil Corporation in its Office of General Counsel.

less respect than ours in international transactions. The old adage of "When in Rome, do as the Romans," is especially applicable, but today qualified with the caveat that the American company, in so doing, does not thereby become free of a burdensome host of extraterritorially applied U.S. laws and regulations. The lawyer should be open-minded to the task of reconciling differences in the laws while, at the same time, seeking to satisfy the client that its proposed activity is legal both at home and abroad.

A primary objective here will be, first, to cover in a general way some of the modern legal and practical considerations as may be encountered by the practicing American lawyer whose client desires to invest abroad in petroleum resources and, second, to briefly describe significant changes in the concession or participation arrangements with various countries (as concern their petroleum resources) as have evolved over the past half-century. The emphasis will be on the current situation and status of such arrangements. It will not be possible in this single chapter to furnish a complete or detailed consideration of these matters on a country-by-country, or even on an area-by-area basis of classification. Any attempt to classify countries into geographical area or political affinity groupings for such a purpose would be fraught with inaccuracies. This is because there are many dissimilarities to be encountered irrespective of how one seeks to classify. This applies even to those relatively underdeveloped countries which were formally colonies having a common colonial heritage in language, law, custom, and the like.

While the scope of this chapter will be confined to that of petroleum resources investment abroad, many of the legal and practical factors to be considered in the earlier portion may be seen equally applicable to hard rock mineral exploration and development abroad. Nevertheless, it is important to note that foreign country laws and regulations governing mineral exploration and mining are normally very different and have arisen under unrelated circumstances in most cases.

§ 7.02   Changing Conditions Affecting Foreign Investment

Three important considerations affect foreign investment in the 1980's:

(1) From the late 1970's to the mid-1980's, American petroleum companies, especially the small and medium-sized independents, sharply curtailed or discontinued new undertakings in foreign exploration ventures. Even the major companies have generally followed this trend. Those of the independents who were convinced in the late 1960's and into the 1970's that the high risks and expensive capital outlays for foreign exploration and development would be overshadowed by large rewards, came to recognize in time that their earlier expectations were not attainable in most cases. Quite apart from the global oil recession and oversupply situation in the three years or so leading up to 1985, it appears that many host governments, including those of some of the most developed countries, brought about increasing disincentives to exploration in the form of changes in laws and applicable regulations or in their tax regimens. These, in turn, resulted in an instability and uncertainty in various countries that was nonresponsive to the foreign risk-taking policies of the companies.

Inherently, and on the basis of past experience, the political and economic risks of foreign petroleum and mining ventures often exceed those of other kinds of ventures abroad. This was true to some extent even before the declining worldwide availability of petroleum (in relation to increasing demand in the 1970's) came to be used as a political weapon by some host countries. This is due not only to the very high-risk nature of oil and mining ventures, but also a company's recovery of investment in these days may require ten or twenty years to achieve. In the course of time, the ground rules (re local laws, regulations, taxation, etc.) of particular countries might have changed to such an extent that investors could be faced with a different set of economic or political parameters from what they considered initially in undertaking these projects. One example of this is where a host country, following the making of a petroleum discovery by a company and its expenditure of substantial sums, enacts a policy delaying the development of the field or severely restricting the production rate to levels that defeat time/use of money ratios on which the investment depends from an economic standpoint.

In general, it would seem that many foreign governments, once they have achieved their own objectives in the encouragement of investment for the discovery and initial development of their petroleum resources, become disinclined to appreciate, or to be particularly concerned about, the special needs and realities of private investors and companies who are required not only to show favorable returns on investment within reasonable timeframes but, in respect to foreign ventures, to show even higher levels of reward for the much higher levels of risk and capital expenditure involved. One needs to bear in mind that the only major source of risk funds available for foreign ventures is that of the private sector.

(2) Coming into the latter half of the 1980's, however, a brighter picture is emerging. This will be considered in some detail later on and it is the result of what appears to be a growing competitiveness among some of the major producing areas to create new incentives for the restimulation of their exploratory and development programs. Much of this is the consequence of several years of global recession, falling prices, oversupply of petroleum products and other significant factors. Whether or not American companies will favorably respond is no doubt dependent on general economic conditions and viability of the petroleum industry itself.

(3) The worldwide rise of nationalism in the past few decades has affected the nature and kind of relationships that may be entered into with foreign governments as concerns the exploration and exploitation of their natural resources, and these aspects are more fully treated below in reference to the evolution of foreign license or concession grants.

§ 7.03 The Approach to Foreign Ventures

Legal representation of petroleum and mining companies abroad involves many of the same practical considerations generally applicable to companies in other lines of activity that carry on foreign business. While the emphasis may well differ from that which applies to companies engaged in manufacturing, marketing, and distribution of a product or in the performance of a service, yet even these aspects are frequently involved in the activities of a petroleum or mining company. The practitioner should, therefore, be prepared to relate to the special legal requirements to be imposed on his client in a given host country, including those that may pertain to the question of repatriation of capital investment and profits, taxation, exchange control restrictions (as might impede return on investment or the free conversion of currencies), corporate or partnership registration requirements, restrictions on exports or imports, labor laws, and the like. Use of local counsel, accounting firms, bankers, and other specialists can be most helpful in providing guidance and in obtaining information on current requirements and policies of the host country in all of these important aspects.

§ 7.04   The Foreign Petroleum Joint Venture

In order to minimize and to spread the cost and high risk of loss, it is not uncommon for two or more companies to participate together on a joint venture basis in foreign oil, gas, or mining projects. There are still major companies that prefer to carry on alone in overseas activities, but this is becoming less important for many reasons, including that of a greater political and economic risk factor in many countries around the world. Small or medium size independent companies sometimes join together with as many as half a dozen or more companies for this purpose. Quite often, they will participate jointly with one or more local host country participants and, in growing instances, this will include a governmentally owned or controlled natural resource company of the host country. Indeed, it may be (and frequently is) a requirement of the host country that government owned entities have a significant, if not a majority, joint venture participation in order for a company to apply for and to obtain concession or other contractual participation rights in respect to their natural resources. In still other countries, as we shall consider, the relationship with the host country may be more in the nature of a servicing contractor to a government entity which exercises both operational and regulatory authority.

§ 7.05 Joint Venture Considerations

In the formation of a participation group for any overseas venture, there are a number of important practical considerations. A great deal of thought needs to be given to the composition and structuring of a foreign joint venture. This requires the making of appropriate inquiries of and between the proposed participants in order to ascertain whether they will be suitable financially, technically, and in various other respects to each other as well as to the licensing or granting authority of the foreign government. As a general rule, the foreign government will scrutinize and have to be satisfied as to each participant. In some countries, there are varying kinds and degrees of sophistication in one or more important aspects that pertain to local investment, participation, and criteria on which petroleum rights may be granted.

In addition to an evaluation of political and economic risks of a general nature, each participant should fully apprise itself of local petroleum and tax laws, operational costs in the area of interest, accounting and banking matters, repatriation rights, exchange control restrictions (if any), and the existence of requirements to employ and train nationals, export and import restrictions, and many other requirements of the host country which may affect a decision to undertake a financial commitment. It is to be emphasized that the respective individual requirements or needs of each participant do not always concern or harmonize with the others in one or more of these respects. It is far better to know of this in advance of the formation of a participant group.

Before entering into a commitment with a foreign government, the participation group of companies customarily enter into a joint venture participation agreement among themselves. This should include, among other things, an adequate understanding of the nature and kind of oil, gas or mining rights to be applied for and obtained in the foreign area, the designation of one of them to be operator for the group, the respective percentage ownership interests of each participant in the venture, the confidentiality of geophysical and well-drilling data purchased or otherwise acquired for the group, and the nature and amount of work to be performed or funds to be expended. One of the difficulties encountered in the framing of these agreements, in the first place, has to do with the extent of their obligation as may be required to be incurred by the host government. Before awarding the concession or other contractual rights, it is possible the host government may impose additional work obligations than those which are set forth and agreed initially among the participating parties.

One should not assume that what is suitable for one company would be acceptable to another in the matter of structuring their coparticipation in a proposed foreign petroleum venture. Complications may arise if one or more of the participants happens to be an individual or a partnership rather than a corporation. Some host countries do not grant rights or enter into participation arrangements with an individual or other entity that is not taxable locally as a corporate entity. Apart from the transitory nature of the membership of some partnerships, host countries may be concerned with their jurisdiction to tax profits from the venture that are to be received by nonresident participants over whom they may have no tax enforcement and collecting authority. In the case of a corporation, however, a registered branch or subsidiary of a corporation is almost always subject to the local tax net.

Quite often the participants will simply cover their respective contractual rights and obligations on the basis of a preliminary agreement and leave to future negotiation the rather lengthy and complex provisions which would govern their joint activities in the event of an award and discovery of petroleum within the area of interest. This is not, of course, the recommended practice from the legal standpoint, as they could later completely disagree on important facets of a development program or in many other important aspects, such as the drilling of non-obligation wells, the marketing and disposition of their respective shares of petroleum as and when produced, the right to select a new Operator, voting procedures, the assignability of rights, and so on. Yet, those who approach it from a pragmatic standpoint argue that, without an early assurance from the host government that the group may be successful in obtaining a concession or other rights in an area of joint interest, the time and expense of finalizing contractual details between them may be deferred to a later time. In any event, the joint venture parties should have a clear understanding of the financial limits each will accept in terms of a work program and funds to be expended. The problem of setting forth a specific financial limitation on the amount to be spent in respect to work to be performed is that estimates of costs in advance, especially drilling costs in remote areas or in an ocean environment, are frequently incorrect and vary widely. In some instances, one or more of the parties may desire to have the right to withdraw from the venture in the event that the concession offered for award by the government calls for a higher commitment than contemplated originally, or if it includes an area of a different size or quality than proposed. In such a case, the other parties are usually given a preferential right to acquire the portion of the withdrawing party or parties on a pro-rata basis.

§ 7.06 Strategies in Applying for Petroleum Rights

The granting of foreign rights to explore for and to produce petroleum is, subject to a few exceptions, based on governmental discretion and not on an auction for cash basis to the highest bidder. Even so, in certain countries, there may be a set or prescribed cash payment or initial expenditure to be made on or after the award of such rights. Such cash expenditures are often expressed in terms of a minimum amount to be expended on the license or concession within a specified period of time. In some countries, the license or concession may require both the payment of an initial sum for the right granted as well as require the making of specific expenditures on geophysical work and for the drilling of one or more wells.

Almost invariably, a cautious approach is taken in the submittal of proposed work programs or in making of other commitments to a foreign government in applying for petroleum rights, especially in yet unproven areas. In the case of minerals, there may have been only an initial discovery of an ore body and, in the case of oil and gas, there may be nothing more than that of a favorable geologic or geophysical report of a regional nature indicating the possible presence of oil or gas bearing sediments or structures. In either case, the aim is to limit one's initial obligation to the foreign government (as the usual owner of the natural resource) to that which permits the advancing of capital funds in ascending conditional stages, with a reservation of a right to disengage from all future obligation if the next higher commitment stage would appear to be economically unfeasible. For example, the company might agree to perform certain regional and detailed seismic work in the proposed area of interest, and to drill at least one well on any prospective structure. Quite obviously, there should be no obligation to drill more than one well if the drilling of the first well on a prospect should geologically disprove the productive potential of the area or the geologic structure. If, however, promising shows of petroleum are indicated in the drilling of a first well, the obligation beyond that should be limited to the drilling of only such appraisal wells as may be necessary to delineate the field and evaluate the commercialization of the structure. If such further appraisal drilling does not indicate an economic feasibility of the project, there should be no further obligation to develop and the owners of the concession should then be free to relinquish the area of grant, or at least that part of the same which has been proven to be unproductive in commercial quantities.

In some countries, the right to assign or "farm-out" petroleum or mineral rights granted by the host government may require the granting of advance approval. This may be most difficult to obtain as, for example, in the case of United Kingdom continental shelf licenses. Local law and policy on this subject could be very important to the investing companies. Even where restrictive assignability practices are adopted as a matter of policy, it is likely that the host government would allow limited or qualified security interest transfers in the case of a commercial discovery and the need arises for obtaining borrowed funds with which to finance operation and development.

§ 7.07 Joint Operating Agreements

The form and content of Joint Operating Agreements between participating companies to govern their long-range activities in foreign oil and gas ventures and operations are not standarized. It is necessary to pattern the provisions in a manner consistent with the particular laws, regulations, and idiosyncrasies of the host country. This frequently requires very special clauses which are tailored, for example, to relate to specific work programs, the surrender or relinquishment of acreage, to provisions for assignment or sub-lease of rights (in whole or in part), sole risk or independent operation provisions (to be effective when less than all parties desire to participate in a given nonobligatory well or project within the concession area), rights to dispose of production in the event one or more of the parties does not have a current market, and to a number of other provisions that will often vary in terms from the more usual provisions of agreements in use, for example, on-shore or off-shore the United States. Carefully drafted clauses need also to be included which deal with the possibilities of war, expropriation, or other extraordinary or *force majeure* events which may seriously affect the rights of the parties in the concession area in consequence of governmental or other action. Further, because of the high risk and liability factor involved in many of these operations, considerable attention should be given to insurance provisions as they relate to various specialized categories of risk, especially with respect to offshore drilling and development operations. Special provisions should also be incorporated which deal with the choice of law to govern, the arbitration of disputes, if agreed, and currency exchange problems as may arise among the various participating companies.

§ 7.08   Resource Ownership and Title

Generally, the ownership of the petroleum or mineral resource itself and the authority to grant the right to explore and to produce in foreign countries is in the government itself. This simplifies title searches and questions of the nature usually encountered in private ownership situations. Even so, this does not excuse one from a thorough examination of relevant government laws, regulations, and records as may be available. In any event, it is important to satisfy oneself that the host country law adequately permits the awarding authority of the government to issue the rights in question and that the same have not been previously covered by grant to other parties. The manner of checking governmental records for these purposes may vary from country to country and quite often one finds that the records are not open to the public in the usual sense, if at all. Then, too, it is important to determine that the host government is not involved in an actual or potential territorial dispute with another government in relation to the particular area of interest.

In recent years, there have been a number of such jurisdictional disputes and a great many of them involve offshore continental shelf areas. The Geneva Convention of 1958[1] merely established a principle of equidistance as a general guide which the ratifying nations bordering on the seas should follow in establishing their respective subsea boundaries in continental shelf areas lying outside their historic territorial waters. This Treaty was not ratified by all nations to which it could have application. Moreover, even those ratifying have had difficulties in following or in interpreting how to apply the principle in many situations. For example, questionable interpretations have arisen over irregular coastlines. This has resulted in numerous bilateral agreements establishing median subsea boundary lines, such as between Norway and the United Kingdom, to establish a median line to divide their respec-

---

[1] Convention on the Continental Shelf, *opened for signature*, April 29, 1958, 15 U.S.T. 471, T.I.A.S. No. 5578, 499 U.N.T.S. 311 (effective June 10, 1964).

tive national shelves.[2] The agreements relate specifically to the seabed and petroleum deposits that may underlie the same, rather than involving navigation or fishing rights which are frequently the subject of unrelated treaties. There are areas of the world, particularly in offshore areas, where a boundary dispute has been a recent occurrence. An example is that of the Greek-Turkish dispute in the Aegean Sea.[3] Another example is an offshore area between Australia and Indonesia, in the so-called Jibiru Basin, where drilling activity is imminent. It is, of course, always possible that a nonsignatory to the Convention might take issue with the rights of seabordering countries who have entered into agreements in keeping with the Convention; however, under customary international law the exercise of sovereignty is not likely to be disputed so long as the relevant bordering countries have the requisite power to defend their own national interests as expressed in their agreements against outside intervenors.

On the establishment of their continental shelf median lines by agreement or otherwise, most of the nations enacted their own separate petroleum laws and regulations governing their respective shelf areas. Under many of these laws, as well as in the bilateral shelf agreements, consideration was given to the possibility that natural deposits of petroleum resources might be found to straddle common median seabed boundary lines with other nations bordering on the same sea. The relevant provisions usually called for the sharing of such a common deposit on equitable principles but were otherwise not specific on important details. Unlike hard rock minerals, oil and gas in an underground reservoir is fugacious in nature so that the drilling of a well or wells on one side of a common median boundary line into a common subsea deposit will likely drain oil and gas from the other side of the median line that is subject to entirely different laws and regulations of another jurisdic-

---

[2] Agreement between the government of the United Kingdom of Great Britain and Northern Ireland and the government of the Kingdom of Norway relating to the Delimitation of the Continental Shelf between the two countries, June 25, 1965, (1967) Gr. Brit. T.S. No. 71 (Cmd. 2757).

[3] See Aegean Sea Continental Shelf, Interim Protection, [1976] I.C.J. 3 (Greece v. Turkey).

tion. The reality of this problem is best demonstrated in the North Sea, particularly between the United Kingdom and Norway. The first such common deposit discovered was that of the Frigg Gas Field which, while being discovered on the Norwegian side of the median line, extended beyond and over into the United Kingdom sector. Since then, several other such large common deposits of oil have been discovered. To resolve the various intricate problems posed by the exploration and exploitation of these deposits, fieldwide Unitization Agreements have been made between the participating companies and approved by the respective governments.[4]

§ 7.09 Nature of Rights Granted

In the context of nationalism, it has become politically inexpedient for foreign governments to enter into arrangements for the exploration and development of their natural resources which grant an ownership interest in the resource itself. As to be discussed later on, this has materially impacted on the form and content of licensing or concession agreements. Even those licenses to produce petroleum from the United Kingdom in the North Sea, for instance, grant only the right to drill and, upon discovery, merely to take away the product or proceeds derived therefrom.

In undertaking to acquire participation rights in certain foreign countries, it should be recognized that differing legislation may pertain to onshore as distinguished from offshore exploration and development. The United Kingdom, Canada, and Australia are good examples of this. In some cases, radical differences are not found as between the separate legislative

---

[4] *See* Horigan, J.E., "Unitization of Petroleum Reservoirs Extending Across Sub-Sea Boundary Lines of Bordering States in the North Sea," 3 Int'l Bus. Law. 401 (1975). *See also* a paper originally presented by the author at the Second Annual European Meeting of the Society of Petroleum Engineers of AIME in London in 1973, and subsequently published in 7 Nat. Resources Law. 67 (1974); Rainder, "Oil and Gas Deposits Across National Frontiers," 73 Am. J. Int'l L. 215 (1979); and Onorato, "Apportionment of an International Common Petroleum Deposit," 25 Int'l & Comp. Law L.Q. 324 (1977).

requirements of onshore and offshore, except as it relates to the fundamental operational and activity differentials to be taken into account in the differing environments. On the whole, however, there are significant differences, such as the size of the areas within which rights are granted, the commitments required for drilling, development, and production, pollution controls, and other terms of dissimilarity.

§ 7.10 Special U.S. Tax Considerations

It is beyond the scope of this essay to cover specific United States tax considerations applicable to investments in foreign oil and gas ventures. Nevertheless, it is important to note that tax considerations, both those of the United States and the foreign host government, often govern the structuring of company's participation and, in some instances, the decision itself on whether or not to invest. Care should be exercised in the planning of a coparticipation joint venture arrangement from the United States tax point of view, particularly to avoid the usual unintended consequence of creating an association taxable as a corporation. The usual criteria apply. Each participant will normally wish to preserve the right to report its own income, depreciation, losses, and expenditures as an individual entity separate and apart from its coventurers. Over the years, the petroleum licensing or tax laws of a foreign host government have presented compatibility problems to the American company from a U.S. tax standpoint. A good example has been the former United Kingdom licensing requirement that only registered United Kingdom corporations could apply for and be issued a license. To avoid this problem legally and to gain desired U.S. tax treatment, it was necessary for a long time for American companies to structure their participation whereby the required United Kingdom corporation became, in effect for U.S. purposes, a shell entity and the American company, by special contract with the United Kingdom corporation applicant, the true investor of economic substance. A somewhat different problem that caused even greater structuring complexity was encountered by corporate licensing requirements on the continental shelf of The Netherlands. Further, the transition away from the more traditional concession or licensing terms in a number of countries to that of so-called Production Sharing Contracts or to service contracts, has required careful consideration of U.S. tax consequences from the standpoint of relevant terms and provisions to be incorporated in such contracts. This was to ensure that, for U.S. purposes at least, the true economic interest in the subject matter resides in the American company.

In many instances, companies have found it desirable to seek and obtain advance United States Internal Revenue Service rulings in respect to various kinds of coarrangements. It should be further noted that special United States tax laws and regulations apply to petroleum companies and their activities which differ in some ways from those applicable to companies engaged in other kinds of businesses. Also, special tax laws, regulations, and rulings apply to international oil and gas operations. For instance, the Tax Reduction Act of 1975 introduced three new terms entitled "foreign oil and gas extraction income," "foreign oil related income," and "foreign oil related loss." Generally from a United States tax standpoint, there is no longer percentage depletion on foreign petroleum production and it may be critical to investment that the foreign tax credit, as well as exploration and development expenditures, include the right to elect for deduction of intangible well-drilling and operating costs, and that this be treated favorably in line with the companies' intentions.

§ 7.11   Financing of Foreign Ventures

The financing of foreign petroleum ventures is a subject of its own and will not be covered here in any detail. Several observations should be made, however, because of their practical importance. Each individual participating company in a joint venture abroad should be prepared to rely on its own source of investment funds, rather than on borrowed funds, at least through the making of an acquisition of a concession or license and, thereafter, through the exploratory and appraisal drilling stages of a required work program. This includes, *inter alia,* the cost of administrative overheads, initial fees or bonuses for the granting of a license or other contractual right, the acquisition of geophysical and geological work relative to the area or areas of interest, annual periodic payments as may be due under the terms of grant, management fees (if any), contract services, expenses incurred in the event of the establishment of a foreign office, and the registration of a branch or a subsidiary corporation in the host country, and a host of related expenses and charges which are quite familiar to the industry. Upon establishing recoverable resources in commercial quantities, however, it is frequently necessary, even in the case of the major oil companies, to borrow funds with which to finance the project. Until this point of commercially proven recoverable reserves has been reached, as a practical matter, there is not sufficient asset to stand on its own as security for a loan to carry the project into the development stages.

The vast majority of financings over the past decade and a half have been made on a "project" basis with the project itself, in the form usually of carved-out production payments, serving as a repayment vehicle. The scope of the financial requirements for a given project may vary considerably depending on a number of circumstances, including whether or not the discovery is onshore or offshore, the remoteness of the area, the availability of contract services and equipment, costs of labor, transportation, and communication. There are enormous variations in anticipated costs in various offshore continental shelf areas around the globe. The drilling of wells in the North Sea, for instance, usually involves greater costs than the drilling of wells in the Gulf of Mexico or offshore in the Java Sea in Indonesia. There is a definite relationship to the character and severity of the ocean environment, water and formation depths involved, the nature and kind of drilling equipment and rigs that are to be engaged, the accessibility to labor skills and technology, shutdown time due to storms, breakdown in operational equipment or function, and the like. Frequently, it is difficult to determine the length of time it will take to drill a well and the drilling contractor today ordinarily charges on a daily basis for the use of offshore drilling rigs. In

1970, in the North Sea, the average drilling cost for a dry hole was approximately $2.5 million. By 1979 this average drilling cost alone ranged around $5 to $7 million per well. By 1985, a cost of $10 million was not uncommon. The cost of development of a field, following an interesting discovery, can be enormous in locations like the North Sea. For instance, Phillips Petroleum Company's Ekofisk Field in Norwegian waters cost the company over $4.5 billion before they were able to produce a single barrel of commercial oil or a cubic foot of gas. The development of other large fields in the North Sea have ranged from $1.5 to $4 billion. Banks or other lending institutions have to satisfy themselves against a number of risks. This includes those risks which have to do with the duration and validity of the concession or license, political and economic factors of the host country, the nature of the production facilities for development, the character of the market and of the discovered petroleum reserves (in terms of production payout), and all of these should point most favorably to an adequate servicing of the project loan over a period of time. Depending on the circumstances and risks involved, backup parent company guarantees may be (and usually are) required.

Under more stable governments, there have been fewer problems in obtaining the necessary finance. However, many areas have become increasingly problematic and much more difficult for this purpose. It is important, in any case, for the participating parties to be aware of the problems they may later encounter in obtaining finance before undertaking the venture.

The lawyer should be especially aware of the restrictions or inadequacies in current legislation in the country of interest. In some cases, as in the United Kingdom and Norway, special legislative and regulatory changes have to be approved in order to permit the banks and lending institutions to obtain rights in the nature of a security interest in the project and in the production proceeds as would furnish protection against contingencies as could adversely affect loan security. Further, licensing provisions ordinarily include broad powers of the government to revoke all rights on the occurrence of stated conditions of default. Not only do such conditions require special handling from the security standpoint, but it is also important to recognize that most foreign concessions do not grant an ownership interest in the petroleum reserves in-place, but rather grant merely the right to drill and produce so long as the license remains in good standing in compliance with the terms and conditions of its issuance. This contrasts with the usual form of oil and gas lease in the United States which ordinarily allows the lessee to continue the lease in full force and effect so long as oil and gas is produced in paying quantities upon the making of the required rental, royalty, or other payments.

The financiers must content themselves with governmental understandings and agreements which will assure them of a continuity in the life of the license and of the rights to produce for the period necessary to have a full repayment of the principal and interest on the loan. There are a number of other questions which could affect the title (and hence the security) of concessions which will not be considered here.[5]

§ 7.12 Reference Literature

There is a growing spectrum of literature available to those interested in pursuing this subject in greater detail on either an area-by-area or a country-by-country basis and, to a very limited extent, this is reflected in the authorities cited in this chapter. Because of long-term activity and a common background historically in relation to the discovery and development of substantial reserves of oil, there is more accumulated literature on the Middle East than other areas of active current interest. This is changing rapidly, however, due primarily to the successful efforts and writings sponsored by the Energy Sections of The International Bar Association (IBA) and the Law Association for Asia and the Western Pacific (LAWASIA). Although much broader in scope of coverage than energy and

---

[5] See, e.g., Sanchez, J., "Foreign Investment in a Changing World: Banking Arrangements and Associated Financial Conditions," Spec. Institute on International Minerals Acquisition and Operations (1974); see also Ns. 10 and 11 infra.

natural resource topics, the annual Institute in Dallas on *Private Investment Abroad* sponsored by the International and Comparative Law Center of the Southwest Legal Foundation normally produces several excellent published papers on developments in this area. Additionally, there have been recent publications that are rather comprehensive in scope. Noteworthy in this respect is a 1984 publication on the subject of *Petroleum Licensing: A Comparative Study* by Prof. Peter Cameron of the University of Dundee in Scotland.[6] It focuses mainly on Northwest Europe, Asia and the Pacific, including China, and North America. From the same University, Prof. Terence Daintith, in addition to other works, has written on related subjects,[7] and Prof. Cameron's work as mentioned adds still other select bibliography of current interest.[8]

The International Bar Association and the LAWASIA Research Institute jointly published papers that were presented in 1982, at Singapore on *Energy Law in Asia and the Pacific.*[9] In 1984, a very successful conference sponsored by the Energy Section of LAWASIA, again in Singapore, produced excellent papers which updated the energy law and policies of each of the countries in the widespread region of Asia and the Western Pacific. No doubt these papers will make their appearance in publication form in due course.

Although somewhat dated now by events, as well as by governmental policy and regulatory changes, the publications of two legal institutes sponsored by the Rocky Mountain Mineral Law Foundation in the Fall of 1974 and 1975 were for a time the best sources of entry material for the American lawyer who

---

[6] Cameron, Peter, *Financial Times Business Information Ltd.* (1984).

[7] Daintith, Terence (ed.), *The Legal Character of Petroleum Licenses: A Comparative Study*, (1981).

[8] Barrows, Gordon H., *Worldwide Concession Contracts and Petroleum Legislation*, (1983); Clapham, Murray C., "Legal Aspects of Foreign Investment in Oil and Mining," 7 Int'l Bus. Law. 115-19 (1979); Horigan, J.E., *Foreign Participation in Domestic Oil and Gas Ventures*, in Proceedings of the 28th Annual Institute of the Rocky Mountain Mineral Law Institute, 1983, at pp. 969-1019; Turner, Louis, *Oil Companies in the International System* (3d edition 1983); and Vock, D., "The Evolution of the Legal Relationship Between International Petroleum Mining Companies and Host Countries," 11 Int'l Bus. Law. 244-46 (1983).

[9] *Energy Law in Asia and the Pacific* (1982).

desired actively to engage in an international energy and minerals practice. The first of these institutes[10] comprised seventeen papers presented by recognized experts in the field who separately covered the legal aspects of oil, gas, and mining activities throughout the world on an area-by-area basis. This included the Middle East, the North Sea, Africa, Latin America, Australia, Indonesia, Canada, and certain other foreign operational areas. Inclusively, the papers gave consideration to U.S. tax, banking and associated financial arrangements, marketing, supply, transportation, labor, and other relevant factors involved with foreign petroleum exploration and development activities. The second institute[11] was differently oriented but fully complementary to the first in its emphasis on both foreign and domestic offshore exploration, drilling and development. Its scope included the detailing of the nature and kinds of contractual arrangements which are pertinent to such activities, including joint venture participation agreements, contracts relating to drilling and development of a field, and ancillary services or support contracts. It also touched on practical and logistical problems, environmental concerns, admiralty law applications, risk and insurance clauses, as well as special tax and financing considerations. As in the case of the first institute, each paper was presented by an expert with actual experience in such field or area of activity.

Another excellent and fairly recent source of information in particular reference to then current laws and policies in respect to both petroleum and minerals in Norway, Southeast Asian nations, and Australia is to be found in a special issue of *The International Business Lawyer,* published in March 1979, and based on the papers presented at a symposium at Cambridge University in England.[12] It contains an indepth summary of oil and gas policies as reflected in systems of taxation

---

[10] Special Institute on International Minerals Acquisition and Operations Law (Rocky Mountain Mineral Law Foundation, November 1974).

[11] Special Institute on Offshore Oil, Gas and Mineral Exploration and Development (Rocky Mountain Mineral Law Foundation, November 1975).

[12] *Energy and Natural Resource Law,* Int'l Bus. Law. (Special Issue, March 1979).

in the above mentioned nations, in addition to the United States system of taxation.

As a parting note to the foregoing sections, it should be emphasized that the lawyer is often called upon to assist in the nonlegal evaluation of the political and economic risk of the local host country. This is frequently a highly important judgment factor and the lawyer's broad experience can be most helpful. It includes the question of stability of the government and the matter of continuity of governmental policies as may apply in the future. In every sense of the word, the lawyer is helpful to his client in a number of ways that may be viewed as extraordinary or unusual in comparison to domestic United States law practice, and his analysis is sometimes important to the making of a foreign investment decision.

§ 7.13   Effect of Modern Trends on Foreign Petroleum Investment

The nature of petroleum exploration and production arrangements between host countries and the oil companies has radically changed in the course of time. Those who would still portray the companies as one-sided exploiters of another nation's natural resources simply cling to old relics of the past and are out of tune with late 20th century realities. This will become evident to the reader as we briefly sketch the general character of arrangements over time.

Indeed, in the course of a half-century, the shifting sands of fortune on this subject have brought forth a picture that would today be quite unrecognizable to earlier negotiators of host nations and of the oil companies themselves. Prior to World War II and (subject to exceptions) extending up into the 1960's, the bargains struck between the companies and a number of host countries, particularly with underdeveloped countries, may arguably be viewed retrospectively as one-sided in favor of the companies. The other side of the coin to such a view, however, would reflect on the high level of economic and political risk in some of the developing countries and the almost complete absence within such countries of an independent wherewithal in technology, know-how, skills, and experience to discover and to develop their own indigenous petroleum resources.

The more classical form of foreign concession, to be reviewed below, typical in the earlier arrangements, eroded in time into contractual arrangements that have reflected a rising fervor of state nationalism and a high degree of governmental participation in the results of discovery and development by the companies. In other words, a more "balanced" *quid pro quo.* Yet, as discussed previously in Section 7.02, above, there remains in this new modern context a measure of political and economic uncertainty and instability that has contributed, commencing in the early 1970's, to a pronounced decline in interest in foreign exploration in various areas of the world by U.S. companies who, after all, are the source of American foreign investment funds.

The traumatic events of 1979, including the fall of the Shah of Iran and the ensuing pinch in oil supplies, the rapid multifold increase in prices established by the Organization of Petroleum Exporting Countries (OPEC), global inflation, and the then increasing energy demands of the Western world, all served to rekindle an urgent need on the part of U.S. companies for the discovery of new sources of petroleum both at home and abroad.

These events, however, occurred at a time when a host of disincentives for foreign exploration plagued the petroleum industry. As indicated previously, the stimulus to American company investment abroad over the years in the search for new sources of petroleum has been the prospect of achieving such rewards from successful discovery as would overshadow the large financial and political risks involved. In overall historical terms, the incentive has been more than sufficient to meet these criteria and a company's losses in specific foreign locations have been, in general, adequately counterbalanced by gains at other locations. This is especially true with the major companies who have, over the years, spread their participation actively around the globe into a number of prospective risk areas. The smaller and medium-sized exploration companies are comparative newcomers to the scene, commencing around the mid-1960's, and are far less diversified in their foreign investment activities and holdings.

Even before the changing events of 1979, many of the non-major or independent companies had become (starting about 1975) disenchanted with the high risks of foreign participation arrangements. Some withdrew completely, and others did so on a limited or selective basis. From a purely financial standpoint, the ability of the small or medium-sized independent exploration and producing company to attract capital for participation in foreign areas had greatly diminished. These include many companies that had, over the years, accounted for so much of the domestic U.S. discoveries of petroleum deposits and who held out promise of significantly enhancing global supplies, that is, absent crippling disincentives. The novelty is that this has never been adequately appreciated, if at all, by foreign licensing host-country governments in the fashioning of their petroleum laws, regulatory, and taxation regimens, save for a few exceptions such as in the United Kingdom's North Sea in the 1964-73 and 1983 periods.

Even some host countries, because of domestic political or economic factors, were taking positions by the mid-1970's that dampened the zeal of the independents and, to some extent, of the major companies as well. A few foreign governments considered policies which would seek to disallow the remission abroad of what were deemed to be "excessive profits." This was expressed, in some cases, in the form of a "renegotiation" of contract terms with the oil companies, or simply by the introduction of special taxation which, while not intending to fully discourage the participation of those companies having needed expertise, technology, and capital, had the effect of rendering their participation much less attractive than seemed to be the case (to the investor) initially. This could be justified by the host governments in some cases without directly incurring the criticism of debasement of the sanctity of contract. One writer has referred to these trends as a form of "subtle nationalization."[13]

---

[13] Tocher, J., "Patterns and Trends in Agreements with Foreign Countries" in Spec. Inst. on International Minerals Acquisitions Law and Operations (Rocky Mountain Mineral Law Foundation, November 1974).

Various instances could be cited where the host government, by undertaking renegotiation of contract, went so far as to cause a withdrawal of certain companies because the new terms were considered to be too discouraging and unreasonable. For example, Indonesia probably went too far in renegotiating the terms of its production sharing contracts in the mid-1970's. This was coupled with an adverse IRS ruling in the United States on tax considerations which served to drive away some of the enthusiasm which had made this area of the world most attractive for exploration. On the whole, however, the rates of return on investment in a number of producing countries continue to be deemed "reasonable," to the host country and perhaps "tolerable" to the participating companies, even though arguably not in the context which original company investment risks were taken. Then, too, in less developed countries and in certain of the countries of the Middle East, the risks to foreign investment have been substantially aggravated by direct expropriation or nationalization in some cases. In still others, the idea of sanctity of contract, which was founded on sound principles of international law, is not recognized. Rather, the contract is regarded as a relationship, instead of a commitment, and is good in duration only so long as such relationship remains satisfactory.

The global side effects from the traumatic events of 1979, particularly inflation and balance of payments problems arising from the OPEC cartel's high prices on energy costs, contributed to or resulted in economic recession in a number of countries. The hardest hit were those with a heavy reliance on imported oil and with difficult foreign debt structures. Indeed, the cartel's imposition of control over and maintenance of the high cost of oil produced by its member countries affected all of the countries of the free world in one degree or another. Prices of oil everywhere, including that produced by non-cartel countries, rose to OPEC pricing levels.

From 1979 to the mid-1980's, the effect of foreign petroleum exploration by these events was not seen as negative overall. The higher prices obtainable from discovery and production, as measured against pre-1979 prices, had largely offset the effects of recession and decline in global demand for petroleum products. The prime test or inducement to exploration abroad continued to be based (apart from geology) on the terms of foreign licensing or concession rights and the relevant laws, taxation and regulatory policies of the respective governments, to say nothing of political and economic risk factors.

Commencing in 1984, however, various signs began to emerge that all was not well with OPEC and its domination of global oil pricing. Prices began to decline notwithstanding "best efforts" on the part of leading OPEC member producers to hold the line as against some of its nonconforming members.

A combination of factors have contributed to what appears at the mid-1980 mark to be a serious challenge to OPEC's past domination of world petroleum events. These include an oversupply of crude oil production due to the effects of recession in consuming countries, enhanced discovery and production of crude oil from non-OPEC member countries (most notably being the United Kingdom and Norway in the North Sea), and conservation practices and uses of some forms of alternate energy sources (most notably in the U.S.). This is not consistent with OPEC's 1979 scenario which called for ever-increasing market demand and prices coupled with decreasing global supplies of petroleum.

From a foreign investment standpoint, the international petroleum industry in the 1985-1990 era is faced with a host of paradoxes that are unresolvable through advance predictability. Will oil supplies from the Middle East remain dependable as in the past? Will the economic recovery in the industrial nations, commenced in the 1983-84 period, continue and, if so, will this rectify the oil oversupply situation of 1985? Will OPEC disintegrate or lose such control over high oil production price maintenance as would render foreign investment uneconomic to the oil companies in relation to the terms of petroleum licensing requirements, taxation, and the like, of foreign governments? In a renewed free market demand context of oil supply and consumption, assuming a diminished OPEC cartel influence, will demand sufficiently increase to firm-up prices and profitability margins?

Relatively recent trends toward law, policy, or taxation improvements in the terms of license or other participation arrangements are in response to declining expenditures and budgets worldwide of many companies. Significant improvements have either been enacted or are under consideration in certain of the producing countries, notably in the United Kingdom, Canada, and in the Western Pacific (*e.g.*, Indonesia, Thailand, and the Philippines). These may serve to ease some of the uncertainties created by the above mentioned paradoxes of the late 1980's; but there still remain many other countries around the globe that are presently unattuned to changing events in exploration activity.

§ 7.14 Nature of Foreign Concessions and Licenses

While still used loosely within the petroleum industry to refer to most any kind of agreement or license with a foreign government to explore for and to develop its petroleum resources, the term "concession" has actually become more restricted and even deemed inapplicable in relation to many of the arrangements that have evolved or significantly altered over the course of time. Such other arrangements have included the Production Sharing contract and the so-called Service contracts, each of which are to be found in nonstandardized versions. The somewhat typical attributes of each will be briefly considered later on:

Essentially, one might fairly categorize the modern-day concession as including leases and licenses issued by foreign governments—but to recognize that these are considerably evolved and, in many ways, substantially different in terms from the historic concessions to be reviewed in the next section. The basic thread of similarity lies in the fact that they involved the granting of a right for a period of time to enter on a defined area to explore for, drill, and to produce oil or gas, but with the host government retaining royalties and the right to collect taxes in varying forms.

Gordon H. Barrows divided world petroleum arrangements into two major types: (1) concessions, and (2) contracts, and would distinguish the concession as having the feature whereby *all* the oil goes to the concessionaire.[14] This is certainly a typical distinction but with a few modifications here and there as, for example, in the United Kingdom and in the Netherlands, where state-owned entities have in the past exercised a regulatory control or a call on some portion of oil or gas production. Prof. Peter Cameron advances the view that the term "license" is preferable to "concession" as a generic term, but makes the point that the differences in terminology conceal a similarity in substance.[15] He then draws a further distinction as between Production Sharing contracts and Service contracts (risk and non-risk varieties).[16]

It is evident that any consideration of the early evolution of foreign petroleum arrangements should not be intended to serve as a means of obtaining a clear understanding of present day arrangements which, in many particulars, are radically different from those from which they evolved. Thus, an historical study of the evolution of foreign participation agreements may be deemed less important than in the past. However, such a study does help in our understanding of the present state of affairs.

§ 7.15 Early Petroleum Concessions

The present day relationships between many of the earlier host producing countries and exploration companies are significantly different in nature from those in existence in the first half of the century. For our purposes here, it would seem appropriate to render only a brief sketch of those historical relationships which evolved in the pre-World War II era. With the end of World War II, noted Professor Keith W. Blinn, "a new specie" of relationship came into evidence which was marked by a rising wave of sovereign national independence

---

[14] Barrows, Gordon H., "World Petroleum Legislation Review" 22 Exploration and Economics of the Petroleum Industry 307-360 (1984).

[15] *See* Cameron, N. 6 *supra*, at pp. 5-6.

[16] *Id.* at pp. 9-14.

and the development of new patterns.[17] The early oil concession agreement which originated in 1901 in Persia set a pattern which was subsequently followed by various other Middle Eastern States. Blinn has called attention to the simplicity and general uniformity of these concessions, describing their chief characteristics to include largeness in size (thousands of square miles), long in duration (oftentimes fifty years or more), and financially founded on a royal payment to the host government which was tied to the value of gold for a ton of crude oil, in addition to the payment of modest bonuses and periodic rentals which increased with time and competition.[18]

The major companies involved in these early day activities were quite free in their budgeting of expenditures and in the conduct of operations. Wellhead ownership of oil followed the traditional United States leasehold pattern. These arrangements were more than welcomed at the time when one takes into account that the host countries, for the most part, were economically underdeveloped and unaware of the then industrial world, lacking in the necessary capital, technology, skill, transportation, and marketing capability, and sorely needing the foreign companies if they were to improve their economies and to develop on their own. In turn, the companies were prepared to take the risks of both a political and economic nature far away from home. This is not to say that, in retrospect, a number of these earlier concession agreements were not one-sided even in the face of risks and uncertainties.

The royalty payable under the early oil and gas concession was usually fixed in amount and not related to future levels or production. In a few instances there may have been a profit sharing component, but it was small in comparison to overall profit. Since the oil companies controlled both the production and transportation, as well as the downstream marketing of the product, it was difficult to determine the extent of their profit margins. Further, the companies ordinarily invoked low

---

[17] Blinn, Keith R., "Production Sharing Agreements for Petroleum and Minerals" in Symposium on Private Investors Abroad 309 (Southwest Legal Foundation's International and Comparative Law Center, 1978).

[18] *Id.* at 306.

pricing policies for crude oil production on which royalty payable to the government was calculated.

§ 7.16 Comparisons to Leasing Practices in the U.S.

Before reviewing the nature of changes in concession agreements that were introduced in the post-World War II era and, in the process, to see how these changes may be measured in an overall context, it may be helpful to the reader to briefly consider in advance the contrasting nature of oil and gas lease agreements entered into in the United States during the same post-World War II period. From this it may readily be seen that substantive shifts have occurred favoring foreign governments in concession terms when compared with an American model.

Such a comparison requires some qualification in that, unlike foreign concessions and licenses, most oil and gas leases in the U.S. (outside of offshore areas and some Rocky Mountain states) are granted by private owners of the petroleum rights; however, leases covering federal or state government owned lands and petroleum rights are not significantly different in terms of size, duration, royalty, taxation rates, etc. Negotiations are always involved on private leases. Other procedures, including competitive bidding, apply on federal and state offshore and on some onshore leases.

While the terms of leases in the United States have evolved in form and content over the past fifty years or so, the general terms and provisions (from the early 1950's onward) are essentially very much the same in terms of duration, royalty and rental obligations, and in many important provisions. While it is true that lease terms may well be (and frequently are) more favorable to the lessor where leases are negotiated in producing areas, yet the essential nature of the oil and gas lease in so-called wildcat or semi-proven areas is much the same today as that found in leases of twenty-five or thirty years ago. Often, the difference lies in the amount of bonus consideration paid at the time of execution of the lease and the royalty payable to the lessor may, for instance, range as high as 25 percent rather than the usual 12.5 percent payable in the ordinary leasing situation. Characteristically, oil and gas leases in the United States embrace a much smaller sized area than those covered in foreign concessions, but the point to be made here simply is that there has been no general dissatisfaction or claim of "unfairness" with respect to these leases over the course of time. The amount of bonus payable for the execution of a lease in unproven areas is usually very modest and the annual rentals payable for the privilege of delaying the commencement of drilling operations are minimal. The leases are generally for a primary period ranging from three up to ten years, and so long thereafter as oil or gas is produced in paying quantities. Federally regulated price controls over oil were completely removed in 1981, and controls over gas prices were partially removed effective January 1, 1985. Federal taxation, in the form of the Windfall Profit Tax, effective March 1, 1980, is high on oil production in various categories and considered discriminatory against the petroleum industry. When measured against these standards, one is in a better position to measure the greater economic risk involved on the part of oil companies in making investments abroad in foreign concessions.

§ 7.17 Post-World War II Patterns

Following World War II, new patterns began to emerge and the motivation for change, according to Blinn, may be attributed to various factors, including a substantial increase in demand for petroleum in and among the developed industrial countries, an increase in competition among them for supplies, and the establishment of a better bargaining position on the part of the host countries. This led the host countries to seek greater profits and to improve on the terms and conditions of their concession grants.[19]

The post-World War II history of relationships between producing countries of the world and oil companies were classified by James T. Jensen into four distinct time periods up to the

---

[19] Blinn, N. 17 *supra*, at pp. 309-10.

year 1974.[20] The first such classification covered the period prior to 1954; the second period extended from 1954 to 1960; the third period from 1960 to 1970, and the fourth period from 1970 to 1974.

During the first such period as mentioned, the government of Venezuela achieved a fifty-fifty profit sharing split with the oil companies in 1948. This was followed in 1950 by an agreement reached between Saudi Arabia and the Arabian American Oil Company for the same fifty-fifty profit split, but expressed in terms of a 50 percent income tax on the profits of the producing company and with the tax liability computation allowing for the royalty as a credit. As noted by Blinn, the allocation of costs, the pricing of petroleum, and the production schedules remained within the exclusive domain of the producing companies.[21] Subsequent developments to 1954 led to a growing dissatisfaction with this new arrangement, primarily because of a drop in the government-take on profits in consequence of increased production and an erosion in the price. Further, a dispute arose in 1951 between British Petroleum (formerly Anglo-Iranian Oil Company) and the government of Iran which led to the formation of the latter of the National Iranian Oil Company (NIOC) to take over the former's properties in Iran. During the course of the dispute, the oil industry formed the Iranian Consortium of International Oil Companies and made it almost impossible for NIOC to sell its oil in world markets.[22]

The fifty-fifty profit sharing principle remained generally in effect in the Middle East during the second period from 1954 until 1960 and oil continued to sell at posted prices at which the profit margin was calculated for tax purposes.[23] According to James D. Tocher, the prices were tied to crude oil prices in the United States and, as U.S. prices rose, the foreign government take per barrel rose with it. A crude oil price increase in the United States at the time of the 1957 Suez crisis benefited

---

[20] Jensen, James T., "International Oil—Shortage, Cartel or Emerging Resource Monopoly?," 7 Vand. J. Transnational L. 335 (1974).

[21] Blinn, N. 17 *supra*, at p. 310.

[22] Tocher, Ns. 10 and 13 *supra*.

[23] *Id.*

the posted prices in the Middle East; however, increased production caused an erosion of prices and this over supply led to a discounting of posted prices and a deterioration of host country revenue.[24]

As further noted by Tocher, the in-fighting over posted prices led to the establishment of OPEC near the beginning of the third period of classification as mentioned. The initial objective of this organization was to restore crude oil prices to the previously prevailing level. The creation of OPEC also permitted the member countries to maintain a common front in seeking artificially to hold posted prices above the world market price.

During the third period, in 1962-63, OPEC introduced a "royalty expensing" program which had the effect of increasing the rate of tax. By this and other forms of taxation, Tocher noted that the split between the company and the government by 1970 was more in the order of 75–25 percent favoring the government over the companies.[25]

While the large reserves of petroleum in the Middle East and the North African nations of Libya and Algeria caused more attention to be given to changes being introduced in the 1960's in their concession agreements, we should not overlook that significant trends were also emerging in other developing areas of the world during the same period. From the historical standpoint, the expression of national sovereignty and the desire of ownership by host countries of their natural resources was evident in many countries, particularly in Venezuela. Across the world in Indonesia, a fresh concept of foreign participation rights evolved in the mid-1960's with the so-called Production Sharing contract. These concurrent events will be discussed later.

The fourth period of classification of Jensen, 1970–1974, was marked by various efforts on the part of OPEC countries to increase the tax rate and even to nationalize the industry as in Libya or in Venezuela. Led by Libya in September 1970, OPEC countries demanded an increase in the posted price of

---

[24] Blinn, N. 17 *supra*, at pp. 310-11.
[25] Tocher, Ns. 10 and 13 *supra*.

petroleum,[26] even to the extent, as in Libya, of bringing about nationalization unless the companies came to its terms of settlement. Iran quickly followed this lead and the companies either had to capitulate on the terms as prescribed or suffer the consequences of nationalization.[27] The result was the Tehran Agreement of 1971, raising posted prices, generally establishing a 55 percent tax rate, and a consequential substantial increase in government take.[28]

Tocher would interrupt Jensen's fourth period by interposing, retrospectively, events which commenced with the Yom Kippur War and the Arab boycott in 1973, as the beginning of a fifth periodic classification. This additional period, having commenced with the producer boycott in 1973, reflected several important characteristics, including that of a complete reversal of the marketing boycott against Iran which occurred during an earlier period into a producing country boycott of the oil companies themselves. The oil companies were thus faced with an entirely different situation than in the past. In the place of the earlier arrangements the host countries exercised control, not only of their own natural resources in terms of national sovereignty, but also over the posted prices and this carried forward into the exertion of some influence in the downstream marketing activities of the companies.

It may well be said that a sixth periodic classification arose in 1979 with the Egyptian-Israeli Treaty, the fall of the Shah of Iran, and the complex set of chaotic events which followed rapidly in the supply and market situation in the Middle East and, to some extent, in certain other producing countries with membership in OPEC. This almost total reversal in bargaining position stunned the economies of the importing countries of the Western World. The importing countries were never faced with such a dilemma. They were overtaken by events which were not altogether foreseeable and, at the same time, were quite ill-prepared in terms of long-range planning.

Since Middle Eastern countries control more than an estimated one-half of the known free world's supplies of oil, the

---

[26] Blinn, N. 17 *supra*, at p. 311.
[27] *Id.* at pp. 311-312.
[28] *Id.* at p. 312.

fate of OPEC in the latter half of the 1980's is quite relevant to this overall discussion. This is especially so when one considers that some significant oil producers outside of the Middle East have also been counted as OPEC members in varying degrees of loyalty.

So long as there are host countries having need of the technology, capital, and markets which are available to the importing countries, foreign venture arrangements will continue to be made as will allow for a reasonable rate of return, however, this may be defined or structured. It may be hoped that serious forms of nationalization, as in Libya in the early 1970's, or of British Petroleum's oil production in Nigeria in 1979, or of foreign producing company interest in Iran in the same year, are a thing of the past and may give way to more practical considerations. The foregoing is not to say, however, that politically or economically motivated concepts of nationalism have been confined to explosive areas, such as the Middle East. Indeed, nationalistic fervor flourished earlier to an extent in Mexico and Argentina in the 1950's. Brazil established the government owned Petobras during that time, and one of the first Service contracts (discussed as to format below) was awarded in Argentina in 1958, even though with far less government control over production and related operations.

§ 7.18 Modern Petroleum Licenses and Concessions

Following along with the concepts of the "concession" and "license" referred to earlier in Section 7.14, as distinguished generally from the Production Sharing and Service contracts which will be discussed later, basic similarities are still to be found in many modern forms, e.g., the grant of right to enter on a defined area or areas for a specified period of time, to explore for and to drill for the extraction of petroleum, and for the state to receive royalty and tax payments. The similarities begin to fade away, however, in the modern context which includes (generally) more restricted areas and periods of duration, initial bonus and periodic license payments in a number of countries, imposition of timely expenditure requirements on the license (including geologic, geophysical, and the drilling of one or more wells), greater administrative and regulatory burdens (reporting, disclosure, accounting, employment of local nationals, use of local contractors and supplies, etc.), higher royalty payments and taxes of various kinds, restrictions on transfer of rights, close control over the means of conducting operations, restrictions on the sale terms and disposition of production outside the host country, and (increasingly) state or local private company equity participation.

Although it is beyond the scope of this chapter to outline concession or licensing requirements on a country-by-country, or even on an area-by-area basis, the reader may nevertheless pursue such an investigation through a number of publications outside of the making of direct inquiries with host government agencies themselves. This would surely include the previously referenced and comprehensive Barrows' *Worldwide Concession Contracts and Petroleum Legislation,*[29] Peter Cameron's *Petroleum Licensing: A Comparative Study, 1984,*[30] *The 1984 International Petroleum Encyclopedia,*[31] and Terence Daintith's *The Legal Character of Petroleum Licenses: A Comparative Study.*[32]

§ 7.19   Role of State-Owned Petroleum Companies

Today, national or governmentally owned oil companies are found in a great many producing countries. There are far too many to enumerate for purposes of this chapter, much less to discuss in any detail. They are briefly considered here because of the role they play in interfacing with the private oil companies in Production Sharing contracts, in Service contracts, and under some concession or license arrangements. These governmentally owned entities have arisen for various reasons, not alone as a manner of pure expression of nationalistic feeling. Many of them were formed, as in Indonesia, Brazil, and

---

[29] Barrows, N. 8 *supra. See also* N. 14 *supra.*
[30] Cameron, N. 6 *supra.*
[31] Pennwell Publishing Co., Tulsa, 1984.
[32] Daintith, N. 7 *supra.*

in certain bordering states to the North Sea, to participate as joint venturers with experienced companies, predominantly American, in order that they might closely ally with those having the technology, skills, and expertise needed to gain for themselves the measure of independence necessary for playing a greater role in the development of their own resources in the course of time. The functional role played by these entities with respect to the conduct of operations has also varied. The same may be said with respect to equity participation as concerns some producing countries. As mentioned, the extent to which these entities have attained the requisite expertise and technological skills has had some bearing on the form of their contractual relationships with producing companies. In some cases, where they do not reserve a participating interest initially, national owned entities may back-in to a participation status with the oil companies on an optional basis after discovery of petroleum. This has been a rather typical feature of the laws of the Netherlands and Norway and, until recently, in the United Kingdom.

The oil companies have, in many instances, voiced objection to state-owned concerns from a number of standpoints. For one thing, they find themselves participating quite often with competing companies or groups of companies in seeking to obtain license or other contractual rights with respect to the same area. Confidential data and information of one company or group is difficult to preserve, it is thought, where the participating state company has access to information common to all of the companies or groups in which it participates. The oil companies have also complained that the state entities may become involved in the decision and operating process which may lead to the making of proposals which are not consistent with the financial aims and geological prognoses of the companies. The importance of this problem is not to be underestimated inasmuch as the local host government may well have differing goals and long-range concepts which are quite inconsistent with those of the participating oil companies. One of the fears, of course, is that the government-owned companies, in the course of time, will develop the expertise and experience that will make the oil companies somewhat redundant.

§ 7.20   Service Contracts

According to Tocher, the so-called Service contract first originated in Iran in 1966 when the French company ERAP became a contractor to the government company NIOC and undertook to perform technical, financial and other services for the account of NIOC.[33] From the point of view of the companies, Service contracts have often resulted in a much reduced profit. In most instances, the effect of Service agreements has not been to eliminate the producing companies from the host country involved, but rather to subvert their prior dominance and control into that of a more subservient position in terms of profits, operations, and in the development of the host country resources. In the typical Service contract, the oil company investor serves much like a general contractor in performing certain exploration and drilling work in a designated area, but it receives no payment unless a discovery is made and a sufficient amount of production is obtained. Ordinarily, the investor-company's payment takes the form of a percentage of profits for a per barrel fee which can be graduated according to the size of discovery, risk-capital invested or other factors.

Professor Cameron appropriately divides Service contracts into two principal types: risk and non-risk or pure Service contracts.[34] In the former, all risk and small incentive is with the oil company contractor. If there is no discovery, the contract terminates without any reimbursement and if production is obtained the contractor gets its expenses reimbursed with interest and a risk fee[35] as its profit, subject to higher taxation on higher fees. Countries with this kind of contract include Brazil and Argentina. The non-risk type are found in some Middle East countries, Venezuela, and in certain other areas—mostly (according to Cameron) where the companies had previously held developed and producing concessions that were later converted by the host government into such contracts. The contracts are non-risk in the sense that the contrac-

---

[33] Tocher, Ns. 10 and 13 *supra.*
[34] Cameron, N. 6 *supra,* at pp. 12-14.
[35] *Id.* at p. 12.

tor previously recouped its investment before conversion. The contractor is paid a flat fee for services, usually on a per barrel basis, and may have a right to purchase some portion of production.[36]

It should be further noted that both Service contracts and Production Sharing contracts (discussed below) have had a rather complex history with American company participants due to the extraterritorial reach of the U.S. tax regimen which undertakes to apply tax laws abroad on the inept framework of petroleum leasing rights in the U.S. The companies have had to assure, in order to justify investment, that these contracts conform in certain ways to meet these requirements, somewhat in the manner as discussed in Section 7.10 above.

§ 7.21 Production Sharing Contracts

The first Production Sharing contract emerged in Indonesia in the mid-1960's. In form and, to some extent, in content, it had its roots in an earlier form of Indonesian agreement known as the "work agreement." A brief review of the Indonesian format should serve to acquaint the reader with the general nature of these contracts. It is a form of Service contract in which the state-owned petroleum company entity, Pertamina, has the contractual right to an active participating role in a host of ways. Its importance needs to be underscored because it has since become a model (albeit in modified form) in a number of areas around the world. During the period that the first Production Sharing contract was being negotiated in Indonesia, OPEC had been established, but, as an organization, it was more concerned at the time with improving the sharing of profits by member host countries and in obtaining substantial increases in prices. Service contracts of the nature now in vogue had not yet gained general acceptance, except to the extent that the Production Sharing contract itself included within its framework the concept of a servicing or contractor relationship in which later versions evolved.

It is appropriate to state briefly some of the more pertinent

---

[36] *Id.* at p. 13; Barrows, N. 7 *supra*.

provisions. It should be noted at the outset, that it significantly departed from the usual terms of earlier foreign concessions around the world. The first such contract, covering a large segment of the Java Sea, was awarded by Pertamina (the state oil company) to a small independent oil company, *i.e.*, Independent Indonesian American Petroleum Company (later merged into the Natomas Company). It was acquired largely through the persistent efforts of two competent independent oil men of the United States, Lawrence W. Barker and Donald Todd. The independents scored a victory over major companies in being awarded this first offshore grant in Indonesia. It was a contract forged in clear recognition of Indonesia's independence and its Oil & Gas Law of 1960 which brought into play a broad interpretation of Article 33 of the Indonesian Constitution of 1945 providing that "land and water and the natural resources contained therein shall be controlled by the state and utilized for the greatest welfare of the people."[37] The terms were rather severe and contrary to industry practices in a number of respects. It required that, in its practical application, the company would assume a high level of trustworthiness and confidence as to how Pertamina would administer the contract in the future. While Pertamina reserved management control, in effect, this meant joint management.[38] Essentially, the sharing of production rather than of profit is a major feature. The oil company is cast in the role of a foreign contractor whereby it agrees to bear all costs which are recoverable up to 40 percent of annual production if and when oil was produced, and the remaining production to be divided between them on the basis of 65 percent to Pertamina and 35 percent to the oil companies. The title to contractor's equipment entering Indonesia for the operation becomes that of Pertamina. In addition to requiring that all data be furnished to Pertamina, it was agreed that a percentage of the production would be contributed to the domestic market; that local participation would be offered to Indonesian nationals, and rather strong provisions required the employment and training of Indonesians on a preferential basis. It was also agreed

---

[37] *See* Clapham, N. 8 *supra*, at p 115.
[38] *Id.* at 116.

that Pertamina would pay the foreign company's taxes as a part of the consideration. It was not long thereafter before the major companies entered the scene to obtain similar contracts, especially in view of the successful discovery of oil in the Java Sea by Natomas.

The terms negotiated or even "renegotiated" by Pertamina, as well as those elsewhere engaging in the use of modified forms of the Production Sharing contract, are far less favorable to the oil companies. In recent years, the cost recovery up to 40 percent of annual production as in the old sharing arrangement had been eliminated by Pertamina and new formulations call for a higher split to Pertamina. For the recovery of capital costs, companies with remaining proven reserves of seven years or less of production have seven years to recoup. Companies with proven reserves of more than seven years can depreciate their capital investments over fourteen years. Non-capital costs, including exploration and intangible drilling costs, are expensible without limitation within the year in which incurred.[39] The contracts are for a term of thirty years unless no oil is discovered after ten years, but parts of the concession area are subject to mandatory relinquishment after three, six, and ten years. Needless to say, new contract terms as mentioned brought about a severe lack of confidence, particularly during the period from 1975 onward on the part of the oil companies. Further exploration effort was discouraged. In some measure, this can be attributed to the position taken by the Internal Revenue Service of the United States to the effect that the companies could not expense as royalty payments the sums assumed by Pertamina in lieu of taxation. To some extent this was set aside by a Revenue Ruling in 1976, but this was made applicable only to Production Sharing contracts made prior to the year 1976. Meanwhile, Pertamina has since attempted to regain the confidence of companies interested in the area by offering more attractive sharing arrangements in areas that had previously been reserved exclusively for Pertamina and to provide more attractive treatment of exploration costs and sharing terms in less prospective areas.

It is to be noted that contracts of this nature, as well as the

---

[39] *Id.*

Service contracts as described, otherwise contain many other provisions that bear a resemblance to the concession or license provisions.

§ 7.22 Conclusion

The international lawyer representing American natural resources companies abroad is required to perform a multitude of diverse services and functions. Assuming a reasonable grasp of the basic subject matter to start, the lawyer must have an acute sense of the long-term objectives, financial capabilities, and tax situation as applicable not only to the client but also to those companies with whom it may coventure in seeking to obtain concession or other rights in a given foreign host country. From this, the lawyer must interface with local host country law and regulations concerning concessions or other forms of contract arrangements. In addition, it is important to engage local expertise as needed to be satisfied that the client's objectives will not be seriously impaired and are compatible with existing or potential laws, policies, and regulations of the host country covering a wide range of subjects. The minimization of risk and the maximization of resource yield is, of course, the objective of the international lawyer.

The political and economic risks of foreign petroleum and mining ventures often exceed those of other kinds of ventures abroad. In part, the exploration for oil and minerals, even on the domestic scene, is most speculative and high risk as to anticipated results. Since private capital is the only available source of American funds to support these ventures, it is evident that a great many foreign host countries have somehow failed to show an appropriate level of concern as to the special needs and realities of private investment in the structuring and improvision of their petroleum and tax legislation and regulatory schemes. Nevertheless, coming into the latter half of the 1980's, there appears to be a growing competitiveness among some of the major producing areas to create new incentives for the restimulation of their exploratory and development programs. Much of this is the consequence of several years of global recession, falling prices, over supply of petroleum products and other significant factors.

The nature of petroleum exploration and production arrangements between host countries and the oil companies has radically changed in the course of time. This is evident when one compares the earlier forms of concession agreements with the types of arrangements in vogue today. Modern contractual arrangements reflect that foreign host governments have become zealous and nationalistic in respect to their natural resources in ways that have altered significantly in many countries the nature of the arrangements themselves. The international petroleum industry in the 1985–1990 era is faced with a host of uncertainties and paradoxes, but so long as the need continues on the global scene for the development of additional supplies, together with the need in most of the host producing countries for the technology, skills, and know-how of the oil companies, it is felt that the incentives so necessary to foster these objectives will be provided and contractual and concession arrangements appropriately modified to meet the realities of the time. Prudent contract construction on the part of the international lawyers will assist in providing a high degree of stability to foreign natural resource investment.

CHAPTER 8

Forum-Selection and Choice-of-Law Clauses in International Contracts

VED P. NANDA*

---

*Professor of Law and Director, International Legal Studies Program, University of Denver Law Center.

Appendix 8A: Sample Choice-of-Law and Choice-of-Forum
          Clause

§ 8.01   Introduction

An attorney counseling a client engaged in or entering into
international contracts[1] should advise the client that it would
be desirable to designate a specific and exclusive forum for
resolution of possible disputes arising from the contract. Similarly, it would be desirable to stipulate the applicable law to
govern the parties' rights and duties. Failure to agree in advance on forum and choice of law is likely to cause uncertainty
and confusion in case of disputes for two reasons: (1) there are
no universally accepted rules regarding jurisdiction under
conflict of laws, and, consequently, several courts may be authorized to hear a controversy with multijurisdictional contacts;[2] and (2) divergent approaches are used by various
jurisdictions to select the applicable law to resolve possible
disputes pertaining, for example, to a contract's validity or
interpretation, issues of performance, and parties' capacity
and, therefore, different outcomes may be reached in different
countries and even in different courts in the same country.[3]

Choice of law is particularly important in some transactions
such as International Letters of Credit, where national laws
differ substantially.[3.1] Differing national laws concerning burdens of proof and remedies may be outcome-determinative in
many cases, yet some lawyers not only neglect to include
choice-of-law clauses in their transaction, but often fail to
argue forcefully for a favorable choice of law before a court
during litigation.[3.2] However, there seems to be an emerging
trend in favor of automatic inclusion of such clauses in stan-

---

[1] *See generally* Delaume, "What Is an International Contract? An American and a Gallic Dilemma," 28 Int'l & Comp. L.Q. 258 (1979).

[2] *See generally* R. Weintraub, *Commentary on the Conflict of Laws* 90-
221 (2d ed. 1980).

[3] *See generally id.* at 348-97.

[3.1] *See, e.g.,* Note, "The Conflicts of Law in International Letters of Credit," 24 Va. J. Int'l L. 171, at 172 (1983).

[3.2] *Id.*

dardized documents in some transactions.[3.3] In other cases, such as transfer of technology transactions, it may be desirable to select a forum that will minimize the introduction of public policy concerns into the dispute.[3.4] Still, it is not possible always to insulate a transaction from the application of the stipulation of certain laws through a forum-selection or choice-of-law clause. For example, such a clause would not affect a U.S. court's jurisdiction in an antitrust case.[3.5]

Counsel should also note the choice-of-law aspects of suing foreign governmental corporations. The Foreign Sovereign Immunities Act (FSIA)[3.6] makes no blanket provision requiring the application of U.S. law on the merits, and it does recognize that international law can play a role in determining choice of law.[3.7] In some cases, courts have avoided difficult questions under the FSIA by applying the act of state doctrine, which has been described as a super choice-of-law rule.[3.8]

The following discussion is designed to acquaint the practitioner with recent developments regarding the use of contractual stipulations in international contracts and to offer some guidelines concerning their effectiveness. The focus of the inquiry is on the United States law.

[3.3] *Id.* at 199-200.

[3.4] *See, e.g.*, Nelson, "Planning for Resolution of Disputes in International Technology Transactions," 7 B.C. Int'l & Comp. L. Rev. 269 (1984).

[3.5] Regardless of a contractual clause, U.S. courts will weigh factors of fairness and comity to determine whether to apply U.S. law. *See, e.g.*, Note, "The Use of Interest Analysis in the Extraterritorial Application of United States Antitrust Law," 16 Cornell Int'l L. J. 147, 153-5 (1983).

[3.6] 28 U.S.C. §§ 1330, 1332(a)(2)-(4), 1391(f), 1441(d), 1602-11 (1976); Pub. L. No. 94-583, 90 Stat. 2891.

[3.7] Crockett, "Choice of Law Aspects of the Foreign Sovereign Immunities Act of 1976," 14 Law & Policy in Int'l Bus. 1041, 1051-52 (1983).

[3.8] *Id.* at 1054, citing Kirgis, "Act of State Exceptions and Choice of Law," 44 U. Colo. L. Rev. 173 (1972). *But see* First National City Bank v. Banco Para El Comercio, 103 S. Ct. 2591 (1983), in which case the U.S. Supreme Court held that rules of liability that govern private individuals are to be applied to foreign states, but that issues not involving liability are to be determined by federal law.

§ 8.02   Choice of Forum Clauses

[1]   U.S. Law and Practice

[a]   The Supreme Court Decisions

Until the Supreme Court's decision in 1972 in the *Bremen v. Zapata Off-Shore Co.*,[4] U.S. courts followed the traditional common law rule in refusing to give effect to the parties' choice of forum, since the outcome was perceived to be to "oust" the jurisdiction of an otherwise competent court.[5] The rationale was two-fold: (1) the parties cannot by agreement in the contract alter the jurisdiction of courts, and (2) such contractual stipulations are violative of public policy. The Court viewed the real issue not to be "ouster" of jurisdiction but of upholding the expectations of the parties by giving effect to "the legitimate expectations of the parties, manifested in their freely negotiated agreement by specifically enforcing the forum clause."[6]

By eliminating uncertainties regarding the place of suit by forum selection in advance, such contractual stipulations were found by the Court to constitute an "indispensable element in international trade, commerce, and contracting."[7] The Court approved of what it called a recent trend in adopting "a more hospitable attitude" toward choice-of-forum clauses, and called upon federal district courts sitting in admiralty to follow it as "the correct doctrine."[8] The Court established a reasonableness test to determine the validity of forum-selection clauses, as it held that "such clauses are prima facie valid and should be enforced unless enforcement is shown by the resisting party to be 'unreasonable' under the circumstances."[9]

Bremen upheld a forum-selection clause stipulated in a contract between a U.S. corporation, Zapata, and a German com-

---

[4] 407 U.S. 1 (1972).

[5] For a brief review, *see* Gilbert, "Choice of Forum Clauses in International and Interstate Contracts," 65 Ky. L.J. 1, 11-19 (1976).

[6] 407 U.S. at 12.

[7] *Id.* at 13-14.

[8] *Id.* at 10.

[9] *Id.*

pany, Unterweser, to tow a drilling rig from Louisiana to Italy. The Court found that the forum-selection clause which required that any dispute arising from the agreement be submitted before the High Court of Justice in London was agreed upon "in an arm's length negotiation by experienced and sophisticated"[10] businessmen. After a storm damaged the rig in the Gulf of Mexico it was towed back to Florida where Zapata, ignoring its contract agreement to litigate "any dispute arising" in the English courts, sued Unterweser in personam and Unterweser's tug, the Bremen, in rem. Both the district court and the Fifth Circuit Court of Appeals, sitting en banc, refused to enforce the clause.[11] The Supreme Court vacated the fifth circuit opinion and remanded for reconsideration, concluding that the forum-selection clause "should control absent a strong showing [by a compelling and countervailing reason] that it should be set aside."[12] Such a strong showing could be made and consequently the clause would not be enforced if it were invalid "for such reasons as fraud or overreaching,"[13] or if the enforcement would be "unreasonable and unjust," or contrary to a strong public policy of the forum.[14]

Subsequently, in 1974, in *Scherk v. Alberto-Culver Co.*,[15] a case involving an international commercial contract between a U.S. corporation and a German national, the Supreme Court upheld the validity of an arbitration clause which was claimed to be unenforceable since it was in violation of Section 10(b) of the Securities Exchange Act of 1934.[16] The Court cited *Bremen*, observing that "[a]n agreement to arbitrate before a specified tribunal is, in effect, a specialized kind of forum-selection clause. . . . The invalidation of such an agreement . . . would not only allow the respondent to repudiate its sol-

---

[10] *Id.* at 12.

[11] In re Unterweser Reederei, Gmbh, 296 F. Supp. 733 (M.D. Fla. 1969), *aff'd,* Zapata Offshore Co. v. M/S Bremen, 428 F.2d 888 (5th Cir. 1970), *aff'd on rehearing* (en banc), Zapata Offshore Co. v. M/S Bremen, 446 F.2d 907 (5th Cir. 1971).

[12] 407 U.S. at 15.

[13] *Id.*

[14] *Id.*

[15] 417 U.S. 506 (1974).

[16] 13 U.S.C. § 78 j (b) (1970).

emn promise but would, as well, reflect a 'parochial concept that all disputes must be resolved under our laws and in our courts. . . .' "[17] The Court again emphasized the need for contractual predictability: "A contractual provision specifying in advance the forum in which disputes shall be litigated and the law to be applied is, therefore, an almost indispensable precondition to achievement of the orderliness and predictibility essential to any international business transaction."[18] It held, therefore, that "the agreement of the parties in this case to arbitrate any dispute arising out of their international commercial transactions is to be respected and enforced by the federal courts. . . ."[19]

The Supreme Court rendered another landmark decision in 1985, *Mitsubishi Motors Corp. v. Soler Chrysler-Plymouth, Inc.*,[19.1] holding that an antitrust dispute between a Puerto Rican corporation and a Japanese corporation was subject to arbitration under the Federal Arbitration Act[19.2] and a forum-selection clause embodied in an agreement between the parties. The clause read: "All disputes, controversies or differences which may arise between [Mitsubishi] and [Soler] out of or in relation to Articles I-B through V of this Agreement, or for the breach thereof, shall be finally settled by arbitration in Japan in accordance with the rules and regulations of the Japan Commercial Arbitration Association."[19.3]

The pertinent facts were that in October 1979, Soler Chrysler-Plymouth, Inc. (Soler), a Puerto Rican corporation, entered into a distributorship agreement with Chrysler International, S.A. (Chrysler), a Swiss corporation and a wholly owned subsidiary of Chrysler Corporation, for distribution by Soler into Puerto Rico of cars made for Chrysler by Mitsubishi Motors Corporation (Mitsubishi), a Japanese corporation. Soler also entered into a separate "sales procedure agreement" with

---

[17] 417 U.S. at 519 (note omitted).
[18] *Id.* at 516.
[19] *Id.* at 519-20.
[19.1] 105 S. Ct. 3346 (1985).
[19.2] 9 U.S.C. § 1 *et seq.*
[19.3] 105 S. Ct. at 3349.

Chrysler and Mitsubishi, which embodied the forum-selection clause in question.

After Soler was unable to meet sales quota, Mitsubishi brought an action against Soler in the United States District Court for the District of Puerto Rico under the Federal Arbitration Act and the Convention on the Recognition and Enforcement of Foreign Arbitral Awards (New York Convention).[19.4] Mitsubishi sought arbitration and recovery of storage charges and penalties on cars ordered by Soler but unshipped. Subsequently, it initiated arbitration proceedings before the Japan Commercial Arbitration Association. Soler counterclaimed, invoking the Sherman Antitrust Act,[19.5] alleging that Mitsubishi and Chrysler had conspired to divide markets in restraint of trade. It also invoked other federal and Puerto Rican statutes.

The federal district court recognized the practice of the federal courts of appeals to follow *American Safety Equipment Corp. v. J.P. Maguire & Co.*[19.6] in holding that under domestic law antitrust issues are not arbitrable. It, however, held, citing *Scherk* that the "international character of the Mitsubishi-Soler undertaking required enforcement of the agreement to arbitrate even as to the antitrust claims."[19.7] The First Circuit[19.8] endorsed the doctrine of *American Safety* and reversed the district court for compelling arbitration on antitrust issues because of the international nature of the contract. The Supreme Court granted certiorari "primarily to consider whether an American court should enforce an agreement to resolve antitrust claims by arbitration when that agreement arises from an international transaction."[19.9]

The Court first addressed the question whether the arbitration clause encompassed the statutory counterclaims of Soler. The Court said:

> By agreeing to arbitrate a statutory claims, a party does not

---

[19.4] 21 U.S.T. 2517, T.I.A.S. No. 6997.
[19.5] 15 U.S.C. § 1 *et seq.*
[19.6] 391 F.2d 821 (2d Cir. 1968).
[19.7] 105 S. Ct. at 3351.
[19.8] 723 F.2d 155 (1st Cir. 1983).
[19.9] 105 S. Ct. at 3353.

forego the substantive rights afforded by the statute; it only submits to their resolution in an arbitral, rather than a judicial, forum. It trades the procedures and opportunity for review of the courtroom for the simplicity, informality, and expedition of arbitration. . . . Having made the bargain to arbitrate, the party should be held to it unless Congress itself has evinced an intention to preclude a waiver of judicial remedies for the statutory rights at issue.[19.10]

On the second and the more significant question for the present discussion, that of arbitrability in the international context, the Court referred to *Scherk* in holding that

concerns of international comity, respect for the capacities of foreign and transnational tribunals, and sensitivity to the need of the international commercial system for predictability in the resolution of disputes require that we enforce the parties' agreement, even assuming that a contrary result would be forthcoming in a domestic context.[19.11]

The Court further noted:

The Bremen and *Scherk* establish a strong presumption in favor of enforcement of freely negotiated contractual choice-of-forum provisions. Here, as in *Scherk*, that presumption is reinforced by the emphatic federal policy in favor of arbitral dispute resolution. And at least since this Nation's accession in 1970 to the [New York] Convention, . . . that federal policy applies with special force in the field of international commerce.[19.12]

Next, the Court addressed the holding of *American Safety* and concluded that the core of the doctrine of that case is "the fundamental importance to American democratic capitalism of the regime of the antitrust laws."[19.13] It noted that the "treble-damages provision wielded by the private litigant is a chief tool in the antitrust enforcement scheme, posing a crucial de-

---

[19.10] *Id.* at 3355.
[19.11] *Id.*
[19.12] *Id.* at 3356-57.
[19.13] *Id.* at 3358.

terrent to potential violators."[19.14]

In addressing this concern the Court said that "[t]here is no reason to assume at the outset of the dispute that international arbitration will not provide an adequate mechanism."[19.15] Acknowledging that although an international tribunal has no direct obligation to vindicate statutory dictates of states, the Court said that the "tribunal, however, is bound to effectuate the intentions of the parties."[19.16] It continued: "Where the parties have agreed that the arbitral body is to decide a defined set of claims which includes, as in these cases, those arising from the application of American antitrust law, the tribunal therefore should be bound to decide that dispute in accord with the national law giving rise to the claim."[19.17]

Further, the Court said:

> Having permitted the arbitration to go forward, the national courts of the United States will have the opportunity at the award enforcement stage to ensure that the legitimate interest in the enforcement of the antitrust laws has been addressed. The Convention reserves to each signatory country the right to refuse enforcement of an award where the "recognition or enforcement of the award would be contrary to the public policy of that country."[19.18]

The Court noted that "it would not require intensive inquiry to ascertain" that the tribunal considered and decided the antitrust claims.[19.19] Thus, such inquiry would not pose any challenge to the integrity of the arbitral process.

In its concluding comments the Court said:

> As international trade has expanded in recent decades, so too has the use of international arbitration to resolve disputes arising in the course of that trade. The controversies that international arbitral institutions are called upon to resolve have increased in diversity as well as in complexity. Yet the potential

---

[19.14] *Id.*
[19.15] *Id.* at 3359.
[19.16] *Id.*
[19.17] *Id.*
[19.18] *Id.* at 3360.
[19.19] *Id.*

of these tribunals for efficient disposition of legal disagreements arising from commercial relations has not yet been tested. If they are to take a central place in the international legal order, national courts will need to "shake off the old judicial hostility to arbitration," . . . and also their customary and understandable unwillingness to cede jurisdicction of a claim arising under domestic law to a foreign or transnational tribunal. To this extent, at least, it will be necessary for national courts to subordinate domestic notions of arbitrability to the international policy favoring commercial arbitration.[19.20]

The Court, citing *Scherk* required "this representative of the American business community to honor its bargain . . . by holding this agreement to arbitrate 'enforce[able].' "[19.21]

[b] Federal Court Decisions

It should be noted that lower federal courts have extended the *Bremen* holding to non-admiralty cases as well as cases involving only domestic corporations.[20] To illustrate, a federal district court in 1979 cited *Bremen's* rationale to decline jurisdiction in a domestic controversy, and to relegate the parties to the forum in which they agreed to litigate. It observed that *Bremen's* holding should not be limited to federal district courts sitting in admiralty, because it was convinced that "the principle is applicable to all forum-selection agreements."[21]

[19.20] *Id.*

[19.21] *Id.* at 3361.

[20] *See, e.g.,* Coastal Steel Corp. v. Tilgham Wheelabrator Ltd., 709 F.2d 190 (3d Cir.), *cert. denied,* 104 S. Ct. 349 (1983); Bense v. Interstate Battery System of America, Inc., 683 F.2d 718 (2d Cir. 1982); In re Firemen's Fund Insurance Cos., 588 F.2d 93 (5th Cir. 1979); Taylor v. Titan Midwest Construction Corp., 474 F. Supp. 145 (N.D. Tex. 1979); Full-Sight Contact Lens Corp. v. Soft Lenses, Inc., 466 F. Supp. 71 (S.D.N.Y. 1978); St. Paul Fire and Marine Ins. Co. v. Travelers Indemnity Co., 401 F. Supp. 927 (D. Mass. 1975); Spatz v. Nascone, 368 F. Supp. 352 (W.D. Pa. 1973), *aff'g,* 364 F. Supp. 967 (W.D. Pa. 1973); In-Flight Devices Corp. v. Van Dusen Air, Inc., 466 F.2d 220 (6th Cir. 1972).

[21] In Public Water Supply Dist. v. American Ins. Co., 471 F. Supp. 1071 (W.D. Mo. 1979), the court upheld a forum-selection clause in the performance and payment bond executed by the parties, citing *Bremen* rationale

In 1982, a federal circuit court applied the *Bremen* rationale to *Bense v. Interstate Battery System of America, Inc.*,[21.1] a case which involved an antitrust claim. The facts were that a franchisee, following termination of his franchise, brought an action in Vermont against a Texas corporation, alleging violations of section 1 of the Sherman Antitrust Act and section 3 of the Clayton Antitrust Act. Enforcing the forum-selection clause of the franchise agreement, which limited venue "of any suits or causes of action arising directly or indirectly from this AGREEMENT . . . [to] Dallas County, Texas," the district court dismissed the complaint for lack of proper venue. The liberal venue provision of section 12 of the Clayton Act provides:

> Any suit, action, or proceedings under the antitrust laws against the corporation may be brought not only in the judicial district whereof it is an inhabitant, but also in any district wherein it may be found or transacts business; and all process in such cases may be served in the district of which it is an inhabitant, or wherever it may be found.[21.2]

Observing that the forum-selection agreement was "part of the bargain into which [the franchisee] freely entered,"[21.3] the circuit court approved a policy of enforcing contractual forum-selection clauses unless "it clearly can be shown that enforcement 'would be unreasonable and unjust, or that the clause was invalid for such reasons as fraud or overreaching.' "[21.4]

In a 1984 decision, the Second Circuit dismissed an action brought by a Dutch investor against Dutch citizens charging securities fraud in connection with the plaintiff's acquisition of U.S. real estate. The court relinquished jurisdiction as it upheld a forum- and law- selection clause in *AVC Nederland B.V. v.*

---

requiring the court "to decline jurisdiction and to relegate the parties to the forum in which they agreed to litigate." (*Id.* at 1071-72).

[21.1] 683 F.2d 718 (2d Cir. 1982).

[21.2] 15 U.S.C. § 22.

[21.3] 683 F.2d at 722.

[21.4] *Id.* at 721-22.

Atrium Investment Partnership.[21.5] The court relied on *Bremen* and *Scherk,* deciding that reasonable choices by the parties should be given effect when the foreign elements of the transaction were "sufficiently meaningful," despite the fact that the chosen forum was unlikely to apply U.S. securities law. The court said:

> While the United States may have an interest in encouraging foreign investment in American real estate which is furthered by extending the protections of the securities laws to securities issued in such transactions, *Scherk* implies that this interest does not require that foreign investors be allowed to escape from a forum-selection/choice-of-law clause in an agreement executed in their own country with their fellow nationals.[21.6]

In the analagous context of the enforcement of an arbitration clause in a contract, in *Tai Ping Ins. Co., Ltd. v. M/V Warschau,*[21.7] the fifth circuit upheld a contractual provision which provided that any disputes were to be referred to a three-person arbitration board in London. The clause specified how the three-person panel should be selected, and also required that the arbitrators be "commercial men experienced in shipping."[21.8] The controversy centered around the district court's order to stay the arbitration pending the litigation in federal court.[21.9] In holding that the district court's action was improper, the court of appeals stated that "duplication of effort, redundant testimony and the possibility of inconsistent findings," were among the risks contemplated by the parties in striking the bargain.[21.10] The court went on to cite the Supreme Court's statement in *Bremen* that arm's length negotiations were to be upheld by the courts.[21.11]

[21.5] Fed. Sec. L. Rep. (CCH) ¶91,584, at 98985 (2d Cir., July 19, 1984).

[21.6] *Id.* at 158.

[21.7] 731 F.2d 1141 (5th Cir. 1984).

[21.8] *Id.* at 1143.

[21.9] Tai Ping Ins. Co. v. Vessel M/V Warschau, 556 F. Supp. 187 (E.D. La. 1983).

[21.10] 731 F.2d at 1145.

[21.11] *Id.*

[c] Restatement (Second) and the Model Choice of
     Forum Act

The pertinent provision in *Restatement (Second) of the Conflict of Laws*[22] is Section 80, according to which "[t]he parties' agreement as to the place of the action cannot oust a state of judicial jurisdiction, but such an agreement will be given effect unless it is unfair or unreasonable."

Similarly, the Model Choice of Forum Act[23] provides a court with a broad range of discretion. Under section 3 of the Act, the forum-selection clause is to be enforced unless (1) the court is required by its own law to hear the case; (2) the plaintiff cannot secure effective relief in the other state; (3) the other forum is substantially inconvenient; (4) the clause "was obtained by misrepresentation, duress, the abuse of economic power, or other unconscionable means"; and (5) if "it would for some other reason be unfair or unreasonable to enforce the agreement."

[d] Exceptions to the Enforcement of Forum-Selection
     Clauses

Bremen and *Scherk* have provided guidelines for the enforcement of a forum-selection or arbitration clause in an international contract. Restatement (Second) and the Model Choice of Forum Act contain similar guidelines. Since the presumption is that of validity, a challenge to the enforcement of such a clause will be successful only on limited grounds,[24] such

---

[22] Restatement (Second) of Conflict of Laws § 80 (1971). (Hereafter Restatement Second.)

[23] *Model Choice of Forum Act* (National Conference of Commissioners on Uniform State Laws, 1968). For the text, *see* Reese, "The Model Choice of Forum Act," 17 Am. J. Comp. L. 292 (1969).

[24] In City of New York v. Pullman, Inc., 477 F. Supp. 438 (S.D.N.Y. 1979), *aff'd*, 662 F.2d 919 (2d Cir. 1981), *rehg. denied*, Sept. 28, 1981, *cert. denied*, 102 S. Ct. 1038 (1982). the court noted from the *Bremen* decision: "Agreements entered into by knowledgeable parties in an arm's-length transaction that contain a forum selection provision are enforceable absent a showing of fraud, overreaching, unreasonableness or unfairness" (*Id.* at 441, n.10). *See*

as: (1) substantial inconvenience, or denial of an effective remedy; (2) fraud, overreaching, or unconscionable conduct; (3) violation of public policy, or otherwise the transaction being unfair, unjust or unreasonable.

In a 1984 case, *Santamauro v. Taito do Brasil Industria E Comercia*, [24.1] a federal district court cited *Bremen* and *In re Fireman's Fund Insurance Cos.*[24.2] in upholding forum-selection clauses in an assignment agreement and articles of association of a business entity domiciled in Brazil and established under Brazilian law. The agreement mandated that disputes were to be settled in Brazilian courts. The court noted that

> [t]he burden is on the party resisting enforcement of the clause to prove that the choice was unreasonable, unfair or unjust, or to show that the clause is invalid by reason of fraud or over-reaching or that enforcement would contravene a strong public policy of this forum.[24.3]

[i]   Substantial Inconvenience or Denial of an Effective Remedy

Under *Bremen*, the contention that the selected forum is inconvenient will not suffice. The party challenging the validity of a forum-selection clause has to overcome the strong presumption that the contractual stipulation is reasonable, and according to the Supreme Court it will be a heavy burden.[25] The inconvenience has to be of such a substantial nature that the party will "for all practical purposes be deprived of his day in court. Absent that, there is no basis for concluding that it would be unfair, unjust, or unreasonable to hold that party to his bargain."[26] Usually, the parties who have freely negotiated an international commercial contract are supposed to have

---

also Coastal Steel Corp., *supra* N. 20, 709 F.2d at 202-04; Bense, *supra* N. 20.

[24.1] 587 F. Supp. 1312 (E.D. La. 1984).

[24.2] 588 F.2d 93 (5th Cir. 1979).

[24.3] 587 F. Supp. at 1314.

[25] 407 U.S. at 18-19.

[26] *Id.* at 18.

foreseen the amount of inconvenience likely to result from litigating in the chosen forum.[27] However, in *Copperweld Steel Co. v. Demag-Mannesmann-Bohler*,[28] a federal district court found substantial inconvenience as the basis of its decision not to enforce a forum-selection clause in a contract stipulating the jurisdiction of the supplier's main office (West Germany) for any dispute resolution. The court distinguished *Bremen* since West Germany in this case, unlike England in *Bremen*, was not a neutral forum.[29] In the court's words, it was unreasonable to enforce the clause, since:

> [T]he casting plant, the performance of which is in dispute, is located here. We foresee the necessity to examine the plant in detail. The plant was constructed by a Pennsylvania firm, all of whose employees are here. Did the defect occur in construction? All of the people who operated the plant are here. Did they operate it improperly? All of the plant's customers are here. If they refused the product, why did they do so? How can these people be made available in Germany? There is no process there to compel their attendance at trial even if they could be transported to Germany. What of the language difficulties? Of course, the German engineers will be inconvenienced and they will have language difficulties we assume, but we think it will be of some advantage to them to have the contractor and the operating people available for obvious reasons.
>
> We remain convinced that in this particular case plaintiffs could not adequately try their case if forced to proceed in Germany and thus perhaps could not obtain a fair and complete hearing . . . because of the obvious impracticality of conducting the litigation in Germany.[30]

The *Demag* court seems also to have considered language as one of the factors in assessing the reasonableness of forum-selection clauses, as it observed that the litigation before a German court "would require translation with its inherent

---

[27] *Id.*

[28] 54 F.R.D. 539 (W.D. Pa. 1972), *reh.*, 347 F. Supp. 53 (W.D. Pa. 1972), *reh.*, 354 F. Supp. 571 (W.D. Pa. 1973), *aff'd*, 578 F.2d 953 (3d Cir. 1978).

[29] 347 F. Supp. at 54.

[30] *Id.*

inaccuracy,"[31] especially since "almost all witnesses are English speaking."[32] It is submitted that the use of language as a basis for finding a forum-selection clause unenforceable would be a misreading and misapplication of *Bremen's* standards, for under the *Bremen* analysis, the parties could have foreseen the amount of inconvenience likely to result from litigating in Germany.

Viewed in this light, it was appropriate that another federal district court dismissed a plaintiff's claim that he was not aware of a forum-selection clause which mandated that any controversy be resolved in West Germany.[33] The court upheld the clause in an employment contract between a German corporation and a New Yorker. The plaintiff's contention which the court rejected was that as the contract was written in German and he did not understand German, he would not have entered into the contract had he been aware of the clause.[34] The court would not come to the aid of a negligent businessman.

The third circuit court of appeals, in *Coastal Steel Corp. v. Tilgham Wheelabrator Ltd.*,[34.1] cited with approval the *Bremen* formulation that the party objecting to the enforcement of forum-selection clause has the burden of proving substantial difficulty of litigating in the agreed-upon forum. The court enforced the clause conferring exclusive jurisdiction upon English courts, despite the fact that the equipment in dispute and some witnesses were present in the United States. The court found that the inspection of the American plant was not necessary to the case, that each party would be equally inconvenienced in obtaining counsel in the other forum, and that some witnesses would be inconvenienced by litigation in either forum.[34.2] The court said that these factors were in "equipoise,"[34.3] and the American corporation had not carried its burden of showing substantial inconvenience if the agreement were enforced.

---

[31] 54 F.R.D. at 542.
[32] *Id.*
[33] Gaskin v. Handel, 390 F. Supp. 361 (S.D.N.Y. 1975).
[34] *Id.* at 366.
[34.1] 709 F.2d 190 (3d Cir. 1983), *cert. denied*, 104 S. Ct. 349 (1983).
[34.2] 709 F.2d at 203-04.
[34.3] *Id.* at 204.

[ii] Fraud, Overreaching or Unconscionable Conduct

If a court finds that the forum-selection clause was obtained by unconscionable means, it is likely that the court will refuse to enforce the clause on the ground that there was absence of any real agreement between the parties. For example, in a recent decision by a federal district court, a forum-selection clause was held to be unenforceable since it was contained in what the court found to be an adhesion contract.[35] In another recent decision by a federal district court,[35.1] jurisdiction with respect to attachment of a vessel and undertaking was challenged by reliance on a forum-selection clause contained in a bill of lading, which provided that all disputes arising out of the bill of lading shall be determined in Korea "to the exclusion of the jurisdiction of the courts of any other country."[35.2] Citing *Bremen,* the court upheld the clause as "prima facie valid and enforceable absent some indication of fraud or overreaching or proof that enforcement would be unreasonable under the circumstances."[35.3] The court noted, however, in a footnote that it

> does not favor forum selection clauses, particularly when the forum chosen favors the drafting party. Bills of lading are commonly carrier-drafted documents that leave the shipper little bargaining power. In short, there is very little to distinguish them from a contract of adhesion which gives substantial advantage to the drafting party. Nonetheless, the United States Supreme Court and the Ninth Circuit Court of Appeals have ruled that such clauses are enforceable. The court is bound by this authority and is not at liberty to alter or deny its impact on the action at bar.[35.4]

---

[35] Bank of Indiana Nat'l Ass'n v. Holyfield, 476 F. Supp. 104, 108 (S.D. Miss. 1979).

[35.1] Teyseer Cement Co. v. Halla Maritime Corp., 583 F. Supp 1268 (E.D. La. 1984).

[35.2] *Id.* at 1271.

[35.3] *Id.*

[35.4] *Id.* n. 1.

[iii]   Violation of Public Policy or Otherwise the
        Transaction Being Unfair, Unreasonable or Unjust

A second circuit case, *Indussa Corp. v. S. S. Ranborg*,[36] illustrates the public policy exception. The court held that the
forum-selection clause contravened the lessening of liability
provision of the Carriage of Goods at Sea Act (COGSA).[37] The
court said:

> [F]rom a practical standpoint, to require an American plaintiff
> to assert his claim only in a distant court lessens the liability of
> the carrier quite substantially, particularly when the claim is
> small. Such a clause puts "a high hurdle" in the way of enforcing
> liability, . . . an effective means for carriers to secure settlements
> lower than if cargo could sue in a convenient forum. . . . A clause
> making a claim triable only in a foreign court would almost
> certainly lessen liability if the law which the court would apply
> was neither the Carriage of Goods by Sea Act nor the Hague
> Rules. Even when the foreign court would apply one or the
> other of these regimes, requiring trial abroad *might* lessen the
> carrier's liability since there could be no assurance that it would
> apply them in the same way as would an American tribunal
> subject to the uniform control of the Supreme Court, and § 3(8)
> can well be read as covering a potential and not simply a de-
> monstrable lessening of liability.[38]

However, in *Bense v. Interstate Battery System of America,
Inc.*,[38.1] the second circuit court of appeals indicates that the
Indussa public policy exception will be construed narrowly.
The court in *Bense* first noted that both *Indussa* and *Krenger
v. Pennsylvania R. Co.*[38.2] were decided prior to *Bremen*.[38.3]
Further, both cases involved specific statutory provisions
which forbade agreements to limit liability, the Carriage of
Goods By Sea Act in *Indussa* and the Federal Employers' Lia-
bility Act in *Krenger*. The court found no comparable provi-

---

[36] 377 F.2d 200 (2d Cir. 1967).
[37] *See* § 1303(8), in 42 U.S.C. §§ 1300-1315.
[38] 377 F.2d at 203-04.
[38.1] 683 F.2d 718 (2d Cir. 1982).
[38.2] 174 F.2d 556 (2d Cir.), *cert. denied*, 338 U.S. 866 (1949).
[38.3] 683 F.2d at 722.

sion in the antitrust statutes and refused to infer such a provision merely from the statutes' liberal venue provisions.[38.4]

In a 1984 case, *Lien Ho Hsing Steel Enterprise Co. v. Weihtag,* [38.5] the Ninth Circuit upheld a forum-selection clause in a marine insurance policy designating Rotterdam as the exclusive forum for any disputes under the policy. The court found the plaintiff's contention without merit that the clause should be invalidated because of the "overweening bargaining power" on the part of the insurers. Also, the court rejected the plaintiff's claim that the Hawaii statute extending personal jurisdiction to persons contracting "to insure any person, property, or risk located within this State at the time of contracting,"[38.6] be construed to have established a strong public policy that insurance cases must be tried in Hawaii despite a claim in the insurance contract to the contrary.

In several areas of law, uncertainty prevails as to the extent of the reach of public policy exception by courts to invalidate a forum-selection clause. Such areas include securities law, antitrust legislation, labor law and patents.[38.7] To illustrate, in *Lake Communications, Inc. v. ICC Corp.,*[38.8] the Ninth Circuit upheld a district court's refusal to submit antitrust issues to arbitration while it directed submission to arbitration of issues as required by the arbitration agreement, involving any unresolved disputes relating to the contract in question. The agreement provided that such dispute "shall be arbitrated in Korea, under the rule of the Republic of Korea and in accordance with the rules of procedure of the Korean Commerical Arbitration Association."[38.9] In response to the appellees' contention that "all claims were subject to arbitration and all court proceedings should be either dismissed or stayed until arbitration was completed,"[38.10] the court observed in a footnote:

Appellees contended in the district court that under the deci-

---

[38.4] 683 F.2d at 720, 722.
[38.5] 738 F.2d 1455 (1984).
[38.6] Hawaii Rev. Stat. § 634-35 (a)(4)(1976), cited in 738 F.2d at 1460.
[38.7] *See* Delaume, *supra* N. 1, at 217-76.
[38.8] 738 F.2d 1473 (9th Cir. 1984).
[38.9]*Id.* at 1476.
[38.10] *Id.* at 1478.

sion in *Scherk v. Alberto-Culver Co.*, . . . even antitrust claims must be arbitrated if they fall within an arbitration agreement in an international commercial contract. However, appellees did not appeal the district court's order permitting continued litigation of the antitrust claims. In any event, *Scherk* is not controlling here. The rationale for refusing to refer antitrust claims to arbitration does not apply to claims under federal securities laws. . . . The nonarbitrability of antitrust claims stems from a variety of public policy considerations, including protection of the public interest in a competitive national economy. *Scherk* and its predecessor, *Wilko v. Swan*, . . . were concerned with protection of a right of action granted an individual under federal securities laws. Even though the international nature of the dispute may be sufficient basis for enforcing an arbitration agreement relinquishing an individual remedy granted by the federal securities laws, it is insufficient to override the strong public policies favoring judicial enforcement of the antitrust laws. *Soler-Chrysler-Plymouth*, 723 F.2d at 166-68.[39]

In another recent case, *Coastal Steel Corp. v. Tilgham Wheelabrator Ltd.*,[39.1] the Third Circuit found that even though a legislative policy of disfavoring forum-selection clauses in bankruptcy cases could be discerned, since "the Congress, in enacting a broad protective federal jurisdiction provision, adopted a policy of facilitating the collection and distribution of debtor estates,"[39.2] a forum-selection clause would be enforced when it was in a contract made by the parties prior to the bankruptcy proceedings. The court noted that a bankruptcy trustee takes the contracts as he finds them. Consequently, at least absent clear Congressional intent to the contrary, the institution of title 11 proceedings was only one factor to be considered in determining whether enforcement of the provision would be unreasonable.[39.3] The court said:

Nothing in the legislative history of the Bankruptcy Code has been called to our attention suggesting that Congress intended to make a change in the public policy favoring forum selection

---

[39] *Id.* n. 3.
[39.1] 709 F.2d 190 (3d Cir. 1983), *cert. denied*, 104 S. Ct. 349 (1983).
[39.2] 709 F.2d at 202.
[39.3] *Id.*

clauses which is manifested in the Federal Arbitration Act
... , or in the common law announced in the *Bremen* and similar
state and federal cases. Section 1471(b) does not announce a
contrary public policy.[39.4]

Under the broad rubric of "unfair, unreasonable or unjust,"[40] a court might consider factors not discussed earlier to
conclude that a forum-selection clause is not to be enforced.
For example, a forum-selection clause which is not phrased in
mandatory or exclusive terms may be struck.

In *McDonnell Douglas Corp. v. Islamic Republic of Iran,*[40.1]
defendants invoked *Bremen* and *Scherk* to argue that the
forum-selection clause in the agreement to be upheld. The
clause stipulated that "[a]ny difference or dispute from the
execution of the contract that may not be settled amicably
should be settled through the Iranian courts."[40.2] The plaintiff
contended that in contrast with the language of the forum-
selection clauses upheld in *Bremen* and *Scherk,* the language
of the clause, "should be settled," was merely preferential and
not obligatory or mandatory. The U.S. district court agreed
with the plaintiff's contention, holding that the clause "must
be considered as expressing only a preference between the
two available fora. . . . Therefore, while the forum selection
clause must be given some weight in the determination of the
issues presented, it need not be considered as presumptively
binding as the clause at issue in *The Bremen.*[40.3] In another
case,[41] which arose in a domestic setting, a federal district
court distinguished the case from *Bremen,* where the court
had found that "the parties specified with particularity that
the London Court of Justice must hear the suit."[42] The court
invalidated the forum-selection clause because as contrasted
with *Bremen,* there was "no such unequivocal agreement to

[39.4] *Id.*

[40] *See* Gilbert, N. 5 *supra.*

[40.1] 591 F. Supp. 293 (E.D. Miss. 1984).

[40.2] Article XV of the Basic Ordering Agreement, cited *id.* at 301.

[40.3] *Id.* at 303.

[41] Int'l Assoc. of Bridge, Structural and Ornamental Iron Workers v. Koski
Construction Co., 474 F. Supp. 370 (W.D. Pa. 1979).

[42] *Id.* at 371.

submit" to the selected jurisdiction.[43]

[e] Changed Circumstances

In negotiating the settlements of the United States-Iranian claims the U.S. government insisted on the inclusion of a provision in the 1981 Declaration Concerning the Settlement of U.S.-Iranian Claims under which the Claims Tribunal is to take into account "changed circumstances" in deciding the enforceability of forum-selection clauses in contracts previously concluded with Iran or Iranian nationals.[43.1] Without this provision the applicable clause in the Declaration excludes from the Tribunal's jurisdiction "claims arising under a binding contract between the parties specifically providing that any disputes thereunder shall be within the sole jurisdiction of the competent Iranian courts . . . ."[43.2] The following two factors constitute the rationale of the "changed circumstances" provision.[43.3] First, the parties, at the time of the contract, could not have foreseen the deep-rooted changes subsequently brought about by the Iranian revolution. It would be manifestly unfair to enforce such a clause since the post-Revolution Iranian judicial system is so different from that contemplated by the parties, and also, because of the likely prejudice in Iran against America and American economic interests. Second, the argument has been advanced that it would be futile to resort to Iranian courts because they cannot provide "the requisite international minimum standard of justice" as recognized under customary international law.[43.4] The Claims Tribunal could consider these two factors under the Declaration.[43.5]

It may be noted that U.S. courts have refused to enforce

---

[43] *Id.*

[43.1] Art. V of the Declaration of the Government of Democratic and Popular Republic of Algeria Concerning the Settlement of the Claims by the Government of the United States and the Government of the Islamic Republic of Iran, *reprinted in* 20 Int'l Legal Materials 230 (1981).

[43.2] Art. II, para. 1, *id.*

[43.3] *See* Note, 16 Geo. Wash. J. Int'l L. & Econ. 335, 337 (1982).

[43.4] *Id.*

[43.5] *Id.* at 375.

forum-selection clauses with Iran for a variety of reasons. To illustrate, in *Itek Corp. v. First National Bank,*[43.6] the reason given by the court for its action was that no adequate remedy would be available in an Iranian forum. In *American Bell International v. Islamic Republic of Iran,*[43.7] the court decided it would be futile to bring a case in an Iranian forum. Similarly, in *McDonnell Douglas Corp. v. Islamic Republic of Iran,* [43.8] the court held that even if the forum-selection clause contained in the agreement can be considered mandatory, "it would not be enforced because of changed circumstances in the forum state."[43.9]

[2] Other Approaches

[a] Regional and Multilateral Conventions

Under the auspices of the European Economic Community, the Convention on Jurisdiction and the Enforcement of Judgments in Civil and Commercial Matters[44] was signed in September 1968. Article 17 of the convention recognizes forum-selection agreements with some qualifications. Article 17 reads in part:

> If, in a written agreement or an oral agreement confirmed in writing, the parties, at least one of which is domiciled in a Contracting State, designate a court or courts of a Contracting State that are to decide an existing or future dispute arising out

---

[43.6] 511 F. Supp. 1341 (D. Mass. 1981), *vacated on other grounds,* 704 F.2d 1 (1st Cir. 1983).

[43.7] 474 F. Supp. 420 (S.D.N.Y. 1979).

[43.8] 591 F. Supp. 293 (E.D. Miss. 1984).

[43.9] *Id.* at 308.

[44] For the translated text of the Convention, *see* 8 Int'l Legal Materials, 229-44 (1969). *See also* Pryles and Trindade, "The Common Market (E.E.C.) Convention on Jurisdiction and Enforcement of Judgments in Civil and Commercial Matters — Possible Impact Upon Australian Citizens," 48 Aust. L.J. 185 (1974).

of a particular legal relationship, such court or courts shall have exclusive Jurisdiction over such disputes. [45]

Among other pertinent conventions which enforce forum-selection clauses, the following deserve special mention: the 1923 Protocol on Arbitration Clauses,[46] the 1927 Convention on Execution of Foreign Arbitral Awards,[47] the American Convention on Private International Law adopted in Havana in 1928,[48] the Treaty on International Civil Law signed at Montevideo in 1940[49] and its Protocol,[50] the 1958 U.N. Convention on the Recognition and Enforcement of Foreign Arbitral Awards,[51] and the 1961 European Convention on International Commercial Arbitration.[52]

---

[45] 8 Int'l Legal Materials, *supra* N. 44, at 235.

[46] Protocol on Arbitration Clauses, *signed at* Geneva, Sept. 24, 1923, in force July 28, 1924, 27 L.N.T.S. 158. The text is contained in 20 Am. J. Int'l L. Supp., Official Documents 194 (1926).

[47] Convention on the Execution of Foreign Arbitral Awards, *signed at* Geneva, Sept. 26, 1927, in force July 25, 1929, 92 L.N.T.S. 302. The text is contained in 27 Am. J. Int'l L. Supp. 1 (1933).

[48] *See* 4 M. Hudson, *Int'l Legislation* 2279 (1931).

[49] *See* 37 Am. J. Int'l L. Supp., Official Documents 141, 149 (art. 56) (1943).

[50] *See id.* at 152 (art. 5).

[51] *Done at* New York, June 10, 1958, T.I.A.S. No. 6979, 21 U.S.T. 2518, 330 U.N.T.S. 38. Article II of the convention reads:

Article II

1. Each Contracting State shall recognize an agreement in writing under which the parties undertake to submit to arbitration all or any differences which have arisen or which may arise between them in respect of a defined legal relationship, whether contractual or not, concerning a subject matter capable of settlement by arbitration.

2. The term "agreement in writing" shall include an arbitral clause in a contract or an arbitration agreement, signed by the parties or contained in an exchange of letters or telegrams.

3. The court of a Contracting State, when seized of an action in a matter in respect of which the parties have made an agreement within the meaning of this article, shall, at the request of one of the parties, refer the parties to arbitration, unless it finds the said agreement is null and void, inoperative or incapable of being performed.

[52] *See* U.N. Economic Commission for Europe, Doc. E/ECE 423, E/ECE Trade 48 (1961). For the translated text, *see* 13 Am. J. Comp. L. 160-61 (1964).

[b] Approaches of Selected Countries

Where, in the setting of an international contract, a case is brought before an English court in breach of an exclusive forum-selection agreement, the court is likely to grant a stay at the request of the defendant "unless strong cause for not doing so is shown."[53] The burden is on the plaintiff to prove such strong cause. In exercising its discretion, the court considers several factors, including: the availability of the evidence; the relative convenience and expense of trial between the English and foreign courts; parties' relationship with England and the other country; whether the law of the foreign court applies; whether "the defendants genuinely desire trial in the foreign country, or are only seeking procedural advantages; [w]hether the plaintiffs . . . would be prejudiced by having to sue in the foreign court because they would: (i) be deprived of security for their claim; (ii) be unable to enforce any judgment obtained; (iii) be faced with a time-bar not applicable in England; or (iv) for political, racial, religious or other reasons be unlikely to get a fair trial."[54] Arbitration agreements are given similar deference in English courts.[54.1]

Under this fourth rationale, English courts have treated the subject of changed circumstances in a few cases. For example, in a 1939 Chancery case, *Ellinger v. Guiness, Mahon & Co.*,[54.2] the court refused to enforce a forum-selection clause that would have required the plaintiff, an expatriate German Jew, to pursue his claim in Nazi Germany. The court reasoned that it would be unlikely for the plaintiff to obtain adequate representation and a free trial in Germany, while in his travel there his life and liberty would be at great risk. More recently, in a 1979 case, *Carvalho v. Hull Blyth (Angola) Ltd.*,[54.3] the court of appeals refused after the Marxist revolution in Angola, to recognize a forum-selection clause which would have required

---

[53] *The Eleftheria*, [1970] P. 94 at 99.
[54] *Id.* at 100.
[54.1] For a concise analysis, *see* Pyrles, "Comparative Aspects of Prorogation and Arbitration Agreements," 25 Int'l & Comp. L. Q. 543, 556-61 (1976).
[54.2] [1939] 4 ALL E. R. 16 (Ch.).
[54.3] [1979] 3 ALL E. R. 280 (C.A.).

a Portugese plaintiff to sue in an Angolan court "as the sole Court competent to adjudicate to the exclusion of all others." As earlier in *Ellinger*, the court noted that it would be unlikely for the plaintiff to receive a fair trial in Angola, that the plaintiff would have difficulty in obtaining adequate representation there, and that traveling there would threaten his safety. Australia and Canada generally follow the British practice.[55] In a recent comparative study of forum-selection clauses, a commentator has observed that, subject to certain qualifications, "there is a fairly wide acceptance of the effectiveness of such agreements. . . ."[56] He concludes that, "as a general rule," contractual exclusion of domestic jurisdiction is considered effective not only in France and West Germany, but also in several other European countries, such as Austria, Switzerland, Belgium, the Netherlands, the Scandinavian countries, and in some nonEuropean states as well.[57]

§ 8.03 Choice-of-Law Clauses

[1]   U.S. Law and Practice

Where the parties to a transnational contract have stipulated a choice-of-law provision, the courts will usually enforce the agreement to apply the parties' chosen law.[58] The rationale for such enforcement is the need for certainty so as to protect the expectations of the parties and for predictability of a certain result, no matter where the case is brought for litigation. The policy consideration reflected in this approach is that

---

[55] *See* N. 54.1 *supra.*

[56] *Id.* at 568.

[57] *Id.* at 570-71. *See also* Delaume, *supra* N. 1, at 271-76, Lenhoff, "The Parties' Choice of a Forum: "Prorogation Agreements," 15 Rutgers L. Rev. 414, 439-90 (1961); Perillo, "Selected Forum Agreements in Western Europe," 13 Am. J. Comp. L. 162 (1964); Schwind, "Derogation Chances in Latin America," *id.* at 167; Eek, "The Contractual Forum: Scandinavia," *id.* at 173; and Coven & Da Costa, "The Contractual Forum: Situation in England and the British Commonwealth," *id.* at 179.

[58] *See generally* Reese, "Choice of Law in Torts and Contracts and Directions for the Future," 16 Colum. J. Transnat'l L. 1, 19-22 (1977).

competent parties have a right to freely enter into contract in such a manner as would best promote their respective business interests,[59] although obviously each state has a legitimate interest in regulating the conduct of business conducted within its borders or affecting its citizens. Thus, as a general rule, parties with capacity to contract are afforded wide latitude to determine the terms of their contract. Since lawyers would normally draft transnational contracts with the law of a particular jurisdiction in mind, it seems desirable to allow the parties to a transnational contract to specify in the contract the applicable law and to uphold the choice-of-law provisions in transnational contracts.

[a] Restatement (Second) of Conflict of Laws

The pertinent section of *Restatement (Second)* is Section 187 which provides in part:

§ 187. Law of the State Chosen by the Parties

(1) The law of the state chosen by the parties to govern their contractual rights and duties will be applied if the particular issue is one which the parties could have resolved by an explicit provision in their agreement directed to that issue.

(2) The law of the state chosen by the parties to govern their contractual rights and duties will be applied, even if the particular issue is one which the parties could not have resolved by an explicit provision in their agreement directed to that issue, unless either

(a) the chosen state has no substantial relationship to the parties or the transaction and there is no other reasonable basis for the parties' choice, or

(b) application of the law of the chosen state would be contrary to a fundamental policy of a state which has a materially greater interest than the chosen state in the determination of the particular issue and which, under the rule of § 188,

---

[59] Restatement (Second), § 187, Comment e.

would be the state of the applicable law in the absence of an effective choice of law by the parties.

Section 188 prescribes the "most significant relationship" test. Thus, the two limitations to the parties' choice of law are: (1) the chosen state has no substantial relationship to the parties or the transaction and there is no other reasonable basis for the parties' choice; and (2) the parties' choice-of-law would violate a "fundamental public policy" of a state whose interest in the determination of the particular issue is greater than that of the state whose law was chosen.

Under the *Restatement (Second)* approach the courts will not give effect to a choice-of-law provision if the consent of a party to its inclusion was obtained by "improper means, such as by misrepresentation, duress, or undue influence or by mistake."[60] Regarding the issues the parties could have determined by explicit agreement directed to a particular issue, the official comment suggests that the rule "is a rule providing for incorporation by reference and is not a rule of choice of law."[61] Furthermore, "most rules of contract law are designed to fill gaps in a contract which the parties could themselves have filled with express provisions. This is generally true, for example, of rules relating to construction, to conditions precedent and subsequent, to sufficiency of performance and to excuse for nonperformance, including questions of frustration and impossibility. As to all such matters, the forum will apply the provisions of the chosen law."[62] In official comment on section 187(2), *Restatement (Second)* identifies issues the parties could not have determined by explicit agreement as those involving the capacity, formalities, and substantial validity.[63] Usually the chosen law would still be applied even "when to do so would require some disregard of some local provision of the state which would otherwise be the state of the applicable law."[64]

---

[60] Restatement (Second), § 187, Comment b.

[61] *Id.*, Comment c.

[62] *Id.*

[63] *Id.*, Comment d.

Restatement (Second) offers the following rationale for this approach:

> Prime objectives of contract law are to protect the justified expectations of the parties and to make it possible for them to foretell with accuracy what will be their rights and liabilities under the contract. These objectives may best be attained in multistate transactions by letting the parties choose the law to govern the validity of the contract and the rights created thereby. In this way, certainty and predictability of result are most likely to be secured. Giving parties this power of choice is also consistent with the fact that, in contrast to other areas of the law, persons are free within broad limits to determine the nature of their contractual obligations.[65]

Restatement (Second)'s response to the objection that to give the parties this power of choice would be tantamount to making legislators of them is that the "forum in each case selects the applicable law by application of its own choice-of-law rules."[66]

A "substantial relationship" exists when one of the parties is domiciled or has his principal place of business in the chosen state, or the chosen state is the place of contracting, or the state where performance of one of the parties is to take place.[67] However, the parties may have a reasonable basis for choosing a state with which the contract may have no substantial relationship. The *Restatement (Second)* gives an example of contracting "in countries whose legal systems are strange to them as well as relatively immature," when the parties should be able to choose a law on the ground that it is sufficiently developed and that they know it well.[68] The rationale is that "only in this way can they be sure of knowing accurately the extent of their rights and duties under the contract."[69]

On the second exception, that of public policy, *Restatement*

---

[64] *Id.*

[65] *Id.*, Comment e.

[66] *Id.*

[67] *Id.*, Comment f.

[68] *Id.*

[69] *Id.*

(Second) emphasizes in a comment that the application "of the chosen law will be refused only (1) to protect a fundamental policy of the state which, under [the most significant relationship rule] would be the state of the otherwise applicable law, provided (2) that this state has a materially greater interest than the state of the chosen law in the determination of the particular issue."[70] The determination of the question whether a given policy is a fundamental one will be according to the forum's legal principles.[71] The policy in order to be fundamental has to be a substantial one. The official comment adds: "Except perhaps in the case of contracts relating to wills, a policy of this sort will rarely be found in a requirement, such as the statute of frauds, that relates to formalities. . . ."[72]

As should be evident by a review of the *Restatement (Second)* rules, under this approach contracting parties have substantial freedom for a choice-of-law provision to govern their transaction. The basic purpose is to allow the parties to realize their expectations. The Reporter of the *Restatement (Second)* recently "reiterated that, in the majority of instances, application of the chosen law will be sought in order to fill a gap in the contract which the parties could have covered by explicit provision. . . . [I]t is only in the exceptional case that one must face the problems that are involved when the question is whether the chosen law should be applied to govern an issue that does not lie within the contractual capacity of the parties."[73]

The *Restatement (Second)* formulation has been criticized on several grounds, including the following: (1) The objectives the *Restatement (Second)* strives to serve by enforcing the party autonomy rule—the protection of the parties' justified expectations and predictability—are better served by "validating the contract whenever it is reasonable to do so. The rebuttable presumption that is preferable in terms of the needs of the business community is that the contract and all its provisions are valid, not merely that the choice-of-law clause is val-

---

[70] *Id.*, Comment g.
[71] *Id.*
[72] *Id.*
[73] *Supra* N. 58, at 26.

id."[74] (2) As to matters beyond the contractual capacity of the parties, a much more restrictive view is desirable, limiting "the effect of an express choice to those issues that do not involve a strong policy of the forum or another concerned state."[75] (3) Since the "substantial relationship test requires some factual contacts, without which section 188 would be the operative section," in this area the *Restatement (Second)* is too restrictive of party choice. Perhaps the wording "substantial relationship" should be changed to a "reasonable interest" or a "reasonable concern" test to give attorneys wider latitude and greater security in party stipulation.[76] (4) *Restatement (Second)* does not address "the function of time, *i.e.*, to which point in time does a court look to a jurisdiction to apply the proper law. . . . [T]he time factor may have important consequences, especially if the relevant law has changed since the date of execution in any of the concerned jurisdictions."[77]

[b] Uniform Commercial Code

The pertinent provision in UCC governing contractual choice of law is § 1-105(1), which provides that "when a transaction bears a reasonable relation to this state and to another state or nation the parties may agree that the law either of this state or of such other state or nation shall govern their rights and duties. . . ."[78] The "reasonable relation" limitation on choice-of-law seems similar to the *Restatement (Second)* ap-

---

[74] R. Weintraub, *supra* N. 2, at 357 (note omitted).

[75] See Sedler, "The Contracts Provisions of the Restatement (Second): An Analysis and a Critique," 72 Colum. L. Rev. 279, 298 (1972). *See also* Cavers, "Symposium: Conflict of Laws Round Table—The Value of Principled Preferences," 49 Texas L. Rev. 211, 221-22 (1971).

[76] *See* Weinberger, "Party Autonomy and Choice-of-Law: The Restatement (Second), Interest Analysis and the Search for a Methodological Synthesis," 4 Hofstra L. Rev. 605, 616 (1976).

[77] *Id.* at 640.

[78] *See generally* Prebble, "Choice-of-Law to Determine the Validity and Effect of Contracts: A Comparison of English and American Approaches to the Conflict of Laws," 58 Cornell L. Rev. 433, 532-36 (1973).

proach.[79] Section 2-3-2 of the UCC deals with unconscionable choice-of-law provisions which the courts might refuse to enforce. Similarly, although the UCC does not explicitly state a public policy limitation on the choice-of-law provisions, it is a fair assumption that the courts would not enforce a provision that violates a fundamental public policy of the forum. Also, despite the absence of an explicit statement in the UCC regarding the matters of validity, as distinguished from construction of a contract, the *Restatement (Second)* and the UCC approaches seem to be similar and the party autonomy would embrace "issues ordinarily beyond the contractual capacity of the parties."[80]

[c] **Recent Judicial Decisions**

In a New York case concerning the issue of the validity of a termination provision in a "dealers' contract,"[81] a federal district court, applying the New York State law, invalidated a choice-of-law clause according to which Indiana law was to govern the contract's interpretation. Plaintiff, a Puerto Rican corporation, had sought the application of Puerto Rican law. Despite the fact that the defendant was headquartered in Indiana with facilities in Indiana, had shipped, processed, and did the paper work in Indiana on the plaintiff's orders for merchandise, the court cited the New York Court of Appeals' suggestion in a prior case that "the parties' intention and stipulation as to the law governing their contract is but one factor, albeit a weighty one, in deciding the ultimate question— namely, which jurisdiction has the most significant contacts with the matter at issue."[82] However, the basis of the decision seems to be, in the court's words: "the application of Indiana law would frustrate the fundamental policy expressed in the

---

[79] *See* Restatement (Second), § 187(2)(a), Comment f.

[80] R. Weintraub, *supra* N. 2, at 357.

[81] Southern Intern Sales v. Potter & Brumfield Div., 410 F. Supp. 1339 (S.D.N.Y. 1976).

[82] 410 F. Supp. at 1341 (footnote omitted).

Puerto Rican Dealers' Contracts Act."[83] Subsequently, in *La-Beach v. Beatrice Foods Co.*,[84] a federal district court, sitting in New York, referred to the New York Court of Appeals' holding in prior cases that "while the parties' choice-of-law is to be given considerable weight, the law of the jurisdiction with the 'most significant contacts' is to be applied."[85] In that case, the plaintiff was appointed Managing Director of the Nigerian operations of the defendant. The contract, a letter agreement, contained a clause that it was to be "construed and governed by the laws of the State of Illinois, regardless of the fact that the performance of [plaintiff's] duties [was to] take place principally in Nigeria."[86] The court rejected the plaintiff's claim that the validity of the release was to be resolved under Nigerian law. The court found that Illinois was the jurisdiction with the most significant contacts.[87] Based upon that finding the court held that the rights and duties of the parties were to be governed by the law of Illinois.[88]

In a case involving a 1974 dealer's contract, which contained a choice-of-law clause that the agreement should be governed by and construed in accordance with the laws of Massachusetts, the clause was held to be unenforceable in Puerto Rico on the ground that the strong public interests behind the pertinent Puerto Rican statute "expressly held that the right afforded thereby are not subject to waiver."[89] Earlier in *Nakhleh v. Chemical Construction Corp.*,[90] a federal district court sitting in New York, cited with approval the *Restatement (Second)* provisions regarding public policy pertaining to the validity of a contract, especially comment (d) to Section 187 regarding the meaning of "fundamental"—that a policy must be substantial to qualify as fundamental—and concluded that the New

---

[83] *Id.*
[84] 461 F. Supp. 152 (S.D.N.Y. 1978).
[85] *Id.* at 155-56.
[86] *Id.* at 154.
[87] *Id.* at 156.
[88] *Id.*
[89] Pan American Computer Corp. v. Data Gen. Corp., 467 F. Supp. 969, 970 (D. Puerto Rico 1979), *aff'd*, 652 F.2d 215 (1st Cir. 1981).
[90] 359 F. Supp. 357 (1973).

York Statute of Fraud did not represent such a policy.[91] The question pertained to the validity of an oral finders' contract.

A federal district court, sitting in Colorado, enforced a choice-of-law clause in an employment contract, wherein plaintiff, a physician, agreed with an international recruiting and hospital management company that the agreement pertaining to his employment in Saudi Arabia "would be construed in accordance with the laws of Saudi Arabia."[92] The clause read: "Disagreement shall be construed in accordance with the Laws and Regulations of the Kingdom of Saudi Arabia."[93] The court said: "The evidence indicates that Dr. Pirkey signed the contract with full knowledge of its contents. In fact not only the choice-of-law provision but several other provisions of the contract made reference to the applicability of Saudi Arabian Rules and Regulations. Further, there is an absence of any evidence that Dr. Pirkey protested the inclusion of such provision in the contract at the time he signed it or at any other time prior to the initiation of the section."[94] The court did not consider the provision under the contract to be contrary to a fundamental policy of Colorado.[95]

In a procedurally complicated case, the fourth circuit by a split decision limited the application of a choice-of-law clause in contracts between a machinery parts corporation and its salesmen.[95.1] Each contract included a restrictive covenant under which the salesman agreed not to compete with the corporation for two years after the salesman's termination, and a provision specifying that the contract would be construed in accordance with the laws of Ohio, the headquarters of the corporation. The salesmen involved in the suit were employed in several southern and southeastern states, and had left employment with Bowman, the plaintiff, and signed contracts with a competitor. Bowman sued for tortious interference with

---

[91] *Id.* at 360.

[92] Pirkey v. Hospital Corp. of America, 483 F. Supp. 770, 771 (D. Colo. 1980).

[93] *Id.* at 772.

[94] *Id.* at 773.

[95] *Id.* at 774.

[95.1] Barnes Group Inc. v. C & C Products, Inc., 716 F.2d 1023 (4th Cir. 1983).

contract.[95.2] Since a necessary element of such a claim is an enforceable contract, a key issue in the case was whether the restrictive covenants were enforceable. The district court had found the provisions enforceable under Ohio law. The lead opinion for the fourth circuit, however, recognized that

> parties cannot by contract override public policy limitations on contractual power applicable in a state with materially greater interests in the transaction than the state whose law is contractually chosen. . . . While contemporary doctrine recognizes a sphere of party autonomy within which contractual choice-of-law provisions will be given effect, it also limits the extent to which deft draftmanship will be allowed to bypass legislative judgments as to basic enforceability or validity. . . . [The *Second Restatement*] provides that a contractual choice-of-law clause will not be given effect . . . when "application of the law of the chosen state would be contrary to a fundamental policy of a state which has a materially greater interest than the chosen state in the determination of the particular issue and which . . . would be the state of the applicable law in the absence of an effective choice of law by the parties." [Citations and footnotes omitted.][95.3]

The court went on to find that under Alabama law the restrictive covenant would be unenforceable, and that this was a fundamental policy of that state.[95.4] Since this policy was in serious conflict with the Ohio policy, the choice of Ohio law would be disregarded with respect to the Alabama salesmen. Even though the laws of Louisiana, South Carolina and Maryland may have differed in degree from Ohio law, there was no serious conflict, so it was proper to apply Ohio law to those claims.[95.5] Consequently, the court affirmed in part and reversed in part the district court's judgment.[95.6]

[95.2] *Id.* at 1026-27.

[95.3] *Id.* at 1029.

[95.4] *Id.* at 1030-32.

[95.5] *Id.* at 1032.

[95.6] This decision was the result of a split: one judge would have found for the plaintiff on all claims by applying Ohio law and the third judge would have found for the defendant on all claims by applying the law of the other jurisdictions and finding a fundamental public policy against covenants not

[2] Other Approaches

Among other countries, England,[96] France,[97] and Germany[98] would enforce a choice-of-law clause on the rationale that the party autonomy should govern.

Among the applicable multilateral conventions, the Hague Convention on the law applicable to international sales of goods,[99] provides in Article 2: "A sale shall be governed by the domestic law of the country designated by the Contracting Parties. Such designation must be contained in an express clause, or unambiguously result from the provisions of the contract." So long as the parties can show reasonable relation or substantial connection they may choose the law of any country which is best suited to their transaction.[100] Article 6 of the Convention contains the public policy limitation. Another convention that has a bearing upon the choice-of-law rules is the Convention on the Law Applicable to Agency drafted in 1976.[101] The recent EEC convention accepts the freedom of choice as its fundamental principle; in Article 3 it states that a "contract shall be governed by the law chosen by the parties."[102] There is no requirement that the law chosen must have relationship with the parties, the facts of the contractual

---

to compete in each jurisdiction. *See id.* at 1035 and 1037. In the lead opinion the claim against the Louisiana salesman was also reversed because that state does not provide a case of action for tortious interference, and the contractual choice-of-law provision could not be used to alter the law controlling a tort action against a person not a party to the contract. *Id.* at 1032, n. 25.

[96] *See* Prebble, *supra* N. 78, at 503-06.

[97] *See* Blom, "Choice of Law Methods in the Private International Law of Contract," 16 Can. Y.B. Int'l Law 230, 231-53 (1978).

[98] *See id.* at 253-75.

[99] For translated text, *see* 1 Am. J. Comp. L. 275 (1952). 74 Yale L. J. 463 (1965).

[100] G. Delaume, *Transnational Contracts—Applicable Law and Settlement of Disputes* § 1.06 (1980). *See also* Bolgar, "Status of Hague Conventions," 23 Am. J. Comp. L. 280, 282-84 (1975).

[101] Diamond, "Conflict of Laws in the EEC," 32 Current Legal Problems 155, 158 (1979).

[102] *See generally,* Diamond, *supra* N. 101; Nadelmann "Impressionism and Unification of Law: The EEC Draft Convention on the Law Applicable to Contractual and Non-Contractual Obligations," 24 Am. J. Comp. L. 1 (1976).

situation, or the surrounding circumstances.[102.1] The parties may select the law applicable to the whole or a part only of the contract.[103] The Convention provides that "the existence and validity of a choice-of-law, like the existence and validity of the contract itself or of any other term in it, is to be determined by applying the law that would have been applicable if a choice or contract or term in question were valid."[104] The Convention also provides in Article 3(2): "The parties may at any time agree to subject the contract to a law other than that which previously governed it, whether as a result of an earlier choice under this Article or of other provisions of this Convention."[105]

A recent notable development is the drafting of two conventions which supply the applicable substantive law for the resolution of various issues concerning international contracts for the sale of goods. The U.N. Convention on Contracts for the International Sale of Goods[106] and the Draft Convention on Agency in the International Sale of Goods[107] are similar in their application, and will be discussed together.

The conventions apply rather than the internal law of any country, if the following conditions are met. The parties must have places of business in different states.[108] Although a place of business is not specifically defined in either convention,[109] the conventions do provide a solution to the problem of multiple places of business, in which case, for the purpose of the convention, the place of business is to be the place of business

---

[102.1] For a criticism of this aspect of the Convention, see R. Weintraub, "How to Choose Law for Contracts and How not to: The EEC Concention," 17 Tex. Int'l L.J. 155 (1982).

[103] Diamond, supra N. 101, at 159.

[104] Id. at 161-62.

[105] Id. at 165.

[106] U.N. Doc. A/CONF. 97/18, April 10, 1980, reprinted in 19 Int'l Legal Materials 668 (1980) [Hereafter Contracts Convention.] See generally Dore, "U.N. Convention on Contracts for the International Sales of Goods," 77 Am. J. Int'l L. 521 (1983).

[107] Draft Convention on Agency in the International Sale of Goods, reprinted in 1983 Revue de Droit Uniform 3 [Hereafter Agency Convention].

[108] Contracts Conv. art. 1(1); Agency Conv. art. 2(1).

[109] See Note, 69 Iowa L.R. 209, at 218-19 (1983).

that has the closest relationship to the sale.[110] If there is no place of business then the reference is to the habitual residence.[111] Also, nationality and civil or commercial nature of the parties are to be ignored in determining the application of the conventions.[112] If the places of business are in different states, then the conventions apply if both states are contracting states (to the convention), or if choice-of-law rules would apply the law of a contracting state.[113]

The conventions only apply to the sale of goods. Neither convention explicitly defines sales of goods; instead the conventions exclude certain transactions from their application.[114] It has been suggested that the policy of the conventions[115] implies that "goods" be broadly interpreted to further the ends of the conventions.[116]

The object of the conventions is to provide a uniform law applicable to the sale of goods or to agency in the sale of goods.[117] Both conventions allow the parties to exclude the application of the convention or vary the application of its provisions.[118] However, in the Convention on Contracts for the International Sale of Goods it is uncertain whether this exclusion can be implied;[119] in the Agency convention it seems that such an exclusion can be implied in some instances.[120]

---

[110] Contracts Conv. art. 10(9); Agency Conv. art. 8(9).

[111] Contracts Conv. art. 10(6); Agency Conv. art. 8(6).

[112] Contracts Conv. art. 1(3); Agency Conv. art. 2(3).

[113] Contracts Conv. art. 1(1); Agency Conv. art. 2(1).

[114] Generally, the conventions exclude auctions and activities of stock and commodity exchanges. The Contracts Convention also excludes sales of ships and aircraft, most consumer goods and electricity. See Contracts Convention art. 2; Agency Conv. art. 3(1).

[115] I.e., promoting uniformity, Contracts Conv. art. 7; Agency Conv. art. 6.

[116] See supra N. 109, at 227-28.

[117] Contracts Conv. art 7; Agency Conv. art. 6.

[118] Contracts Conv. art. 6; Agency Conv. art. 5.

[119] See supra N. 109, at 235-39; Dore and DaFranco, "A Comparison of the Non-Substantive Provisions of the UNCITRAL Convention on the International Sale of Goods and the Uniform Commercial Code," 23 Harv. Int'l L. J. 49, at 53 (1982).

[120] This is true between the agent and principal but the convention is as ambiguous as the Contracts Convention on the type of exclusion that must exist in the contract with the third party. Agency Conv. art. 5.

§ 8.04   Conclusion

As the preceding discussion shows, it will be desirable to include both forum selection and choice-of-law clauses, while drafting a transnational contract. The general policy to uphold contracts, validate them and meet the expectations of the parties is being accepted by many courts as a basic policy in transnational contracts. However, it should be reiterated that if a stipulation is made this alone appears to be insufficient to make section 187 (2) (a) of Restatement (Second) operative, for substantial relationship must be demonstrated by additional means. Factual contacts indicating substantial relationship are usually present in transnational contracts. In any event, without such a stipulation, uncertainty is likely to be compounded.

Appendix 8A: Sample Choice-of-Law and Choice-of-Forum Clause

This contract (is made and) shall be construed (interpreted) according to the laws of _____, and any controversy arising under or in relation to this contract shall be settled (by arbitration and to be held) in _____. The courts and authorities of _____ shall have exclusive jurisdiction over all controversies which may arise under or in relation to this contract, especially with respect to the execution, interpretation, and compliance of this Agreement, the parties hereto waiving any other venue to which they might be entitled by virtue of domicile, habitual residence or otherwise.

CHAPTER 9

Antitrust Aspects of International Business Operations

THEODORE L. BANKS*

---

*Corporate Counsel, Dart & Kraft, Inc., Northbrook, Illinois; B.A., Beloit College, J.D. University of Denver College of Law. My thanks to Cheryl Banks and Howard Hoosin who reviewed portions of this paper and provided valuable suggestions. The opinions expressed herein are solely those of the author, who bears responsibility for any errors.

The businessman who ventures forth from his home country for the first time, whether as buyer or seller, has a multitude of new problems to confront, including the risk of antitrust violations. Yet, there are no simple rules that can be propounded under which all such risk can be avoided. One cannot assume that the laws of foreign countries will be the same as those of the United States, nor can one assume that overseas operations by an American or foreign corporation will necessarily be free of the risk of running afoul of the U.S. antitrust laws. Because of their special importance to the American businessman, this chapter will emphasize the essential points of the antitrust laws of the European Economic Community and the United States, and will touch upon selected aspects of the antitrust laws of other countries. Certainly, however, the businessman or attorney who contemplates international operations is usually well-advised to consult with expert counsel at both ends of the transaction prior to investment of significant time or capital.

§ 9.01   Introduction

Enforcement of certain types of antitrust laws is a phenomenon peculiar to the United States. Not only are antitrust laws enforced more vigorously in the U.S. than elsewhere, but many countries encourage precisely the kind of conduct prohibited by American legislation. Antitrust laws are regarded as an unaffordable luxury by many developing nations, and even

countries like France[1] and Italy lack the kind of national antitrust laws that are more-or-less well accepted in the U.S. while
Japan and Germany, which acquired antitrust laws as part of
their post-World War II reconstruction, have originally
showed relatively little interest in vigorously enforcing these
alien (*i.e.*, American) concepts, their laws have developed to
the point where they can have a significant impact on business
activities.[2]

If the U.S. antitrust laws were limited to controlling the
conduct of Americans and others only when there were both
actions and effects in the United States, they would not be
especially noteworthy. However, the American laws have
been uniquely used, with even greater intensity in recent
years, to attack certain practices occuring not only inside, but
also outside of the U.S., where there is a perceived effect on
the domestic or *foreign* commerce of the United States.[2.1]
Until the early 1950s, such actions were generally limited to
challenging cartels,[3] but the government enforcers have now
broadened their scope, concentrating on the activities of U.S.
or foreign firms, wherever such activities may occur,[4] when-

---

[1] The Napoleonic Code of 1808 did include a one-sentence condemnation
of price-fixing. *See* 769 Antitrust & Trade Reg. Rep. (B.N.A.) [hereinafter
"A.T.R.R."] D1 (June 12, 1976).

[2] The West German Federal Cartel Office has attempted to change its
image recently. Wolfgange Karte, as President of the Cartel Office, has
asserted that Germany's merger control provisions are the most highly perfected anywhere, including "the U.S., our model of antitrust legislation."
Colitt, "West German Cartel Office Takes on Banking Giants," Financial
Times 3 (June 21, 1979). An agreement was signed in 1976 to provide for
cooperation between the U.S. and West Germany in antitrust matters. 772
A.T.R.R. D1 (July 13, 1976). U.S. and Japanese officials have met to establish
procedures to coordinate antitrust enforcement. 960 A.T.R.R. A-8 (June 5,
1980).

[2.1] For more information on the jurisdictional limits of U.S. antitrust laws,
see Chapter 10, *infra*.

[3] International Economic Report of the President (1974), Trade Reg. Rep.
(CCH) [hereinafter "T.R.R."] ¶ 50,262.

[4] Interview with John H. Shenefield, Assistant Attorney General, 843
A.T.R.R. AA-1 (Aug. 3, 1978).

---

ever there is some impact upon the United States.[4.1]

It should be noted that this trend of expansion has included not only antitrust laws, but also banking, shipping, securities, and tax laws. But because of its direct and powerful force, foreign antitrust enforcement often tends to command greater attention by businessmen and attorneys than some of these other laws.[5]

In 1976, new legislation[6] gave the Department of Justice[7] (DOJ) the power to sue foreign governments (as well as private corporations) for their anticompetitive behavior. To pursue this power, the DOJ has attempted to take depositions abroad, and to demand documents overseas, even from third parties having only a slight business link with the defendant in the case. In spite of the friction this has caused with some of our allies,[8] it sometimes appears that there is not a great deal of sympathy at the DOJ for the foreign policy ramifications of its actions.[8.1] Former Attorney General Griffin Bell has said that this new mode of conduct was justified, since, in the past, the U.S. had been extending comity more than it had been receiv-

---

[4.1] United States v. Aluminum Co. of America, 148 F.2d 416 (2d Cir. 1945).

[5] American Bar Association, *Antitrust Law Developments* at 354 (1975).

[6] Hart-Scott-Rodino Antitrust Improvements Act of 1976, P.L. 94-583 (Sept. 30, 1976), 90 Stat. 1383; Foreign Sovereign Immunities Act, 28 U.S.C. § 1330, P.L. 94-583 (Oct. 21, 1976), 90 Stat. 289.

[7] Although the Department of Justice (DOJ) has been active in the area of international enforcement of the antitrust laws, the Federal Trade Commission (FTC) also has certain international authority.

[8] Some joint activities, such as rate setting by shipping conferences, may be legal abroad, but illegal in the U.S. 1008 A.T.R.R. A6 (April 2, 1981). The United Kingdom retaliated for the antitrust actions brought against a number of European shipping companies for rate fixing. Even though the companies decided to settle with the DOJ (and paid fines of $6.1 million), the fixing of rates on shipping routes would not have been illegal in Britain. Legislation was enacted on March 20, 1980 to prevent enforcement in Britain of U.S. antitrust judgments. "Clipping the Wings of U.S. Trust-Busters," World Business Weekly 25 (Oct. 19, 1979); "Britain Says to Go Home," The Economist 79 (Sept. 15, 1979); 922 A.T.R.R. A30 (July 12, 1979); 950 A.T.R.R. F1 (April 10, 1980).

[8.1] However, foreign policy considerations were the major restraints on the DOJ in its pursuit of the international uranium cartel. 943 A.T.R.R. A1 (Dec. 13, 1979).

ing it in return.[9]

Behind this increase in antitrust enforcement activity, is the philosophy that free and fair competition is the best means to stimulate economic progress and higher living standards.[10] The DOJ sees its function as one of "competitive advocacy" in international trade, and has stated that it will work against protectionist trends, even if this means opposing other U.S. government agencies, such as the International Trade Commission.[11] Although a former DOJ official advocated repeal of the Webb-Pomerene Act,[12] which allows formation of "cartels" for export activity, contrary to this approach has been the push in Congress to expand the antitrust exemption for export cartels. The Export Trading Company and Foreign Trade Antitrust Improvements Act of 1982,[12.1] which is discussed, *infra*, would allow banks to participate in export trading activities.

The DOJ articulated specific facts of its enforcement policy with the release of its international enforcement guidelines in 1972 and 1977.[13] These guidelines, which are discussed throughout the chapter, were designed to clarify the DOJ's view of the U.S. antitrust laws since unclear case law had caused many U.S. businessmen and lawyers to become too conservative in their overseas activities. The DOJ stated that it will seek to promote competition with a two-fold end: (1) protecting the consumer by allowing the economy to benefit from imports or the entry of foreign firms into the United

---

[9] "Antitrust Tensions With Europe," *Dun's Review* 102 (May 1978).

[10] International Economic Report of the President, *supra* N. 3.

[11] T.R.R. ¶50,371.

[12] Shenefield interview, *supra* N. 4, at AA3. Because Webb-Pomerene has been little used he argued that repeal would not matter, and the DOJ business review letter procedure (per 28 C.F.R. § 506) could be used instead. The DOJ guidelines encourage the use of this procedure rather than blanket reliance on the Guidelines. Although companies have been reluctant to use the BRP, the DOJ's record shows that it handles requests seriously and expeditiously.

[12.1] Pub. L. 97-290, 96 Stat. 1233, 12 U.S.C. §§ 1841-3, 635a-4, 372, 15 U.S.C. §§ 6A, 45(a)(3).

[13] Memorandum of the Department of Justice Concerning Antitrust and Foreign Competition, Trade Reg. Rep. ¶ 50,129 (Jan. 25, 1972); Department of Justice, *Antitrust Guide for International Operations* (1977), 799 A.T.R.R. E-1 (Feb. 1, 1977). (Hereinafter "DOJ guidelines.")

States; and (2) protecting U.S. exports and foreign investment by allowing each U.S. firm to compete on its own merits.[14] One should be cautioned, however, against over-reliance on statements of enforcement policy such as the guidelines. The views of the DOJ at any given time may differ from those of the FTC or ITC. Also, a change in administration may significantly alter the thrust of enforcement policy. Finally, private litigation, which represents the majority of antitrust activity, may not be influenced by government opinions.

§ 9.02 Specific Areas of Antitrust Law

[1] Monopolization and Restraint of Trade

[a] "Rule of Reason" vs. *Per Se* Violations

Although it is not the purpose of this publication to present a detailed review of the U.S. antitrust laws, it should be noted that the concepts of these laws that affect international operations have been largely derived from cases involving domestic commerce. For example, § 1 of the Sherman Act[15] appears to prohibit all restraints of trade. Yet, it was recognized early on that some restraints are reasonable and should be allowed,[16] while other restraints are presumed to be always detrimental to competition (*per se* unreasonable) and therefore illegal. Such *per se* violations include price fixing, allocations of customers, group boycotts, resale price maintenance, and certain tie-in sales.[17] However, antitrust law is difficult in that, in non-*per se* situations, there are very few objective criteria to determine legality. Traditionally, in a "rule of reason" evaluation, the courts will examine the restraint to see (1) if there is a significant adverse effect on competition; (2) the nature of the justification, (3) whether that justification could be achieved in a less anti-competitive way; (4) whether the restraint is merely ancillary to a lawful main purpose; (5) if the scope and duration of the restraint are greater than necessary to achieve the main

---

[14] DOJ guidelines at E2.

[15] 15 U.S.C. § 1.

[16] Standard Oil Co. of New Jersey v. United States, 221 U.S. 1 (1911).

[17] Catalano, Inc. v. Target Sales, Inc., 446 U.S. 643 (1980); Northern Pac. Ry. v. United States, 356 U.S. 1, 5 (1958); DOJ guidelines, at El.

purpose; and (6) if the entire agreement is reasonable, either alone or in combination with other circumstances.

The rule of reason approach to antitrust analysis has gained favor since the *Sylvania*[18] decision, which removed most vertical restraints (*e.g.*, in a manufacturer-distributor relationship) from the *per se* category. The absence of *per se* rules means that consistency is difficult to accomplish, since decisions are based on such factors as economic evidence and the size of the market participants. Thus, apparently identical fact situations may provide opposite verdicts.

The DOJ has taken the position that the rule of reason approach (as opposed to a *per se* approach) will normally be utilized in evaluating international marketing arrangements, since there are special justifications for certain international activities that are not applicable to the domestic market, and since there is less certainty regarding the adverse effects on U.S. commerce when international activities are involved.[19] Yet the DOJ also advises U.S. firms not to participate in foreign activities that might be considered *per se* unreasonable at home, even if a foreign sovereign directs such conduct.

Therefore, the fact that an agreement or act is international in character is probably not enough to remove it from the risk of a U.S. antitrust violation. A court will analyze the nature of the industry involved, including the history and rationale for the restraints under scrutiny.[20] For example, the otherwise innocent act of constructing a plant may be unlawful if its purpose is to harass or foreclose competition in export or import trade.[21] So, while not every act may be *per se* illegal, the effects and motivation of a potentially anti-competitive action must be carefully reviewed.

The rule of reason analysis is especially important in international business arrangements, since they frequently do not fit the pattern of any familiar domestic business agreements. The

---

[18] Continental T.V., Inc. v. GTE Sylvania, Inc., 433 U.S. 36 (1977).

[19] DOJ guidelines, at E1.

[20] National Society of Professional Engineers v. United States, 435 U.S. 679 (1978).

[21] FTC v. Eastman Kodak Co., 274 U.S. 619, 629 (1929); United States v. Aluminum Co. of America, 148 F.2d 416, 431 (2d Cir. 1945); J. Van Cise, *Understanding the Antitrust Laws* 263 (1976).

case of *Hunt v. Mobil Oil Corp.*[21.1] is an example of such a unique arrangement. In 1971, oil companies operating in Libya signed the Libyan Producers' Agreement (LPA) to share the burden of any government-imposed production cutbacks by supplying the injured party with crude oil. As local governments exerted more control over oil production, difficulties in implementing the LPA increased. Hunt's firm was nationalized, which triggered a series of lawsuits regarding these events. A claim that other oil companies conspired to have Hunt nationalized was barred by the act-of-state doctrine.[22] The remaining claims alleged a conspiracy to injure Hunt through the use of the production-sharing agreement.

Although the agreement was approved by the Departments of State and Justice, the court rejected the defendants' argument that the agreement is automatically exempt from antitrust scrutiny. The court also dismissed the defendants' counterclaims, but appears to have accepted virtually everything else from defendants' argument. This is both a reflection of the merits of plaintiffs' case, and another indication that when novel rule-of-reason analysis is indicated, skillful advocacy can go far in convincing a judge of the reasonableness of an arrangement.

One clause of the LPA limited the amount of crude available to a firm to that quantity adequate to supply existing customers. Rather than being a resale restraint, the court determined that the clause was an "entitlement condition"[23] designed to determine the amount of crude to be supplied. Another clause of the LPA ("dimes clause") allowed producers to pay $0.10 per barrel rather than supplying crude. Hunt alleged, but failed to prove, a conspiracy to injure Hunt by utilizing the dimes clause rather than providing crude. In the end, the court referred Hunt's claim to the arbitration as stipulated in the LPA.

[21.1] 465 F. Supp. 195 (S.D.N.Y. 1978), *aff'd*, 610 F.2d 806 (2d Cir. 1979).
[22] 410 F. Supp. 10 (S.D.N.Y. 1976), *cert. denied* 434 U.S. 984 (1977).
[23] 465 F. Supp. at 216.

[b] Boycotts and Horizontal Price Fixing

An agreement among suppliers or customers to fix prices or boycott a company are examples of one of the *per se* violations.[24] For example, using a common sales agent within the U.S. to coordinate sales and prices of competitors would be a violation.[24.1] Even though allegations of world-wide conspiracies may be involved, normal pleading and practice rules generally apply. To sustain a claim that defendant's conduct violated § 1 of the Sherman Act, a plaintif must be able to prove that (1) defendants contracted, combined or conspired, (2) that the combination produces anti-competitive effects within the relevant market, (3) that the objects of the conduct pursuant to the conspiracy were illegal, and (4) that plaintiff was injured as a result of the conspiracy.[24.2] A plaintiff must be within the target area of the illegal conduct. When oil refiners decided to stop buying oil from Libya, an indirect customer of the companies could not maintain an action under § 1 of the Sherman Act for a group boycott.[24.3]

But, what happens if a foreign government orders a U.S. company to stop dealing with another U.S. company? The DOJ has outlined such a case, and has taken the position that comity between nations does not require a U.S. corporation, even if it is operating on foreign soil to commit a *per se* violation.[25] Where a course of conduct was merely authorized by a foreign government, and not compelled, U.S. antitrust liability is more likely.[25.1] The DOJ does admit, however, that its rather hard position is contrary to the decision in *Interamerican Refining*

---

[24] Klors, Inc. v. Broadway-Hale Stores, Inc., 359 U.S. 207 (1959).

[24.1] United States v. Societe Nationale des Poudres et Explosifs, Consent Decree, T.R.R. ¶ 45,080 (D.N.J. 1980).

[24.2] Martin B. Glauser Dodge Co. v. Chrysler Corp., 570 F.2d 72 (3d Cir. 1977), *cert. denied,* 436 U.S. 913 (1978).

[24.3] Long Island Lighting Co. v. Standard Oil Co. of California, 521 F.2d 1269 (2d Cir. 1975), *cert. denied,* 423 U.S. 1073 (1976).

[25] DOJ guidelines at E14-E15.

[25.1] Continental Ore Co. v. Union Carbide & Carbon Co., 370 U.S. 690 (1962), *but see* Occidental Petroleum Corp v. Buttes Oil & Gas Co., 461 F.2d 1261 (9th Cir. 1972), *cert. denied,* 409 U.S. 950 (1973).

Corp. v. Texaco Maracaibo, Inc.,[26] although it argues that the case was wrongly decided, and no exemption should be provided for acts outside the sovereign territory.[27] The U.S. Attorney General has also ruled that export restraints on cars imposed by a foreign government would not violate the U.S. antitrust laws where the conduct was compelled by the foreign government.[27.1] Given this divergence of opinion, until such time as Congress or the Supreme Court addresses the issue, the American legal ramifications will be uncertain.

Application of one of the *per se* rules to international transactions is usually relatively straightforward, which does provide some degree of guidance in determining which agreements may be impermissable under U.S. law. Where acts take place on foreign soil, the safer course would be to follow the DOJ position, since courts have held that U.S. laws apply, so long as there is more than an insignificant effect on the foreign or interstate commerce of the U.S.[27.2] In *Sanib Corp. v. United Fruit Co.,*[28] United Fruit ceased selling bananas to Sanib in Honduras, allegedly pursuant to a conspiracy formed in Honduras. The court held that such conduct, although taking place entirely outside of the U.S., stated a cause of action under the U.S. antitrust laws. Similarly, in *Continental Ore Co. v. Union Carbide,*[28.1] the Sherman Act was held to apply to the Canadian subsidiary of a U.S. corporation where its activities were part of a U.S.-based conspiracy to monopolize shipments from the U.S. to Canada.

The Justice Department gives *Pacific Seafarers, Inc. v. Pacific Far East Line, Inc.,*[29] as an example of the type of concerted illegal conduct it will pursue. Plaintiff's business was

---

[26] Interamerican Refining Corp. v. Texaco Maracaibo, Inc., 307 F. Supp. 1291 (D. Del. 1970).

[27] DOJ guidelines at E15.

[27.1] Opinion of the Attorney General, May 7, 1981, T.R.R. ¶ 63,998.

[27.2] Montreal Trading Ltd. v. Amax, Inc., 661 F.2d 864 (10th Cir. 1981); Conservation Council of Western Australia, Inc. v. Aluminum Co. of America, 518 F. Supp. 270 (W.D. Pa. 1981).

[28] Sanib Corp. v. United Fruit Co., 135 F. Supp. 764 (S.D.N.Y. 1955).

[28.1] Continental Ore, *supra* N. 25.1.

[29] Pacific Seafarers, Inc. v. Pacific Far East Line, Inc., 404 F.2d 804 (D.C. Cir. 1968), *cert. denied,* 393 U.S. 1093 (1969).

developed around the concept of using older vessels to ship cement and fertilizer from Taiwan and Thailand to South Viet Nam at a more competitive price. Since the purchases of cement and fertilizer were subsidized by payments from the U.S. government, at least 50 percent of the cargo had to be transported on U.S.-flag vessels. Defendants were members of the American-flag Berth Operators (AFBO), which set the rates for these shipments, and did not welcome price competition. Defendants made numerous attempts to block plaintiff's entrance to the business. When these efforts failed, rates were dropped to almost half their prior level. Plaintiff went out of business, and prices rose to "substantially higher levels than those prevailing before plaintiff sought to enter the trade."[30]

Plaintiff filed suit under §§ 1 and 2 of the Sherman Act after being denied relief at the Federal Maritime Commission. The District Court dismissed the suit since there was no claim of restraint of foreign commerce, but the Court of Appeals disagreed, finding that a cause of action was stated. The facts showed that plaintiff was injured by the defendants' conspiracy, and, in the court's opinion, that actual imports to or exports from the U.S.A. were not necessary to find injury to foreign commerce. Since the entire enterprise was dependent on, and motivated solely by, subsidies from the U.S. government, there was an "ongoing and substantial nexus to the United States" to support application of the Sherman Act.

Pacific is a good example of the traditional type of forbidden conduct that will not escape U.S. liability even if it occurs outside of the United States. Government enforcers scrutinize the activities of cartels carefully, and appropriately concentrate their efforts in this fashion, since such price fixing and market allocation systems are *per se* violations of § 1 of the Sherman Act.[31] However, as in domestic transactions, an

---

[30] 404 F.2d at 809.

[31] Weiner, "International Joint Ventures and Section One of the Sherman Act: Per Se as the Meaningful Standard," 23 American U.L. Rev. 689, 794 (1974). Foreign companies that fix prices at the encouragement of their governments may not be amenable to suits under the American antitrust laws. When the price of uranium quadrupled in 1974-75, Westinghouse Electric Co. reneged on its long-term uranium supply contracts with its reactor customers. The reactor customers sued Westinghouse, and Westing-

agreement not to sell products in certain countries ancillary to the sale of a business will be allowed, provided the restraint is reasonable in scope and duration.[31.1]

Even when foreign governments are involved, cartel-type activities will not necessarily be protected.[31.2] An opinion[32] by the Commission of the European Communities[33] indicates sensitivity to this area of U.S. law. The Commission was engaging in joint consultations with various sectors of the European economy to review possibilities for increasing production efficiency. In response to inquiries from subsidiaries of U.S. corporations, the Commission stated that it would not make an agreement with the U.S. antitrust authorities, since even though such consultations were standard practice in dealing with E.E.C. problems, U.S. subsidiaries, concerned with U.S. antitrust laws, may decline to participate.[34]

The boycott by certain Arab countries of companies with Jewish or Israeli contacts may have U.S. antitrust consequences. An American firm, or a foreign firm controlled by an American company,[35] that participates in the boycott by, for example, refusing to buy component parts from a "blacklisted" company, will incur the risk of both a Sherman Act criminal charge from the DOJ, and a civil suit from the injured compa-

---

house sued seventeen domestic and twelve foreign uranium producers alleging price fixing. But the foreign companies have refused to accept service of process or appear in court, and, in some cases, have enacted blocking or "clawback" statutes in retaliation. Although most of the cases were settled prior to trial, the blocking statutes remain on the books.

[31.1] Thoms v. Sutherland, 52 F.2d 592 (3d Cir. 1931).

[31.2] For example, although joint setting of shipping rates is legal throughout most of the world, there may be no U.S. antitrust immunity for such actions. *See supra* N. 8 and 906 A.T.R.R. A5 (March 22, 1979).

[32] Q&A 109/78, issued by Comm. 6/12/78, T.R.R. No. 339 (June 20, 1978).

[33] Hereinafter "Commission." The Commission is responsible for administering the antitrust laws of the EEC which will be covered at length in § 9.03[3], *infra*.

[34] *Supra* N. 32.

[35] Finagrain, a Swiss subsidiary of Continental Grain Co., paid $20,000 in civil penalties for illegally certifying that commodities sold to Iraq were not of Israeli origin, and that Finagrain was not affiliated with any blacklisted company. Huffman, "Top Fine Buoys Anti-Boycott Effort," *Legal Times of Washington* 2 (Sept. 3, 1979).

ny. Also, the Department of Commerce and the Internal Revenue Service[36] have elaborate reporting requirements (covered in detail in Chapter 13) to detect (and penalize for) participation in the boycott. The initial legislation and enforcement efforts softened the demands of the boycott countries from requiring negative certificates (no Israeli goods) to positive certificates (certificate of origin), and a corresponding reduction in enforcement by the various U.S. authorities.

In *United States v. Bechtel Corp.*[37] Bechtel was challenged by the DOJ under § 1 of the Sherman Act, alleging that its refusal to deal with blacklisted U.S. corporations restricted interstate and foreign commerce. Bechtel settled with the government on terms more onerous than required by the subsequently enacted regulations. Bechtel's challenge to this settlement was dismissed,[38] and thus there is some question remaining as to the extent of antitrust liability for compliance with the boycott. However, as enforcement of these regulations declines, this area should be come less controversial. In any event, substantive compliance with the Commerce and IRS regulations should insulate a company from antitrust exposure since they effectively prevent participation in a boycott.

Regardless of compliance with boycott regulations, private actions may be filed by American companies who believe they are injured by the boycott. For example, a suit was filed by a "Jewish-owned" company that manufactures bus seats against several large U.S. bus manufacturers. The complaint charged that the bus manufacturers backed-out of a $2.9 million contract for seats for buses that were to go to Saudi Arabia since the firm was on the Arab blacklist. The suit alleged that a rival

---

[36] Export Administration Act Amendments of 1977, 50 U.S.C. § 2403(1)(a), P.L. 95-52 (1977); Ribicoff Amendments to the Tax Reform Act of 1976, 26 U.S.C. § 999, P.L. 94-455 (1976). For a discussion of the various policy conflicts regarding the Arab Boycott, *see* 72 Proc. A.S.I.L. 80 (1978). Also, there are state boycott laws that may not be pre-empted by the federal statutes, such as the one in California. 794 A.T.R.R. A12 (Dec. 21, 1976).

[37] Civ. No. 76-99 (N.D. Cal., January 16, 1976); T.R.R. ¶ 64,429. Under the settlement, Bechtel agreed to submit the names of all potential subcontractors to the Arab nations, and not act as a "gatekeeper" by excluding any companies. 796 A.T.R.R. A17 (Jan. 11, 1977).

[38] 648 F.2d 660 (9th Cir. 1981).

seat manufacturer (which eventually got the contract) advised the Saudi Arabian government of the Jewish ownership of the company which resulted in the termination of the deal.[39]

[c] Attempts to Monopolize

Often, a scheme may be condemned as illegal not because a specific practice is necessarily violative of the law, but because an examination of the totality of circumstances surrounding and constituting the scheme indicates a violation. Section 2 of the Sherman Act[40] prohibits monopolies or attempts to monopolize any line of domestic or foreign commerce of the U.S.[41] In *United States v. General Electric Co.*,[42] G.E. dominated the market for certain newly-developed hard metal products by entering into a number of patent licenses from the foreign owners. These licenses, combined with G.E.'s patents and licenses it granted in turn (which contained clauses fixing prices, controlling unpatented products, and requiring cross-licensing), were found to violate §§ 1 and 2 of the Sherman Act. G.E. had agreed with the original license owner on which markets it could serve (and at what prices) and purchased competitors in order to preserve its market control. In spite of the fact that patents were involved, which gave the owner of license limited monopoly rights, the abuse of those rights resulted in antitrust violations.[43]

---

[39] Metzger, "Jewish Firm Takes on Giants," Crain's Chicago Business 1 (February 26, 1979). The case was ultimately settled, and since the file was sealed, we will probably never know the outcome.

[40] 15 USC § 2.

[41] Iberia Airlines charged Boeing with attempting to monopolize export commerce in commercial jet aircraft sold to Spain. The complaint alleged that, in the course of negotiations for the sale of aircraft, certain fraudulent misrepresentations were made in furtherance of a scheme to monopolize this market. Iberia, Lineas Aereas de Espana, S.A. v. The Boeing Co., No. 80-0244 (D.D.C. Jan. 28, 1980), A.T.R.R. A-12 (Jan. 31, 1980).

[42] United States v. General Electric Co., 80 F. Supp. 989 (S.D.N.Y. 1948).

[43] *See* A. Neale, *The Antitrust Laws of the U.S.A.* 351 (2d ed. 1970). The control of technology is being examined by the FTC and DOJ as one way a dominant company can maintain control of a market. High R&D spending may be viewed as anticompetitive by those agencies when undertaken for the purpose of keeping competitors out of the market.

The line of foreign commerce to be monopolized in a § 2 charge may be in the traditional form, involving a product imported into the U.S. In *United States v. Sisal Sales Corp.*,[44] the sole importer of sisal (used to make twine) conspired with the sole exporter, a Mexican corporation, controlled both supply and price, and eliminated all competition.

In *United States v. Eastman Kodak Co.*,[45] Kodak obtained control over the entire supply of imported raw paper used for the manufacture of photographic printing paper, and refused to sell to other manufacturers. Tying up this supply resulted in the demise of several competitors, and this result, combined with Kodak's acquisition of several competitors and distributors, constituted monopolization under § 2.

A service may also be the monopolized line of foreign commerce, as it was in *Thomsen v. Cayser.*[46] In *Thomsen*, defendants conspired to monopolize shipping routes between New York and South Africa by granting favorable rates to customers who dealt with them and by using "fighting ships" to undercut competitors.

As an illustrative example[47] of monopolization, the DOJ constructs the case of the acquisition of a small German corporation which owns U.S. patents by a competing U.S. corporation with a 50 percent market share. Section 2 may be violated by such an acquisition, the DOJ asserts, since the acquiring company had "monopoly power" (its 50 percent market share), if it purchased the German company for the purpose of creating or maintaining that monopoly power.[48] Although the earlier cases spoke in terms of the traditional monopolization of a market (all or virtually all of it), today a 50 percent market share, when combined with an intent to monopolize, may be enough to violate § 2. Thus, a company with a small market share has more freedom to undertake "restrictive" agreements than does the corporation with a larger market share.

Market share figures are rough guides at best, however. In

---

[44] United States v. Sisal Sales Corp., 214 U.S. 268 (1927).
[45] United States v. Eastman Kodak Co., 226 F. 62 (W.D.N.Y. 1915).
[46] Thomsen v. Cayser, 243 U.S. 66 (1916).
[47] DOJ guidelines Case B at E5.
[48] *See* United States v. Grinnell Corp., 384 U.S. 563, 571-72 (1966).

Outboard Marine Corp. v. Pezetel, [49] an agency of the Polish Government achieved a 35 percent share of the electric golf cart market in the U.S., and, in so doing, was accused of violating §§ 1 and 2 of the Sherman Act by an American manufacturer forced out of business. In denying a motion to dismiss, the U.S. District Court (D. Del.) held that while a 35 percent market share would not sustain a monopoly charge, the requisite intent to monopolize could be inferred from the market share when it was obtained through the use of territorial restraints in the distribution process. However, many courts do not assume that the mere fact that a firm has a large market share will automatically bring all aggressive (but otherwise legal) behavior under the bar of § 2 of the Sherman Act.[49.1]

[2] Dealing with Customers and Suppliers

A seller of goods is free to deal or refuse to deal with whomever he chooses, so long as his decision is not motivated by illegal considerations.[49.2] In many instances, customers allege that the seller refused to deal when the customer refused to adhere to restraints imposed by the seller. Distribution cases of this type are frequently resolved at the Court of Appeals level, and, even though the balance is probably in favor of the manufacturer, the costs and delays of trial and appeal often dictate the need for careful planning, restrained programs, and, frequently, out-of-court settlements.[49.3] Although international distribution agreements typically refer the resolution of disputes to a designated arbitration panel, U.S. courts will not allow this method to resolve antitrust claims between the par-

---

[49] 461 F. Supp. 384 (D. Del. 1978).

[49.1] Berkey Photo, Inc. v. Eastman Kodak Corp., 603 F.2d 623 (2d Cir. 1979), *cert. denied,* 444 U.S. 1093 (1980); California Computer Products, Inc. v. IBM Corp., 613 F.2d 727 (9th Cir. 1979).

[49.2] United States v. Colgate & Co., 250 U.S. 300 (1919).

[49.3] In Taubler v. Girard, 655 F.2d 991 (9th Cir. 1981), a French winemaker terminated a California distributor after only one shipment. Although the District Court dismissed the distributor's suit, the Ninth Circuit determined that the one sale was enough to confer jurisdiction, due to an "intent" to do business in the state.

ties. Because of the interest in protecting competition, as a matter of public policy, antitrust claims may not be decided by arbitration.[49.4] Therefore, in an antitrust claim by a terminated dealer in Puerto Rico against a Japanese manufacturer and its U.S. distributor, the international nature of the distribution agreement was held not to alter the application of the U.S. policy against arbitration of these claims.[49.5]

United States antitrust law currently distinguishes between horizontal restraints (agreements between actual or potential competitors) and vertical restraints (agreements between customers and suppliers), with a decided bias in favor of the reasonableness of the vertical restraint. When an enhancement of inter-brand competition can be shown as a result of a supplier's intra-brand restraints, a reasonableness analysis is appropriate.[50] However, resale restraints imposed on a horizontal basis would come under the *per se* prohibition.[51]

In spite of these distinctions, attempts to restrain where or how a customer disposes of product, or other restraints, such as tying contracts, should be approached with caution.[52] Al-

---

[49.4] American Safety Equipment Corp. v. Hickok Manufacturing Co., 391 F.2d 821, 68 Trade Cas. ¶ 72,387 (2d Cir. 1968).

[49.5] Mitsubishi Motors Corp. v. Soler Chrysler-Plymouth, Inc., 84-1 Trade Cas. ¶ 65,774, 46 A.T.R.R. 29 (1st Cir. 1983).

[50] Continental T.V., Inc. v. GTE Sylvania, Inc., 433 U.S. 36 (1977). Although *Continental* may limit DOJ activity at present, private lawsuits are always a risk where a restraint, even if "reasonable," is imposed. Pacific Coast Agricultural Export Ass'n v. Sunkist Growers, Inc., 1973 Trade Cas. (CCH) ¶ 74,523 (N.D. Cal. 1973).

[51] United States v. Topco Associates, Inc., 405 U.S. 596 (1972).

[52] The DOJ filed suit against Mercedes-Benz of North America, alleging that it conspired to restrain trade in violation of § 1 of the Sherman Act by conditioning the grant of a franchise upon the purchase of replacement parts exclusively from Mercedes. This agreement allegedly restrained competition in the market for Mercedes replacement parts. United States v. Mercedes-Benz of North America, Inc., 517 F. Supp. 1369 (N.D. Cal. 1981). Yet, in Reisner v. General Motors, 511 F. Supp. 1167 (S.D.N.Y. 1981), General Motors stopped selling body parts to an Italian automobile manufacturer when it started using Ford engines. The court granted summary judgment for the defendant, since there was a failure to show the essential elements of tying, including conditional sales.

though now overruled, the *Schwinn*[53] opinion, which held that once a person transfers title to a product he parts with all rights to control, still commands much judicial sympathy, both in the U.S. and Europe.[54] Therefore, great care should be exercised here.

When analyzing antitrust risks attendant to selling operations, one should start with the assumption that distribution outside of the U.S. will present no U.S. antitrust problems so long as no restraints on U.S. commerce are imposed, even where competition in a foreign market is eliminated.[55] Restraints imposed outside of the U.S. would avoid U.S. antitrust scrutiny both as a matter of U.S. competition and as a tenet of international law,[56] so long as there is no impact on commerce in the U.S. A restraint on a U.S. distributor from exporting to compete with an exclusive foreign distributor will state a Sher-

----

[53] United States v. Arnold, Schwinn & Co., 388 U.S. 365 (1967).

[54] In Timken Roller Bearing v. United States, 341 U.S. 593 (1951), it was held that licensing of a trademark would be illegal if it were part of a scheme to allocate national markets and prevent international competition. The same rule was adopted by the E.E.C. in Grundig Verkaufs G.m.b.H. & Establissements Consten v. Commission des Communautes europeenes [1975] C.J. Comm. E., Case No. 73/74, Comm. Mkt. Rep. (CCH) ¶ 8335. DOJ case J, which discusses an exclusive distributorship, was written prior to *Continental T.V.*, and therefore is overly conservative. While exclusive distributorships are not *per se* illegal, when they run for very long time periods, or are between competing firms that control a market, there may be problems proving the reasonableness of such restraints. Vertical restraints that do not serve to increase interbrand competition arc imposed by firms with significant market power, or are designed to fix resale prices, are also suspect.

[55] Timken Roller Bearing v. United States, *supra*. For a suggested form of international sales contract, *see* Davran, "An International Distribution Agreement," 3 ALI-ABA Course Materials J. 113 (1979).

[56] American Banana Co. v. United Fruit Co., 213 U.S. 347 (1909); Branch v. F.T.C., 141 F.2d 31 (7th Cir. 1944); Taubler v. Girard, *supra* N. 49.3. It should be noted that egregious conduct overseas, while not otherwise admissable in U.S. litigation, might be used as evidence of other activities within U.S. jurisdiction. United States v. Aluminum Co. of America, 148 F.2d 416 (2d Cir. 1945); Bausch Machine Tool Co. v. Aluminum Co. of America, 172 F.2d 236 (2d Cir. 1954); J. Van Cise, *Understanding the Antitrust Laws* 247 (1976).

man Act cause of action.[56.1] Specialized laws, such as the Automobile Dealer's Day in Court Act, may also cover the activities of foreign corporations selling into the U.S.[56.2] Furthermore, many U.S. laws encourage exports,[56.3] and the legislative history of many antitrust laws reflects an intent not to prohibit incidental U.S. restraints connected with foreign sales.[57] Section 2(a) of the Robinson-Patman Act,[57.1] does not

(*Text continued on page 9-19*)

[56.1] Todhunter-Mitchell & Co. v. Anheuser-Busch, Inc., 375 F. Supp. 610 (E.D. Pa.), *modified,* 383 F. Supp. 586 (E.D. Pa. 1974).

[56.2] Sunrise Toyota, Ltd. v. Toyota Motor Co., Ltd., 55 F.R.D. 519 (S.D.N.Y. 1972).

[56.3] Some laws do limit exports, particularly with regard to military or high-technology items. For these items, approval for sale must be received from the Department of Commerce under the Export Administration Act.

[57] Mandeville Island Farms, Inc. v. American Crystal Sugar Co., 334 U.S. 219 (1948); United States v. Frankfort Distilleries, Inc., 324 U.S. 293 (1945); United States v. Aluminum Co. of America, *supra* N. 55. A "direct and substantial" effect on U.S. commerce is needed to satisfy the jurisdictional requirements, and much litigation can be devoted to defining the degree of substantiality necessary. United States v. U.S. Alkalai Export, 86 F. Supp. 59 (S.D.N.Y. 1949); United States v. The Bayer Co., 135 F. Supp. 65 (S.D.N.Y. 1955). There will be a U.S. violation when the restraint can be shown to (1) affect U.S. commerce, (2) be direct and substantial, and (3) be unreasonable. Sanib v. United Fruit, 135 F. Supp. 764 (S.D.N.Y. 1955).

[57.1] 15 U.S.C. § 13(a).

proscribe price discrimination in foreign sales, since the Act requires that comparable sales at different prices be made for goods sold for use, consumption or resale within the U.S. Therefore, sales made at a higher price to an exporter are not violative of the Act.[57.2] However, an indirect purchaser of imported goods may maintain an action under § 2(f) of the Act against a direct-buying competitor if plaintiff's wholesaler is the victim of discriminatory pricing.[57.3]

If it can be shown that a restraint, although substantial, was essential to the conduct of business overseas, then it may pass the rule of reason test.[58] However, it will not be an adequate defense to assert that a restraint reflects the customary method of doing business abroad, such as by participation in a cartel,[59] for participation in a foreign cartel will be attacked if there are

---

[57.2] "(T)he focus of the Act is on where the goods are going, not where the parties are located." Fimex Corp. v. Barmatic Products Co., 429 F. Supp. 978 (E.D.N.Y. 1977), aff'd, Dkt. 77-7235 (2d Cir. Oct. 7, 1977); Zenith Radio Corp. v. Matsushita Electrical Indust. Co., 402 F. Supp. 244 (E.D. Pa. 1975).

[57.3] Paceco, Inc. v. Ishikawajima-Harima Heavy Industries Co., Ltd., 468 F. Supp. 256 (N.D. Cal. 1979).

[58] Restraints that have met the rule of reason tests include granting of exclusive rights, United States v. Necchi Sewing Machine Sales Corp., 1958 Trade Cas. (CCH) ¶ 68,957 (S.D.N.Y. 1958); United States v. Imperial Chemical Industries, Ltd., 105 F. Supp. 215 (S.D.N.Y. 1952); United States v. Schering Corp., 1940-43 Trade Cas. (CCH) ¶ 56,179 (S.D.N.Y. 1941); restraints on product use, Tri-Continental Financial Corp. v. Tropical Marine Enterprises, Inc., 265 F.2d 619 (5th Cir. 1957); P. Lorillard Co. v. Weingarden, 280 F. 238 (W.D.N.Y. 1922); and covenants not to compete ancillary to the sale of a product, Thoms v. Sutherland, 52 F.2d 592 (3d Cir. 1931); United States v. American Type Founders, 1958 Trade Cas. (CCH) ¶ 69,065 (D.N.J. 1958). Of course restraints imposed overseas, even if legal under U.S. law, may violate local laws. Outboard Marine Corporation's Norway subsidiary was found to have violated Norway's pricing laws by introducing a two-tiered pricing system. Notwithstanding OMC's argument that this method of distribution was customary, the Norwegian Price Council ruled that because of OMC's position with 25 percent of the Norwegian market (and 50 percent of the world market), its preferential pricing structure to exclusive dealers penalized consumers by reducing competition. "Competition Decision in Norway Puts Consumer Interests First," Business Europe 110 (April 6, 1979).

[59] United States v. National Lead Co., 63 F. Supp. 513 (S.D.N.Y.) aff'd, 332 U.S. 319 (1947).

effects in the U.S.,[60] such as raising the price of imports or excluding products from the domestic market.[60.1] Joint efforts to fight a foreign cartel may also give rise to allegations of price fixing.[60.2]

The DOJ gives the example[61] of an MNC with various foreign subsidiaries with part ownership by foreign governments and others. Although the U.S. parent controls the business, each subsidiary has an exclusive sphere of operation. This is examined in light of the *Timken* case,[62] where Timken was charged under Sherman Act § 1 with restraint of trade. Timken had various agreements going back to 1909 with European competitors and part-owned companies to limit competition in the bearing market. Common ownership of a company is not an automatic defense to an antitrust charge, since Timken was found to have eliminated competition in the U.S. and abroad

---

[60] Branch v. FTC, *supra*, N. 55; FTC v. The Eastman Kodak Co., 7 F.2d 994 (2d Cir. 1925), *aff'd*, 274 U.S. 619 (1927); United States v. Concentrated Phosphate Export Ass'n, Inc., 393 U.S. 199 (1968); United States v. Pacific & Arctic Co., 228 U.S. 87 (1913). A suit was filed by the International Association of Machinists challenging the Organization of Petroleum Exporting Countries (OPEC) for price fixing in violation of the Sherman Act. The defendants failed to appear, and a hearing was ordered under the Foreign Sovereign Immunities Act, 28 U.S.C. § 1068(e), which prohibits a default judgment against a foreign nation unless there is a proof of the claim against the defendant. The case was dismissed under the "Act of State" doctrine, since, under this approach, there is no adjudication of politically sensitive disputes which require the courts to judge the legality of sovereign acts of foreign states. International Ass'n of Machinists & Aerospace Workers v. Organization of Petroleum Exporting Countries, 477 F. Supp. 553 (C.D. Cal. 1979), *aff'd*, 649 F.2d 1354 (9th Cir. 1981), *cert. denied*, Dkt. 81-645 (U.S. Jan. 11, 1982). From an antitrust standpoint, it would appear to have otherwise been a reasonable cause of action, but, given the political sensitivity in the area, there is yet no international antitrust consensus condemning the practice of cartelization.

[60.1] Where the reason for the business failure can be tied to the incompetence of the plaintiff, no conspiracy will be presumed. Pan Islamic Trading Corp. v. Exxon Corp., 632 F.2d 539 (5th Cir. 1980), *cert. denied*, Dkt. 81-167 (U.S. Oct. 13, 1981).

[60.2] Long Island Lighting Co. v. Standard Oil Co., *supra* N. 24.3; Hunt v. Mobil Oil Co., 410 F. Supp. 10 (S.D.N.Y. 1975); Lefrak v. Arabian American Oil Co., 487 F. Supp. 808 (S.D.N.Y. 1980).

[61] DOJ Guidelines Case A at E3-E4.

[62] Timken Roller Bearing v. United States, *supra*, N. 54.

through its practice of negotiating restrictive agreements, and subsequent solidifying of these agreements by stock purchases in the competing companies. The DOJ distinguishes the facts in its example, since there was no anticompetitive agreement predating the corporate relationship.

The DOJ cites with approval the opinion of the 1955 Attorney General's Study[63] that a parent corporation may allocate territories or set prices for subsidiaries it fully controls. The DOJ would apply the same test where a U.S. corporation has a minority share, but, after a factual inquiry, is determined to effectively control the company.[64]

Agreements to divide world markets between manufacturers and potential competitors may also violate the Sherman Act.[64.1] In *Engine Specialties, Inc. v. Bombardier, Ltd.*,[65] the First Circuit affirmed a jury verdict of $485,000 in damages, in a holding that the defendant had engaged in a horizontal market allocation by inducing the supplier to break its distribution contract with the plaintiff and substitute the defendant. Since Bombardier failed to object to jury instructions that treated the parties as competitors, they were precluded from raising this issue on appeal. The Court also ruled that calling the new arrangement a "joint venture" would not avoid a *per se* test, although the Court did not discuss the fact that *Timken* (which it cited) dealt with actual, not potential, competition.

Although beyond the scope of this section, mention should be made of the possibility of running afoul of U.S. antitrust and other laws through certain "improper" payments. These payments may be considered legitimate sales commissions, gifts, or bribes, depending on the circumstances. The Foreign Corrupt Practices Act,[66] which prohibits "corrupt" payments to foreign government officials (except minor functionaries)

---

[63] *The Attorney General's National Committee to Study the Antitrust Laws* 35 (1955).

[64] This was the case in United States v. Citizens & Southern National Bank, 422 U.S. 86 (1975), where a 5 percent share gave control.

[64.1] *See, e.g.,* the consent decree entered in United States v. Addison-Wesley Publishing Co., 76-2 Trade Cas. ¶ 61,225 (S.D.N.Y. 1976).

[65] 605 F.2d 1 (1st. Cir. 1979), *cert. denied,* 100 S. Ct. 2964 (1980).

[66] Foreign Corrupt Practices Act of 1977, 15 U.S.C. § 78a, P.L. 95-213, 91 Stat. 1494.

caused a considerable amount of fear among U.S. corporations when it was first passed due to its apparent blanket prohibitions, internal auditing requirements, and criminal penalties. Until more cases are litigated, the precise conduct allowed or prohibited under the Act will be unclear. Most major U.S. corporations are taking a conservative position and, in spite of fears of competitive disadvantage, there has been little evidence of actual transactions aborted due to the Act.[67]

Other statutes may also be used to attack questionable overseas payments. The FTC settled a number of cases pending against aircraft manufacturers under the FTC Act[68] and § 2(c) of the Robinson-Patman Act[69] for payments made by the aircraft manufacturers to induce purchase of their products. Even though the consent decrees allow payments for normal business expenses and business gifts (under $1,000), the FTC noted with apparent satisfaction that its terms were more stringent than the Foreign Corrupt Practices Act.[70] In a DOJ action, Gulfstream American Corporation pled guilty to making false statements on forms used by the Commerce Department to calculate the U.S. balance of payments. The DOJ alleged that the "Shipper's Export Declaration" was false since, in stating the value of airplanes sold, the "commissions" paid to agents were not deducted. Although defense lawyers question whether the charges would have stood up had the case gone to trial, this approach provides a very broad range of possible targets, since many exports require filing of the form in question (Commerce 7525-V). Thus, even if a practice is legal and accepted in the foreign country, it may still violate

---

[67] A survey by *Business Week* indicated that many companies have overreacted to the law, and needlessly prohibited even those payments allowed under the Act. "Misinterpreting the Antibribery Law," Business Week 150 (Sept. 3, 1979); *see also* McManis, "Questionable Corporate Payments Abroad: An Antitrust Approach," 86 Yale L.J. 215 (1976); Note, "Disclosure of Payments to Foreign Government Officials Under the Securities Acts," 89 Harv. L. Rev. 1848 (1976).

[68] 15 U.S.C. § 45.

[69] 15 U.S.C. § 13(c).

[70] Lockheed Corp., File No. 761-0074, Consent Order to Cease & Desist, Dkt. C-2942, Trade Reg. Rep. (CCH) ¶ 21,454 (Aug. 17, 1978).

U.S. laws.[71]

To enhance the competitive position of U.S. firms selling abroad, and limit any antitrust uncertainty that might have caused U.S. companies to back away from a foreign venture, the Export Trading Company Act was passed in 1982.[71.1] The law allows certain banking companies to form export trading companies, or hold equity interests in ones formed by others, whereas previously banks were not allowed to become involved in such non-banking activities. The Act also clarifies the impact of the U.S. antitrust laws, by limiting the coverage of the Sherman and Federal Trade Commission Acts to only such conduct, or unfair methods of competition, having a "direct, substantial, and reasonably foreseeable effect" on domestic commerce, import trade, or a U.S. company's export trade. A certification procedure has been established, through which individuals or companies may apply to the Departments of Justice and Commerce for an exemption from any criminal or civil antitrust action against export trading conduct specified in the application.[71.2]

The original estimates of the number of trading companies that would be formed under the Act were "unrealistic" according to Donald Zarin, former Commerce Department official.[71.3] Some applications for certification have been received even though it was plain that no antitrust protection was needed, with the applicant perhaps hoping to use the certification as an advertising tool. The most beneficial part of the law is Title IV, which contains the language clarifying the jurisdictional scope of the antitrust laws. Export activities, based on reported cases, seem to present somewhat less antitrust uncertainty than do domestic distribution practices, but if the law

---

[71] Hager, "DOJ Unveils New Payments Device," *Legal Times of Washington* 1 (Jan. 8, 1979). All exports from the U.S. require a license from the Office of Export Administration, which may or may not be automatically available. Birenbaum & Alford, "Trying to Reverse a Trade Deficit That's Impinging on U.S. Economy," National L.J. 21 (July 30, 1979).

[71.1] *Supra*, N. 12.1.

[71.2] The rules are found at 48 Fed. Reg. 15937 (April 13, 1983); Trade Reg. Rep. ¶ 50,446.

[71.3] 47 A.T.R.R. 204 (Feb. 2, 1984).

has a mild stimulative impact on U.S. exports it will have been helpful.

Finally, mention should be made of the Webb-Pomerene Act,[72] passed in 1918, which allows competing U.S. firms[73] to form export associations to promote the export sales of their products.[74] Such an association will be exempt from the antitrust laws, provided that (1) there are no restraints imposed on U.S. domestic trade, or any effect on U.S. prices; and (2) the association does not restrain the export trade of any U.S. competitor of the association.

As with all statutory exemptions, the provisions are read narrowly and must be followed precisely.[75] In *United States v. Minnesota Mining & Mfg. Co.,*[76] four U.S. firms (constituting four-fifths of the abrasives industry) formed a Webb-Pomerene company. In certain countries, the company set up local manufacturing subsidiaries. The court ruled that since there were virtually no U.S. exports to the countries where the manufacturing occurred, the company was acting as an unlawful combination to restrict exports, and therefore lost the protection of the Act.

As a practical matter, the Act is in little use today, with only about 5 percent of U.S. exports being transacted under its protection. Few U.S. companies showed a willingness to undertake common efforts with their competitors, perhaps reflecting their consideration of the importance of brand-name differentiation. Many Webb-Pomerene companies are used to sell such undifferentiated goods as raw materials or agricultural commodities. Department of Justice officials have complained about Webb-Pomerene, and the National Commission for the Review of Antitrust Laws and Procedures proposed that Webb-Pomerene should be re-examined by Congress. If

---

[72] 15 U.S.C. § 61.

[73] The Act does not permit agreements with foreign competitors. United States v. U.S. Alkalai Export Ass'n, Inc., *supra,* N. 57.

[74] The Act does not cover licensing agreements or the sale of services.

[75] Sales made pursuant to U.S. foreign aid regulations are not automatically entitled to the Webb-Pomerene exemption where the sellers agree on prices prior to submitting bids. United States v. Concentrated Phosphate Export Ass'n, *supra* N. 60.

[76] 92 F. Supp. 947 (D. Mass. 1950).

the statute is retained, the Commission recommended that it be amended to include services, and that the antitrust immunity for export associations be made contingent on a showing of particularized need.[77] Laws like Webb-Pomerene create uncertainty, since joint activities under the Act may violate foreign antitrust laws, and U.S. companies sometimes complain about joint activities abroad that would be allowed at home under Webb-Pomerene. The DOJ has stated, however, that it will not challenge members of a foreign export association for conduct the U.S. would permit under Webb-Pomerene.[77.1]

[3] Licensing

Because many products are not suitable for export, some companies attempt to exploit their technology by licensing their patents, trademarks, and secret know-how. The methodology of licensing is discussed in detail in Chapter 6. Licensing is mentioned here since certain practices may be of concern to the U.S. antitrust authorities (or to private parties who perceive an injury) when the license imposes some restraints on U.S. commerce.[77.2] A simple license, without restraining where the licensed goods could be sold, at what price, or in what quantity, would probably raise no antitrust con-

---

[77] *Report to the President & the Attorney General of the National Commission for the Reform of Antitrust Laws & Procedures,* Jan. 22, 1979, 897 A.T.R.R. Spec. Supp. at 85. The DOJ urged the Commission to recommend complete repeal Webb Pomerene, but was unsuccessful. 892 A.T.R.R. A16 (Dec. 7, 1978). Yet, shortly after these positions were taken, Congressional activity to increase the antitrust exemptions for export associations began with enthusiasm, as indicated by the passage of S.B. 734 by a vote of 93-0 in the Senate in April 1981. *See also* Gribbin, "Export Cartels: Report of the Committee of Experts on Restrictive Business Practices of the O.E.C.D.," 21 Antitrust Bull. 341 (1976).

[77.1] 807 A.T.R.R. A24 (March 29, 1977); 242 Daily Report for Executives (BNA) [hereinafter "DER"] L1 (Dec. 17, 1981).

[77.2] *See* American Bar Association Section of Antitrust Law Monograph No. 6, "United States Antitrust Law in Patent and Know-How Licensing" (1981); Wallace, "Overlooked Opportunitites—Making the Most Out of U.S. Antitrust Limitations on International Licensing Practices," 10 Int. Law. 275 (1976).

cern.[77.3] Yet, since a "simple license" is rarely used these days, the practitioner must contend with the very complex and inconsistent body of case law that has developed here. Decisions are very fact-specific, and difficult to distill into hard rules of law. Further, the enforcement policies of the DOJ tend to fluctuate, varying between the application of firm rules of prohibited conduct (the "Nine No-Nos"[77.4]) to a somewhat more relaxed reasonableness standard.[78]

The law does favor exploitation of patent and trademark rights, but since these statutorily granted monopolies are themselves restraints on trade, attempts to capitalize on these restraints must be done with care.[78.1] Patent, trademark or know-how licenses cannot be used as a "cover" for a scheme to restrain trade.[79] Certain licensing practices are *per se* illegal, such as restrictions on resale, mandatory package licensing, collecting royalties after patents have expired, and collecting royalties on sales of unlicensed products.[80] Other practices are

---

[77.3] United States v. United Engineering and Foundry Co. (consent decree), 1952-53 Trade Cas. (CCH) ¶ 67,378 (W.D. Pa. 1952).

[77.4] "Licensing Practices: Myth or Reality," Remarks by Bruce Wilson, United States Department of Justice (Jan. 21, 1975).

[78] "Current Antitrust Division Views on Patent Licensing Practices," Remarks by Abbot Lipsky, United States Department of Justice, T.R.R. ¶ 50,434 (Nov. 5, 1981).

[78.1] Brownell v. Ketcham Wire & Mfg. Co., 211 F.2d 121 (9th Cir. 1954).

[79] For example, a license cannot be used to hide a price-fixing conspiracy, United States v. General Electric Co., 80 F. Supp. 989 (S.D.N.Y. 1949); or to cover an otherwise illegal territorial allocation, Holophane Co. v. United States, 119 F. Supp. 114 (N.D. Ohio 1954); *aff'd per curiam,* 352 U.S. 903 (1956); or to exclude a foreign company from the U.S., United States v. Singer Mfg. Co., 374 U.S. 14 (1963).

[80] A process patent may give the patent holder some rights to control resale of unpatented goods made from the licensed process. The distinction between a product and process patent may no longer be enough to make this type of restraint *per se* unreasonable. *Compare* Robintech, Inc. v. Chemindus Wavin, Ltd., 628 F.2d 142 (D.C. Cir. 1980) *with* Ethyl Corp. v. Hercules Powder Co., 232 F. Supp. 453 (D. Del. 1964), *and* United States v. Studeingesellschaft Kohle, m.b.H., 81-2 Trade Cas. ¶ 64,394 (D.C. Cir. 1981). *See also* Brulotte v. Thys Co., 379 U.S. 29 (1964) [royalties on expired patents]; United States v. Line Material Co., 333 U.S. 287 (1948) [price fixing]; International Salt Co. v. United States, 332 U.S. 392 (1947) [tie-in to non-patented products]; United States v. Krasnov, 143 F. Supp. 184 (E.D. Pa. 1956), *aff'd per curiam,* 355 U.S. 5 (1957) [licensee veto arrangement].

evaluated under a reasonableness standard, which seeks to determine (1) whether there is a lawful primary purpose to the agreement (such as the public interest in widespread use of the industrial property); (2) whether the restraint is necessary and ancillary to this lawful primary purpose;[81] (3) whether there are any less restrictive alternative restraints that would enhance competition, and (4) whether there is an anticompetitive effect caused by the restraint.[81.1]

When a foreign license is involved, there must also be a direct and substantial effect on U.S. commerce before a violation can be found.[82] Although a court may excuse a restraint it feels has a *de minimus* effect on U.S. commerce,[83] there is little in the way of judicial guidance to indicate the dividing line between *de minimus* and "direct and substantial."[83.1]

Experience has shown that some restraints (such as output restrictions and tie-in clauses) while not *per se* unreasonable are viewed as being so restrictive that they are almost impossible to justify. A license should not be used to allocate markets among competitors,[84] or in an attempt to secure a monopoly

(*Text continued on page 9-27*)

---

[81] United States v. E.I. duPont deNemours & Co., 118 F. Supp. 41 (D. Del. 1953), *aff'd* 351 U.S. 377 (1956); Foundry Services Inc. v. Beneflux Corp., 110 F. Supp. 857 (S.D.N.Y.), *rev'd on other grounds,* 206 F.2d 214 (2d Cir. 1953). A bare assertion that the restraint is "merely ancillary" to the lawful main purpose will not succeed without strict proof. United States v. Bayer Co., Inc., 135 F. Supp. 65 (S.D.N.Y. 1955).

[81.1] Platt Saco Lowell Ltd. v. Spindelfabrik Suessen-Schurr, 78-1 Trade Cas. ¶ 61,898 (N.D. Ill. 1977).

[82] United States v. General Electric Co., 82 F. Supp. 753 (D.N.J. 1949), *modified,* 115 F. Supp. 835 (D.N.J. 1953).

[83] Alfred Bell & Co. v. Catalda Fine Arts, Inc., 1951-52 Trade Cas. (CCH) ¶ 62,893 (2d Cir. 1951).

[83.1] United States v. Westinghouse Electric Corp., 471 F. Supp. 532 (N.D. Cal. 1978), *aff'd,* 548 F.2d 642 (9th Cir. 1981), appeared to allow jurisdiction merely because the revenues earned by a foreign license came back into the U.S.

[84] United States v. Imperial Chemical Industries, Inc., 100 F. Supp. 504 (S.D.N.Y. 1951); General Talking Pictures Corp. v. Western Electric Co., 305 U.S. 124 (1938); Dunlop Co. v. Kelsey-Hayes Co., 484 F.2d 407 (6th Cir. 1973), *cert. denied,* 415 U.S. 917 (1974). In Mannington Mills, Inc. v. Congoleum Industries, Inc., 610 F.2d 1059 (3d Cir. 1979), the court held that a cause of action was stated under § 1 of the Sherman Act where a patent holder terminated a licensee at the request of other licensees.

in a given market.[85] Depending on the size and market share of the licensee and licensor, and the effect on present and potential competition, certain limitations may be placed on the areas in which the license is used, such as field of use restraints which limit the licensee to a particular product use, provided the limitations are reasonable in time and scope.[86] Although the DOJ may not like field of use restrictions, they are generally legal, on the theory that since the patent holder could refuse to give any license at all, even a limited license increases competition.[86.1]

The foregoing discussion has assumed that a license would cover a package of rights—patent, trademark, know-how, and copyright. It should be noted that when only a trademark license is granted, the power to restrict ultimate disposition of the trademarked product is even further limited. Tying requirements, or import/export restraints will be very difficult to justify, unless a strong connection to protection of product quality is shown.[87] The DOJ has stated that it does not favor

---

[85] United States v. Singer Mfg. Co., 314 U.S. 174 (1963); Zenith Radio Corp. v. Hazeltine Research, Inc., 395 U.S. 100 (1969). However, a long-standing patent and technology license between Westinghouse and Mitsubishi was found not to violate the antitrust laws, as the court determined there was no intent to carve-up world markets. United States v. Westinghouse Electric Corp., *supra* N. 83.1.

[86] United States v. E.I. duPont deNemours, *supra*, N. 81; Scapa Dryers, Inc. v. Abney Mills, 269 F.2d 6 (5th Cir.), *cert. denied*, 361 U.S. 901 (1959); Brownell v. Ketcham Wire & Mfg. Co., 211 F.2d 121 (9th Cir. 1954); Melard Mfg. Co. v. Chase Brass & Copper Co., 1959 Trade Cas. (CCH) ¶ 69,595 (N.D. Ill. 1959); United States v. C.D. Caulk Co., 126 F. Supp. 693 (D. Del. 1954). Market divisions that serve no purpose apart from restraining competition will not be allowed. United States v. Fisons, Ltd., Civil No. 69C1530 (N.D. Ill.), 1972 Trade Cas. (CCH) ¶¶ 73,790, 73,794.

[86.1] *Compare* General Talking Pictures Corp. v. Western Electric Co., 304 U.S. 175 (1975) *with* the remarks of Roland Donnem, T.R.R. ¶ 50,111 (1969); United States v. Ciba-Ceigy Corp., 508 F. Supp. 1157 (D.N.J. 1979); *and* United States v. Westinghouse Electric Corp., *supra* N. 83.1.

[87] Speech by Joel Davidow, U.S. Department of Justice, Antitrust Division, Policy Planning Office, to United States Trademark Association, "Evolving International Issues Concerning Trademark-Competition Problems," (May 12, 1978), Comm. Mkt. Rep. (CCH) ¶ 10,050, noting trends in US, EEC & OECD. *See also* Jones, "Executive's Guide to Antitrust in Europe," Harvard Bus. Rev. 106, 115 (May 1976).

broad licensing of trademarks, since it may dilute the quality of the product or cause confusion as to the source.[88] If only know-how is being licensed, courts will uphold restraints that are reasonably ancillary to the license. Since a licensor of know-how lacks statutory patent protection, the extent to which a territorial restraint will be considered reasonable will depend on the degree to which the subject matter of the license is substantial, whether the restraint is limited to the life of the know-how, and whether the restraint is limited to products made with the know-how.[88.1]

In *United States v. National Lead Co.*,[89] the court reviewed a series of agreements that effectively controlled the world supply of titanium pigments. These agreements, which were not limited in duration or by the scope of the patents, provided that no company could import the product into the United States without National Lead's consent, and that National Lead would refrain from sales outside the western hemisphere. National Lead and other companies had divided the world into assigned markets, and the court held that the combination constituted a classic violation of § 1 of the Sherman Act. Even though these agreements may have been excessive, the case does not automatically prohibit every U.S. patent owner from granting a license with export restrictions. Such a restraint may be illegal under foreign law,[90] and, while this is not determinative, it may be one factor in a rule-of-reason evaluation of the agreement.[91] As noted above, the size of the companies involved will play a part in a rule-of-reason analysis, and a small company will be allowed a more restrictive agreement,[92] up to

---

[88] Speech by Douglas Rosenthal, U.S. Department of Justice, Antitrust Division, Foreign Commerce Section, to Practicing Law Institute, Seventeenth Annual Advanced Antitrust Law Seminar, "International Trade & the Antitrust Laws," (December 1, 1977), Antitrust & Trade Reg. Rep. (BNA) No. 842 at A9 (Dec. 8, 1977).

[88.1] Shin Nippon Koki Co., Ltd. v. Irvin Industries, Inc., 49 A.D.2d 528 (1st Dept. 1975), 75 Trade Cas. ¶ 60,347.

[89] 63 F. Supp. 513 (S.D.N.Y. 1945), *aff'd*, 332 U.S. 319 (1947).

[90] *See* discussion of licensing under EEC law, § 9.03[2][c] *infra.*

[91] United States v. Watchmakers of Switzerland Information Center, 133 F. Supp. 40 (S.D.N.Y. 1955).

[92] Foundry Services, Inc. v. Beneflux Corp., *supra* N. 81.

some invisible point where the restraint becomes unreasonable or *per se* illegal.

In *National Lead,* one method used to divide the world into separate markets was the fictitious sale of a nonexistent foreign business together with the granting of a restrictive license of patents and know-how. This type of covenant was found not to be reasonably ancillary to a lawful principal purpose, since there initially was no foreign business for disposal. The only purpose served by the license was the restraint of trade.[93]

Another method of world market allocation is through the use of parallel patents in different countries. When the DOJ reviewed this practice in 1972,[94] they opined that U.S. law allowed a patent owner to grant rights under a foreign patent, but not under the parallel U.S. patent, that prevented the licensee from importing that product into the U.S.[95] The licensor may be able to similarly restrict the use of unpatented know-how to a certain area if the know-how is very closely related to the patent.

Even though one owner of a patent may be able to separate his licenses into separate markets, there is little sympathy for similar attempts by a group of patent holders. Such horizontal conspiracies to confine the participants to certain markets are usually viewed as *per se* violations of § 1 of the Sherman Act,[96] although it may be possible for a number of very small companies to band together in this way.

The DOJ has expressed its concern with licensing restraints in its public statements,[97] and by extensive treatment in its guidelines. The DOJ has set forth what it alleges to be five *per se* violations: (1) licensor requiring the licensee to purchase non-patented products; (2) one licensee getting a veto over

---

[93] 63 F. Supp. at 524, *citing* United States v. Addyston Pipe & Steel Co., 85 F. 271 (6th Cir. 1898), *aff'd,* 175 U.S. 211 (1899); Greater New York Live Poultry Chamber of Commerce v. United States, 47 F.2d 156 (2d Cir.), *cert. denied,* 283 U.S. 837 (1931).

[94] Department of Justice Memorandum, "Antitrust and Foreign Commerce," released January 25, 1972, Trade Reg. Rep. (CCH) ¶ 50,129.

[95] Dunlop Co. Ltd. v. Kelsey Hayes Co., *supra* N. 84.

[96] Hazeltine Research, Inc. v. Zenith Radio Corp., 401 U.S. 321 (1971); United States v. Singer Manufacturing Co., 314 U.S. 174 (1963).

[97] *Supra* Ns. 87, 88.

other licensees; (3) a mandated resale price; (4) collecting a royalty on an expired patent; and (5) mandatory exclusive grant-back of improvement patents.

In Case E of its guidelines,[98] a U.S. corporation with 22 percent of a transistor market (ranking number three), enters into a joint venture and licensing agreement with a Japanese company in order to market its product in Japan. Due to the lower manufacturing costs in Japan, which might disrupt other export markets, the Japanese joint venture will not export to the U.S. or certain designated countries. Although such a joint venture would not eliminate competition, since the participants in the above facts are not competing,[99] the Japanese partner might be a potential entrant to the U.S. market. If the U.S. corporation were large enough to have a substantial degree of market power, the presence of the potential entrant might be a restraint on the abuse of this market power. If the joint venture were structured to nullify this threat,[100] or if the resultant joint venture would tend to dominate the market (and come under the bar of § 7 of the Clayton Act), the DOJ would be concerned.

The territorial restraint in the license is more important, however. Balancing the anticompetitive effects with the business justification, a moderate competitive restraint would be acceptable if the main purpose is a legitimate business objective, and the restraint is reasonably necessary to achieve the main purpose.[101] Taking all of these facts together, the DOJ says (in Case E) that it would challenge this agreement[101.1] since it would permanently exclude the Japanese company from the United States, and would enhance the strength of the U.S. company, which is already a leading firm in a concentrat-

---

[98] DOJ guidelines, Case E at E8.

[99] United States v. Monsanto Co., consent decree, 1967 Trade Cas. (CCH) ¶ 72,001 (E.D. Pa. 1967). The DOJ noted in a footnote that it will challenge international joint ventures that eliminate competition, United States v. Mitsui Petrochemical Industries Ltd., C.A. 4667-73 (D. Del. 1973), 1973 Trade Cas. (CCH) ¶ 74,530.

[100] United States v. Penn-Olin Chemical Co., 378 U.S. 158 (1964).

[101] United States v. Third National Bank, 390 U.S. 171 (1968).

[101.1] Its position may be contrary now in light of *Continental T.V., supra* N. 19; remarks of Lipsky, *supra* N. 77.4.

ed market. A more reasonable (and, presumably, acceptable) agreement could be structured by limiting the time period to a term just long enough for the Japanese company to develop its own know-how. The DOJ's suggestion may be a bit short-sighted from the businessman's viewpoint, since there would be little incentive for any corporation to share its technology on a short-term basis, and then be faced with a new competitor without having received what it felt to be adequate compensation for its contribution to the venture.[101.2] Further, there may be little incentive to engage in licensing when the licensor will be faced with competing imports.[101.3]

In its Case F,[102] the DOJ gives the situation of the hypothetical small U.S. corporation that grants a twenty-year know-how license to a German company. The U.S. corporation will be able to export licensed products to Germany, but the German company will not export its products to the U.S. The German company will only use certain U.S. components in the manufacturing process, and the finished goods will bear the U.S. trademark. With negotiation of a similar agreement in Japan, the German company agrees not to export to East Asia.

The DOJ states that although the U.S. corporation is small, the export prohibition and territorial restraints would be challenged since the time period is too long. The DOJ suggests again, for know-how licenses, a time period equal to the reverse-engineering period. A patent license would have a built-in definition of a reasonable time period: the life of the patent. A pure know-how license, the DOJ would argue, is very close to a license fee collected on expired patents, unless limited in time to some reasonable period. The DOJ would challenge arrangements utilizing a series of reciprocal restraints where the know-how was insubstantial and there appeared to be a

---

[101.2] Also, there is no requirement that the licensee be economically capable of developing new products without infringing the licensor's patents, so long as the initial patent grant is legal. United States v. Westinghouse, *supra* N. 83.1.

[101.3] Bleeke and Rahl, "The Value of Territorial and Field of Use Restraints in the International Licensing of Unpatented Know-How: An Empirical Study," 1 N.W.J. Int. L. & Bus. 450 (1979).

[102] DOJ guidelines, Case F at E10.

scheme to carve-up the world into separate markets.[103]

In this example, the license requiring a tie-in to specified U.S. products would be *per se* illegal according to the DOJ, if the license were sufficiently valuable to confer monopoly power in a given domestic market.[104] However, the legality of such a license in a foreign market could not be determined without examining whether there were any effects on U.S. commerce.[105] The DOJ would be concerned if other U.S. sellers could not compete for the tied items, or if the German company was eliminated as a potential entrant to the U.S. market. Exclusion of overseas sellers from certain overseas markets would be allowed since this is not an act in U.S. commerce.

To protect its tie-in clause, the U.S. corporation would need to prove that the tie-in was essential to protect its interest in the related goodwill and technology.[106] Once again, the DOJ's suggested maximum term is the time necessary to reverse-engineer the product, since after that point the tie-in requirement would be difficult to justify. But a longer time period would be allowed where smaller competitors or very heavy investments are involved.[107]

Doing business with less-developed countries (LDCs) presents special problems. In Case G,[108] the DOJ discusses a U.S. company that wants to do business in an LDC, but cannot export. A license is granted to a local company to manufacture

---

[103] United States v. Imperial Chemical Industries, Ltd., 100 F. Supp. 504 (S.D.N.Y. 1951).

[104] International Salt Co. v. United States, 332 U.S. 392 (1947).

[105] The restraints may be illegal under local laws, such as §§ 20, 21 of the Law Against Restraints in the Federal Republic of Germany and § 57 of the U.K. Patent Act.

[106] United States Steel Corp. v. Fortner Enterprises, Inc., 429 U.S. 610 (1977); Dehydrating Process Co. v. A.O. Smith Corp., 292 F.2d 653 (1st Cir. 1961); Advance Business Systems and Supply Co. v. SCM Corp., 415 F.2d 55 (4th Cir. 1969).

[107] United States v. Jerrold Electronics Corp., 187 F. Supp. 545 (E.D. Pa. 1960), *aff'd per curiam*, 365 U.S. 567 (1961). Recent enforcement talk suggests that the DOJ has moved away from this position, and would allow greater flexibility with regard to tie-ins. Remarks of Lipsky, *supra* N. 77.4 at 6.

[108] DOJ guidelines Case G at E11.

under patents and know-how, but since the LDC restricts royalty payments, the U.S. corporation requires the local company to purchase its supplies from the U.S., and licenses additional patents that are not used.

Although the goal of trying to get some money out of the LDC seems reasonable, this is not enough to justify what the DOJ characterizes as illegal restraints. The DOJ argues that the product tie-in would be illegal *per se* if done in the U.S.; it would be illegal overseas if competing U.S. exports were possible, and other U.S. sellers were therefore foreclosed from making sales to the LDC. Although the DOJ does not discuss it, more analysis is necessary before this method of financially justifying LDC investment should be rejected. If the LDC corporation is related to the U.S. company, more restrictions may be legally imposed by the U.S. company. The market share of the U.S. company, and the effect on its competitors (their relative size, whether they could or are currently doing business in the LDC) would need to be examined to fairly evaluate whether there is any competitive impact.

If the Case G agreement were negotiated between U.S.-based companies, there would be a strong likelihood of litigation. Mandatory licensing of a package of patents is illegal *per se* in the U.S., since it denies any choice to the licensee in selecting the patents in the package. Thus by forcing the licensee to take an undesired patent in order to get the desired patent, another illegal tie-in may be created.[109] However, if the patents in the package must be used together (blocking patents), then a rule of reason analysis is appropriate.[110]

One additional clause often inserted into patent licenses is the requirement of exclusive grant-backs to the licensors of all improvements discovered by the licensee. While such grant-backs are not illegal *per se*,[111] they can violate the antitrust laws if they go beyond the term of the licensed patent,[112] and the DOJ has sometimes threatened to treat these clauses as *per se*

---

[109] United States v. Loew's Inc., 371 U.S. 38 (1962).

[110] Standard Oil v. United States, 283 U.S. 163 (1931).

[111] Transparent-Wrap Machine Corp. v. Stokes and Smith Co., 392 U.S. 637 (1947).

[112] Brulotte v. Thys Co., 379 U.S. 29 (1964).

offenses.[113] Once again, the DOJ's statements must be viewed in perspective. The Department cannot determine what is a *per se* offense, only Congress or the Supreme Court can. Although grant-back clauses certainly reduce the incentive for licensees to engage in their own research, they are still evaluated under the rule of reason.

The more narrow the grant-back, however, the less likelihood of a challenge. For example, the obligation to grant back a new patent that does not need to be used with the original patent, might be seen as excessive.[114] To the extent a U.S. corporation owns or controls a foreign company, however, this type of clause may be seen as a reasonable benefit of ownership. And, the effect on competitors must be examined to see if there is any injury that would sustain enforcement action.

[4] Imports

Restriction or unfair trade tactics connected with how imported goods arrived or are sold in the U.S. may violate the antitrust laws as would any other domestic transaction.[114.1] In addition to the antitrust laws already discussed, certain laws have been enacted that deal only with imports. Section 73 of the Wilson Tariff Act of 1894[115] prohibits combinations, contracts, and conspiracies with the intent to restrain trade or increase the price of items imported into the U.S. The law essentially duplicates the prohibitions of the Sherman Act,[116]

---

[113] DOJ guidelines, Case I at E13. *Compare* the contrary position of the International Trade Commission, In re Reclosable Plastic Bags, No. 337-TA-22 (Jan. 17, 1977), Antitrust & Trade Reg. Rep. (BNA) No. 801 at A3 (Feb. 15, 1977). Recent DOJ policy has shifted here also. Remarks of Lipsky, *supra* N. 77.4 at 9.

[114] United States v. Wisconsin Aluminum Research Foundation, consent decree, C.A. No. 69-C-316 (W.D. Wis. 1969), 1970 Trade Cas. (CCH) ¶ 73,-015.

[114.1] *See, e.g.,* Glazer Steel Corp. v. Yawata Iron & Steel Co., Ltd., 56 F.R.D. 75 (S.D.N.Y. 1972).

[115] 15 U.S.C. § 8; Fosburgh v. California & Hawaiian Sugar Refining Co., 291 F. 29 (9th Cir. 1923).

[116] United States v. Sisal Sales Corp., 274 U.S. 268 (1927).

but makes certain that imports are specifically covered.[117]

Gaining more attention recently have been the antidumping statutes. Beginning with the Revenue Act of 1916,[118] a number of statutes[119] have made it unlawful to import items into the U.S. at less than their actual market value or wholesale price where produced or exported.

Section 337 of the Tariff Act[119.1] prohibits unfair acts in connection with importation that prevents the establishment of a U.S. industry, substantially impairs a present U.S. industry, constitutes a restraint of trade, or infringes a U.S. patent.[119.2] Trademark owners may also seek to exclude importation of

---

[117] Reliable Volkswagen Sales & Service Co., Inc., v. World-wide Automobile Corp., 182 F. Supp. 412 (D.N.J. 1960). Importation of products that infringe U.S. patents may be prohibited if the importation injures an industry that is efficiently operated in the U.S. However, a recent decision of the ITC (No. 337-TA-90, Jan. 1980) ruled that, in spite of an infringement, the importation of the products in question would be in the public interest, since they were necessary for the manufacture of fuel-efficient automobiles. The I.T.C. essentially applies standards consistent with the case law under the Sherman Act. In re Certain Electronic Audio Equipment, No. 337-TA-7, 759 A.T.R.R. A20 (April 2, 1976). However, criminal violation of the Wilson Tariff Act are punishable only as misdemeanors with maximum fines of $5000 and one year imprisonment.

[118] Act of Sept. 8, 1916, ch. 463, 39 Stat. 756, 15 U.S.C. §§ 71-77, 19 U.S.C. §§ 1333, 1335. See Mundheim, "Developments in Antidumping Law," 34 Bus. Law. 1831 (1979).

[119] Antidumping Act of 1921, 19 U.S.C. §§ 160, 1337, 1671(c), 1673(e), 2251, as amended by the Trade Act of 1974, P.L. 93-618, 88 Stat. 1978 (January 3, 1975), 19 U.S.C. § 1337, and Trade Agreements Act of 1979, P.L. 96-39, 93 Stat. 144 (July 26, 1979), 19 U.S.C. § 2501 et seq. which provides that "unfair methods of competition and unfair acts in the importation of articles into the United States . . . are declared unlawful. . . ." A private right of action for parties injured by dumping is available, but there is only one reported case, and it was not decided on the merits. H. Wagner & Adler Co. v. Mali, 74 F.2d 666 (2d Cir. 1935).

[119.1] 19 U.S.C. § 1337 et seq.

[119.2] Additional provisions of the 1916 Act allow for a double duty on goods with exclusive dealing provisions attached to them. It has been held illegal to limit imports by imposing royalties on amounts produced over a quota. United States v. Aluminum Corporation of America, 148 F.2d 416 (2d Cir. 1945). The Trade Agreements Act of 1979 established new standards for dumping cases, and a timetable under which the Commerce Department and the ITC must act after they receive a complaint.

items bearing a trademark registered with U.S. Customs. The intent of the law is to prevent counterfeit items from coming into the U.S., but the status of "grey market" imports, where a genuine item comes in through unauthorized distribution channels, is unclear. A private plaintiff with a complaint about unfair imports may pursue a remedy in the I.T.C. rather than the federal courts. Proceedings must be completed within twelve-to-fifteen months, which limits dilatory tactics, but the only remedies available are exclusion or cease and desist orders.[119.3] Since the creation of the I.T.C. in 1974, its mandate has been gradually expanded to cover the entire range of antitrust and consumer protection claims.[119.4] This creates certain conceptual problems, since the antitrust laws are designed to protect competition, while the trade laws are invoked by one competitor who feels he has been injured.[119.5] The Treasury Department, the International Trade Commission, and the Commerce Department also enforce these laws, and can impose countervailing duties on these goods in order to eliminate the advantage they may have gained by an exporter's subsidy.[119.6] Private parties may also petition the Customs Service to change the classification of competing imported goods under Section 51C of the Tariff Act of 1930.

Legal actions challenging imports tend to fluctuate with the political and economic climate in the U.S. Relatively few antidumping actions were commenced until 1969, but more activity has occurred since that time.[119.7] The controver-

---

[119.3] A private party who receives a favorable decision from the I.T.C. may lack standing to participate in an appeal notwithstanding the risk of reversal. Krupp Int'l, Inc. v. United States Int'l Trade Comm'n, 626 F.2d 844 (C.C.P.A. 1980).

[119.4] Ward, "The Tariff Act of 1930—Sec. 337: An Antitrust Ugly Duckling," 27 Antitrust Bull. 355 (1982).

[119.5] Applebaum, "Are U.S. International Trade and Commerce Conduct Laws in Harmony with Traditional Antitrust Laws & Policy?" 49 Antitrust L.J. 1207 (1980).

[119.6] Under § 201 of the 1921 Act, retroactive duties may be assessed on all imported goods found to have been sold into the U.S. at less than fair value. Timken Co. v. Simon, 539 F.2d 221 (D.C. Cir. 1976); see also 20 Int. Leg. Mat. 186 (1981).

[119.7] For the regulations of the U.S. and E.E.C. regarding antidumping and countervailing duties, see 19 Int. Leg. Mat. 429 (1980).

sies surrounding this area were brought into focus by the
Zenith[120] case. In 1970, Zenith had attempted to protect its
U.S.-produced products from lower-priced Japanese competitors by filing a complaint with the Commissioner of Customs.
The petition sought the imposition of countervailing duties
against Japanese products, claiming that the Japanese Government's remission of certain indirect taxes on exported goods
was a "bounty or grant" under the terms of the statute. Although the antidumping provisions were upheld as constitutional,[121] in January, 1976 the Commissioner of Customs
denied Zenith's request.[122] Zenith appealed to the Customs
Court and won a reversal of the Commissioner's ruling.[123] A
further appeal to the Court of Customs and Patent Appeals
brought another reversal, this time in favor of the Government,[124] holding that not every tax remission is a "bounty or
grant" that should trigger countervailing duties. Although the
U.S. Supreme Court sustained the finding of the Appeals
Court, and the right of the U.S. to settle claims under the Tariff
Act of 1930 was upheld.[124.1] Zenith pursued a private action
against virtually the entire Japanese consumer electronics industry.[125] Zenith's private action was initially dismissed by the

---

[120] Zenith Radio Corp. v. United States, 437 U.S. 443 (1978).

[121] Zenith Radio Corp. v. Matsushita Electric Industrial Co., Ltd., 402 F.
Supp. 251 (E.D. Pa. 1975).

[122] 41 Fed. Reg. 1298 (1976).

[123] Zenith Radio Corp. v. United States, 430 F. Supp. 242 (Cust. Ct. 1977).

[124] United States v. Zenith Radio Corp., 506 F.2d 1209 (C.C.P.A. 1977).

[124.1] Zenith Radio Corp. v. United States, 509 F. Supp. 1282 (Ct. Int. Tr.
1981).

[125] Zenith alleged a worldwide conspiracy to destroy the domestic consumer electronics industry in the United States by selling products for substantially less than their market value or wholesale price in Japan. Among
preliminary findings, the court decided that Zenith had a right to a jury trial,
notwithstanding the complexity of the issues raised. In re Electronic Products Antitrust Litigation, M.D.L. No. 189 (E.D. Pa. June 6, 1979). The
Antidumping Act of 1916 required the products under consideration to be
comparable, and most of the products imported into the U.S., the court
found, differed from those sold in Japan, 494 F. Supp. 1161, 1190 (E.D. Pa.
1980). The court also decided that the rule in *Illinois Brick* should not be
read to bar a suit by a manufacturer on the theory that the damages were
actually suffered by the manufacturer's distributors. (E.D. Pa. May 5, 1980),
Antitrust & Trade Reg. Rep. (BNA) at A-11 (May 29, 1980), and it also ruled

District Court, but the dismissal was reversed by the Third Circuit as to all defendants except Sony. The final status is currently unclear.[126] The DOJ has opposed any attempts to pursue antidumping remedies,[129] arguing that it favored U.S. consumers getting goods at low prices, and that a complainant would need to prove that the dumper had the power to monopolize the U.S. market by predatory pricing.[130]

The DOJ also questions the legality of private parties settling antidumping cases. Such settlement discussions may amount to price-fixing or quantity-fixing arrangements, which violate § 1 of the Sherman Act. The procedures set forth in the appropriate statutes must be followed, and use of the threat of filing an antidumping complaint cannot be used to begin price-fixing discussions.[131]

---

that the 1953 Treaty of Friendship, Commerce and Navigation between the U.S. and Japan did not repeal the provisions of the 1916 Antidumping Act. 494 F. Supp. 1246 (E.D. Pa. 1980). Defendant's motion for summary judgment on all counts was granted, the Court ruling that there was no evidence from which a jury could find an agreement or converted action with respect to exports to the U.S. that could have injured Zenith. In spite of the voluminous record before the court, it was willing to grant a dismissal prior to a full trial on the theory that the defendant suffered no injury, rather than any rule of reason justification. 513 F. Supp. 1100 (E.D. Pa. 1981).

[126] Trade Reg. Rep. No. 626, Extra Edition (Dec. 3, 1983); Greene, "One to Watch," Forbes 114 (Feb. 13, 1984).

[Next footnote is 129.]

[129] Address by Joel Davidow, U.S. Department of Justice, to Polish Institute of State & Law, *Legal Times of Washington* 21 (June 26, 1978).

[130] The DOJ has followed a policy of not proceeding against members of foreign export associations if their conduct would be allowed in the U.S. under Webb-Pomerene. The DOJ opposes the use of § 337 as a "second shot" against imports after a dumping case has failed. Letter from Ass't Attorney General Baker to Sen. Kennedy, Antitrust & Trade Reg. Rep. (BNA) No. 807 at A24 (March 29, 1977); *see also*, Plaut, "Why Dumping is Good for Us," Fortune 212 (May 5, 1980).

[131] United States v. Socony-Vacuum Oil Co., 310 U.S. 450 (1949); *see also* speech by Alexander Sierck to World Trade Institute, Trade Reg. Rep. (CCH) at 4 (Sept. 17, 1979). The DOJ views its "competitive advocacy" role as possibly requiring a limitation of the powers of the I.T.C. in the dumping area to avoid protectionism. Speech by John Shenefield to ALI-ABA Course on International Antitrust Law, 1978-1 Trade Cas. (CCH) ¶ 50,371. The

The Treasury Department and International Trade Commission, responding either to DOJ pressure or to their own economic philosophies, have been somewhat intermittently active in this area and the future effectiveness of these statutory remedies appears in doubt.[132] Since the Supreme Court has spoken, it would appear that a home government rebate of indirect taxes will not trigger countervailing duties, but the possibility that an exporter who unilaterally decides to charge more for his goods abroad than in the United States may still risk violation of these laws, especially if the market power mentioned by the DOJ can be shown.

The major limit on import freedom may come not from antitrust laws, but rather from conventional politics. Faced with an economic downturn in the short run, or a perceived long run alteration of our economy, interest groups will turn to lobbying. Various bills have been introduced calling for imported products (such as automobiles) to contain a specified percentage of U.S. components, or for retaliation against countries that do not grant U.S. products "substantially equivalent market access."[132.1] Although organized labor in the U.S. has officially supported free trade since 1946, at least since 1967

F.T.C. has also entered the picture, with a study on the costs and benefits to the U.S. economy of various import restrictions. *See* Antitrust & Trade Reg. Rep. (BNA) No. 925 at A-18 (Aug. 2, 1979).

[132] On a bilateral basis, governments sometimes arrange "orderly marketing agreements" which are voluntary quotas to restrain imports. The question of whether such agreements may be exempt from U.S. antitrust laws is not resolved. Consumers Union of U.S., Inc. v. Kissinger, 506 F.2d 136 (D.C. Cir. 1974), *cert. denied*, 421 U.S. 1004 (1975). For a discussion of orderly marketing agreements, *see* 72 Proc. A.S.I.L. 1 (1978). Private parties who feel threatened by imports are usually quite willing to abandon their efforts to obtain imposition of countervailing duties if they receive assurances that the government will negotiate to avoid "market disruptions" (*i.e.*, limit imports). For example, three groups of Florida vegetable growers withdrew their complaint that Mexico was selling vegetables below-cost after assurances from U.S. officials to negotiate the matter. The Treasury Department was then able to end its antidumping investigation, which, some feared, would have seriously disrupted relations between the countries. Washington Food Report, No. 2311 at 1 (July 21, 1979); *see also* letter of John H. Shenefield regarding Presidential negotiations to limit imports. T.R.R. ¶ 50,422 (Dec. 29, 1980).

[132.1] See., e.g., 97th Cong., S. 2094.

they have pushed for restraints on certain imports.[132.2]

[5] Joint Ventures

Where the resources of one firm seem inadequate to capitalize on the opportunities available in multinational operations,
a joint venture between two (or more) companies is frequently
utilized. In spite of the popularity of the joint venture, there
is no specific controlling statute, and few cases directly on
point, to guide us as to the relevant antitrust considerations.

Advocates of joint ventures argue that they should be favored as procompetitive, since they minimize risk and allow
for participation in markets by companies that might otherwise have been deterred. Yet it certainly is possible that a joint
venture might be used as a method of avoiding the nuisance
of competition between parties in a foreign market.[133] If the
parties to a joint venture engaged in conduct traditionally held
to be *per se* illegal (such as a price-fixing agreement), then of
course the agreement would be illegal. The use of the joint
venture format, like a licensing agreement, carries with it no
insulation from the U.S. antitrust laws.[134] Some early cases[135]
even lead to some speculation that all joint ventures would be
attacked, but the lack of significant federal enforcement ef-

---

[132.2] Colvin & deKieffer, "A Legal & Economic Analysis of the Quota
Provisions of the Proposed Fair Trade & Investment Act of 1972," 6 Int.
Law. 771 (1972); "Domestic Content Legislation Linked in Senate to Japa-
nese Beef Quotas," 2 Inside U.S. Trade 1 (Feb. 17, 1984).

[133] United States v. Imperial Chemical Industries, 100 F. Supp. 504
(S.D.N.Y. 1951); United States v. Minnesota Mining & Mfg. Co., 92 F. Supp.
947 (D. Mass. 1950).

[134] At a press conference held Sept. 26, 1978, President Carter spoke
favorably of the ability of joint ventures to expand U.S. exports. Antitrust &
Trade Reg. Rep. (BNA) No. 882 at A4 (Sept. 28, 1978). The DOJ responded
by committing to answer business review letters regarding international
joint ventures within thirty days in order to remove the antitrust uncertainty
that has constrained such efforts in the past. Trade Reg. Rep. (CCH) ¶ 8559,
and by issuing its Guidelines on Research Joint Ventures.

[135] Timken Roller Bearing v. United States, 83 F. Supp. 284 (N.D. Ohio
1949), *modified & aff'd*, 341 U.S. 593 (1951); United States v. Minnesota
Mining & Mfg. Co., *supra* N. 133.

forts since 1951 has dispelled that notion.[136] Nearly all international joint ventures will be analyzed under the rule of reason, and will usually pass antitrust scrutiny so long as its purpose or effect is not to restrain trade or create a monopoly.

In *United States v. Imperial Chemical Industries,*[137] a series of patent and know-how licenses were shown to have been granted with the purpose of dividing world markets. Joint ventures were formed between the competitors to control the market for explosives and other chemicals in countries where the competitors (principally duPont and ICI) did not already operate. The Court determined that the initial purpose in forming the ventures was to avoid and prevent competition, and therefore was illegal.[138]

The leading U.S. case involving international joint ventures, *Timken Roller Bearing Co. v. United States,*[139] unfortunately failed to set clear standards in this area. Although the Justices of the Supreme Court seemed to be unable to agree on the facts of the case, it appears that a U.S. firm combined with its British and French affiliates, after its key patents had expired, to fix prices and allocate certain markets. The agreement was found to violate § 1 of the Sherman Act, by eliminating competition and restricting imports into and exports from the U.S. Certain foreign firms were acquired by Timken, which was found to be part of the restrictive scheme. Normally, a foreign branch owned or controlled by a U.S. corporation would incur no antitrust risk by exclusively supplying one market, since there would not be an agreement between two parties involved. There was some evidence presented to the District Court that another shareholder, Michael Dewar, actually con-

---

[136] Davidow, "Extraterritorial Application of U.S. Antitrust Laws in a Changing World," 8 Law & Policy Int'l Bus. 895, 898 (1976).

[137] *Supra* N. 133.

[138] *Id.* The remedy decreed was compulsory licensing of the patents at reasonable royalty rates. *Id.* at 105 F. Supp. 215 (S.D.N.Y. 1952). Covenants not to compete with a joint venture in a certain market may be allowed if it can be proved that the purpose of the restraint is the development of new business. United States v. E.I. duPont deNemours & Co., 118 F. Supp. 41, 220 (D. Del. 1953).

[139] *Supra,* N. 135.

trolled the foreign companies, not Timken.[140] Whatever the nature of the violation, the Court did not call it *per se* illegal, but rather said that the "aggregation of trade restraints . . . are illegal."[141]

It is also possible that a long-term joint venture will be considered to violate the acquisition controls imposed by § 7 of the Clayton Act.[142] It is not entirely clear how § 7 may be used to control international ventures, since the Act only covers acquisitions of the assets of other corporations "where in any line of commerce in any section of the country, the effect of such acquisition may be substantially to lessen competition or tend to create a monopoly." Nevertheless, if there is an effect on U.S. competition, the Clayton Act may be involved. *United States v. Penn-Olin Chemical Co.*,[143] looked at whether both parties to a joint venture would have entered a market individually. If so, the venture would probably be illegal and would be similar to a cartel. If the participants would not have entered the market at all, the agreement will be acceptable (barring any other improper restraints). If only one party would have entered the market, the agreement may be illegal under the theory that potential competition was eliminated.

The DOJ responded negatively to a proposed joint venture between General Electric and Hitachi to produce televisions in the United States. Although Hitachi had a small U.S. market share (1.6 percent color; 2.5 percent B&W), the DOJ announced that it would challenge the arrangement since it would, in their view, "eliminate significant existing and potential competition" between the participants. So, as far as the DOJ is concerned, the mere addition of a foreign partner to a joint venture is no insulation from a DOJ challenge, if there is

---

[140] 83 F. Supp. 284, 311 (N.D. Ohio 1949).

[141] 341 U.S. at 598.

[142] Celler-Kefauver Antimerger Act of 1950, ch. 1184, 64 Stat. 1125, 15 U.S.C. § 18. International acquisitions and mergers are discussed in detail in § 9.02[6], *infra*.

[143] 378 U.S. 158 (1964), *aff'd on remand* 389 U.S. 308 (1967). Penn-Olin, however, dealt with the application of § 7 to domestic joint ventures.

evidence that the foreign company could enter the U.S. market alone.[144]

The DOJ responded positively, however, to a proposed joint venture between RTE Corp. (U.S.) and Zellweger Uster Ltd. (Swiss) to manufacture and distribute certain electrical equipment. The business review letter noted that since the U.S. partner had never contemplated entry into the market and the Swiss partner would leave the market if the joint venture did not proceed, competition was not reduced.[144.1]

An F.T.C. complaint challenging a joint venture between Brunswick Corp. and Yamaha Motor Co. was, at first, dismissed by an administrative law judge, based on his finding that the "actual procompetitive effects" would outweigh the anticompetitive effect of "the temporary removal of Yamaha from the edge of the market." Even though the judge concluded that Yamaha would have eventually entered the outboard motor market, the addition of a new competitive force (*i.e.*, the joint venture) was a more important aid to competition than the existence of Yamaha on the fringes of the market as a potential entrant. The Commission reversed the ALJ, and concluded that Yamaha was an actual potential entrant, the agreement foreclosed the likely entry of Yamaha into the market, and that the collateral agreements between Brunswick and Yamaha were an unlawful restraint of trade. On remand, the ALJ determined that the joint venture should be terminated to restore Yamaha to its 1972 position as an actual potential entrant to the market.[145]

The Eighth Circuit Court of Appeals affirmed the decision[145.1] on liability, noting that the application of the potential competition doctrine was appropriate in light of the concentrated market, the feasibility of Yamaha's entry, and the procompetitive effects of Yamaha's entry.[145.2]

---

[144] Trade Reg. Rep. (CCH) No. 362 at 3 (Dec. 4, 1978). Should a balance of payments problem continue for the U.S., it is possible that political pressures may relax the DOJ's enforcement views regarding ventures that may reduce imports into the U.S.

[144.1] 1027 A.T.R.R. A26 (Aug. 13, 1981).

[145] In re Brunswick Corp., Dkt. 9028 T.R.R. ¶¶ 21,623, 21,740.

[145.1] 657 F.2d 971 (8th Cir. 1981).

[145.2] United States v. Marine Bancorporation, Inc., 418 U.S. 602 (1974). Four firms with a 99 percent market share met the concentrated market requirement of Marine.

9-43

The DOJ has provided two hypothetical situations dealing with joint ventures in its recent guide.[146] In Case C,[147] a consortium of U.S. firms was formed to bid on a Latin American project, since a smaller group could not handle it. Starting with the proposition that any joint venture between competitors has an antitrust risk,[148] the DOJ would assign less risk to a one-shot venture than a long term agreement, since there will be less tendency in the short-term venture to reduce the participant's zeal for competition outside of the venture. For further protection, the personnel working on the joint venture might well be separated from the firms' other activities.

Three major factors are considered in the DOJ's antitrust analysis: (1) Does the creation of the joint venture unreasonably restrain competition? (2) Should the unreasonable collateral restraints to the joint venture be removed even if the venture is allowed? (3) Is the joint venture a "bottleneck monopoly" which, because of its importance to the relevant market, must be opened to all competitors on reasonable and non-discriminatory terms?

With a more permanent joint venture, the DOJ threatens to treat the agremeent as a merger in the market covered. However, since § 7 of the Clayton Act would probably not be applicable to operations overseas, the arrangement would be analyzed under § 1 of the Sherman Act. Normally, the DOJ will not challenge a venture where competition is reduced in a foreign market only, even if U.S. exports may be involved.[149] The term of the agreement, the amount of financial invest-

---

[146] It should be noted again that while the DOJ guidelines are a helpful tool to understand the U.S. antitrust laws, they are not the "law." Rather, they are one agency's conservative view of the law, which, when taken together with statutes, cases, and economic data, can be used to analyze the antitrust risks inherent in a given agreement.

[147] DOJ guidelines, Case C at E6.

[148] Timken Roller Bearing v. United States, *supra* N. 133; United States v. Minn. Mining & Mfg., *supra* N. 132.

[149] John Shenefield, former head of the DOJ Antitrust Division, urged businessmen not to assume that there is necessarily anything anticompetitive in forming a joint venture for the purpose of competing abroad. Shenefield encouraged the use of the DOJ's expedited business review procedure to resolve any doubts about a proposed venture. Speech to National Governors Association (Seattle, June 6, 1979), Trade Reg. Rep. (CCH) No. 389 at 5.

ment required, and whether complementary skills are required, will bear upon the reasonableness of the venture.[150]

On the facts proposed by the DOJ, the venture would not deal with an essential facility that would create a bottleneck monopoly.[151] If the remaining U.S. firms could form a competing consortium to bid on the project, this would be helpful.[152] Encouragement of the venture by U.S. government officials (presumably other than those in the Antitrust Division of the DOJ) will not provide an automatic antitrust exemption, but will be evidence of good faith among the parties.[153]

(Text continued on page 9-45)

---

[150] United States v. Morgan, 118 F. Supp. 621 (S.D.N.Y. 1953).

[151] Silver v. N.Y. Stock Exchange, 373 U.S. 341 (1963); Assoc. Press v. United States, 326 U.S. 1 (1945); United States v. Terminal R.R. Ass'n of St. Louis, 224 U.S. 383 (1912). No case has ever held a short-term joint venture to be a bottleneck monopoly.

[152] Worthen Bank & Trust Co. v. Nat'l Bankamericard, Inc., 485 F.2d 119 (8th Cir. 1973).

[153] United States v. Socony Vacuum Oil Co., 310 U.S. 150 (1940).

In Case D,[154] a joint research project between a U.S. and a British corporation (neither of whom is dominant in their market) is formed to develop a process to extract a metal. If the research is fruitful, the U.S. corporation would get exclusive marketing rights in North America, and the British company would get the EEC and former British colonies. After repeating the three-part analysis used in Case C, the DOJ notes that there would not be a bottleneck monopoly problem under these facts, and the narrower the scope of the joint venture (both as to time and subject), the less likely it would be to inhibit competition.

It is generally accepted that through competition, companies are encouraged to develop new products. However, this venture would, in the DOJ's view, eliminate competition in the development of a new process. The next question to ask, then, is whether either of the companies would have undertaken the project alone, or whether this course would have been too expensive. The inability of one party to finance the project, and the existence of a considerable number of other firms in the field, indicates that any elimination of competition by the venture would not be substantial.

However, the granting of exclusive territories may violate the Sherman Act as a horizontal conspiracy.[155] If the arrangement is not *per se* illegal, then it would be subject to a rule of reason analysis, to see if the restraint were reasonable in scope and necessary to the legitimate purposes of the joint venture.[156]

Thus, it can be observed that an antitrust analysis of a joint venture is similar to the testing of a license agreement. If the *per se* practices are avoided, the market position and the restrictions of the proposed agreement must be examined together to see if an antitrust risk is present.

If the companies have some degree of market power, the joint venture, to pass antitrust muster, should be a necessary prerequisite to market entry. Legal risk is minimized by keep-

---

[154] Case D at E7.

[155] United States v. Topco Associates, Inc., 405 U.S. 596 (1972).

[156] United States v. Addyston Pipe & Steel Co., 85 F. 271 (6th Cir. 1898), *aff'd*, 175 U.S. 211 (1899).

ing the venture's scope and duration only long enough to accomplish its purposes. The parties should be aware that the venture will be scrutinized by enforcement agencies, customers, suppliers and competitors for any sign that it may be engaging in conduct apart from its legitimating purpose.[157]

[6]   International Acquisitions and Mergers

As noted in the preceding section, both § 1 of the Sherman Act and § 7 of the Clayton Act control mergers and acquisitions. Section 7, which is a civil statute primarily enforced by the Federal Trade Commission, prohibits the acquisition of the stock or assets of a corporation engaged in commerce, "where in any line of commerce or in any activity affecting commerce in any section of the country, the effect of such acquisition may be substantially to lessen competition or tend to create a monopoly."[158] Since the statute requires both firms to be engaged in U.S. commerce, and an adverse effect to be felt on some part of the U.S. market, most acquisitions of foreign corporations will not be challenged by the DOJ or FTC if there is a foreclosure of exports or foreign consumers are hurt, there must be an elimination of actual or potential competition in a U.S. market.[159] Section 7A of the Clayton Act,[159.1] added in

---

[157] Brodley, "Joint Ventures and the Justice Department's Antitrust Guide for International Operations," 24 Antitrust Bull. 337 (1979).

[158] 15 U.S.C. § 18.

[159] United States v. Aluminum Co. of America, 91 F. Supp. 333 (S.D.N.Y. 1950). A U.S. corporation is virtually free to do what it wants abroad, so long as there are no effects on U.S. commerce, but it may not use a foreign subsidiary to deceive customers, or as an instrument of an unlawful agreement. Timken Roller Bearing Corp. v. United States, 341 U.S. 593 (1951); Kiefer-Stewart Co. v. Joseph E. Segram & Sons, Inc., 340 U.S. 211 (1951); United States v. Arkansas Fuel Oil Corp., 1960 Trade Cas. (CCH) ¶ 69,619 (N.D. Okla. 1960); United States v. Minn. Mining & Mfg. Co., 92 F. Supp. 947 (D. Mass. 1950). An acquisition overseas is more likely to be challenged where the U.S. firm dominates its market, and the only probable source of new competition is from the foreign markets, or, in an extension of the concept of protecting small business, if a small U.S. exporter were somehow foreclosed by the acquisition. United States v. Von's Grocery Co., 384 U.S. 270 (1966). The DOJ threatened suit if General Electric acquired the cat-

1976, which required notification of the D.O.J. and F.T.C., and a waiting period before consummation of certain acquisitions, may also cover acquisitions of or by foreign firms. Detailed regulations govern the reporting of international mergers,[159.2] and they should be consulted if it appears that the transaction value will exceed $10 million in sales or assets.

The potential competition analysis may be utilized by government enforcers to evaluate acquisitions when a foreign firm is already engaged in U.S. commerce. Enforcement activity may be triggered by positive answers to all of the following questions: (1) Is the relevant market highly concentrated? (2) Is the foreign firm one of a small group of potential entrants? (3) Does the foreign firm have incentives to enter the U.S. market? (4) Does the foreign firm have the capability to enter the U.S. market?[160] Countering any of these assertions will probably defeat the application of the potential competition.[160.1]

Since there are no *per se* rules here, the facts surrounding international merger cases, and the economic evidence that can be developed from those facts, is probably more important than the legal approaches or concentration guidelines used by the courts. For example, even if there is a "reasonable probability of eventual entry," if no procompetitive benefits are provided by a firm as a potential entrant, an acquisition will be

---

scanner business of Thorn-EMI, since G.E. was already in the business in the U.S. The deal was allowed to proceed after assurances by G.E. that certain assets would not be acquired. 444 T.R.R. 3 (June 27, 1980).

[159.1] *Supra* N. 6.

[159.2] 16 C.F.R. §§ 802.50 *et seq.*

[160] DOJ guidelines at E5. In United States v. Standard Oil Co., 253 F. Supp. 196 (D.N.J. 1966), Standard, which had large Canadian potash holdings, was prevented from acquiring the Potash Company of America. The court ruled that Standard would have entered the U.S. market independently, had it not made the acquisition. An injunction to block the acquisition of the largest domestic manufacturer of nuclear medical imaging equipment by Siemens Corp. was denied. Even though Siemens manufactured the same equipment in Germany, there was no "reasonable probability" that it would enter the U.S. market de novo, nor was it perceived as a potential competitor. Siemens Corp. v. United States, 621 F.2d 499 (2d Cir. 1980).

[160.1] United States v. Marine Bancorporation, Inc., *supra* N. 145.2.

allowed. In *BOC International Ltd. v. FTC*,[161] the Second Circuit allowed a British company to acquire an American producer of industrial gases, holding that the potential entry theory requires a showing of some degree of certainty that the acquirer will enter a market. The mere assertion of "ephemeral possibilities" that a firm might enter a market at some undetermined date in the future will not support a § 7 charge.

If the acquired firm (or foreign joint venture partner) operates in the U.S., or is a potential entrant into the U.S. market, the transaction will be evaluated as any other domestic merger,[162] but may require the use of the Sherman Act to obtain jurisdiction. Where the acquired foreign firm is a major source of supply to U.S. companies, the antitrust analysis should include a consideration of whether competitors have alternate supply sources available.[163]

Other countries may evaluate the assistance an acquisition might provide to foreign trade, but this would not necessarily help support the pro-competition arguments for a U.S. acquisition if other indicia are negative. The theory is that the U.S. market is large enough to provide both efficiency and competition, while other countries have such a small domestic market that they must rely on exports to survive.

Even where the government will decide not to attack an acquisition due to a minimal effect on U.S. commerce, private parties who believe they have been injured will not be deterred. For example, in *International Telephone & Telegraph*

---

[161] BOC International Ltd. v. FTC, 557 F.2d 24 (2d Cir. 1977).

[162] In United States v. Joseph Schlitz Brewing Co., 253 F. Supp. 129 (N.D. Cal.), *aff'd per curiam*, 385 U.S. 37 (1966), the DOJ stopped an acquisition by Schlitz of a Canadian brewer that controlled a California brewer that competed with Schlitz. *See also* Litton Industries, Inc., Dkt 8778, Trade Reg. Rep. (CCH) ¶¶ 20,267, 20,233 (1973). In United States v. Gillette Co., 406 F. Supp. 713 (D. Mass. 1975), Gilette was forced to set-up a new company for the purpose of selling Braun razors in the U.S., and then to divest the company. Gilette was allowed to keep the European Braun operations, and could distribute Braun's non-shaving products in the U.S. Because Braun sold non-shaving products in the U.S. prior to the acquisition, the F.T.C. was able to assert jurisdiction under § 7.

[163] Dresser Industries, Order Dismissing Complaints, Dkts. 7095, 7096, Trade Reg. Rep. (CCH) [1963-65 T.B.] ¶ 16,513 (1963).

Corp. v. General Telephone & Electronics Corp.,[164] I.T.T. brought an action against G.T.E. under §§ 1 and 2 of the Sherman Act and § 7 of the Clayton Act, alleging, *inter alia,* that G.T.E.'s acquisition of various manufacturers of telephone equipment resulted in a vertically integrated corporation that foreclosed certain foreign markets to competitors who were unable to sell the equipment they manufactured to the telephone companies owned by G.T.E. G.T.E. counterclaimed, asserting that I.T.T.'s vertical integration and ownership of equipment manufacturing plants and telephone companies in the Virgin Islands, Puerto Rico, South America, and Europe foreclosed the export trade of G.T.E. and violated the Sherman and Clayton Acts. I.T.T. responded with an amended complaint, alleging that the acquisition of a Canadian firm by G.T.E. foreclosed I.T.T.'s export sales. Although both parties failed to prove actual foreclosure, the Court noted that such an action could be maintained as a matter of law, if the evidence were available to support it.[165]

In theory, acquisition of suppliers or customers (vertical mergers) may be illegal, but are usually perceived as leading to economic efficiency. Although competition for customers is reduced, it is unlikely that many vertical mergers will be litigated in the next few years.[165.1]

Where a U.S. firm is acquired by a foreign firm, the same general considerations apply,[166] but political and economic

---

[164] 351 F. Supp. 1153 (D. Hawaii 1972), *rev'd on other grounds,* 518 F.2d 913 (9th Cir. 1975).

[165] *Id.*

[165.1] Calnetics Corp. v. Volkswagen of America, Inc., 532 F.2d 664 (9th Cir.), *cert. denied,* 429 U.S. 940 (1976); United States v. Aluminum Ltd., 1965 Trade Cas. ¶ 71,366 (D.N.J. 1965).

[166] In a Consent Order, Bayer A.G. agreed to divest the U.S. assets it acquired from Miles Laboratories that manufactured allergenic extracts. At the time of the acquisition, Bayer had a 35 to 40 percent market share and Miles 12 percent. Consent Order to Cease and Desist, File No. 7910119, 95 F.T.C. 254 (1980). The F.T.C. issued a complaint to block the proposed acquisition of Harnischfeger Corp., a manufacturer of cranes and related products, by Mannesmann A.G., a West German competitor. The complaint alleged that, since the two firms are competitors, the acquisition would reduce competition in the affected markets, which were already concentrated. Trade Reg. Rep. (CCH) ¶ 21,616 (Oct. 1, 1979).

pressures may be more significant here in influencing the enforcement agencies to challenge the acquisitions.[167] For example, SKF of Sweden acquired two U.S. bearing manufacturers, one in 1955 and one in 1960. The FTC investigated in 1960, and decided to take no action. Subsequently, SKF Industries (the U.S. subsidiary) and Federal Mogul Corp. (a U.S. firm), made a buy-sell agreement to allow Federal to market certain SKF bearings.

In 1975, the FTC decided to challenge the 1955 and 1960 acquisitions (and some foreign acquisitions), and the Federal Mogul agreement, as eliminating competition. The administrative law judge ruled that the FTC could not now challenge the old acquisitions since there was no effect on U.S. competition. But he also ruled that the distribution arrangement was anti-competitive. Since Federal stopped manufacturing certain items and backed out of a proposed Japanese joint venture, and SKF Industries abolished its U.S. marketing department and transferred its business to Federal, there were found to be a *per se* unlawful allocation of markets.

On appeal, the F.T.C. upheld the finding that the *per se* rule

---

[167] On August 17, 1978, the DOJ filed a complaint under § 7 of the Clayton Act challenging the acquisition of Blandin Paper Co. (Minnesota) by British Columbia Forest Products, Ltd. The complaint alleged that the acquisition will substantially lessen competition in the production and sale of coated groundwood paper. United States v. British Columbia Forest Products, Ltd., Civ. No. 4-78-357 (D. Minn.), Trade Reg. Rep. (CCH) ¶ 45,-078, case 2650 at 53,729. The FTC negotiated a consent order whereby Nestle, S.A. agreed to divest a frozen-food plant it acquired in 1973 as part of its acquisition of Stouffer Foods. The FTC issued a complaint in 1975 alleging that the acquisition would substantially reduce competition in the frozen entree market between Stouffer and Libby, McNeil & Libby, a subsidiary of Nestle. Under the agreement, Nestle is prohibited until 1985 from acquiring any frozen food concern with annual sales of $10 million without prior FTC approval. In re Nestle Alimentana, S.A., Dkt. 9003, Consent Order to Cease and Desist (April 24, 1979), Trade Reg. Rep. (CCH) ¶ 21,560. The acquisition of U.S. banks by foreign companies gave rise to a bill in Congress proposing a six-month moratorium on foreign takeovers of American banks. Testimony by Deputy Assistant Attorney General Donald Flexner before the Senate Banking Committee on July 16, 1979 made it clear that, as far as the DOJ was concerned, the nationality of the acquiring party was a "neutral factor" and the appropriate concern was with the effect on competition. *Legal Times of Washington* 20 (July 23, 1979).

was appropriate, since 1) SKF and Federal were direct competitors at the time of their agreement; 2) one competitor, SKF, was eliminated from the market; and 3) SKF was expressly precluded from re-entering the distribution market.[168] As can be seen, the complexion of a case can be altered by the way it is characterized. What might strike a businessman as SKF's reasonable efforts to salvage something out of a failed U.S. venture became transformed by the FTC into a conspiracy to eliminate competition.

Mergers between foreign corporations will not necessarily escape U.S. antitrust problems if they do business in the U.S. In *United States v. Ciba Corp.*,[169] the proposed merger between two Swiss chemical companies was attacked based on an adverse effect on their respective U.S. subsidiaries. The case was settled through a consent decree ordering divestiture of certain overlapping U.S. operations, even though there would have been little the DOJ could have done to un-do the merger between the Swiss parents.

The DOJ, in Case B,[170] provides the example of a U.S. corporation with a 50 percent market share, that plans to acquire a German firm with a small market share and negligible U.S. sales.[171] Clayton § 7 would not be applied here, since there are no U.S. sales by the German company. However, the DOJ asserts that if the German firm held patents in the U.S., they might be enough to constitute participation in U.S. commerce for purposes of Clayton Act § 7. Or, the U.S. acquisition might be treated as a grant of an exclusive patent license to the U.S. firm under Sherman § 1, or as an attempt to monopolize under

---

[168] In re SKF Industries, Dkt. 9046, Antitrust & Trade Reg. Rep. (BNA) No. 925 at A-1 (Aug. 2, 1979).

[169] 1970 Trade Cas. (CCH) ¶¶ 73,269, 73,319 (consent decree, S.D.N.Y. 1970).

[170] DOJ guidelines, Case B at E5.

[171] The DOJ has frequently been successful in obtaining "corrective" divestitures when U.S. companies have acquired foreign firms with little or no U.S. sales. *See, e.g.,* United States v. Merck & Co., Consent Decree, 80-81 Trade Cas. ¶ 63,682 (S.D. Cal. 1980); United States v. Gould, Inc., T.R.R. ¶ 45,080, Case No. 2794; United States v. Ibstock Johnson, Ltd., T.R.R. ¶ 45,080 Case No. 2781. The willingness of the firms to settle these cases, however, may have seemed due as much to the perceived value of their acquisitions as to the strength of the government's legal case.

Sherman § 2. So, even if a preliminary analysis shows no U.S. business by a foreign acquisition target, the buyer should be aware that aggressive government agencies may look for any excuse, no matter how flimsy it may seem to the defendant, to assert their powers.

Even if an outright merger does not occur, a U.S. and a foreign company that compete in the U.S. may violate § 8 of the Clayton Act[172] if they share common directors. For example, the FTC issued a complaint against Borg-Warner Corp. and Bosch G.m.b.H. charging an unlawful interlock. The two firms had two directors in common, and were also competitors in the manufacture of auto parts.[173]

§ 9.03   Antitrust in the Common Market and Elsewhere

[1]   Introduction

There is clearly no consensus on any universal principles of antitrust law that should be applied throughout the world, nor is there any consistent position on how far U.S. (or other nation's) laws go in covering acts or effects that occur outside of the U.S. or other nation's territories. The U.S. takes the position that its international antitrust enforcement policies are consistent with accepted principles of international law,[174] but the result has been that some actions which have been brought are arguably within its international law power, but cannot be justified in terms of protecting U.S. commerce.[175]

One response to the dilemma of how to advise foreign managers as to antitrust considerations has been to quote U.S.

---

[172] 15 U.S.C. § 19.

[173] FTC Dkt. 9120, T.R.R. ¶ 21,724.

[174] United States v. Aluminum Co. of America, 148 F.2d 416 (2d Cir. 1954); Restatement (2d) of Foreign Relations Law § 18 (1965).

[175] In Calnetics Corp. v. Volkswagen of America, Inc., 353 F. Supp. 1219 (C.D. Cal. 1973), U.S. law was applied to prevent the importation of Volkswagens from Germany with air conditioners based on alleged infringements in Germany.

law.[176] Unfortunately, some countries may be either more or less restrictive than the U.S. in certain situations, even if there is not a major problem with application of their laws beyond the national borders. Plus, if you attempt to evaluate corporate conduct in a foreign country in terms of U.S. law, you may be faced with entirely different philosophical approaches that will add to differing opinions as to whether an MNC has abused its power.

For example, European countries look to the general concept of "restrictive business practices" to see if a firm with a dominant market position has violated the law by charging an excessively high price or earning an unconscionable profit.[177] The U.S. would not attempt to control prices in this way, but rather would look to see if a monopoly existed. LDCs will concentrate on intra-corporate or parent-subsidiary relationships and restrictions, especially where limits are imposed on exports.[178] Faced with a crucial need to increase its foreign reserves, and promote domestic development the emerging country will carefully examine any agreements that prevent attainment of these goals.

The legal niceties that could be used to accomplish such restraints in the U.S. will simply not work in many countries. Licensing agreements in the U.S. are tested on the basis of whether the agreement exceeds the scope of the patent or trademark.[179] But the developing state will reject the international law concept of patents, including the treaties covering patents, on the theory that since the MNCs make enough

---

[176] For example, while there is no *per se* ban on price-fixing in the E.E.C., they have stated that they will examine U.S. concepts, but of course remain free to develop their own solutions as necessary. Imperial Chemical Industries, Ltd. v. Commission des Communautes europeenes, Case No. 48/69, [1971-73 T.B.] Comm. Mkt. Rep. (CCH) ¶ 8161 (1972). The E.E.C. appears to have adopted the U.S. concept of the "effects" doctrine for extraterritorial application of antitrust law. Bequelin Import Co. v. G.I. Import-Export, S.A., Case No. 22/71, [1971-73 T.B.] Comm. Mkt. Rep. ¶ 8149 (1971), but has nothing comparable to the foreign commerce clause of the Sherman Act.

[177] Davidow, "Extraterritorial Application of U.S. Antitrust Law in a Changing World," Antitrust & Trade Reg. Rep. (BNA) No. 769 at D-1 (June 22, 1976).

[178] UNCTAD Rep. TD/B 398 (1972).

[179] International Salt Co. v. United States, 332 U.S. 392 (1947).

money elsewhere, they will not be allowed to use this system to prevent the maximum economic benefit to the LDC.[180]

Another reality of doing business in the many LDCs is the ever-present political instability. A practice acceptable to one government may be highly exploitative in the eyes of a successor government. Special economic arrangements, which may run the gamut from bribes to special training classes, may make an otherwise unacceptable practice suddenly of no concern to the current rulers.

At the risk of oversimplification, it would seem that operations in LDCs should be justified on the basis of how much they benefit the LDC. To say that a given arrangement is "legal" under American antitrust concepts will not be a very compelling argument to a government attempting to maximize every available resource in the development of its economy.

Because of the huge volume of local laws that would be covered if every state's antitrust laws were to be outlined,[181] and because of the constantly changing political and economic situation, this part will concentrate on the antitrust law, of the European Economic Community, and provide a brief summary of antitrust laws in selected countries. As stated before, the best overall advice is to check with local counsel before embarking on any projects in a foreign country.

[2] The Antitrust Laws of the European Economic Community

[a] Article 85 of the Treaty of Rome

In the aftermath of World War II, attempts to unify the European states began with establishment of the Coal and Steel Community in 1951. The success of this treaty, which created a common market for coal and steel by the elimination of tariff barriers, led to the formation of the European Eco-

---

180 *UNCTAD: The Role of the Patent System in the Transfer of Technology to Developing Countries* (1973).

181 For further information *see* B. Hawk, *United States, Common Market and International Antitrust* (1979).

nomic Community (EEC)[182] and European Atomic Energy Community in 1957. The goal of the EEC is to create a single economic system by removal of public trade barriers (tariffs) and private barriers (restrictive agreements). Although many sections of these treaties control trade, as do national "antitrust" laws, emphasis will be placed on Articles 85 and 86 of the 1957 Treaty of Rome as the most important guidelines to European trade.

"Free trade," as advocated in the U.S., is not viewed quite the same way in Europe. The European tradition is strongly protectionist[183] in that each national government has traditionally attempted to protect local industries from foreign competition. Where there were not adequate laws (prior to the EEC), small businesses would bond together in cartels for mutual protection (and mutual benefit. While the Treaty of Rome eliminated many traditional restrictive practices, a new "protectionism" developed,[184] aimed at allowing almost any practice that could be said to further the goal of creating a common market. Certain practices that lessen competition between members may be allowed (on the theory that the agreement strengthens the EEC as a whole), whereas such

---

[182] Treaty Establishing the European Economic Community, done at Rome, March 25, 1957, 298 U.N.T.S. 47. Current members of the EEC are Belgium, France, the Federal Republic of Germany, Greece, Italy, Luxembourg, the Netherlands, Denmark, Great Britain, and Ireland.

[183] The protectionist tendency continues in spite of EEC attempts to eliminate distortions to free competition in Europe. The growing practice of government ownership or subsidization of certain industries has generated complaints from non-subsidized competitors. Article 90 of the Treaty of Rome states that public ventures are subject to Articles 85 and 86, provided the competition rules do not defeat the "particular task assigned" to the public undertakings. With this loophole, it is unclear how far the Commission can go both legally and politically in attempting to control local government distortion of competition. See "An E.E.C. Finger in the State Pie," The Economist 50 (January 20, 1979). Economic problems tend to create more pressure for protectionism. "Let us have no more silly or extreme talk of free trade for the sake of free trade. Let us see what we have to do for our own industry." Michael Walsh, European Parliament Committee on External Economic Relations, Dun's Business Monthly 94 (Oct. 1981).

[184] Wolff and Pugliese, "European Antitrust Law: the Development of Protectionism within the Common Market," 178 The Legal Intelligencer 1 (May 19, 1978).

agreements may be prohibited between outsiders.[184.1]

Article 85[185] prohibits business practices between enterprises that affect trade between member states, with a purpose or effect of preventing, restricting, or distorting competition in the common market, including (but not limited to) price

---

[184.1] Furthermore, strains within the economies of the member states have led to the use of various local barriers to free movement of both goods and people. Lewis, "Common Market After a Quarter Century: An Unworkable Jigsaw Puzzle?" *New York Times* 4 (Feb. 22, 1984); Gelb, "Test of Wills in the Common Market," 67 *The New Leader* 5 (Jan. 9, 1984); Hermann, "Backward Glance at a Year of Protectionism," *Financial Times* 4 (Jan. 9, 1984).

[185] Article 85 states:

"1. The following practices shall be prohibited as incompatible with the Common Market: all agreements between undertakings, all decisions by associations of undertakings and all concerted practices which are liable to affect trade between Member States and which are designed to prevent, restrict or distort competition within the Common Market or which have this effect. This shall, in particular, include:

(a) the direct or indirect fixing of purchase or selling prices or of any other trading conditions;

(b) the limitation or control of production, markets, technical development or investment;

(c) market-sharing or the sharing of sources of supply;

(d) the application of unequal conditions to parties undertaking equivalent engagements in commercial transactions, thereby placing them at a competitive disadvantage;

(e) making the conclusion of a contract subject to the acceptance by the other party to the contract of additional obligations, which, by their nature or according to commercial practice, have no connection with the subject of such contract.

"2. Any agreements or decisions prohibited pursuant to this Article shall automatically be null and void.

"3. The provisions of paragraph 1 may, however, be declared inapplicable in the case of:

—any agreement or type of agreement between undertakings,

—any decision or type of decision by associations of undertakings, and

—any concerted practice or type of concerted practice which helps to improve the production or distribution of goods or to promote technical or economic progress, while allowing consumers a fair share of the resulting profit and which does not:

(a) subject the concerns in question to any restrictions which are not indispensable to the achievement of the above objectives;

(b) enable such concerns to eliminate competition in respect of a substantial part of the goods concerned."

fixing, production limits, market allocation, and tying agreements. Agreements prohibited by the Article are declared
void. Certain otherwise-prohibited practices are allowed, however, if they contribute to improving the production[186] or distribution of goods, promote economic or technical progress,
give benefits to consumers, use only indispensable restrictions,
and do not eliminate competition.

While private suits are theoretically possible to enforce the
Articles, albeit without treble damages, this tactic is not the
preferred method as it is in the U.S.[186.1] The main enforcer is
the Commission of the European Communities ("Commission"), headquartered in Brussels, which has broad powers to
investigate allegations of violations of Articles 85 and 86
brought to it by individuals.[187] Although the Commission can
initiate its own investigations, it usually acts in response to a
complaint. Cease and desist orders can be imposed, and, for
willful or negligent violations, penalties of up to one million

---

[186] The benefits, however, must be on an EEC-wide basis. Attempts by
one member state to bolster a particular industry in that state may violate
Article 85. For example, the Commission was asked to investigate certain
regional development grants by the Belgian government that were made
available to a wallpaper manufacturer. Merritt, "E.E.C. Fair Trading
Probe," *Financial Times* 4 (December 28, 1978).

[186.1] In order to ease the pressure on an overburdened Commission staff,
Competition Commissioner Frans Andriessen urged, in a speech delivered
on Jan. 10, 1984, that private plaintiffs take their claims to national courts.
Although there is great reluctance to initiate this practice, it appears that
France, Great Britain, and Germany already recognize the right of private
parties to recover damages for violations of the Rome Treaty. 46 A.T.R.R.
145 (Jan. 19, 1984).

[187] Concerns over the Commission's practice of not disclosing all of the
evidence it had in its possession, and certain other peculiarities in its conduct
of investigations, led a group of European attorneys to call for an open trial
to replace the current closed investigatory hearings. Hermann, "EEC Competition Policy on Trial," *Financial Times* 10 (March 27, 1980). The Commission has used surprise "raids" on corporate headquarters to obtain
documents without giving the target company the chance to produce them
voluntarily. National Panasonic (UK) v. Comm'n, Case No. 136/79 (1980).
After the uranium cartel cases were begun in the U.S., the U.S. attempted
to obtain certain documents in the U.K. A British court refused to produce
the documents, based on self-incrimination, whereupon the Commission
staff seized all of the documents for its own investigation.

units of account or 10 percent of the previous year's sales can be imposed. The highest fines are sought for export restraints and horizontal restraints such as quotas; there appears to be somewhat more leniency on vertical restraints.

The European Court of Justice in Luxembourg can review Commission decisions, and the Court has the power to increase as well as decrease fines. A private plaintiff may bring an action in a national court (which is empowered to apply Articles 85 and 86) at the same time the matter is being investigated by the Commission.[188]

Four elements must be proven to establish a violation of Article 85: (1) an agreement, (2) between enterprises, (3) that affects trade, and (4) distorts competition in the common market. As with the U.S. antitrust statutes, each key word of Article 85 (and 86) has required judicial interpretation. An "agreement" that violates the Article, need not be in the form of a written contract. Concerted action by the parties involved, or the mere continuance of the effects of a contract that is no longer in force will come under the Article.[189] Both horizontal and vertical agreements are covered.[190]

"Enterprises" (or "undertakings") as it sometimes may be translated) covers all commercial entities that have a degree of independence. Accordingly, the Article would not be applicable to an agreement between a parent and subsidiary where the subsidiary was not independent and the agreement concerned allocation of tasks between the parent and sub-

---

[188] Belgische Radio en Televisie v. SABAM, [1974] C.J. Comm. E., Case No. 127/73, 1974-1 Rec. 51, [1974 T.B.] Comm. Mkt. Rep. (CCH) ¶ 8268.

[189] EMI Records Ltd. v. CBS United Kingdom, Ltd., [1976] C.J. Comm. E. Case No. 51/75, 1976-5 Rep. 811, [1977 T.B.] Comm. Mkt. Rep. (CCH) ¶ 8350.

[190] Grundig-Verkaufs G.m.b.H. & Establissements Consten v. Commission des Communautes europeenes, [1966] C.J. Comm. E. Case Nos. 56/64, 58/64, 12-4 Rec. 429, Comm. Mkt. Rep. (CCH) ¶ 8046. The Commission will strongly oppose horizontal arrangements which restrict competition, even if they do not directly involve exchange of price information. They may, however, allow cartels to operate when an agreement has been notified to the Commission under Art. 85(3). Members of a cartel may be able to get an injunction against price cutters if an agreement has been properly notified. Com. Mkt. Rep. ¶ 8646.

sidiary.[191] In a decision regarding a cancelled broadcast of a LaScala opera, Unitel, which had exclusive contracts with four singers, declined to participate in the Commission's investigation, claiming that singers were not "enterprises," and that the contracts should be exempt since there was no effect on member states. The Commission ruled that artists become enterprises when they perform commercially, and the worldwide broadcast provided sufficient effect on member states to come under the Commission's scrutiny.[192]

The agreement as a whole will be reviewed by the Commission to see if there is an indirect or direct effect on current or future trade. Both goods and services are covered,[193] and, as noted above, this includes operatic concerts and television broadcasts. An agreement that could have some detrimental effect in the future will be illegal, even if there is an immediate beneficial effect.[194] Even if an agreement is confined to one country, if it may affect trade outside of that state, it is within the scope of the Article.[195]

"Competition" is not clearly defined in the Articles, nor in the cases. The change in competitive structure resulting from the elimination of a competitor has been held to "affect" trade

---

[191] Centrafarm B.V. and Adriaan de Peijper v. Sterling Drug, Inc., [1974] C.J. Comm. E. Case No. 15/74, 1974-6 Rep. 1147, [1975 T.B.] Comm. Mkt. Rep. (CCH) ¶ 8246. See Forcione, "Intra-Enterprise Conspiracy under the Antitrust Regulations of the Common Market," 25 Bus. Law. 1419 (1970). Also, an agreement with a sales agent (in contrast to an independent distributor) is not covered by Article 85.

[192] RAI/Unitel, O.J. Comm. E. (No. L157) 39 (June 15, 1978); Comm. Mkt. Rep. (CCH) ¶ 10,054.

[193] Grundig-Verkaufs, supra N. 190. Insurance is also covered. Industrial Fire Insurance, O.J. L80/36 (March 26, 1982); Nuovo Cegan, O.J. C281 (Oct. 18, 1983).

[194] Id. An agreement ancillary to the sale of a business restricting further scientific research by the seller violated Art. 85(1) since the only legitimate object of a non-compete clause is "to secure to the buyer the transfer of the full commercial value of the transferred undertaking." In re Reuter/BASF O.J. No. L/254 at 40 (Sept. 17, 1976), 784 A.T.R.R. A22.

[195] Groupement des Fabricants de Papiers Peints de Belgique v. Commission des Communautes europeenes, [1975] C.J. Comm. E. Case No. 73/74, 1975-8 Rep. 1491, Comm. Mkt. Rep. (CCH) ¶ 8335.

between member states.[196] The Commission has announced that it will not pursue agreements it feels present a *de minimus* distortion of competition, based on market share and value of sales. But the EEC concept of competitive restraints is different from that applied in the U.S., since the Commission actively seeks cooperation between small and medium-sized companies if it will help them compete against larger companies.[197] For example, a sales company operated jointly by French and British firms was granted an exemption from Art. 85(1) since the Commission felt it would aid competition against the dominant Japanese and German manufacturers.[197.1] The main concern seems to be whether the goal of European integration is frustrated by an agreement that limits a party (presumably not a small corporation) to one (or more) states within the EEC. Thus the result is one of encouraging free trade within the EEC, but allowing restrictive agreements between smaller companies, or for ventures outside of the EEC only.

[b]   Article 86

The abuse of economic power by one or more enterprises having a dominant position in a product or geographic market is prohibited by Article 86.[198] To prove a violation of the Arti-

---

[196] I.C.I. & Commercial Solvents Corp. v. Commission, [74 T.B.] Com. Mkt. Rep. ¶ 8209 (E.C.J. 1974).

[197] *E.g.*, specialization agreements. In re Prym-Beka, [73-75 T.B.] Com. Mkt. Rep. ¶ 9609 (Com. 1973).

[197.1] In re Nachet, 42 A.T.R.R. 220 (Jan. 28, 1982). A ten-year joint venture between Iveco and Rockwell to manufacture axels was approved based on technological advances and the benefits to the local economy. 45 A.T.R.R. 284 (Aug. 18, 1983); Com. Mkt. Rep. ¶ 10,509.

[198] Article 86 states:

"Any improper exploitation by one or more undertakings of a dominant position within the Common Market or within a substantial part of it shall be deemed to be incompatible with the Common Market and shall be prohibited, in so far as trade between Member States could be affected by it. The following practices, in particular, shall be deemed to amount to improper exploitation:

cle, one must show (1) a dominant position, (2) in a defined geographic or product market, (3) by one or more enterprises, (4) within the EEC, (5) where such power is abused, and (6) with an effect on trade between member states.[199] Until the last few years there was not much activity under Article 86, but a spate of recent cases have provided some guides as to the limits of acceptable conduct.

"Dominant position" takes into consideration market share, strength of competitors, market behavior, and the overall size of the enterprise. A market share of 30 percent or more is necessary, but market share alone is not conclusive. In *Continental Can*,[200] indices of dominance were the power to behave

(a) the direct or indirect imposition of any unfair purchase or selling prices or of any other unfair trading conditions;

(b) the limitation of production, markets or technical development to the prejudice of consumers;

(c) the application of unequal conditions to parties undertaking equivalent engagements in commercial transactions, thereby placing them at a commercial disadvantage;

(d) making the conclusion of a contract subject to the acceptance by the other party to the contract of additional obligations which by their nature or according to commercial practice have no connection with the subject of such contract."

[199] Abuse in non-member countries may also violate Art. 86. Greenwich Film Production v. SACEM, Comm. Mkt. Rep. (CCH) ¶ 8567 (1980). Carl, "The Common Market Judgments Convention—Its Threat and Challenge to Americans," 8 Int. Law. 446 (1974).

The fine of 50,000 units of account (£20,833) imposed upon Hugin Kassaregister AB by the Commission for abuse of dominant position, O.J. No. L22 (Jan. 27, 1978) at 23, [76-78 T.B.] Comm. Mkt. Rep. (CCH) ¶ 10,007, was overturned by the Court of Justice. Hugin Kassaregister AB v. Comm'n, [1979] C.J. Comm. E. Case No. 22/78, Comm. Mkt. Rep. (CCH) ¶ 8924. Lipton's Cash Registers, Ltd., had complained to the Commission when Hugin had refused to sell it spare parts. The Commission determined that Hugins 12 percent market share in the EEC (13 percent in Britain) was dominant, and the refusal to sell parts, an abuse. However, the Court said that while Hugin's position might be dominant, there was no evidence that Lipton's had ever attempted (or might attempt in the future) to expand its business beyond the U.K. Therefore, there was no effect on intra-community trade. The unit of account is established based on a "basket" of the currencies of the member states. [73-75 T.B.] Com. Mkt. Rep. ¶ 9739.

[200] Continental Can Co. v. Commission des Communautes europeenes, [1973] C.J. Comm. E. Case No. 6/72, 1973-2 Rec. 215, [1971-73 T.B.] Comm. Mkt. Rep. (CCH) ¶¶ 9481, 8171.

9-61

independently of suppliers and competitors, technological predominance, a wide product line, the diverse locations of manufacturing facilities, the availability of necessary production equipment, and access to international money markets to obtain capital. United Brands Corp.[201] had a 40 percent share of the banana market in the EEC, and 45 percent in the geographic market investigated. Although the next largest competitors also had some degree of market power (with shares of 20 percent and 12 percent), UBC was dominant because, in addition to its market share, it had a well-established trademark, sales in all member states, vertical integration, production and marketing strength, ownership of banana transport facilities, and extensive know-how and financial power. Thus, a number of factors will be examined together to see if an enterprise has the power to impede competition, and be considered "dominant."[201.1]

The determination of relevant market is of course closely tied to the question of dominance. The product market has been defined as the market for the identical products, products which are viewed as identical or interchangeable by consumers,[202] or those products which, while not identical, have a certain degree of interchangeability.[203]

While one enterprise alone may violate Article 86 (unlike Article 85), several enterprises, which individually do not have a dominant position, may also violate Article 86 by acting together. Legally independent companies, acting in a group (such as a joint venture or a trade association) to serve the same economic purpose and taking the same market positions, can

---

[201] United Brands Co. v. Commission des Communautes europeenes, [1978] C.J. Comm. E., Case No. 26/76, 1978-2 Rec. 207, Comm. Mkt. Rep. (CCH) ¶ 8429.

[201.1] A joint venture between VW and MAN to produce trucks was allowed since a new product would be created, and the two firms had only a 4.5 percent market share in the E.E.C. 46 A.T.R.R. 144 (Jan. 19, 1984).

[202] Sirena S.R.L. v. Eda G.m.b.H., [1971] C.J. Comm. E. Case No. 40/70, 15 (1971-1) Rec. 309, Comm. Mkt. Rep. (CCH) ¶ 8101.

[203] Where there was some interchangability between simple and composed fertilizers, the two constituted one market. Kali und Salz AG v. Commission des Communautes europeenes, [1975] C.J. Comm. E. Case Nos. 19/74, 20/74, 1975-4 Rep. 499, Comm. Mkt. Rep. (CCH) ¶ 8284.

be viewed as dominant.[204] The members of an oligopolistic market will probably not be automatically treated as dominant unless there is some parallel conduct.[205] Although the activity must take place somewhere within the EEC, operations confined to one member state may be considered a substantial enough part of the EEC to meet the jurisdictional requirements.[206]

Anticompetitive conduct as specifically defined in Article 85 (such as tying contracts), or the erection of other artificial barriers to competition, will constitute the abuse of a dominant position. When a company obtains a position of dominance it becomes subject to higher standards of conduct and certain practices are closed to it that may be available to non-dominant enterprises.[206.1] For example, a refusal to supply products or raw materials by a dominant firm may be an abuse when competition from the customer may be eliminated.[207]

In 1974, the Commission began an investigation of IBM,

---

[204] Deutsche Grammophone G.m.b.H. v. Metro S.B. Grossmarkte G.m.b.H. & Co., [1971] C.J. Comm. E. Case No. 78/70, XVii (1971-5) Rec. 487, Comm. Mkt. Rep. (CCH) ¶ 8106. Subcontracting is covered by specific guidelines, O.J. Comm. E. (C1) 2; Comm. Mkt. Rep. (CCH) ¶ 10,103.

[205] Schlieder, "Recent Developments in the European Community," 31 Rec. Bar Ass'n N.Y.C. 315, 323 (1976); Jones, "A Primer on Production and Dominant Positions under EEC Competition Law," 7 Int. Law. 612 (1973).

[206] Gesellschaft fur musikalische Auffuhrungs ("GEMA"), O.J. Comm. E. (L 134) 15 (June 20, 1971), [1970-72 T.B.] Comm. Mkt. Rep. (CCH) ¶ 9348; Loyrette, "Dominant Size and Merger Under Article 86 of the Rome Treaty," 27 Bus. Law. 531 (1972).

[206.1] Loyalty discounts for exclusive dealing were held to be an abuse of dominant position in the Hoffmann-LaRoche case, 26 C.M.L.R. 211 (1979).

[207] I.C.I. and Commercial Solvents Corp. v. Commission des Communautes europeenes, [1974] C.J. Comm. E. Case Nos. 6/73, 7/73, 1974-3 Rep. 223, [1974 T.B.] Comm. Mkt. Rep. (CCH) ¶ 8209; see also General Motors Continental N.V. v. Commission, No. 26/75, 755 A.T.R.R. A18 (E.C.J. 1976). A "bottleneck monopoly," where companies are denied access to a service may also violate Art. 86. British Telecommunications abused its dominant position by denying access to other companies who wanted to transmit telex messages. O.J. L/360 (Dec. 21, 1982). Similarly, when the only copyright management company in Germany refused to contract with non-resident artists, it was challenged by the Commission. Gessellschaft zur Verwertung [GVL] v. Commission, Case. No. 7/82.

based on complaints from eight competitors.[207.1] Allegations were made that IBM, with between 53 to 60 percent of all mainframe computers in Europe, violated Art. 86 by only selling its components together with its software, which prevented competitors from selling products compatible with IBM products. The Commission sent IBM a letter with a 1000-page statement of objections in December 1980. While it did not request any major structural changes, it did want IBM to separately price the main memory and software, and sell IBM programs to owners of non-IBM equipment. After requesting certain documents from the Commission, IBM filed suit[207.2] in the European Court of Justice, accusing the Commission of failing to consult other commissioners before issuing a "complaint," and that the "complaint" itself was too vague. The Court refused to block the proceeding,[207.3] ruling that while a proceeding under Art. 173 may be brought for a declaration that acts of the Commission are void, a binding legal action is necessary to be reviewable. The 1980 letter was not a decision, and therefore there was no need for evaluation of substantive issues.

The defensive registration of a trademark by a dominant firm may be a violation of Art. 85 or 86 when the firm knows or should have known that the mark is being used by a competitor.[207.4] Price discrimination may be evidence of abuse where it is significant and cannot be justified on "objective" grounds.[208] As of 1973, a merger or acquisition (called a "concentration" in the EEC) will be an abuse of power if it actually or potentially eliminates competition.[209]

[207.1] *See* Business Week 104D (Jan. 26, 1981).

[207.2] Case No. 60/81, Comm. Mkt. Rep. ¶ 10,303.

[207.3] Comm. Mkt. Rep. ¶ 8708 (Nov. 11, 1981).

[207.4] Osram, G.m.b.H., 42 A.T.R.R. 228 (Jan. 28, 1982).

[208] Deutsche Grammophone, *supra* N. 204; United Brands, *supra* N. 201. Prices in excess of product cost do not necessarily indicate an abuse of a dominant position, since a corporation may have the right to recoup research and development costs. Comm. Mkt. Rep. ¶ 10,236.

[209] European Ballage Corp. v. Commission des Communautes europeenes, [1973] C.J. Comm. E. Case No. 6/72, 1973-2 Rec. 215, Comm. Mkt. Rep. (CCH) ¶ 8209.

[c] Licensing of Industrial Property Rights

This section is intended as an introduction to the antitrust considerations surrounding the exploitation of intellectual property rights (which include patents, trademarks, copyrights, and know-how). A complete business and legal guide to intellectual property ("IP") is given elsewhere in the volume.

Until recently, licensing agreements were used as a legal method to assign exclusive territories to various licensees, and keep out competing goods from other licensees. Since IP rights were created by each member state, local laws would allow exclusion of goods manufactured under a patent in another country that would infringe the local licensee's patent rights. Realizing that continuance of this practice would defeat the overriding purpose of integrating Europe into one market, the EEC set out to eliminate these agreements by vigorously enforcing Articles 85, 86, 30-36, and 222[210] (where appropriate), and by the drafting of a new EEC Patent Convention,[211] that allows patented goods to flow into any country, once marketed in one country.

Even prior to the new patent treaty, the principle had emerged that trademarks could not be used to divide the EEC into different markets regardless of local law. In *Sirena S.r.l.v. Eda G.m.b.H.*,[212] it was held that a trademark owner or licensee cannot block the importation of an item with the same trademark if the manufacturer had the right to use the mark in the country where it was produced.[212.1] Sirena was given an

---

[210] Articles 30-36 eliminate quantitative restrictions on imports and exports between E.E.C. member states. *See* Comm. Mkt. Rep. (CCH) ¶¶ 321-352. Article 222 makes it clear that each state's system of property ownership is not affected by the treaty. *See* Comm. Mkt. Rep. (CCH) ¶ 5261. *See* Callman, "The Law of Unfair Competition in the Member States of the European Economic Community," 7 Int. Law. 855 (1973); Jones, "Fundamentals of International Licensing Agreements & Their Application in the European Community," 7 Int. Law. 78 (1973).

[211] Convention on the Grant of European Patents, Oct. 5, 1973, Comm. Mkt. Rep. (CCH) ¶ 5503.

[212] *Supra* N. 202.

[212.1] Similarly, *see* Van Zuylen Freres v. Hag A.G. [74 T.B.] Comm. Mkt. Rep. ¶ 8230 (E.C.J. 1974); Advocaat Zwarte Kip [73-75 T.B.] Comm. Mkt. Rep. ¶ 9669 (Comm. 1974); Sirdar-Phildar [74-75 T.B.] Comm. Mkt. Rep. ¶

exclusive trademark license for Italy, while Eda had the exclusive license for Germany from the same U.S. company. Eda attempted to sell the product in Italy, and was challenged by Sirena in the Italian court, which referred the matter to the Commission. The Commission determined that trademark licenses should be approached on a "rule of reason" basis, by examining all of the facts surrounding the agreement, such as whether consumers will be misled. However, attempts to isolate national markets through the use of a trademark license will not be allowed.

In spite of this holding it may still be possible for a trademark owner to bar the importation into the EEC of trademarked products that have their origin outside of the EEC.[213] Similar rules regarding the exhaustion of patent rights were applied in the *Centrafarm* case.[214]

Although naked attempts to carve out exclusive markets within the EEC will be difficult, some ancillary restraints are possible. One starts from the proposition that under Article 85 an exclusive license is not a *per se* violation, and the possession of monopoly IP rights is not a *per se* violation of Article 86. Yet, these rights can be the basis for violations of both articles if improperly applied.[215]

In its Official Notice on Patent Licensing Agreements,[216] and in some subsequent cases,[217] the Commission specifically

---

9741 (Comm. 1975); Commission v. Pfizer, Inc., Case No. 1/81 (E.C.J. Dec. 3, 1981).

[213] EMI Records Ltd. v. CBS United Kingdom, Ltd., *supra* N. 189.

[214] Centrafarm B.V. and Adriaan de Peijper v. Sterling Drug, Inc., *supra* N. 191.

[215] Davidson/Happich, O.J. Eur. Comm. (No. L143) 31 (June 23, 1972), Comm. Mkt. Rep. (CCH) ¶ 9512; Kabel und Metallwerk/Luchaire, O.J. Eur. Comm. (No. L222) 34 (July 24, 1975), [1973-75 T.B.] Comm. Mkt. Rep. (CCH) ¶ 9761.

[216] Official Notice on Patent Licensing Agreements, O.J. Comm. E, (No. 139) 2922 (Dec. 24, 1962), Comm. Mkt. Rep. (CCH) ¶ 2698 (1962). Regarding proposed changes, *see* Handler & Blechman, "An American View of the Common Market's Proposed Group Exemption for Patent Licenses," 14 Int. Law. 403 (1980), and 995 A.T.R.R. A7 (Jan. 1, 1981).

[217] Burroughs/Geha, O.J. Eur. Comm. (L13) 53, [1970-72 T.B.] Comm. Mkt. Rep. (CCH) ¶ 9512 (Dec. 22, 1971); Burroughs/Deplanque, O.J. Comm. E. (L13) 50, [1970-72 T.B.] Comm. Mkt. Rep. (CCH) ¶ 9485; Davidson/

allowed the imposition of the following ancillary restraints in non-exclusive licenses: (1) prohibition on sublicenses, (2) confidentiality of know-how, (3) minimum quantity to meet demand, (4) quality standards, (5) use of trademark to show origin, (6) arbitration clauses, (7) minimum royalties, (8) nonexclusive grant-backs of improvements.

Conversely, certain ancillary restraints are probably illegal, including: (1) prohibitions on contesting the validity of the licensor's patents, (2) extension of agreements and royalty payments beyond patent expiration,[218] (3) non-competition clauses, (4) tying clauses, except where a necessary part of the license, (5) restrictions on price or maximum quantity produced, (6) unreasonable export prohibitions, (7) exclusive grant-back clauses, (8) excessive secrecy periods for know-how.[218.1] To violate the articles, there must be more than a *de minimus* likelihood that the restraint will affect competition in the EEC.[219] The proposed revision to the licensing regulation would relieve parties from the requirement of notifying the Commission in advance. Agreements would be entitled to automatic exemptions even if they included such restraints as national exclusivity clauses for manufacturing, field-of-use clauses, and restraints on sublicenses. However, export bans would not be allowed if either party's sales were over 100 million units of account. Volume restrictions, post-expiration royalties, and price controls would make the agreement ineligible for the block exemption.[220]

Happich, *supra* N. 215; Raymond/Nagoya, O.J. Comm. E. (L143) 39, Comm. Mkt. Rep. (CCH) ¶ 9513 (June 23, 1972).

[218] In AOIP/Beyrard, O.J. Comm. E. (No. L6) 8 (Dec. 18, 1975), [1976-78] Comm. Mkt. Rep. (CCH) ¶ 9801, the license had no time limit, and could be unilaterally extended with improvement patents. This would have forced the licensee to pay royalties even though his competitors could produce essentially the same product without paying royalties. *See also* Comm. Mkt. Rep. (CCH) ¶ 10,224.

[218.1] An excessively long license may be objectionable. Linde A.G., Comm. Mkt. Rep. ¶ 10,321.

[219] Raymond/Nagoya, *supra* N. 217.

[220] Draft Regulation on Patent Licensing Agreements, O.J. Comm. E. (L58) (March 3, 1979), Comm. Mkt. Rep. Euromarket News (CCH) 2 (March 26, 1979); Comm. Mkt. Rep. (CCH) ¶ 10,118. When the new regulations finally take effect, they will replace the Notice on Patent Licensing Agree-

Examples of the Commission's view of license restraints were provided by three 1978 decisions.[221] In the first case, the "Persil" detergent trademark was owned by Unilever in England and France, and by Henkel elsewhere. Each agreed not to contest the other's mark. Unilever, however, sold Persil at lower prices, and this disturbed Henkel, so the parties worked out an agreement to limit competition. A distributor complained about this unfair restraint on the free movement of goods, and the problem was solved by packaging the Henkel-Persil in red and the Unilever-Persil in green, without the distribution restraints.

In the second case, the owners of the "Campari" trademarks executed license agreements that contained quality control provisions and a prohibition against selling competing products outside of allotted territories. This agreement was allowed since it was found to serve legitimate ends, and did not unduly restrict trade in the EEC.[222]

The final case involved the "Penneys" trademark claimed by both Penneys, Ltd., a Dublin textile manufacturer, and J.C. Penney, Inc., the U.S. department store chain. The Commission approved a 1976 agreement allowing both companies to use the mark, since this was the least restrictive alternative, and the free movement of goods in the Community was not hampered. These considerations apparently outweighed the risk of the possibility of consumer confusion.

---

ments. In the case of Windsurfing International, Inc., 45 A.T.R.R. 393, Comm. Mkt. Rep. ¶ 10,515, O.J. No/L229 (Aug. 20, 1983), a manufacturer attempted to control marketing of its products by prohibiting attachment of patented rigging to other manufacturers' sailboards. No sales of spare rigging parts separate from the board was allowed, and license fees were collected based on the price of the entire board. A fine of 50,000 ECUs was imposed for the attempt to use the limited patents to restrain sales of the entire product.

[221] Information Memo. from Commission No. p-17 (Feb. 1978); Comm. Mkt. Rep. (CCH) ¶ 10,026.

[222] Reg. 67/67, O.J. Comm. E. (57) 849 (March 25, 1967), Comm. Mkt. Rep. (CCH) ¶ 2727.

[d]   Distribution

A company that wishes to sell its goods in the E.E.C. has the
choice of using a direct sales network, employing a distributor,
or licensing its technology to allow others to make and sell the
goods.[222.1] A manufacturer who uses a sales agent (as distinguished from an independent distributor)[223] can impose certain restrictions without violating Article 85(1) regarding
agreements between enterprises. However, the Article may
be violated when a number of sellers use a common sales
agency that sells at a uniform price,[224] unless adequate justifications can be adduced.[224.1] Restrictions in distribution agreements may be approved by the Commission if only export sales
are involved,[225] or if they take place in only one state and are
not likely to affect trade between member states.[226]

Although it is generally said that, given the exemptions of
Article 85(3), there are probably no *per se* rules in the EEC, the
Commission laid down some rather tough rules against restrictive distributorship agreements in the *Grundig-Consten*
case.[227] Grundig appointed Consten as its exclusive distributor
in France, with an exclusive trademark license. Consten was

[222.1] Jones, "Practical Aspects of Commercial Agency & Distribution
Agreements in the European Community," 25 Bus. Law. 543 (1972); Chard,
"The Economics of Exclusive Distribution Arrangements with Special Refer-
ence to E.E.C. Competition Policy," 22 A.T. Bull. 405 (1980).

[223] *Id.* In the EEC, an agent acts as an auxiliary of its principal, bears no
economic risk and is generally paid a percentage commission. A distributor
is an independent enterprise that buys goods for its own account and makes
a profit based on sales.

[224] Kali and Salz AG, *supra* N. 203; *Floral, GmbH,* Comm. Mkt. Rep.
(CCH) ¶ 10,184 (Dec. 1979).

[224.1] Negative clearance granted for formation of joint distribution companies. S.H.V.-Chevron [73-75 T.B.] Comm. Mkt. Rep. ¶ 9709; Rank-Sopo-
lem [73-75 T.B.] Comm. Mkt. Rep. ¶ 9707.

[225] SAFCO, O.J. Comm. E. (L13) 44 (Jan. 7, 1972), [1970-72 T.B.] Comm.
Mkt. Rep. (CCH) ¶ 9487. The Commission approved the standard distribution agreement used by Robert Krups which contained some restrictions it
felt were reasonable. Comm. Mkt. Rep. (CCH) ¶ 10,223. But, a ban on
exports from one member country to another will be a violation. Comm.
Mkt. Rep. ¶ 10,352.

[226] Article 85 (1), *supra* N. 185.

[227] Grundig-Consten, *supra* N. 190. *See also* 80 Harv. L. Rev. 1594 (1967).

prohibited from exporting, as were all other Grundig distributors, from their respective countries. Imports into France would violate the trademark license held by Consten. The Court of Justice ruled that the agreement violated Article 85 by restricting competition and therefore frustrating the purpose of the EEC: economic integration. The trademark license (of the mark "GINT") only served to limit trade and not to indicate product quality, since the mark "Grundig" was already affixed to the goods. Even though the agreements admittedly increased trade in the items, the Court ruled that a violation occurred where there was proof of intent to restrict competition.

Although it was at first thought that *Grundig-Consten* prohibited all exclusive distributorships, later cases relaxed the rule. Each agreement must be evaluated on its merits, and consideration will be given to the nature of the product, the quantity involved, the restrictions imposed, the size and strength of the parties,[227.1] and whether one contract or a series are involved.[228] Also, Regulation 67/67[229] granted a block exemption to certain exclusive distributorships, so long as the

---

[227.1] NBIM (Michelin's Dutch subsidiary) was fined 680,000 ECUs by the Commission for abuse of its dominant position. A bonus (rebate) system tended to discourage dealers from using competing manufacturers and kept newcomers from entering the market. Comm. Mkt. Rep. ¶ 10,340. Johnson & Johnson was fined 200,000 ECUs for prohibition of exports. Comm. Mkt. Rep. ¶ 10,277.

[228] Maschinenbau/Ulm, Case No. 55/65, XII (4) Rec. 337, [1961-66 T.B.] Comm. Mkt. Rep. (CCH) ¶ 8047.

[229] *Supra* N. 222. The Regulation is scheduled to expire at the end of 1982, and a new draft should encourage parallel imports. Comm. Mkt. Rep. ¶ 10,314. The Commission fined Kawasaki (U.K.) $130,000 for prohibiting its dealers from exporting motorcycles to other EEC countries. The Commission confirmed that there was a high variance in price from country to country, which was the original cause for a consumer, Mrs. Mary Putz, to initiate the investigation. When Mrs. Putz discovered that prices in the U.K. were 30 percent less than in Belgium (her home), she travelled to the U.K., only to find the dealers refusing to sell her a motorcycle for export. "On Your Bike," The Economist 106 (Dec. 16, 1978). A similar housewives' protest in Japan against the high prices of televisions led to Japanese government intervention, and the reduction of prices. Thompson, "Antitrust and the Multinational Corporation: Competition or Cartels," 8 Int. Law. 618 (1974).

agreement allowed parallel imports or re-exports.[229.1] The Court of Justice has refused to set down rigid rules to evaluate franchises or selective distribution cases, and has shown a willingness to defer to national courts based on the impact to the local economy.[229.2]

New regulations to replace 67/67 took effect on July 1, 1983.[292.3] Under Regulation 1983/83, manufacturers may grant exclusive territories to distributors, but the Commission will scrutinize agreements between competitors, except small firms. In order to guarantee price competition, the agreements should allow for parallel imports. The restrictions allowed under 67/67 are continued under 1983/83 if they are "generally speaking indispensible if improvement in the distribution of goods sought through the exclusive distribution is to be obtained." Exclusive purchasing agreements, covered under Regulation 1984/83, may foreclose competing sellers, and are thus limited to five years, except for gas stations and pubs. A decided preference was expressed for objective criteria by which to judge distributors, and a refusal to supply a long-standing distributor will be suspect.[292.4]

Resale price maintenance will generally not be attacked by the Commission if it occurs only in one state. However, if such an agreement has the effect of affecting trade between member states, Article 85 will be violated.[230] Even if no specific agreement is involved, concerted practices may be evidence of prohibited conduct. In *I.C.I. and Commercial Solvents,*[231] increases in the price of dyes throughout the EEC on the same

---

[229.1] *See, e.g.*, Public Prosecutor v. Dassonville, [75 T.B.] Comm. Mkt. Rep. ¶ 8276 (E.C.J. 1974); Van Vliet v. Fratelli Dalle Grode [75 T.B.] Comm. Mkt. Rep. ¶ 8314 (E.C.J. 1975).

[229.2] S.A. Lancome v. Etos B.V., Case No. 99/79, Comm. Mkt. Rep. ¶ 8714 (1981); Anne Marty S.A. v. Estee Lauder, S.A., Case No. 33/79, Comm. Mkt. Rep. ¶ 8713 (1981); Comm. Mkt. Rep. ¶¶ 10,235-10,236.

[292.3] Comm. Mkt. Rep. ¶ 10,496.

[292.4] Ferrier, "Exclusive Dealing Agreements in View of the New E.E.C. Regulations," Int. Bus. Law. 33 (Jan. 1984).

[230] Deutsche Philips G.m.b.H., O.J. Comm. E. (L293) 40, [1973-75 T.B.] Comm. Mkt. Rep. (CCH) ¶ 9606.

[231] I.C.I. and Commercial Solvents Corp., *supra* N. 207.

day provided the impetus for the Commission to pierce corporate veils and attribute the actions of subsidiaries to the parent.

Special product requirements may allow for more restrictive distribution arrangements. BMW[232] appointed wholesalers for its vehicles, with responsibility for an assigned territory. The wholesalers in turn appointed retailers, subject to approval by BMW. Both the wholesalers and the retailers were obligated not to sell BMWs to anyone other than private customers or other authorized dealers. The Commission accepted BMW's argument that the restrictions were necessary since an automobile is a complex item needing repair, the quality of service must be high, and close ties between the manufacturer and dealers help assure consistent service. The BMW agreement, while not applicable to all complex distribution systems, has been used as a pattern by others, and will probably be acceptable to the Commission.[233]

An enterprise without a dominant position is free to choose its customers or to refuse to deal under EEC law.[234] A problem

---

[232] Bayerische Motoren Werke, A.G., O.J. Comm. E. (L29) 1 (Dec. 17, 1974), [1973-75 T.B.] Comm. Mkt. Rep. (CCH) ¶¶ 9701, 9617. BMW's Belgium subsidiary and dealers lost their appeal to the Court of Justice which attempted to overturn a decision of the Commission finding a violation of Art. 85. The dealers and BMW Belgium had agreed to prevent re-export of the cars out of Belgium, which had been occurring due to the price differential. Even though some of the dealers may have been unaware that they violated the law, the Court found this assertion not to be a defense to the charge. The fines ranged from 150,000 UA (BMW Belgium) to 1000 UA (individual dealers). BMW Belgium, S.A. v. Commission, Case Nos. 32/78, 36-82/78, Comm. Mkt. Rep. (CCH) ¶ 10,008 (E.C.J. July 12, 1979); ¶ 8548 (E.C.J. 1980). The restraints on sales of Hasseblad cameras, and the discriminatory service polices based on whether the cameras were purchased at a discount, were a violation, and fines of over $700,000 were imposed. Comm. Mkt. Rep. ¶ 10,356; 42 A.T.R.R. 227 (Jan. 28, 1982).

[233] Omega Louis Brandt et Freres, S.A., O.J. Comm. E., (L242) 22 (Oct. 30, 1970). [1970-72 T.B.] Comm. Mkt. Rep. (CCH) ¶¶ 9346, 9396; Parfums Marcel Rochas Vertriebs v. Bitsch, [1970] C.J. Comm. E. Case No. 1/70, XVI Rec. 515, [1971-73 T.B.] Comm. Mkt. Rep. (CCH) ¶ 8102.

[234] Some national laws, such as France, limit these rights. If the Commission does not grant a form negative clearance or exemption, a restrictive distribution agreement on which it takes no action may be challenged in local courts. Bruno Giry and Guerlain S.A., Case Nos. 253/78, 3/79, Comm. Mkt. Rep. ¶ 8712 (E.C.J. 1981); Anne Marty S.A., *supra* N. 229.2

might arise, as it would under United States law, if the decision to accept or reject a dealer was made after consultation with other dealers.[235] Thus, the safest course would be to choose dealers based on uniform objective quality criteria which are necessary to adequate distribution and are applied without discrimination to all interested parties. In the *SABA*[236] case, the nature of the product (electronic components) was examined to see if all of the conditions were necessary. It was determined that the requirement of the maintenance of a six-month inventory was not justified by the needs of adequate distribution, but the agreement would get an exemption. When the agreements were reviewed again in 1983, they were again granted an exemption based on the need for technically sophisticated products to have a specialized retail network. The Commission did require SABA to establish objective criteria for accepting or terminating dealers, and to decide on applications within a four-week period.[236.1]

The Commission has scrutinized manufacturers who have established networks of exclusive dealerships, but to the extent the products require special treatment, exemptions under Article 85(3) may be possible.[237] The factors to be considered, which must be applied on an objective basis, include: (1) a high quality and expensive product; (2) limited number of potential customers; (3) flexibility for local preferences; (4) service and warranty programs; (5) dealers with technical skill;[237.1] (6) cooperation between manufacturer and dealer; and (7) a contract designed to improve the efficiency of distribution and pass to consumers their fair share of benefits. It is fairly clear now that the Commission is more kindly disposed to firms that show a degree of willingness to modify their agreements ac-

---

[235] Schlieder, *supra* N. 205 at 320.

[236] SABA, O.J. Comm E. (L28) 19 (Dec. 18, 1975), [1976-78 T.B.] Comm. Mkt. Rep. (CCH) ¶ 9802.

[236.1] 46 A.T.R.R. 206 (Feb. 2, 1984); Comm. Mkt. Rep. ¶ 10,487; O.J. C/140 (May 28, 1983).

[237] Kodak, O.J. Comm. E. (L147) 24, [1970-72 T.B.) Comm. Mkt. Rep. (CCH) ¶ 9378. Regulations were proposed to exempt auto distribution and service contracts from the competition laws. Comm. Mkt. Rep. ¶ 10,493.

[237.1] Metro S.B.-Grossmarkte, Comm. Mkt. Rep. ¶ 8435; L'Oreal v. De Nieuwe A.M.C.K., Case No. 31/80. Comm. Mkt. Rep. ¶ 8715 (E.C.J. 1982).

cording to the Commission's suggestions.[238]

[e]   Imports, Exports and the Free Movement of Goods

As noted previously, the underlying goal of EEC competition policy is the economic integration of the member states. The Commission's emphasis, therefore, is on eliminating restrictive practices that hinder the free movement of goods between member states.[239] The free movement concept pervades all other aspects of the Commission's policy, and although the Articles make reference to an "affect competition" test (which sounds similar to the U.S. jurisdictional requirement), free movement of goods is actually the test. In this respect, the Commission is as concerned with the restraints imposed by member states that hinder free movement as they are with private agreements that have a similar effect.[239.1]

---

[238] For example, in reviewing the agreement the jewelry firm Murat planned to use with retailers, the Commission approval required the removal of an antibootlegging agreement (i.e., a prohibition of resale to unapproved retailers). The revised version allowed sales to retailers who met specified objective criteria. 46 A.T.R.R. 144 (Jan. 19, 1984).

[239] Grundig/Consten, *supra* N. 190; Vereeniging von Cementhandelaren v. Commission des Communautes europeenes, [1972] C.J. Comm. E. Case No. 8/72, XVIII (1972-6) Rec. 977, [1971-73 T.B.] Comm. Mkt. Rep. (CCH) ¶ 8179.

[239.1] Article 30 of the Treaty of Rome bars import quotas or national laws having a similar effect. When local provisions obstruct the free movement of goods, they will be overturned. A special committee has been formed to investigate the use of "technical barriers" (usually dealing with health or safety) to protect domestic industries from competition. *See e.g.*, Herbert Gilli, Case No. 788-79, Comm. Mkt. Rep. ¶ 8683, on Italian restrictions on imported vinegar. The European Court of Justice ruled that Dutch and German regulations regarding the alcohol content and labeling of imported beverages may not be used to prevent imports. Barriers to intra-EEC trade are allowable, according to the Court, only if they are absolutely necessary. C.J. Comm. E., Case No. 120/78 (1979); Case No. 27/80 (1982); Comm. Mkt. Rep. ¶¶ 8543, 8688, 8602, 8721, 10,342. Attempts to restrain customers from traveling within the E.E.C. to purchase an automobile where it is cheapest have generated an investigation from the Commission. "Two Victories for Cheaper Cars," The Economist 37 (Oct. 24, 1981); Comm. Mkt. Rep. ¶ 10,361; *see also* the discussion on pricing in the EEC at § 9.03[2][g], *infra*.

Member states, for example, have been asked to stop using "certificates of origin" for goods moving within the E.E.C., where the certificates were used to block the free movement of goods.[239.2]

Further evidence of the difference of the free movement test from the U.S. competition test can be found in EEC treatment of the "butter ships." In order to aid farming and unify prices, EEC regulations increased certain food prices in some states. At the same time, to stimulate exports, a subsidy for some foodstuff exports was granted. To avoid the high prices at home, as many as 130 ships, mostly based in North German ports, would sail into international waters where they would sell their butter and meat, and then return the shoppers and their purchases home. Numerous regulations to curtail this practice were attempted, and the E.C.J. ruled that the exemptions from the EEC pricing controls would not apply where the international travel to purchase goods was "purely symbolic."[239.3]

In the *Centrafarm*[240] decision, Sterling Drug had parallel patents for the drug "Negram" in England and Holland.[240.1] Negram sold at a low price in England (where prices were controlled by the government), and a private firm bought the drug there and resold it in Holland for less than Sterling charged. Sterling complained of patent and trademark infringement, but the Commission held that (1) Sterling had

---

[239.2] Comm. Mkt. Rep. ¶ 10,344.

[239.3] Downay, "EEC Court Rules Against Butter Ships," *Fin. Times* 18 (Feb. 15, 1984); "Rules for the Bending," The Economist 50 (Feb. 18, 1984). The Commission attacked the sixteenth century German law that, by forbidding the consumption of beer that contained anything but water, hops, malt and yeast, had prohibited the importation of beer from other countries that contained preservatives. Yerkey, "European Court to Strike Down German Beer Restraints," 51 Advertising Age 1 (Jan. 23, 1984). The refusal of Ford Werke A.G. to supply its German dealers with right-hand drive cars (for export to England) was challenged when Ford applied for an exemption for its distribution system. The Commission believed that the possibility of parallel imports from Germany was an important factor in promoting competition in England. 46 A.T.R.R. 93 (Jan. 12, 1984).

[240] Centrafarm, *supra* N. 191.

[240.1] Art. 36 of the Rome Treaty allows certain restraints to protect intellectual property rights.

exhausted its IP rights by marketing the product in England, and (2) enforcement of Sterling claims would be contrary to encouraging free movement of goods as provided by Articles 30-36.

Similarly, in *Merck & Co., Inc. v. Stephan B. V.*[240.2] the E.C.J. ruled that a patent holder cannot block the importation of low-priced goods when the product was originally marketed by the proprietor of the patent.

Agreements that have an indirect or potential effect of hindering the free movement of goods are examined under a "rule of reason" test, with an analysis based on the facts surrounding each such agreement.[241] Some restraints may cross national boundaries, but be excused on the basis of their *de minimus* effect on the EEC as a whole.[242]

Agreements dealing only with exports or trade entirely outside of the EEC are not covered by Article 85,[243] since there is presumably no effect on trade between member states.[244] In general terms, an express provision against reexports, or sales back into the EEC (assuming that the free movement of goods within the EEC is not otherwise affected), may still be acceptable.[245]

The Commission's position is somewhat more aggressive regarding agreements that restrict imports into the EEC. In this area, Article 85 may be applied to conduct outside of the EEC if there are effects within the EEC, and foreign firms will be held liable for the actions of their subsidiaries in the EEC.[246] It would probably be fair to expect the Commission to expand its "effects" approach in the future to cover more restraints

---

[240.2] Case No. 187/80, Comm. Mkt. Rep. ¶ 8707 (1981).

[241] American Bar Association, Antitrust Law Developments 383 (1975). For example, a royalty organization could not demand that importers of records into Germany make up the difference between the royalty paid elsewhere and the rate charged in Germany. GEMA, Case Nos. 55,57/80, Comm. Mkt. Rep. ¶ 8246 (Jan. 20, 1981).

[242] Volk v. Ets. T. Vervaecke, s.p.r.l., [1969] C.J. Comm. E. Case No. 5/69, XV (1969-4) Rec. 295, [1967-70 T.B.] Comm. Mkt. Rep. (CCH) ¶ 8074.

[243] Kodak, *supra* N. 237; Omega, *supra* N. 233; BMW, *supra* N. 232.

[244] Kabelmetal/Luchaire, *supra* N. 215.

[245] Raymond/Nagoya, *supra* N. 217.

[246] Imperial Chemical Industries, Ltd., *supra* N. 246.

that are normally imposed outside the EEC, so that any foreign agreements that does somehow affect the free movement of goods in the community will not escape on a "technicality." As in the U.S., duties may be imposed on goods that are "dumped" into the EEC.[247]

[f] Mergers and Acquisitions

EEC merger law can still be summed-up by reference to one case, *Continental Can.*[248] Before the case is examined, mention should be made of Article 66 of the Coal and Steel Treaty,[249] which encourages mergers among coal and steel producers. This policy of merger encouragement by the Commission, which is also applied in certain other industries, is part of the Commission policy of rationalizing the EEC economic structure by eliminating overcapacity.[250] The Commission is

---

[247] Reg. 459/68 (OJ 1979 No. L 196/1); Reg. 1681/79, Euromarket News (CCH) at 2 (Aug. 14, 1979); Toyo Bearing Co., Ltd., No. 113/77, Comm. Mkt. Rep. ¶ 8574 (1980). An antidumpting duty was imposed on certain U.S.-made synthetic fibers, on the theory that government controls on the price of crude oil in the U.S. kept the export price of the fibers below what would otherwise have been the fair market value. O.J. No. L.114 at 37 (May 3, 1980), however, the Commission would not authorize formation of a cartel, purportedly in response to pressures from imports, to exchange price or product information. Comm. Mkt. Rep. ¶ 10,234. Regulations on antidumping and countervailing duties for the U.S. and the EEC are reprinted at 19 Int. Leg. Mat. 429 (1980).

[248] Continental Can, *supra* N. 200. Although discussions regarding the promulgation of a merger control statute have continued since 1973, the EEC Council has been unable to agree on its terms. Comm. Mkt. Rep. (CCH) ¶ 10,178 (Dec. 1979). "While national trustbusters in the UK and Germany go softly, softly, the Commission's project of a European merger control is now more than 'pie in the sky.'" Hermann, *supra* N. 184.1

[249] Treaty establishing the European Coal and Steel Community, done at Paris, April 18, 1951, Comm. Mkt. Rep. (CCH) ¶ 101.35. For example, the plan of three Italian companies to set-up a joint undertaking to lease a bankrupt steel plant was approved by the Commission. 1042 A.T.R.R. A14 (Dec. 3, 1981).

[250] The Commission approved the merger between Peugeot-Citroen and Chrysler Europe, noting no violation of Art. 86, and determining that the merger was in keeping with EEC policies to eliminate redundancy in European industry, and increase the ability to compete with Japanese manufac-

concerned with restraints on trade that may occur in the course of a divestiture, and has acted to limit the time period of noncompetition clauses. Although it was believed that Art. 85(1) would not apply to these clauses based on the Reuter/ BASF decision in 1976,[251] the Commission revised the terms of the sale of the Luycks division by the Dutch company Nutricia. Considering such factors as whether a transfer of goodwill or a trademark license was involved, a four-year period may be the maximum, and the geographic territory covered may be limited to only the actual market the company operated in at the time of the sale.[252]

However, the situation is different when a dominant firm (not in the coal or steel industry) makes an acquisition, or when a merger will create a dominant firm. The action against Continental Can was the first time the EEC had asserted that it had authority under Article 86 to attack acquisitions, and its position (with some qualification) was sustained in the Court of Justice.

Continental Can, which is the largest can manufacturer in the world (it ranks second in the U.S.) began the process by acquiring a German firm (based in Brunswick) that had 70 percent of the market for metal cans for meat and fish. Continental then attempted to buy the shares of the largest Benelux can company through a public tender offer. The Commission announced that the acquisition would violate Article 86, but Continental Can went ahead. The next day the Commission issued its complaint charging that the acquisition, by itself, was an abuse of dominant position. No other abusive behavior was charged.

The Commission ruled against Continental Can on this theory and was partially sustained by the Court of Justice. The Court agreed that the acquisition would have been abusive exploitation had Continental Can been in a dominant position, but the Commission had used the wrong relevant market. Although Continental Can may have had 80 percent of the

turers. O.J. Comm. E. (C5), Written Question No. 567/78 (Jan. 8, 1979), Comm. Mkt. Rep. (CCH) ¶ 10,106.

[251] *Supra*, N. 194.

[252] 46 A.T.R.R. 205 (Feb. 2, 1984); O.J. No. L. 376/22 (Dec. 31, 1983).

meat and fish container market, cans are cans, and Continental Can's overall market share of 20 percent was not enough to constitute a dominant position.

In the aftermath of this decision, Commission officials began work on merger regulations that would define the criteria for acceptable regulations. After a long gestation period, various drafts were issued that would require companies with annual sales in excess of one billion ECUs to provide advance notice to the Commission of their merger plans. Pre-notification would be optional if the combined sales are between 750 million and 1 billion ECUs. If the combined sales would be less than 750 million ECUs, or less than 20 percent of the EEC or a "substantial part," no notification would be necessary. The Commission could block the consummation of mergers if an enterprise would obtain or reinforce a position of market dominance which hampers effective competition in the EEC or a substantial part of it.

Even though the proposed threshhold may offer an element of certainty heretofore lacking, local laws still provide the greatest obstacle to mergers in Europe, particularly when one party is a foreign corporation. In any event, the proposed rules were met with a less than enthusiastic response, and, as of this writing have not been adopted.

The Commission has also proposed rules that would allow for joint ventures to conduct research and development projects. A blanket exemption would be granted for certain ventures, but for agreements involving two of the top three firms in an industry, or if the parties have combined sales over 500 million ECU, approval must be sought. Since approvals that were sought in the past were subject to lengthy delays, an expedited procedure will now be followed.[252.1]

[g] **Pricing**

While there is no specific price discrimination statute in

[252.1] O.J. Comm. E. (Jan. 21, 1984).

Europe similar to the Robinson Patman Act in the U.S.,[253] the Commission has asserted broad powers in this area, including the right to regulate prices where necessary.[254] The Commission kept all of its options open in early cases, by holding that different prices in different member states for the same item could be evidence of restrictive practices,[255] at the same time it held that identical prices for the same item could also be evidence of concerted activity.[256] The retail prices of some items (such as automobiles) vary widely with the EEC, but the Commission for many years paid little attention to this area.[257] However, unfair pricing practices seem to make the Commission more willing to start an Art. 86 proceeding against corporations who otherwise do not seem to be dominant.[258]

A 1949 agreement that fixed the resale prices for books sold in Belgium and the Netherlands was challenged by the Commission. Although this practice was defended on the basis of allowing greater freedom of expression, and the prevention of loss leaders, the ECJ was not persuaded. Even if the laws of the

---

[253] Art 85(1)(D) does prohibit agreements which apply "dissimilar conditions to equivalent transactions with other trading parties, thereby placing them at a competitive disadvantage," however, an agreement reinforcing the price discrimination (such as a prohibition of exports) is required to bring the matter under the ambit of Art. 85. Distillers Co., Ltd. v. Commission, [1980] E.C.R. 2229, [1980] 3 C.M.L.R. 121 (E.C.J. 1980).

[254] Rather than impose outright price controls, the Commission generally investigates differences in prices to see if there is an abuse of a dominant position, such as in the drug industry investigation. Written Question No. 916/77, O.J. Comm. E. (C98) 9 (April 24, 1978); Written Question No. 398/78, O.J. Comm. E. (C251) 18 (Oct. 23, 1978), Comm. Mkt. Rep. (CCH) ¶¶ 10,093, 10,094. The Commission can also move against national price control laws. Comm. Mkt. Rep. ¶ 10,282.

[255] Deutsche Grammophone G.m.b.H., *supra* N. 204; *Grundig-Consten*, *supra* N. 54. Pioneer Electronic Europe was fined a total of 7 million units of account (approximately $10 million) when the Commission determined that its pricing and distribution system was used to prevent the free movement of goods. Comm. Mkt. Rep. (CCH) ¶ 10,185 (Jan. 1980), "Quadrophonic Fine," The Economist 36 (Dec. 22, 1979); Wyles, "EEC Levies Record Fine," *Financial Times* 1 (Dec. 18, 1979).

[256] Imperial Chemical Industries, *supra* N. 207.

[257] "The Common Scandal of the Uncommon Market," Economist 56 (Sept. 19, 1981).

[258] Imperial Chemical Industries, *supra* N. 207; Hugin, *supra* N. 199.

member states would allow these "fair trade" agreements, Art. 85(1) was violated, and the agreement would be invalidated.[258.1]

Competitor's complaints may rouse the Commission into action. In *Akzo Chemie UK*,[258.2] a competitor complained that predatory prices by Akzo had hampered its efforts to expand into other markets. The Commission ordered Akzo to raise its prices 15 to 20 percent, and thereafter lower its prices only to meet a competitor's price.

A Dutch association of farm equipment importers prohibited its members from granting rebates to customers in excess of 25 percent. No exemption for this practice was granted under Art. 85(3), since the group accounted for 90 percent of the farm equipment imported into the Netherlands, and there was no benefit to consumers from the arrangement.[258.3]

Specific pricing practices were part of the Commission's case against Kodak.[259] The Kodak distribution system allowed a customer to purchase products anywhere in Europe, but he had to be invoiced through his local distributor at local prices. The Commission insisted this condition be removed, which allowed some degree of price competition to be inserted into the Kodak distribution system.

The intricate pricing and supply system used by Hoffman-LaRoche[260] was also challenged by the Commission. Hoffman, which had between 47 and 95 percent of the market for seven groups of vitamins, required its twenty-two largest distributors to purchase all or most of their vitamins from Hoffman, at Hoffman's prices. In exchange, Hoffman would pay a "fidelity rebate," varying from 1 to 20 percent, to the distributor. Under the "English clause" of the agreements, Hoffman would offer to meet the price of other manufacturers, or allow the customer to purchase from the competitor.

[258.1] Vereniging ter Bevordering Von Het Vlaamsche Bockwezen v. Commission, No. 43/82, 46 A.T.R.R. 277 (1984).

[258.2] 45 A.T.R.R. 530 (Oct. 6, 1983), Comm. Mkt. Rep. ¶ 10,517.

[258.3] Vimpoltu, Comm. Mkt. Rep. ¶ 10,504; 45 A.T.R.R. 346 (Sept. 1, 1983).

[259] Kodak, *supra* N. 237; Canenbly, "Price Discrimination and EEC Cartel Law," 17 Antitrust Bull. 269 (1972).

[260] F. Hoffman-LaRoche & Co., A.G., [1976-78 T.B.] Comm. Mkt. Rep. (CCH) ¶ 9853.

The Commission determined that Hoffman had taken undue advantage of its dominant position by charging an excessively high price, hampering the customer's freedom of choice, and by discriminating against certain customers. According to the Commission, the market shares in themselves were not determinative, but the facts, when taken together, indicated an abuse of a dominant position.[261] The fidelity bonus system was determined to be discriminatory, and a violation of Art. 86(c) since it was not a true quantity discount. Different prices had been charged to two customers buying the same quantity of an item if one customer also dealt with other suppliers. The offer to meet competitive prices enabled Hoffman to cut its prices at its choosing, and therefore strengthen its dominance in an "abusive" way.

In February 1979, the European Court of Justice affirmed the Commission's finding of dominance in six of the seven markets, agreed that the "loyalty discount"[262] limited competition, but lowered the fine from 1,100,000 to 732,000 deutschemarks. With the decision, it is now clear that Art. 86 covers abuses of dominant position that not only injure actual customers and competitors, but also limit market entry by potential competitors.[263]

In 1978, protracted litigation regarding United Brands' (UBC) pricing and distribution system was finally resolved in the Court of Justice.[264] UBC was found to be dominant in the

---

[261] A similar challenge to Hoffman's pricing by the German Federal Cartel Office was overturned by the Supreme Civil Court for failure to prove abuse of a dominant position. Comm. Mkt. Rep. (CCH) ¶ 31,142 (1980).

[262] Cumulative discounts that were not cost-justified were the basis of the Commission's attack on the rebated practices of Michelin's Dutch subsidiary. However, since the penalty was levied for abuse of a dominant position, it raises the possibility that a non-dominant firm could engage in a similar practice without violating the law; *supra*, N. 227.1.

[263] "The Vitamin Giant Which Would Brook no Competitor," The Economist 58 (Feb. 17, 1979). Another issue in the case was the fact that the Commission was able to make its case against Hoffman based on company documents provided by a former employee. Although removal of the documents by the employee led to his conviction under the applicable Swiss law, that did not bar their use in this case.

[264] United Brands, *supra* N. 201.

banana market with 40 to 45 percent[265] of the market in Denmark, Germany, Ireland, Netherlands, Belgium, and Luxembourg.[266] In addition to its market share, UBC's dominance derived from its vertical integration (it controlled both the growing and shipping of the bananas) and heavy advertising that created a consumer preference for its "Chiquita" brand. The bananas, which were shipped into Europe at two ports with little cost difference, were sold to distributors at prices that varied by as much as 50 percent from 1971-1974.

The Court found that Art. 86 was violated when, as part of its scheme to control the pricing and conduct of its distributors, its long-standing Danish distributor was terminated for participating in an advertising campaign for a competitor (Dole). The effect of the cut-off, said the Court, was to discourage other distributors from carrying competing brands. UBC's prohibitions on re-sale were also found to be an abuse of its dominant position. Although UBC argued that these restraints were merely to protect the quality of its trademarked product, the Court determined that they were primarily intended to confine a distributor to a local market.

UBC argued that dissimilar prices to distributors were due to market forces beyond its control, but the Court rejected this and found the price discrimination to be violative of Art. 86. But the Court in turn rejected the Commission's finding that UBC had charged excessive prices, noting that there had been no rise in banana prices in real terms in almost twenty years. UBC's arguments that its European operations were unprofitable from 1971-1976 did not make much of an impression, however. The Court thought that a dominant firm could afford to take losses for a while in order to solidify its position, which is somewhat similar to the predatory price cutting theory applied (and disputed) in the U.S.

The net result of the UBC case is the entrenchment of the

---

[265] Previous cases dealing with Art. 86 violations had required a 50 percent market share for "dominance." The 40 percent figure used here may be indicative of the Commission's plans for other Art. 86 cases, although it has repeatedly stated that market share alone will not be conclusive.

[266] France, Italy, and England were excluded from the market definition due to special import arrangements in those countries.

Robinson-Patman concept in the EEC. Although language regarding discriminatory terms has always been in the Treaty of Rome, uniform prices had never really been expected. Although the goal of the Commission is the furtherance of the economic integration of Europe, the differences in local markets, taxes, and currencies will interfere with prices for the immediate future. The Commission has stated that while it will attack price differences as low as 5 percent, it will concentrate its efforts on "considerable price differences [which are] without substantial justification."[267]

The marketing practices of UBC did not fit the U.S. definition of monopoly power, which contemplate the ability to control prices. UBC was subject to pressure from its competitors, including price wars and the elasticity of demand for bananas (consumers could always switch to other fruits). But it would appear that the combination of a large market share (40 percent or more), strong brand name, and arbitrary price differences will incur the risk of Commission action. Attempting to utilize the market power of the brand name to restrain distributors may be a violation in itself. However, it would not appear that every price difference will need to be justified to the penny based on the narrow U.S. defenses of cost justification or meeting competition. Provided that the price differences are not totally arbitrary, and do not result in excess profits, the Commission still appears willing to listen to reasonable explanations.

[h] Exemptions and Negative Clearances

Although the Commission has reserved to itself broad powers to regulate trade, it has also openly expressed a willingness to use a "double standard" of sorts, by allowing restrictive agreements in situations it feels would ultimately further the goals of the EEC. Article 85(3) specifically contemplates the granting of exemptions to arrangements that might otherwise violate the Article when they improve production and promote technical progress, as long as there is no elimination of

---

[267] *See, supra* N. 184.

competition in a substantial part of the market.[267.1]

The provisions of Article 85(3) were implemented by Regulation 17, issued by the Commission in 1962.[268] The parties to a potentially anticompetitive agreement can apply to the Commission for a "negative clearance," that is, a request to the Commission, based on the facts presented, for the Commission not to intervene. An injured party can also apply to the Commission to see if the agreement in question violates Articles 85 or 86. If negative clearance is not granted, it is still possible to petition for exemption under the language of Article 85(3). A petition for an Article 85(3) exemption has the effect of suspending the imposition of fines on an illegal agreement until such time as the Commission has acted upon the request. The Commission also has the power to find all or part of the agreement invalid, and levy fines up to 1 million units of account (more than $1.2 million).[268.1]

Negative clearances are usually given in individual cases, but published notices have the effect of providing blanket approval for similar arrangements. As with any bureaucracy, the Commission was unable to cope with the thousands of applications it received after Regulation 17 was announced, so it established a policy of providing group exemptions to give the benefits of Article 85(3) without actual notification if cer-

---

[267.1] Dietz, "Enforcement of Antitrust Laws in the E.E.C.," 6 Int. Law. 742 (1972).

[268] Council Reg. No. 17/62, O.J. Comm. E. (204) 62 (March 6, 1962), Comm. Mkt. Rep. (CCH) ¶ 2401. The Commission has interpreted the provisions of Article 17 very expansively, and has used the language to act on requests for "interim" measures prior to the conclusion of an investigation, similar to injunctive relief to prevent violations of Art. 85 or 86. Camera Care, Ltd. v. Commission, Case No. 792/79, [1980] 1 C.M.L.R. 334, Comm. Mkt. Rep. ¶ 8645. Under Art. 14 of Reg. 17, the Commission can also examine books and records, take copies or extracts from books, ask for immediate oral explanations, enter any premises, land or means of transport. No warnings need to be given, nor any request for voluntary cooperation. Panasonic, Case No. 134/79, Comm. Mkt. Rep. ¶ 8682 (E.C.J. 1981).

[268.1] Although the Commission denies that it engages in "plea bargaining," it admits that it may negotiate a reduced fine where a company cooperates with an investigation. Written Question No. 2006/82, O.J. No. C 118/21 (May 3, 1983).

tain criteria are met.[269] Regulation 1983/83,[270] as discussed earlier, provides a block exemption for certain purchase and supply agreements, and certain exclusive distributorships that are justified on the basis of increasing sales. Exclusive distributorships that do not meet the requirements of 1983/83 may still quality for an exemption.[270.1]

U.S. firms should be aware that the participation in an arrangement that has received negative clearance may still violate U.S. law. Thus, before entering into such an arrangement, the firm should determine whether there will be any effect on U.S. commerce. Conversely, U.S. firms that rely on the Webb-Pomerene Act to protect export activities from U.S. antitrust violations should be aware that such concerted activities may violate EEC laws, or those of other countries.

Agreements that were in existence prior to the promulgation of Regulation 17 are treated as provisionally approved when noticed. New agreements, however, may be challenged in national courts which will not defer the cases while the Commission is considering the agreement,[271] and agreements found to be illegal are void *ab initio.* However, there is a method to obtain some consistency in the application of EEC antitrust law in national courts. Under Article 177, a national court considering a breach of contract case can seek an advisory opinion from the Court of Justice as to the legality of the agreement. The local court can then apply the EEC interpretation to the merits of the case.

The corporation that desires to use a series of standard contracts with other firms can register the blank form with the

---

[269] Blanket exemptions are provided for certain exclusive distributorships and "specialization agreements" aimed at rationalizing production or marketing efforts of small- and medium-size firms. Though anti-competitive, certain types of agreements are justified on the basis of helping participating companies to compete on a world level. Notice on Agreements, Decisions, and Concerted Practices Concerning Cooperation Between Enterprises, O.J. Comm E. (C75, July 29, 1968); Comm. Mkt. Rep. (CCH) ¶ 2699.

[270] *Supra* N. 222.

[270.1] Goodyear Italiana-Euram, [73-75 T.B.] Comm. Mkt. Rep. ¶ 9708 (Comm. 1974); Dyno-Dyne Europair, [73-75 T.B.] Comm. Mkt. Rep. ¶ 9708A (Comm. 1974).

[271] Brasserie de Haecht v. Wilkin & Janssen, Case No. 48/72 [1973] C.J. Comm. E. (1973-2) Rec. 77, [71-73 T.B.] Comm. Mkt. Rep. (CCH) ¶ 8170.

Commission for a blanket approval, to avoid the necessity of submitting each one.[272] Joint research and development projects are generally allowed unless they are between large competitors. But the Commission has been willing to view non-restrictive agreements between competitors with some flexibility.[273] For example, a joint venture to develop and exploit a coal gasification process was approved, even though the participants agreed not to compete among themselves. Noting the high costs of the project, the Commission ruled that the benefits outweighed the costs of lost competition. But the venture had to remove certain parts of the agreement that divided the market and limited competition after a withdrawal from the venture.[273.1]

Acts that could legally be done by a trade association in the U.S., such as exchange of market data and credit information, have been given blanket approval by the Commission.[274] To further the goal of economic integration, small companies have been given permission to execute specialization agreements with competitors.[275] A block exemption for certain patent licenses has been proposed, which would allow some restraints if reasonable in time and territory. The proposal, which is expected to be adopted, would allow the licensor to prohibit sales by a licensee in territories assigned to other licensees.

[3] Australia

Australia has shown its resentment to the extraterritorial enforcement of U.S. antitrust laws, particularly in response to

---

272 Parfums Marcel Rochas Vertrichs, *supra* N. 233.

273 Henkel/Colgate, O.J. Comm. E. (L14) 14 (Jan. 7, 1972), Comm. Mkt. Rep. (CCH) ¶ 9491; SOPELEM/Rank, O.J. Comm. E. (L29) 20 (Jan. 6, 1975), [1973-75 T.B.] Comm. Mkt. Rep. (CCH) ¶ 9707.

273.1 Carbon Gas Technologie, 46 A.T.R.R. 206 (Feb. 2, 1984).

274 *Supra* N. 241, at 385.

275 Reg. 2779/72, O.J. Comm. E. (L285) 46 (Dec. 29, 1971), Comm. Mkt. Rep. (CCH) ¶ 2731; *see also* Press Release No. IP (72) 137 (July 14, 1972), [1970-72] Comm. Mkt. Rep. (CCH) ¶ 9517; Communication, O.J. Comm. E. (C31 Feb. 7, 1978), [1976-78 T.B.] Comm. Mkt. Rep. (CCH) ¶ 10,022.

the uranium cartel litigation. In 1976, it enacted the Foreign Proceedings (Prohibition of Certain Evidence) Act, which blocked production of documents. This law was followed by the Foreign Antitrust Judgment (Restriction of Enforcement) Act of 1979,[276] which provides that when a foreign court renders an antitrust judgment the Attorney General thinks is inconsistent with international law or comity, and recognition of the judgment would adversely affect trade, he may order that judgment unenforceable, or reduce the amount of damages sought. To enhance this power even further, "clawback" legislation was introduced that would allow an Australian firm to recapture damages assessed in U.S. courts.[276.1]

[4] Canada

Anticompetitive and unfair[276.2] conduct is regulated in Canada by the Combines Investigation Act.[276.3] Because the Act is criminal, there has been virtually no activity in restricting mergers and monopolies, although proposals have been made to create a civil merger review board. In the first litigated merger case to reach the Supreme Court of Canada, *Regina v. K.C. Irving, Ltd.*,[276.4] the defendant acquired control over all of the English-language newspapers in New Brunswick. The court ruled that the creation of monopoly power by the merger, even if all competitors were eliminated, did not violate the Combines Act. The Act requires that one was a party to or knowingly, assisted in the formation of a monopoly, and that

---

[276] Royal Assent, March 15, 1979, 18 Int. Leg. Mat. 869; Trade Reg. Rep. ¶ 50,414.

[276.1] 1019 A.T.R.R. A17 (June 18, 1981).

[276.2] Combines Investigation Act, amendments of January 1, 1976, which prohibit misleading advertisements, warranties, pyramid schemes, and other unfair trade practices. 756 A.T.R.R. A23 (March 23, 1976).

[276.3] R.S., c314, s.1. In spite of the similarities between U.S. and Canadian law, there are significant differences in both style and substance. Although the U.S. and Canada pledged cooperation with each other in antitrust matters, agressive antitrust enforcement by the U.S., including attempts to secure evidence from Canadians, caused resentment. Department of Justice Press Release, Nov. 3, 1969, Trade Reg. Rep. ¶ 50,112.

[276.4] (1976) 32 C.C.C. 1, 12 N.R. 458 (S.C.C.), 793 A.T.R.R. A22.

the acquired business thereafter be operated to the detriment of the public. Since there was no change in the markets served by the papers, the Act was not violated.[276.5]

More controversy exists in the area of acquisitions due to the enactment of the Foreign Investment Review Act in 1974. This law requires detailed disclosures whenever a non-Canadian acquires control of a Canadian company. The control of Canada's economy by foreigners is quite sensitive, and the government negotiates each FIRA acquisition to get the best possible "deal" for Canada in terms of local employment and control.[276.6] Many mergers between U.S. companies are not implemented in Canada for a number of years, due to delays involved in the FIRA approval process. This procedure has been criticized as discouraging investments in Canada.[277]

The Combines Act has been enforced more vigorously in the area of price fixing. In *Regina v. Aluminum Co. of Canada, Ltd.*,[278] five Canadian aluminum extruders were indicted for allegedly conspiring to pass-on to customers a 1.2 cents per pound increase. Evidence showed a typed memorandum reflecting an agreement to increase prices, and routine exchange of price lists between the competitors. Yet there was no violation since the price lists were merely points from which the manufacturers negotiated with customers, and the evidence showed that the actual prices charged were different. Mere agreement to pass along cost increases may not violate the Act, since, to prove a lessening of price competition, the common (net) prices must be fixed. The Crown does not need to prove that all competition is eliminated, but that competition is lessened in some substantial way.

However, Levi Strauss of Canada pleaded guilty and was

276.5 *See* Reschenthaler & Stanbury, "A Clarification of Canadian Merger Policy," 22 A.T. Bull. 673 (1977).

276.6 *See, e.g.,* Clark, "Canada-U.S. Trade Relations," Canadian Bus. Rev. 48 (April 1981); Sandler, "What Price Canadianization," Institutional Investor 231 (Jan. 1982).

277 Comments of Denis Mote, 46 A.T.R.R. 145 (Jan. 19, 1984).

278 794 A.T.R.R. A8 (Quebec Sup. Ct. 1976). Similarly, in Regina v. Allied Van Lines, Ltd., 46 A.T.R.R. 31 (Ont. Sup. Ct., Dec. 14, 1983), five van lines were ordered to cease price fixing, and a trade association was ordered to stop acting as a tariff bureau.

fined C$ 150,000 for establishing and enforcing resale prices in violation of § 38 of the Act.[279] The conviction of Hoffman-LaRoche, Ltd. for selling valium at unreasonably low prices for the purposes of lessening competition was sustained by the Ontario Supreme Court.[280] If, however, companies can show that they are acting as agents for the Crown, then they are immune from criminal liability under the Act.[281]

Restrictive distribution practices may also violate the Act. Investigation of Kodak-Canada's marketing and distribution procedures was settled based on the receipt of assurances that Kodak-Canada would grant non-exclusive licenses to qualified photo-finishers. Although Canadian patents gave Kodak effective control of all processing business, 95 percent of the film sold in Canada included processing. Since the criminal penalties under the Combines Act were available, a settlement was preferable.[282]

[5] France

French antitrust laws were strengthened in 1977 with the creation of the Competition Commission which has the power to investigate cases of restrictive business practices, and challenge mergers that might create a dominant market position. Yet little has been accomplished due to continuous political pressure. The acquisitions that were disapproved by the French government apparently have been based largely on the nationality of the purchaser. For example, in 1979-80, the government refused to approve the acquisition of Ducellier by the U.K.'s Lucas, and Thorn Electric was refused permission to purchase Locatel, a television rental company, due to pressure from French television manufacturers.

Although the French Stock Exchange has tightened its rules

---

[279] Regina v. Levi Strauss of Canada, Inc., 902 A.T.R.R. A14 (Feb. 22, 1979).

[280] Regina v. Hoffman-LaRoche, Ltd., 1038 A.T.R.R. A24 (App. Ct., Ont. Sup. Ct. 1981).

[281] Regina v. Eldorado Nuclear, Ltd., Canada S.Ct. (Dec, 15, 1983), 46 A.T.R.R. 28 (Jan. 5, 1984).

[282] 791 A.T.R.R. A6 (1976).

for takeovers,[283] the French Social and Economic Council has reported that the alleged French hostility to foreign takeovers is exaggerated.[284] The foreign investment rules have been loosened somewhat, and now up to FF 5 million per year can be invested without government authority. Approval is required if a foreign group obtains more than 20 percent control of a French firm, but acquisitions by EEC-based firms are given presumptive approval if the Treasury takes no action within two months of notification. Acquisitions by EEC-based companies are evaluated based on a determination of whether the firm is genuinely based in the EEC (other countries cannot channel their investments through an EEC subsidiary[285]), and whether the transaction will endanger the public order, health or national defense.

The attempt by the United States F.T.C. to serve a complaint by mail on a corporation's Paris headquarters,[286] although disallowed by the U.S. courts, resulted in the enactment of a blocking statute. It is now a crime to request or produce business records, even on a voluntary basis, if they are subpoenaed in a foreign antitrust suit.[287]

Although the French government has taken some action against horizontal restraints in its economy,[288] there are some tendencies to preserve the old order, and political pressure against new methods of competition seems to be fairly effec-

---

[283] Comm. Mkt. Rep. ¶ 40,225.

[284] Comm. Mkt. Rep. ¶ 40,223.

[285] This discrimination based on the identity of the shareholder may be contrary to the freedom of establishment provisions of the Treaty of Rome.

[286] F.T.C. v. Compagnie de Saint-Gobain-Pont-a-Mousson, 80-1 Trade Cas. ¶ 63,026 (D.C. Cir. 1979).

[287] 993 A.T.R.R. A7 (Dec. 11, 1980).

[288] The law prohibits concerted action that artificially raises or lowers prices, blocks technical progress or limits free competition. A dominant enterprise may not restrict normal operations of a market. Certain exemptions may be available for conduct in response to a government regulation, or where joint efforts are undertaken to encourage economic progress. A FF 3 million fine was levied for price fixing of household appliances in 1980. In July 1981, a FF 2.8 million fine was imposed on a pharmaceutical trade association for boycotts of generic drugs.

tive.[289] For example, although refusals to deal and selective distribution are nominally prohibited in France,[290] the receptivity of the government to the established order tends to allow certain traditional restraints to continue.[291]

Much French law directly controls profit margins and prices.[292] The application of these laws may result in some inconsistencies,[293] since the pricing laws may be used to promote certain social goals (such as reducing medical costs by not allowing the recapture of R&D expenses in drug sales) rather than encouraging competition. The price legislation may also conflict with Art. 30 of the Rome Treaty.[294]

[6] Germany

Effective antitrust laws were introduced in Germany by the Allied Occupation forces in 1947, but in that short time a highly developed set of statutes has emerged.[295] The basic statute is the Gesetz gegen Wettbewerbsbeschrankungen (GWB), the law against restraints of competition.[296] The law is primarily enforced by the Federal Cartel Office (Bundeskartellamt), with an independent Monopoly Commission (Mono-

---

[289] The government has issued directives on loss leaders to protect manufacturers and consumers from "unscrupulous" discount houses. The Commission de la Consurrence investigated sixteen manufacturers and the Darty discount chain, looking into bait and switch tactics. Political pressure apparently allowed vertical price maintenance in the book industry to be justified on the basis of protecting small sellers.

[290] Comm. Mkt. Rep. ¶ 23,023.

[291] The refusal by certain perfume manufacturers to sell to discount houses was justified on the basis of the need for specially trained sales personnel.

[292] Comm. Mkt. Rep. ¶ 23,005.

[293] Inconsistent results may also be traced to the fact that two enforcement agencies are involved in the competition area, the Direction General de la Concurrence et des relations economiques interieures (General Directorate for Competition and Internal Economic Relations), and the Commission de la Concurrence (Commission for Competition).

[294] 404 Euromarket News 1 (Sept. 4, 1980).

[295] See Riesenkampf, "Recent Developments in German Antitrust Law," 30 Bus. Law. 1273 (1975).

[296] BGBZ I 1081 et seq., passed in 1957, as amended.

polkommission) that reports to the Parliament every two years on industrial concentration trends. Private damages may be recovered only from the time a Cartel Office ruling comes into force (after all court appeals are exhausted), so private suits are of limited value.

The GWB prohibits agreements that may have the effect of restraining competition, such as price fixing, resale price maintenance,[297] and abuse of a dominant position.[298] Small and medium sized firms have more freedom to cooperate among each other, in an effort to support their ability to compete with the large firms in an industry. Exclusive dealing or tying contracts may be found unlawful by the Cartel Office where a significant number of enterprises in a given market are restricted by contracts of this type. However, since these restraints are evaluated under a rule of reason, justifications may be offered. In the *Volkswagen* case,[299] the Cartel Office challenged VW's practice of requiring all dealers to use only factory-approved repair parts. On review, the Supreme Court found that the repair business was economically and technically linked to the new car business, and since customer expected factory quality repairs, and there was not evidence that VW had exploited its power, the restraint was allowed.

Mergers and acquisitions are regulated by a detailed set of controls, most recently amended in 1980.[300] Mergers are subject to control where the acquired firm had sales over DM 50 million. If the acquiring corporation had worldwide sales over DM 2 billion, the Cartel Office must be pre-notified of any acquisition over DM 4 million. A maximum fine of DM 1 million can be levied for failure to notify the Cartel Office, and, while not many mergers are stopped by Cartel Office litiga-

---

[297] GWB §§ 1, 15, 16. "Suggested" resale prices are allowed for branded goods; only in the publishing industry are binding prices permissable.

[298] *See* Stockmann, "Abuse Control over Market Dominating Enterprises," 9 Int. Bus. Law. 384 (1981).

[299] KVO/8/80, Supreme Court, Sept. 22, 1981.

[300] *See* Deringer, "German Control of Mergers and Acquisitions: Application to Foreign Enterprises" (American Chamber of Commerce in Germany, 1981); Comm. Mkt. Rep. ¶ 40,020.

tion,[301] many are aborted after "informal" consultations with the Cartel Office.[302]

The Cartel Office will prohibit a merger if it would create or strengthen a market dominating position (presumed when sales are over DM 2 billion or market share is in excess of 25 percent).[303] The impact of this approach was demonstrated by the attempts of the Cartel Office to halt the merger between Rothmans and Philip Morris. Each of the companies had subsidiaries in Germany, which together would control 31 percent of the German cigarette market. Although the merger of two foreign corporations is considered to be the merger of their subsidiaries, the Berlin Appeals Court ruled that outright prohibition of the foreign merger was too drastic a solution when other remedies were available. The Court affirmed the validity of the Cartel Office's power, but felt that extraterritorial measures may be employed only when there were no domestic alternatives.[304]

The law against unfair competition (Gesetz urber unlauferen Wettbewerb, UWG)[305] allows a competitor to seek damages for acts that offend "good morals," including, *inter alia*, false advertising, deceptive labeling, and commercial bribery. The law does not forbid sales below cost, however, on a theory that the manufacturer's image would be damaged. Loss leaders may be attacked if part of a scheme to injure competitors,

---

[301] Two mergers were forced to halt in 1979; twelve in 1978.

[302] *E.g.*, Phillips reduced its share in Grundig to 24.5 percent based on a Cartel Office opinion.

[303] *See* Comm. Mkt. Rep. ¶ 40,219 (June 1981). In 1978, the Cartel Office disallowed the merger between GKN and Sachs, based on the opinion that the combination of these two corporations would scare away the competitors in the clutch business, even though there was no effect on actual competition by the combination.

[304] Kammergericht, Kart 16/82; Financial Times 21 (Feb. 16, 1984); 46 A.T.R.R. 147 (Jan 19, 1984). The Cartel Office is appealing the decision to the Federal Supreme Court. The Cartel Office ruled against the acquisition of various shoppers' guides, since each of the acquiring newspapers had a market-dominating position in its main distribution area, and acquisition of the shopping guides would eliminate the remaining competition. 46 A.T.R.R. 93 (Jan. 12, 1984).

[305] RGBZ, 1909 page 499; Comm. Mkt. Rep. ¶ 23,525.

which might be the case if retailers offered loss leaders on a long-term basis.[306]

[7] Japan

Japan also received its antitrust laws by virtue of the military occupation following World War II.[307] Antitrust principles similar to those in effect in the U.S. were imposed upon Japan, and were designed to be contrary to the pro-cartel activities of the former Japanese government.[308]

Unreasonable restraints of trade are prohibited in the categories of price fixing, group boycotts, and monopolization. The Fair Trade Commission (JFTC) was established to enforce the Antimonopoly Act, but little happened during the 1950s and 1960s, in part due to the contrary actions of the Ministry of International Trade and Industry, which would issue directives aimed at reducing "excessive" competition in some industries.[309]

Recently, however, the JFTC has ruled that administrative guidance from MITI may cause cartels, and will not be an automatic defense under the Antimonopoly Act.[310] Merger guidelines have been issued pursuant to the JFTC's authority to prohibit acquisitions where a substantial restraint of competition will result. In practice however, few mergers are blocked, due to frequent reports by Japanese companies to the JFTC.

---

[306] Braun v. Groso Markets, Business Europe 58 (Feb. 24, 1984).

[307] "Act Concerning Prohibition of Private Monopoly and Maintenance of Fair Trade," Act No. 54 (April 14, 1947).

[308] See Uekusa, "Effects of the Deconcentration Measures on Japan," 22 A.T. Bull. 687 (1977).

[309] It is still legal to form an anti-recession cartel to keep markets orderly when demand is soft. See 46 A.T.L.J. 502 (1977).

[310] Petroleum Cartel Case, Tokyo High Court (Sept. 26, 1980); JFTC policy statement (March 1981) incorporating views of Court, and urging government agencies to consult with JFTC before engaging in administrative guidance.

[8]   United Kingdom

The modernization of Britain's antitrust statutes also coincided with the end of World War II, with the passage of the Monopolies and Restrictive Practices (Inquiry and Control) Act of 1948.[311] Additional statutes were passed[312] which now puts Great Britain in the position of having a much more detailed set of laws dealing with antitrust and unfair competition than does the U.S.

Monopolies and mergers in the U.K. are reviewed by the Board of Trade, which will refer a matter to the Monopolies Commission if an acquisition will create or strengthen a monopoly (one-quarter market share or greater)[313] or involves assets in excess of £ 5 million. Although pre-notification is not required, most parties to major mergers have done so on a voluntary basis.[314] Certain acquisitions may be allowed to proceed after assurances have been given to the Secretary of State that certain assets will be spun-off or allowed to continue as separate business entities.[315] Trade Secretary John Nott has stated that British policy on mergers will be more "skeptical,"

---

[311] 11 & 12 Geo. 6, Chap. 66.

[312] Monopolies & Merger Act of 1965, Fair Trading Act of 1973, Restrictive Trade Practices Acts of 1956 and 1968, and the Resale Prices Act of 1964, Comm. Mkt. Rep. ¶ 24,002.

[313] The acquisition of one casino by a 29 percent-owned subsidiary of another casino was opposed, since, in practice, the two would control the London casino market. Grand Metropolitan/Trident, 46 A.T.R.R. 146 (Jan. 19, 1984).

[314] Actual pre-notification would go to the Office of Fair Trading which has the power to notify the Monopoly Commission if it objects to the proposed merger. Usually, OFT objection is enough to stop a merger. 1042 A.T.R.R. A13 (Dec. 13, 1981). Political reasons, especially fear of lost jobs, may make the Commission decide to ignore the OFT. Churchill, "A Hiccup in Merger Policy," Financial Times 12 (Nov. 23, 1981); see also Colenutt & O'Donnell, "The Consistency of Monopolies & Merger Commission Reports," 23 A.T. Bull. 51 (1978).

[315] For example, the offer to acquire British Surga by S.W. Berisford was allowed to proceed provided that British Surga was held as a separate subsidiary. 1008 A.T.R.R. A18 (Apr. 2, 1981). The acquisition by Great Universal Stores (40 percent market share) of Empire Stores (7 percent market share) was opposed. 46 A.T.R.R. 146 (Jan 19, 1984). See also Howe, "Rethinking British Merger Policy," 17 Antitrust Bull. 283 (1972).

particularly where "the acquisition of a successful company by a large and unrelated company which is merely shopping around when flush with funds . . . may in reality involve a diminution of competition and no evident efficiency gain."[316]

Certain trade practices and resale price maintenance are regulated by the Restrictive Trade Practices Act of 1976. The Act covers restraints imposed in connection with the prices or quantities of goods purchased, or the persons to whom such goods may be sold. The specified restrictions also include restraints of service and information agreements. The legislation has been criticized as being more concerned with the form of the agreement than its effect on competition.[317]Agreements that fall within the Act are registered with the Director General of Fair Trading, which may remain in effect until reviewed by the Restrictive Practices Court, which may take two to three years. Failure to register an agreement is not illegal, but it may make the restraints contained in the agreement unenforceable.[318]

A number of recent actions have challenged exclusive dealing or restrictive distribution arrangements. The Raleigh bicycle company was challenged on its refusal to sell to discounters.[319] The 72 percent market share of the liquified petroleum gas market held by Calor was found not to be against the public interest, so long as distributors were not required to buy appliances exclusively from Calor, and were not prevented from carrying competing brands of LPG.[320]

The "Protection of Trading Interests Act of 1980" retaliates for the ocean shipping and uranium cases filed in the U.S. A clawback provision enables British firms to recover two-thirds of the damages assessed against them in foreign antitrust actions by making claims against U.S. subsidiaries operating in

---

[316] 602 Euromarket 5 (July 29, 1980).

[317] Marshall, "Concept & Practice of the British Restrictive Practices & Monopolies Law," 8 Int. Law. 59 (Feb. 1980).

[318] See, e.g., 1029 A.T.R.R. A13 (Aug. 21, 1981) regarding the price agreements of British Steel Corp.; and Comm. Mkt. Rep. ¶ 40,213; 42 A.T.R.R. 226 (Jan. 28, 1982). A proposal was introduced to impose criminal sanctions for price fixing. 1000 A.T.R.R. A12 (Feb. 8, 1981).

[319] 42 A.T.R.R. 208 (1982).

[320] 1006 A.T.R.R. A11 (Mar. 19, 1981).

Britain. This clawback law strengthens the previously enacted blocking statutes that prevented compliance with discovery attempts in foreign antitrust cases.[321]

[9] An International Antitrust Law?

Apart from the U.S., the EEC, and a few other countries, there is a wide divergence as to whether there should be international enforcement of antitrust laws. Most governments never attempt to pursue violators beyond their borders, and local enforcement may be negligible.

A decree of international enforcement occurs on a bilateral level, through the formal and informal exchanges of information regarding antitrust violators between officials charged with antitrust enforcement. There are many contacts between the EEC Commission staff and the DOJ, but official policy limits the data exchanged to non-confidential material only. The U.S. and Canada have agreed to consult whenever it appears that the other country's national interest may be affected by an antitrust investigation or case.[322] Antitrust matters are also covered in bilateral[323] or multilateral agreements.[324]

Various international organizations have put forward (or are working on) codes of conduct to govern the practices of MNCs.[325] While these codes are not strictly "antitrust" in nature, they may well provide the foundation for international

---

[321] 935 A.T.R.R. A18 (Oct. 18, 1979); 938 A.T.R.R. A1 (Nov. 8, 1979).

[322] The agreement was reached after a radio patent case, United States v. General Electric Co., 1962 Trade Cas. (CCH) ¶¶ 72,342, 70,428, 70,546 (S.D.N.Y. 1962, consent decrees); DOJ Press Release, November 3, 1969; American Bar Association, Developments, *supra* N. 241 at 379.

[323] *See, e.g.,* Treaty of Friendship, Commerce & Trade between U.S. & Italy, Feb. 2, 1948, Art. 18, ¶ 3, 63 Stat. 2255, T.I.A.S. No. 1965 (eff. July 26, 1949).

[324] GATT 1960 resolution recommending consultations on restrictive business practices. GATT: B.I.S.D. 28 (9th Supp., 1961).

[325] For summaries of the efforts to develop an international antitrust code, *see* Davidow, "Toward an International Antitrust Code," 65 *A.B.A.J.* 631 (1979); Chonce, "Code of Conduct for MNCs," 33 Bus. Law. 1799 (1978).

antitrust guidelines in the future.[326] The Restrictive Business Practices Committee of the Organization for Economic Cooperation and Development (OECD) has been active in developing guidelines of corporate conduct that may be considered similar to international antitrust rules. The Council of the OECD has recommended that member states consult when the interests of another member state may be involved in an antitrust investigation,[327] and the DOJ has acknowledged its adherence to this policy.[328]

The OECD has also attempted to devise substantive rules, and its Code of Conduct urges MNCs not to behave in an anticompetitive fashion or pay bribes. The Code, which is a voluntary guideline only,[329] does not allow use of national antitrust laws to fulfill an MNCs obligations, and also calls upon host countries not to discriminate against MNCs.[330] The OECD has also been developing recommendations regarding restrictions on international movement of trademarked goods, and permissible restrictions on distribution and sale of trademarked goods in contexts such as franchises.[331]

At the U.N., UNCTAD committees have been working in the areas of technology transfer and restrictive business practices.[332] The General Assembly, on December 5, 1980, adopted

---

[326] Joelson, "The Proposed International Codes of Conduct as Related to Restrictive Business Practices," 8 Law & Policy in Int. Bus. 837 (1976).

[327] O.E.C.D. Council Recommendation, adopted Oct. 5, 1967, O.E.C.D. Doc. C(67)53, W. Fugate, *Foreign Commerce and the Antitrust Laws* 554 (2d ed., 1973); 18 Int. Leg. Mat. 1171 (1979).

[328] DOJ guidelines at E6. However, many foreign governments strongly oppose actual attempts to prosecute antitrust violators outside of the U.S. Sen. Mathias introduced a bill into the U.S. Senate (S. 1010, April 25, 1979) to establish a Commission on the International Application of Antitrust Laws to try to deal with these problems.

[329] *See* 18 Int. Leg. Mat. 986 (1979). Although voluntary, as courts cite the guidelines in decisions (as has happened in Belgium, Holland, and before the E.C.J.), they begin to take on the force of law. Bus. Int'l 236 (July 27, 1979).

[330] 766 A.T.R.R. A17 (June 1, 1976).

[331] The O.E.C.D. has also examined the prices MNCs charge their subsidiaries for goods; Halpern, "OECD Report on Transfer Pricing & Multinational Enterprises," 6 Tax Planning International 132 (July 1979).

[332] The U.N. Center on Transnational Corporations adopted a code of conduct on Sept. 14, 1981, covering bribery and withdrawal of investments from South Africa. However, it has not been adopted by the General Assem-

a voluntary code on restrictive practices that would prohibit
(1) agreements or practices that limit access to markets or
unduly restrain competition; (2) price fixing of imports or exports, market allocations, concerted refusals to deal, or collective denials of access to an arrangement crucial to competition;
(3) abuses of dominant position by predatory pricing, discriminatory pricing, and restrictions on imports of validly
trademarked items. State-owned companies are included, and
agreements between parents and subsidiaries are exempt.[333]
Under the UNCTAD restrictive business practices code,[334] a
"Group of Experts" will meet periodically to draft a model
antitrust law.[335] Progress in this area, as well as in technology
transfer regulations, has been minimal.[336]

---

bly, and there is no agreement whether it is binding or voluntary. 1033
A.T.R.R. A8 (Oct. 1, 1981). The Center's function is to help LDCs negotiate
with MNCs and may show some bias toward LDCs in the code it produces.
See also 748 A.T.R.R. A22 (Jan. 27, 1976) and 73 Am. J. Int. L. 519 (1979).

[333] 993 A.T.R.R. A8 (Dec. 11, 1980).

[334] Antitrust & Trade Reg. Rep. (BNA) No. 961 at A-10 (April 24, 1980);
No. 963 at G-1 (May 8, 1980). Officially known as the Set of Multilaterally
Agreed Equitable Principles and Rules for Control of Restrictive Business
Practices."

[335] 1042 A.T.R.R. A5 (Dec. 3, 1981).

[336] The Geneva meeting held April 10, 1981 ended without agreement.
1013 A.T.R.R. A3 (May 7, 1981).

CHAPTER 10

Jurisdictional Problems in the Application of the Antitrust Laws

DAVID K. PANSIUS*

§ 10.01   Introduction

Although the virtually unlimited extraterritorial reach of United States antitrust laws has spawned much comment,[1] as

---

*J.D. University of Denver, 1978; L.L.M. in Taxation N.Y.U., 1979; Attorney, Ku and Pansius, San Jose, CA.

[1] See, e.g., W. Fugate, *Foreign Commerce and the Antitrust Laws*, 20-55 (1973), H. Zwarenisteyn, *Some Aspects of the Extraterritorial Reach of the American Antitrust Laws* (1970); Note, "Extraterritorial Application of the

a practical matter, any antitrust law, if it is to be applied fairly, equitably, and effectively, must be applied extraterritorially as well. For example, the Japanese, hardly noted as being international trust busters, nonetheless made provisions in their antitrust laws for regulating the activities of foreign entrepreneurs which impact on Japanese markets.[2] Customarily, U.S. antitrust legislation expressly provides that foreign, as well as domestic, commerce is within its reach: For example, the Sherman Act applies to "trade or commerce among the several states, or with foreign nations." In like fashion, the Clayton Act incorporates trade with foreign nations in its definition of commerce. The exact circumstances in which such laws will be applied to international commerce is the subject of this first part. The remaining parts of this section will address the sovereignty defenses to subject matter jurisdiction and the unique jurisdictional problems which a litigant may expect if he should bring an international antitrust claim in U.S. courts.

As a practical matter, a U.S. businessman engaged in foreign transactions should never be in doubt as to whether U.S. antitrust laws will be applied to him. In almost all circumstances they will. As will be developed more fully below, the basic test of antitrust jurisdiction is one of effect; will the transaction impact on U.S. commerce, foreign or domestic. Where a U.S. businessman is involved such effect is almost always present.

Exactly what will or will not create the necessary jurisdictional effect will be discussed at length in a later section of the chapter. However, before this somewhat complicated issue is discussed, a more fundamental question to a U.S. enterprise

---

Antitrust Laws," 69 Harv. L. Rev. 1452 (1956); Note, "Sherman Anti-Trust Law: Applicability to Foreign Commerce," 37 Cornell L.Q. 821 (1952); Note, "Application of the Antitrust Laws to Extraterritorial Conspiracies," 49 Yale L.J. 1312 (1940). Beadsang, "The Extraterritorial Jurisdiction of the Sherman Act," 70 Dick. L. Rev. 187 (1966).

[2] *E.g.*, Part II, 86(1) of the Act Concerning Prohibition of Private Monopoly and Maintenance of Fair Trade (Act No. 54, 14 April (1947) provides: "No entrepreneur shall enter into an international agreement or an international contract which contains such matters as constitute unreasonable restraint of trade or unfair business practices." It has been made clear that the term "entrepreneur" includes foreign as well as Japanese persons. Hiroshi Iyori, *Antimonopoly Legislation in Japan*, 53-55 (1969).

will be analyzed first, to wit, does the U.S. antitrust law protect foreign competitors and foreign consumers from antitrust violations by U.S. persons? As the material below indicates, the answer in almost every instance is yes.

§ 10.02   Foreign Party's Standing to Sue

There now seems little debate that the antitrust laws do provide relief to foreign persons against U.S. violators. A United States company, in particular, must recognize that the U.S. antitrust laws are a double-edged sword. The antitrust law may protect U.S. companies and consumers from foreign monopolistic restraints on the foreign commerce of the United States; but, so does it also protect foreign consumers and companies from the monopolistic activities of U.S. corporations. Recent judicial decisions clearly indicate that foreign persons can employ the U.S. antitrust laws to maintain a private cause of action against a U.S. defendant.

In *Waldbaum v. Worldvision Enterprises, Inc.,*[3] a U.S. corporation moved to dismiss an antitrust complaint filed against it by a citizen of South Africa. Specifically, plaintiff charged the defendant company with illegal tying arrangements in the sale of copyrighted video products. The court ruled that the foreign plaintiff had properly stated a cause of action.

> While the purposes of the [Sherman] Act is to benefit United States business and consumers, it is clear that a foreign business or nation is not precluded from bringing an action under the Act when the alleged illegal conduct in addition to having anti-competitive effects in the United States, also harms a foreign business or nation.[4]

The *Waldbaum* decision relied heavily on *Todhunter-Mitchell & Co., Ltd. v. Anhaeuser-Busch, Inc.,*[5] where defendant restricted the wholesale distribution of beer in foreign

---

[3] 1978-2 U.S.Trade Cases ¶ 62,378 (50 N.Y. 1978).

[4] *Id.* at 76,257.

[5] 375 F.Supp. 610 (E.D. Pa. 1974), modified in part. 383 F.Supp. 586 (E.D. Pa. 1974).

markets to certain persons within certain territories. The *Tod-hunter-Mitchell* court also rejected the notion that the Sherman Act cannot be applied to grant relief to a foreign corporation.[6]

The *Todhunter-Mitchell* decision was also relied upon by the court in *Industria Siciliana Asfalti Bitami, S.P.A. v. Exxon Research and Engineering Co.,*[7] where the court permitted a foreign corporation to sue a U.S. corporation based on another alleged illegal tying arrangement. The court concluded that as long as the foreign person suffered injury from those acts which violated the antitrust laws as applied to the foreign commerce of the United States, then the foreign person had standing to sue.[8]

The right of foreign persons to sue has been construed to also include the right of foreign governments to sue for treble damages under the antitrust laws. In *Pfizer, Inc. v. Government of India,*[9] the United States Supreme Court considered whether a foreign sovereign suing on behalf of itself and its citizenry is a person for purposes of the Clayton Act. Noting the expansive remedial purpose of both the Sherman and Clayton Acts, the Court concluded that the foreign governments had standing to bring suit. The Court reached this conclusion in two steps: First, the Court concluded that, as described above, foreign persons may sue private U.S. defendants under the prohibitions of the antitrust laws. The fact that the original intent of the law may have been protectionist did not preclude foreign standing, even on policy reasons. "Treble-damage suits by foreigners who have been victimized by antitrust violations clearly may contribute to the protection of American consumers."[10]

The Court then ruled that the term "person entitled to sue under the Clayton Act" also included foreign sovereigns, based in part on the same belief that the antitrust laws were intended

---

[6] 375 F.Supp. at 624.

[7] 1977-1 U.S. Trade Cases ¶ 61,256 (S.D.N.Y. 1977).

[8] *Id.* at 70,785; *see* A.G.S. Electronics, Ltd. v. B.S.R. (U.S.A.), Ltd., 460 F. Supp. 707 (S.D.N.Y. 1978), *aff'd* 591 F.2d 1329 (2d Cir. 1978)

[9] 98 S.Ct. 584 (1978).

[10] *Id.* at 588.

to be expansively applied. The Court reasoned that to fail to permit a foreign government to sue privately for treble damages would be to deny foreign governments all remedies under the antitrust laws.[11]

If a foreign person may sue a U.S. person under the antitrust laws, then, when jurisdiction is otherwise present, so may a foreign person also sue another foreign person under the antitrust laws. *Joseph Muller Corp. v. Societe Anonyme de Guance et D'Armiment*[12] reached this conclusion. The Second Circuit in that edition permitted a Swiss corporation to sue a French corporation for treble damages under the Sherman Act for alleged price fixing of the transportation of various chemical commodities from the United States to other countries. (*Cf., Raubal v. Engelhard Minerals and Chemicals Corp.,*[13] where the Court denied a foreign plaintiff standing to sue a foreign defendant because the complained of acts did not have the necessary effect on the foreign commerce of the United States.)

§ 10.03   The Effects Test Applied

The willingness of the courts to permit foreign plaintiffs to seek antitrust relief in U.S. courts in itself indicates the broad extraterritorial reach of the U.S. antitrust laws. Nonetheless, there are theoretical and practical limits to the reach of the U.S. antitrust sword. The first, although possibly not the most severe, limitation is that the U.S. court must have the necessary subject matter jurisdiction over the violation. The alleged antitrust violation must have sufficient effect on U.S. commerce before the court will exercise jurisdiction and apply the U.S. law.

Although the effects test of jurisdiction is widely applied, strangely there is no single statement of that test recognized as the definitive expression of extraterritorial antitrust jurisdic-

---

[11] *Id.* at 591.
[12] 451 F.2d 727 (2d Cir. 1971).
[13] 364 F.Supp. 1352 (S.D.N.Y. 1973).

tion.[14] Among the earliest and most attractive standards is the court's reaction in *Hamburg* to a restraint in the ocean transportation of passengers between the United States and Europe: "The agreement *directly* and *materially affects* foreign commerce and is partly intraterritorial because it is to be carried out in part in the United States."[15] The concept of a "direct and material effect," later developed into the concept of "direct and substantial effect" which, at least until the *Timberlane* decision, appeared to be the most popular of the formulations advanced by the courts and the commentators.[16]

The so-called "substantial effects" test has two principle advantages besides its obvious brevity: First, by requiring a substantial effect, the possibility that foreign sovereigns may also have a legitimate interest in a transaction is given some recognition, albeit implied and indirect.[17] As the famous Judge Hand stated in the equally famous *Alcoa* decision: "We should not impute to Congress an intent to punish all whom its courts can catch, for conduct which has no consequences within the United States."[18] Second, to apply a requirement of substantial effect would, at least in language, inject a degree of symmetry into the U.S. antitrust law. Whether or not an intrastate antitrust violation (*e.g.,* a violation occurring entirely within the state of California) is subject to federal antitrust law will depend upon whether the alleged violation has a "substantial effect" on interstate commerce. Consequently, by employing substantial effect, the tests for when intrastate commerce is subject to the antitrust law and when international commerce

---

[14] *See, e.g.,* Timberlane Lumber Co. v. Bank of America, 549 F.2d 597, 610-11 (9th Cir. 1976) [hereinafter cited as *Timberlane*].

[15] United States v. Hamburg-Amerikanische Packet-Fahrtactien-Gesellschaft, 200 F. 806, 807 (S.D.N.Y. 1911), *aff'd* 216 F. 971 (S.D.N.Y. 1914), *rev'd on grounds of mootness,* 239 U.S. 466 (1916).

[16] 549 F.2d at 610. *See, e.g.,* W. Fugate, *Foreign Commerce and the Antitrust Laws* (2d ed. 1973).

[17] 549 F.2d at 611.

[18] United States v. Aluminum Company of America, 148 F.2d 416, 443 (2d Cir. 1945).

is subject to the antitrust law would, at least superficially, be the same.[19]

The substantial effects rule, however, has several drawbacks: First, what is a "substantial" effect as opposed to an insubstantial one? The test really adds little definition beyond the basic concept of effect. Second, the test does not directly address the possible legitimate concerns of foreign governments in the transaction. Even though the U.S. effect may be substantial, the effect in country X may be more substantial.[20] And finally, the analogy to interstate commerce is inappropriate. The distinction between inter versus intrastate commerce derives from the somewhat unique constitutional principles of federalism.[21] The concept of deference to foreign law, however, derives from the fundamental principle of comity: the laws of all nations deserve the respect legitimately demanded by equal participants in the international arena: A kind of international legal "golden rule." Comity, therefore, requires a jurisdictional test which in part balances interests.[22]

---

[19] *See, e.g.,* Hospital Bldg. Co. v. Rex Hospital Trustees, 425 U.S. 738, 743 (1976); Gulf Oil Corp. v. Copp Paving Co., 419 U.S. 186, 195 (1974). Boddicku v. Arizona State Dental Health Ass'n, 549 F.2d 626, 629-30 (9th Cir. 1977).

[20] "An effect on United States commerce, although necessary to the exercise of jurisdiction under the antitrust laws, is alone not a sufficient basis on which to determine whether American authority *should* be asserted in a given case as a matter of international comity and fairness." Timberlane, 549 F.2d at 613 (emphasis in original).

[21] "Since, however, no comparable constitutional problem exists in defining the scope of congressional power to regulate *foreign* commerce, it may be unwise blindly to apply the 'substantiality' test to the international setting. Only respect for the role of the executive and for international notions of comity and fairness limit that constitutional grant." Timberlane, 549 F.2d at 612 (emphasis in original).

[22] *Timberlane* states that the point at which U.S. interests must defer to foreign interests "is not defined by international law." 549 F.2d at 609. This statement might be interpreted to indicate that once some effect on U.S. commerce is shown no overriding principles of international law compel further restraints on extraterritorial jurisdiction. *See also,* United States v. Aluminum Company of America, 148 F.2d 416, 443 (2d Cir. 1945). The principles of "fairness and comity" which requires some deference to foreign interests thus represent the implied intent of Congress—not a constitutional principle limiting Congress' authority to legislate.

This broad view of potential U.S. jurisdiction is likely misleading. The Congress' authority to regulate the foreign commerce of the United States may be limited by the Constitutional command to act within the confines of

The court in *Timberlane Lumber Co. v. Bank of America, N.T.&S.A.,* recognized these shortcomings and proposed instead a test which "balances the foreign interests involved." The court enumerated the following factors to be weighed in the analysis: (1) "the degree of conflict with foreign law or policy"; (2) "the nationality or allegiance of the parties and the locations or principal places of business of corporations"; (3) "the extent to which enforcement by either state can be expected to achieve compliance"; (4) "the relative significance of effects on the United States as compared with those elsewhere"; (5) "the extent to which there is explicit purpose to harm or affect American commerce"; (6) "the foreseeability of such effect"; and (7) "the relative importance to the violations charged of conduct within the United States as compared with conduct abroad."[23] Some courts have found favor with *Timberlane's* approach of balancing jurisdictional facts.[24]

In its 1984 *Timberlane* decision[25] (hereafter *Timberlane II*), the Ninth Circuit was given the opportunity to apply its *Timberlane* balancing test to specific facts. The court reaffirmed the balancing test as part of a three-part inquiry: "Does the alleged restraint affect, or was it intended to affect, the foreign commerce of the United States? Is it of such a type and magnitude so as to be cognizable as a violation of the Sherman Act? As a matter of international comity and fairness, should the

---

international law. Vanity Fair Mills, Inc. v. T. Eaton Co., 234 F.2d 633, 641 (2d Cir. 1956). Pacific Seafarers, Inc. v. Pacific Far East Line, Inc., 404 F.2d 804, 814-15 (D.C. Cir. 1968).

Where it serves one's purpose, the established doctrine of comity should be proffered as a principle of international common law binding on the court. One should recognize however, that the court's obligation to apply international law may create as well as deny jurisdiction, depending upon the international legal principle to be applied. *Compare* Justice Marshall's decision in Rose v. Himely, 8 U.S. (4 Cranch) 241 (1808) *with* his opinion in the Schooner Exchange v. M'Fadden, 11 U.S. (7 Cranch) 116 (1812).

[23] 549 F.2d at 614.

[24] Mannington Mills, Inc. v. Congoleum Corp., 595 F.2d 1287 (3d Cir. 1979); Timberlane Lumber Co. v. Bank of America, N.T. & S.A., 749 F.2d 1378 (9th Cir. 1984); Montreal Trading, Ltd. v. AMAX, Inc., 661 F.2d 864 (10th Cir. 1981).

[25] Timberlane Lumber Co. v. Bank of America N.T. & S.A., 749 F.2d 1378 (9th Cir. 1984).

extraterritorial jurisdiction of the United States be asserted to cover it?"[25.1]

The first two stages of the jurisdictional inquiry merely reformulate the established requirement that the effect in United States commerce be direct, substantial, and foreseeable. The plaintiffs alleged that Bank of America conspired to restrain commerce in the export of lumber from the Honduras into the United States, thus meeting this direct, substantial and foreseeable standard.[25.2]

However, to resolve the comity question, the *Timberlane* balancing test was applied. *Timberlane II* addressed each of the seven *Timberlane I* factors in turn. However, the tone of the court's opinion indicates that certain criteria predominated. First, the court determined that enforcement of the U.S. antitrust law in this case would directly conflict with Honduran law guaranteeing freedom of contract. The volume of commerce involved was substantial as regards Honduras. In contrast, the volume of commerce as regards United States lumber consumption was insignificant. Consideration of the other *Timberlane* factors did not yield any facts that would otherwise indicate a strong U.S. concern in the transaction. As a consequence, considerations of comity dictated that the courts abstain from exercising jurisdiction over Timberlane's claims.[25.3]

§ 10.04 Simplified Balancing Test

Commentators have praised the *Timberlane* and *Mannington Mills* balancing test for their consideration of competing international concerns.[26] From a theoretical standpoint, the seven *Timberlane* factors appear to represent an ideal expres-

---

[25.1] *Timberlane I,* 549 F.2d at 615, quoted in *Timberlane II,* 749 F.2d at 1382-83.

[25.2] 749 F.2d at 1383.

[25.3] *See* 749 F.2d at 1383-86.

[26] *See, e.g.,* Shenefield, "Thoughts on Extraterritorial Application of the United States Antitrust Laws," 52 Fordham L. Rev. 350 (1983); Feinberg, "Economic Coercion and Economic Sanctions: The Expansion of United States Antitrust Jurisdiction," 30 Am. U.L. Rev. 323 (1981).

sion of the elements which should properly define jurisdiction. From a practical standpoint, however, the *Timberlane* and *Mannington Mills* balancing tests may be too complicated. Except in the more obvious cases, one cannot confidently apply so many factors.[26.1] Principles of comity require some form of balancing as distinguished from a one-sided assessment of the substantiality of effect. However, without the benefit of numerous "close" cases to delineate the fine distinctions in the law, cruder expressions of balancing will better serve those involved.

This text's summary of *Timberlane II* illustrates a step by step application of *Timberlane* and *Mannington Mills* that, together with the traditional effects test, may provide a greater degree of certainty.

Step One: Does the alleged conduct have a direct, substantial, and foreseeable effect on United States commerce.[26.2] If not, the inquiry ceases and the court must decline jurisdiction.

Step Two: Is there a conflict with foreign law? If no conflict exists then jurisdiction is present and no further inquiry is required.[26.3]

Step Three: Does the other nation have a substantial interest in the issue? If not, then the U.S. interest in enforcing its anti-

---

[26.1] *See, e.g.,* In re Uranium Antitrust Litigation, 480 F. Supp. 1138, 1148 (N.D. Ill. 1979), *aff'd in part on other grounds,* 617 F.2d 1148 (7th Cir. 1980). *See* Shenefield *supra* N. 26 at 366-69, Dunfee & Friedman, "The Extra-Territorial Application of United States Antitrust Laws: A Proposal for an Interim Solution," 45 Ohio State L.J. 883, 904-905 (1984).

[26.2] This constitutes the statutory requirement under the Foreign Trade Antitrust Improvement Act of 1982, 15 U.S.C. §§ 6(a), 45(a)(3)(A). For example, in Conversation Council of Western Australia, Inc., v. Aluminum Co. of America, 518 F. Supp. 270, 275-75 (W.D. Pa. 1981), an Australian environmental group sued the U.S. parent of an Australian mining company on account of environmental injury in Australia. The court stated that there was no intended effect on U.S. commerce resulting from the acts alleged in plaintiff's complaint. *See* National Bank of Canada v. Interbank Card Ass'n, 666 F.2d 6 (2d Cir. 1981).

[26.3] The Restatement section 40 presumes a conflict with foreign law. If the minimum requirements for jurisdiction are present, and no conflict with foreign law exists there is no reason to decline to exercise jurisdiction. *See* text at Ns. 40-49.5 *infra.*

trust laws requires the exercise of jurisdiction, and no further inquiry is required.[26.4]

Step Four: Is a substantial interest of the United States at issue? If the activity has little significance to the United States, and is not likely to have significance to the United States in the future, then the court should decline to exercise jurisdiction, and no further inquiry is needed.[26.5]

Step Five: If the court has not as yet resolved jurisdiction through steps one through four, then the court faces its most difficult task. Complicated balancing factors may yet determine the outcome.

This text advocates a simplistic approach:

(A) If all parties are U.S. persons, the courts should exercise jurisdiction;
(B) otherwise,
   (i)   if the conduct was intended to affect sales and purchases from or to the United States then jurisdiction should be exercised;
   (ii) otherwise it should not.[26.6]

Such a simplistic approach leaves open the possibility of substantial conflicts with foreign laws. However, absent international agreements regulating the international application of U.S. antitrust laws, such conflict must be accepted as a conse-

---

[26.4] This constitutes a corrollary to step two. Unless the conflict with a foreign jurisdiction is serious there is no need for the U.S. court to "mitigate" its jurisdiction. *See* text at N. 52.3.

[26.5] This reflects the result in *Timberlane II*, and the general policy against lightly interfering in the domestic affairs of foreign states. *See* text at Ns. 49.3-52.2 *infra*.

[26.6] This step attempts to condense the remaining factors of the Restatement, *Timberlane I* and *Mannington Mills* into a more conclusory investigation, tempered with a general policy that whenever jurisdiction is in doubt jurisdiction should be exercised. By focusing on the nationality of the parties, intent, and U.S. imports and exports these tests indirectly address such factors as foreseeability of effect, relative interests of each nation, ability to effect a remedy or enforce compliance, and the degree to which U.S. commerce is directly implicated in the alleged conduct.

quence of the need to uniformly and consistently apply the antitrust law.[26.7]

The effects test by itself is insufficient as it fails to acknowledge foreign law. The balancing test is also insufficient as it cannot deal with situations where strong national interests collide. The simplistic five-step rule, to some degree, reconciles the two tests. A review of the major recent cases illustrates that the results of those cases fit within the five-step approach.

Viewed in terms of the five-step analysis, *Timberlane II's* result can easily be reached. *Timberlane II* found that only a small volume of U.S. commerce was affected. Although substantial enough to meet the initial requirements for jurisdiction, such commerce was too insignificant to overcome the conflict with local Honduran law.[27] Jurisdiction is declined under step three where the United States does not have a strong interest in the matter, and the foreign nation has a strong conflicting interest. The Ninth Circuit focused on the small volume of commerce involved to determine that the U.S. lacked a strong interest in the *Timberlane* case.

One might criticize the Ninth Circuit's exclusive reliance on the existing volume of exports to the United States.[27.1] A plaintiff seeking to avoid *Timberlane II* should point out that, absent the alleged constraints, the volume of U.S. commerce affected would be much greater. If, for example, the alleged restraint involved a new computer chip not yet sold in the United States, an analysis of current computer chip sales volume would be inappropriate and substantially irrelevant.

Generally, unlike *Timberlane II*, when conflicting foreign law is present, most cases will proceed to step five of the jurisdictional inquiry. The recent *Laker Airways* litigation[27.2] illustrates the relative uselessness of the *Timberlane* balancing test in a step five level of conflict of competing policies that

---

[26.7] Dunfee and Friedman, *supra* N. 26.1, at 922-23.

[27] 749 F.2d at 1385-86.

[27.1] The court relied upon lumber consumption figures in the United States for the years 1970 through 1972.

[27.2] Laker Airways v. Sabena Belgian World Airlines, 731 F.2d 909, 915 (D.C. Cir. 1984).

involve substantial international contacts with the competing jurisdictions.

Laker Airways filed suit in federal court against several defendants, including American, British and other foreign airlines. Rather than answering these suits in the United States, some defendants filed suit in the United Kingdom seeking an injunction forbidding Laker from prosecuting its antitrust action against them. Meanwhile, Laker sought an order requesting that the other defendants be restrained from seeking similar relief in the courts of the United Kingdom.[27.3]

Laker's antitrust claim was essentially that certain air carriers conspired to establish predatory pricing policies with the intent and effect of driving Laker out of business.[27.4] Although the details and course of the Laker litigation are complex, the critical issue facing the court was whether the United States should exercise antitrust jurisdiction over certain foreign defendants in view of express declarations by the British government that it would take every effort to thwart any U.S. antitrust proceedings.[27.5]

The court first examined whether the United States had jurisdiction to apply its laws to the conduct. United States jurisdiction is based upon the conduct's alleged effects on commerce in the United States.[27.6] Effects jurisdiction is not "extraterritorial" jurisdiction. Rather, effects jurisdiction acknowledges that acts outside a nation's territory may have the same harmful effect as acts performed inside the territory.[27.7] Since the effect of predatory pricing could be to

---

[27.3] *Id.* at 915, 918-20.

[27.4] *Id.* at 916-17.

[27.5] *Id.* at 914-15, 940.

[27.6] *Id.* at 922. *See* United States v. Aluminum Co. of America, 148 F.2d 416 (2d Cir. 1945); Deutsche Lufthansa Aktiengesellschaft v. Civil Aeronautics Board, 479 F.2d 912, 917 n.9 (D.C. Cir. 1973); Pacific Seafarers Inc. v. Pacific Far East Line, Inc., 404 F.2d 804, 814-15 (D.C. Cir. 1968), *cert. denied*, 393 U.S. 1093 (1969).

[27.7] Certainly the doctrine of territorial sovereignty is not such an artificial limit on the vindication of legitimate sovereign interests that the injured state confronts the wrong side of a one-way glass, powerless to counteract harmful effects originating outside its boundaries which easily pierce its "sovereign" walls while its own regulatory efforts are reflected back in its face. Unless one admits that there are certain vital interests that can be

eventually raise fares to U.S. air passengers, the alleged harmful effect on the United States was clearly present.[27.8] Nonetheless, the court also referred to other harmful effects as well,[27.9] all of which support exercise of jurisdiction under the Sherman and Clayton Acts.[27.10]

However, just as the United States had the right to regulate the conduct in question, so did the United Kingdom.[27.11] This results in concurrent jurisdiction, where both countries have the power to regulate the events that allegedly transpired as a result of the conspiracy.[27.12]

In instances of concurrent jurisdiction the normal practice is to permit parallel proceedings. However, when one court seeks to carve out exclusive jurisdiction for itself, another court can seek to enjoin such proceedings in order to preserve its own jurisdiction. Consequently, the Court of Appeals affirmed the district court's decision to issue an injunction precluding further anti-suit proceedings in the United Kingdom.[27.13]

The defendants argued, in part, that under the balancing tests, the U.S. court should defer to the United Kingdom proceedings. However, the court rejected a balancing approach. Where U.S. domestic law seeks one end, and foreign law seeks to thwart that end, and both jurisdictions have significant interests in the conduct at issue, the balancing approach cannot practically address the problems facing the court.[27.14] Either the factors counterbalance each other, or the factors are so political that the courts are not competent to engage in a

---

affected with impunity by careful selection of the decision making forum, with the results that a country may be forced to rely entirely on the good offices of a foreign state for vindication of the forum's interests—even when vindication of the forum state's own policies—then availability of territorial effects jurisdiction must be recognized. 731 F.2d at 923.

[27.8] *Id.* at 924.

[27.9] Such as injury to U.S. creditors and regulation of airline traffic in the United States. *Id.* at 924-25.

[27.10] *Id.* at 925.

[27.11] *Id.* at 926.

[27.12] *Id.*

[27.13] *Id.* at 926-30.

[27.14] *Id.* at 948.

comparative evaluation.[27.15] The court quoted from the *Uranium Litigation* cases discussed immediately hereafter: "courts are ill-equipped to balance the vital national interests of the United States and the [United Kingdom] to determine which interests predominate."[27.16]

One could argue that if all parties are foreign and all substantial acts occurred outside of the United States, then a U.S. court should decline to exercise jurisdiction. The District of Columbia Circuit seemed to downplay the importance of the fact that the plaintiff was not a United States citizen.[27.17] Nor did the court put particular importance on where certain acts occurred.[27.18] *Laker Airways* apparently takes the position that whenever significant and substantial U.S. interests are at issue, antitrust jurisdiction must be exercised.[27.19]

The court's firm decision to accept jurisdiction may, to some extent, have been a reaction to the United Kingdom's efforts to deny the court's jurisdiction.[27.20] Nonetheless, as in almost all

---

[27.15] The court particularly criticized political factors advanced in the 1981 Restatement, Tentative Draft No. 2, *Id.* at 949.

[27.16] 731 F.2d at 950, quoting In re Uranium Antitrust Litigation, 480 F. Supp. 1138, 1148 (N.C. Ill. 1978). *See* Dunfee and Friedman, *supra* N. 26.1, at 910-15.

[27.17] 731 F.2d at 934-936.

[27.18] *Id.* at 923-24.

[27.19] "Laker seeks to recover for injuries it allegedly sustained as a result of the defendants' conduct in violation of United States antitrust laws. The complaint alleges a conspiracy to drive out of business a corporation permitted by United States treaty to operate within the United States and conducting substantial business here. If Laker's allegations are proved, the intended and actual effect in the United States are clear since Laker, which was carrying up to one out of every seven transatlantic passengers, was subsequently forced into liquidation. Resolution of Laker's lawsuit would further the interests protected under United States law, since American creditors' interests in open forums, and consumers' interests in free competition may be vindicated." *Id.* at 955-56. The court also noted that U.S. courts decline jurisdiction only when the U.S. interests are *de mininis. Id.* at 951.

[27.20] "Unilateral abandonment by the Judiciary of legitimately prescribed national law in response to foreign counter-legislation would not materially advance the principles of comity and international accommodation which must form the foundation of any international system comprised of coequal nation states. The British Government's invocation of the Protection of Trading Interests act to foreclose any proceeding in a non-English forum brought to recover damages for trade injuries caused by unlawful conspiracies is a

international cartel cases, U.S. defendants were involved and, likely as not, U.S. acts were involved as well.[27.21] *Laker*, therefore, followed the result of a number of other courts, to the effect that international cartels in restraint of U.S. trade are subject to antitrust suits in U.S. courts.[27.22]

Consistent with the result in *Laker Airways*, those courts that have applied *Timberlane I*'s balancing test have done so to deny jurisdiction in a *Timberlane II* situation where the interests of the United States in the suit were speculative. The plaintiff in *Montreal Trading Ltd. v. AMAX, Inc.*[28] alleged a conspiracy to limit potash production and drive up prices for potash. Plaintiff was refused supplies of potash in Canada for resale there. The court applied the *Timberlane I* balancing test to deny relief. No United States sales were at issue and any effect on U.S. commerce was speculative and insubstantial.[28.1]

The *Timberlane I* balancing test was applied to pendent

---

naked attempt exclusively to reserve by confrontation an area of prescriptive jurisdiction shared concurrently by other nations. This assertion of interdictory jurisdiction propels into the courts a controversy whose eventual termination is restricted to two unsatisfactory alternatives: (1) either one state or the other will eventually capitulate, sacrificing its legitimate interest, or (2) a deadlock will occur to the eventual frustration of both the states' and the litigants' interests. The underlying goal of the legislation is apparently to compel the United States to cede its claims to regulate those aspects of its domestic economy deemed objectionable by the United Kingdom. However, the possibility of a cooperative, mutually profitable compromise by all affected countries is greatly restricted. Granting recognition to this form of international mechanisms necessary to resolve satisfactorily the problems generated when radically divergent national policies intersect in an area of concurrent jurisdiction." *Id.* at 954-55.

[27.21] *Id.* at 923 n. 33.

[27.22] *See* text at N. 46 *infra.*

[28] 661 F.2d 864 (10th Cir. 1981).

[28.1] *Id.* at 870. It is true that the United States imports potash from Canada, and exports its own potash to various countries. We could speculate that a restraint on trade of any commodity this country imports or exports, or even uses, could have some effect on commerce in the United States. But we believe that neither the Constitution nor the Sherman Act was intended to give such far reaching power. The Department of Justice Antitrust Guide for International Operations suggests that we should not take jurisdiction over foreign activities of United States firms "which have no direct or intended effect on United States consumers or export opportunities," for such jurisdiction would be beyond the scope Congress intended, and "could en-state claims of unfair competition in *Vespa of America Corp. v. Bajaj Auto Ltd.*[29] The dispute surrounded use of formerly licensed technology in manufacturing scooters in India for sale to countries other than the United States. The court denied jurisdiction finding conflict with Indian law and no effect on United States commerce.[29.1]

The Third,[30] Ninth,[31] and Tenth[32] Circuits have advanced balancing formulas as the basis for determining jurisdiction or determining whether jurisdiction would be exercised.[32.1] Other circuits, as exhibited by the *Laker* decision, have been more cautious. The Fifth Circuit in *Industrial Investment Development Corp. v. Mitsui & Co., Ltd.*[33] overturned a district court decision granting summary judgment to the defendant. The court found that the defendant, at that point in the proceedings, had failed to show either a lack of effect on United States commerce or any conflict with foreign law. Relying principally on the direct and substantial effects test, the Fifth Circuit stated: "Competition between two American importers to obtain a source of supply on foreign territory affects the foreign commerce of the United States."[33.1] The court therefore refused to dismiss a complaint alleging conspiracy to

croach upon the sovereignty of a foreign state without any overriding justification based on legitimate United States interest." *Id.*

[29] Vespa of America Corp. v. Bajaj Auto Ltd., 550 F. Supp. 224 (N.D. Cal. 1982).

[29.1] *Id.* at 229.

[30] Mannington Mills v. Congoleum, Inc., 595 F.2d 1287 (3d Cir. 1979).

[31] Timberlane Lumber Co. v. Bank of America, 549 F.2d 597 (9th Cir. 1976); Wells Fargo Co. v. Wells Fargo Express Co., 556 F.2d 406 (9th Cir. 1977).

[32] Montreal Trading Ltd. v. AMAX, Inc., 661 F.2d 864 (10th Cir. 1980).

[32.1] There is a dispute regarding whether the balancing test denies jurisdiction, or denies, on grounds of comity, the exercise of jurisdiction otherwise present. *See, e.g.,* Industrial Investment Development Corp. v. Mitsui & Co., Ltd., 671 F.2d 876, 884 n.7 (5th Cir. 1982), *vacated on other grounds,* 103 S. Ct. 1244 (1983); Vespa of America Corp. v. Bajaj Auto Ltd., 550 F. Supp. 224, 226-27 n.2 (N.D. Cal. 1982). *See* Swan, "International Antitrust: The Reach and Efficacy of United States Law," 63 Or. L. Rev. 177, 203 (1984).

[33] 671 F.2d 876 (5th Cir. 1982), *vacated on other grounds,* 103 S. Ct. 1244 (1983).

[33.1] 671 F.2d at 883.

monopolize the supply of lumber for import into the United States. Although *Timberlane* was cited by the Fifth Circuit, *Timberlane* was not the principal basis for the court's decision.[33.2]

In contrast, the Second Circuit has apparently rejected the *Timberlane* balancing rationale. In *National Bank of Canada v. Interbank Card Association,* the court criticized the *Timberlane* balancing test as permitting jurisdiction when only minimal effect in the United States was present.[33.3] The Second Circuit refused to adjudicate a dispute between Canadian banks regarding Master Charge credit card licensing agreements in Canada since the activities concerned had no anticompetitive effect in the United States.[33.4] The court reached this result even through the licensor was a United States citizen.

The Second Circuit's approach in *National Bank of Canada* does not conform to the five-step analysis posed in this article unless the case is interpreted as holding that the possible effect in the United States was *de minimis.* Since an American licensor was involved, a restraint regarding use of its licenses might have some effect in the United States. Based upon this fact, there might be a basis for jurisdiction, absent conflict with

---

[33.2] *Id.*

[33.3] National Bank of Canada v. Interbank Card Assn, 666 F.2d 6, 8 (2d Cir. 1981). The court stated as follows: "Without questioning the pertinence of the third test identified in Timberland, we conclude that the separate identification of the first two tests may lead unwarrantedly to an assertion of jurisdiction whenever the challenged conduct is shown to have some effect on American foreign commerce, even though the actionable aspect of the restraint, the anticompetitive effect, is felt only within the foreign market in which the injured plaintiff seeks to compete. Building upon the fundamental 'effects' test outlined by Judge Learned Hand in United States v. Aluminum Company of America, 148 F.2d 416 (2d Cir. 1945), we think the inquiry should be directed primarily toward whether the challenged restraint has, or is intended to have, any anticompetitive effect upon United States commerce, either commerce within the United States or export commerce from the United States." *Id.* at 8. *See* Bulk Oil (ZUG) A.G. v. Sun Co., Inc., 583 F. Supp. 1134, 1136-37 (S.D.N.Y. 1983).

[33.4] "The anticompetitive effect of a decline in the number of Canadian cardholders on United States commerce, however, is not clear." 666 F.2d at 9.

foreign law.[33.5] The Second Circuit failed to address the question of conflict with foreign law, although one can note that Canada is one of those jurisdictions that in the past has opposed extraterritorial application of U.S. antitrust laws.[33.6]

The Seventh Circuit also declined to apply *Timberlane's* balancing test in its decision to find jurisdiction in a uranium price fixing scheme. In *In re Uranium Antitrust Litigation*,[34] Westinghouse alleged that twenty domestic and nine foreign corporations conspired to fix the price of uranium. The activities in question were alleged to have occurred throughout the world including the United States. Relying on the "intended effects",[34.1] the court ruled that "concerted conduct both abroad and within the United States intended to affect the uranium market in this country" and provided the basis for jurisdiction.

The district court opinion had failed to find *Timberlane* of use in a situation where strong interests of the United States competed with countervailing foreign interests. The court said:

> Aside from the fact that the judiciary has little expertise, or perhaps even authority, to evaluate the economic and social policies of a foreign country, such a balancing test is inherently unworkable in this case. The competing interests here display an irreconcilible conflict on precisely the same plane of national policy.[34.2]

Although not addressing the district court's view of the balanc-

---

[33.5] The court, perhaps incorrectly, assumed that since the only American actor was a defendant, plaintiff's claim did not allege adverse effect on United States commerce. The court reasoned: "A relevant inquiry is whether Interbank, the only American actor clearly involved in this action, and the business with which it is concerned, would be adversely affected if we do not permit the assertion of jurisdiction. Perhaps the simplest answer to that question is that Interbank is a defendant in this action and presumably is acting in its self-interest. *Id.* at 9.

[33.6] *See, e.g.,* In re Uranium Antitrust Litigation, 617 F.2d 1248 (2d Cir. 1980).

[34] 617 F.2d 1248 (2d Cir. 1980).

[34.1] *Id.* at 1253-54.

[34.2] 480 F. Supp. 1138, 1148 (N.D. Ill. 1979); Shenefield, *supra* N. 26, at 367.

ing test, the Seventh Circuit upheld the district court's decision that jurisdiction should be exercised.[34.3]

Therefore, *Timberlane's* balancing test must be limited to situations where United States' interest in a transaction is minimal. The Second Circuit[35] and the District of Columbia Circuit[36] have viewed the balancing approach with disdain. The Seventh Circuit also appears to ignore *Timberlane* when serious U.S. interests are involved.[37]

§ 10.05   Application of the Five-Step Rule

These disparate approaches to jurisdiction can be reconciled through the five-step analysis suggested earlier. Hereafter, the five-step approach is applied to specific cases.

It is settled that there can be no jurisdiction absent a direct, foreseeable, and substantial effect on U.S. commerce. This principally represents the rule of *Alcoa,* as recently codified by Congress.[37.1] For purposes of this rule, the following comment from *Alcoa* is instructive:

> Almost any limitation of the supply of goods in Europe . . . or in South America may have repercussions in the United States if there is trade between the two. Yet when one considers the international complications likely to arise from an effort in this country to treat such agreements as unlawful, it is safe to assume that Congress certainly did not intend the Act to cover them.[37.2]

[34.3] 617 F.2d at 1255.

[35] National Bank of Canada v. Interbank Card Ass'n, 666 F.2d 6 (2d. Cir. 1981).

[36] Laker Airways v. Sabena Belgian World Airlines, 731 F.2d 909 (D.C. Cir. 1984).

[37] *See* text at Ns. 34 through 34.3 *supra.*

[37.1] *See, e.g.,* H.R. Rep. No. 686, 97th Cong., 2d Sess. 5-6 (1982).

[37.2] United States v. Aluminum Co. of America, 148 F.2d 416, 443 (2d Cir. 1945).

There must be more than an indirect, inconsequential effect on United States commerce. *Montreal Trading*[37.3] and *Vespa of America*[37.4] illustrate examples of de minimis effect on U.S. commerce. *National Bank of Canada*[37.5] supports this rule, provided that one minimizes the significance of the United States licensor in the alleged restraint.

The Southern District of New York, also reached this result in *El Cid Ltd. v. New Jersey Zinc Co.*[38] The plaintiff alleged that the defendant wrongfully denied it gold concessions in Bolivia. As a consequence, the plaintiff could not mine gold, which it could have imported to the United States. Also, the plaintiff alleged that if it had received the concessions, it would have purchased equipment from the United States. The court found these allegations of effect to be speculative and insignificant.[38.1] The court quoted from *Alcoa*, "We should not impute to Congress an intent to punish all whom its courts can catch, for conduct which has no consequence in the United States."[38.2]

Bulk Oil (ZUG) A.G. v. Sun Co. Ltd.,[39] another district court decision from New York, restated the Second Circuit's rejection of the *Timberlane* balancing test. *Bulk Oil* dismissed a U.S. antitrust claim based upon the defendant's compliance with a United Kingdom decree precluding shipment of oil to Israel. The plaintiff had brought suit based upon allegations of group boycott. The court failed to find anticompetitive effect in the United States derived from a boycott of oil shipments from one foreign point to another by foreign shippers, with respect to prospective foreign purchasers.[39.1] Although group boycotts may be per se violations of the antitrust laws, there is no rule stating "that any boycott, anywhere, is presumed to have an-

---

[37.3] *See* text at N. 28 through 28.1 *supra*.
[37.4] *See* text at Ns. 29 through 29.1 *supra*.
[37.5] *See* text at Ns. 33.3 through 33.4 *supra*.
[38] 551 F. Supp. 626 (S.D.N.Y. 1982).
[38.1] *Id.* at 631-32.
[38.2] *Id.* at 629, quoting 148 F.2d at 443.
[39] 553 F. Supp. at 1134 (S.D.N.Y. 1983).
[39.1] *Id.* at 1137.

ticompetitive effects in the United States."[39.2]

If a direct, substantial, and reasonably foreseeable effect is present, the courts will permit a suit unless a conflict with foreign law is present.

A number of pre-*Timberlane* cases illustrate the courts' general willingness to accept jurisdiction when a direct, substantial, and foreseeable effect on United States commerce is present. This test can be readily satisfied when restrictions are aimed directly at the United States market.[40]

Restraints involving the import or export of U.S. goods, services, technology, or contractual privileges generally satisfy the initial effects test of jurisdiction.[40.1] In *Sulmeyer v. Seven-up Co.*,[41] the plaintiff, a bankruptcy trustee of Bubble-Up International Ltd., alleged that the defendant's agreements with foreign bottlers prohibited those bottlers from producing soft drinks of other companies with the same flavor as Seven-up. Based upon the allegation that these restrictions were designed to limit the foreign franchising efforts of Bubble-Up, the court granted jurisdiction. The court cited the following factors in reaching this conclusion: (1) a substantial impact on U.S. commerce was alleged; (2) both plaintiff and defendant were American companies; and, (3) the challenged conduct included actions within the United States. Quoting from *Continental Ore*, the court stated: "A conspiracy to monopolize or restrain the domestic or foreign commerce of the United States is not outside the reach of the Sherman Act just because part of the conduct complained of occurs in foreign countries."[41.1]

In a similar fashion, it is within the jurisdiction of the antitrust law to consider claim that a U.S. company improperly

---

[39.2] *Id.*

[40] *See, e.g.,* Fleischmann Distilling Corp. v. Distillers Co., Ltd., 395 F. Supp. 221 (S.D.N.Y. 1975); Sanib Corp. v. United Fruit Co., 135 F. Supp. 764 (S.D.N.Y. 1955).

[40.1] *See* United States v. Sisal Sales Corp., 274 U.S. 268, 269 (1927); United States v. Singer Mfg. Co., 374 U.S. 174 (1963); Pacific Coast Agricultural Export Ass'n v. Sunkist Growers, Inc., 526 F.2d 1196 (9th Cir. 1975); United States v. General Electric Co., 82 F. Supp. 753, 847 (D.N.J. 1949).

[41] 411 F. Supp. 635 (S.D.N.Y. 1976).

[41.1] Continental Ore Co. v. Union Carbide & Carbon Co., 370 U.S. 690, 704 (1962).

used its advantages in the domistic telex market to attempt to restrain competition in the international telex market.[41.2]

Rather than a U.S. person seeking to restrict the business of a competitor, *Todhunter-Mitchell & Co., Ltd. v. Anheuser Busch, Inc.*[42] addressed the jurisdictional issue, where one party claims that a U.S. person is restricting his own foreign commerce. The Plaintiff was a Bahamaian corporation engaged in the wholesale distribution of liquor and beer in the Bahama Islands. In direct competition with plaintiff was Bahama Blenders, Ltd., another Bahamas corporation. Defendant Anheuser-Busch sold its product to Bahama Blenders, but refused to sell to the plaintiff. In ruling that plaintiff could sue Anheuser-Busch for antitrust violations, the court determined that the acts which constitute the antitrust violation occurred primarily in this country and involved the foreign commerce of the United States with a foreign nation.[42.1]

In *Industria Siciliana Asfalk, Bitami, S.P.A. v. Exxon Research & Engineering Co.*,[43] the plaintiff successfully established jurisdiction in a suit which alleged that the plaintiff was the victim of a reciprocal dealing arrangement with Exxon and Exxon's Italian subsidiary, which required the plaintiff to purchase unwanted engineering services. Exxon argued that the plaintiff was a foreign corporation not engaged in business within the United States and therefore, the alleged injury was wholly without the United States. The court disagreed noting that restraints on the export of engineering services was a restraint upon U.S. commerce. If the plaintiff was coerced into buying an unwanted product because of activity which had the effect of restraining the foreign commerce of the United States, then plaintiff had standing to bring suit, even though its injury may well have been entirely confined to a foreign country.

Even the alleged monopolization of foreign tourist facilities can be subject to a U.S. antitrust action where U.S. tourist trade

---

[41.2] ITT World Communications Inc. v. Western Union Telegraph Co., 524 F. Supp. 702 (S.D.N.Y. 1981).

[42] 375 F. Supp. 610 (E.D. Pa. 1974).

[42.1] 383 F. Supp. 586, 588 (E.D. Pa. 1974).

[43] 1977-1 U.S. Trade Cases § 61, 256 (S.D.N.Y. 1977).

is involved. In the case of *Dominicus Americana Bohio v. Gulf & Western Industries, Inc.*,[44] the court postponed a final determination of jurisdiction until sufficient discovery had taken place. Nonetheless, the court noted that the activities of the United States defendant weighed heavily in favor of jurisdiction.[44.1]

The U.S. status of the defendant can weigh heavily in favor of jurisdiction. The willingness to regulate the U.S. defendant wherever it may do business is further illustrated by *Branch v. FTC*,[45] which applied the Federal Trade Commission Act to foreign commerce of the United States. Branch sold correspondence courses by mail in foreign countries, fraudulently representing that his courses were from an educational institute or university. The court determined that this foreign advertising was an unfair practice injuring U.S. competitors. The injury to U.S. competitors conferred jurisdiction in that: "Congress has the power to prevent unfair trade practices in foreign commerce by citizens of the United States, although some of the acts are done outside the territorial limits of the United States."[45.1]

However, the plaintiff must also take care to allege an effect on U.S. commerce. In *A.G.S. Electronics, Ltd. v. B.S.R. (U.S.A.), Ltd.*, the court denied jurisdiction in an antitrust claim based upon a wrongful termination of a distributorship agreement for the territory of Canada and the Far East. Although the facts seemed similar to *Todhunter Mitchell* discussed *supra*, the court denied jurisdiction because plaintiffs had failed to allege an effect on the exports of the United States.[45.2]

A cartel arrangement regarding the constraint of a substantial portion of the world market will also generally be presumed to have sufficient jurisdictional effect in the United States. The *National Lead* case stated: "No citation of authority is any longer necessary to support the proposition that a combi-

---

[44] 473 F. Supp. 680 (S.D.N.Y. 1979).
[44.1] *Id.* at 688.
[45] 141 F.2d 31 (7th Cir. 1944).
[45.1] 141 F.2d at 35 (emphasis added).
[45.2] 480 F. Supp. 707 (S.D.N.Y. 1981).

nation of competitors, which by agreement divides the world into exclusive trade areas, and suppresses all competition among the members of the combination, offends the Sherman Act."[46] The *National Lead* court took pains to note that the cartel had an immediate impact on U.S. commerce.[46.1] Later cases have substantially ignored an assessment of the probable U.S. effect on the cartel. If a U.S. defendant is found to be a member of a market allocation conspiracy, the appropriate U.S. impact is presumed and all defendants, both foreign and domestic, become subject to the jurisdiction of U.S. courts.[46.2]

The *Alcoa* case involved a cartel arrangement. However, the court's task was complicated by the fact that the principal defendants were foreign citizens. The foreign defendants in *Alcoa* had agreed to a system which effectively imposed quotas upon the production of aluminum in certain foreign countries. This agreement had been in effect for several years and at one time had been amended. The effect of that amendment was to include within the quotas all imports into the United States. Even though the United States was not specifically named in the agreement, this inclusion was sufficient to convey an intent to restrain the foreign commerce of the United States. Having found the necessary intent, the *Alcoa* court then examined whether the arrangement had an effect on U.S. commerce. As the court itself implied, there was no real evidence that the

---

[46] United States v. National Lead Co., 63 F. Supp. 513, 523 (S.D.N.Y. 1945); *See also* United States v. American Tobacco Co., 221 U.S. 106, 184 (1911); United States v. Timken Roller Bearing, 83 F. Supp. 284 (N.D. Oh. 1949); United States v. Imperial Chemical Industries, 100 F. Supp. 504 (S.D.N.Y. 1951); United States v. General Dyestuff, Corp., 57 F. Supp. 642 (S.D.N.Y. 1944).

[46.1] "Clearly this combination affects the interstate and foreign commerce of the United States. No titanum pigments enter the United States except with the consent of Natcoma Lead. No foreign titanum pigments move in interstate commerce without disapproval. No titanum pigment produced by National Lead may leave the ports of the United States for points outside the Western Hemisphere." 63 F. Supp. at 522.

[46.2] *See, e.g.,* United States v. United States Alkali Export Ass'n, 86 F. Supp. 59, 71 (S.D.N.Y. 1949), where the court limited its inquiry to whether the U.S. markets were the specific subject of the cartel agreements without assessing the practical economic effect of the agreements; United States v. Bayer Co., 135 F. Supp. 65 (S.D.N.Y. 1955).

quota agreement had an actual effect on U.S. imports. Nonetheless, the court concluded that a violation of the Sherman Act had occurred. Having found the requisite intent to limit imports through the imposition of quotas, it assumed that the agreement had the effect of so doing, unless the defendants could prove the contrary.[46.3] Since defendants could not prove lack of effect, there was a violation of the U.S. antitrust law.

In the final analysis, the only evidence that *Alcoa* had of a violation of U.S. law was an agreement to restrict output which did not exclude U.S. commerce. The intent to affect U.S. commerce was not explicit, nor were there any factual findings of an effect on U.S. commerce. The alleged violation, a restriction of output, is a severe U.S. antitrust violation constituting a per se offense. Thus, since *Alcoa* is so devoid of factual findings, it implies that the very character of the offense imposed upon a large volume of world commerce may be sufficient to warrant jurisdiction and impose liability.

Zenith Radio Corp. v. Matsushita Electric Industrial Co.[47] provides further support for the argument that the character of the violation will to a great extent determine the willingness of the court to exercise jurisdiction. In that case the plaintiffs, a U.S. electronics firms, alleged that Japanese companies had conspired to take over the consumer electronics market in the U.S. by artificially lowering their export prices. Matsushita argued that the antitrust law could not apply to it since all of its alleged acts took place outside of the U.S. and since it made no sales within the U.S. The court, citing *Alcoa*, disagreed:

> American antitrust laws extend to conduct abroad by foreign corporations, at least when that conduct is intended to affect United States interstate or foreign commerce, when it actually has such effect, and when a balancing of considerations of international comity leads the court to exercise that jurisdiction.[47.1]

The court focused on the fact that although the defendant itself did not sell products in the U.S., it was allegedly part of

---

[46.3] 148 F.2d at 444.

[47] 494 F. Supp. 1161 (E.D. Pa. 1980).

[47.1] *Id.* at 1189.

a conspiracy which did. This was sufficient for jurisdiction. Stated in other terms, the foreign defendant was indirectly involved in what amounted to a potential direct violation of the law — a conspiracy to regulate prices. "Conspiracy" and "price restraints" provided jurisdiction. Therefore, when the foreign defendant intentionally and directly imposes restraints on the sale of goods in the United States, jurisdiction will normally be present.[47.2]

Nonetheless, even when per se offenses are involved, it appears that the restriction must at least be designed to restrain international commerce, if not U.S. foreign commerce, to a significant extent. In *Alfred Bell Co. v. Catalda Fine Arts*,[48] the court also addressed the significance of an English copyright guild agreement to restrict output of published products. The defendant in a copyright action had raised the defense that the plaintiff had violated the antitrust laws through its participation in guild activities. In rejecting this defense, the court noted the following facts:

> Of some 600 or 700 members . . . only "one or two" are in this country; for all that the slender proof shows, their participation in Guild activities may have been limited to the receipt of Guild catalogues; the plaintiff [against whom the defense was being asserted] has no office or assets here, and there is no evidence that it acted here on behalf of the Guild. So far as the evidence discloses, the output restriction was not imposed with sales in the United States in mind. Accordingly, we take it that the restriction was meant to have, and did have, at most, only an incidental peripheral, reference to sales in the United States of America.[48.1]

Significantly, however, the court did not conclude that there was no justifiable antitrust violation. Rather, the court only determined that if an antitrust violation existed, it was not

---

[47.2] Fleischmann Distiling Corp. v. Distillers Co., Ltd., 395 F. Supp. 221 (S.D.N.Y. 1975). A program of price stabilization in Japan coupled with customer allocation in the United States may present an actionable Sherman Act claim. *In re Japanese Electronic Products Antitrust Litigation*, 723 F.2d 238, 306 (3d Cir. 1983).

[48] 191 F.2d 99 (2d Cir. 1951).

[48.1] 191 F.2d at 105-106.

sufficient to act as a defense to plaintiff's claims that defendants had violated the copyright laws.[48.2] Commerce between two foreign points can become subject to U.S. antitrust law when there is sufficient impact on the United States. Consider for example, restraints in international ocean and air transportation. If a U.S. point of origination or destination is involved in the restraint, the courts will readily accept jurisdiction.[48.3] The issues become more complicated, however, when the alleged restraints do not involve traffic to or from the United States. In *Pacific Seafarers, Inc. v. Pacific Far East Line, Inc.,*[49] the plaintiffs alleged restraints in the ocean traffic between foreign ports of goods purchased by foreign governments with U.S. aid. The provisions of the aid program required that U.S. flag vessels be used to transport the purchased goods. Based upon this, the court construed the plaintiff's allegations as presenting "a conspiracy to drive plaintiffs out of the business of selling United States-flag shipping services [which] is a restraint on the United States foreign commerce subject to the Sherman Act."[49.1]

It is not clear whether foreign port to port traffic of foreign persons is also subject to the jurisdiction of U.S. antitrust laws. In *In re Grand Jury Investigation of the Shipping Industry,*[49.2] this issue was discussed. In regard to an investigation of the shipping industry pursuant to the antitrust laws and the shipping act, the court determined that the grand jury had authority to request data on foreign port to port traffic since this traffic could be carrying U.S. goods. Movants had sought to quash the subpoena duces tecum arguing that U.S. antitrust law applied only to the import or export of goods and therefore could not apply to the traffic for which data was sought. The court disagreed, stating that such traffic may have a sufficient effect on the foreign commerce of the United States and, therefore, might be subject to the antitrust laws. Problems

---

[48.2] *Id.*

[48.3] *See, e.g.,* Thomsen v. Cayser, 243 U.S. 66, 88 (1917); United States v. Pacific & Arctic Railway Navigation Co., 228 U.S. 87 (1913); Civil Aeronautics Board v. British Airways Board, 433 F. Supp. 1379 (S.D.N.Y. 1977).

[49] 404 F.2d 804 (D.C. Cir. 1968).

[49.1] *Id.* at 810.

[49.2] 186 F. Supp. 298 (D.D.C. 1960).

involved in extraterritorial discovery are discussed in greater detail in a later section.

It should be noted that the rule of effects jurisdiction will be moderated if there is substantial conflict with foreign law. If the interest of the foreign nation is insubstantial, jurisdiction will be retained, despite the potential for conflict. Otherwise, in the event of substantial conflict with foreign law, jurisdiction will be declined, unless the United States interest in the matter is also important.

This rule overlays *Timberlane* and *Mannington Mills* rule of reason concerns, in addition to the *Alcoa* effects test of jurisdiction. This rule is most efficiently applied by treating the balancing test as a special rule where the courts, due to comity concerns, decline to exercise jurisdiction even though jurisdiction otherwise would be present.[49.3] The best example of the application of this rule is *Timberlane II* where, although jurisdictional effect was present, the interest of the United States in the matter was so clearly outweighed by conflicting foreign law that jurisdiction was not exercised.[49.4] Another example is *Alfred Bell,* where British guild law outweighed the U.S. antitrust interests in a copyright infringement suit.[49.5]

The Lanham Act regarding trademark abuse may not be totally analogous to the U.S. antitrust laws, as it is not clear if the Lanham Act requires substantial effect.[49.6] The Lanham Act cases involving foreign trademarks often appear to turn on the court's assessment of the foreign nation's stake in the trademark at issue. In *Steele v. Bulova Watch Co.,*[50] the plaintiff sought to enjoin the defendant from using the name "Bulova" on watches which the defendant manufactured in Mexico and had successfully defended that name in Mexican courts.

In analyzing the jurisdictional question, the court first noted that Mexico's grant of a trademark did not evidence Mexico's interest in the actual exercise of the trademark privilege. The

---

[49.3] *See, e.g.,* Industrial Investment Development Corp. v. Mitsui & Co., Ltd., 671 F.2d 876, 884 n. 7 (5th Cir. 1982); In re Uranium Antitrust Litigation, 617 F.2d 1248, 1255 (7th Cir. 1980).

[49.4] *See* text at Ns. 25 through 25.3 *supra.*

[49.5] *See* text at Ns. 48 through 48.2 *supra.*

[49.6] *See* text at N. 52 *infra.*

[50] 344 U.S. 280 (1952).

court then determined that Steele's acts had an injurious effect on a U.S. business, noting that many Americans travel to Mexico where they buy spurious Bulova watches. But a crucial fact was the U.S. citizenship and U.S. domicile of defendant Steele. The circuit court quoted from Section 63 of the Restatement of Conflict of Laws:

> A nation recognized as such in the law of nations had jurisdiction over its nationals wherever they may be to require or forbid them to do an act unless the exercise of this jurisdiction involved the violation of the law or public policy of the state where the national is.[50.1]

The court therefore had power to regulate the defendant's acts and, presumably, issues regarding interference in Mexican law would thereby be minimized.

Vanity Fair Mills v. T. Eaton Co., however, involved a foreign defendant rather than a U.S. citizen and yielded a different result. Eaton obtained a Canadian trademark for "Vanity Fair" after the plaintiff, through its advertising, had established the value of that name in Canada. Vanity Fair sought to challenge the validity of Eaton's Canadian trademark. The court refused to accept jurisdiction. The court did not think that Congress intended the Lanham Act to "be applied to acts committed by a foreign national in his home country under a presumably valid trademark registration in that country."[50.2]

The *Vanity Fair* court sought to distinguish *Bulova* on the basis that the Mexican trademark at issue in *Bulova* had been cancelled, and therefore the public policy of a foreign government was not at issue as it was in *Vanity Fair*. The court in *Bulova* made the following comment with respect to the Mexican government's interest in the suit: "It could not be contended that Steele's Mexican trademark placed upon him any duty to use the name 'Bulova'. The Republic of Mexico was not interested in his exercise of the privilege purportedly granted."[50.3]

[50.1] 194 F.2d at 571, *aff'd*, 344 U.S. 280 (1952).

[50.2] 234 F.2d 633, 642 (2d Cir. 1956).

[50.3] 194 F.2d at 571. The circuit court decided before Mexico subsequently invalidated defendant's mark, 344 U.S. at 285. The Supreme Court, noting

The Fifth Circuit decision in *American Rice Inc. v. Arkansas Rice Growers Cooperative Association*[51] has described the *Bulova* decision as holding that "a United States district court has jurisdiction to award relief to an American corporation against acts of trademark infringement and unfair competition consummated in a foreign country by a citizen and resident of the United States."[51.1]

The *American Rice* case set forth a limited balancing test for determining jurisdiction in a trademark infringement case. The principal factors of this test are "the citizenship of the defendant, the effect on United States commerce, and the existence of a conflict with foreign law."[51.2] Although these factors are not exclusive, they are the predominant factors.[51.3]

The *American Rice* court exercised jurisdiction. The defendant was an American corporation. The foreign sales of rice at issue had a substantial impact on United States commerce, and the defendant had failed to establish a legal right to use the mark in Saudi Arabia.[51.4] The court distinguished *Vanity Fair* on the basis that the defendant in that action established a superior trademark right in the foreign jurisdiction.[51.5]

The Ninth Circuit applied the *Timberlane* balancing test to

---

that Mexico had invalidated the mark, stated that "there is no conflict which might afford petitioner a pretext that [Lanham Act] relief would impugn foreign law."

[51] 701 F.2d 408 (5th Cir. 1983).

[51.1] *Id.* at 413.

[51.2] *Id.* at 414.

[51.3] The court cited *Timberlane I,* and Wells Fargo & Co. v. Wells Fargo Express Co., 556 F.2d 406, 428-29 (9th Cir. 1977) (discussed in the text hereafter), as a source of additional factors. *Id.* at 414.

[51.4] "Absent a determination by a Saudi court that Riceland has a legal right to use its marks, and that those marks do not infringe [plaintiff's] mark, we are unable to conclude that it would be an affront to Saudi sovereignty or law if we affirm the district court's injunction prohibiting the defendant from injuring the plaintiff's Saudi Arabian commerce conducted from the United States." 701 F.2d at 415-16.

[51.5] The court stated that Vanity Fair "followed the act of state doctrine, applicable when exclusive rights are confined by the act of a foreign sovereign, the ramifications of which we may avoid." *Id.* at 416. Reference to the act of state doctrine is perhaps too strong. *Vanity Fair* chose to avoid an obvious conflict with foreign law in a dispute in which the defendant was foreign, not a U.S. citizen.

a Lanham Act claim involving foreign commerce. *Wells Fargo & Co. v. Wells Fargo Express Co.*,[52] perhaps incorrectly, stated that "substantial" effect on U.S. commerce is not required so long as the balancing test is satisfied. The factors of citizenship, effect on U.S. commerce, and degree of conflict with foreign law are but a few of the factors to be balanced.[52.1] Noting that some of defendant's foreign marks had already been invalidated by proceedings in various countries, the Ninth Circuit remanded to the district court for further findings of fact.[52.2]

Although distinguishable from Sherman Act claims, the Lanham Act cases illustrate that conflict with foreign law may lead the court to decline jurisdiction which otherwise might be exercised, so long as the United States policy interests in the transaction are not significant. Consequently, as in *Vanity Fair*, where the defendant was foreign, and the mark is a presumably valid foreign mark, jurisdiction, otherwise present due to the substantial effect on commerce, is not exercised.

Mere presence of conflict with foreign law does not require the court to refrain from jurisdiction. If the interest of the foreign nation in the suit is insubstantial then jurisdiction should always be exercised by the U.S. court whenever sufficient jurisdictional effect is present. Illustrating this principle is the *Bulova* case where the court recognized that Mexican interest in the litigation was minimal.[52.3]

If there is a conflict of law, and if the interests of the U.S. and the foreign nation are both substantial, then jurisdiction should be retained, unless foreign parties are involved and the conduct in question was *not* consciously intended to affect sales or purchases from or to the United States.

This author is unaware of any U.S. case which declined to exercise antitrust jurisdiction where the United States interest in the matter was substantial. On the other hand, all cases which have exercised jurisdiction over foreign defendants, despite probable conflict with foreign law, have done so in situations where it could reasonably be inferred that the foreign

---

[52] 556 F.2d 406 (9th Cir. 1977).

[52.1] *Id.* at 428-29.

[52.2] *Id.* at 429.

[52.3] *See* text at Ns. 50-50.1 *supra.*

defendants had deliberately intended to restrain the flow of goods or services into or out of the United States. The restraint was imposed upon the import-export sale itself, not upon some other level of activity such as the manufacturing process.[53]

If only U.S. citizens are involved, then jurisdiction should always be proper,[53.1] absent a special consideration such as the act of state doctrine.[54] The *Laker Airways* case involved an alleged restraint on air traffic into and out of the United States. The court exercised jurisdiction despite vehement objections from the United Kingdom.[55] The *Uranium* case prompted several governments to object to the United States proceedings. The court nonetheless exercised jurisdiction over alleged restraints regarding the import of uranium into the United States.[56]

In *United States v. Watchmakers of Switzerland Information Center, Inc.*,[57] the court found that a Collective Convention designed to regulate the export of Swiss watches throughout the world in general, and the United States, in particular, was a violation of U.S. antitrust laws. The court reached its conclusion despite the fact that the defendant's activities were endorsed by the Swiss government.[58]

United States v. Imperial Chemicals Industries, Ltd. involved restraints on U.S. exports implemented through foreign licensing agreements.[59] The court exercised jurisdiction despite the conflict with British law, and eventually went so far

---

[53] The importance of export-import trade is highlighted in 15 U.S.C. § 6(a).

[53.1] *See* Blackmer v. United States, 284 U.S. 421 (1932); Cook v. Tait, 256 U.S. 47 (1924); United States v. Bowman, 260 U.S. 94 (1922).

[54] *See* discussion of the doctrine of sovereign compulsion in the act of state chapter.

[55] *See* text at Ns. 27.2 through 27.22 *supra*.

[56] *See* text at Ns. 34 through 37 *supra*.

[57] 1963 CCH Trade Cases ¶ 70,600 (S.D.N.Y. 1963).

[58] The court did eventually modify its decree to minimize conflict with Swiss law. 1965 CCH Trade Cases ¶ 71,352 (S.D.N.Y. 1965).

[59] 105 F. Supp. 215 (S.D.N.Y. 1952).

as to order a British defendant to relinquish certain of its British technology rights.[59.1]

Daishowa International v. North Coast Export[60] involved an alleged buyer's cartel organized in Japan with respect to purchases of wood chips in the United States and North America. The court placed minimal emphasis on the *Timberlane* balancing test[61] and exercised jurisdiction in view of "the serious nature of the anticompetitive conduct alleged, and the foreseeability of the harm occurring from the alleged activities."[62] The court downplayed the significance of the defendant's claim that its activities were specifically endorsed by Japanese policy and exempted from Japanese antitrust law.[63]

In sum, the balancing test can provide a basis for the courts to decline jurisdiction where a conflict with foreign law exists, the interest of the foreign nation is substantial, and either the U.S. lacks a substantial interest in the dispute or U.S. imports and exports were not the target of the alleged restraint. Otherwise the courts will exercise jurisdiction whenever there is a direct, foreseeable, and substantial effect on United States commerce.

§ 10.06   Forum Non Conveniens

In addition to lack of jurisdiction a defendant can argue for dismissal of an international antitrust case on the basis of forum non conveniens. Such arguments are rarely successful when an antitrust claim provides the central basis of the complaint. The U.S. policy in favor of enforcing the antitrust laws is so strong that the courts are reluctant to transfer jurisdiction.[64] If the alternative foreign forum lacks a similar antitrust law, transfer

---

[59.1] *Id.* at 228.

[60] 1982-2 CCH Trade Cases ¶ 64,774 (N.D. Cal. 1982).

[61] Note, *"Daishower International v. North Coast Export:* An Alternative Approach in the Judicial Balancing of International Comity Considerations," 15 L. & Pol'y Int'l Bus. 613 (1981) [hereinafter cited as "Alternative Approach"].

[62] 1982-2 CCH Trade Cases ¶ 64,724, at 71,790.

[63] "Alternative Approach," *supra* N. 61, at 625-27.

[64] *See, e.g.,* Laker Airways Ltd. v. Pan American World Airways, 568 F. Supp. 811, 813-14 (D.D.C. 1983).

of the case would leave the plaintiff without an effective meaningful remedy.[64.1] As a consequence at least one court has determined that antitrust suits are not subject to forum non conveniens concerns.[64.2]

§ 10.07 Sovereignty Defenses

Once the requisite U.S. interest has been found so as to permit jurisdiction under the antitrust laws, there remains to be addressed whether consideration of the action might yet be barred by one of the sovereign defenses. Basically, two forms of sovereignty defenses might be raised: (1) *The Defense of Sovereign Immunity:* The defendant named is a foreign sovereign who is granted immunity out of traditional principles of comity; and (2) *The Defense of the Act of State Doctrine:* The defendant named is a private citizen, but the act complained of was the act of a foreign sovereign, or a private defendant acting at the direction of the foreign sovereign which, out of principles of comity, cannot be reviewed by the courts. As will become evident, the geographic territory in which the act takes place or within which sovereign policy is implemented and the commercial character of the act or policies is crucial to the applicability of either defense.

[1] Sovereign Immunity

The once mighty doctrine of sovereign immunity had been eroded over time by the case law to the extent that judicial developments were codified in the "Foreign Sovereign's Immunities Act of 1976." Whereas once a foreign sovereign could not be held liable in U.S. courts for his alleged wrongdoings, under current law a foreign sovereign can be sued for violations of U.S. law incurred in connection with their commercial

---

[64.1] *Id.* at 817.

[64.2] Industrial Investment Development Corp. v. Mitsui Co., Ltd., 671 F.2d 876, 891 (5th Cir. 1982), *vacated on other grounds,* 103 S. Ct. 1244 (1983).

activities occurring within or having a direct effect upon the United States, and for certain other alleged wrongs as well. Section 4(a) of the Act[65] states the general rule that a foreign state is immune from suit, foreign states being defined to include political subdivisions, agencies, and instrumentalities of the foreign state.[66] From this broad grant of immunity are carved certain exceptions, two of which are particularly important for purposes of antitrust cases.

[a] The Commercial Exception

A foreign sovereign is not immune from an antitrust suit in those instances where he is engaged in commercial activities connected with the United States. A case may be brought against a foreign sovereign where "the action is based upon a commercial activity carried on in the United States by the foreign state; or upon an act performed in the United States in connection with a commercial activity of the foreign state elsewhere; or upon an act outside the territory of the United States in connection with a commercial activity of the foreign state elsewhere and that act causes a direct effect in the United States."[67]

The statute further defines commercial activity as follows:

> A "commercial activity" means either a regular course of commercial conduct or a particular commercial transaction or act. The commercial character of an activity shall be determined by reference to the nature of the course of conduct or particular transaction or act, rather than by reference to its purpose.[68]

A commercial activity carried on in the United States means

---

[65] P.L. 94-583 *see*, 4(a).

[66] 28 U.S.C. § 1603(a). *See, e.g.,* Edlow International Co. v. Nuklearna Elektrarna krsko, 441 F. Supp. 827 (D.D.C. 1977) for a discussion of this statutory definition.

[67] 28 U.S.C. § 1606 (a)(2).

[68] 28 U.S.C. § 1603 (d).

an activity having "substantial contact with the United States."[69]

The "commercial exception" described above was applied in *Outboard Marine Corp. v. Pezetel*,[70] to permit suit against a trade agency of the Polish government, which had allegedly violated the Sherman Act, the Wilson Tariff Act, and the Antidumping Act in its method of marketing golf carts to U.S. distributors. As a defense to Outboard Marine's allegations, Pezetel raised the doctrine of sovereign immunity. Pezetel argued that the commercial exception to immunity outlined above was limited to ordinary tort and contract claims and did not extend to antitrust violations. After a brief review of the legislative history, the court concluded that the commercial exception was not so limited and that Pezetel was therefore subject to suit for alleged antitrust violations occurring within the U.S.[71]

In *Pezetel*, however, it was evident that the tortious activity was both commercial and within the territorial confines of the United States. Had the allegedly illegal agreements been with foreign distributors who in turn imported into the United States, it would be more doubtful as to whether the commercial exception to the sovereign immunity doctrine applies. Specifically, no court has yet to consider whether the statutory requirement of "direct effect" applicable to the commercial exception to immunity imposes a test which requires greater, lesser, or equivalent impact on U.S. commerce than does the jurisdictional test of the antitrust laws in general. Logically, as long as the tortious activity was commercial activity, the standard of effect applicable to the commercial exception and the standard of effect applicable to antitrust jurisdiction should be identical.[71.1] If such is the case, then the foreign sovereign's only defense to antitrust action other than lack of jurisdictional

---

[69] 28 U.S.C. § 1603 (e).

[70] 461 F. Supp. 384 (D. Del. 1978).

[71] 461 F. Supp. at 395.

[71.1] Tending to support this conclusion is the following quote from the House Committee Report to the Sovereign Immunities Act: "Neither the term 'direct effect' nor the concept of 'substantial contacts' embodied in section 1603(e) is intended to alter the application of the Sherman Antitrust Act, 15 U.S.C. 1, *et seq.* to any defendant." [1976] U.S. Code Cong. & Adm. News at 6618.

effect is that his allegedly tortious acts were not commercial in character.

Those cases not involving antitrust claims have on occasion applied the effect requirement of the commercial exception to immunity by assessing the alleged acts in terms of the due process and fairness rules of *International Shoe.*[72] Thus, *Carey v. National Oil Corp.*[73] determined that contracts for the purchase of Libyan Oil between a foreign subsidiary of a U.S. company and an agency which was an agency of the Libyan government did not subject that agency or Libya to suit in U.S. courts for the alleged breach of those contracts. The deprivation of oil to foreign companies, even if that oil was to be shipped to the United States, did not create the requisite minimum contacts for jurisdiction under *International Shoe.*

In a much easier case, the court in *Upton v. Empire of Iran*[74] dismissed tort claims filed against the Iranian government for injuries sustained by plaintiffs when a roof of a building in the Tehran airport collapsed upon them. The alleged tortious activities did not satisfy the minimum contact rules of *International Shoe.* However, when the alleged tort arose as part of an airline's commercial traffic into and out of the United States, the requisite effect in the United States is present even though the wrong occurred outside of the United States.[74.1]

The limits of the commercial exception of the Foreign Sovereign Immunities Act have been the subject of much recent litigation. The final rules which emerge will likely be a blend of the minimum contact rules of *International Shoe* and parallels to the "effects" requirements so often necessary for subject matter jurisdiction in many actions, including antitrust cases.[74.2] In the interim it is only necessary to note that few if

---

[72] International Shoe v. Washington, 326 U.S. 310 (1945).

[73] 453 F. Supp. 1097 (S.D.N.Y. 1978).

[74] 459 F. Supp. 264 (D.D.C. 1978); *see* Harris v. VAO, Intourist, Moscow, 481 F. Supp. 1056 (E.D.N.Y. 1979). *But see* In re Rio Grande Transport, Inc., 516 F. Supp. 1155 (S.D.N.Y. 1981) (collision between U.S. vessel and ocean vessel operated by foreign sovereign in international commerce had sufficient effect upon commerce of the United States to warrant jurisdiction.).

[74.1] Sugarman v. Aeromexico, Inc., 626 F.2d 270 (3d Cir. 1980).

[74.2] *See* Texas Trading & Milling Corp. v. Federal Republic of Nigeria, 647

any antitrust actions will be dismissed based upon sovereign immunity. That one case which relied on sovereign immunity to dismiss an antitrust action was modified by the appeals court so that the result rested on the act of state doctrine.[74.3] Most antitrust actions should fall within the commercial exception to sovereign immunity.

[b] The International Law Exception

A foreign sovereign may also be sued where it holds property in the U.S. which was acquired in violation of international law. Thus a case may be brought against a foreign sovereign where "rights in property taken in violation of international law are in issue and that property or any property exchanged for such property is present in the United States in connection with a commercial activity carried on in the United States by the foreign state; or that property or any property exchanged for such property is owned or operated by an agency or instrumentality of the foreign state and that agency or instrumentality is engaged in a commercial activity in the United States."[75]

Under this exception the tortious act itself need not have a direct effect on the United States as long as the "rights in property" illegally appropriated can be traced to the United States or to an agency in the United States. Under this exception, however, the claim against the sovereign must arise from a violation of international law; and the property must have come to the United States in connection with a commercial activity, or the agency holding the property is engaged in a commercial activity in the United States.

As a practical matter, in the antitrust context the most probable violation of international law would be a foreign government's expropriation of property of the plaintiff. In the past such expropriations were not considered to be violations of

---

F.2d 300 (2d Cir. 1981).

[74.3] International Ass'n of Machinists & Aerospace Workers v. OPEC, 477 F. Supp. 553 (C.D. Cal. 1979), *aff'd on other grounds*, 649 F.2d 1354 (9th Cir. 1981).

[75] 28 U.S.C. § 1605 (a)(3).

international law.[76] However, recent court decisions would indicate an increasing willingness by the courts to declare that certain expropriations violate international law.[76.1] As doctrines of international law gain increased recognition in the courts, the international law exception to sovereign immunity will gain vitality.

Another unanswered question is whether a foreign government's violation of a treaty, convention, United Nations' resolution, or other international compact will supply a sufficient international law violation as would render the foreign government subject to suit in U.S. courts. Notably, the United States itself cannot be sued by its own citizens for its violations of international agreements unless they are self-executing or confer rights on citizens of the United States through implementing legislation enacted by Congress.[77]

[c] Suits Involving the United States

Finally, the executive branch of the U.S. government itself may be subject to injunctive suit for its own actions which violate the antitrust laws. The traditional deference afforded the executive in matters concerning international relations may afford the executive no protection where, without Congressional authority, it attempts to alter the commercial relationship between the United States and another country in a manner which violates the antitrust laws.[78]

---

[76] *See, e.g.*, Banco Nacional de Cuba v. Sabbatino, 376 U.S. 398 (1964); Hunt v. Mobil Oil Co., 550 F.2d 68 (2d Cir. 1977); United Mexican States v. Ashley, 556 S.W.2d 784 (Tex. 1977).

[76.1] *See* the discussion in Banco Nacional de Cuba v. Chase Manhatten Bank, 505 F. Supp. 412, 429-32, 435 (S.D.N.Y. 1980), *aff'd* 658 F.2d 875, 891-92 (2d Cir. 1981).

[77] Diggs v. Richardson, 555 F.2d 848 (D.C.Cir. 1976).

[78] *See* Consumers Union v. Kissinger, 506 F.2d 136, 140-41 (D.C.Cir. 1974). *But see* Opinion of the United States Attorney General addressed to Ambassador Yoshio Okawara of Japan, May 7, 1981, 81-1 U.S. Trade Cases ¶ 63,998.

[2] Act of State Doctrine

Whereas principles of sovereign immunity address the sovereign character of the *defendant,* the act of state doctrine addresses the sovereign character of the *acts* which allegedly form an integral part of the antitrust violation. Thus, the act of state doctrine may shelter non-sovereigns, as well as sovereigns, from antitrust suit.

The act of state doctrine has been traditionally stated as follows: "Every sovereign state is bound to respect the independence of every other sovereign state, and the courts of one country will not sit in judgment on the acts of the government of another one within its own territory."[79] Thus, if the allegations of an antitrust suit will require the court to "judge" the acts of another government done within its own territory, then plaintiff's "claim" must be dismissed, as the allegations are such which a court cannot consider. The defense does not apply, however, to acts of a foreign sovereign not exclusively within its own territory.[80]

Particularly in cases involving antitrust claims, substantial debate has arisen as to what type of an inquiry represents "sitting in judgment" on the acts of a foreign sovereign. Two basic schools of thought have emerged: the broad view, derived from the U.S. Supreme Court decision in *American Banana v. United Fruit Co.,*[81] states that a court cannot examine the motives of a foreign sovereign in commiting an act within its territory which may effect a violation of the U.S. antitrust laws. Thus, where a plaintiff alleges that a private person conspired to cause a foreign sovereign to commit an act injurious to plaintiff's business, that allegation cannot be considered by the court; it requires the court to assess the motivation behind a foreign sovereign's action and the act of state doctrine bars such judgment.

---

[79] *Underhill v. Hernandez,* 168 U.S. 250, 252 (1897).

[80] Outboard Marine Corp. v. Pezetel, 461 F. Supp. 384 (D. Del. 1978); Linseman v. World Hockey Ass'n, 439 F. Supp. 1315, 1324 (D. Conn. 1977); United Nuclear Corp. v. General Atomic Co., 629 P.2d 231, 258, 96 N.M. 155 (1980); *see* Civil Aeronautics Board v. British Airways Board, 433 F. Supp. 1379 (S.D.N.Y. 1977).

[81] 213 U.S. 347 (1909).

The narrow view derives from the Supreme Court's decision in *Continental Ore Co. v. Union Carbide & Carbon Co.*[82] and permits a plaintiff to allege that a defendant wrongfully attempted to influence a foreign sovereign to effect a violation of the U.S. antitrust laws. Arguably the narrow view would permit a court to examine the motivation behind a sovereign's act, why the sovereign did what it did.

Both views of the act of state defense recognize the doctrine of sovereign compulsion: A person is not subject to suit for acts commited within a foreign territory ordered or compelled by the sovereign of that territory. The narrow view, however, limits the act of state defense to incidents of sovereign compulsion; thus the defendant must show that he was genuinely compelled by the foreign sovereign before the act of state defense applies. The broad view, however, precludes all analysis of a foreign sovereign's acts and therefore will harbor defendants who have allegedly prompted the sovereign to issue its anticompetitive orders.

The principles of sovereign compulsion aptly illustrate the classic application of the act of state doctrine. For example, in *Interamerican Refining Corp. v. Texaco Maracaibo, Inc.*,[83] plaintiff alleged that defendants engaged in a concerted boycott which was designed to cut off the supply of Venezuelan crude oil to plaintiff Interamerican. Defendants answered by stating that they were compelled to engage in such boycott by Venezuelan regulatory authorities. Following the narrow application of the act of state doctrine as derived from *Continental Ore*, the court noted that defendants neither procured the Venezuelan boycott order, nor did they otherwise voluntarily assist in the promulgation of the boycott regulation.[84] Defendants were genuinely compelled to refuse sales to Interamerican by sovereign Venezuelan authorities. Since a sovereign has the authority to regulate trade within its jurisdiction and since businesses within that jurisdiction must obey such regulations, the court ruled that an antitrust suit cannot be based upon acts directed by a foreign sovereign within that sovereign's territo-

---

[82] 370 U.S. 690 (1962).

[83] 307 F. Supp. 1291 (D. Del. 1970).

[84] *Id.* at 1297.

ry. Furthermore, it is of no consequence that the foreign sovereign's orders may have also violated its own laws. The act of state doctrine precludes a court from sitting in judgment on the acts of a foreign sovereign and therefore prevents a court from considering the validity of the sovereign's acts under its own laws.[85]

Interamerican defines the narrowest possible application of the act of state defense; it remains to explore what the maximum limits of the doctrine are. It is generally accepted that the act of state doctrine applies only to directives of a foreign sovereign, not the sovereign's mere policies. A defendant cannot argue as a defense that its anticompetitive behavior was encouraged by a foreign sovereign. In *United States v. The Watchmakers of Switzerland Information Center, Inc.*,[86] for example, defendants argued that their restrictions on exports to the United States were encouraged by the Swiss government. The court ignored the policies of the Swiss government: "In the absence of direct foreign governmental action compelling the defendants' activities," defendants remained liable for their anticompetitive acts.[87]

What if a defendant persuades a foreign sovereign to commit or order the anticompetitive results which it desires. The issue of "wrongful" influence over a foreign sovereign poses the greatest difficulty for the act of state doctrine and has led to the divergent approaches outlined at the introduction to this section. *Continental Ore Co. v. Union Carbide & Carbon Co.*[88] posed the narrow construction of the act of state doctrine: In order for the act of state doctrine to apply, it must be the foreign sovereign, not the private defendant who effectively imposes restraint on foreign commerce. In *Continental Ore*, the Canadian government had appointed a subsidiary of the U.S. corporation, Union Carbide, to act as its exclusive agent to purchase and allocate vanadium for Canadian indus-

---

[85] *Id.* at 1298.

[86] 1963 Trade Cases, ¶ 70,600 (S.D.N.Y. 1962), *order modified,* 1965 Trade Cases ¶ 71,352 (S.D.N.Y. 1965).

[87] *Id.* at 74,457; *see* United States v. R.P. Oldham Co., 152 F. Supp. 818 (N.D.Cal. 1957).

[88] 370 U.S. at 690.

tries. Continental Ore alleged that Carbide used its exclusive agency to bar Continental's access into the Canadian vanadium market. Both the district and circuit courts denied Continental's claim arguing that since Carbide was the authorized agent of Canada any exclusionary acts were the acts of Canada itself. The Supreme Court overruled the lower courts and held Carbide subject to suit for what was effectively its own private anticompetitive acts. Although Carbide's acts had the approval of Canada, they were not required by Canada, and therefore were not within the act of state defense.[89]

Continental Ore may be distinguished on the basis that Carbide itself implemented the wrongful exclusion, and the Canadian government was involved only because it delegated those powers to Carbide. However, an earlier decision *United States v. Sisal Sales*[90] more specifically addressed the issue as to whether a private party can be liable for wrongfully motivating a foreign sovereign. Plaintiffs in *Sisal* alleged that defendants conspired in the United States to influence the Mexican government to pass discriminatory legislation which would have the effect of eliminating competition in the export of Sisal to the United States. The court determined that plaintiff's allegations presented an instance where by their own acts defendants brought about the prohibited monopoly which eliminated competition in the foreign commerce of the United States. Therefore, the fact that discriminatory foreign legislation aided their efforts was no defense.

Sisal, however, did note that plaintiff's allegations went beyond the limited circumstance where a private party has instigated a foreign sovereign to effect an anticompetitive result. *Sisal* portrayed defendants as engaged in an anticompetitive conspiracy of their own over a number of years, in which a foreign government effectively became the agent of the illegal conspiracy. This illegal conspiracy was sufficient to subject defendants to potential antitrust liability.

As a practical matter, the element of a continuing conspiracy between multiple defendants, as contrasted to the monopolizing efforts of a single defendant who illegally seeks

---

[89] *Id.* at 706
[90] 274 U.S. 268 (1927).

discriminatory foreign governmental action, is of small consequence to the injured plaintiff. As a legal matter, however, the distinction can be important. First, even in domestic antitrust cases, the element of conspiracy dramatizes the defendants' anticompetitive intent and is of substantial assistance to a plaintiff who, absent a conspiracy, must then demonstrate that defendant was illegally monopolizing certain markets. Secondly, where a foreign sovereign actually effects the noncompetitive result, the presence of a conspiracy can permit a court to conclude that defendants illegally sought to restrain trade by influencing a foreign sovereign, without ever having to judge whether the sovereign's action in fact resulted from that action. The presence of a conspiracy substantially relieves the court from the burdens of undertaking a detailed examination of the actual motives behind the acts of allegedly manipulating foreign sovereigns.

The United States Supreme Court used the element of conspiracy as one factor in distinguishing the facts of *Sisal* from the facts presented in its earlier decision in *American Banana.* In *American Banana v. United Fruit Co.*,[91] plaintiff sued for treble damages under the Sherman Act, claiming that United Fruit prompted the government of Costa Rica to seize plaintiff's banana plantation and railway. The Supreme Court dismissed plaintiff's cause of action on two grounds: (1) The alleged effect on United States commerce was insufficient to present a cause of action justiciable under the antitrust laws,[92] a conclusion which of course would not be followed today;[93] and (2) Since Costa Rica acted within its de facto jurisdiction, by virtue of its sovereign power, its act was legal; and therefore, a private party's efforts to prompt that act was legal as well.[94]

---

[91] 213 U.S. 347 (1909).

[92] *Id.* at 355-57.

[93] *See, e.g.*, Dominicus Americana Bohio v. Gulf & Western Industries, Inc., 473 F. Supp. 680, 687 (S.D.N.Y. 1979); Zenith Radio Corp. v. Matsushita Electric Industrial Co., Ltd., 494 F. Supp. 1161, 1184 (E.D. Pa. 1980); In re Uranium Antitrust Litigation, 617 F.2d 1248 (7th Cir. 1980).

[94] *See* 213 U.S. at 357-58. *See also* Foreign Trade Antitrust Improvements Act, 15 U.S.C.A. § 6(a); Eurim-Pharm GmbH v. Pfizer, Inc., 593 F. Supp. 1102 (S.D.N.Y. 1984). Cf. de Atucha v. Commodity Exchange, Inc., 85-1 U.S. Trade Cas. ¶ 66, 608 (S.D.N.Y. 1985).

10-45

Despite appearances, the somewhat rusty *American Banana* decision does not resolve the issue of whether a plaintiff may sue for alleged wrongful motivation of a foreign sovereign. First, *American Banana* can always be distinguished on the basis that the court found that there was insufficient effect on U.S. commerce to justify application of the antitrust laws, and, therefore, its conclusion regarding private persuasion of foreign sovereign acts applies only when there is insufficient effect to permit consideration of the suit anyway. The district court in *Intramerican,* in dicta, drew this exact conclusion. Second, *American Banana* may have been effectively overruled by the Supreme Court itself in its decisions in *Sisal* and *Continental Ore.* Finally, the Supreme Court in *American Banana* did not state that the court was barred from reviewing whether the defendant in fact prompted the foreign sovereign's anticompetitive act. Rather, the Court said that it would be futile to initiate such a review since the presumed legality of the foreign sovereign's act made the private party's persuasion of that act legal as well.[95] The court employed the act of state doctrine to "legalize" Costa Rica's expropriation of plaintiff's business interests. But the court went beyond the act of state doctrine in concluding that the acts of the private citizen were legal as well. As will be discussed below, this seemingly minor point is crucial to the understanding of the application of the act of state doctrine to antitrust cases.

The broadly immunizing result of *American Banana* was broadened further by the Second Circuit in its decision in *Hunt v. Mobil Oil Corp.*[96] The essence of Hunt's complaint was that the major oil companies in Libya, known as the "Seven Sisters," had conspired to cause the government of Libya to nationalize Hunt's Libyan interests. The purpose of the conspiracy was to restrict the Libya oil monopoly to the Seven Sisters. Relying on *American Banana,* the Second Circuit concluded that Hunt failed to present a justifiable claim since the act of state doctrine barred any inquiry into the facts surrounding Libya's expropriation of Hunt. The Second Circuit drew no distinction between inquiring into the motivation of a sover-

---

[95] *See* 213 U.S. at 358.
[96] 550 F.2d 68 (2d Cir. 1977).

eign's act and the legality of that sovereign act. "We conclude that the political act complained of here was clearly within the act of state doctrine and that since the disputed pleadings inevitably call for a judgment on the sovereign acts of Libya the claim is non-justiciable."[97]

Although the decision in *Hunt v. Mobil Oil* has been followed by the district court within the Second Circuit,[98] and may well be the majority view with regard to whether a court may inspect the motivation behind acts of a foreign sovereign, the reasoning, if not the result of *Hunt v. Mobil Oil* should be ignored by future courts. The analysis of *Hunt v. Mobil Oil* is illogical and is even beyond the bounds of the moribund *American Banana* decision upon which the Second Circuit so heavily relied. *Hunt v. Mobil Oil* postulated that to inspect the events prompting Libya's expropriation of Hunt would inevitably require an act of passing judgment on those acts. Clearly such is not the case. A court can quite readily evaluate the motivation behind Libya's actions without going the additional step of commenting on the legality or illegality of Libya's actions. *Underhill,* which best defines the act of state doctrine, prohibits only the process of judging the acts of a foreign sovereign. Nothing in *Underhill* indicates that the Court also intended to prohibit analysis of a foreign sovereign's acts.

In the recent U.S. Supreme Court case, *Dunhill v. Republic of Libya,*[99] the Court ruled that the act of state doctrine did not prohibit suit against a Cuban agency for acts which it committed without sovereign authority. In permitting plaintiff's suit in that action the Supreme Court engaged in extensive analysis of Cuba's sovereign processes in order to determine whether the complained of act resulted from Cuba's sovereign processes.[100] Viewed only in terms of *Dunhill,* the Second Circuit's broad concept of "judgment" cannot be justified. The act of state doctrine precludes judicial consid-

---

[97] *Id.* at 73. *See also* Libyan American Oil Co. v. Socialist People's Libyan Arab Jamahirya, 482 F. Supp. 1175, 1178 (D.D.C. 1980).

[98] *See, e.g.,* Bokkelen v. Grumman Aerospace Corp., 432 F. Supp. 329 (E.D.N.Y. 1977).

[99] 425 U.S. 682 (1976).

[100] *Id.* at 691-93.

eration of whether a foreign sovereign's act is contrary to law; it does not preclude an examination of what its foreign sovereign in fact did and why he did it.

Even *American Banana* avoided the broad construction of the act of state doctrine advanced by the Second Circuit. *American Banana* reasoned as follows: The act of state doctrine necessarily "legalizes" the foreign sovereign's expropriation of plaintiff's property. Since the expropriation was legal, any influence designed to effect a legal act must be legal as well and therefore is not such to support a claim of an antitrust violation. The first conclusion derives from the act of state doctrine. The act of state doctrine derives from principles of comity which force courts to recognize the sovereignity of other states. Therefore, any alterations in the act of state doctrine, and *American Banana's* first conclusion, must be restricted and cautious. The second conclusion, however, is divorced from principles of comity, except possibly when foreign defendants are involved. The second conclusion, that any influence to commit a lawful act is itself lawful, is an application of a particular rule of domestic antitrust law which subsequent to *American Banana* became known as the *Noerr-Pennington* doctrine.

The Noerr-Pennington doctrine states that private parties may conspire to influence public policy and government so that discriminatory legislation or government action is implemented to the conspirator's benefit.[101] Not all influence of government will be so protected. The conspirators' influence must be directed at the decision-making process and should not be "a mere sham to cover what is actually nothing more than an attempt to interfere directly with the business relationships of a competitor."[102] In other words, a businessman may petition government for an advantage over its competitor; but some principles of fairness are required. Domestic antitrust cases abound with examples where defendant's con-

---

[101] Eastern Railroad Presidents Conference v. Noerr Motor Freight, Inc., 365 U.S. 127 (1961); United Mine Workers of America v. Pennington, 381 U.S. 657, 670 (1965).

[102] 365 U.S. at 144.

duct became so outrageous that he lost Noerr-Pennington protection.

In *American Banana*, the court's decision not to examine the motivation behind Costa Rica's expropriation of plaintiff's property, represents an application of Noerr-Pennington principles, not act of state principles. The act of state doctrine did not preclude analysis of the motivating forces behind Costa Rica's act. However, since the act of state doctrine presumes those sovereign acts to be legal, then Noerr-Pennington rules presume that the private party's petition for such acts was legal as well. Consequently, the result in *Hunt v. Mobil Oil* may well be correct, as the Second Circuit there addressed facts virtually identical to *American Banana* except for the additional element of a conspiracy. However, by failing to apply the two-step reasoning of *American Banana* the Second Circuit inflated the act of state doctrine beyond its proper bounds and forfeited an opportunity to define the Noerr-Pennington doctrine as it should apply in modern times to private parties who influence foreign sovereigns to effect restrictions in the foreign commerce of the United States.

Perhaps one can excuse the reasoning of *Hunt v. Mobil Oil*[103] because of the uniquely domestic origins of the Noerr-Pennington rule: This doctrine originated from the constitutional protections which safeguard a person's right to petition government. These same constitutional safeguards may be inapplicable in the foreign setting and therefore create the need for the broad interpretation of the act of state doctrine as employed by the Second Circuit.[104] Logically, however, if a person's right to petition is recognized for purposes of United States laws, then those same rights should be extended to all persons with regard to all sovereigns when United States law is sought to be applied against them.[104.1]

---

[103] *See, e.g.,* California Motor Transport Co. v. Trucking Unlimited, 404 U.S. 508 (1972).

[104] Occidental Petroleum Corp. v. Buttes Gas & Oil Co., 331 F. Supp. 92, 108 (C.D. Cal. 1971), *aff'd,* 461 F.2d 1261 (9th Cir. 1972); *cert. denied,* 409 U.S. 950.

[104.1] *See* Zenith Radio Corp. v. Matsushita Electric Industrial Co., Ltd., 513 F. Supp. 1100, 1155-57 (E.D. Pa. 1981) (trade association efforts to influence U.S. and Japanese legislatures is protected by the *Noerr-Pennington* doctrine).

10-49

In fact, the United States Supreme Court implicitly reached this conclusion in *Continental Ore*. Defendant Carbide had argued that its exercise of its agency powers to exclude Continental Ore from the Canadian vanadium market were immune from suit in part because of the Noerr-Pennington doctrine which protects its right to petition for anticompetitive rulings of a sovereign. The court could have rejected this defense by stating that the Noerr-Pennington doctrine did not apply to restraints by a foreign sovereign, but it did not. The court instead described why the doctrine did not protect defendants in this instance. The Court first summarized the *Noerr* rule to state that the Sherman Act did not apply to government-directed activity "at least insofar as those activities comprised mere solicitation of governmental action with respect to the passage and enforcement of laws."[105] The Court then determined that Carbide's exercise of its agency powers was private commercial activity, not the solicitation of government action, and therefore was outside the bounds of Noerr-Pennington immunity. [106] At least one circuit court has endorsed the application of the *Noerr-Pennington* doctrine to international antitrust cases. [106.1]

Virtually every case involving private anticompetitive influence over foreign sovereigns can be readily resolved by applying the simple rule of *Noerr* as described by the Supreme Court in *Continental Ore:* At least insofar as activities comprise the mere solicitation of governmental action with respect to the passage and enforcement of laws, those activities cannot be the basis of an antitrust suit. Principles of comity require that one's interpretation of such terms as "governmental action" and the "passage and enforcement of laws" be liberally interpreted to include any exercise of policy making functions by a foreign sovereign. Moreover what does and doesn't constitute "mere" solicitation must be further defined by future court decisions. Nonetheless, these simple principles will ex-

---

[105] 370 U.S. at 707.

[106] *Id.* at 707-08.

[106.1] Coastal States Marketing, Inc. v. Hunt, 694 F.2d 1358 (5th Cir 1984); *See* Note, "The *Noerr-Pennington* Doctrine and the Petitioning of Foreign Governments," 84 Colum. L. Rev. 1343-70 (1984).

plain the apparently disparate results reached by the courts as described above.

For example, *American Banana* involved private influence directed toward persuading Costa Rica to expropriate plaintiff. The act of expropriation has universally been regarded as the exercise of public policy by a sovereign. Since the alleged private persuasion was directed at the public policy functions of government, those acts of persuasion are immune from suit. *Hunt v. Mobil Oil* merely represents the identical result as above. The Second Circuit had carefully noted that Libya's expropriation of *Hunt* resulted from its exercise of public policy functions.[107]

Sisal also involved influence of the policy making process. However, in *Sisal* defendants engaged in multiple acts of influence, over an extended period of time, with the unquestioned purpose of achieving an absolute monopoly in the relevant market. Unfortunately the facts in Sisal are very brief. Nonetheless *Sisal* did state that "the United States complain of a violation of their laws within their own territory by parties subject to their jurisdiction, not merely of something done by another government at the instigation of private parties."[108] Defendants in *Sisal* had apparently gone beyond the mere solicitation of legislation.[109]

In *Occidental Petroleum v. Buttes Gas & Oil Co.*,[110] plaintiff alleged that defendants engaged in a conspiracy to misappropriate plaintiff's oil concession in the Persian Gulf by persuading a neighboring Arab state to extend its territorial waters to twelve miles from the customary three miles, thereby engulfing plaintiff's concession obtained from a neighbor. The court in *Buttes Gas* relied on *American Banana*[111] and refused to permit suit.[112] Nonetheless, decisions to extend territorial waters are clearly policy making decisions and efforts to prompt such decisions would thus fall within the *Noerr* immunity as

---

[107] 550 F.2d at 73.
[108] 274 U.S. at 276.
[109] *Id.*
[110] 331 F. Supp at 108.
[111] 331 F. Supp. at 109-110.
[112] *Id.* at 108

described above. Reliance on *Noerr* would have saved the *Buttes Gas* court from expanding the rule of *American Banana* in the same fashion as *Hunt v. Mobil Oil* later expanded that rule.

The Ninth Circuit's decision in *Timberlane Lumber Co. v. Bank of America*,[113] aptly illustrates the ease of analysis afforded by applying Noerr-Pennington to foreign commerce. *Timberlane* found actionable defendants' alleged use of specious claims in the Honduran courts to thwart plaintiff's entry into the local timber industry exporting to the United States. In order to avoid the *American Banana* result the court was forced to temper its concept of the act of state doctrine. No longer were domestic courts forced to defer to all acts of a foreign sovereign within its jurisdiction. Rather, deference must be based upon a "balance of the relevant considerations," the principle consideration being whether the sovereign's act was designed "to give effect to its public interests." The court then determined that the decisions of the Honduran courts were not "acts of state" as would require deference: "A judgment of a court may be an act of state. Usually it is not, because it involves the interests of private litigants or because court adjudication is not the usual way in which the state exercises its jurisdiction to give effect to its public interests."[114]

Timberlane unnecessarily narrowed the act of state doctrine. Although the Supreme Court in *Dunhill* denied act of state protection to a public act of a ministerial sovereign authority, *Dunhill* only stated that act of state requires that the sovereign agency be blessed with the authority to perform the act in question. *Dunhill* did not state that all nonpolicy making agencies of sovereigns are outside the protection of the act of state doctrine. To require that sovereign action be designed to effect the public interest is to further narrow the act of state doctrine in a peculiarly confusing fashion. Presumably every sovereign act is ultimately designed to effect the public interest, thereby making the *Timberlane* definition exceedingly difficult to apply. Secondly, not even the *Timberlane* court would totally permit U.S. judgment regarding the legality of

---

[113] 549 F.2d 597 (9th Cir. 1976).
[114] *Id.* at 607-08.

Honduras' court proceedings, yet technically the *Timberlane* decision creates that potential by stating that the court processes were not acts of state.

The *Timberlane* result can be better reached by applying the two-step analysis of *American Banana*. The Honduran court proceedings were acts of state and are presumed legal by the act of state doctrine. The private parties use of those court proceedings were not legal, however, as they amounted to an abuse of process in violation of the antitrust laws. Since these private actions were not appeals to the policy-making elements of the Honduran government, these actions are *not* immunized from suit by the Noerr-Pennington rule. *Timberlane* meant to establish a rule that a private person cannot employ ministerial procedures of foreign governments to illegally effect an anticompetitive restriction on the foreign commerce of the United States. The Noerr-Pennington rule achieves *Timberlane's* result without torturing traditional concepts of the act of state doctrine.

Had *Hunt v. Mobil Oil* and *Timberlane* employed the *Noerr* rule, the result in the recent district court decision, *Bokkelen v. Grumman Aerospace Corp.*, may have been different. Bokkelen involved an allegation that Grumman breached its agency contract with Bokkelen by causing Brazilian authorities to deny Bokkelen necessary import licenses. The court dismissed the claim by applying the rule of *Hunt v. Mobil Oil*. The denial of the import permit was an act of state into which U.S. courts cannot inquire. Since an inquiry into the motivation behind the act might embarrass the "Executive Branch of the Government," the court was precluded from analyzing the Brazilian act of state. Such an inquiry into Grumman's behavior would amount to passing judgment on an act of state of Brazil contrary to the rule of *Hunt v. Mobil Oil*.

Had *Hunt v. Mobil Oil* employed *Noerr* analysis a different result could easily have been envisaged. *Bokkelen* would have been forced to examine whether the denial of the import license was an act of public policy or a ministerial act resulting from the illegal urgings of defendant Grumman. If the former, the *Noerr* rule may protect Grumman as it was petitioning for the "passage and enforcement of laws." If ministerial, *Timber-*

lane would apply and Bokkelen's claims would be justiciable. Moreover, since *Bokkelen* involves a breach of contract case, quite possibly an effort to influence Brazil in policy matters could well be actionable if Grumman expressly promised Bokkelen to the contrary. The broad application of *Hunt v. Mobil Oil* precluded even this basic inquiry, however.

Similarly, in *Clayco Petroleum Corp. v. Occidental Petroleum Corp.*, [114.1] the Ninth Circuit retreated from its *Timberlane* decision and employed *Hunt* analysis to avoid investigation of the alleged use of illegal bribes to acquire an oil concession. In so doing the court tacitly endorsed illegal activity proscribed by congressional legislation.[114.2] Use of *Noerr-Pennington* inquiry into the legality of sovereign motivation would have at least required the court to weigh the significance of U.S. antibribery legislation.

Illustrating the confusion which resulted from the courts' failure to use Noerr-Pennington analysis is the decision in *Industrial Investment Development Corp. v. Mitsui & Co., Ltd.*,[115] which reached a result directly opposite to the result in *Bokkelen*. In that case the court, relying on *Timberlane,* permitted an inquiry into the motivation behind Indonesia's denial of a logging permit. Defendant had allegedly conspired to see that plaintiffs were denied the permit. The court determined that the act of state doctrine did not bar plaintiff's suit. The court was not going to evaluate the sovereign acts of the state of Indonesia; the court was merely going to determine why Indonesia acted the way it did. The court would only pass judgment on the private acts of the defendant; it would determine if defendant's illegally descriptive acts caused damage to plaintiff. In *Mitsui* the court was forced to expend great effort distinguishing its facts from such cases as *Hunt.* Had the courts relied on *Noerr* analysis it would have been clear that the inquiry was proper. The only issue would be if the public policy of the sovereign was so involved as to "legalize" defendant's acts motivating the sovereign. Since the denial of the

---

[114.1] 712 F.2d 404 (9th Cir. 1983), *cert. denied,* 464 U.S. 1040 (1984).

[114.2] *See* The Foreign Corrupt Practices Act of 1977, 15 U.S.C. §§ 78dd-1 *et seq.*

[115] 594 F.2d 48 (5th Cir. 1979).

permit was a ministerial act, based upon traditional *Noerr* principles, defendant's acts could yield antitrust violations.[116]

The District Court of New York reached the same conclusion distinguishing its Circuit's decision in *Hunt v. Mobil Oil*. That court stated: "In order to trigger application of the act of state doctrine, the government act at issue must be a public one such as a legislative enactment, regulatory decree, or executive use of the police powers."[116.1] The requirement of some law-making involvement effectively defines the act of state doctrine in terms of the *Noerr* doctrine.

Mannington Mills, Inc. v. Congoleum Corp.[116.2] repeats the distinction between law-making functions and administrative functions. In *Mannington Mills*, the Third Circuit determined that the act of state doctrine did not preclude an antitrust action based upon defendant's alleged fraudulent procurement of foreign patents. The government act of granting the patent did not preclude judicial examination of how the private party obtained the patent. "The granting of patents per se, in substance, ministerial activity, is not the kind of governmental action contemplated by the act of state doctrine. . . ."[116.3]

Stated in terms of the *Noerr* rule: Defendant did not solicit

---

[116] *Id. See also* Mannington Mills, Inc. v. Congoleum Corp., 595 F.2d 1287 (3d Cir. 1979); Dominicus Americana Bohio v. Gulf & Western Indus. 1979-2 CCH Trade Cases ¶ 62,757 (S.D.N.Y. 1979).

However, in some instances it may be difficult to draw the line between a ministerial act and public policy. In Northrop Corp. v. McDonnell Douglas Corp., 498 F. Supp. 1112 (C.D. Cal. 1980), the court ruled that a competitor's alleged influence, contrary to mutual contract, regarding military sales to foreign governments was protected by the act of state doctrine. It would seem that any unfair influence might be viewed as ministerial and subject to review. At least the court should be permitted to review if the defendant violated its contract with plaintiff by seeking to influence foreign governments. The *Northrop* case is perhaps not instructive regarding the act of state doctrine. The case was based principally on a mutual contract between Northrop and McDonnell Douglas and the court had ruled the contract void as contrary to the antitrust law.

[116.1] Dominicus Americana Bohio v. Gulf & Western Industries, Inc., 473 F. Supp. 680 (S.D.N.Y. 1979).

[116.2] 595 F.2d 1287 (3d Cir. 1979).

[116.3] 595 F.2d at 1294.

the passage or enforcement of law, activity which is sheltered from antitrust prosecution. Rather, defendant sought to abuse the administrative processes of government in order to effect a restraint of trade. Defendant's alleged fraudulent procurement of patents was not directed at the law-making functions of government and was therefore not subject to antitrust immunity.[116.4]

From the above discussion, several conclusions can be drawn regarding the application of the act of state doctrine and sovereign immunity doctrines to antitrust suits.

Where an antitrust restraint is implemented within the United States that restraint will be subject to suit regardless of whether the tortfeasor is or is not a foreign sovereign, and regardless of the sovereign character of the act.

If a sovereign seeks to implement anticompetitive policy within the United States that policy will not be protected by the act of state doctrine since the act was implemented outside the territorial confines of the foreign sovereign's jurisdiction. Where a foreign sovereign engages in wrongful commercial activity that too will not be subject to protection if implemented within the United States since commercial activity is not subject to the rules of sovereign immunity.

Where a foreign sovereign acts within his own jurisdiction then the possibility arises for a sovereign immunity or act of state defense. When a private party has been named defendant, he may claim the act of state defense if the act complained of by plaintiff was compelled by the foreign sovereign within that sovereign's jurisdiction. A private party may also petition the public policy elements of a foreign sovereignty for favorable anticompetitive action within as yet undefined bounds of fairness and not be subject to antitrust penalties. However, a private party may not employ the ministerial elements of a foreign sovereignty to an anticompetitive end without running some risk of antitrust liability.[116.5]

[116.4] The identical conclusion was reached in Forbo-Giubiasco, S.A. v. Congoleum Corp., 516 F. Supp. 1210, 1217 (S.D.N.Y. 1981).

[116.5] *See* Williams v Curtiss-Wright Corp., 694 F.2d 300 (3d Cir. 1982), where, although declining to focus on ministerial acts, the court upheld potential antitrust liability regarding alleged wrongful influence of military procurement decisions.

The unanswered questions revolve predominantly around whether a foreign sovereign itself may be liable under U.S. antitrust laws for acts which it commits outside the United States, but having a direct effect on U.S. commerce. Where there is sufficient effect on U.S. commerce sovereign immunity rules will not protect the foreign sovereign from suit if his activity is commercial in character. For purposes of sovereign immunity, commercial activity can include a regular course of commercial conduct as well as a particular commercial transaction or acts. The *Pezetel* case discussed earlier did not really question that marketing arrangements by a commercial element of the Polish Government were commercial activities within the meaning of the statutory exemption from sovereign immunity. What if that same Polish agency sought to fix the price of its products with other importers? Or what if foreign governments sought to restrict output and fix the price of oil; are these acts actionable under U.S. antitrust laws?

Disregarding issues of sovereign immunity, such acts by foreign sovereigns outside the United States would seemingly be immune from suit based upon the act of state doctrine. However, the act of state doctrine contains a commercial exception as well. If this exception for the act of state doctrine is as unqualified as the exception for sovereign immunity apparently is then it would appear that even OPEC itself would be subject to potential U.S. antitrust liability.

The commercial exception to the act of state doctrine arose from *Dunhill v. Republic of Cuba*,[117] noted above. In *Dunhill* certain cigar importers mistakenly paid for cigar shipments by sending the money to the Cuban government instead of the now-expropriated owners of the cigar factories. When the importers tried to get their money back their demands were ignored. The Court faced the question of whether the Cuban refusal was a non-justiciable act of state. In a plurality opinion the court ruled that purely commercial obligations of a government or its commercial instrumentality were not within the protection of the act of state doctrine. Public acts remain subject to protection and U.S. courts will not judge the legality of this act. Purely commercial acts of a sovereign, however, will

---

[117] 425 U.S. at 682.

remain subject to suit. The Court determined the Cuban agency which ignored the requests for payment, lacked authority to commit a sovereign public act.[118] Nonetheless, the Court refused to rest its holding on this fact and held the commercial character of the act itself precluded an act of state protection.[119] This last aspect of the opinion outlining the commercial exception was agreed to by only four of the nine judges and is thus of doubtful precedential value.

Hunt v. Mobil Oil, however, nonetheless considered the commercial exception as viable law. Stating the requirement for the applicability of the commercial exception to be whether the government has descended to the level of an entrepreuner, the Second Circuit determined that Libya's expropriation of Hunt's properties was not a purely commercial action and was thus not within the commercial exception to act of state immunity.[120] Normal businesses do not possess the power to expropriate and therefore that act should not be considered as commercial. Similarly in the *Bokkelen* case the court noted that the granting and denial of import licenses was also not normally a business function so it too would not fall within the *Dunhill* commercial exception.[121]

The scope and impact of the commercial exception to the act of state and sovereign immunity doctrines therefore remains substantially undefined. Recent decisions hint at greater acceptance of the commercial exception.[121.1] However, the commercial exception will likely be limited in application to specific commercial incidents, not broad-based commercial policies. There can be no doubt that OPEC agreements have a direct impact on the United States, are commercial in nature,

---

[118] 425 U.S. at 695.

[119] 425 U.S. at 706.

[120] 550 F.2d at 73; *see* D'Angelo v. Petroleos Mexicanos, 422 F. Supp. 1280, 1286 (D. Del. 1976); United Mexican States v. Ashley, 556 S.W.2d 784 (Tex. 1977).

[121] 432 F. Supp. at 333-34.

[121.1] *See, e.g.,* Behring International, Inc. v. Imperial Iranian Air Force, 474 F. Supp. 396, 401 (D.N.J. 1979); Sage Int'l v. Cadillac Gage Co., 534 F. Supp. 896, 906 (E.D. Mich. 1981); National American Corp. v. Federal Republic of Nigeria, 448 F. Supp. 622 (S.D.N.Y. 1978), *aff'd,* 597 F.2d 314 (2d Cir. 1979).

and that these cartel arrangements are agreements which private businesses themselves would perform if the antitrust laws had not precluded such arrangements. Neither can it be doubted that the OPEC agreements are reached by foreign sovereigns in order to advance the public policies of such sovereigns. Does the element of public policy preclude application of the commercial exception and grant those commercial acts of policy, act of state protection? Significantly, although not a basis of the commercial exception language of the opinion, the *Dunhill* majority had painfully noted that the complained of act was ministerial in character, and thus would provide a ready basis for distinguishing *Dunhill* from OPEC-like cartels.

In *International Association of Machinists and Aerospace Workers v. OPEC,*[121.2] the Ninth Circuit faced this very question. Unfortunately, the court ignored the decision in *Dunhill* and instead relied upon the policy expressed in *Banco Nacional de Cuba v. Sabbatino*[121.3] in favor of judicial abstenance whenever a question involves serious foreign policy concerns. In this fashion the court avoided a detailed analysis of the act of state doctrine.

In its comments the court down-played the importance of the commercial element of the activity: "While purely commercial activity may not rise to the level of an act of state, certain seemingly commercial activity will trigger act of state considerations."[121.4] This was the court's only reference to the commercial exception in *Dunhill,* and consequently *Association of Machinists* adds little to defining the limits of *Dunhill.*

It could be said that *Association of Machinists* limits *Dunhill's* commercial exception to purely commercial ventures.[121.5] Such a distinction is incapable of application, since any act by a sovereign, regardless of how mundane, involves some public element simply because a sovereign performed it, and, as a result, cannot be purely commercial.

If *Dunhill* is to be distinguished when applied to OPEC it

121.2 649 F.2d 1354 (9th Cir. 1981).
121.3 376 U.S. 398 (1964).
121.4 649 F.2d at 1360.
121.5 *See* Hunt v. Mobil Oil, 550 F.2d 68, 73 (2d Cir. 1977).

must be because the acts complained of are legislative in character and not ministerial. As noted earlier in the text, *Dunhill's* commercial exception applied only to ministerial acts.

Undoubtedly the meaning of *Dunhill's* commercial exception will be the subject of much future litigation. A whole body of law analogous to the *Noerr*-Act of State rules may be developed. In antitrust cases, however, it will be the rare instance where a foreign sovereign is sued for an antitrust violation based upon only a ministerial act as would come within the *Dunhill* commercial exception.

Perhaps an international law exception, rather than a commercial exception to act of state, will be more appropriate when a foreign sovereign is sued for violation of the antitrust laws. If the plaintiff can convince the court that a violation of international law has occurred, then neither the act of state doctrine nor sovereign immunity should protect the defendant sovereign.[122] It is difficult to imagine international antitrust principles so accepted as to become international law. Yet as cases such as those described in this chapter proliferate, accepted rules of international commerce must eventually develop.

---

[122] The district court (477 F. Supp. 553 (C.D. Cal. 1979)) never addressed the act of state issues but instead determined that the sovereign immunity law precluded plaintiff's claims. OPEC was not within the commercial exception since it was exercising control over the removal of a prime natural resource, a traditional sovereign function. The court then reasoned that the act of determining together how each sovereign is to perform these acts is also a sovereign act. The Ninth Circuit declined to rule that OPEC failed to fall within the commercial exception under the sovereign immunity law.

The approach of the circuit court in relying on the act of state doctrine is superior to the district court's reliance on sovereign immunity. The OPEC acts were certainly commercial in character. Sovereign immunity is not concerned with the degree of public policy involvement in the commercial act. The act of state doctrine is concerned with the public policy element, however, and thus the act of state doctrine was the proper basis for denying jurisdiction.

§ 10.08 Remedial Sanctions Imposed Upon Foreign Defendants

The deference owed foreign sovereigns raises important international antitrust issues other than the narrower question of liability. For example, act of state considerations may often limit the remedial sanctions which a U.S. court can impose upon a foreign defendant.

As a practical matter, the success to a litigant of an antitrust action may turn on the nature of the strictures imposed upon the antitrust violator. Where a plaintiff seeks more than monetary damages which can be satisfied out of the foreign defendant's property held in the United States, that plaintiff may find himself in a position where he "wins the battle, but loses the war." A U.S. court may find jurisdiction over the foreign defendant, and may further find that the foreign defendant is indeed violating the U.S. antitrust laws. But, if the court's sanctions impose or require conduct outside the territorial jurisdiction of the United States, the court and the plaintiff face the likely prospect that the remedial solution prescribed by the court will be ignored by the defendant.

An apt illustration that the court's practical jurisdiction to impose sanctions may not extend as far as its jurisdiction to hear the complaint is the case of *United States v. Imperial Chemicals Industries, Ltd.*[123] As part of its remedial order, the court ordered that neither defendant du Pont nor its British co-defendant Imperial Chemicals Industries (ICI) could themselves assert their non-United States patents to bar exports from the United States, nor could they assign these patent rights to others so that the assignee could assert these exclusive rights.[124] British Nylon Spinners claimed a contractual right to purchase certain exclusive patent rights of ICI. If ICI fulfilled these contractual obligations and conveyed the patents to British Nylon Spinners, they would be in violation of the U.S. court order. Indeed, the court in *ICI* specifically referenced the patents to be transferred to British Nylon Spinners and required that non-exclusive licensing provisions be substituted for exist-

---

[123] 105 F. Supp. 215 (S.D.N.Y. 1952).
[124] *Id.* at 236.

ing agreements.[125] British Nylon Spinners sued to enforce ICI's
contractual obligation, presenting the British court with the
issue of whether an American court can alter a British contract
concerning British patent rights.

The British court ignored the U.S. court order and upheld
the rights of British Nylon Spinners.[126] The court initially determined that British law governed the performance of the
British contract. The court then concluded that these contractual obligations are not unenforceable because they subsequently have been determined to have violated the public
policy of a friendly court. The court, therefore, required ICI
to execute an exclusive license to British Nylon Spinners, contrary to the order of the United States court.

The U.S. court had relied upon its in personam jurisdiction
over ICI to order ICI to relinquish certain of its British patent
rights. ICI had argued that British public policy precluded the
U.S. court from partially dismantling British patents. The U.S.
court denied the conflict stating: "we observe that, acting on
the basis of our jurisdiction in personam, we are merely directing ICI to refrain from asserting rights which it may have in
Britain, since the enforcement of those rights will serve to
continue the effects of wrongful acts it has committed within
the United States affecting the foreign trade of the United
States."[127] Of significance, the British court order only frustrated the U.S. court order to the extent that it affected rights of
British nondefendants. Nonetheless, the *ICI* case illustrates
that the U.S. court is subject to some limitations in the sanctions it may decree.

Defining the remedial limits of a U.S. court's extraterritorial
antitrust jurisdiction becomes further complicated when the
U.S. order frustrates the long-recognized public policy of a
foreign government, but where the order is not explicitly contrary to the law of that foreign government. Such a conflict
arose in *United States v. Watchmakers of Switzerland Infor-*

---

[125] *Id.* at 231-32.
[126] British Nylon Spinners, Ltd. v. Imperial Chemical Industries, Ltd.,
[1955] ch. 37. *See* [1952] A.E.L.R., Vol. 2, at 780.
[127] 105 F. Supp at 228.

mation Center, Inc.[128] The court in that case found that a Collective Convention designed to regulate the export of Swiss watches and the technology to make such watches throughout the world in general, and the United States in particular, was in violation of U.S. antitrust laws. The defendants argued that these "wrongful" activities had the approval of the Swiss Government. But, as was discussed *supra* in the section concerning the act of state doctrine, the fact that a foreign government approves an act is no defense unless the foreign government has the authority to, and does in fact, compel that act.

The *Watchmakers* court then issued an order which in practical effect was designed to limit and regulate the Swiss trade associations so that the Swiss associations could not impose volume or other restrictions upon the importation of Swiss watches by U.S. firms and their subsequent resale in the United States. The Swiss government then responded by issuing specific regulations regarding the export of Swiss watch parts. The U.S. court, citing the *ICI* case and its aftermath discussed *supra*, then modified its decree, so as to expressly permit the defendants to comply with these regulations.[129]

§ 10.09   Venue and Personal Jurisdiction

It is insufficient for the court to merely have subject matter jurisdiction over the suit. The forum must also have sufficient contact with the defendant so as to satisfy the due process requirements of personal jurisdiction and proper venue. In antitrust suits involving foreign defendants, the crucial legal issue resolves to one of venue.

Fortunately for the plaintiff, the antitrust defendant is typically a corporation. In private antitrust actions against corporate defendants, a special liberal venue provision is applicable. Section 12 of the Clayton Act provides:

> Any suit, action, or proceeding under the antitrust laws against a corporation may be brought not only in the judicial district

---

[128] 1963 Trade Cases 70,600 (S.D.N.Y. 1963).
[129] 1965 Trade Cases 71,352 (S.D.N.Y. 1965).

whereof it is an inhabitant, but also in any district wherein it may be found or transacts business and all process in such cases may be served in the district of which it is an inhabitant, or wherein it may be found.[130]

A corporation is "found" in a district if the corporation is doing or carrying on business of any substantial character in that district.[131] What constitutes business of a substantial character for purposes of the antitrust laws has been subject to divergent interpretation. The most vexing issues arise when a plaintiff seeks to subject a foreign parent to the jurisdiction of the court by reason of the activities of the parent's subsidiary in that district. The majority rule derives from *United States v. Scophony Corp.*[132] and liberally interprets what is business of a substantial character. In *Scophony* a foreign parent was subject to suit in a district by reason of the activities of its majority-owned, but not wholly-owned, subsidiary. The thrust of the *Scophony* court was to ignore the formal separation of the companies and to instead distinguish between subsidiaries held for investment purposes and subsidiaries owned so that the parent corporation can exploit the U.S. market.[133] If the subsidiary falls into the latter category, then the subsidiary's activities will subject the foreign parent to venue and personal jurisdiction. To draw this distinction the court will examine the nature of the parent's control over the subsidiary, specifically, is that control "sufficient to influence and control those decisions which might involve violations of the antitrust laws."[134]

Some courts have painfully enumerated a number of factors to be examined in assessing whether the requisite parental

---

[130] 15 U.S.C. 22 (1970).

[131] United States v. Scophony Corp., 333 U.S. 795, 810 (1948); Hitt v. Nissan Motor Co., 399 F. Supp. 838, 840 (S.D. Fla. 1975).

[132] 333 U.S. 795 (1948).

[133] *Id.* at 810-811. *See* Bulova Watch Co., Inc. v. K. Hattori & Co. Ltd., 508 F. Supp. 1322, 1341 (E.D.N.Y. 1981).

[134] 399 F. Supp. at 842; *See also* Sunrise Toyota Ltd. v. Toyota Motor Co., 55 F.R.D. 519 (S.D.N.Y. 1972); Audio Warehouse Sales, Inc. v. U.S. Pioneer Electronics Corp., 1975 Trade Cases 60,213 (D.D.C. 1975).

control exists.[135] For the most part, however, these factors are irrelevant. Where a court applies the broad rule derived from Scophony, it also applies the following corollary. A plaintiff need not show that a parent controls the day-to-day affairs of a company in order to subject the foreign parent to venue and personal jurisdiction.[136] When the test is whether there is control as would influence decisions which might involve antitrust violations, the plaintiff need only demonstrate that the parent can influence the major business decisions of the domestic subsidiary. One can imagine few parent-subsidiary relationships where such influence does not exist and is not exercised,[137] particularly where the subsidiary performs services for the parent.[138] As a practical matter, a plaintiff pleading venue will cite facts which satisfy the factors enumerated by the courts. Usually, the very nature of the parent-subsidiary relationship will be sufficient to supply facts which satisfy these factors.

A plaintiff's task becomes far more complicated, however, where the court ignores *Scophony* and requires that the plaintiff demonstrate that the foreign parent manages the daily affairs of the domestic subsidiary. Relying on cases which predated *Scophony, Williams v. Canon, Inc.*, for example, requires that the plaintiff "demonstrate that the parent both controls and *manages* the subsidiary."[139] The additional requirement of management imposes the need to show that the parent exercises day-to-day control over the domestic subsidi-

---

[135] *See* the factors described in Zenith Radio Corp. v. Matsushita Electric Industrial Co., 402 F. Supp. 262, 327-28 (E.D. Pa. 1975); *See also* United States v. Diebold, Inc., 1978-1 U.S. Trade Cases 61,831 (N.D. Ohio 1976).

[136] 399 F. Supp. at 842; *See also* In re Electric & Musical Industries, Ltd., 155 F. Supp. 892 (S.D.N.Y. 1957); In re Siemans and Halske A.G., 155 F. Supp. 897 (S.D.N.Y. 1957).

[137] But *see also* O.S.C. Corp. v. Toshiba America, Inc., 491 F.2d 1064 (9th Cir. 1974).

[138] Waldron v. British Petroleum Co., 149 F. Supp. 830 (S.D.N.Y. 1957). Zenith Radio Corp. v. Matsushita Electric Industrial Co., Ltd., 402 F. Supp. 262 (E.D. Pa. 1975).

[139] 432 F. Supp 376, 380 (C.D. Cal. 1977) (emphasis in original).

ary.[140] Contrary to the result reached by courts employing *Scophony,* one can imagine only a few instances where the parent's control is likely to be so extensive as to amount to the management of the subsidiary's daily affairs. The factual factors cited by plaintiff in *Williams* almost certainly would have satisfied the control requirements of courts employing the broad *Scophony* rule. The minority rule requiring daily management appears to be predominant in the Ninth Circuit.[141]

Venue imputes to the parent because of the parent's control over its subsidiary. It follows that the acts of a domestic parent will *not* subject the foreign subsidiary to venue as the foreign subsidiary does not control the domestic parent.[142] Nonetheless, if the domestic parent performs acts for the foreign subsidiary as its agent in the district in which venue and jurisdiction is sought, then the foreign subsidiary may become subject to venue and jurisdiction in that district.[143] Where brother-sister companies are involved, the question of control is subsumed into a broader issue: Is each brother company but one division in a functionally integrated larger international enterprise? Where such integrated activities are found the activities of the domestic brother will subject the foreign brother to venue and jurisdiction.[144]

Disregarding the presence or absence of related companies, a foreign defendant may always be subject to venue and personal jurisdiction based upon its own activities in a district. The courts will place particular importance on whether defendant sold goods in the district, the substantiality of those sales, and

---

[140] *Id. See* Caribe Trailer Systems, Inc. v. Puerto Rico Maritime Shipping Authority, 475 F. Supp. 711 (D.D.C. 1979).

[141] *See, e.g.,* Kramer Motors, Inc., v. British Leyland Ltd., 1980-1 Trade Cases 63,261 (9th Cir. 1980); 491 F.2d at 1064; Hayashi v. Sunshine Garden Products, Inc., 285 F. Supp. 632 (W.D. Wash. 1967), *aff'd,* 396 F.2d 13 (9th Cir. 1968). *But see* Cascade Steel Rolling Mills, Inc. v. Itoh & Co. (America) Inc., 499 F. Supp. 829 (D. Ore. 1980).

[142] Industrial Siciliana Asfalt v. Exxon Research & Engineering, 1977-1 Trade Cases 61,256 (S.D.N.Y. 1977).

[143] *See* S.C.M. Corp. v. Brother International Corp., 316 F. Supp 1328 (S.D.N.Y. 1970).

[144] United States v. Watchmakers of Switzerland Information Center, 134 F. Supp. 710 (S.D.N.Y. 1955); *see* Industrial Siciliana Asfalt v. Exxon Research and Engineering, N. 142 *supra.*

the manner in which such sales were executed.[145] Failure to show a substantial physical presence in the district, generally indicates lack of contact with that jurisdiction.[146]

Once the issue of venue has been established, the issue of personal jurisdiction has been resolved as well. Once venue has been found, the fact that the defendant conducted business, or that it committed tortious acts, within the district will be sufficient to satisfy the minimum contacts requirements of *International Shoe*.[147] The absence of venue will also generally indicate that those minimum requirements necessary to satisfy the process may be absent as well.[148] Of course, such conclusions with respect to personal jurisdiction also presume that the relevant requirements regarding service of process have been satisfied as well.[149] More than the mere ownership of a U.S. subsidiary will be required. Nonetheless, the presence of a subsidiary in a district generally brings such accompanying parent-subsidiary interaction as will subject the foreign parent to jurisdiction in the district.[150] Similarily, the mere presence of defendant's property in the district will generally be insufficient to establish personal jurisdiction.[151]

§ 10.10 Extraterritorial Discovery

Antitrust cases are noteworthy for the volumes of discovery typically required in order to properly prosecute and defend an action. In cases involving restraints on international commerce, documents and witnesses required by plaintiff or de-

---

[145] 399 F. Supp 838; Hoffman Motors Corp. v. Alfa Romeo S.P.A., 244 F. Supp. 70 (S.D.N.Y. 1965).

[146] 432 F. Supp. at 376.

[147] 399 F. Supp at 838, 402 F. Supp. at 260; Waldron v. British Petroleum Co., 149 F. Supp. 830 (S.D.N.Y. 1957).

[148] 399 F. Supp at 850.

[149] Shaffer v. Heitner, 433 U.S. 186 (1977); Amoco Overseas Oil v. Compagnie Nationale Algerienne de Navigation, 459 F. Supp. 1242 (S.D.N.Y. 1978).

[150] Cannon Manufacturing Co. v. Cudahy Packing Co., 267 U.S. 333 (1925); 432 F. Supp at 376.

[151] Fed. R. Civ. Proc. 26.

fendant may be located in another national jurisdiction. If the foreign jurisdiction, for whatever reason, chooses to protect such documents or witnesses from the U.S. court proceedings, an extremely delicate conflict arises. Ultimately, a plaintiff seeking to impose antitrust liability against a foreign defendant may be forced to abandon its litigation because actions of a foreign sovereign bar the availability of crucial and necessary testimony. In this regard consideration of foreign blocking legislation is crucial.

Before a document can be discoverable, it must be relevant to the litigation. As with domestic issues, this concept of relevancy is to be given a broad interpretation. Frequently, a party may argue that documents relating to foreign business activities are not discoverable as these business activities do not relate to the foreign commerce of the United States. This argument will not bar the discovery of the documents: "Evidence of anticompetitive conduct relating only to foreign commerce not involving the United States is admissible where such conduct shows links in a chain designed to control the commerce of a substantial part of the world, including the foreign commerce of the United States."[152] Since relevancy can't really be judged until the document is examined, almost all documents relating to foreign commerce become discoverable,[153] particularly when the party subject to discovery is a United States citizen.[154]

Once determined that the sought after documents are relevant to the proceeding, the documents become discoverable even if located in a jurisdiction other than the United States. The United States court will order discovery of the documents and it is incumbent upon the burdened party to attempt to produce such documents even where it may be potentially violating foreign law in doing so.[155] Thus, in *Arthur Anderson*

---

[152] Duplan Corp. v. Deering Milliken, Inc., 397 F. Supp. 1146 (D.S.C. 1974).

[153] *Id.* at 1188.

[154] In re Grand Jury Investigation of the Shipping Industry, 186 F. Supp. 298 (D.D.C. 1960).

[155] The courts will nonetheless order discovery based upon the following provisions of Section 39 of the Restatement of Foreign Relations:

and Co. v. Finesilver,[156] the Tenth Circuit ignored an earlier line of cases which had implied that a court cannot order discovery if production of the documents would cause a party to violate foreign law.[157] Where a real or potential conflict with foreign law exists the proper procedure is to nonetheless order discovery. It then becomes the duty of the party subject to discovery to attempt to resolve that conflict in a manner which will permit discovery. Should those attempts be unsuccessful, the courts must balance the interests of the respective jurisdictions in assessing what further orders, if any, should be imposed.[158]

As a practical matter, the strength of a discovery order can be no greater than the sanctions which the court is willing to impose for its violation. The willingness of the court to impose sanctions will turn on two broad considerations: (1) The nature of the conflict between U.S. interests and the foreign sovereign's policy which deters discovery, and (2) the nature of the efforts made by the party subject to discovery to seek the foreign sovereign's acquiescence to that party's compliance to

---

39. Inconsistent Requirements Do Not Affect Jurisdiction

(1) A state having jurisdiction to prescribe or to enforce a rule of law is not precluded from exercising its jurisdiction solely because such exercise requires a person to engage in conduct subjecting him to liability under the law of another state having jurisdiction with respect to that conduct.

(2) Factors to be considered in minimizing conflicts arising from the application of the rule stated in Subsection (1) with respect to enforcement jurisdiction are stated in 40.

See in re Westinghouse Electric Corp. Uranium Contracts Litigation, 563 F.2d 992, 997 (10th Cir. 1977); Arthur Anderson & Co. v. Finesilver, 546 F.2d 338, 342 (10th Cir. 1976), *cert. denied,* United States v. First National City Bank, 396 F.2d 897, 901 (2d Cir. 1968).

[156] 546 F.2d at 338.

[157] *See, e.g.,* First National City Bank of New York v. Internal Revenue Service, 271 F.2d 616 (2d Cir. 1959), *cert. denied,* 361 U.S. 948; Ings v. Ferguson, 282 F.2d 149 (2d Cir. 1960); Application of Chase Manhatten Bank, 297 F.2d 611 (2d Cir. 1962).

[158] *See, e.g.,* In re Uranium Antitrust Litigation, 480 F. Supp. 1158 (N.D. Ill. 1979); In re Westinghouse Electric Corp. Uranium Contracts Litigation, 563 F.2d 992 (10th Cir. 1977); *see also* United States v. Vetco, 644 F.2d 1324 (9th Cir. 1981).

the U.S. courts discovery order. To a certain extent the nature of the subject party's efforts to obtain waiver, and the foreign sovereign's response to those efforts, will highlight the exact nature and degree of the policy conflict resulting from the discovery order.

In attempting to assess the nature of the intersovereign conflict and the degree to which the U.S. discovery order should yield to foreign interests, the courts rely heavily on the Restatement of Foreign Relations, Section 40. That section outlines five factors to be considered:

40. Limitations on Exercise of Enforcement Jurisdiction.

Where two states have jurisdiction to prescribe and enforce rules of law and the rules they may prescribe require inconsistent conduct upon the part of a person, each state is required by international law to consider, in good faith, moderating the exercise of its enforcement Jurisdiction, in the light of such factors as:

(a)   Vital national interests of each of the states,
(b)   The extent and the nature of the hardship that inconsistent enforcement actions would impose upon the person,
(c)   The extent to which the required conduct is to take place in the territory of the other state,
(d)   The nationality of the person, and
(e)   The extent to which enforcement by action of either state can reasonably be expected to achieve compliance with the rule prescribed by that state.[159]

Where a violation of the United States antitrust laws is involved, the United States' interest in discovery is afforded the greatest importance.[160] In *First National City Bank*, a U.S. defendant sought protection from discovery in an antitrust case based upon the alleged strong German policy in favor of bank secrecy and a contractual provision to that effect. The court noted that there was no statute requiring bank secrecy in Germany nor were there any criminal sanctions to be im-

---

[159] *See* 396 F.2d at 897, 902; United States v. Vetco, 644 F.2d 1324, at 1330-31.

[160] 396 F.2d at 902-03; American Industrial Contracting Inc. v. Johns-Manville Corp., 326 F. Supp. 879 (W.D. Pa. 1971).

posed on bank personnel if such secrets were revealed. The court further commented that Germany had raised no objections that pursuit of the subpoenas would injure its public interests. The court concluded by commenting that the bank's potential loss of foreign business was not a legitimate factor to be weighed against the need for discovery; and, the bank's breach of its contractual promise of secrecy would impose minimal civil liability. Since the foreign sovereign's policy interests in maintaining secrecy were minimal at most, the court found the bank to be in contempt for failure to comply with the subpeonas issued by the trial court.[161]

However, the U.S. interest in enforcing the antitrust law can be overcome, particularly when the information sought is cumulative in nature. The Westinghouse litigation presents this contrasting situation.

The plaintiff, Westinghouse, sought documents which were subject to the protective provisions of the Canadian Uranium Information Security Regulations promulgated under the authority of Canada's Atomic Energy Control Act. The plaintiff had caused letters rogatory to issue to the Ontario Supreme Court seeking assistance in obtaining the documents and the deposition of a Canadian defendant. The Ontario court refused citing the above-noted legislation and potential restraints on Canadian Sovereignty if plaintiff's request was granted. The defendant then sought permission of the Canadian Minister of Energy, Mines, and Resources to release the company's records located in Canada. The Minister denied the request. The Tenth Circuit concluded that the defendant's good faith effort to seek a permissable means of discovery precluded the trial court from citing defendant for contempt. Defendant sought waiver from the applicable regulation and there was no evidence that defendant sought the imposition of the regulation in order to avoid discovery. Given the express policy concerns of Canada, as outlined in the Ontario court decision, the "balance of interests" weighed against sanctions for failure to comply with the discovery order.[162] The court also noted that

---

[161] 396 F.2d at 903-05.

[162] In re Westinghouse Uranium Contracts Litigation, 563 F.2d 992 (10th Cir. 1977).

much of the information sought by plaintiffs had been obtained already in the discovery of other defendants.

In a case which did not involve antitrust allegations, the United States Supreme Court has also ruled that a party was not in contempt for failure to produce documents "confiscated" by the Swiss government in order to insure compliance with its panel laws regarding the secrecy of banking records where that party sought waivers which, if obtained, would have permitted release of the documents.[163]

As noted earlier, however, the mere existence of a foreign penal law precluding discovery will not necessarily afford relief to a party subject to discovery. The subject party must show that the law will likely be applied so that real probable sanctions will result.[164] Moreover, the *Arthur Anderson* case, discussed above, implicitly imposes a requirement that a party subject to discovery actively seek waiver of the prohibitive provisions before foreign law can be used as a defense to a contempt motion.[165] Cases which have deferred to foreign prohibitions without a showing of an effort to obtain waiver have noted that the information sought was basically irrelevant to the uses in litigation.[166]

Even where contempt is inappropriate other sanctions may be imposed, although the sanctions must fit "the crime." In a case involving the maritime laws the court in *Calcutta East Coast of India and East Pakistan/U.S.A. Conference v. F.M.C.*,[167] determined that the failure of certain conference members to comply with subpoenas issued in a single rate proceeding did not permit the Federal Maritime Commission to cancel the entire conference agreement. Notably, the district court had earlier held that the conference members had not been in contempt for failure to comply with the subpoenas

---

[163] Societe Internationale Pour Participations Industrielles et Commerciales v. Rogers, 357 U.S. 197 (1958).

[164] 326 F. Supp. at 879.

[165] *See* United Nuclear Corp. v. General Atomic Co., 96 N.M. 155, 629 P.2d 231 (1980); Note, "Discovery of Documents Located Abroad in U.S. Antitrust Litigation," 14 Va. J. Int. L. 747 (1974).

[166] Trade Development Bank v. Continental Insurance Co., 469 F.2d 35 (2d Cir. 1972).

[167] 399 F.2d 994 (D.C. Cir. 1968).

since foreign law banned disclosure and the members had in good faith sought waiver from the antidisclosure rules.[168]

Calcutta raises the as yet unresolved issue as to what is the evidentiary effect of the legitimate inability to produce documents. Where the party failing to comply with discovery is the plaintiff, the trial court may well draw negative evidentiary inferences from the lack of complete disclosure by the plaintiff. The U.S. Supreme Court so noted in *Societe International* when it permitted plaintiff to maintain its action despite its failure to comply with the trial court's discovery order:

> This is not to say that petitioner will profit through its inability to tender the records called for. It may be that in a trial on the merits, petitioner's inability to produce specific information will prove a serious handicap in dispelling doubt the Government might be able to inject into the case. It may be that in the absence of complete disclosure by petitioner, the District Court would be justified in drawing inferences unfavorable to petitioner as to particular events.[169]

Where a defendant, rather than a plaintiff, cannot comply with a discovery order due to foreign antidisclosure rules the practical evidentiary effect is less clear. The unavailability of documents may well create doubts which will reduce the weight of a defendant's evidence, but, unless the contempt remedy is appropriate, defendant's inability to produce documents should not raise any presumption that plaintiff's factual allegations are true. This was implied by the Tenth Circuit in *Westinghouse* which noted the availability to Westinghouse of other evidence which would enable it to present its claim, thereby mitigating its need for discovery with respect to the particular documents at issue.[170] Indeed to create presumptions from the inability to produce documents would be to impose a sanction far worse than the customary fine resulting from the contempt citation, and would therefore be inappropriate. Indeed, if the information sought from a defendant is essential to the litigation the U.S. court may be forced to im-

---

[168] *Id.* at 996 n.4.
[169] 357 U.S. at 212-13.
[170] 563 F.2d at 999.

pose contempt sanctions despite contrary foreign law and defendant's good faith effort to comply with the discovery order.[170.1]

Finally, with respect to all pretrial matters, the litigants should be aware of the ability to consolidate multidistrict litigation involving the same factual issues into a single proceeding.[171]

[170.1] *See* In re Grand Jury Proceedings, 532 F.2d 404 (5th Cir. 1976); Pansius, "Resolving Conflicts with Foreign Non Disclosure Laws: An Analysis of the *Vetco* case," Denver J. Int'l L. & Pol'y (forthcoming 1982).

[171] 28 U.S.C. 1407 (1970); In re Uranium Antitrust Litigation, 1978 Trade Cases 62,251 (Panel on Multidistrict Litigation 1978).